Roman Drama and its Contexts

Trends in Classics –
Supplementary Volumes

Edited by
Franco Montanari and Antonios Rengakos

Scientific Committee
Alberto Bernabé · Margarethe Billerbeck
Claude Calame · Philip R. Hardie · Stephen J. Harrison
Stephen Hinds · Richard Hunter · Christina Kraus
Giuseppe Mastromarco · Gregory Nagy
Theodore D. Papanghelis · Giusto Picone
Kurt Raaflaub · Bernhard Zimmermann

Volume 34

Roman Drama
and its Contexts

Edited by
Stavros Frangoulidis, Stephen J. Harrison and
Gesine Manuwald

DE GRUYTER

ISBN 978-3-11-058068-6
e-ISBN (PDF) 978-3-11-045650-9
e-ISBN (EPUB) 978-3-11-045558-8
ISSN 1868-4785

Library of Congress Cataloging-in-Publication Data
A CIP catalog record for this book has been applied for at the Library of Congress.

Bibliografische Information der Deutschen Nationalbibliothek
The Deutsche Nationalbibliothek lists this publication in the Deutsche Nationalbibliografie; detailed bibliographic data are available on the Internet at http://dnb.dnb.de.

© 2016 Walter de Gruyter GmbH, Berlin/Boston
This volume is text- and page-identical with the hardback published in 2016.
Logo: Christopher Schneider, Laufen
Typesetting: PTP Protago-TEX-Production, Berlin
Druck und Bindung: CPI books GmbH, Leck

♾ Printed on acid-free paper
Printed in Germany

www.degruyter.com

In grateful memory of
Daniel Iakov
(1947–2014)

Preface

The present volume is published in loving memory of Daniel Iakov, a leading scholar in Greek drama and Greek Lyric poetry and an inspiring presence at the Aristotle University of Thessaloniki for over 40 years. As David Konstan succinctly put it, "He is affectionately remembered for his immense learning, his profound wisdom and equally vast humanity."

The collection brings together 33 papers on Roman Drama, most of which were first presented at a conference on *Roman Drama and its Contexts* held by the Department of Classics at the Aristotle University of Thessaloniki from May 29 to June 1, 2014.

Due to the wide variety of texts, topics and approaches presented at the conference and in this volume, editorial standardization was limited to bringing manuscripts in line with the overall *Trends in Classics* house style. Beyond that, contributors were free to use the most appropriate format for references and quotations in their papers, observing UK or US spelling and punctuation conventions as they preferred.

We would like to thank all invited speakers, chairs and participants for an eventful conference, which raised many stimulating ideas and generated lively responses. Much of the conference's success was due to the assistance of departmental colleagues, research assistants and both graduate and undergraduate students.

Warmest thanks also go to our sponsors: The British Council at Thessaloniki; the Archdiocese of Athens; University Studio Press; the Aristotle University Research Committee; and the Department of Philology.

We are most grateful to the Welfare Foundation for Social and Cultural Affairs (KIKPE) and especially to its vice chairman Manos Dimitrakopoulos, for support in organizing the Roman Drama conference in particular and for continuous assistance provided to the *Trends in Classics* conferences in general.

The Aristotle University Research Dissemination Center and its PR Office Director Mr. Dimitrios Katsouras are to be thanked for hosting the event and offering much-needed practical assistance during the conference. We would also like to express our thanks to Dr. Polyxeni Adam-Veleni, Director of the Thessaloniki Archaeological Museum, for allowing us to use the museum auditorium as a conference venue. Dr. Adam-Veleni and Prof. Ioannis Tzifopoulos kindly offered conference participants a guided tour of the fascinating exhibition: "Letters from the 'Underground': Writing in Methone, Pieria late 8th early 7th century BCE", hosted by the Archaeological Museum.

We are very much indebted to our co-organizers Professors Theodore Papanghelis, Richard Hunter and Antonios Rengakos for helping us run a successful conference.

A special debt of gratitude goes to both Franco Montanari and Antonios Rengakos, General Editors of *Trends in Classics*, for their constant interest and support, as well as for their eagerness to include this collection of papers in the *Trends in Classics* – Supplementary Volumes series.

Last but not least, at De Gruyter we would like to thank John Whitley, Project Editor, and especially Lucas Meinhardt, Production Editor in Classics and Ancient Studies, for their meticulous editorial work at various stages of the publication process.

Stavros Frangoulidis
Stephen Harrison
Gesine Manuwald

Table of Contents

Preface —— VII

Gesine Manuwald and Stavros Frangoulidis
Introduction: Roman Drama and its Contexts —— 1

Part I: Roman Comedy

Richard Hunter
Some Dramatic Terminology —— 13

Alessandro Schiesaro
Bacchus in Roman Drama —— 25

Niall W. Slater
Speculating in Unreal Estate: Locution, Locution, Locution —— 43

Amy Richlin
The Kings of Comedy —— 67

Alison Sharrock
Genre and Social Class, or Comedy and the Rhetoric of Self-aggrandisement and Self-deprecation —— 97

Martin T. Dinter
Sententiousness in Roman Comedy – A Moralising Reading —— 127

Ioannis M. Konstantakos
Plautus' *Aulularia* and Popular Narrative Tradition —— 143

Sophia Papaioannou
Plautus Undoing Himself – What is Funny and What is Plautine in *Stichus* and *Trinummus*? —— 167

Kathleen McCarthy
Prologues between Performance and Fiction —— 203

David Christenson
All's Well That Ends Well? Old Fools, Morality, and Epilogues in Plautus —— 215

T. H. M. Gellar-Goad
Plautus' *Curculio* and the Case of the Pious Pimp —— 231

C. W. Marshall
The Young Man in Plautus' *Asinaria* 127–248 —— 253

Robert Germany
Civic Reassignment of Space in the *Truculentus* —— 263

Catherine Connors
Nothing to do with *Fides*? The Speaker of the Prologue and the Reproduction of Citizenship in Plautus' *Casina* —— 275

Katerina Philippides
Symmetrical Recognitions in Plautus' *Epidicus* —— 289

Mario Telò
Basket Case: Material Girl and Animate Object in Plautus's *Cistellaria* —— 299

Bernhard Zimmermann
Elements of Pantomime in Plautus' Comedies —— 317

Part II: Roman Tragedy

Gesine Manuwald
History and Philosophy in Roman Republican Drama and Beyond —— 331

Timothy J. Moore
Music in Roman Tragedy —— 345

Cedric Littlewood
Seneca, Horace and the Poetics of Transgression —— 363

Christopher Trinacty
Tragic *Translatio*: *Epistle* 107 and Senecan Tragedy —— 379

Stavros Frangoulidis
Seneca's *Agamemnon*: Mycenaean Becoming Trojan —— 395

David Konstan
When Reason Surrenders its Authority: Thyestes' Approach to Atreus' Palace —— 411

Lauren Donovan Ginsberg
History as Intertext and Intertext as History in the *Octavia* —— 417

Part III: Reception of Comedy and Tragedy

Ruth Rothaus Caston
Terence and Satire —— 435

Dorota Dutsch
How to Do Things with Words – and Pictures: Text and Image in the Parisian Terence —— 453

Michael Fontaine
Is the Story of *Susanna and the Elders* Based on a Greek New Comedy? —— 471

Antony Augoustakis
Terence's Comedies in the *Terentius Christianus*: The Case of *Naaman* —— 489

Evangelos Karakasis
Petronian Spectacles: The Widow of Ephesus Generically Revisited —— 505

Theodoros Antoniadis
Furor and Kin(g)ship in Seneca's *Thyestes* and Valerius Flaccus' *Argonautica* (1.700–850) —— 533

Emily Gowers
Noises Off: The Thyestes Theme in Tacitus' *Dialogus* —— 555

Roland Mayer
Seneca's Ted Hughes —— 573

Stephen Harrison
Seneca's *Thyestes*: Three Female Translators into English —— 585

Notes on Contributors —— 601

General Index —— 607

Index locorum —— 617

Gesine Manuwald and Stavros Frangoulidis
Introduction: Roman Drama and its Contexts

The title of this volume (and the conference on which it is based) takes its inspiration from the fact that, while interest in 'Roman drama' is flourishing, Roman drama, or rather individual Roman dramatic genres and poets, tend to be looked at in isolation or only within particular contexts. Therefore, this collection aims to break out of this cycle, which is the result of the development of the history of scholarship over the last 200 years or so.

A noticeable characteristic of research on Roman drama is that, apart from a few introductions and brief overviews,[1] there is little scholarship on 'Roman drama' (in contrast to, e.g., Roman epic); instead there is scholarship on the Republican comic poets Plautus and Terence, on the imperial tragedian Seneca and on Roman dramatic fragments (with varying intensity according to dramatic genre). Of course, different dramatic genres, different periods of composition and whether or not a work of literature has been transmitted in full pose different questions and require different approaches; and it is difficult to sketch developments over the course of ancient Roman drama because of the major changes between the Republican and the early imperial periods and the loss of almost all drama from Augustan times.[2] Still, all these works combine to represent what is called 'Roman drama' and might benefit from being considered together and in context.

The reason why the various elements of Roman drama used to be looked at separately (and often by different scholars) is perhaps that historically different approaches were chosen for each of them: the plays of Plautus and Terence were compared with assumed Greek models or used to reconstruct them; the tragedies of Seneca were compared with classical Greek tragedies, mainly those by Euripides; and for the fragments the key focus was on establishing a text and reconstructing plays, again often in comparison with underlying Greek dramas. There was then, originally, a common denominator, namely the comparison with Greek drama, since Roman drama (like much else in Roman literature) was regarded as a 'translation' of its Greek counterpart; therefore Roman drama was sometimes assigned little literary value, and, because of the assumed small difference between the two, Greek and Roman material was often used indiscriminately to reconstruct plays, while other scholars tried to separate Greek and Roman elements in existing scripts. One could argue that this approach of modern scholars

---

[1] See e.g. Beare 1964; Manuwald 2011.
[2] But see Tarrant 1978.

was the Romans' own 'fault' to some extent since, for instance, writers of comedies often mention the Greek models used in their prologues, and there were discussions among Roman playwrights and early scholars, such as Cicero, about the best ways of transposing works of Greek literature into Latin. Also, Roman literary drama was introduced by an official decision in 240 BCE, just after the end of the First Punic War, on the basis of Greek drama, to demonstrate, among other things, Rome's culturally advanced position. But a careful examination of these pieces of evidence, as has now been attempted, reveals that for Roman writers it was common practice to base their own dramas on Greek precedents, but that in the process they transformed them and adapted them for a Roman public.

In line with the development of approaches of modern literary theory, intertextuality and theories of translation in particular, views on the relationship between Greek and Roman drama have changed significantly in recent decades, and scholars now talk of 'Romanization' and identify Roman elements in Roman drama. Moreover, the scope of aspects addressed has widened, and it has been questioned whether comparison with Greek drama is the best way to understand the characteristics of Roman plays and whether trying to segregate Greek and Roman elements (which often is impossible to do accurately in the absence of sufficient material on either side) is indeed relevant. So, many scholars are now looking at the plays in the form in which they have been transmitted and ask questions on their performance, their dramatic structure and meaning.[3] With the increasing interest in reception, later plays, especially those from the Renaissance onwards, based on Plautus, Terence and Seneca are finding renewed attention (while such an approach can obviously be applied only to completely preserved plays).[4]

For the different areas this means that research on Senecan tragedy has now addressed the following questions: the dramas' time of composition, their relationship to the emperor(s) in power at the time, their potential links to Seneca's philosophical works, their metrical and linguistic structure, comparison with classical Greek tragedy, performability and performance,[5] the role of the chorus, characterization of protagonists and reception. As regards the Republican period Plautus and Terence are the most popular objects of research.[6] The themes explored in relation to their works illustrate the general tendencies sketched. All

---

3 See e. g. Leigh 2004.
4 See e. g. Segal 2001; but see already von Reinhardstoettner 1886.
5 See e. g. Harrison 2000.
6 See e. g. Duckworth 1952; Konstan 1983; Hunter 1985; Lowe 2008; Augoustakis/Traill/Thorburn 2013; Fontaine/Scafuro 2014.

the completely preserved plays are now well served by translations into modern languages and commentaries.

The fragments of Roman drama have been edited frequently,[7] and there have been debates on the constitution of the text, particularly since the 19th century. However, the focus in those early discussions was mainly on establishing a comprehensible text (often with heavy use of conjecture) and reconstructing plots (often on the basis of assumed Greek originals). Because of this approach and because Greek-style 'comedy' and 'tragedy' were regarded as the more elevated and more important dramatic genres, researchers mainly focused on those, while other Roman dramatic genres, such as *fabula praetexta*,[8] *fabula togata*, Atellana and mime,[9] tended to be neglected.[10] In recent decades, however, it has been recognized that, even if the remains of these further dramatic genres are meagre and there is often not a single complete example, they are distinctive to Roman dramatic literature, and one therefore needs to find out about them as much as one can, to get an idea of the full panorama of Roman drama and put genres like comedy and tragedy into their dramatic context.

Still, a substantial amount of research on Republican dramatic fragments focuses on Roman tragedy.[11] Besides improving editions and commentaries, scholars now ask broader questions about the role of tragedy in Roman culture, about its characteristics in relation to Greek plays and prominent motifs and formal aspects, and, as far as possible, about the impact of performance contexts and the relationship to the audience.

For the Republican period, the only period for which complete plays are known to have been performed in open theatres at public festivals, there has also been research on the practicalities of theatre business, including the dates and length of festivals, the role and composition of the audience, the selection of plays, the arrangement of rehearsals, the position of impresarios, the size of theatre companies, payments and the use of costumes and masks.[12]

---

[7] In addition to the critical editions by Ribbeck (1871/1873, 1897/1898), the Republican dramatic fragments are still most easily accessed in Warmington's Loeb edition (1935/1936), though the fact that his edition only includes 'tragedy' and 'comedy' may have influenced the scholarly focus.
[8] See e. g. Manuwald 2001.
[9] See e. g. Panayotakis 2010.
[10] For brief overviews of the major Republican playwrights see the relevant entries in Suerbaum 2002.
[11] See e. g. Erasmo 2004; Boyle 2006; for bibliography see Manuwald 2001 (2004); Goldberg 2007.
[12] See e. g. Beacham 1991; Marshall 2006; on Roman theatre buildings see e. g. Sear 2006.

What has not been done much so far is combining these different aspects and approaches, i. e. studying the various dramatic genres collectively and looking at Roman drama beyond its generic confines. The essays in this volume do not claim to remedy the situation completely and to look at all possible 'contexts' (which is hardly achievable even for a substantial collection). But, together, these contributions show a number of ways in which Roman drama could fruitfully be explored by going beyond concentrating on individual poets or plays. The title of this volume may recall Eric Csapo's and William J. Slater's *The Context of Ancient Drama* (1995): but that book offered a selection of texts illustrating the contexts in which ancient, mainly Greek, drama took place, while the present collection makes an effort to interpret Roman drama within a wide range of contexts.

Contributors were free to interpret 'contexts' in whichever way they wished and to choose the poets, plays, fragments or themes that they wanted to put into 'context'. The result is a series of representative case studies, covering the period from almost the beginning of Roman drama to its reception until the 20th century as well as including Plautus, Terence, Seneca and fragmentary playwrights. There are still few studies on dramatic genres beyond tragedy and comedy, and discussions of fully preserved plays dominate; but the variety of contexts suggested outweighs this potential limitation. The contexts touched upon include: a variety of literary and formal aspects, the structure of plays, the generic, especially comic, tradition, the plays' intertextual and intergeneric frameworks both among the different forms of Roman drama and beyond, the role of translation, the literary discourse among contemporaries and/or later authors, the impact of ritual and performance space, the relationship to contemporary historical, cultural and religious developments, the contemporary professional and moral context, engagement with historical and social developments, the reception of plays after antiquity.

In greater detail, the 33 papers in this collection on Roman drama, more specifically on Roman comedy and tragedy, address the following 'contexts'.

The first main section of the volume is devoted to Roman comedy. By means of a theoretical discussion of issues of literary criticism, Richard Hunter explores the historical development of two important dramatic terms, *fabula* and *comoedia*; on that basis he examines the dramatic self-awareness of comic discourse in the early Republican period.

Several contributions contextualize Roman comedy within its historical and social background. Alessandro Schiesaro focuses on the role of Bacchus in the context of early Roman drama: he looks at allusions to Bacchic cult and myth in Plautus, the end of whose career coincided with the famous episode of the Bacchanalia decree in 186 BCE, and analyses both Virgil's account of the rustic origins of tragic performances in Greece and Rome at *Georgics* 2.380–86 and Horace's discussion of similar topics in *Epistles* 2 and the *Ars poetica*. With respect to Plautus' *Mostellaria* Niall W. Slater argues for the presence of three houses (two real and one unreal), substantiating a contrast between an old-fashioned traditional exchange economy and a novel monetary system of transaction with reference to slaves and houses. He also claims a parody of philosophical discourse in the case of Philematium's mirroring at the beginning of the play, which also functions as a narrative prolepsis of the illusionary house of the slave's scheme. Amy Richlin reads invocations of Hellenistic kings as a verbal means for acquiring and asserting power on the part of the powerless; these may also function as a way of venting anger yet again on the part of the socially inferior. In examining Plautus' *Persa* Alison Sharrock challenges the traditional view, which reads the controlling slave as the meta-dramatic *persona* of the poet, although the *servus fallax* constitutes one of the major innovations of Plautus' creation. For *Aulularia*, however, Sharrock explores how and why Plautus identifies with slaves and not with citizens of meagre means. Moving on to Terence, Martin Dinter examines moralizing maxims and *sententiae* in Terentian comedy from both the historicizing and the dramatic perspectives. He shows that the maxims function as part of a Terentian poetics of character delineation and, through the aid of a sixteenth-century compilation of Terentian *sententiae*, associates comic moralizing with Catonian discourse, ancient theoretical discussions of *sententiae* and the manner in which these may reflect an author's character.

The next two papers deal with Plautus' relationship to Greek models, discussing Plautine innovation and originality as well as Plautus' deconstruction of dramatic norms. Ioannis Konstantakos argues that Plautus' *Aulularia* dramatizes a folk fable belonging to tale-type ATU754 ("Happy Poverty"). This folktale is linked to other Aesopic material (e. g. fable 225 Perry about a miserly character). For Konstantakos such a dramatic mixture is owed to the Greek model and may not be understood simply in terms of Plautine innovation. Sophia Papaioannou examines the ways in which Plautus undermines and deconstructs comic generic elements established as such by himself: *Stichus* and *Trinummus* are used as case studies and are shown to diverge significantly from earlier Plautine comic rules.

The framework of a drama, i. e. its prologue and epilogue, is studied in the following two papers. Kathleen McCarthy analyses the prologues of Plautus' *Menaechmi* and *Captivi* and demonstrates their antithetical function: the prologues both disrupt the illusion of the fictional world and draw the audience into it. This disruption of the dramatic illusion is achieved through the arbitrariness of the plot, whereas plot exposition and the concomitant engagement of the audience with the fictional world are achieved through the actors' ambiguous relationship to the spectators. David Christenson concentrates on the epilogues of three *senex amator* plays: Plautus' *Asinaria*, *Casina* and *Mercator*. Christenson argues that these epilogues are consistent with their plays' moral conservatism and do not exhibit a spirit of comic freedom, as suggested in earlier scholarship. The piece also reassesses the figure of the *matrona* in Plautine dramas involving a *senex amator*: the comic *matrona* functions not only as a character blocking her husband's erotic pursuits, but also as an idiosyncratic comic heroine.

Attention then turns to dramatic characterization in the context of dramatic tradition. T. H. M. Gellar-Goad challenges the *communis opinio* that sees Cappadox in Plautus' *Curculio* as a typical comic villain. Gellar-Goad underscores the religious piety the pimp exhibits throughout the comedy and therefore argues for the individuality of the *leno* character, marked out against all other professional pimps of Plautine comedy. Against the *communis opinio*, which understands 'The Young Man' at Plautus, *Asinaria* 127–248 as Diabolus, C. W. Marshall puts forward new arguments in favour of identifying him as Argyripus.

The topic of comedy's affinity with ritual structures and topography is studied next. On the basis of Athens' incursion into Rome, as suggested by the prologue to Plautus' *Truculentus*, Robert Germany argues for a form of a comic re-appropriation of the so-called *indictio belli* ritual: in both instances Roman space becomes foreign for a period of time, to be watched, engaged with and finally obliterated. Within this framework it is also claimed that the initial staging of *Truculentus* would most probably have been performed during the *Ludi Apollinares*, close to the *columna bellica*. Catherine Connors revisits the issue of the divinity's identity in the prologue to Plautus' *Casina*. By examining Plautine topography and the Temple of Fides within the *Casina*, she concludes that Fides is the goddess of the prologue.

A further group of papers investigates aspects of dramaturgy and staging and thus considers the plays in their performance context. Adopting a dramaturgical approach, Katerina Philippides shows the artful construction of Plautus' *Epidicus* in the face of claims for the opposite: she demonstrates the masterful dramatic symmetry (of monologues, dialogues, positive and negative recognition scenes) evidenced throughout the play. Mario Telò argues for a symbolic value in the case of the *cistella* in Plautus' *Cistellaria*. For Telò, in the fourth act of the play, the affectionate exchange of the casket between the various dramatic characters brings out its symbolism as representing the baby-girl; this symbolism also enables a meta-dramatic reading of the casket in terms of the comic plot and its temporal layers. Bernhard Zimmermann looks at the possible influence of early forms of Roman pantomime on Plautine comedy. The author convincingly demonstrates this through a thorough examination of the Plautine corpus, considering the way the movements and behavior of a *dramatis persona* are described by another character on stage.

The second main section, on tragedy, starts with discussions of early Latin tragic production. The essay by Gesine Manuwald presents the first systematic attempt to show how drama was integrated into the literary and intellectual tradition at Rome. Manuwald demonstrates this view through correspondences between drama and the areas of philosophy and history in both content and linguistic form. Timothy Moore examines the metrical relationship of tragedy and comedy: as in comic dramas, in tragedies too metrical diversity is used as a means for musical contrast between tragic characters. However, tragic diction resorts to sung metres more often than comic language, for expository reasons. Despite the fact that tragedy becomes less musical over time, still it is shown that even early imperial tragedy significantly avails itself of musical moments.

With respect to the Senecan corpus from the imperial period, two papers explore intertextuality and the art of translation. Cedric Littlewood traces the presence of Horatian lyric in the choral odes in two of Seneca's tragedies, *Thyestes* and *Medea*. He concludes that the Senecan poetics of criminal excess can best be contextualized in – and run counter to – the discourse of Horatian lyric, often marked by a rhetoric of piety, which determines what may be appropriately expressed within the genre. Using Seneca's translation of a poem by Cleanthes in *Ep.* 107 as a paradigm of the most explicit translation methodology, Christopher Trinacty examines Seneca's translation of Greek material in his *Epistulae morales* and his tragedies. Reading the *Troades* and *Phaedra* confirms the view that Seneca features translations as opportunities for metaliterary reflection and poetic *aemulatio*.

A group of papers deals with literary motifs informing tragic plots. Stavros Frangoulidis explores the interplay between the Mycenaean and the Trojan perspectives running through Seneca's *Agamemnon*: events at Argos are represented against the background of the Trojan past. The representation of current events at Argos in terms of Troy and therefore the past adds a distinctly Trojan-Roman touch and consequently serves as an indication of the playwright's originality in handling a mythical plot. David Konstan views Tantalus' surrender to thirst and hunger in Seneca's *Thyestes* as anticipating Thyestes' approach to Atreus' palace. Through a detailed comparison of the episodes Konstan sheds light on the Stoic theory of motivation and the manner in which appearances (*species*, *phantasiai*), combined with pain and suffering, delineate the limits of the Stoic rational approach towards human desires.

Lauren Donovan Ginsberg adds a study of the *praetexta Octavia*, transmitted among the corpus of Seneca's plays, but probably written later, in the Flavian period. Using the hermeneutics of intertextuality and cultural literary memory, Ginsberg focuses on the riots described as following Nero's divorce in this play: Nero, the messenger, the chorus and the prefect are all made to view the revolution through the parameters of Virgil's *Aeneid* and Lucan's *Bellum civile*. Such a perception, according to Ginsberg, allows the *Octavia* poet to point to important links between the Neronian riots and the civil wars of the late Republic that helped the Julio-Claudians come to power.

The final main section investigates various aspects of the reception of Roman comedy and tragedy and thus looks at various chronological contexts. Attested reception starts as early as Lucilius: Ruth Caston examines Lucilian satire from the perspective of its relationship to Terence, advancing the view that Horace's *Satires* have misled us about a number of important links between Terence and Lucilian satire. These comic 'intrusions' into Lucilius' satire are evidenced by metrical and thematic similarities, but also through common moral themes, such as decadence and secrecy, as well as Greek terminology concerning hypocrisy and status.

Moving beyond the Republican period, Dorota Dutsch surveys the miniatures of actors wearing costumes and masks in the Carolingian manuscripts of Terence. By a close examination of the first few scenes of Terence's *Andria* in the Parisian manuscript (B. N. 7899) Dutsch claims that the miniatures act as a visual dramatic commentary, both learned and humorous, on the play in performance. The combination of text and image evidences the way in which ancient performance tradition was received in late antiquity.

The next couple of papers look at aspects of reception in the early modern period. Michael Fontaine concentrates on Johannes Burmeister (1576–1638). In 1622 this Baroque poet laureate adapted Plautus' *Casina* into a comedy entitled *Susanna*, based on the tale of Susanna and the Elders in Daniel 13. Fontaine first offers a reconstruction of the lost neo-Latin play to demonstrate the inherently comic features of the biblical Susanna story, associated with the New Comedy of Diphilus of Sinope, as known from a variety of sources (fragments as well as Plautus' *Casina*, *Rudens* and *Amphitruo*). Fontaine further suggests that the author of the biblical Susanna story probably transformed an oral story according to a Hellenistic-Jewish dramatic form rather than in line with the poetics of Hellenistic-Roman comedy. Antony Augoustakis examines the ways in which Terentian comedy is received in terms of both language and themes by the Dutch playwright Cornelius Schonaeus (1540–1611). By focusing mainly on *Naaman*, Augoustakis sheds light on Schonaeus' objective, namely to Christianize Terence and replace pagan moralism with Christian ethics.

Evangelos Karakasis covers the reception of both comedy and tragedy, considering the ways in which Petronius' tale of the Ephesian *matrona* is informed by comedic, mimic and tragic discourses. Female fickleness is thus proven to exist on an inter-generic level.

With regard to the reception of tragedy Theodoros Antoniadis studies the notion of revenge and reciprocity in crime as intertextual markers of Senecan discourse on Valerius Flaccus. Emily Gowers traces *Thyestes* plots in Latin literature, i.e. the mythic cores involving Thyestean banquets, and pays particular attention to the tragedian Curiatius Maternus in Tacitus' *Dialogus de oratoribus*. Gowers argues that Maternus describes creation by employing the metaphors of pregnancy and delivery already intrinsic in *Thyestes* tragic plots.

The volume ends with two papers exploring the reception of Senecan tragedy in the form of adaptation or translation. Roland Mayer looks at the features of Seneca's *Oedipus* that might have been appealing to Ted Hughes, given the fact that he took on the adaptation of Seneca's drama fortuitously. Based on Hughes' preface, Mayer argues that Hughes' interest in anthropology may have made Seneca's apparent primitivism attractive to him, while the tragedian's obsession with fate and his focus on the grotesque fits Hughes' sensitivities as a poet. By dwelling mainly on the divergences in rendering the same passages from the original, Stephen Harrison sheds light on the variant translation strategies pursued by three different female writers in their respective verse translations of Seneca's *Thyestes*: that by Ella Isabel Harris in *The Tragedies of Seneca* (1904), the first English verse translation of all the Senecan plays, that by the poet Jane Elder (1982) and that by the dramatist Caryl Churchill (1995).

As this overview shows, even though obviously not exhaustive, the large number of papers in this collection, by scholars with different backgrounds, interests and approaches, illustrates the wide range of potential contexts in which Roman drama can be viewed. It is hoped that thereby further research on these or similar contexts will be encouraged and eventually lead to a more integrated picture of Roman drama.

Bibliography

Augoustakis, A., Traill, A., Thorburn, J. E. (2013), (eds.), *A Companion to Terence*, Chichester/Malden (MA).
Beacham, R. C. (1991), *The Roman Theatre and its Audience*, London.
Beare, W. (1964, 3rd edn), *The Roman Stage. A Short History of Latin Drama in the Time of the Republic*, London.
Boyle, A. J. (2006), *An Introduction to Roman Tragedy*, London/New York.
Csapo, E., Slater, W. J. (1995), (eds.), *The Context of Ancient Drama*, Ann Arbor.
Duckworth, G. E. (1952), *The Nature of Roman Comedy. A Study in Popular Entertainment*, Princeton (N. J.); Second Edition. With a Foreword and Bibliographical Appendix by R. Hunter, Norman/Bristol 1994.
Erasmo, M. (2004), *Roman Tragedy: Theatre to Theatricality*, Austin (Texas).
Fontaine, M., Scafuro, A. C. (2014), (eds.), *The Oxford Handbook of Greek and Roman Comedy*, Oxford.
Goldberg, S. M. (2007), 'Research Report: Reading Roman Tragedy', *IJCT* 13, 571–84.

Harrison, G. W. M. (2000), (ed.), *Seneca in Performance*, London.
Hunter, R. L. (1985), *The New Comedy of Greece and Rome*, Cambridge/London/New York/ New Rochelle/Melbourne/Sydney.
Konstan, D. (1983), *Roman Comedy*, Ithaca (N. Y.)/London.
Leigh, M. (2004), *Comedy and the Rise of Rome*, Oxford.
Lowe, N. J. (2008), *Comedy*, Cambridge (Greece & Rome, New Surveys in the Classics 37).
Manuwald, G. (2001), *Fabulae praetextae. Spuren einer literarischen Gattung der Römer*, München.
_____ [2001 (2004)], 'Römische Tragödien und Praetexten republikanischer Zeit: 1964–2002', *Lustrum* 43, 11–237.
_____ (2011), *Roman Republican Theatre*, Cambridge.
Marshall, C. W. (2006), *The Stagecraft and Performance of Roman Comedy*, Cambridge.
Panayotakis, C. (2010), (ed.), *Decimus Laberius. The Fragments*, Cambridge.
von Reinhardstoettner, K. (1886), *Spätere Bearbeitungen plautinischer Lustspiele*, Leipzig (Die klassischen Schriftsteller des Altertums in ihrem Einflusse auf die späteren Litteraturen 1); repr. Hildesheim/New York 1980.
Ribbeck, O. (1871), (ed.), *Scaenicae Romanorum poesis fragmenta. Vol. I. Tragicorum Romanorum fragmenta, secundis curis rec.*, Leipzig (repr. Hildesheim 1962).
_____ (1873), (ed.), *Scaenicae Romanorum poesis fragmenta. Vol. II. Comicorum Romanorum praeter Plautum et Terentium fragmenta, secundis curis rec.*, Leipzig.
_____ (1897), (ed.), *Scaenicae Romanorum poesis fragmenta. Vol. I. Tragicorum Romanorum fragmenta, tertiis curis rec.*, Leipzig.
_____ (1898), (ed.): *Scaenicae Romanorum poesis fragmenta. Vol. II. Comicorum Romanorum praeter Plautum et Syri quae feruntur sententias fragmenta, tertiis curis rec.*, Leipzig.
Sear, F. (2006), *Roman Theatres. An Architectural Study*, Oxford.
Segal, E. (2001), *The Death of Comedy*, Cambridge (MA)/London.
Suerbaum, W. (2002), (ed.), *Handbuch der Lateinischen Literatur der Antike. Erster Band. Die Archaische Literatur. Von den Anfängen bis Sullas Tod. Die vorliterarische Periode und die Zeit von 240 bis 78 v. Chr. (HLL 1)*, München (HbdA VIII.1).
Tarrant, R. J. (1978), 'Senecan Drama and its Antecedents', *HSPh* 82, 213–63.
Warmington, E. H. (1935), (ed.), *Remains of Old Latin. Newly Ed. and Transl. Vol. I. Ennius and Caecilius*, London/Cambridge (Mass.) (rev. and repr. 1967; several repr.) (LCL 294).
_____ (1936), (ed.), *Remains of Old Latin. Newly Ed. and Transl. Vol. II. Livius Andronicus, Naevius, Pacuvius and Accius*, London/Cambridge (Mass.) 1936 (repr. 1957, with minor bibliographical additions; several repr.) (LCL 314).

Part I: **Roman Comedy**

Richard Hunter
Some Dramatic Terminology

The history of the word δρᾶμα has been written many times,[1] but in this short paper I want to pick away at some of the implications of the usage of it and related terms in Greek and, then, to consider how Roman dramatists adapted Greek terminology in their plays. This study should be seen as a contribution to the history of the development of the language of criticism in Rome.

The origin of the word δρᾶμα is for these purposes less important than its 'flavour'. The earliest extant occurrences are probably Herodotus' two references to Phrynichus' famous play on 'The capture of Miletus' as a δρᾶμα (6.21.2), perhaps (and I offer this speculation hesitantly) because δρᾶμα was a more 'pan-Hellenic', less parochially Attic, term than τραγωιδία, which is what Phrynichus' play of 493 BC presumably was; δρᾶμα thus came more 'naturally' to Herodotus of Halicarnassus than did τραγωιδία, and would have seemed more natural also to a pan-Hellenic audience.[2] Herodotus in fact never uses τραγωιδία or κωμωιδία. As for Aristophanes, who uses the word frequently, it is well known that δρᾶμα in the extant comedies seems always to refer to tragedy, but of equal interest at least is the identity of those who use the word. In the *Frogs*, which seems the natural place to start, it will not surprise that the word is only found in the mouth of Aeschylus (1021) and Euripides (920, 923, 946–7), and in *Thesmophoriazousai* we similarly find it used by Agathon's servant (52), Agathon himself (149, 151, 166), and once by Euripides' old relation as he ponders which 'drama' (of Euripides) he will use to get Euripides to come to his aid (849); this scene shows the old man as not just an expert in Euripides' plays, but also as well versed in the 'newfangled' language of criticism. In the *Acharnians*, Euripides himself uses the word (470), but most instructive of all perhaps is Dicaiopolis' plea to him:

> ἀτὰρ τί τὰ ῥάκι'; εἰς τραγωιδίας ἔχεις
> ἐσθῆτ' ἐλεινήν; οὐκ ἐτὸς πτωχοὺς ποιεῖς.
> ἀλλ' ἀντιβολῶ πρὸς τῶν γονάτων σ', Εὐριπίδη,
> δός μοι ῥάκιόν τι τοῦ παλαιοῦ δράματος. 415
> δεῖ γάρ με λέξαι τῶι χορῶι ῥῆσιν μακράν·
> αὕτη δὲ θάνατον, ἢν κακῶς λέξω, φέρει.
>
> Aristophanes, *Acharnians* 412–17

---

1 Cf. Richards 1900, and further bibliography in Austin-Olson on Ar. *Thesm.* 52.
2 Strabo 14.1.7 cites the Alexander-historian, Callisthenes, as also recording (*FGrHist* 124 F30) that Phrynichus ὁ τραγικὸς staged (δρᾶμα ἐποίησε) the capture of Miletus; it is unclear whether Callisthenes is following Herodotus.

> But why these rags? The wretched clothes are for your tragedies? No wonder you create beggars! But please, Euripides, by your knees, give me some rag of the old drama. I have to deliver a long speech to the chorus, and if I speak badly, the reward will be death.

The 'tragic' nature of τραγῳδία determines its use here alongside 'piteous clothing',[3] but when Dicaiopolis tells Euripides that he needs 'some rag from/of an old drama', because he has to deliver 'a long *rhesis* to the chorus' it is clear that he appeals to Euripides with the kind of 'theatrical' language that will precisely carry weight with the tragedian. Whether or not we should see here a comic poet, 'Aristophanes-Dicaiopolis', appealing to the solidarity of a tragic fellow-craftsman may be debated, but what should, I think, be clear is that the language, while not 'technical' in the sense of language not understood by anyone except a practitioner, carries nevertheless a kind of professional flavour. δρᾶμα is a word that playwrights use. I am reminded somewhat of the way pilots tell you over the intercom about the 'aircraft', rather than 'the aeroplane' or even 'the plane', or about 'the airfield' rather than 'the airport'; these are ordinary words which everyone understands, but they are only (or mainly) used by those in the profession.[4]

Little can be added from the fragments of the rest of Greek comedy, but it is worth noting that δρᾶμα appears in the famous fragment of Antiphanes' *Poiesis* (fr. 189), perhaps spoken by 'Poiesis' herself or by 'Komoidia', pouring scorn on the habits of tragic poets ἐν τοῖς δράμασιν, and in Ecphantides fr. 3 K-A (probably the earliest fragment to contain the word), in which a character (a poet?) claims that he is ashamed 'to make τὸ δρᾶμα Megarian'. Elsewhere, we find the word (again) in connection with Euripides (Strattis fr. 1, Telecleides fr. 41, Diphilus fr. 74), and at Euphron fr. 1.35 a pretentious cook draws a distinction between δρᾶμα and παίγνιον; the distinction may there too characterise a professional interest. Fragments never, of course, give everything away, and it can hardly be claimed that δρᾶμα was never used in comedy (or indeed at Athens) entirely 'neutrally', perhaps even in the Aristophanic play or plays entitled Δράματα.[5] So too, the conclusions to be drawn from the fact that δρᾶμα seems never to appear

---

3 Cf. also τραγῳδία at *Peace* 148.
4 For a rather more sophisticated analysis of the range of such language in comedy cf. Willi 2003: Chap. 3; on p. 60 Willi discusses the very relevant class of words which are understood, but not normally used by, non-specialists.
5 At Ephippus fr. 16.1 Διονυσίου δράματα are the object of scorn, and there seems no reason why τραγῳδίας could not have been substituted (cf. esp. Ar. *Knights* 401). An interesting case is Adesp. Com. 51 K-A ἤδη δὲ λέξω τὸν λόγον τοῦ δράματος, which Wilamowitz (*Kleine Schriften* IV (Berlin 1962) 157–8) argued to come from a Menandrean metrical hypothesis, rather than from a play itself; the matter must, however, be considered quite uncertain.

in what survives of Menander are certainly debatable; it might be thought unsurprising that it is indeed explicitly τραγωιδία against which κωμωιδία continues to measure itself (cf., e. g., *Aspis* 329, *Epitr.* 325, 1125, *Samia* 590),[6] as in Dicaiopolis' famous claim that 'τρυγωιδία also knows what is just' (Ar. *Ach.* 500). δρᾶμα was subsequently to have a full life as a word of grammarians, writers of dramatic *hypotheseis* and so on, but it seems never to have been fully adopted on to the dramatic stage itself.

When we move forward to Roman comedy, where *fabula* might be thought the nearest equivalent for δρᾶμα, it may be sensible to work backwards from Terence to Plautus, and to begin not in fact with *fabula*, but rather with *comoedia*. The latter term occurs only once in Terence outside the prologues, at *Hecyra* 866:

> placet non fieri hoc itidem ut in comoediis
> omnia omnes ubi resciscunt. hic quos par fuerat resciscere
> sciunt; quos non autem aequomst scire neque resciscent neque scient.
>
> Terence, *Hecyra* 866–8

I don't want it to be like in comedies where everyone learns everything. In this case those who should find out know; those who have no need to know will neither learn nor know.

Although *fabula* in the sense of 'play' never, I believe, occurs in Terence outside the prologues, there seems no reason to doubt that here *fabulae* could have taken the place of *comoediae*; we may, however, ask what the choice of the Greek word, which may of course have appeared in Apollodorus' Greek play, lends to this very 'metatheatrical' passage.[7] What is *not* at stake here, I think, is Greek κωμωιδία vs Roman *fabula*, a contrast which – to anticipate – we shall see in Terence's prologues; the Roman audience are likely to see themselves, not Greek audiences and institutions, as the subject of the joke here. Rather, I suggest, *comoediae* is here used as the unmistakably theatrical, and hence distancing, 'formal' term: *this* action, so Pamphilus insists, is not going to be like an artificial performance on the stage, as far removed from 'real life' as *comoediae* is (in origin) from the Latin language. In 'real life' some people do remain in the dark and it is not the case that, as happens in comic drama, 'everybody gets to know everything'; it is almost as though 'everybody gets to know everything at the end' is one of the generic criteria for comedy, and this term here thus points to a rather sophisticated play with the dramatic illusion,[8] or whatever we want to call such effects. The fact that Terence nowhere uses *comicus*, *tragicus*, or *tragoedia*

---

[6] Cf., e. g., Hunter 1985, 118–21, 134–5.
[7] The matter is not really discussed in Goldberg's recent commentary.
[8] Cf. Bain 1977, 212 n. 3.

reinforces the suspicion that *comoediae* at *Hecyra* 866 carries a very distinctive charge.

If we move to the prologues, we find that *comoedia* can reinforce the 'Greekness' of a Greek title (*Phormio* 26, *HT* 4–5), and can indeed stand in contrast to a Latin adaptation designated as *fabula* (*Ad.* 6–7), a distinction we do not, I think, find in Plautus.[9] On the other hand, the *fabulae* which Terence's alleged opponents claim should not be 'contaminated' (*Andria* 16) seem to be Greek plays, rather than Roman adaptations (cf. *HT* 16–7), and in the same prologue it is *comoediae* which Terence looks forward to composing in the future (*Andria* 26, contrast *quas fecisset fabulas*, v. 39). This last seems in fact to be something of an exception to general practice, as *fabula* is essentially the default term for 'play' (including Terence's plays) in the prologues (cf. *Eun.* 23–5, 33–4, *Hecyra* 1, *Phormio* 4, *Ad.* 11 (with reference to Diphilus' play)). The terminology is clearly fluid enough for the case of *Andria* 26 to carry little or no significance, but given that Terence is apparently so sparing with the term *comoedia*, we should at least keep an open mind here. I wonder in fact whether Terence is not making something of a statement about the nature of his drama: he will continue to write in both Greek and Roman (vv. 18–21) traditions, and the use of the borrowed Greek term thus carries a charge. Everything we think we know about Terence and the context in which he wrote at Rome makes that 'Hellenising' claim a very pointed one.

When we move to Plautus, who is much less sparing with the term *comoedia*, no very clear distribution emerges, but it may again be possible to discern some interesting patterns. Unlike in Terence, of course, Plautine characters freely use both *fabula* and *comoedia*, thus giving, as is well known, a much more 'metatheatrical' flavour to Plautine plays; it is not difficult to show that the two terms can be virtually interchangeable, but also that the Greekness of *comoedia* can be activated when Plautus (or the prologue-speakers) desire it, as for example at *Menaechmi* 7:

> atque hoc poetae faciunt in comoediis:
> omnis res gestas esse Athenis autumant,
> quo illud uobis graecum uideatur magis;
> ego nusquam dicam nisi ubi factum dicitur.   10
> atque adeo hoc argumentum graecissat, tamen
> non atticissat, uerum sicilicissitat.
>
>   Plautus, *Menaechmi* 7–12

---

9 Note a case such as *MG* 84–7, where *comoedia* might be thought to reinforce the Greek title Ἀλαζών, but seems also to be used of the Latin play being acted; *Casina* 31–3 presents a similar case.

> This is what poets do in comedies: they declare that everything takes place in Athens, just so you will think it more Greek; as for me, I won't say it took place anywhere except where it is said to have happened. Therefore, this plot Grecises, but does not Atticise so much as Sicilise.

comoediis here introduces the 'Greek theme' of the following verses. *fabula* is by contrast, as it is in Terence, the neutral, unmarked term. This is particularly clear from the several instances where *fabula* is used when a character (or the whole troupe) declares at or near the end that 'the play is over', or words to that effect, cf. *Cas.* 1006, *Merc.* 1007, *Most.* 1181, *Poen.* 1370, *Pseud.* 1335, *Rud.* 1421, *Truc.* 967. Only once does *comoedia* appear in such a position, and this case seems telling:

> nunc, quod postremum est condimentum fabulae,
> si placuit, plausum postulat comoedia.
> Plautus, *Poenulus* 1370–1

> Now, as the last seasoning for the play, if you liked it, the comedy asks for your applause.

The *uariatio* of terms (*fabula* ~ *comoedia*) might be thought to suggest that the two terms are here strictly synonymous, but it might be suggested that *fabula* here refers to standard theatrical practice (applause at the end), whereas *comoedia* reminds the audience of the jolly time they have had, a pleasure which they can return by their applause.

The case of the Plautine prologues is notoriously problematic, and notoriously fascinating, for more than one reason. Whatever view we take of the history of the Plautine text, we all but certainly have, particularly in the prologues, the work of a number of different poets/troupe-managers, whatever you want to call them; in these circumstances, any search for consistency in semantic usage must be a very cautious one, and any proper consideration of the matter would have to take this into account. Here I will limit myself to brief remarks on a couple of passages, before turning to the plays themselves.

When the difference between tragedy and comedy is at stake, then of course *comoedia* and related terms are inevitably chosen. The prologist of the *Captiui* refers to the play about to be acted as a *fabula* (52, 54), but then turns to the virtues of what the audience are about to see:

> profecto expediet fabulae huic operam dare.
> non pertractate facta est neque item ut ceterae: 55
> neque spurcidici insunt uersus, immemorabiles;
> hic neque periurus leno est nec meretrix mala
> neque miles gloriosus; ne uereamini,

> quia bellum Aetolis esse dixi cum Aleis:
> foris illic extra scaenam fient proelia. 60
> nam hoc paene iniquomst, comico choragio
> conari desubito agere nos tragoediam.
>
> Plautus, *Captiui* 54–62

It will certainly be to your advantage to pay attention to this play. It is not composed in a very familiar style nor is it like other plays. It contains no dirty verses which are not for repetition. Here there is no perjured pimp nor wicked courtesan nor boastful soldier. Don't be afraid because I said that the Aetolians and the Eleans are at war; the battles will take place over there off-stage. It would almost be an outrage for us with our comic gear suddenly to try to put on a tragedy.

Warfare belongs with tragedy, not comedy.[10] The theme of 'decent comedy' returns at the very end of the play (1029–34):

> spectatores, ad pudicos mores facta haec fabula est,
> neque in hac subigitationes sunt neque ulla amatio 1030
> nec pueri suppositio nec argenti circumductio,
> neque ubi amans adulescens scortum liberet clam suom patrem.
> huius modi paucas poetae reperiunt comoedias,
> ubi boni meliores fiant.

Spectators, this play was composed with chaste morals: it contained no illicit sex, no love-story, no supposititious child, no fraudulent extraction of money, no young man in love setting free a prostitute without his father knowing. Poets find few comedies of this kind, in which the good become better.

Here, at first glance, *fabula* and *comoedia* might be thought exactly interchangeable, particularly as 1030–2 describe the typical plot elements of a comedy. Nevertheless, it may be worth suggesting that *ubi boni meliores fiant* at least gestures towards rather different ideas of what kind of a representation comedy is; this is not, of course, to suggest that Plautus (or a Greek poet) has in mind, for example, Aristotle's ideas of comedy normally being an imitation of 'the worse' (*Poetics* 1448a11–7, cf. 1453a30–8), but a sense of generic definition does seem to resonate here in the marked term *comoediae*. In the case of the famous prologue of the *Amphitruo*, the matter seems clear:

> nunc quam rem oratum huc ueni primum proloquar, 50
> post argumentum huius eloquar tragoediae.
> quid? contraxistis frontem, quia tragoediam
> dixi futuram hanc? deus sum, commutauero.

---

10 The argument is a very old one, cf., e. g., Isocrates, *To Nicocles* 48–9.

> eandem hanc, si uoltis, faciam iam ex tragoedia
> comoedia ut sit omnibus isdem uorsibus. 55
> utrum sit an non uoltis? sed ego stultior,
> quasi nesciam uos uelle, qui diuos siem.
> teneo quid animi uostri super hac re siet:
> faciam ut commixta sit: <sit> tragicomoedia.
> nam me perpetuo facere ut sit comoedia, 60
> reges quo ueniant et di, non par arbitror.
> quid igitur? quoniam hic seruos quoque partes habet,
> faciam sit, proinde ut dixi, tragicomoedia.
>
> Plautus, *Amphitruo* 50–63

First I'll tell you the request I have come here to make and then I will explain the plot of this tragedy. What? You're frowning because I said that this would be a tragedy? I'm a god, I'll change it. If you like, I'll make this same play not a tragedy but a comedy, with the very same verses. Do you want that or not? Silly me! Of course I know what you want, as I'm a god. I understand your desires in this matter. I'll make it a mixture: let it be a tragicomedy. I don't think it would be right for me to make it a comedy outright when kings and gods will appear. What then? As a slave has a role here, I'll make it, just as I said, a tragicomedy.

Here 'generic definition' is clearly at issue, and this will, I think, shed light on a passage later in the same prologue:

> ipse hanc acturust Iuppiter comoediam.
> quid? admirati estis? quasi uero nouom
> nunc proferatur, Iouem facere histrioniam; 90
> etiam, histriones anno cum in proscaenio hic
> Iouem inuocarunt, uenit, auxilio is fuit.
> praeterea certo prodit in tragoedia.[11]
> hanc fabulam, inquam, hic Iuppiter hodie ipse aget,
> et ego una cum illo. nunc <uos> animum aduortite, 95
> dum huius argumentum eloquar comoediae.
>
> Plautus, *Amphitruo* 88–96

Jupiter himself will have a role in this comedy. What? You're surprised? As if we were now doing something new, making Jupiter an actor. Last year, right here on this stage, the actors called on Jupiter and he came and helped them. Moreover, he certainly appears in tragedy. To repeat: Jupiter himself will have a role in this play, and myself alongside him. Now pay attention while I tell you the plot of this comedy.

Here we might well think that vv. 88 and 94 are a very clear case of the interchangeability of *comoedia* and *fabula*, but I would suggest that the formal term in v. 88 triggers the generic joke which follows, so that *fabula* in v. 93 shows that

---

[11] Leo's deletion of this verse is very attractive.

the whole matter is closed: this is now just 'a play' and the issues of its genre settled, or perhaps rather no longer important (the 'generic' joke has now been played out). On his second run through the idea of Jupiter appearing as a character, Mercury avoids having to deal with a surprised audience reaction by using the neutral term *fabula*; one can imagine that considerable emphasis was in fact given to *fabulam* by the actor playing Mercury. Far, in this instance, from being interchangeable, *comoedia* and *fabula* are in fact potently different.

In turning to the plays themselves, I begin with a famous piece of mockery by the slave Stasimus in *Trinummus*:

> non enim possum quin exclamem: eugae, eugae, Lysiteles, πάλιν.
> facile palmam habes: hic uictust, uicit tua comoedia.
> hic agit magis ex argumento et uorsus meliores facit.
>
> Plautus, *Trinummus* 705–7

> I can only exclaim: well done, well done, Lysiteles! Encore! You easily carry off the prize; he's beaten, your comedy has won! This chap follows the script more closely and makes better verses.

The mocking use of Greek, and the theatrical terms with which Stasimus expresses himself, here make *comoedia* (or should we print κωμῳδία?) much more pointed than *fabula* would have been; the slave is comparing alternative 'performances', and suggesting that both are 'posed' and artificial (cf., e. g., *Pseudolus* 1080–3, 1239–41). Here again, then, *comoedia* functions as the marked term which emphasizes the distance between a 'performance' and 'real life'. Over one hundred and thirty years ago, in a famous discussion of such phenomena, Friedrich Leo drew a distinction within Roman comedy between references to plays and matters theatrical of the kind which people do make 'in real life', and which do not (as we, glossing Leo, might say) 'break the dramatic illusion', and those which make it clear and explicit that the spectators are watching a play; Leo classed *Trinummus* 705–8 in the former category.[12] We would not, I think, today make such a straightforward distinction, or at least not in those terms and/or without considerable nuancing, but Leo's other claim that *Trinummus* 705–8 is very likely to be a 'faithful' adaptation from the Greek original does deserve a moment's attention. Leo claimed that the verses referred to Greek, not Roman, practices. Again, it is a measure of the change that has come over the study of Roman comedy that, even were this true, it would no longer be thought to be a convincing demonstration of 'Greekness'. In fact, however, that claim is at best uncertain. This passage represents one of three references in Roman com-

---

[12] Leo 1883, 561–2.

edy to contests between actors, and the other two occur in Plautine prologues (*Amph.* 69, *Poen.* 37); there is also a reference in a Terentian prologue to the *palma* available for anyone involved in *ars musica* (*Phormio* 17). The onus of proof would in fact seem to be on those who see Greek practice here.[13]

Stasimus' justification of his award of the palm to Lysiteles is itself not without interest. He claims that Lysiteles' acting 'follows the script' more closely (I think that this is what *ex argumento* means – or is it 'contributes to the plot'?), and that he produces 'better verses'. We seem to have here a pairing somewhat analogous to Terence's famous claim in the prologue of the *Andria* about Menander's *Andria* and *Perinthia*:

> Menander fecit Andriam et Perinthiam.
> qui utramuis recte norit ambas nouerit: 10
> non ita dissimili sunt argumento, [s]et tamen
> dissimili oratione sunt factae ac stilo.
>
>   Terence, *Andria* 9–12

> Menander composed an *Andria* and a *Perinthia*. Anyone who knows one of them, knows them both; it's not the plots which are different, but rather they are composed with different verbal manner and style.

However tendentious that assertion, and however familiar in Greek criticism and rhetoric the distinction between 'plot' and 'verbal elaboration' might be,[14] we might at least wonder whether we catch here echoes of a developing Roman critical discourse, and one which was fostered precisely by the fact that early Latin literature (and, of course, most notably drama) was precisely a literature of translation and adaptation. It is such a literature which puts pressure on *inuentio*, and which draws particular attention to the various elements which may be the object of imitation and elaboration; the quality of *oratio* or *stilus* moves 'centre stage' (so to speak) when one is moving from one language to another (think, to go no further, of Catullus' translations of Sappho and Callimachus). If there is anything to this, then this critical discourse comes to Rome not (or not principally) from the Greek critical heritage, but rather from the very practice of Roman writing.

The *Trinummus* passage has suggested that Plautus could (at need) use *comoedia* to stress 'comedy' as something set apart as an artificial performance, with its own motifs and rules. It seems natural to move from there to the famous instance[15] of *Mostellaria* 1149–51:

---

13 Cf. Brown 2002, 234, Jory 1988, Maurach on *Poen.* 37 (non-committal).
14 Cf., e. g., Jocelyn 1967, 24.
15 Cf., e. g., Bain 1977, 211–12.

> *Theopropides.* quid ego nunc faciam?
> *Tranio.* si amicus Diphilo aut Philemoni es,
> dicito eis, quo pacto tuos te seruos ludificauerit:
> optumas frustrationes dederis in comoedias.
>
> Plautus, *Mostellaria* 1149–51

comoedias *Kassel*: comoediis

> *Theopropides.* What am I to do now? *Tranio.* If you're a friend of Diphilus or Philemon, tell them how your slave fooled you. You'll give them marvellous bamboozlements for their comedies.

Almost every possible permutation of answer has been given to the question of whether these verses of the *Mostellaria* come from Plautus' Greek model or not,[16] but – if I was a betting man – I would have a small wager on the fact that, whatever the Greek text had at this point, there was no reference to 'comedy'. This is there in the Roman text not just to remind Plautus' audience of who Diphilus and Philemon are, but also precisely to reinforce the 'theatricality' of what Tranio is saying: his deception was so brilliant it deserves to be commemorated in art. The only other occurrence of *frustratio* in our extant corpus of Plautus is in Jupiter's second prologue to the *Amphitruo* and this may be thought to support the suggestion made here:

> nunc Amphitruonem memet, ut occepi semel,
> esse adsimulabo, atque in horum familiam
> frustrationem hodie iniciam maxumam;   875
> post igitur demum faciam res fiat palam
> atque Alcumenae in tempore auxilium feram
> faciamque ut uno fetu et quod grauida est uiro
> et me quod grauidast pariat sine doloribus.
>
> Plautus, *Amphitruo* 873–9

Now, as I once started, I'll pretend myself to be Amphitruo, and today I'll throw the highest degree of bamboozlement into this family. After that, I will finally make everything plain and I'll help Alcmena just when it's needed: I'll bring it about that, in one painless birth, she has both her husband's child and mine.

Almost immediately before this, Jupiter has explained the reason for his appearance:

---

16 Cf. Bain loc. cit., Williams 1983, 215 (resurrecting the idea that Plautus found only Diphilus in the original).

> ego sum ille Amphitruo, cui est seruos Sosia,
> idem Mercurius qui fit, quando commodumst,
> in superiore qui habito cenaculo,
> qui interdum fio Iuppiter, quando lubet;
> huc autem quom extemplo aduentum adporto, ilico   865
> Amphitruo fio et uestitum immuto meum.
> nunc huc honoris uostri uenio gratia,
> ne hanc incohatam transigam comoediam.
>
>   Plautus, *Amphitruo* 861–8[17]

I am that Amphitruo, whose slave is Sosia, but who is also Mercury when it suits. I live in the upper storey, and when I take the fancy, I sometimes become Jupiter. Whenever however I have occasion to come here, I immediately become Amphitruo and I change my clothes. I've come here now out of respect for you, so as not to bring this comedy to a premature end.

That this second prologue is a highly 'metatheatrical' moment within the comedy hardly requires discussion (Jupiter also makes a joke about changing his costume (866) and addresses the audience directly (867)); my guess would be that *frustratio* itself had some kind of theatrical resonance,[18] as though *frustratio* and *faciam res fiat palam* (*Amph*. 876) represented the Roman comic equivalent of Aristotelian δέσις and λύσις. Tranio's advice to Theopropides in the *Mostellaria* comes, then, pointedly at the time when the *frustrationes* are set aside and the typical comic ending of reconciliation and revelation take over. Greek equivalents for the language of *frustratio* are, of course, not hard to find,[19] but it is less important here to wonder about 'Plautinisches im Plautus' than to feel a developing Roman language in which the literariness of comedy, and no doubt tragedy also, could be discussed.

I have in these brief remarks taken two different, but I hope complementary, approaches to teasing out the development of a Roman critical discourse, centred on the adaptation of Greek comedies to the Roman stage. The picture is inevitably a very partial one, and our sight is blocked as often as it is allowed glimpses of searchable terrain. What matters, I think, is that there is indeed searchable terrain, and progress seems possible as long as we ask the right questions.

---

17 The sense of v. 868 must be something like De Melo's 'so as not to bring this comedy to a premature end', but the expression is at least awkward (which presumably led to Havet's *ut* for *ne*), cf. Christensen ad loc., making the nice suggestion that Jupiter is also suggesting that he has not arrived as a closing *deus ex machina*.
18 Cf. Christensen ad loc. Very similar are Mercury's words to the audience at vv. 470–8.
19 Cf. ταραχή in Tyche's prologue at Men. *Aspis* 137.

Bibliography

Bain, D. (1977), *Actors and Audience*, Oxford.
Brown, P. (2002), 'Actors and Actor-Managers at Rome in the Time of Plautus and Terence', in: P. Easterling and E. Hall (eds.), *Greek and Roman Actors*, Cambridge, 225–37.
Hunter, R. (1985), *The New Comedy of Greece and Rome*, Cambridge.
Jocelyn, H. D. (1967), *The Tragedies of Ennius*, Cambridge.
Jory, E. J. (1988), 'Publilius Syrus and the Element of Competition in the Theatre of the Republic', in: N. Horsfall (ed.), *Vir Bonus Discendi Peritus. Studies in Celebration of Otto Skutsch's Eightieth Birthday*, London, 73–81.
Leo, F. (1883), '*Lectiones Plautinae*', *Hermes* 18, 558–87 [= *Ausgewählte kleine Schriften* (Rome 1960) 13–33].
Richards, H. (1900), 'On the Word Δρᾶμα', *CR* 14, 388–93.
Willi, A. (2003), *The Languages of Aristophanes*, Oxford.
Williams, G. (1983), 'Roman Poets as Literary Historians. Some Aspects of *imitatio*', *ICS* 8, 211–27.

Alessandro Schiesaro
Bacchus in Roman Drama

1

The story of Bacchus in Roman drama is one dotted by fragmentary texts and often elusive contexts, an unpromising set-up which encourages theories, suggestions and even projections. While Hellenists can discuss with a wealth of arguments, and a distinguished set of authorities, from Aristotle to Nietzsche, whether drama has nothing, or much, or all, to do with Dionysos, students of Roman literature must make do with more limited evidence, chiefly because the fragments of the Republican tragediographers are tantalizing at best.

Important recent work has done much to problematize the relationship between Dionysus and Athenian drama, and fresh critical approaches to Nietzsche's *Birth of Tragedy*, a book which we may well exorcise, but cannot possibly ignore, has also contributed to loosening the connection.[1] All these developments must be taken into account as we move into Roman territory, but two factors mark a fundamental difference. To begin with, while Roman theatre has direct access to 5th-century Greek originals, it arises in a different cultural milieu, that of 3rd-century central and southern Italy, with a set of theatrical practices, texts and genres which are substantially different from their counterparts in Golden Age Athens. To give just one obvious example, by this time actors are unquestionably the *technitai* of Dionysus, a guild-model which Rome imports as early as Livius Andronicus hails from Tarentum.[2] Secondly, as it begins to develop its own tragic and comic theatre, Roman authors confront a cultural phenomenon which over the past two hundred years had undergone significant changes and formed its own internal taxonomies and theories, including the enormous success of Euripides' *Bacchae* as the most powerful reflection on the nature of the theatrical experience.

There are several areas in which the need to flesh out and assess the presence and role of Dionysos-Liber-Bacchus in a Roman theatrical setting is especially strong, and I will single out but a few in a much longer list. The first, related to the *Urgeschichte* of theatre itself, centres upon the connection ancient authors establish between the god and the very origin of performances. The second, and partly connected one, is the hope of reaching back, through the skilful peeling off of

---

[1] Silk-Stern 1981 remains invaluable, as is now Porter 2000.
[2] Jory 1970, 226–8.

various layers of commingled traditions, to the point in time at which Liber, Bacchus and Dionysus, each with his own features and lineage, met and mixed, perhaps conferring upon Roman theatre a meaningful connection with an indigenous culture and cultic sphere. The organisation of theatrical performances and the existence of guilds under the god's patronage forms a third, significant point of interest.

In this paper, however, I have opted to focus, rather than on Bacchic themes and texts, on three moments in the history of Latin literature in which the theoretical self-reflection, direct or indirect, about the relationship between Bacchus and theatre is especially significant: the connection between archaic drama and the repression of the Bacchanalia in 186 BCE, and the role assigned to Bacchus in the reconstruction of early drama and related genres in Virgil and Horace.

2

An understanding of Bacchus in early Roman drama must negotiate a path between a relative paucity of direct literary evidence and an over-abundant amount of information about the Bacchanalian affair of 186 BCE. The inevitable result has been to seek in Livy's extensive account of the historical events surrounding the *senatus consultum* the elements otherwise missing in the literary texts, or to read those available in the light suggested by the historian's own version of the events.

Working back from the events of 186 as told by Livy, it is tempting to take references to Bacchus in earlier or contemporary texts as negative reflections of the cult or at least of some of its aspects, even as evidence that a growing disquiet was mounting until the consuls took decisive action. Indeed, as some scholars have influentially argued, this 'pejorative image' of the cult went as far as to 'predispos[e] the Romans towards persecution before the consul denounced the cult in 186'.[3]

Recent historiography paints a more nuanced picture of those events and especially of Livy's retelling of them. His reconstruction is, on the face of it, a rather straightforward, if fascinating, account of the repression of rites which threaten political and social upheaval. Had the consuls not intervened with unprecedented firmness, the spread of the cult would have torn apart the fabric of the *res publica*, subverting the structure of the family and the state. Upon closer inspection, however, almost nothing in this account is actually straightforward or, for

---

3 Rousselle 1987, 193.

that matter, ordinary:⁴ the political danger of the rites is perhaps more feared than real;⁵ Bacchanalian observance represents neither an unprecedented attraction to foreign rites nor a real menace for the *pax deorum*;⁶ official attacks against foreign rites, moreover, are on the whole not in keeping with Roman practice.⁷ We do not know much about the spreading of Bacchic rites before 186, but there is no reason to believe that the cult was either novel or new, suddenly springing up or causing particular problems just around that time.⁸

In his relentless critique of the received opinion, Erich Gruen has questioned whether the action of the Senate and the consuls in 186 should be read as the inevitable response to the growing popularity of a cult which had been festering for some time. He argues that much the opposite appears to have happened: in a moment of heightened power struggle between emerging individual leaders buoyed by significant successes in the East and the Senate, the latter, represented by the consul Postumius, seized upon the matter as a *casus belli* in order to 'exhibit senatorial authority, to declare dominion in Italy, to distinguish collective interest from individual excesses, and to distance itself from some of the manifestations of Hellenism'.⁹ After all the cult, which must have been around for a while,¹⁰ was not altogether banned or rooted out, but subjected to the control of the Senate, in a display of power which was as much symbolic as it was real.¹¹

Gruen's radical approach downplays the unease authorities must have felt towards a rite they could not control,¹² but his scepticism encourages a more open-ended interpretation of the references to Bacchus and Liber in pre-186 theatre.

---

4 Gruen 1990 provides what is to my knowledge the most persuasive interpretation of Livy's narrative and of the events of 186. My take on the matter is based on his work. On the exceptional nature of many of the actions reported by Livy see esp. 39–47.
5 Gruen 1990, 47.
6 Gruen 1990, 48; Beard-North-Price 1998, 1.93, who, however, point out that the ecstatic and unregulated nature of the growing cult must have been genuinely problematic to the Roman authorities (95 and n. 84), and its social implications unwelcome (95–6). On the traditional tolerance on foreign cults see North 1979, 87–9.
7 Gruen 1990, 39.
8 Gruen 1990, 49–50, 75. The lack of evidence for any particular upsurge of the popularity of Bacchic rites in the years before 186 weakens the attempts to connect them with specific historical events, such as the consequences of the Hannibalic wars: Gruen 1990, 49.
9 Gruen 1990, 72–3.
10 This is much the sense we get from Augustine's notices about the Bacchanalia at *De civ. dei* 6.9 and 18.13, which go back to Varro: see Tarditi 1954, 274.
11 Gruen 1990, 75–6.
12 A point stressed by Takács 2000.

None of the passages drafted into the service of a teleological reading of the events and their causes actually supports the interpretation proposed, even less so if we read them without being unduly influenced by Livy's tale. A few examples drawn from Plautus, who mentions Bacchic rites in nine of his plays,[13] including the aptly named *Bacchides*, will suffice to clarify this point.[14] In general, Plautus refers to the Bacchae and their rites incidentally, often in hyperbolic comparisons with the current predicament of his characters which are difficult to take as a serious criticism of the cult, let alone as an expression of fear about it. From a short remark in the *Miles gloriosus*, for instance, we gather that the secret nature of Bacchic rites could be alluded to as a matter of course (1016): *MI. cedo signum, si harunc Baccharum es.* ('MILPHIDIPPA Give me a password, if you are one of these Bacchantes.')[15] In *Menaechmi*, Menaechmus II feigns madness in order to escape (828–39), and he does so by evoking Bromius and his call to the wild: *euhoe atque euhoe, Bromie, quo me in silvam venatum vocas?* (835).[16] Congrio, in the *Aulularia* (406–14), laments that he has fallen into a *bacchanal coquinatum* (408) when he has been beaten up. The destroyed ship at the beginning of *Vidularia* is, metonymically, Pentheus himself, torn asunder by the Bacchae: *eiusdem Bacchae fecerunt nostram navem Pentheum.*[17]

Casina (978–81) offers the only reference we can directly connect with the repression of 186:[18]

> CHA. non amas me? CLE. quin responde, tuo quid factum est pallio?
> LY. Bacchae hercle, uxor ... CLE. Bacchae? LY. Bacchae hercle, uxor ...
> MY. nugatur sciens,
> nam ecastor nunc Bacchae nullae ludunt. LY. oblitus fui.
> sed tamen Bacchae ... CLE. quid, Bacchae? <LY.> sin id fieri non potest ...
>
> CHALINUS You don't ... love me? CLEOSTRATA Come, come, answer me. What has become of your cloak? LYSIDAMUS Oh Lord, my dear, some Bacchantes ... CLEO. Bacchantes? LY. Oh Lord, my dear, some Bacchantes ... MYRRHINA That's nonsense, and he knows it. Why, goodness me, there are no Bacchante revels now. LY. I forgot that, but, just the same, some Bacchantes ... CLEO. What? Bacchantes? LY. Well, if that's impossibile ... (transl. Nixon)

---

13 Not including *Cist.* 156–9, where the statement that *fuere Sicioni iam diu Dionysia* is of a different nature. Cf. Rousselle 1987 and Flower 2000.
14 Pailler 1988, 229–38; Gruen 1990, 150–2.
15 Cf. also lines 854–8. Unless otherwise stated, I quote from Lindsay's *OCT*.
16 *euhoe euhoe* is a widely accepted emendation for the transmitted *eubi atque heu*, which Gratwick 1993, 110 retains in the text within *cruces*. The reference to Bacchus is in any case explicit.
17 *Vidularia* fr. I Lindsay = I Monda = 12 Calderan (whose comment *ad loc.* is useful).
18 MacCary 1975.

Even so, the passage appears to be carrying no great sense of urgency or drama. Lysidamus haltingly tries to justify the loss of his cloak by repeating *Bacchae hercle, uxor* – the absence of a verb suggesting the anguish caused by his fictitious ordeal at the hands of violent Bacchae, a feature so well-known that it is explicitly mentioned by Sosia in *Amphitruo* with *non scis*? (702–4). But, as his wife's friend Myrrhina quickly retorts, this is no time for the Bacchae to be up to any trick.

Overall, in spite of what many editors are inclined to believe, it is difficult to take these references seriously,[19] if nothing else in the light of the context in which they figure. The negative aspects of the Bacchic rites which they imply are part and parcel of the tradition: ecstasy, female over-excitement, an aura of mystery. We can interpret them as indications of deep-seated anxiety only in the retrospective light of the repression of 186 and the great ado Livy makes about it. Also, they seem typologically of a single cloth, with no discernible variations in general outlook between plays of arguably different dates. It should quickly be added, however, that this scepticism does not add weight to the opposite, if altogether less popular thesis, that Plautus was an enthusiastic follower of Bacchic rites.[20]

Rather than criticism or endorsement of Bacchic cults, Plautus shows an early awareness of the metatheatrical connotations of the god and his actions. In the *Mercator*, for instance, Charinus makes the connection explicit: *Pentheum diripuisse aiunt Bacchas: nugas maxumas / fuisse credo, praeut quo pacto ego diuorsos distrahor* (469–70 'They say the Bacchantes tore Pentheus to pieces: mere trifles compared with the way I'm rent and riven!'). *Aiunt* represents what in other contexts we are apt to label an 'Alexandrian footnote',[21] which highlights the metaliterary implications of the words.

They are equally evident in a well-known passage from *Curculio*, the ode to *uinipollens lepidus Liber* 'lovely Bacchus, Lord of Wine' (114) delivered by Leaena (96–109), who, suitably bribed, allows for the plot to get under way. The woman carries a suggestive name, doubly so: it evokes Lenaeus (and Λῆναι), but lionesses are also regular members of Dionysus' cortège. *Euax* at 98, in spite of Varro's gloss,[22] establishes an explicit link to the Bacchic atmosphere. At night, the god attracts (*prolicit*) the old woman away, and her final promise to follow him, *persequar*, seals her status as a Bacchant of sorts, indeed we are reminded of

---

19 Flower 2000, 27.
20 Gruen 1990, 152 n. 146.
21 The term goes back to Ross 1975, 78, cf. Hinds 1998, 1–5.
22 *LL* 7.93 *Euax verbum nihil significat, sed effutitum naturaliter est ...*

sequi deum at the end of Horace's most 'Bacchic' ode, 3.25. Several further examples could be adduced, and I refer for this and other instances to Dorota Dutsch's excellent treatment, which highlights the pervasiveness of the Bacchic issue in Plautus as a privileged locus for the problematization of gender roles and theatricality.[23]

For Plautus, the mastertext of engagement with Dionysiac themes is Euripides' *Bacchae*, a repository of insights into the nature of theatre. The play enjoyed great popularity in Greece and Magna Graecia, and while earlier discussions of its impact on *Amphitruo* posited the existence of a Southern Italian intermediary, perhaps by Rhinton of Tarentum, Niall Slater[24] has convincingly argued that the contact was probably direct. In this most unusual of Plautine plays, the metatheatrical dimension is key. So is the exploration of themes and concerns which we may well term 'Bacchic': the shifting boundaries between genders; the problematic nature of personal identity, which is subject to splitting and doubling; or the related issue of dressing up and changing costumes, which is linked to ritual features of the Dionysiac cult and in this context portends disaster and death, as Seneca's Thyestes will find out at his own peril.[25] Since I have chosen to focus on issues of literary history I cannot do justice to this line of argument, which would deserve a detailed treatment. There can be no doubt, however, that a grammar of Bacchic themes spans a large number of dramatic texts and fragments, and is closely connected with the very essence of the tragic experience as a locus for exploding certainties and exploring the uncanny.[26]

3

Let us go back to Livy for a moment. Rather than looking to Plautus for confirmation of the social and political implications of the Bacchanalian affair of 186, it is probably useful to do the opposite. For all its high political stakes, Livy structures his account in terms which are strikingly close to narrative models, so much so that it has been labelled a 'roman-feuilleton'.[27] Novelistic elements are

---

23 Dutsch 2008, 149–85.
24 Slater 1990.
25 Segal 1982, 169–70.
26 On the metadramatic aspects of Accius' *Bacchae* see now Zimmermann (2002). Ribbeck (1875) 569–76 is still useful.
27 Although, as Beard-North-Price 1998, 93 point out, 'some of the fiction may well go back to the second century itself', rather than being the product of Livy's pen. Cf. Gruen 1990, 64: 'the entire course of events smacks of a staged operation'. Suspicions stemming from the novelistic

much in evidence, with the love story between Ispala and Aebutius providing a focal point, esp. in 39.10, where the sexual implications of Bacchic licence resonate. Others have argued that Livy may have drawn from a drama about the affair.[28] I shall leave this suggestion aside, but I would like to draw attention to some specific theatrical elements of the narrative, which in general terms mirrors the story of the arrival and rejection of the cult of Dionysus as we know from Euripides' *Bacchae* as well as, we presume, from the Republican fragments. The *sacrificulus et vates* who arrives from Greece in Etruria and then in Rome[29] recalls the γόης ἐπῳδός of *Ba.* 234, and the subsequent description of the orgiastic, nocturnal rites is unsurprisingly similar. The development of the action is neatly subdivided into a sequence of scenes and dialogues, including the rhesis of the main witness, Ispala herself, who appears in front of the consul Postumius as the messenger does in *Bacchae*. Both ἄγγελοι are worried that their words may attract a punishment (perhaps, as Hispala suggests, an Euripidean *sparagmos*)[30], and both are reassured in similar terms (*Ba.* 672; Liv. 39.12.3). A theatrical element finds its way in Hispala's account of the rites: she claims that those who refused to take part in the impious deeds requested of them by the Bacchants were tied to machines which made them disappear into secret caves, as if they had been snatched by the gods, *rapti a dis* (39.13.13).[31] As it happens, archaeological evidence does confirm that such Bacchic temples existed,[32] but it is also clear that these *machinae*[33] are none other than the devices employed to stage the appearance of the *deus ex machina*, a pattern here neatly reversed to conjure up the opposite effect. Indeed, Dionysos' appearance at the beginning of *Bacchae* may well have been staged precisely in this manner.[34]

---

flavour of some aspects of Livy's account go back to the 19th century: see Tarditi 1954, 272–3. Cova 1974 is good on the literary and dramatic overtones, about which see Walsh 1996, who, however, ignores Cova's important contribution.
28 See Walsh 1996, contra Flower 2000, 30–1.
29 Livy 39.8.3–4 (I follow Briscoe's Teubner text): *Graecus ignobilis in Etruriam primum uenit nulla cum arte earum quas multas ad animorum corporumque cultum nobis eruditissima omnium gens inuexit, sacrificulus et uates; nec is qui aperta religione, propalam et quaestum et disciplinam profitendo, animos errore imbueret, sed occultorum et nocturnorum antistes sacrorum.*
30 Livy 39.13.5: *magnum sibi metum deorum occulta initia enuntiaret, maiorem multo dixit hominum esse, qui se indicem manibus suis discerpturi essent.*
31 Livy 39.13.13: *raptos a dis homines dici quos machinae inligatos ex conspectu in abditos specus abripiant; eos esse qui aut coniurare aut sociari facinoribus aut stuprum pati noluerint.*
32 Pailler 1976.
33 On these devices see Di Benedetto-Medda 1997, 19–22, 33. A *machina* is required at the end of Seneca's *Medea*, but its use is likely in Republican theatre as well: Boyle 2006, 187–8.
34 Di Benedetto-Medda 1997, 21.

The potential parallelism is intriguing for an act of commission and one of omission. Just like the Bacchic cult, Livy argues that drama itself came to Rome from Etruria, a detail which, as we will see in a moment, is signally absent in other Augustan discussions of the issue, even those dependent on the same source as Livy. Conversely, his important chapter on the origins of drama assigns no role to Bacchus.

4

A century and a half after the Bacchanalian affair unfolded, Virgil opens the Augustan cultural debate on Bacchus and poetry with a semi-incidental discussion about the origins of Roman drama under the aegis of the god towards the end of *Georgics* 2. In a book which is entirely dedicated to this god Virgil expands at 380–96 on a compact, if intriguing, exercise in comparative literary history, which is introduced in quasi-Ovidian fashion into a rather different context:

> non aliam ob culpam Baccho caper omnibus aris   380
> caeditur et ueteres ineunt proscaenia ludi,
> praemiaque ingeniis pagos et compita circum
> Thesidae posuere, atque inter pocula laeti
> mollibus in pratis unctos saluere per utres;
> nec non Ausonii, Troia gens missa, coloni   385
> uersibus incomptis ludunt risuque soluto,
> oraque corticibus sumunt horrenda cauatis,
> et te, Bacche, uocant per carmina laeta, tibique
> oscilla ex alta suspendunt mollia pinu.
> hinc omnis largo pubescit uinea fetu,   390
> complentur uallesque cauae saltusque profundi
> et quocumque deus circum caput egit honestum.
> ergo rite suum Baccho dicemus honorem
> carminibus patriis lancesque et liba feremus,
> et ductus cornu stabit sacer hircus ad aram   395
> pinguiaque in ueribus torrebimus exta colurnis.

for no other crime is it that a goat is slain to Bacchus at every altar, and the olden plays enter on the stage; for this the sons of Theseus set up prizes for wit in their villages and at the crossways, and gaily danced in the soft meadows on oiled goatskins. Even so Ausonia's swains, a race sent from Troy, disport with rude verses and laughter unrestrained, and put on hideous masks of hollow cork, and call on you, Bacchus, in joyous song, and to you hang waving amulets from the tall pine. Hence every vineyard ripens in generous increase; fullness comes to hollow valleys and deep glades, and every spot towards which the god has turned his comely face. Duly, then, in our country's songs we will chant for

Bacchus the praise he claims, bringing him cakes and dishes; the doomed he-goat, led by the horn, shall stand at the altar, and the rich flesh we will roast on spits of hazel. (transl. Fairclough-Goold).

In the first five lines, dealing with Greece and specifically with Athens, Virgil packs together in a very compressed form a number of different elements: a) the sacrifice of a goat to Bacchus, i. e. Dionysus; b) the beginning of *ludi* connected with the sacrifice (the *et* at line 381 would admittedly deserve a separate discussion), i. e. the rural Dionysia; c) the institution of prizes around villages and crossroads; d) finally, a description of *askoliasmos*, a ritual dance carried out around the inflated skin of a goat and also part of the Dionysia.

The passage mixes together different stages of evolution, different genres and even different countries, providing in the process a number of aetiological suggestions which are never spelled out explicitly. The setting is Athenian, but the opening reference to Bacchus at 380 introduces a Roman theme, and the mention of *pagos* and *compita* at 382 would perhaps have reminded Romans of their own Paganalia, Liberalia and Compitalia festivals.[35] As for genres, *saluere per utres* describes *askoliasmos*, but *proscaenia* at 381, which Mynors regards as humorous,[36] makes it difficult to restrict the reference to this practice, given its technical connotation, especially when coupled with *ludi*. The notion, too, that *praemia ... ingeniis* refers to *askoliasmos*, being reserved, as Mynors puts it, for 'gifted members of the rustic community', is stretched. In fact, Donatus has no difficulty paraphrasing 'prizes which stimulated the minds of learned men to write'.[37] Rather than restricting his interest to *askoliasmos*, Virgil appears to be connecting together tragedy, comedy and dancing under the overall patronage of Dionysus/Bacchus.

As he switches to early Rome Virgil describes a primitive dramatic form, the *Fescennina carmina*, adding an interesting reference to the use of *oscilla*, masks, which again provide a proleptic reference to further stages in the evolution of theatrical performances.

Tracing the sources of Virgil's passage is a complicated affair. Meuli's comprehensive treatment in 1955 suggests that the direct source is Varro's lost book on Roman theatre mentioned by Jerome, *De scaenicis originibus*, although one detail, the 'punishment' of the billygoat as a danger to vines, occurs in an extant

---

35 Thomas 1988, 1.227. Contra Mynors 1990, 149.
36 Mynors 1990, 149.
37 *De comoedia* 5.7 (p.68 Kaibel) *nec deerant praemia quibus ad scribendum doctorum prouocarentur ingenia*.

fragment of *Res rusticae*.[38] Behind Varro he surmises Eratosthenes, the author, among many other things, of a tract on *On Old Comedy* (Περὶ τῆς ἀρχαίας κωμῳδίας),[39] whose theory on the origins of Greek drama Varro may have learnt from a scholion to Aratus. Indeed, Virgil would represent a key source for reconstructing the 'Erastothenic theory', which differs substantially from Aristotle's well-known take on the issue in the *Poetics*. Severe difficulties arise, as Pickard-Cambridge pointed out long ago,[40] in the reconstruction of a theory for which the one extant testimony is a line of Eratosthenes' aetiological poem *Erigone* (*Erigona* fr. xxxii Hiller = 22 Powell = 4 Rosokoki) transmitted by Hyginus[41] –'In Icaria, where they first danced around the goat' (Ἰκαριοῖ, τόθι πρῶτα περὶ τράγον ὠρχήσαντο) –, and a very problematic line at that.[42]

But if the general Varronian ascendance of this account is likely, as indeed is the case for Livy as well, some elements are not incompatible with Aristotle's own theory, such as the spontaneous nature of early dramatic activity, which Aristotle calls 'extemporary' (1449a9 αὐτοσχεδιαστικῆς), and Virgil conveys through the

---

[38] 1.2.18–20 (text Heurgon, Budé) *quaedam enim pecudes culturae sunt inimicae ac ueneno, ut istae quas dixti caprae. haec enim omnia nouella sata carpendo corrumpunt, non minimum uites atque oleas. [19] itaque propterea institutum diuersa de causa ut e caprino genere ad alii dei aram hostia adduceretur, ad alii non sacrificaretur, cum ab eodem odio alter uidere nollet, alter etiam uidere pereuntem uellet. sic factum ut Libero Patri, repertori uitis, irci immolarentur, proinde ut capite darent poenas; contra ut Mineruae caprini generis nihil immolarent propter oleam, quod eam quam laeserit fieri dicunt sterilem: eius enim saliuam esse fructuis uenenum; [20] hoc nomine etiam Athenis in arcem non inigi, praeterquam semel ad necessarium sacrificium, ne arbor olea, quae primum dicitur ibi nata, a capra tangi possit. nec ullae, inquam, pecudes agri culturae sunt propriae, nisi quae agrum opere, quo cultior sit, adiuuare, ut eae quae iunctae arare possunt.*
[39] The fragments are collected by Strecker 1884 and now Bagordo 1998.
[40] Pickard-Cambridge 1962, 72–4. His scepticism is endorsed by the author of the most recent treatment of this line, Broggiato (2014).
[41] Hyginus, *de astronomia* 2.4.2 (text Le Boeuffle, Budé, but I quote Eratosthenes' line according to Powell): *nonnulli hunc Icarum Erigones patrem dixerunt, cui propter iustitiam et pietatem existimatur Liber pater uinum et uitem et uuam tradidisse, ut ostenderet hominibus quomodo sereretur, et quid ex eo nasceretur; et, cum esset natum, quomodo id uti oporteret. qui cum seuisset uitem et diligentissime administrando floridam facile fecisset, dicitur hircus in uineam se coniecisse et quae ibi tenerrima folia uideret, decerpsisse. quo facto Icarum irato animo tulisse eumque interfecisse, et ex pelle eius utrem fecisse ac uento plenum praeligasse, et in medium proiecisse suosque sodales circum eum saltare coegisse. itaque Eratosthenes ait:* Ἰκαριοῖ, τόθι πρῶτα περὶ τράγον ὠρχήσαντο.
[42] The key περὶ τράγον is an emendation by Johann Soter (1534) for the mss. περιστραγον **D**, περιστρατον **Eg** and πεστρατον **G** (Ἰκαριοῖ is also an emendation, by Hiller). See Broggiato 2014 for a detailed discussion of the text and the numerous emendations proposed. She finally endorses περὶ τράγον after offering a fresh explanation of how the sigma could have found its way in the text (the change from gamma to tau in τράγον is easily accounted for, and τράγον would be *difficilior*).

image of rustic early festivals happening *inter pocula* (383) and yielding *incompti versus* (386); the connection with Dionysus/Bacchus, which Aristotle packs into his reference to dithyrambs as the source of tragedy and phallic dances as that of comedy; the key role of dancing in the early stages of evolution, when this type of poetry was 'rather fit for dancing' (1449a23 ὀρχηστικωτέραν), before iambic trimeters replaced tetrameters, note line 384 *unctos saluere per utres*; perhaps even the suggestion, implicit *in pagos* and *compita circum* (382), that comedy emerged from performances held by travelling actors 'around the villages', (1148a36 κατὰ κώμας).[43]

Virgil's account, is as 'ideological' as Aristotle's, and in the end cannot help much as a source about the origins of Greek, and even of Roman theatre. Its overall import, however, is clear. Virgil has no hesitation in placing the whole spectrum of dramatic performances under the tutelage of Bacchus, and in identifying a significant source for their beginning in spontaneous, often licentious *carmina*. In so doing he achieves a double objective, as he manages to connect Roman theatre with its prestigious Greek ancestors while stressing that it is also rooted, almost independently, in the spontaneous practices of the simple but creative rustic life of early Italy. The description of its inhabitants as both *Ausonii ... coloni* and a 'a people sent from Troy' (385) encapsulates this double approach to identity and originality. *Ausonii*, a name which is used here for the first time in extant Latin, were the indigenous Latins and Rutulians,[44] before they mixed with any foreign people, which in any event were Trojans rather than Greek. Unlike Livy, Virgil makes no mention of Etruria as a cultural intermediary.

5

The almost total absence of Bacchus – a veritable 'absent presence' in Horace's discussions of the origins of drama is all the more intriguing given Virgil's precedent, but his systematic focus on a comparison with Greece is also markedly different.

Epistle to Augustus 139–55 rewrites the *Georgics*' account of the birth of *fescennina*:

---

43 1448a36, quoted by Thomas on 380–3, cf. Mynors on 382, who connects *pagos* with *komodia* but does not quote Aristotle.
44 Horsfall on 7.723, *EV* s. v.

agricolae prisci, fortes paruoque beati,
condita post frumenta leuantes tempore festo 140
corpus et ipsum animum spe finis dura ferentem,
cum sociis operum pueris et coniuge fida,
Tellurem porco, Siluanum lacte piabant,
floribus et uino Genium memorem breuis aeui
Fescennina per hunc inuenta licentia morem 145
uersibus alternis opprobria rustica fudit,
libertasque recurrentis accepta per annos
lusit amabiliter, donec iam saeuus apertam
in rabiem coepit uerti iocus et per honestas
ire domos impune minax. doluere cruento 150
dente lacessiti; fuit intactis quoque cura
condicione super communi; quin etiam lex
poenaque lata, malo quae nollet carmine quemquam
describi: uertere modum, formidine fustis
ad bene dicendum delectandumque redacti. 155

the farmers of old, a sturdy folk with simple wealth, when, harvesting the grain, they sought relief at holiday time for the body, as well as for the soul, which bore its toils in hope of the end, together with slaves and faithful wife, partners of their labours, used to propitiate Earth with swine, Silvanus with milk, and with flowers and wine the Genius who is ever mindful of the shortness of life. Through this custom came into use the Fescennine licence, which in alternate verse poured forth rustic taunts; and the freedom, welcomed each returning year, was innocently gay, till jest, now growing cruel, turned to open frenzy, and stalked amid the homes of honest folks, fearless in its threatening. Stung to the quick were they who were bitten by a tooth that drew blood, even those untouched felt concern for the common cause, and at last a law was carried with a penalty, forbidding the portrayal of any abusive strain. Men changed their tune, and terror of the cudgel led them back to goodly and gracious forms of speech. (transl. Fairclough).

The setting is the same, that of a rustic post-harvest feast characterised by a quasi-Epicurean reliance on simple pleasures. Bacchus is almost evoked at line 144, only to be passed over: these early farmers offered sacrifices to major deities, such as a pig to Tellus, replacing Virgil's much more evocative billygoat, milk to Silvanus and wine to Genius. Bacchus lurks behind the mention of wine and the reference to Silvanus, a deity often associated with Pan and somewhat redolent of Bacchus' own delight in the wildness of the countryside (and note the evocative *libertas* at 147).

But why is the god whom Virgil so emphatically associates with the emergence of early poetry removed from this primal scene? A first hint at a possible answer comes as the epistle describes the fruit of these early labours: not drama as such, but *fescennina carmina* marked from the onset by *licentia* and soon morphing into 'cruel taunts' (148–9 *saeuus ... / ... iocus*) and open rage (149 *in rabiem*) worthy of being sanctioned by law, a strongly negative view of the 'unrestrained laughter' mentioned by Virgil (386 *risu soluto*).[45] This autochthonous form of literary expression ends up in a blind alley. Rome will have a chance to get acquainted with theatre proper only after *Graecia capta* offered an attractive model for imitation and, following the Punic wars, Romans began to study in earnest Sophocles, Thespis and Aeschylus and to try their hand at translating. This they did with good results, being by nature *sublimis* and *acer* and displaying a natural propensity for a daring tragic style (166 *spirat tragicum satis et feliciter audet*), but, unfortunately, they failed to pay enough attention to the need for a very controlled and polished style as only *labor limae* could achieve. Horace thus emphasizes a contrast between Greece and Rome dependent not on the strength of inspiration, but on the severity of stylistic self-restraint, hardly a Bacchic forte. The god's absence in this context neatly contrasts his significant presence in other parts of Horace's oeuvre, especially the *Odes*, where he stands as the symbol of the desire to keep the polished and compact form of the *carmina* open to his liberating inspiration.

Ars poetica offers a similar, perhaps even starker assessment. Again, Bacchus is not named, but the inventor of tragic poetry, Thespis, is portrayed with his face coloured with must, and it will be only thanks to Aeschylus that decorum prevails on the stage, at least on the tragic stage, because archaic Greek comedy features the same excessive abuse which characterizes both *fescennina* and *palliata*. Rescue for the genre, at Rome, comes from an unexpected quarter: not the judicious poring over of Greek models, but, in a quasi-Callimachean move, the abandonment of their *uestigia* and the decision to celebrate *domestica facta* (287) both in *praetextae* and in *togatae*. Even the Romans' lack of natural inclination to *labor limae* is presented here as a remediable shortcoming (289–94): once this is eliminated, Rome can aspire to achieve in matters literary the same *gloria* which its military prowess already attracts.

The downplaying of Bacchus' role in the creation and development of drama is also made more noticeable by the fact that he is not completely absent from the *Epistles*. In 1.19 Horace states boldly that poetry is the preserve of winedrinkers, and poets form part of the cortège of the god together with Satyrs and Fauns – he mentions Homer and Ennius, but the latter qua epicist rather than playwright. Similarly, in the epistle to Florus he is referred to, incidentally, as patron of the poets, *scriptorum chorus*, who love the woods and seek from him rest and shade as opposed to the uninspiring noise of the city (*ep.* 2.2.77–8). In 2.1 his civilizing role is even wider, if, together with Romulus, Castor and Pollux he is responsible for steering mankind onto the path that leads to the end of wars and the establishment of boundaries and cities.

---

45 *Solutus* reinforces the metrical naïveté already conveyed by *versibus incomptis*.

Bacchus, or at least his *praeceptor* Silenus, does play a significant role in the *Ars* precisely where we would least expect it after his overall marginalization in the more predictable contexts. At *Ars* 220–50 Horace expands on satyric drama, arguing that this was created by the same author and at the same time as tragedy, and goes on to suggest that this is a viable genre in the Rome of his time. He has nothing against transitioning from the seriousness of tragedy, which he represents as a decorous lady, to the 'laughing' and 'clever-tongued' (*risores* and *dicaces*) Satyrs, especially since by that time spectators are likely to be 'drunk' and 'lawless' (224 *potus et exlex*). There are limits, however, to be observed. The transition cannot be bathetic, and the kings and heroes of tragedy cannot suddenly disappear into smoky taverns. Satyr drama, too, should conform to the golden rule of middle style, avoiding exclusive reliance on *inornata et dominantia nomina* (234) and striving to maintain a stylistic distinction between bawdy characters such as those of Caecilius' comedies and *Silenus, custos famulusque dei ... alumni* (239).

Here Bacchus's name is silenced, the nameless god is transformed into an innocuous ward, and Silenus is portrayed not as a drunken member of his retinue but as a respectable old sage, while the Fauni, 'dragged from the woods into the theatre' (244 *siluis deducti*), will have to refrain from *inmunda ... ignominiosaque dicta* (247). Such expressions offend the sensibilities of *equites*, well-born men and the wealthy, much as they appeal to sellers of fried chickpeas. Remarkably, Horace suggests as a viable option for Roman writers the composition of satyric *exodia* adhering to the middle style which are based on a double taming of Dionysiac inspiration: first the removal from their habitual countryside setting of Bacchic characters such as the Satyrs or Fauni (the countryside being the preferred setting for Bacchic inspiration in the *Odes*), and then their counterintuitive reconfiguration as characters which could rein in the disruptive potential of a drunken audience and steer it away from excessive vulgarity.

Horace's downplaying of Bacchus is in part predictable, in part perplexing. It is in keeping with his negative evaluation of archaic comedy, especially Plautus, whom he regards as a sloppy writer, far removed from the qualities and the models which are foremost in his hierarchy of taste. But even if we allow for a slightly ironic tone in the statement about Satyrs, the correlation he establishes between social standing and stylistic level still introduces a contrast between Bacchus' role in a social setting such as the theatre and the Bacchus of lyric poetry. The strictures against the Bacchic dimension of dramatic performances are couched in social terms – after all the fluid boundaries between poetic and social excess could be problematic in that context – but they hark back to a fundamental cultural opposition. In the world of lyric Bacchus is a positive source of emotion and inspiration for the enthused poet, but this is the Bacchus of Archilochus and Alcaeus, the medium for a transcendence of human boundaries in search of a heightened state of cognition and a more powerful poetic expression. The uniqueness of personal, even aristocratic inspiration is well removed from the potential rowdiness of *licentia*, particularly after *Graecia capta* has had time to work a pervasive impact on the style and practice of elevated poetry.

Bacchus and Liber are almost never mentioned outside the *Odes*, where they figure prominently.[46] But in the *Odes* Horace attempts a bold fusion between Dionysiac inspiration and Callimachean refinement for which he could find a suggestion in Lucretius' *De rerum natura*,[47] surely not in the early playwrights and not in Virgil's (or Tibullus')[48] Bacchus, who foregrounds a nostalgic aura of primitive spontaneity. If the reinvention of Latin literature under the sign of Greek influence had to be made the turning point in the history of Latin letters, and the aristocratic models of Greek literature acquire a unique position, then no nostalgia is possible for early rustic festivals and *incompti versus*. This time at least Bacchus and Liber must abandon the stage.

Acknowledgements

I am very grateful to Theodore Papanghelis, Stavros Frangoulidis, Richard Hunter, Stephen Harrison and Antonios Rengakos, who organised the Thessaloniki conference, as well as to Andrea Cucchiarelli and Fiachra Mac Góráin, who have read a draft of this paper and offered valuable criticism and suggestions.

Bibliography

Bagordo, A. (1998), *Die antiken Traktate über das Drama. Mit einer Sammlung der Fragmente*, Stuttgart-Leipzig.
Batinski, E. (1991), 'Horace's Rehabilitation of Bacchus', *CW* 84, 361–77.
Brink, C. O. (1962), 'Horace and Varro', in: *Varron* (Entretiens Hardt 9), Vandoeuvres-Genéve 1962, 175–206.
Broggiato, M. (2014), 'Eratosthenes, Icaria and the Origins of Tragedy', *Mnemosyne* 67, 885–99.
Casquero, M.-A. M., (2004), 'Plauto y el dios de la libertad y del vino: Líber-Dioniso-Baco', *Minerva* 17, 104–24.

---

[46] *Carm*. 1.12.22; 1.16.7; 1.18.7; 1.32.9; 2.19.7; 3.8.7; 3.21.21; 4.8.34; 4.12.14; 4.15.26; *Sat*. 1.4.89; *Epist*. 1.19.4; 2.1.5. See Batinski 1991.
[47] Schiesaro 2009, 70–1.
[48] See Georgics 2.255–8: *agricola et minio suffusus, Bacche, rubenti | primus inexperta duxit ab arte choros. | huic datus a pleno, memorabili munus, ouili | dux pecoris hirtus; duxerat hircus oues.*

Cova, P. V. (1974), 'Livio e la repressione dei Baccanali', *Athenaeum* 52, 1974, 82–109.
Cucchiarelli, A. (2011), 'Virgilio e l'invenzione dell''età augustea' (Modelli divini e linguaggio politico dalle 'Bucoliche' alle 'Georgiche')', *Lexis* 29, 229–74.
Di Benedetto, V., Medda, E. (1997), *La tragedia sulla scena. La tragedia greca in quanto spettacolo teatrale*, Turin.
Dutsch, D. M. (2008), *Feminine Discourse in Roman Comedy: On Echoes and Voices*, Oxford.
Fabre-Serris, J. (2009) 'Figures romaines de Dionysos à la fin du Ier siècle av. J.-C.', in: R. Duits, F. Quiviger (eds.), *Images of the Pagan Gods. Papers of a Conference in Memory of Jean Seznec*, London, 281–96.
Flower, H. (2000), '*Fabula de Bacchanalibus*: The Bacchanalian Cult of the Second Century BC and Roman Drama', in: G. Manuwald (ed.), *Identität und Alterität in der frührömischen Tragödie*, Würzburg, 23–35.
Freyburger, G. (2013), 'Liber-Bacchus dans la poésie augustéenne: du passé de Rome au temps d'Auguste', in: O. Devillers, G. Flamerie de Lachapelle (eds.), *Poésie augustéenne et mémoires du passé de Rome*, Paris-Bordeaux, 93–9.
Fuhrer, Th. (2011), 'Inszenierungen von Göttlichkeit. Die politische Rolle von Dionysos/Bacchus in der römischen Literatur', in: R. Schlesier (ed.), *A Different God? Dionysos and Ancient Polytheism*, Berlin-Boston, 373–89.
Gallini, C. (1963), 'Il travestismo rituale di Penteo', *Studi e materiali di storia delle religioni* 34, 211–28.
Gratwick, A. S. (1993), (ed.), *Plautus, Menaechmi*, Cambridge.
Gruen, E. S. (1990). 'The Bacchanalian Affair', in: *Studies in Greek Culture and Roman Policy*, Berkeley-Los Angeles-London, 34–78.
Hiller, E. (1872), *Eratosthenis carminum reliquiae*, Leipzig.
Hinds, S. (1998), *Allusion and Intertext. Dynamics of Appropriation in Roman Poetry*, Cambridge.
Jory, E. T. (1970), 'Associations of Actors in Rome', *Hermes* 98, 224–53.
La Penna A. (1963), *Orazio e l'ideologia del principato*, Turin.
Longo, A. (2004–2005), 'Concezioni e immagini dell'ispirazione poetica in Orazio', *Incontri trestini di filologia classica* 4, 429–78.
MacCary, W. T. (1975), 'The *Bacchae* in Plautus' *Casina*', *Hermes* 103, 459–63.
Mac Góráin, F. (2013), 'Virgil's Bacchus and the Roman Republic', in: J. Farrell, D. Nelis (eds.), *Augustan Poetry and the Roman Republic*, Oxford, 124–45.
―――― (2014), 'The Mixed Blessings of Bacchus in Virgil's *Georgics*', *Dictynna* 11, 2–14.
Massa-Pairault, F. H. (1984), 'Image et sens politique du thiase des tragiques latins à Ovide', in: *L'association dionysiaque dans les sociétés anciennes*, Rome, 199–226.
Mazzoli, G. (2011), 'Il vino nelle commedie di Plauto', *Sandalion* 32-33 [2009–2010], 43–56.
Meuli, K. (1955), 'Altrömischer Maskenbrauch', *MH* 12, 206–35 (= *Gesammelte Schriften*, Basel / Stuttgart 1975, 1.261–82).
Miller, J. F. (1991), 'Propertius' Hymn to Bacchus and Contemporary Poetry', *AJP* 112, 77–86.
Montanari, E. (1984), 'Figura e funzione di Liber pater nell'età repubblicana', in: *Studi e materiali di storia delle religioni* 8, 245–264 (now in Id., *Identità culturale e conflitti religiosi nella Roma repubblicana*, Rome 1988).
Mynors, R. A. B. (1990), (ed.), *Virgil, Georgics*, Oxford.
North, J. A. (1979), 'Religious toleration in Republican Rome', *PCPS* 25, 85–103.
O'Brien-Moore, A. (1924), *Madness in Ancient Literature*, Weimar.
Pailler, J.-M. (1976), '"*Raptos a diis homines dici* ..." (Tite-Live xxxix, 13): les Bacchanales et la possession par le nymphes', in: *Mélanges J. Heurgon*, Rome, 2.731–42.

_____ (1988), *Bacchanalia: la répression de 186 av. J.-C. à Rome et en Italie*, Rome.
Pickard-Cambridge, A. (1962), *Dithyramb Tragedy and Comedy*, revised by T. B. L. Webster, Oxford².
Porter, J. I. (2000), *The Invention of Dionysus: An Essay on the Birth of Tragedy*, Stanford.
Ribbeck, O. (1875), *Die römische Tragödie im Zeitalter der Republick*, Leipzig (reprinted Hildesheim 1968).
Ross, D. O. (1975), *Backgrounds to Augustan Poetry: Gallus, Elegy and Rome*, Cambridge.
Rousselle, R. (1987), 'Liber-Dionysus in Early Roman Drama', *CJ* 82, 193–8.
Sauron, G. (2007), 'L'actualité des Bacchantes d'Euripide dans les conflit idéologiques de la fin de l'époque hellénistique', in: F. H. Massa-Pairault, G. Sauron (eds.), *Appropriation et représentation du monde d'Alexandre à Cèsar*, Rome, 247–62.
Schiesaro, A. (2009), 'Horace's Bacchic Poetics', in: L. B. T. Houghton, M. Wyke (eds.), *Perceptions of Horace. A Roman Poet and His Readers*, Cambridge, 61–79.
Scullion, S. (2002), '"Nothing to do with Dionysos": Tragedy Misconceived as Ritual', *CQ* 52, 102–137.
Segal, Ch. (1982), *Dionysiac Poetics and Euripides' Bacchae*, Princeton.
Sharrock, A. (2009), *Reading Roman Comedy: Poetics and Playfulness in Plautus and Terence*, Cambridge.
Silk, M. S., Stern, J. P. (1981), *Nietzsche on Tragedy*, Cambridge.
Slater, N. (1990), 'Amphitruo, Bacchae, and Metatheatre', *Lexis* 5–6, 101–25.
Smith, R. A. (2007), '"*In vino civitas*": the Rehabilitation of Bacchus in Vergils' "Georgics"', *Vergilius* 53, 52–86.
Solmsen, F. (1942), 'Eratosthenes as Platonist and Poet', *AJP* 73, 192–213.
_____ (1947), 'Eratosthenes' *Erigone*: A Reconstruction', *TAPA* 78, 252–75.
Stevens, J. A. (1999), 'Seneca and Horace: Allegorical Technique in two *Odes* of Horace (*Hor. C.* 2. 19 and Sen. *Oed.* 403–508)', *Phoenix* 53, 281–307.
Stewart, Z. (1958), 'The *Amphitruo* of Plautus and Euripides' *Bacchae*', *TAPA* 89, 348–73.
_____ (1960), 'The god Nocturnus in Plautus' *Amphitruo*', *JRS* 50, 37–43.
Strecker, C. (1884), *De Lycophrone Euphronio Eratosthene comicorum interpretibus*, Greifswald.
Takács, S. S. (2000), 'Politics and Religion in the Bacchanalian Affair of 186 BCE', *HSCP* 100, 301–31.
Tarditi, G. (1954), 'La questione dei Baccanali a Roma nel 186 a. C.', *PP* 9, 265–87.
Thomas, R. F. (1988), (ed.), *Virgil, Georgics*, Cambridge.
Trevizam, M., Raimundo, R. de F. M. (2011), 'Papéis de Baco em Geórgicas II: figuraçao poética, religiosidade e história do teatro', *Nuntius Antiquus* 7, 79–103.
Walsh, P. G. (1996), 'Making a Drama out of a Crisis: Livy on the *Bacchanalia*', *G&R* 43, 188–203.
Waszink, J. H. (1948), 'Varro, Livy and Tertullian on the History of Roman Dramatic Art', *Vigiliae Christianae* 2, 224–42.
Wyler, S. (2008), 'Réhabilitation de Liber: ambiguïtés de la condamnation des images dionysiaques, de "l'affaire" des Bacchanales à Actium', in: S. Benoist, A. Daguet-Gagey (eds.), *Un discours en images de la condamnation de mémoire*, Metz, 229–44.
_____ (2013), 'An Augustan Trend Towards Dionysos: Around the 'Auditorium of Maecenas', in: A. Bernabé, et al. (eds.), *Redefining Dionysos*, Berlin-Boston, 541–53.
Zimmermann, B. (2002), ''Accius' und Euripides' *Bakchen*', in: S. Faller, G. Manuwald (eds.), *Accius und seine Zeit*, Würzburg, 337–43.

Niall W. Slater
Speculating in Unreal Estate: Locution, Locution, Locution

Every play makes a world – and every play makes a different world. Plautus's *Mostellaria* is in many ways a typical Roman comedy, with a young man in love spending money he doesn't have to buy the girl of his dreams out of slavery while depending on the slave Tranio to make it all come out alright somehow. In other ways it is a surprising play, built not only in a quiet residential quarter but also in a turbulent world of commerce and exchange. The *Mostellaria* is a tale of three houses – two of them partially visible on stage and a third embodied in Philolaches, the hapless 'hero' of the piece. The master plotter of the piece, the slave Tranio, makes a market in all these houses and in the process makes the world of the play.

Like all but two of Plautus's plays, we do not know exactly when the *Mostellaria* premiered. It has been argued that, on average, the amount of song in his plays (as opposed to spoken dialogue) increased in course of Plautus's career, and by that standard the *Mostellaria* is likely to be a later play, after 200 B.C. My interpretation of the play will not depend closely upon its dating,[1] but I would like to argue that its deep involvement in a world where property is readily bought and sold makes ever more sense the later we go in Plautus's lifetime. Roman theatre officially began in 240 B.C. in the celebrations for the end of the First Punic War, the war that gave Rome its first overseas province, the rich island of Sicily. The Second Punic War in turn took a tremendous toll on Roman resources, but it also ended with a victory that pumped more and more money into the Roman economy. Rome had a money economy well before the Punic Wars, but even centuries later not everyone lived in the money economy. The Roman ideal remained the self-sufficient small farmer, who grew virtually everything he needed for himself and his family and needed to participate in a wider economy only to acquire metal, tools, and other specialized goods by barter or money. There was a sharp and significant divide between a rural agricultural barter economy, where land was largely inherited, and an urban monetary economy in which property was increasingly bought and sold.

---

[1] Buck 1940, 85–7 dates the play to 193 B.C. (or soon thereafter) based on the reference to a public *porticus* in verses 908–9, as the first such structure in Rome was built by the aediles then; Schutter 1955 suggests at the *Megalenses* of that year. For further discussion of the date, see Leach 1969, 328 and n. 1.

The *Mostellaria* opens with the embodiment of these two different worlds in two feuding slaves, Grumio and Tranio.[2] Grumio the country slave sees himself as loyal to his old master, the head of the household, and appalled by the corruption into which the city slave Tranio has led his young master, Philolaches, the son of the house. Grumio appears only here, but his loud and abusive quarrel with Tranio allows Plautus to fill the audience in on some essential background information while warming them up with lots of insult comedy. The old master, Theopropides, has been gone on business for three years, and in the interval he charges that Tranio has corrupted Philolaches in every possible way:[3]

> nunc, dum tibi lubet licetque, pota, perde rem,   20
> corrumpe erilem adulescentem optumum;
> dies noctesque bibite, pergraecamini,
> amicas emite liberate, pascite
> parasitos, obsonate pollucibiliter.
> haecine mandavit tibi, quom peregre hinc it, senex?   25

> Now, while you want to and while you can, drink, squander,
> ruin our fine young master.
> Drink up day and night, live like Greeks,
> buy girlfriends, free them; entertain
> the entourage; hire the fancy catering.
> Is this what the old man trusted to you when he went abroad?[4]

As the scene ends, Grumio returns to the country farm, never to reappear, while Tranio heads down to the Piraeus to buy fish for dinner, presumably a luxury variety, emphatically joining the world of commerce as a consumer.

The stage is thus left empty for the appearance of the young man they have been arguing over, Philolaches. He introduces himself to us in a monologue that develops a single image at considerable length: he compares himself to a house,

---

[2] The staging is controversial here: does Grumio arrive at this moment from the country to confront Tranio, as Sonnenschein 1907, 60 and more recently Mariotti 1992 suggest, or is he driven out of the house mid-argument as most others suggest? Certainty is impossible, but if Tranio is staged as the driving force, expelling his enemy, as Perutelli 2000, 19–20 argues, by this exclusion Tranio links himself not just to the city but very specifically to the house itself. Cf. Frangoulidis 2014, esp. 127–8, for the implied contrast between Greek and Roman values as well.

[3] Cf. briefly Segal 1974, 98–9; when Grumio charges that 'your example and your teaching have done this' (*virtute id factum tua et magisterio tuo*, 33), he effectively says that the slave's *virtus* has deprived the young master of his own *virtus*. See also Della Corte 1972, 21–3 on Stoic elements in Grumio's characterization.

[4] Texts of Plautus are from de Melo 2012, translations mine unless otherwise noted.

well constructed by the original builders, his parents, but ruined by the lack of maintenance by a lazy tenant who then moves in:

> atque ubi illo immigrat nequam homo, indiligens 105
> cum pigra familia, immundus, instrenuos,
> hic iam aedibus vitium additur, bonae cum curantur male;
> atque illud saepe fit: tempestas venit,
> confringit tegulas imbricesque: ibi
> dominus indiligens reddere alias nevolt; 110
> venit imber, perlavit parietes, perpluont,
> tigna putefacit, perdit operam fabri:
> nequior factus iam est usus aedium.

> And when some worthless man moves in there, careless,
> together with a lazy household, dirty, a slacker,
> then the rot gets into the house, a good house but badly cared for,
> And that happens a lot: a storm comes,
> it breaks the tiles and gutters. Then
> the careless owner doesn't want to replace them.
> Rain comes in, soaks the walls, drenches through,
> rots the timbers, destroys the builder's edifice.
> The house becomes less habitable.

Note that this is a family house, inhabited not just by the feckless owner (*nequam homo, indiligens*) but a lazy household (*pigra familia*) as well: the building's ruin is a group project. Further on in the speech, Philolaches goes back and forth about the responsibility for its destruction: first it is his own fault entirely, then that of the destructive power of rain pouring through and rotting the structure:

> postea quom immigravi ingenium in meum, 135
> perdidi operam fabrorum ilico oppido.
> venit ignavia, ea mihi tempestas fuit,
> mi adventu suo grandinem imbrem[que] attulit;
> haec verecundiam mi et virtutis modum
> deturbavit detexitque a med ilico; 140
> postilla optigere me neglegens fui.
> continuo pro imbre amor advenit, pluit in corpus meum,
> is usque in pectus permanavit, permadefecit cor meum.

> After I moved into my own character,
> I destroyed the builders' work there completely.
> The easy life came in: that was my storm,
> it brought me hail and rain on its arrival.
> It whirled away my modesty and modicum of manhood
> and unroofed me utterly.
> After that, I didn't care about re-roofing myself.

Immediately Love arrived in place of rain, rained right into my body.
He seeped right into my breast and soaked my heart.

The storm that ruined him arrives on stage hereafter in the person of his girlfriend, Philematium, talking with her servant, and the eavesdropping Philolaches makes the connection explicitly:

> PHILOL.   O Venus venusta,
> haec illa est tempestas mea, mihi quae modestiam omnem
> detexit, tectus qua fui; tum mihi Amor et Cupido
> in pectus perpluit meum, neque iam umquam optigere possum:
> madent iam in corde parietes, periere haec oppido aedes.   165

> Philolaches. O charming Venus, there's my storm,
> the one that unroofed all my modesty,
> as much roof as I had; then Love and Desire
> rained right through my breast, and I can't ever cover up again:
> the walls of my heart are drenched, this house is completely done for.

The scene between the two women both adds to our background information and paints their characters in strong contrast. Philematium seems very young, charming, and grateful to Philolaches, who has bought her out of slavery to be his courtesan. The old servant Scapha is a former courtesan who tries to persuade the girl, based on her own experience, that she should use Philolaches solely for her own monetary advantage, because no woman's charms will last forever. Once again then, two very different systems of exchange are embodied for us on stage: the hardened Scapha speaks as the survivor and advocate of thoroughly monetized, pay-as-you-go relations between men and women, while Philematium lives in a world of reciprocal love[5] – for which her eavesdropping lover, Philolaches, would gladly exchange family and everything he owns:

---

[5] As part of a larger argument for parody of the *Odyssey* in this play, Janka 2004, 65–7 treats Philematium as 'eine Art Penelope unter den Hetären' (65). The qualification is worth noting; while like Penelope she is indeed interested in her own *fama*, Philematium sees a clear connection between her reputation and her financial success: *ut fama est homini, exin solet pecuniam invenire./ego si bonam famam mihi servasso, sat ero dives* (228–9, 'A person's reputation helps her find funds. If I keep my good reputation, I'll be rich enough.') Owens 2001 believes that Philematium becomes aware that Philolaches is eavesdropping and thus suggests (223): 'The courtesan assumes her Roman persona immediately after overhearing her admirer and removes it after Philolaches reveals himself at the end of the scene.' Though the scene certainly could be played this way, I am doubtful that it was so originally; nonetheless, the disagreement between Scapha and Philematium offers an intriguing female counterpoint to the Tranio/Grumio feud that opens the play.

> PHILOL. Siquidem hercle vendundust pater, venibit multo potius,
> quam te me vivo umquam sinam egere aut mendicare. 230
> SC. Quid illis futurum est ceteris qui te amant? PHILEM. Magis amabunt,
> quom <me> videbunt gratiam referre <bene mere>nti.
> PHILOL. Utinam nunc meus emortuos pater ad me nuntietur,
> ut ego exheredem meis bonis me faciam atque haec sit heres.

> Philol. If I have to sell my father, he'll be sold much sooner
> than I'll ever let you be in want or beg while I'm alive.
> Scapha. What'll happen to your other lovers?
> Philem.   They'll love me more,
> seeing me grateful to a man who deserves well.
> Philol. If only my dad's death were announced to me right now,
> so that I could disinherit myself and make her my heir.

So far there is nothing very much out of the ordinary in this scene: the jokes are standard ones to appeal to a Roman audience, and the young man's eagerness to kill off his father for the benefit of his girlfriend would offer a familiar Oedipal thrill.

The scene then takes a turn to something much less familiar, as Philematium asks for her mirror to make herself up nicely for meeting Philolaches. Because such scenes are familiar to us from later Roman literature,[6] we may miss some of the touches here:

> PHILEM. Cedo mi speculum et cum ornamentis arculam actutum, Scapha,
> ornata ut sim, quom huc adveniat Philolaches voluptas mea.
> SC. Mulier quae se suamque aetatem spernit, speculo ei usus est: 250
> quid opust speculo tibi, quae tute speculo speculum es maxumum?
> PHILOL. Ob istuc verbum, ne nequiquam, Scapha, tam lepide dixeris,
> dabo aliquid hodie peculi tibi, Philematium mea.

> Philem. Give me my mirror and jewel box at once, Scapha,
> so I'm all decked out when my darling Philolaches arrives.
> Scapha. Only a woman who worries about herself and her age needs a mirror.
> Why do you need a mirror? You're the mirror for the mirror yourself.
> Philol. For saying that, Scapha, not for free and so nicely,
> I'll give a bonus today – to you, my Philematium.

On one level, Scapha is simply complimenting the beauty of her mistress: she argues that only an older woman could need a mirror, not the young and beautiful Philematium, and some of her later lines, when she advises her against using make-up, support the idea of flattery here as the primary interpretation.

---

[6] Think only of Ovid's advice on using mirrors in the *Ars Amatoria* 3.136, 681.

Even so, Scapha's second line, the one that prompts the praise from the eavesdropping Philolaches, is a bit puzzling: in what way can Philematium be a mirror for the mirror, and the greatest mirror at that? Wolfgang de Melo in his new Loeb edition suggests in a note that the line is:

> A compliment on her complexion and especially her clear eyes; she can show the mirror more than the mirror can show her.[7]

English language commentators on this passage like to quote Shakespeare, either Ophelia on Hamlet before his madness, 'The glass of fashion and the mould of form' (*Hamlet*, Act 3, Scene 1, 153), or Lady Percy on Hotspur 'He was indeed the glass/Wherein the noble youth did dress themselves. (*Henry IV, Part 2*, Act 2, Scene 3, 22).[8] Yet this is a touch anachronistic. Today mirrors are very basic and unremarkable technology, but they have only been common and cheap since the nineteenth century – our silvered mirrors do not go back in the West before the Venetians in the sixteenth century, where they were familiar to nobility such as Hamlet and Hotspur, but not to the groundlings. Greek and Roman mirrors were polished metal, silver as we shall find in the *Mostellaria* scene, or bronze – and the latter in particular offered a dark and dim reflection.

We ought also to suspect a hint of parody here of both philosophical use of mirrors and of the mirror's rivalry with art and artistic representation. The philosophical use of mirrors was already a cliché in the next generation of Roman comedy and subject to parody.[9] In Terence's *Adelphoe*, old Demea talking to the slave Syrus boasts how he gives his son such good advice:

> DE. ...nil praetermitto: consuefacio: denique
> inspicere tamquam in speculum invitas omnium
> iubeo atque ex aliis sumere exemplum sibi.
> hoc facito. SY. Recte sane. DE. Hoc fugito. SY. Callide.   (*Adelphoe*, 414–7)

---

[7] de Melo 339 n. 4. This seems to follow Leo's notion that Philematium is in competition with the mirror; in his edition Leo offers as a parallel Meleager, *AP* 5, 143: ὁ στέφανος περὶ κρατὶ μαραίνεται Ἡλιοδώρας· αὐτὴ δ' ἐκλάμπει τοῦ στεφάνου στέφανος (cited in Fuchs 1944, 142 n.). The notion of the mirror may change the quality of the rivalry here, however.

[8] Fay 1902 *ad* 251, Sonnenschein 1907 *ad* 251. Fay 1902 and Merrill 1972 take *speculo* as 'dative of the person judging,' thus personifying the mirror, which makes Philolaches' perception of the mirror as a rival perhaps more plausible.

[9] One of the fullest accounts of the use of mirrors for philosophic self-examination appears in Apuleius's *Apology* 13–6. Apuleius traces back to Socrates himself the notion that flaws in one's character showed themselves in one's appearance, so a mirror could be used to study self-correction, although no actual philosophic text gives any hint of this until well after Plato. That some version of this idea was about in popularized philosophy already in the Hellenistic period seems clear from the jokes in Terence discussed here.

Dem. I never turn a blind eye. I teach him good habits. Above all I tell him to look into the lives of others as if into a mirror and to take from them an example for himself. 'Do this,' I say.
Syr. Quite right.
Dem. 'Avoid that.'
Syr. Splendid. (trans. Barsby)

Moments later, Syrus parodies this into cooking advice:

> conservis ad eundem istunc praecipio modum:
> hoc salsumst, hoc adustumst, hoc lautumst parum:
> illud recte: iterum sic memento. Sedulo
> moneo, quae possum pro mea sapientia:
> postremo tamquam in speculum in patinas, Demea,
> inspicere iubeo et moneo quid facto usus sit. (*Adelphoe*, 424–9)

I instruct my fellow slaves on the same principles as yours. 'Too salty,' I say. 'A bit burnt. Not clean enough. Just right: be sure to do the same next time.' I do my best to advise them with such wisdom as I have. Above all I tell them to look into the saucepans as if into a mirror, Demea, and I advise them what lessons to learn.[10]

Back in the *Mostellaria* scene then, Philematium is certainly superior in beauty to the image in her mirror – but we must not forget the hidden observer Philolaches, who is gazing at her – as if into a mirror – and drawing conclusions very different from those a father or philosopher might want him to.

After Scapha persuades her mistress not to apply any make-up or perfume, Philematium hands the mirror back – but first kisses it:

> PHILEM. Cape igitur speculum. PHILOL. Ei mihi misero, savium speculo dedit.   265
> nimis velim lapidem, qui ego illi speculo diminuam caput.
> SC. Linteum cape atque exterge tibi manus. PHILEM. Quid ita, obsecro?
> SC. Ut speculum tenuisti, metuo ne olant argentum manus:
> ne usquam argentum te accepisse suspicetur Philolaches.
> PHILOL. Non videor vidisse lenam callidiorem ullam alteras.   270
> ut lepide atque astute in mentem venit de speculo malae.

> Philem. Take the mirror then.
> Philol.   Oh me! She's kissed the mirror!
> I wish I had a stone to smash that mirror's head.
> Scapha. Take a towel and scrub your hands.
> Philem.   Why, please?
> Scapha. Since you held the mirror, I worry your hands might smell of silver;
> Don't let Philolaches suspect you've taken money from somewhere.

---

10 See Goldberg 2005, 150–1 on this discussion.

> Philol. I don't think I've ever seen a sharper madam anywhere.
> How smart and neatly that witch thought about the mirror!

Probably the performer here can play the kiss as an approval of the perfection of her own beauty without the addition of any cosmetics. For the eavesdropping Philolaches, however, the mirror becomes a rival, which he would like to destroy.[11] Scapha then tries to ward off a different interpretation of the mirror as evidence of a rival: we learn that the mirror is made of silver (perhaps then an expensive gift from Philolaches) when she warns against leaving the smell of silver as a trace on the girl's hands, which Philolaches might take as evidence of receiving money from a rival. Philolaches then ironically approves of the precautions of the clever old woman!

A good bit of commentary on this scene focuses on the so-called 'problem' of staging out in the street a scene that would most naturally take place indoors.[12] If we were particularly interested in chasing the lost Greek play that may stand behind Plautus's version, we could speculate about Plautine expansion, or the possible staging of the Greek scene on the *ekkyklema*, the rolling platform that could 'reveal' interior scenes.[13] Yet Plautus put or kept this scene in his Roman version for a purpose, a purpose which centers around one very visible and central prop, the mirror, and culminates with the rejection of the mirror in favor of Philematium herself. We shall leave mirrors for the moment, but they will be back.

Philolaches leaves his concealment and addresses the two women. Problems of staging continue. Philematium speaks as though the party now begins in the street:

> PHILEM. Age accumbe igitur. cedo aquam manibus, puere, appone hic
>   mensulam.
> vide, tali ubi sint. vin unguenta?
> PHILOL.   Quid opust? cum stacta accubo.   (308–09)
>
> Philem. Come on, lie back. Some water for our hands, slave, put the little table
>   here.

---

11 Fuchs 1944, 142–3 n. 3 notes how the threat to the object in the beloved's hand is a comic innovation over the simple wish in Greek epigram or lyric to be an object near the beloved (including a mirror! ἐγὼ δ' ἔσοπτρον εἴην, ὅπως ἀεὶ βλέπῃς με, *Carmina Anacreontica* 22 Preisendanz), while the form is thoroughly Plautine in animating the inanimate mirror (Fraenkel 2007, 75 = Fraenkel 1922, 106).
12 See for example Duckworth 1952, 126–7, arguing for 'unity of place' in the plays.
13 Grimal 1976, esp. 377–82 discusses the possibility that the Greek original represented a house with a πρόθυρον, a kind of porch, at the front, where both Philematium's make-up scene and the subsequent party might be more realistically set, but Plautus does not pause over these details with his audience.

See where the dice are. Do you want some perfume?
Philol.   What for? With my Obsession already next to me.

Is this vivid imagination, or have unnamed and unremarked servant figures brought dining couches and tables out into the street?[14] In a few more lines, Philolaches' already tipsy friend Callidamates and the latter's girlfriend Delphium stroll in and join the party. In the midst of lots of verbal and presumably also visual slapstick from the reeling Callidamates, Delphium gives him some advice:

DEL. Cave modo, ne prius in via accumbas,
quam illi, ubi lectus est stratus, concumbimus.   326–7

Del. Just watch that you don't lie down in the street before
we stretch out together, where the couch is laid.

The party then does apparently get going in the street in front of the house.

This extraordinary scene, which looks much more like a celebration at the end of a play rather than one near its beginning is interrupted by Tranio running back onto the stage with the dire news that, of course, Philolaches' father has just returned to town.[15] With lots more physical comedy, Tranio succeeds in moving the whole party of revelers into Philolaches' house with orders not to make a sound and locks them all inside. This exchange with another servant hints at the scheme Tranio is already improvising:

SPHAE.   Iussit maximo
opere orare, ut patrem aliquo absterreres modo,
ne intro iret ad se. TR. Quin etiam illi hoc dicito,
facturum <me>, ut ne etiam aspicere aedis audeat,
capite obvoluto ut fugiat cum summo metu.
clavem cedo atque abi intro atque occlude ostium,   425
et ego hinc occludam.– iube venire nunciam.
ludos ego hodie vivo praesenti hic seni
faciam, quod credo mortuo numquam fore.
concedam a foribus huc, hinc speculabor procul,
unde advenienti sarcinam imponam seni.   430
Sphae. He told me to beg you desperately
to scare away his father somehow so that he won't go inside.

---

14 As Katerina Philippides reminds me (pers. comm.), we have direct evidence for such silent servant figures in the mosaics of Menander's *Synaristosae* (on which see Slater 2014), the source for Plautus's *Cistellaria*.

15 For the relation of Tranio's monologue here to his opening confrontation with Grumio, see Averna 1977.

Tr. Sure; tell him I'll contrive
not only that he won't dare to peek in the house
but run away in terror with his head covered up.
Give me the key, go in, and lock the door;
I'll lock it from outside. Let him come now.
I'll put on a show for the old man today, while he's here alive,
that I'm sure he'll never get when he's dead.
I'll step back from the door and spy from here
how I can pull the wool over the old man's eyes when he arrives.

Tranio's promise to send the old man running with his head covered will soon be fulfilled. He takes up the performatively powerful position of eavesdropper to spy from a distance (*speculabor procul*, perhaps a military metaphor[16]) as the father arrives home – only to discover that where home *is* has become a question.

Theopropides begins with ironic thanks to Neptune and a curse upon himself if he ever ventures onto the sea again.[17] Tranio's scheme is to convince the old man that his house is not just empty but haunted – by an angry ghost he might have disturbed by knocking on the door:

> TH. ... pultando [pedibus] paene confregi hasce ambas <foris>.
> TR. Eho an tu tetigisti has aedis? TH. Cur non tangerem?   454–5
> quin pultando, inquam, paene confregi foris.   456
> TR. Tetigistin? TH. Tetigi, inquam, et pultavi. TR. Vah. TH. Quid est?
> TR. Male hercle factum. TH. Quid est negoti? TR. Non potest
> dici, quam indignum facinus fecisti et malum.
> TH. Quid iam? TR. Fuge, obsecro, atque abscede ab aedibus.   460
> fuge huc, fuge ad me propius. tetigistin foris?

> Th. I almost broke both both leaves of the door with my pounding.
> Tr. Oh, no, you touched the house?
> Th. Why not touch it? I said, I almost broke the doors with pounding.
> Tr. You really touched it? Th. I did – and pounded. Tr. Oh, woe!
> Th. What's up? Tr. A dire deed! Th. How so? Tr. I can't say
> what an awful and evil deed you've done.
> Th. And so? Tr. Flee, I beg you, get away from the house.
> Hither flee, flee nearer to me. You really touched the doors?

---

16 For other military language and a discussion of successive 'siege' scenes in the play, see Philippides 1999.
17 For Janka 2004, 68–9, this scene is key to setting Theopropides up as an Odysseus *manquè*: the survivor of Poseidon/Neptune's wrath, but also a gullible and superstitious fool who is putty in the hands of the real master manipulator in the play, Tranio.

Tranio proceeds to spin a richly detailed story of a guest murdered in the house years before, who then appeared to Philolaches in a dream and told him the whole story. As a result, Philolaches has had to vacate the house. This is a great ghost story – until the drunken and unruly partygoers inside the house forget their instructions and call out, whereupon Tranio even weaves that into his tale of horror:[18]

> INTVS. Heus, Tranio. TR. Non me appellabis, si sapis.   515
> nihil ego commerui, neque istas percussi fores.
> INTVS. Quaeso – <TR. Cave verbum faxis. TH. Dic> quid segreges
> <sermonem. TR. Apage hinc te. TH. Quae res> te agitat, Tranio?
> quicum istaec loquere? TR. An quaeso tu appellaveras?
> ita me di amabunt, mortuom illum credidi   520
> expostulare quia percussisses fores.
> sed tu, etiamne astas nec quae dico optemperas?
> TH. Quid faciam? TR. Cave respexis, fuge, [atque] operi caput.
>
> [From inside]. Hey, Tranio!
> Tr.   You won't call my name, if you're reasonable.
> I've done nothing wrong, and I didn't hit the door.
> [From inside]. Please –
> Tr.   Don't say a word.
> Th.   Tell me why you're cutting off
> the conversation.
> Tr.   Get ye hence!
> Th.   What's bothering you Tranio?
> Who are you talking to?
> Tr.   Please, did you call?
> For the love of the gods, I thought the dead man
> cried out because you'd pounded the door.
> But are you really still standing there and not doing what I say?
> Th. What should I do?
> Tr.   Don't look back, run, and cover your head.

Within a few more lines, Theopropides flees.

Tranio's troubles are just beginning, however. The moneylender Misargyrides, who advanced Philolaches the cash to buy his girlfriend's freedom, arrives – and with a cavalier disregard for offstage time,[19] Theopropides re-appears, claiming he met the man who sold him the house originally, and this man denies any

---

18 For a brief discussion of Tranio's 'subversive perception' of the old man's belief in ghosts, see Slater 1993, 121–2. Cf. Frangoulidis 2014, 130–5 for the very intriguing suggestion that the party itself, once moved inside, is the 'ghost' of previous revelry.
19 On this gap and possible stage management of the Greek original, see Barton 1972 and Lowe 1985, 8–9.

knowledge of any murder. Before we continue with the details of the plot, it is worth remarking on some implications of this claim for the world of the *Mostellaria*. Theopropides' house is not an old, ancestral family residence: he bought it and can even locate the buyer again. In contrast to the world of the country, then, the city (nominally Athens, since its port is Piraeus, but performatively Rome, with its Latin-speaking inhabitants) is a highly mobile economy – financed by a money supply so excessive that the moneylender's key problem is finding anyone to take his loans. Misargyrides' very first lines are:

> MIS. Scelestiorem ego annum argento faenori
> numquam ullum vidi quam hic mihi annus optigit.
> a mani ad noctem usque in foro dego diem,
> locare argenti nemini nummum queo.   535

> Mis. I've never seen a worse year for lending money at interest than this year that's hit me. From morning to late at night I wear away my day in the forum, but I can't lend even one silver coin to anybody.

The moneylender Misargyrides has come to collect the interest on the money he lent to young Philolaches. Tranio struggles to keep him away from Theopropides, but the father eventually figures out that his son indeed owes a substantial amount of money. Tranio's ingenious explanation is that the son used it to put down a deposit on a new house:

> TH.   Responde mihi: 635
> quid eo est argento factum? TR. Salvom est. TH. Solvite
> vosmet igitur, si salvomst. TR. Aedis filius
> tuos emit. TH. Aedis? TR. Aedis. TH. Euge, Philolaches
> patrissat: iam homo in mercatura vortitur.
> ain tu, aedis? TR. Aedis inquam. sed scin quoius modi?   640
> TH. Qui scire possum? TR. Vah. TH. Quid est? TR. Ne me roga.
> TH. Nam quid ita? TR. Speculoclaras, candorem merum.

> Th. Answer me: what's happened to the money?
> Tr. It's safe. Th. Then pay him
> yourselves, if it's safe. Tr. Your son has bought
> a house. Th. A house? Tr. A house. Th. Well done! Philolaches
> takes after his dad; he's a man with a turn for business.
> A house, you say? Tr. A house, I say. But, do you know what kind?
> Th. How can I? Tr. Wow! Th. What does 'wow' mean? Tr. Don't ask.
> Th. Why's that? Tr. A mirror-bright one, pure radiance.

Tranio's description of the house as *speculoclaras* has provoked some puzzlement. Some editors print it as two words: Fay then explains *speculo* as a dative of judgement, as though 'even a mirror would call the house splendid.'[20] De Melo and others, including the *Oxford Latin Dictionary*, take it as a unique instance of a Plautine compound meaning 'bright as a mirror.'[21] In either case, it is quite a novel formulation – and one that the audience, whether consciously or subconsciously, will connect with the shining stage property last seen at the center of Philematium's scene. The mirror-bright house is the fantasy object of desire with which Tranio tempts the old man, the vision that his son has turned into the kind of smart businessman he wants him to be – a mirror image, in fact, of the old man himself. Theopropides is thoroughly delighted with the prospect.

Tranio's problems grow worse when Theopropides wants to see the actual house, not just a verbal image. Tranio first claims not to remember where the house is – then offers this aside:

> TR.   Quid ego nunc agam,
> nisi ut in vicinum hunc proximum <rem conferam>,
> eas emisse aedis huius dicam filium?
> calidum hercle esse audivi optimum mendacium.   665
> quidquid dei dicunt, id decretumst dicere.

> Tr. What should I do now other than refer the business to our next-door neighbor and say that this is the house his son bought? I've heard your best lie is one that's served up piping hot. I'm resolved to say whatever the gods tell me.[22]

This of course is the other house on the stage – and Theopropides wants to inspect it immediately.

Tranio then approaches the neighbor Simo. His brilliant idea is to tell Simo that old Theopropides wants to build an addition to his house, part of a plan for marrying off his son. He will warn Theopropides against discussing the sale with Simo, however, alleging that Simo now regrets a bad deal he can't get out of. Tranio can thus keep two false tales spinning in the air at the same time. It helps, of course, that Simo seems to have watched the goings on next door in Theopropides' absence with envious amusement, as the young man partied his fortune away.[23] Now the father is home, and Simo asks at first with malicious curiosity:

---

[20] Fay 1902, 119 *ad* 645. This is also the text of Leo.
[21] *OLD* s. v.; cf. Merrill 1972, 92 *ad* 645. So also Lindsay 1905.
[22] Janka 2004, 75 even suggests this reference to 'whatever the gods say' functions as an appeal to the Muses for poetic inspiration, very much in keeping with Tranio's role as poet-improviser of the plot.
[23] As Stärk 1991, 121 says of Simo: 'Er ist ein Voyeur, der sich am flotten Treiben im Haus des Philolaches ebenso weidet wie an der nun bevorstehenden Züchtigung (vv. 722–43).'

SI	Numquid increpitavit filium?	750
TR. Tam liquidust quam liquida esse tempestas solet.		
nunc te hoc orare iussit opere maximo,		
ut sibi liceret inspicere hasce aedis tuas.		
SI. Non sunt venales. TR. Scio equidem istuc. sed senex		
gynaeceum aedificare volt hic in suis		755
et balineas et ambulacrum et porticum.		
SI. Quid ergo somniavit?		

Simo.   Has [your master] thundered at his son?
Tranio. He's as calm as calm weather can be.
Now he wants me to ask you most urgently
to let him inspect your house.
Si. It's not for sale. Tr. Yes, I know that. But the old man
wants to build women's quarters here in his house
and baths and a walkway and portico.
Si. So what has he been dreaming about?

Simo sets up a brief return to the storm imagery so important to Philolaches' monologue on love as the storm that ruined his house, when he asks the boy if his father stormed or thundered (*increpitavit*, 750) at him.[24] With his play on *liquidus*, Tranio calms the storm – but the notion that the good weather (*tempestas*[25]) could easily turn stormy again remains near the surface. When Simo asks why his neighbor is so interested in architecture, he regards it as a dream (*somniavit*[26]), not a serious plan, and that image will recur later.

The scene that follows is Tranio's *tour de force* as architect of the plot and real estate agent extraordinaire. Plautus uses the architect image elsewhere.[27] Here Tranio invents 'some architect' who praised Simo's house to Theopropides as the basis for the house tour:

---

24 In Plautus, *Amph.* 1077, after Amphitruo has been struck down by Jupiter's thunderbolt and then revives, he says *totus timeo, ita med increpuit Iuppiter* (I'm completely terrified, the way Jupiter thundered me down). While the verb *increpo* quickly moves to include stormy language, the underlying natural image remains very much alive.
25 *tempestas* originally derives from *tempus* and can simply mean time or season: when Grumio tells Tranio right at the beginning that he will get in trouble 'in a short time' (*cis hercle paucas tempestates*, 18), the storm has not yet arisen – as it does the moment Philolaches comes on stage for his monologue.
26 The manuscripts at 757 actually read *quid conconsomniavit*. *quid consomniavit* will not scan, and *quid ergo somniavit* is Leo's solution, but the double-prefixed verb might make an intriguing Plautine invention for the case – since so many other things will double in this play.
27 *Miles* 901–2, 915, 919, 1139; *Poenulus* 1110.

> nam sibi laudavisse hasce ait architectonem 760
> nescio quem exaedificatas insanum bene;
> nunc hinc exemplum capere volt, nisi tu nevis.

> For he says some architect praised your house
> to him as insanely well built;
> now he wants to use it as a model house – unless you object.

One does have to be careful of over-translating here. 'Insanely' as an adverb sounds almost painfully modern, but it is attested elsewhere in Plautus.[28] Edwin Fay even suggests that *insanus* might be a term especially appropriate to architecture, since Cicero in the *Pro Milone* 53 refers to the vast substructures (*insanas illas substructiones*) of Clodius's house that could hide a thousand thugs.[29] Here it certainly suggests to Simo that Theopropides is a little cracked on the subject of houses – and the audience will likely remember that turn of phrase when at the end of the tour inside the house, in ring-compositional fashion, Theopropides himself will praise Simo's house:

> TR. Cuius modi gynaeceum? quid porticum? TH. Insanum bonam.
> non equidem ullam in publico esse maiorem hac existimo. (908–9)

> Tr. What sort are the women's quarters? How about the portico? Th. Insanely good.
> I don't think there's any bigger than this anywhere in public.

In between Tranio demonstrates his ability to make two different houses appear to the two old men – and indeed to incorporate them into the very fabric of this fantasy real estate. The visible part of the house of course is the exterior doorway on the stage. Modern reconstructions of the Plautine temporary stage often frame these doorways with exterior posts, based on vase representations of South Italian Greek stages and later wall paintings. Thus the audience may see actual wooden posts, although Leach and others suggest they are rather to be imagined to be part of the *porticus* inside the house, thus supposedly visible through the door to the onstage characters but not the audience.[30] This allows Tranio, as he spins his story, to turn the two old men first into doorposts themselves:

> TR. Age specta postes cuius modi,
> quanta firmitate facti et quanta crassitudine.

---

28 Chrysalus in *Bacchides* 761 undertakes an 'insanely great enterprise' (*insanum magnum molior negotium*); cf. *Miles* 24, where a dish makes 'insanely good eating' (*estur insanum bene*).
29 Fay 1902 *ad* 761.
30 Leach 1969, 327 and n. 1.

> TH. Non videor vidisse postis pulchriores. SI. Pol mihi 820
> eo pretio empti fuerant olim. TR. Audin 'fuerant' dicere?
> vix videtur continere lacrimas. TH. Quanti hosce emeras?
> SI. Tris minas pro istis duobus praeter vecturam dedi.
> TH. Hercle qui multo improbiores sunt quam a primo credidi.
> TR. Quapropter? TH. Quia edepol ambo ab infimo tarmes secat. 825
> TR. Intempestivos excisos credo, id eis vitium nocet.
> atque etiam nunc satis boni sunt, si sunt inducti pice;
> non enim haec pultiphagus opifex opera fecit barbarus.
> viden coagmenta in foribus? TH. Video. TR. Specta, quam arte dormiunt.
> TH. Dormiunt? TR. Illud quidem, ut conivent, volui dicere. 830
> satin habes? TH. Vt quidquid magis contemplo, tanto magis placet.

> Tr. Here, look at the fashion of the doorposts, what solid workmanship and how thick!
> Th. I don't think I've seen more beautiful posts. Si. By Pollux,
> I paid quite a price for them – once.
> Tr.   Do you hear that "once?"
> He can hardly keep from crying.
> Th.   How much did you pay for them?
> Si. I gave three minas for the two of them, freight extra.
> Th. By Hercules, they're a lot worse than I thought at first.
> Tr. How so?
> Th.   Because woodworm has undermined both from below.
> Tr. I think they were untimely cut, that's their problem.
> They're good enough now, if you slap some pitch on.
> no porridge-eating barbarian did this work.
> Do you see the door joints?
> Th.   I do.
> Tr.   See how snug they nap together.
> Th. "Nap?"
> Tr.   "Snap together," I meant to say.
> Got it?
> Th.   The more I look, the more I like.

The jokes here not only play on the *senes* as old, worm-eaten blockheads but, as Lowe points out, the reference to coating them with pitch suggests a particularly nasty Roman form of execution.[31]

Tranio's imagination then decorates the house with a still-life fresco of birds that only he can see:

> TR. Viden pictum, ubi ludificat cornix una volturios duos?
> TH. Non edepol video. TR. At ego video. nam inter volturios duos
> cornix astat, ea volturios duo vicissim vellicat.

---

[31] Lowe 1985, 24.

quaeso huc ad me specta, cornicem ut conspicere possies. 835
iam vides? TH. Profecto nullam equidem illic cornicem intuor.
TR. At tu isto ad vos optuere, quoniam cornicem nequis
conspicari, si volturios forte possis contui.
TH. Omnino, ut te absolvam, nullam pictam conspicio hic avem.
TR. Age, iam mitto, ignosco: aetate non quis optuerier. 840

Tr. Do you see the painting, where a crow is making a fool of two vultures?
Th. By Pollux, I don't.
Tr.   But I do: between the two vultures
there's a crow standing, and he plucks the two of them in turn.
Look over at me so you can spot the crow.
Do you see him already?
Th.   I don't see any crow at all there.
Tr. Well, you look toward the two of you, since you can't spot
the crow, maybe you can see the vultures.
Th. Alright, already, I give up, I don't see any painted bird here.
Tr. Fine, okay, I understand: you can't see because of your age.

Leach suggests that such a still-life scene would be highly unusual in a domestic context at Rome this early,[32] though not unknown in Hellenistic painting. It may be another expression of Tranio's ability to *pergraecari*, as well as making him the artist and the old men the expressions of his art.

Let me offer one more speculation about the once much-discussed dog at the end of this little sequence. When Theopropides is finally ready to go in, he spots a dog inside – and is afraid to enter. It takes both Tranio and Simo to reassure him before he crosses the threshold – whereupon Simo leaves. It is extremely unlikely that the dog is played by a dog: actors know better than to share the stage with real animals, if they can help it. While Thompson argued for a stuffed dog, earlier opinion largely divided between assuming that the audience was meant to imagine a real but unseen dog or an equally invisible artistic representation, but one like Tranio's description of the bird painting.[33] The comic impact of an imagined dog, however, would not be as strong as one with a real visual presence. I do wonder if the joke here might be that, while there is no painting of birds on the stage backdrop, there might be a painting of a guard dog – maybe even labelled CAVE

---

[32] Leach 1969, 327. The view of Knapp 1917, 144–6 that the painting is to be imagined on the exterior of the house seems quite unlikely, in Plautus's time or indeed much later.

[33] Thompson 1890. An earlier version of this paper was given at a conference on the *Mostellaria* at the State University of New York at Binghamton, and I am most grateful to John Starks for his invitation there. Starks produced and directed his own translation of the play there under the title, *The Ghoul Next Door*, and a stuffed dog was indeed a great success in that performance. For the dog in an imagined mosaic, see Sonnenschein 1907 *ad* 850, in a painting Knapp 1917, 147–8.

CANEM – and the audience knows that a painted dog is not about to attack anyone.[34] Finally, we might contemplate just here the title of the play, if indeed *Mostellaria* is the original title. While we regularly translate it *The Ghost Story*, its root, the diminutive *mostellum*, does not solely mean 'little ghost' but little *monstrum*, apparition, sign, and monster. The dog in Simo's house may be the precise parallel to the imagined ghost in Theopropides' house – and neither is a real *monstrum*.

While Tranio and Theopropides tour the interior of Simo's house, two slaves show up on stage, looking for their drunken master Callidamates at Theopropides' house. Under the conventions of Roman comedy, only after he has sent Tranio away does Theopropides spot them banging on the door of his supposedly haunted house:

> PIN.   Pergam pultare ostium.
> heus, reclude, heus, Tranio, etiamne aperis? TH. Quae haec est fabula?
> PIN. Etiamne aperis? Callidamati nostro adversum venimus.
> TH. Heus vos, pueri, quid istic agitis? quid istas aedis frangitis?
> PHAN. Heus senex, quid tu percontare ad te quod nihil attinet?   940
>
> Pinacium.   I'll persist in pounding the door.
> Hey, unlock this, hey, Tranio, open the door.
> Theo.   What's the story here?
> Pin. Won't you open the door? We've come for our master Callidamates.
> Theo. Hey, you slaves, what are you doing there? Why are you beating down the doors?
> Phaniscus. Hey, old man, why are you sticking your nose in what's none of your business?

Tranio's fantasy houses now begin crashing down. When Theopropides claims the house is empty, he gets a shock:

> PHAN. Non hic Philolaches adulescens habitat hisce in aedibus?   950
> TH. Habitavit, verum emigravit iam diu ex hisce aedibus.
> PIN. Senex hic elleborosust certe. PHAN. Erras pervorse, pater.
> nam nisi hinc hodie emigravit aut heri, certo scio
> hic habitare. TH. Quin sex menses iam hic nemo habitat. PIN. Somnias.
>
> Phan. Doesn't young Philolaches live here in this house?
> Theo. He did, but he moved from this house ages ago.
> Pin. This old man is definitely off his meds. Phan. You're way off, dad.

---

34 Knapp 1917, 147 notes the parallel to Encolpius's misadventures with the painted dog in Trimalchio's entrance hall in Petronius, *Sat.* 29.1, but does not suggest a connection. I think a deliberate nod to Plautus on Petronius's part would not be at all out of place in so theatrical a setting as Trimalchio's house. For Fay 1903, 251, the *Mostellaria*'s dog is reminiscent of Cerberus, with Tranio/Hermes leading a distinctly unheroic Theopropides/Heracles past the entrance, and such Underworld connections fit the *Satyrica* as well. Philippides 1999, 92–93 suggests the dog may be an avatar of Simo's wife here.

> Unless he moved out of here yesterday or today, I know for sure
> he lives here. Theo. Nobody's lived here for six months now. Pin. You're dreaming.

As the slaves fill in the details, the old man wakes up from his dream house purchase to the nightmare reality: his son has bought a slave girl, not a house. Left alone on stage, Theopropides realizes that he has no idea where he is. He confronts the returning Simo, trying to figure out how Tranio has duped them both, and they retreat to Simo's house to plan what to do.

This leaves the stage empty for the return of a disgusted Tranio. He tried to get his master and the party out of the house by the back way, but they have ignored and shut him out. In fact, they are reminding him that he is property:

> ubi ego me video venire[35] in meo foro   (1051)
>
> When I saw that I was being sold in the market ...

He also hears Theopropides coming out of the other house in time to hide and eavesdrop – and the result is that he knows the game is up. Theopropides plans to chain and torture him with the help of slaves borrowed from Simo.[36] When they do confront each other, though, Tranio manages to elude capture and takes refuge at the altar. Theopropides unsurprisingly fails to trick him into leaving the altar and rages at him:

> TH. Iam iubebo ignem et sarmenta, carnifex, circumdari.
> TR. Ne faxis, nam elixus esse quam assus soleo suavior.   1115
> TH. Exempla edepol faciam ego in te. TR. Quia placeo, exemplum expetis?
> TH. Loquere: quoius modi reliqui, quom hinc abibam, filium?
> TR. Cum pedibus, manibus, cum digitis, auribus, oculis, labris.

---

35 A fuller picture using this image appears at *Bacchides* 814–5, where the slave Chrysalus tells old Nicobulus: *o stulte, stulte, nescis nunc venire te;/atque in eopse astas lapide, ut praeco praedicat* (you fool, you fool, you don't know you yourself are being sold, and you're standing on the very block while the auctioneer calls the bids).

36 Do these *lorarii* appear on stage? Fay 1902, Sonnenschein 1907, and Collart 1970 all list these mute performers among the *dramatis personae* for this scene (Sturtevant 1925 and Merrill 1972 do not), but Theopropides tells them to hide inside the doorway of Simo's house (*ilico intra limen isti astate*, 1064), presumably so Tranio will not see them – so should the audience? Modern productions tend to include them just to enrich the stage picture, but they are arguably as or even more imaginary than the guardian dog. Moreover, as Thomas Jenkins has pointed out to me (pers. comm.), they are effectively different slaves in different stories: either the slaves that Theopropides claims he himself wishes to examine under torture to expose Simo's financial misdealings or the torturers Theopropides wishes to use against Tranio. Both are creations of the fictions they are embedded in.

Theo. I'll surround you with fire and kindling, you jailbird.[37]
Tran. Don't: I'm much more savory boiled than roasted.
Theo. I'll make an example of you! Tran. I'm so great, you want me as your example?
Theo. Tell me, what kind of son did I leave here when I went away?
Tran. One with feet, hands, fingers, ears, eyes, lips.

The discussion of 'examples' ties up a long chain of images in this play, beginning with Philolaches' use of the *exemplum* that a man is just like a house (lines 90, 103), through Tranio's insistence that his master wants to use Simo's house as an example for building (lines 762–3), to Theopropides promising to tell Simo the examples of how Tranio made a fool of him (*quis med exemplis hodie ludificatus est*, 1040). When Tranio deliberately misunderstands what kind of example Theopropides wants to make of him, however, I think more than punning is going on – as seen in the next exchange. What kind of a son did he leave? A human one, with four of five senses (touch, hearing, sight, taste) – and not a house.

There is no denying that Plautus wraps this play up quickly and arbitrarily. Finally sobered up, Callidamates re-appears as the ambassador for his embarrassed friend Philolaches.[38] He offers to be arbitrator between father and son – and father and slave. He persuades Tranio off the altar[39] and takes it for a seat of judgement himself. As Theopropides rages on, Tranio suggests one possible ending:

> TH. Quid ego nunc faciam? TR. Si amicus Diphilo aut Philemoni es,
> dicito eis, quo pacto tuos te servos ludificaverit: 1150
> optumas frustrationes dederis in comoediis.

> Theo. What will I do now? Tran. If you're a friend of Diphilus or Philemon,
> tell them how your slave played you:
> you can put your best bamboozlements into comedies.

---

[37] My translation here is influenced by the speculative but intriguing argument of Fontaine 2009, 174–6 that in the Greek original Tranio might have been explicitly labeled a βωμολόχος, a jackdaw or 'altar-lurker,' a scavenger perched on the altar.

[38] Many commentators find it odd that Philolaches does not face his father himself here (though if Parker 1989, 242 is right that 'the *servus callidus* ... is in large measure a figure for the *adulescens* himself,' the son's absence may not be felt as much by the Roman audience). Janka 2004 (esp. 69–70) suggests that Philolaches is a failed Telemachus, unable to grow up, and Callidamates a quasi-*deus ex machina* (cf. Duckworth 1952, 180 and n. 9, a '*homo ex machina*'), negotiating like Athena for an end of strife at the end of the *Odyssey*. Frangoulidis 2014, 137–8 offers a much more positive view of Callidamates as successfully negotiating a real compromise between the 'Greek' mores of the son and the previously much stricter Roman mores of the father.

[39] And why did he flee there in the first place? Because his fool of a master, Theopropides, terrified him into doing so when he appeared from the house (*inscitissimus/adveniens perterruit me*, 1135–6). In effect, Theopropides is the latest *monstrum* to pop out of the house (Thomas Jenkins, pers. comm., has suggested to me that 'stupidity [is] the real *monstrum* of the play').

Callidamates finally offers the truly persuasive argument for forgiveness: he and unnamed friends will band together to pay off Philolaches' debts for the girl and the parties. Theopropides is still unwilling to forgive Tranio for his role – until Tranio points out:

> TR. Quid gravaris? quasi non cras iam commeream aliam noxiam:
> ibi utrumque, et hoc et illud, poteris ulcisci probe. (1178–9)

> Tran. Why get so upset? As if I won't commit some other crime tomorrow!
> Then you can avenge both, today's and tomorrow, properly.

Whether such an argument could possibly convince a Roman slave owner is not the point. Tomorrow is another day, in which Tranio and Theopropides, like the Roadrunner and Wile E. Coyote, will play the same *ludus* over and over again.[40] With a quick appeal for applause to the audience, the play is done.

And yet the *Mostellaria* – the ghost story without a ghost in it – is not just any and every Roman comedy, nor Tranio every *servus callidus*. Tranio has an extraordinary ability to understand the desires that motivate others and to make them see things that are not there. He is a builder of dream castles, a top agent in the world of unreal estate. He shows Theopropides a fantastic house bargain, in which the old man sees both profit and the image of his son as a smart real estate speculator – but he and Simo cannot see the reflection of themselves in the image of a house no less material than the one Theopropides thinks he has acquired. Fictionally the play takes place in an elsewhere, in Athens, so that world may look like a fantasy Greek housing bubble, until Callidamates bails out the market at the end, but it is more than a little caught up in the tides of new money sloshing through the Roman economy in the wake of the first two Punic wars. And if we in the audience look carefully, we may find a few distorted images of ourselves in the reflections looking back from the play.

Acknowledgements

I am deeply grateful to Professors Rengakos, Frangoulidis, and the organizing committee for the invitation to the conference and to the participants there for the most rewarding and rich discussion. My earlier thoughts on this play benefitted especially from comments by John Starks and Thomas Jenkins, the final version from Stephen Harrison's keen eye. The errors that remain are, alas, mine own.

---

[40] See the classic discussion of the Tranio/Theopropides scene in Segal 1987, 160–1.

Bibliography

Averna, D. (1977), 'Un monologo plautino (*Most.* 348 sgg.)', *Pan* 5, 79–89.
Barton, I. M. (1972), 'Tranio's Laconian Key', *G&R* 19, 25–31.
Buck, C. H. (1940), *A Chronology of the Plays of Plautus*, Baltimore.
Collart, J. (1970), *T. Maccius Plautus: Mostellaria*, Paris.
Della Corte, F. (1972), 'La commedia della fantasima', in: *Opuscula* II. Genoa [= *Dioniso* 15 (1952), 49–56], 17–24.
Duckworth, G. (1952), *The Nature of Roman Comedy*, Princeton.
Fay, E. W. (1902), *T. Macci Plauti Mostellaria*, Boston, New York, Chicago.
_____ (1903), 'Further Notes on the *Mostellaria* of Plautus', *AJP* 24, 245–77.
Fontaine, M. (2009), *Funny Words in Plautine Comedy*, Oxford.
Fraenkel, E. (2007), *Plautine Elements in Plautus,* tr. Tomas Drevikovsky and Frances Muecke, Oxford [= *Plautinisches im Plautus*, Berlin, 1922].
Frangoulidis, S. (2014), 'Renewal and Compromise in Plautus' *Mostellaria*', in: I. N. Perisynakis and E. Karakasis (eds.), *Plautine Trends: Studies in Plautine Comedy and its Reception*, Berlin and Boston, 127–39.
Fuchs, H. (1944), 'Zur Putzszene der Mostellaria', *Hermes* 79, 127–48.
Goldberg, S. (2005), *Constructing Literature in the Roman Republic*, Cambridge.
Grimal, P. (1976), 'La maison de Simon et celle de Théopropidès dans la Mostellaria', in: *L'Italie préromaine et la Rome républicaine: mélanges offerts à Jacques Heurgon*, vol. 1, Rome, 371–86.
Janka, M. (2004), 'Jenseits der Plautus-Analyse: Die *Mostellaria (Gespensterkomödie)* als komisch verkehrte *Odyssee*', in: M. Janka (ed.), *ΕΓΚΥΚΛΙΟΝ ΚΗΠΙΟΝ (Rundgärtchen): Zur Poesie, Historie und Fachliterature der Antike*, Munich and Leipzig, 55–77.
Knapp, C. (1917), 'References to Painting in Plautus and Terence', *Classical Philology* 12, 143–57.
Leach, E. W. (1969), '*De exemplo meo ipse aedificato*: An Organizing Idea in the *Mostellaria*', *Hermes* 97, 318–32.
Lowe, J. C. B. (1985), 'Plautine Innovations in the *Mostellaria* 529–857', *Phoenix* 39, 6–26.
Mariotti, I. (1992), 'La prima scena della Mostellaria di Plauto', *Museum Helveticum* 49, 105–23.
Merrill, F. R. (1972), *Titi Macci Plauti Mostellaria*, London.
Owens, W. (2001), 'Plautus' Satire of Roman Ideals in *Rudens, Amphitruo*, and *Mostellaria*', in: E. Tylawsky and C. Weiss (eds.), *Essays in Honor of Gordon Williams*, New Haven, 213–27.
Parker, H. (1989), 'Crucially Funny or Tranio on the Couch: The *Servus Callidus* and Jokes about Torture', *TAPA* 119, 233–46.
Perutelli, A. (2000), 'Il tema della casa nella *Mostellaria*', *Maia* 52, 19–34.
Philippides, K. (1999), 'Contrasting Houses, Contrasting Values: An Interpretation of Plautus' *Mostellaria* Based on Mirror Scenes', in: B. Zimmermann (ed.), *Griechisch-römische Komödie und Tragödie III (Drama* 8), Stuttgart and Weimar, 67–112.
Schutter, K. H. E. (1955), '*De Mostellariae Plautinae actae tempore*', in: P. de Jonge (ed.), *Ut pictura poesis: studia Latina Petro Iohanni Enk septuagenario oblata*, Leiden, 174–183.
Segal, E. (1974), 'The Business of Roman Comedy', in: G. K. Galinsky (ed.), *Perspectives of Roman Poetry*, Austin, 93–103.
_____ (1987), *Roman Laughter: The Comedy of Plautus*, 2nd ed, New York.

Slater, N. W. (1993), 'Improvisation in Plautus', in: G. Vogt-Spira (ed.), *Beiträge zur mündlichen Kultur der Römer* (*ScriptOralia* 47, series A, vol. 11), Tübingen, 113–24.

―――― (2014), 'The Evidence of the Zeugma *Synaristosai* Mosaic for Imperial Performance of Menander', in: S. Douglas Olson (ed.), *Ancient Comedy and Reception: Essays in Honor of Jeffrey Henderson*, Berlin, 366–74.

Sonnenschein, E. A. (1906), 'The Dog of the *Mostellaria*', *CR* 20, 440.

―――― (1907), *Titi Macci Plauti Mostellaria*, 2nd ed., Oxford.

Stärk, E. (1991), '*Mostellaria* oder *turbare* statt *sedare*', in: E. Lefèvre, E. Stark, and G. Vogt-Spira (eds.), *Plautus barbarus: sechs Kapitel zur Originalität des Plautus*, Tübingen, 107–140.

Sturtevant, E. H. (1925), *Titi Macci Plauti Mostellaria*, New Haven.

Thompson, E. S. (1890), 'Notes', *Classical Review* 4, 381.

Amy Richlin
The Kings of Comedy

pauper, mendicus, rex, parasitus, hariolus

Plautus, *Menaechmi* 76

Behind the door in the backdrop lives a potential cast of characters, as the prologue-speaker of *Menaechmi* says.[1] What is that king doing in the middle of the line, and in such dubious company? The king surrounded by poor man, beggar man, sponger has everything to do with the history behind the *palliata*: political, literary, popular, theatrical. The kings of comedy are both rulers and comedians, real and performed, subject and object; they mark the distance between high and low; they live in the space between dates and the *longue durée*. And sometimes their stories chalk the outline of what happens when free speech hits violent force.

Kings in Plautus: Ζεῖ ὁ βασιλιὰς Ἀλέξανδρος

Philip II had a daughter, Thessalonike, by a Thessalian wife, so that she was Alexander's half-sister.[2] She was married to Alexander's brutal successor in Macedon, Cassander, who founded the city now called Thessaloniki and named it after her; she died in 295 at the hand of one of her sons. The story goes that Alexander once made her immortal, so that, when she tried to drown herself in the sea at the news of his death, she turned into a mermaid. For centuries she would stop passing boats and ask her question: ζεῖ ὁ βασιλιὰς Ἀλέξανδρος; The sailors had to answer, ζεῖ καὶ βασιλεύει καὶ τὸν κόσμο κυριεύει – 'He lives, and is king, and rules the world' – or she would turn into a gorgon and wreck their ship. The *palliata* developed in a world still ruled by Alexander's kingship, especially in popular culture; just as Alexander, Thessalonike, mermaids, and gorgons live

---

1 Many thanks to Stavros Frangoulidis for his kindness and patience, and for the warm hospitality of the Eighth *Trends in Classics* Conference at Thessaloniki. Reading with Kristin Mann made me think about fables and their readers; thanks also to Dana Fields and S. Douglas Olson for allowing me to see work in progress, and to Olson for an essential unreality check; to Hans Bork, Douglas Fraleigh, and Brent Vine for linguistic bibliography; and especially to Arthur Eckstein for sharing his knowledge of real kings. Dedicated to Jeffrey Henderson, who introduced me to Aristophanes and got me started on the road to comedy.
2 For the historical Thessalonike, see Athenaeus 13.557c; Pausanias 8.7.7, 9.7.3; Carney 2000, 155. For the story, see Mitakidou/Manna 2002, 96.

side by side in this story, so kingship itself belongs in the 200s BCE to a cognitive world where history and story merge. In that world, after all, history-writers, story-tellers, comedians, and collectors lived side by side, where we find them assembled by Athenaeus in his own collecting-box, four centuries later.³

The plays of Plautus have certain kings in mind: Agathocles of Sicily (*Men.* 409–10, *Mos.* 775, *Ps.* 532) and his line (*Men.* 409–12); Alexander (*Mil.* 777, *Mos.* 775); Antiochus (*Poen.* 694); Attalus (*Per.* 339, *Poen.* 664); Darius (*Aul.* 86); Demetrius (*Cornicula*, frg. 61); Jason (*Ps.* 193); Philip (*Aul.* 86, 704, *Per.* 339); and Seleucus (*Mil.* 75, 948–51). Most of these king-names could denote any member of a dynasty, and to an audience in central Italy in the late 200s BCE these names would call to mind, among other things, the kings currently in the news: Demetrius II of Macedon (ruled 239–229); Philip V of Macedon, with whom the Romans were at war both during the Second Punic War and immediately afterwards (214– 205, 200–196); Attalus I, who ruled from the 230s to 197; Antiochus the Great, who reigned from 223–186 BCE, and whose outrageous life is the centerpiece of John Ma's essay on Hellenistic kings (2003). These king-names are associated with places at once exotic to a native of central Italy and familiar to a substantial number of slaves in this period: the Near East, Macedon, and Sicily. At the same time, stories of earlier comedians are interwoven with stories of the kings who ruled in the East and in Sicily from the 300s into the 200s, and these stories, too, could have accompanied the eastern slaves sold across the Latin language line into central Italy in the 200s. But even if the Plautine king references derive from some original Greek text (and Fraenkel did not think they did), the meaning of these kings and their locations would have been considerably different for an audience and players in third-century BCE Italy, as the *palliata* developed.⁴ The Near East stands for a particular range of meanings in Plautus, associated with trade, conquest, and escape from slavery or poverty. The king-names have similar associations.

---

3 For a related approach, see Hägg 2012, 99–147, a chapter entitled 'Popular Heroes: The Slave, the King, the Poet'. The slave is Aesop, the king is Alexander, and the poet is Homer, rather than the much humbler poets who will appear below; Hägg poses the whole as a study in what he calls 'open biography', following David Konstan's ideas on 'open texts'. Openness is also the point at issue here. On the merging of history and story in accounts of *parasiti*, see Tylawsky 2002, 66–77; cf. Gabba 1981, and below.
4 For extended discussion of kings in Plautus, see Fraenkel 2007, 11–14, 127–33, 291–92 nn. 26– 30, 342–45 nn. 97–113, 410–12 (Addenda).

Speakers in the plays sometimes appear not to have a specific king in mind; rather, each name means 'proverbially powerful king'. The unnamed Slave of Lyconides in *Aulularia*, clutching Euclio's pot of gold, shows how kings' gold stands for the jackpot, the winning lottery ticket, the ticket out of here (701-04):

> picis divitiis, qui aureos montis colunt,
> ego solus supero. nam istos reges ceteros
> memorare nolo, hominum mendicabula:
> ego sum ille rex Philippus. o lepidum diem!

> I alone surpass in wealth the griffins
> who live in the Golden Mountains. Those other kings –
> I don't even want to name them, that bunch of beggarmen:
> I am King Philip himself. Oh charming day!

His words epitomize the associations of kings in the *palliata*: wealth; the exotic East; and the transformation of slave into king – from the very bottom to the very top. Moreover, as in the *Menaechmi* prologue, the Slave here juxtaposes kings and beggars. The 'King Philip' he means is Philip II, whose gold coinage clinks through the plays, but Philip's reality here is on the same plane as that of the griffins and of the 'Golden Mountains', proverbially located in Persia (the griffins come from much farther away). Fraenkel pointed to the way in which lines like this conflate history with myth (2007, 11-12):

> Whether the parallel is taken from myth or history makes no difference to Plautus, as the passage just quoted from *Aulularia* shows, putting both [myth and history] next to each other. ... It must further be said that Philip of Macedon, too, is mentioned in Plautus in only very stereotyped expressions. ... There is a strong impression that for Plautus he was not the actual king of Macedon, the father of Alexander, but merely the eponym of the *Philippum aurum* ... which was familiar to the Romans at an early date, as prosody demonstrates.

He argues here that such seemingly topical references were part of what he calls 'Mediterranean lore of the Hellenistic period'. The point is that the historical Philip II turned into a gold coin well before the *palliata* got going; the King Philip in *Aulularia*, then, evokes Philip V only by a kind of syllepsis. It must be emphasized that a joke like this about Philip II does not belong to those hurt worst by Chaeronea (338), still within living memory as the *palliata* took shape in the early 200s. This joke comes from lower down and far away. It was clear to Fraenkel that stories circulated not only with the trade in decorated objects from the south to central Italy, but with the trade in human beings: 'one must not forget that the numerous Greek slaves and freedmen in Rome had brought with them the wondrous tales of their people and undoubtedly found eager listeners'. The tales changed focus and meaning as they traveled (2007, 66-67). Indeed, later Roman cultural commentators complained that elite children's minds were warped by the tales told them by their slave attendants; in the *palliata*, *nutrices* are not only represented within plays as taking their charges to the theater (*Cur.* 643–45), but are also addressed directly from the stage, along with the babies they are nursing (*Poen.* 28–31). 'What every child knows' is the basic ingredient of every culture; oral culture, in any case, reaches everyone within earshot.

Kings are named onstage in a limited range of contexts. They show up in the sarcastic *mirum quin* formula as an impossible model, like the king that a cat can look at. 'Strange that I wouldn't sell you on account of King Philip or Attalus, rather than on my own account, since you're mine', says Saturio in response to his daughter's protest (*mirum quin regi' Philippi caussa aut Attali/te potius vendam quam mea, quae sis mea*, *Per.* 339–40); 'Strange that Jupiter wouldn't turn me into King Philip or Dareus on account of you, triple-witch', says the miser Euclio (*mirum quin tua me caussa faciat Iuppiter/Philippum regem aut Dareum, trivenefica*, *Aul.* 85–86). These kings are fantasy figures and appear here as part of common parlance. In both cases, a relatively recent name is paired with a legendary name: Philip (which one?) with the imposing figure of the king who sent the Magna Mater to Rome in 204 BCE (Livy 29.11, 14); Philip (which one?) with the antique figure of Darius (so also Fraenkel 2007, 12). Each is there to point a sharp contrast with the lowly speaker – a *parasitus*, a poor man; a man selling his daughter for the price of a meal, a man with nothing in his house worth guarding. Kings exemplify what they are not.

Philip II is also present onstage by metonymy in his eponymous gold coinage; the figure of 'three hundred golden Philips' is cited eight times in *Poenulus* alone. Soldiers have Philips; to top them all, Curculio, masquerading as a soldier's freedman, says his soldier, on his way back from India, has stopped in Caria to arrange for a seven-foot statue of himself made 'out of Philip's gold' (*ex auro Philippo*), a perfect monument to his fantastic conquests (*factis monumentum suis*; *Cur.* 437–41). For a slave, famous kings are a byword for luxury; the *vilicus* in *Poenulus*, scamming the pimp, says he wants to go 'where I can be taken care of more delicately than the eyes of King Antiochus are taken care of' (*ubi ego curer mollius/quam regi Antiocho oculi curari solent*, 693–94). Best known to readers of the plays are the scenes in which slaves boast of their achievements, comparing themselves favorably to kings, as Tranio claims his own 'immortal deeds' (*facinora immortalia*) will outdo those of 'Alexander the Great' and Agathocles (*Mos.* 775–77); these kings exist on the same plane as Agamemnon and Ulysses when Chrysalus invokes them for the same purpose (*Bac.* 940, 946, 949–52 *mendicans*, 962–65). The Slave of Lyconides makes the same use of Philip and the griffins. The distance between slave and king is precipitous; Simo says to Pseudolus that, if Pseudolus brings off his coup, he will outdo King Agathocles in *virtus*, but that, if he fails, there is no reason why Simo, his owner, should not send him to the mill (*Ps.* 531–34).

Soldiers onstage, on the other hand, speak of kings as employers, or (boastfully) as actual opponents in battle. The soldier in *Miles* claims to be recruiting mercenaries as a favor to King Seleucus (75–77, 948–50); the slave Palaestrio asks him, 'Why don't you mind your own business instead of Seleucus's?' (*quin tu tuam rem cura potius quam Seleuci*, 951) – more sarcasm, designed to take him down a peg. Someone in *Cornicula* worked as a mercenary for Demetrius for ten years (frg. 61). The Advocati in *Poenulus* make up a story that the *vilicus* has been a mercenary in Sparta, working for King Attalus (663–64); the real Attalus I was active as Rome's ally against Philip V in both the First and Second Macedonian Wars. The Sicyonians, who had already set up a statue to him in their agora ten cubits high, subsequently voted him a golden statue – the kind of thing that inspired the fantasy of the soldier's statue in *Curculio*.[5] The *parasitus* Artotrogus describes the soldier in *Miles* as 'kingly in beauty' (*forma regia*, 10) and as victor over a general with golden armor (15–16), and Palaestrio says of this soldier that he claims that he surpasses the beauty of Alexander (777); again here, the line blurs between the mythic past of Homer (is this Paris?) and the already-legendary past of Greek conquest (is it Alexander the Great?). The same thing happens when the pimp Ballio says that people will call him 'King Jason' (*regem Iasonem*, *Ps.* 193); his wish conflates an actual king of (grain-rich) Thessaly in the generation before Philip II with the Iasion of mythology, consort of Demeter, recalling Fraenkel's concept of 'Mediterranean lore'.[6] Conversely, the entirely mythical King Pterela in *Amphitruo* is defeated by Amphitruo in single combat (*Am.* 252), a significant achievement in Roman terms and topical in and after 222 BCE, when Marcellus won the *spolia opima* at Clastidium (see Christenson 2000, *ad loc.*, and on Naevius's play *Clastidium*). Pterela's name is also funny – starts with a spit – which must be why he and his 'golden saucer' (*patera aurea*) appear so often (*Am.* 260–61, 413, 415, 419, 534–35, 746, 760, 769–92). Roman names do not start with *Pt-*; 'Ptolemy' does, however, and a string of kings named Ptolemy impinged on both Greek comedians and Italian politics in the 200s BCE.

Often, however, soldiers are not so specific, and Stasimus in *Trinummus* worries that he and his bankrupt owner will have to go 'to Asia or Cilicia' (599) and fight for 'some king' (*aliquem ad regem*, 722). The *rex* is the polar opposite of the

---

5 Plb. 21.20.3, 22.8.10, Livy 26.24.8–11 (helping Rome, 211 BCE); Livy 31.25.1, 31.33.2, 31.44.1–47.3, 32.8.9–16 (helping Rome, 200–198 BCE); Plb. 18.16 (the statues at Sicyon). See Ma 2013, 119 n. 40; 'gold statues' were gilded, not made of solid gold (Ma 2013, 116, 253–54).
6 Fraenkel, however, took this King Jason to be 'a slip' (2007, 23); 'rich Iasion' comes out of 'a rich complex of legends from Hellas' (44). For Jason of Pherae, king of Thessaly in the 370s, see Xenophon, *Hellenika* 6.1.5–16: boasting that his country has so much food that he can export grain, 6.1.11; cf. 6.4.29, a donation of a thousand cattle for sacrifice.

poor man, the beggar, and the slave, and all these low characters call themselves *rex* onstage when feeling grand; they say they are acting, or walking, or feasting 'like a king', using the Latin/Greek hybrid form *basilice*. The pimp Lycus, echoing Ballio, says *rex sum* (*Poen.* 671). What is less easy to explain, *parasiti* refer to their patrons as *reges*, and at this point things get more complicated.

Where did they come from?

In Roman comic texts from Plautus to Juvenal, *rex* means 'rich man', a word conventionally spoken by someone who identifies as not-rich: a relational term. When the *parasitus* Ergasilus speaks of *meus rex* (*Capt.* 92), he makes it clear that this is the man at whose dinner table he hopes to keep eating (cf. *As.* 919, *St.* 455). The oddity of this arrangement is not staged as odd in the plays, but it is marked by the fact that *rex* is a Latin word and *parasitus* is not, and indeed it is hard to translate *parasitus*. Fraenkel was troubled by this lexical inconcinnity, as he was by the word *basilice*, and gave it some thought.[7]

He reasons: Whereas 'the king and queen', who indeed show up as a couple in Plautus, belong to the world of folktales and children's games, *basileus* in Greek comedy refers to actual kings, especially kings in the East, especially those after Alexander (2007, 127–28). But *basileus* in Greek comedy does not denote the person who feeds a *parasitus*. Even *basilice*, in Latin, refers more to the qualities of folktale kings than to the qualities of rulers like Antiochus, and Fraenkel thought that Plautus, or someone before him in central Italy, might first have coined the term as *regie* (2007, 131, 411). 'For Roman sensibilities ... even in Republican times, the concept of *rex*, with all its associations, has a different, richer import than *basileus* had for the Athenians' (132). He instances Roman cult functions, and architectural landmarks like the *regia*, past which inhabitants of the city would have walked every day. In sum (133),

> The king who incorporates might and magnificence, and the *rex* and *regina* as a couple, were familiar symbols to the Romans. They spoke of king and pauper, of king and queen as we do. Thus the words from *Stichus* (133): *placet ille meus mihi mendicus: suos rex reginae placet* ('my beggar pleases me: her king pleases the queen') are not a covert allusion to political conditions in Athens but a figure of Roman daily speech with a hint of the fairy tale.

---

7 On the *rex* in Naevius, *Tarentilla* frg. 72–74R, see Wright 1974, 45–6, citing the discussion by Harsh 1936, who critiques, Fraenkel on this point. Harsh brings in some of the material from Athenaeus discussed below, alongside later evidence.

He might have added that the speaker of this line is a young woman defending her marriage, in defiance of her father's wishes. The old man has asked her and her sister, 'Am I going to let you be the wives of beggar husbands?' (*mendicis ... viris*, 132). Her replies to him insist that married love remains constant in poverty or wealth (*paupertate* vs. *olim in divitiis*, 134) and that her father married her to a husband (*viro*) and not to cash (*argento*, 136). Again, *rex* and *mendicus* are polar opposites. For her, 'king and queen' equals 'husband and wife', but also 'rich man and wife' (what she is not). Conversely, the guilty husband Lysidamus calls his wife *mea Iuno* and himself *tuo Iovi* (*Cas.* 230): flattery (cf. Fraenkel 2007, 69).

Then where did this *rex* acquire a *parasitus*? The *parasitus* was a robustly developed character in Greek comedy, and his shtick is taken over by the *palliata*, but it seems impossible that a social institution as fully fleshed-out as the *parasitus-rex* relationship could have worked onstage in cities where no similar institution existed: this is not a foreign institution, a literary import, in need of subtitles. Fraenkel suggested that, as with the *palliata* as a whole, a Greek costume clothed a local custom (2007, 343 n. 101):

> Perhaps even then Roman gentlemen of distinction occasionally had clowns or jongleurs about them who used this expression which was then transferred to the Greek παράσιτοι ('parasites'). Most odd is the *parasitus* whom Cato (*Agr.* 5.4) puts in the house of a Roman estate overseer.

Parasiti in Greek comedy had a stock list of skills, among which was making jokes; the most developed *parasiti* in Plautus all make jokes. As historians of Greek performance have pointed out, Hellenistic kings and tycoons had comedians as members of their entourages (Panayotakis 2014, 379–80; Tylawsky 2002, 66–67); if Fraenkel was right, the word *rex* belonged to a parallel custom that grew up on its own in central Italy, where the part of the *parasitus* belonged to the *scurra* (target of a slam by a *parasitus* at *Cur.* 296: self-reflexive, like the rest of this speech?). Otherwise, the adoption of such performers into great households in Rome in the 200s would have been a move similar to the adoption by Roman magistrates of honorific monuments, like the *columna rostrata* of C. Duilius (standing in the Forum, it commemorated Duilius's victory as consul in the naval battle of Mylae in 260). Both practices might be described as 'behavioral calques': the lexical difference caused by translation represents a real difference in meaning, on the ground.[8] Certainly the *parasiti* onstage are not associated with any markedly great houses; they eat in the kitchen or eat leftovers, rather than barging in on formal dinners; and in *Persa* the *parasitus* sponges off a slave – just like the *para-*

---

[8] For a comparable argument, see Bettini (2012, 32–60), on translation as transformation.

situs of the *vilicus* in Cato. (Saturio calls the slave Toxilus, who feeds him, not *rex* but *mi Iuppiter/terrestris* – 'my earthly Jupiter', *Per.* 99–100.) Indeed, Cato also warns against letting your *vilicus* have a *hariolus*, taking us back to the *Menaechmi* prologue.⁹

I will repeat here an observation of the archaeologist Ted Robinson on the theatrical vase paintings that circulated from Greece to Sicily to southern Italy to Campania before 300 BCE (2004, 207):

> It is perhaps time ... to consider the perspectives that some decades of post-colonial theory may offer for the general situation in South Italy. Two factors emerge very clearly. Firstly, a colonial society (such as the Greeks in South Italy) is inevitably changed in its transferral to foreign shores. And ... [w]hen it comes to their neighbours, recent studies have demonstrated that those aspects of Greek culture which appeared amongst the Italians were extremely unlikely simply to have been passively accepted. Material culture does not work like that. Foreign objects and concepts tend to be brought into existing value systems and are reinterpreted and used for the benefit of the adopters, usually to send messages to others within their own societies.

This principle is fundamental to what I have elsewhere referred to as 'the traffic in shtick' (Richlin forthcoming b). Jokes and comedians moved around the Mediterranean, sometimes with the slave trade, changing their meanings (but not their structures) from place to place, from time to time; they significantly changed their meanings as they shifted from Greek into Latin.

Then what about the *names* of kings in Plautus? Where does this kind of name come from?

Not from Old Comedy, although a wonder-tale like the one from *Aulularia* features in *Acharnians* (61–128), when the Athenian ambassadors return from a fabulous visit with the King of Persia, who uses the Golden Mountains as a latrine (82). They bring back with them the 'King's Eye' Pseudartabas (91–94): the ultimate source of the 'eyes of King Antiochus' in *Poenulus*? Nor do the Plautine kings come from Roman legendary history: there are no Tarquins in the *palliata*, and not even Servius Tullius, whom we might expect. Nor do they come from Roman tragedy, although, like Greek tragedy, it is full of kings. Euripides' Telephus lends his beggar costume to Dikaiopolis in *Acharnians* – a king who became a beggar,

---

9 See Dalby 1998, 69 on the *Chaldaei* who also appear at Cato, *Ag.* 5.4 as hangers-on of the *vilicus*, along with *haruspices* and augurs: 'Cato provides the earliest evidence that these Eastern magic-makers were at work in rural Italy. Roughly contemporary are the first occurrences of 'Chaldees' trading as magicians or astrologers in Aramaic literature (*Daniel* 1.4 and elsewhere) and in Greek'. See below on the Book of Daniel; Eastern wonder-working was to play a role in the First Sicilian Slave War in the 130s, led by Eunus, a slave from Apamea in Syria.

he was at home in comedy – but, while Ennius produced a *Telephus*, his character is not borrowed by the *palliata*. Mercurius in *Amphitruo* says flatly that kings do not belong in comedy (59–63):

> sit tragicomoedia:
> nam me perpetuo facere ut sit comoedia,   60
> reges quo veniant et di, non par arbitror.
> quid igitur? quoniam hic servos quoque partis habet,
> faciam sit, proinde ut dixi, tragicomoedia.

> Let it be a tragicomedy.
> Indeed, for me to make it an outright comedy,   60
> where kings come, and gods – I don't think that's right.
> What then? Since a slave also plays a part here,
> I'll make it, like I said, a tragicomedy.

Comedy belongs to slaves: literally true, in central Italy in the 200s, as I have argued elsewhere (Richlin 2014b).

With current events, we are getting warmer – closer to a view of kings from below. The pages of Livy's third decade are full of kings: kings of Macedonia, kings of Epirus (Pyrrhus was in Italy as the *palliata* was forming), kings in the East, kings of Egypt, kings of Africa, kings of Sicily. Embassies from the Ptolemies were in Rome in 273 BCE and again in 203; just possibly, an embassy also came from Seleucus II (reigned 246–225).[10] The Numidian king Syphax, says Livy, would have been paraded in Scipio's triumph in 201 BCE, if he had not died first; as it was, he had a grand public funeral. And indeed Polybius says Syphax *was* in Scipio's triumph, as Livy grudgingly concedes (30.45.3–5; Plb. 16.23.6). The kings of Sicily were of pressing interest to the *plebs* from the First Punic War onwards; in 216, Hieron II presented the beleaguered Romans with a golden statue of Victory, a shipload of grain, and reinforcements (Livy 22.37.5; Weinstock 1957, 221). His death, and the deeds of his three wicked daughters, affected the course of the Second Punic War and led to the sack of Syracuse, Marcellus's *ovatio*, and the display of loot, which, as Polybius said, moved the original owners to hatred (Plb. 9.10.7–10; Livy 26.21.7–

---

10 In line with Fraenkel's idea of kings as part of the city landscape, Katherine Welch (2003) argued that the *Atrium Regium* that burned down in the Forum fire of 210 was an early basilica, built to deal with the royal delegations that visited Rome in the 200s, as was the Graecostasis. Margaret Miles (2008, 87) accepts this interpretation in the course of her argument on the display of loot and grand imported materials. It is certainly the case that the wars of the 200s involved visits from royal delegations, for example the one from Hieron II that brought the gifts mentioned below, or one from Syphax in 210 BCE (Livy 27.4.5, *legati ab rege Syphace*). For a list of embassies and sources, see Welch 2003, 26, with details and reservations in Burton 2011, 105–08.

13, 29–32). Here we might fit in the list of the kings of Sicily at *Menaechmi* 409–12, which Fraenkel saw as different in kind from the other king-names in Plautus (2007, 11). Onstage, the prostitute Erotium aligns her recognition of Menaechmus, and his parentage, with the royal patriline (*Men.* 407–12):

> non ego te novi Menaechmum, Moscho prognatum patre
> qui Syracusis perhibere natus esse in Sicilia,
> ubi rex Agathocles regnator fuit et iterum Phintia,   409–10
> tertium Liparo, qui in morte regnum Hieroni tradidit,
> nunc Hiero est?

> Don't I recognize Menaechmus, sprung from his father Moschus,
> you who are said to have been born at Syracuse in Sicily,
> where King Agathocles was the ruler, and then Phintias,   409–10
> third, Liparo, who gave the kingdom to Hiero on his death,
> and now Hiero is [ruler]?

This is a sort of genealogy *puttanesca*. Agathocles, as seen above, made a big impression on popular memory, so that he could be cited as a byword for *virtus*, bloody leader of mercenaries though he was (King of Sicily 304–289 BCE); Hieron was indeed ruler of Syracuse 'now', in that Hieron II ruled there from 269–215. On the other hand, Phintias (tyrant of Acragas 288–279), was not related to Agathocles, and Liparo, as far as anyone can tell, never existed, although he sounds like the Lipari Islands, site of a major Roman naval defeat in the First Punic War. This king-list, then, might be summed up as a list of names that sound Sicilian, produced by an onstage character who is not an historian, for an audience most of whom could tell she was talking nonsense but who might not have been able to do better themselves. And she emphatically repeats the Latin form of 'king' – *rex*, *regnator*, *regnum*: domesticating them.

Even if Plautus's king-names are not copied directly from some Greek comedy, could this usage come from literature in some other way? If this usage is, as Fraenkel suggested, folkloristic, does it have literary cousins? Subliterary? The pair 'king and queen' in the 200s BCE did not evoke only folktales; in Alexandria, at least, the king and queen were real, so that we might expect to find them in Herodas, or in Theocritus, or in the fragments of Machon. But the real king and queen appear together only briefly (Theocritus, *Idyll* 15.23–24), in a conversation between two women; when the lust-crazed Bitinna in Herodas' *Mimiambi* swears by the queen (τὴν τύραννον, 5.77), this is probably a goddess; otherwise, not in comic performance. Machon's *Chreiai*, however – verse anecdotes about *parasiti* and other low-lifes – feature plenty of kings. All three writers played a part in the traffic in shtick: Theocritus moving from Syracuse to Alexandria, Herodas repeating jokes that show up in Plautus, Machon commodifying the tales of itinerant comedians.[11] But they did not export the king and queen.

We might expect to find kings in fables, a major folk form, and indeed what might be called 'kingness' is a recurring structural element in fables, although not as often as you would think. *Aesopica* 124, for example, tells the tale of the fox and the crow, and how the fox flatters the crow into dropping a piece of meat: 'You should definitely be king of the birds', says the fox (ὡς πρέπει αὐτῷ μάλιστα τῶν ὀρνέων βασιλεύειν). Fables are preoccupied precisely with the distance between high and low that appears in the king/beggar and king/slave contrast in the *palliata*; 'king' in a fable means 'high/powerful/violent', and in the fable of the fox and the crow the sense 'high' is underlined by the physical placement of the two animals. Scholars are divided in their interpretation of this aspect of fables: subversive or conservative? Do fables preach rebellion or resignation?[12] Most pertinent here is the polyvalence of fables as a form, a quality they share with jokes and comedy: the teller is covered by the multiplicity of possible interpretations, as well as by the form's sheer lowness.

Fables, however, very rarely mention any historical personage by name; pointed stories about real people certainly existed, by the thousand, but were understood to be a different form (see Gow 1965, 12–14). Yet king-names do appear in one of the central texts in the history of fables, the *Life of Aesop*, and here we find an evident cousin to the *palliata*.[13] Although scholars date this text, in its current form, to the 100s CE, the king-names very obviously belong to a much earlier time, or to no-time: Dionysius of Byzantium (79–80), Croesus king of Lydia (92–100), King Lycurgus of Babylon (101–23), and Nectanebo king of Egypt (105). Chapters 101–23 are recognized as a version of the Ahiqar Romance, an Aramaic tale dating before 500 BCE. As in the *palliata*, these kings have certain attributes in common, chiefly wealth: Dionysius is the owner of a buried treasure; Croesus was a byword for wealth and is historically associated with gold coinage; Nectanebo has a splendid court (112–15); Lycurgus (Aesop tells Nectanebo) has

---

[11] On shtick shared by Herodas and Plautus, see Richlin forthcoming b; on Machon, see further below.
[12] For discussion of fables before the 200s BCE, see duBois 2003, 170–77 (conservative); Forsdyke 2012, 9, 59–73 (polyvalent, possibly subversive); Hall 2013 (polyvalent); Holzberg 2002, 16 (conservative: Aesop 'definitely does not personify ... the common people's spirit of rebellion against oppressive rule'); Kurke 2011 (different meanings for different audiences); Mann 2015, 35–98 (subversive); Rothwell 1995 (strongly associated with slaves and the lower classes; several later discussions are indebted to this one). For later fables, see esp. Henderson 2001 on polyvalent kings in Phaedrus; also Fields in progress.
[13] Reference here is to the translation by Lloyd W. Daly in Hansen 1998, 111–62, based on *Vita G*.

winged men working for him (116), and sets up a golden statue of Aesop (123). Also as in the *palliata*, their reality is somewhat compromised: Croesus and Nectanebo were not contemporaries, while Dionysius belongs in Sicily, and Lycurgus does not belong in Babylon, although Babylon rings with kings. Unlike real kings, the ones in the *Life* compete with one another by way of riddles and diplomacy, for which they need the services of wise men like Aesop, and in the *Life*, after he is freed from slavery, Aesop travels around from king to king – the very model of an itinerant wise man, like Solon in the tale of Solon and Croesus or Daniel in the Book of Daniel.[14]

I bring up Daniel with intent. On a time-line stretching from 700 to 300, first we have Nebuchadnezzar (ruled 605–562), Chaldaean king of the Neo-Babylonian empire; then Croesus, king of Lydia 560–547, until he was unseated by the Persians under Cyrus, founder of the Achaemenid Empire (ruled from the 550s-530); then Belshazzar, the last king of Babylon (ruled 553–539), who also lost his kingdom to Cyrus; then Darius, third king of the Achaemenid Empire (ruled 522–486 BCE), the king who lost at Marathon; then Nectanebo I, founder of the last native dynasty of Egypt (ruled 379/8–361/0 BCE). Just as Aesop and Solon advised Croesus, and Croesus, as the legend goes, advised Cyrus instead of dying on the pyre, so Daniel, during the Babylonian captivity, advised first Nebuchadnezzar and then Belshazzar. Like Joseph with his unidentifiable Pharaoh, Daniel served as an interpreter of Nebuchadnezzar's dream (Dan. 2); as the Sicyonians would later do for Attalus, Nebuchadnezzar set up a giant golden statue of himself, which Daniel's fellow captives Shadrach, Meshach, and Abednego refused to worship, then enduring the fiery furnace without injury, a deed which Christian martyrs would later emulate (Dan. 3). For Belshazzar, Daniel famously interpreted the writing on the wall, which, like Croesus's Delphic oracle, should have taught Belshazzar to be careful (Dan. 5). But kings in these stories always find out the hard way. Like the *Life of Aesop*, the Book of Daniel was compiled at a later date – the Maccabean period, in the mid-160s BCE, when the Jews were resisting Antiochus IV Epiphanes – and it is believed that chapters 7–12 date to that period. The early chapters, however, are thought to belong to Aramaic folktales that go back at least to the Babylonian captivity, when the Jews suffered forced relocation: Shadrach, Meshach, and Abednego bore names given them by their captors (Dan. 1: 6–7).

---

14 On the Ahiqar Romance and the *Life of Aesop*, see Kurke 2011, 176–85; Winkler 1985, 279–80. See Winkler 280 on 'the indifference of storytellers to the tight grids of history and geography': 'Popular narrative gives famous names to its characters with no thought for chronology and changes them according to the fluctuations of what is currently famous among those with minimal education' (cf. Hägg 2012; see n. 3, above). On Solon and Croesus, see West 2003. On the Book of Daniel, see Hartman/Di Lella 2005, esp. 55–61 on the 'Romance of the Successful Courtier'.

The Book of Daniel has a long history as inspiration for resistance movements, and the parallels between Daniel and Aesop raise the question of the association between king stories and the Near East, and between king stories and the slave trade.[15]

Niklas Holzberg casually suggested that fables circulated into Greece through the slave trade with the Near East (2002, 15):

> It would, after all, be safe to say that the narrative texts brought from Mesopotamia only circulated in very rare cases as actual reading material, because the books of wisdom were written in a foreign language. It is much more reasonable to assume that, between the eighth and fifth centuries B.C., Greek familiarity with originally Babylonian fable literature was based almost exclusively on oral tradition. And who better to tell such fables than natives of the Near East now living in Greece, for example, educated citizens from the towns of Asia Minor who had been carried off as slaves?

It is unclear why Holzberg thought a person would need to be educated, or indeed a citizen, to understand fables like the tale of the fox and the crow or to tell tales about Aesop and the kings.[16] Those already enslaved were, historically, more likely than others to be carried off as slaves. Aesop, in the *Life*, starts out as a slave – a mute, agricultural slave – who then regains his voice (by divine intervention), poses a threat to the slave overseer, and is sold (like Joseph) to a slave trader who happens by; with other slaves in the trader's inventory, he is marketed first in Ephesus and then in Samos (17–20). In the *Life*, he is a Phrygian; elsewhere he is said to have been a Thracian or Lydian; and Holzberg lists the ethnic labels applied to fables in Greek texts: Libyan, Egyptian, Carian, Cyprian, Lydian, Phrygian, Cilician, Sybarite. The geographic jump into the western Mediterranean is a shock; the list hopscotches from mid-central and coastal Anatolia to the coast of Africa, and so to southern Italy. This is a significant geography.

Holzberg's argument anticipated a major development in the scholarly debate on ancient slavery. Did the Athenians, in fact, engage in a slave trade with the Near East – with the Anatolian- and Semitic-speaking peoples of Turkey and the Levant, and farther inland? Moses Finley argued that those cultures were not 'slave societies' in the technical sense, and historians have looked, like Finley, to the Black Sea trade (see Shaw 1992, 20). But recent work by David Lewis (2011) has demonstrated the commonness of eastern slaves in classical Attica; and Saskia Roselaar has placed Italian traders in the eastern Mediterranean in the early 200s (2012, 153–54; cf. Kay 2014, 13–14, 190, 198). If stories traveled with

---

[15] On Daniel and resistance, see Wessinger 2011 passim.
[16] See Forsdyke 2012, 59–73, 82–85 on slaves as carriers both of fables and of stories about Aesop.

slaves, then there were plenty of carriers in mainland Greece, and others who could have been carried all the way back to Italy. Not that transmission always has to be so direct; stories must also have filtered through language membranes in the hybrid cultures of Ionia and Anatolia, by way of intermarriage as well as slavery. Mothers and grandmothers tell stories, as well as *nutrices*. Fables must have come into Greek by this kind of osmosis as well as by the violent disruption of the slave trade.

Lewis's case depends, first of all, on slave names in Attic inscriptions, and he argues that ethnic names were probably 'bestowed after purchase in Attica and formulated to reflect a slave's (perceived) ethnic origin' (2011, 96) – if anything, ethnicities are underrepresented by re-naming, as some slaves were given Greek names. Among the names he first surveys from the manumission inscriptions in Hellenistic Delphi (97), there can be discerned a disturbing fashion for naming slaves after kings of the appropriate ethnicity: so Ἀλέξανδρος τὸ γένος Μακεδόνα; Σέλευκος τὸ γένος Σύρον, a name which reappears among the freedman guests at Trimalchio's dinner party. Compare 'Midas' in Aristophanes' *Wasps* (433). This practice, in turn, would undergo a violent re-claiming in the slave uprisings from the 130s onward, where slave leaders took on the names of real kings, as Eunus took the name Antiochus. Slaves were also named for luxury goods. Slaves named Λίβανος appear not only at Delphi but at Naupactus, the first identified as Syrian, the second as Arabian (Lewis 2011, 97); the name's geographic association is, then, outweighed by the fact that frankincense came from both places, so that one sort of expensive commodity bears the name of another – jarring, in *Asinaria*, where the slave Libanus boasts of his ability to bear pain.

Trade was wide in reach and grasp. Lewis, taking Old Comedy to be a useful caricature of Athenian reality, points out that the name Μάνης, which 'can be found in inscriptions from all over Asia Minor', was used by Pherecrates as a generic term for 'slave'; it is also the name of a mythical king (Hdt. 1.94.3).[17] Among the main sources of slaves, Lewis lists Paphlagonia, Caria, Lydia, Cilicia, and Syria, as well as Thrace, strongly recalling Holzberg's list of ethnic adjectives associated with fables. Lewis's Attic epigraphic sources are the Attic stelae, the inscriptions from Laureum, and the naval list, hence largely male, but he also uses Balbina Bäbler's catalogue of non-Greek gravestones, which include nurses and *paidagogoi*: more than half are persons from the Near East (Lewis 2011, 104). The selling of children into slavery, a common backstory in Plautus (*Captivi, Curculio, Persa, Poenulus, Rudens*), already appears in the 300s in Antiphanes'

---

[17] Lewis 2011, 97, 99. See Tordoff 2013, 24–27 for cautions on the relationship between slave onomastics onstage and in reality; not detrimental to Lewis's case.

Neottis: a trader brought a Syrian boy and his sister to Athens, where they were sold at auction (fr. 166 K–A). The label 'Syrian', Lewis observes, might have included Jews; in a discussion of the centrifugal trade '*away* from the Aegean world', he cites 'Theodorus of Tarentum, peddling his wares (good-looking young boys) in the Levant during Alexander's invasion', although this comes from Plutarch (*Alex.* 22; Lewis 2011, 109). So even the story of Daniel could have echoed as far as Italy. Both Aesop and his fables seem to have done so, if Ennius cited Aesop when he retold the fable of the lark and the farmer in his *Saturae*, as Gellius does.[18]

Philip Kay, in a brief account of the economic history of the 200s BCE in Rome, lists the assets of 'Rome's aristocratic plutocracy' (2014, 16–17) and instances the words for 'specialized workers' in Plautus as evidence for contemporary industry (229): a useful reminder that luxury goods are as familiar to the cleaners as they are to their owners. That trade with the Near East was part of the life of the audience of the *palliata* is strongly suggested by the arrival of the ship at *Stichus* 374–89, with its mixed cargo of silver, gold, cloth, purple dye, *lecti* with ivory and gold trim, Babylonian tapestries (*Babylonica et peristroma, tonsilia et tappetia*), musical slave-women, perfumes, and comedians (*parasiti*). The ship is newly arrived *ex Asia* (367). The old man in *Mostellaria* is just back from Egypt (440, 994); Egyptian and Syrian slave-women can be bought as drudges (*Mer.* 415); it is *Aegyptini* who carry the buckets around the Circus at the *ludi* (*Poen.* 1291). The soldier in *Truculentus* is a Babylonian (84, 202, 392, 472), although he talks like a Roman soldier (491). Ballio, threatening to beat his slaves piebald, says their bodies will be so multi-hued (*Ps.* 146–47):

> ut ne peristromata quidem aeque picta sint Campanica
> neque Alexandrina beluata tonsilia tappetia
>
> that not even Campanian tapestries are so embroidered,
> nor those Alexandrian cut-velvet carpets with the animal designs.

This is a joke, and a joke about beating; the audience has to have seen these things, or at least have a good idea of what they are.[19] Livy says that, after the Romans took Capua (210 BCE), the confiscated goods of the local magistrates were sold at Capua, while all Campanian free persons now subject to sale, among

---

18 Gell. 2.29.3–16, 20; see Courtney 1993, 13–16. Gellius quotes only two lines from Ennius's version of the fable; they are in *versus quadratus*, a choice that links them to several Roman popular oral forms.
19 Fraenkel considers this passage briefly among his examples of 'Mediterranean lore of the Hellenistic period' (2007, 12–14).

them some of these dignitaries and their families, would be sold at Rome (*libera corpora quae venum dari placuerat Romam mitti ac Romae venire*, 26.34.11). So some people sitting in the audience would have known these tapestries as trade goods, some as part of a former local identity.

All these elements matter if kings like those Aesop served are to reach central Italy in the 200s. There are certainly traces of Near Eastern child-minders in Attica, not only in Bäbler's inscriptions but in comic texts: the woman with the wineskin/baby in *Thesmophoriazousai* identifies the slave next to her, the one actually holding the baby, as her τίτθη (608–09), and later addresses this slave-woman as Μανία, an ethnic name that identifies her as Phrygian (739, 754).[20] Kinesias in *Lysistrata* enters with his baby, carried by a slave whom he addresses as Μάνης (908). In Theocritus *Idyll* 15 (late 270s BCE), the slave-woman whom Praxinoa assigns to stay home and mind the baby is named Φρυγία (42–43); Praxinoa and her friend Gorgo are identified as Syracusan women living in Alexandria. Another slave nurse lies among the lost pieces of Herodas, *Mimiambi* 9 – again, a scene of women together.

We must ask, then: if Athenian babies were, often enough, tended by slaves from the Near East, and this is one way in which Aesop and his fables reached the Greek mainland, why does it not show in the language? Especially in the language of comedy? Greek comic vocabulary is funny through coinages and wordplay, with a vivid mix of food, drink, and concrete objects in everyday use. Hybrid it is not: this is a huge difference from the comic language of Naevius and Plautus. Is it that, like the boy's sister in Antiphanes' *Neottis*, future wet-nurses were sold young, so that they lost their birth language and soaked up their owners' language before they ever told a story to a child? Stephen Colvin usefully points out, however, that 'although many slaves in Athens were foreign, ... it does not seem to have been part of the convention of the comic stage to characterize slaves' language as foreign' (2000, 292–93).[21] The paucity of Semitic, even Anatolian loan-words in Greek is well known; Greek just seems to have been a much less porous language than Latin (Janse 2002, 334). Momigliano argued that, in the early Hellenistic period, 'trends of thought emerged which reduced the distance between Greeks and non-Greeks', but that 'the intellectual influence

---

20 See Lewis 2011, 98–101. Cf. the *hetaira* named 'Mania' in Machon (188–210 Gow = Ath. 13.578b–d): Machon says 'it is shameful for a woman to have a Phrygian name/especially a *hetaira* from the middle of Hellas', 191–92; Gow takes her name to be the Greek 'Mănia', a pejorative nickname like others given to *hetairai*. Her story is discussed in Kurke 2002, 43–44.
21 See *contra* Sells 2013, who takes some of Colvin's material to indicate a 'language barrier' between owners and slaves. For Athenian perceptions of Phrygian speech, see duBois 2003, 210–11, on Euripides' *Orestes*.

of the barbarians was, however, felt in the Hellenistic world only to the extent to which they were capable of expressing themselves in Greek' (1971, 7). Not that we would need texts to see the degree to which Greek culture was influenced by the East, and the long history of this influence, as Sarah Morris has amply shown (1989, 1992). For our purposes, it must be significant that one of the few Greek words that linguists agree has a Semitic root is χρυσός: gold.[22]

What makes convention? How does the stage diverge from the street? It was not part of the Italian convention, either, to differentiate slaves' speech from their owners'; in the 200s, the Latin they speak is more or less the same: hybrid. I would put forward as a hypothesis that the lack of bilingual vocabulary in Greek comedy demonstrates that the people who made Greek comedy were different in kind – in experience – from the people who made the *palliata*, as their audiences were different from the people who watched the *palliata*. Both comedians and audience, in Italy, were hybrid, inflected by wars and mass enslavements. This brings us back to the *parasitus* and his *rex*.

The stories mice tell about cats

A great part of the fabric of Athenaeus's *Deipnosophistae* is made up of jokes, and much of Book 6 is taken up with stories about jokers: *parasiti* and *kolakes* – flatterers. All these stories are set in double quotation marks, as they are quoted from their reading by characters in this scrapbook symposium (the 'inner dialogue'), as well as by the character Athenaeus in the frame narrative (the 'outer dialogue'). So we have, not Machon, but "Machon".[23] Within this double framework, the stories are both fictionally fictional (excerpted from the eight hundred plays of Middle Comedy the long-winded Democritus says he has read, amidst a colossal run of fish stories, 8.336d–e) and fictionally nonfictional (excerpted from many histories, biographies, and collections of anecdotes, often specifically collections of humorous anecdotes); to this latter group I will here add the stories about the *kithara*-player Stratonicus and a few stories about the piper Dorion (Book 8), the stories of *gelôtopoioi* and *planoi* (Book 14), and the story of the poet Sotades (Book 14). These stories are 'historical' in that their characters once really existed, but, as with much grander histories, we always have to ask what they

---

22 On this issue, see also Jasanoff/Nussbaum 1996 (rebutting Martin Bernal); Hawkins 2010 (focusing on Anatolian languages). On gold, see Jasanoff/Nussbaum 1996, 197; it belongs to a lexical group associated with trade (types of cloth; spices; containers; commercial terms).
23 On the structure of the *Deipnosophistae* and its speakers, see Wilkins 2000b.

were for, and we are hampered by the fact that they are fragments, dislodged from their original context and embedded in someone else's story.[24] Some *parasiti* appear in both historical and comic fragments; all comic stories, as noted above, have multiple meanings. Madeleine Henry points out that many of the comic fragments as well as the anecdotes are preserved in Athenaeus and nowhere else: a sample skewed by food (2000, 508). Douglas Olson has shown, moreover, that the prose excerpts in Athenaeus are pervasively distorted, either by Athenaeus himself or by some intermediate source, so that elements in any story may be later add-ons (2015). What we have of the 200s BCE is a stitched-together Frankenstein's monster. Let's listen to it sing 'Puttin' on the Ritz'.

Elizabeth Tylawsky titled her book on the *parasitus* tradition *Saturio's Inheritance*, a title that captures three fundamental points: (a) the *parasitus* in Plautus has no *maiores*, although, like Plautine slaves, he lays claim to them; (b) the *parasitus* in Plautus is the direct descendant, or cousin, of *parasiti* in (Athenaeus's) Greek comedy, from Epicharmus in the 400s to Diodorus in the 200s, with the same self-identifying monologues, the same kinds of nicknames bestowed by 'the young men', and similar skill sets; (c) the Greek *parasiti* left a fungible legacy in the form of jokes. When Ergasilus, Gelasimus, and Saturio refer onstage to 'my jokebooks', this inheritance is part of the contents; as Saturio tells his daughter (*Per.* 392, 394–96),

> librorum eccillum habeo plenum soracum.
> ...
> dabuntur dotis tibi inde sescenti logei
> atque Attici omnes; nullum Siculum acceperis: 395
> cum hac dote poteris vel mendico nubere.
>
> Look, I've got a storage basket full of books.
> ...
> You'll have a dowry from here of six hundred *logei*,
> and all Athenian ones, you won't get a single Sicilian one: 395
> with this for a dowry you could even marry – a beggar.

A trade joke, contrasting the big time with the small time.

Another stop on the comic circuit was Alexandria, which draws special attention from the Naucratite Athenaeus and one of his characters, Plutarchus of

---

24 Leslie Kurke argues that the *Chreiai* of Machon have been invisible to historians partly because of the customary division between history and fiction (2002, 59, 62) – a false one, especially since, as Emilio Gabba pointed out (1981), readers of history after Alexander liked this line blurred. On the problems with reading fragments, see Stephens 2002.

Alexandria. Thus the writer Machon becomes a pivotal figure in Saturio's lineage, living at Alexandria in the mid-200s, where 'Athenaeus' says he produced his own comedies (14.664a).[25] In the inner dialogue, Plutarchus claims Machon as a native son and sets Machon's epitaph amidst his catalogue of *parasiti* (Ath. 6.241e–242a); there, Machon is a worthy follower of Old Comedy. In his *Chreiai*, as Athenaeus selected them, Machon retailed stories in which *parasiti* and other low-lifes say something funny, often in connection with a βασιλεύς, and Leslie Kurke argues that Machon in his own time was writing political verse: not just a collection of anecdotes, but marked by meter as something more. Certainly a book in iambic trimeter about comedians is a self-reflexive joke.[26] Gow thought that Machon's stories would have had practical value for professional comedians (1965, 24), and Kurke agrees (2002, 26), calling them 'jokes that appear to be composed for more casual streetcorner performances – whether by Machon himself or circulated anonymously' (2002, 61).

More precisely, the *Chreiai* are a simulacrum of standup, as Herodas' *Mimiambi* are a simulacrum of street mime; both constitute 'love and theft', in the sense outlined by Eric Lott, whereby a performer steals a low form that is not his own, but which he loves.[27] In Machon's case, at least, he had some claim to be writing the stories of people like himself – comedians – although lower down in the food chain. Comic performers, then, were commodified both in themselves and in the form of anecdotes – items to be collected in Hellenistic collections – just as comic actors circulated in the form of souvenirs, cheap terracotta figurines, for fans who could not afford bronzes.[28] Even their masks were sold in terracotta: double simulacra. At

---

25 This detail about Machon comes up in the fadeout to Book 14, as the voice of Athenaeus as narrator of the outer dialogue merges with that of the last named speaker, Aemilianus (14.662f).
26 Kurke argues that Machon's *Chreiai* are specifically a sendup of the lost *Chreiai* of Demetrius of Phaleron (2002, 41–44); *chreiai* are supposed to be morally improving, which Machon's, as Gow observed, are not: 'highly unsuitable for the schoolroom' (1965, 14).
27 Lott 1993, 17–18. Gow takes Machon's stories to have come partly from other collections, with an admixture of oral sources from Alexandria involving the Ptolemaic court (1965, 19–21). Cf. Wilkins 2000a, 86 on comedy and anecdotes as 'mutually nourishing genres'.
28 On jokebooks as commodities, see the seminal discussion in Beard 2014, 204–09, 274–75; Richlin forthcoming b. Beard takes Hellenistic collections like Machon's not to be jokebooks per se, disagreeing with Gow's assessment, and argues that the commodification of jokes and comedians was an entirely Roman practice, born of Roman imperialism. This is clearly not so, although the practice certainly worked differently in central Italy than it had in the Greek-speaking world. Although there is little shtick in Menander, an exchange from Antiphanes' *Soldier* is full of funnyman/straight man setups (Ath. 6.257d–f, a tall tale comparable to Plautus *Poen.* 470–90); Athenaeus incorporates three different versions of the one about the *parasitus* kept by an old woman, two of which come from Machon (246b–c), cf. Gow 1965, 14. On Hellenistic anecdote collections in Athenaeus, see Dalby 2000.

times they commodified themselves, viz. the title of Plautus's *Addictus*. Athenaeus's joking *hetairai* are also bodies for sale, both in the stories they inhabit, and, as Henry says, as 'one of the objects to be enjoyed at [Athenaeus's] symposium' (2000, 504). Conversely, a *parasitus* could be insulted as a former prostitute (Lark's rival snipes, 'I remember when a Lark cost an obol', 6.241e), and this usage is marked in the Plautine nicknames 'Peniculus' (*Men.* 77) and 'Scortum' (*Capt.* 69, for Ergasilus; unsubtle). The mixed cargo of the ship in *Stichus* explains the mixed personnel in Athenaeus, where *parasiti*, musicians, and prostitutes all work the crowd. In this context, the namelessness of most Italian actors and jokers in this period must be significant, locating them outside the written collection circuit. The *parasiti* in the *palliata* bear a strong resemblance not only to the central slaves, as Fraenkel remarked (2007, 344 n. 105), but to the comedians who, together, made the *palliata*, and to playwrights like Plautus, who was himself the subject/object of a Hellenistic life-story.[29] As such, they are the descendants of the real comedians who appear in Athenaeus's stories, many of whom, as he tells it, were dependents of kings.

A comedians' timeline running from Homer to Machon and the *palliata* in the 200s would include these high points: Irus the beggar in Odysseus's hall (Tylawsky 2002, 7–16) and the blame poets discussed by Gregory Nagy and Ralph Rosen; the description of a *parasitus* attributed to Epicharmus in the 480s or so, if this is genuine; the *Kolakes* of Eupolis in 421 and the *Parasitos* of Alexis (Tylawsky 2002, 43–51, 60–61); the many *parasitoi, gelôtopoioi,* and *kolakes* onstage in Greek comedy and, offstage, associated with kings, tyrants, and rich men in the 300s through the 200s BCE; and the *parasiti* in the *palliata*. All those between Homer and Plautus are known mainly through Athenaeus, for whom, as Tim Whitmarsh argues (2000), these parasites and kings were a figure for the Greek intellectual's relationship to the Roman power structure during the Second Sophistic (Dana Fields (in progress) argues that Phaedrus's fables negotiate a similar power imbalance). In somewhat the same way, the *Life of Aesop* is known to

---

29 On the historically liminal status of the woman comic, see Richlin 2014a, 67; Athenaeus's *hetairai* encroach on the role of the *mima*. On overlaps between the commodified bodies of *parasiti* and slaves, see Richlin forthcoming a. Kurke is throughout dismissive of Henry's 1992 analysis of the objectification of *hetairai* in Athenaeus's stories, but *aulêtrides* like Lamia, in a story within this text, are said to be routinely auctioned off as part of the fun (13.607d), and a political message does not override all other meanings. Nor was ancient sexual abuse 'obvious' before 1992 (cf. Kurke 2002, 57 n. 107). Indeed, the *deipnosophistai* have stories about *hetairai* in place of any *hetairai* of their own (see Wilkins 2000b, 540 n. 9). Both the inner and outer narratives are at times intensely misogynistic; see Henry 2000. On Plautus's biography, see Richlin forthcoming a; on the slippage between onstage slave, comedian, and the figure of the playwright Plautus, Richlin 2014b, 186–87. Cf. Wilkins 2000a, 72: 'The jests may often be at his own expense, but the poet, even the comic poet, may share something of the parasite's role'.

us from its incarnation in the Second Sophistic, but attests to stories stretching back to the fifth century BCE. So we can expand the kings' timeline above to take in their advisers, or clowns, and we get a series of analogies: Belshazzar is to Daniel as Croesus is to Aesop, as Callias is to Philippus the *gelôtopoios* in Xenophon's *Symposium*, as Nicocles (or Nicocreon) is to Stratonicus, as Ptolemy (which one?) is to Sotades and Lark, as the *rex* is to the *parasitus*, as emperors are to sophists. And perhaps as the Metelli were to Naevius. What the stories about all these paired relationships have in common is that the person with less power sometimes scores off the person with more power, or tries to, a phenomenon that reaches its apex in Philostratus's *Lives of the Sophists*; Athenaeus, then, lies midway between Lucian's *Paid Companions* and Philostratus, with the fiction of the *Deipnosophistae* placing him, an Egyptian, at a dinner hosted by the Roman he depends on. In a meta-moment at the start of Book 14, the host's provision of comedians cues a conversation about *gelôtopoioi* and *planoi*, a sort of return of hospitality (14.613c-616e). As in fables, the relationship of low to high is viewed from the perspective of the low man; these stories are not written by kings. These are the stories mice tell about cats.

Athenaeus's Plutarchus surprisingly reports that, although one source says Alexis invented the character of the *parasitus*, in fact Epicharmus, in *Hope or Wealth*, already has a full-blown example (6.235e–236b). This puts the character back around the 480s, and in Sicily, well before the extant plays of Old Comedy. The speech Plutarchus quotes from Epicharmus includes shtick, in the form of two jokes about coming to dinner uninvited that make use of what Eckard Lefèvre calls 'die Technik der bedeutungsvollen Pause' (2001, 112, 117). This *parasitus* says part of his job is to generate laughs (ποιέω πολὺν/γέλωτα); he engages in flattery (ἐπαινέω); he fears he will meet the city guards, and will be thankful if all they do is whip him (an element that reappears in the slave Sosia's entrance speech in *Amphitruo*, 153-62 – much expanded); when he gets home, he will sleep with no blankets (ἄστρωτος), an element that reappears at the end of the slave Gripus's big song in *Rudens* (937–37a, *sed hic rex cum aceto pransurust/et sale sine bono pulmento*, 'but this king is going to eat lunch with vinegar and salt, without any good bit of meat'). The conventionality of these elements makes it hard to believe that Epicharmus invented them, just as the element of shtick in the tiny fragments of Livius Andronicus makes it hard to believe he wrote the first-ever *palliata*.[30] Shtick like this is part of a comedian's stock in trade.

---

[30] Epicharmus's *parasitus* is treated as a genuine part of his *oeuvre* by Bosher 2014, 86–87. For shtick in Livius, see Richlin forthcoming b.

The *parasiti* in Plutarchus's comic fragments often speak of their talent for σκῶμμα, both dishing it out and taking it; like the *parasiti* in Plautus, they brag about how much of a beating they can take. Like Epicharmus's *parasitus*, they claim to be funny.[31] Once Plutarchus moves on to examples of real-life *parasiti*, however, he soon zooms in on *parasiti* whose job it was to be funny for kings, and this theme continues when Democritus turns the conversation to *kolakes* (6.248c). In some stories, this was a risky business. Plutarchus begins at 6.244f with Sostratus, *parasitus* of Antiochus the Great; Euagoras the hunchback, *parasitus* of Demetrius Poliorcetes; Phormio, *parasitus* of Seleucus (probably Seleucus I Nicator, d. 281 BCE); after him, Democritus continues through 6.262a.[32] In the course of this discussion, by my rough count, the two speakers mention thirty-four kings, eighteen of whom belong to the century after Alexander; notable earlier kings include Philip II and Dionysius I and II, tyrants of Syracuse. Most of the names on Plautus's list are also in Athenaeus's stories.

Athenaeus's *parasiti* travel; Machon tells in the *Chreiai* how Archephon sailed to Egypt from Attica, where he was invited to dinner by King Ptolemy (probably Ptolemy II Philadelphus, ruled 283–246 BCE).[33] Polybius, says Democritus, records that Philip V had a *kolax* named Heracleides of Tarentum (6.251d–e); he was a long way from home, expelled by war.[34] The *parasitus* nicknamed Lark (*Korydos*) is the center of several strings of Plutarchus's stories (6.241a–242b, 245d–246a), some of which also bring him to Alexandria, and Plutarchus refers to a whole book of his jokes put together by Lynceus (6.241d).[35] But no one traveled more than the *kithara*-player Stratonicus; in one story, someone even asks him why he travels so much (8.350e). Stories stitched together by Democritus (8.347f–348a, 348c–352d), including a long excerpt from Machon's *Chreiai* (348e–349f), put him in Mylasa, Pella (twice), Abdera, Pontus (twice), Corinth, Cyprus, Ephesus, Byzantium (twice), Side, Phaselis in Pamphylia (twice), Rhodes (twice), Alexandria, Teichious in Milesia,

---

31 On these stock characteristics of *parasiti*, see Tylawsky 2002, 65, 120–22; Wilkins 2000a, 71–86; also Damon 1997, 23–36, merging Greek and Roman *parasiti*. Some characteristics of Greek *parasiti* vanish in the *palliata*.

32 For the dates here and below, I am chiefly indebted to Olson (2008), who identifies all the kings as much as possible, along with many of the performers and writers.

33 Ath. 6.244b–d = Machon 25–45 Gow, see Gow 1965, 10. Cf. discussion in Kurke 2002, 51–55, arguing that Archephon's choice in fish has to do with the loss of Athenian civil liberties. For itinerant performers in general, see Hunter/Rutherford 2009 (restricted to serious performance).

34 The late excerptor of Polybius (13.4) incorporates a description of Heracleides as a former male prostitute, of banausic parentage, exiled from Tarentum due to his dealings with the Romans during the Second Punic War. The accusation of having been a prostitute was an invective commonplace; see above on Lark.

35 See also Tylawsky 2002, 67–73 on the *parasitus* Chaerephon, the one most frequently attested.

Aenus, Heracleia (twice), Leucadia, Ambracia, Maronesia, Cardia, and Sicyon (twice). These points, plotted on a map, take him around the eastern Mediterranean from Alexandria to Thessaly, with a detour to the south shore of the Black Sea; he spent some time on the mainland, where he traveled as far west as the coast of Aetolia; no further. Democritus likes his sarcastic retorts; many of them slam other musicians, but he also said nasty things about the places he visited, and bad bath attendants, and bad teachers: generic jokes. His *parrhêsia* is said to have been the cause of his death, though at the hands of different kings of Cyprus: drowned by Nicocreon king of Salamis on Cyprus in 332/1, because at a drinking party he called attention to the queen's attempt to conceal a fart (8.349e–f, from Machon); a generation earlier, forced to drink poison by Nicocles king of Cyprus, because he mocked the king's sons (διὰ τὸ σκώπτειν, 8.352d, another source).[36] When he 'sailed to Pontus' to visit King Berisades (8.349d; king of Thrace 358–357/6), he is said to have stayed 'a long time'; the combination of a real, datable king with timeless time is typical of the life-stories that emerge from these anecdotes. In another story (8.350c), he argues about *kithara*-playing with King Ptolemy; the earliest one would be Ptolemy I Soter, whose reign began in 305. In Plautus's *Rudens*, the slave Gripus sings that he wants to sail all around, just like Stratonicus (932–33, *mihi navem faciam atque imitabor Stratonicum;/oppida circumvectabor*, 'I'll make me a ship and imitate Stratonicus; I'll sail all around the towns'). Stratonicus, then, was a legend long after his time and far beyond his travels, remembered for his free tongue and his freedom of movement.

He was not alone. The itinerant poet Sotades in the 280s–270s, inventor of cinaedic verse, was notorious for his nasty verses about kings. He met his end, as the story goes, after abusing Ptolemy II Philadelphus and his wife: drowned in the original pair of concrete overshoes (Ath. 14.620e–621b).[37] We would like to know what Ennius made of him in his *Sota* (see Courtney 1993, 4–7). The *aulêtês* Dorion, like Stratonicus, is said to have had a witty run-in with Nicocreon, and Democritus reports his jokes as collected by Machon (8.337c–d), Lynceus (337d–f), and Aristodemus, in his *Geloia Apomnêmoneumata* (337f–338b). In this last story he has a 'crooked foot' – he is κυλλόποδος, like Hephaistos – and as such is one of several comedians who are described as deformed, including Euagoras (seen above, 6.244f) and Ptolemy's interlocutor Alcenor (244d), both described as κυρτός. Hephaistos, as all know who know Homer, was always good for a laugh. This suggests an additional dimension to the comic costume, which imposed a

---

36 On Stratonicus, see also Gilula 2000; Kurke 2002, 30, on the fart story.
37 So Olson reasonably interprets the text's 'tossing him into a lead jar' (2011, 139).

kind of deformity on the actors' bodies, as the masks certainly imposed grotesquerie on their faces.³⁸

Of the kings in Athenaeus, some are said to collect jokers, and some are said to be jokers themselves (many grouped at 6.260a–261c). Kings in stories sometimes make their own jokes, and a *kolax* of Philip II complains about being upstaged (6.248e); Machon, in the *Chreiai*, has Demetrius Poliorcetes make a very dirty joke about his 'royal head' (187 Gow = Ath. 13.577f, βαλάνου ... βασιλικῆς). Collectors include Ptolemy IV Philopator (246c–d) as well as Philip II (260a–c). Philip was said to love βωμολοχία and to be a βωμολόχος himself (260a, b); Dionysius I of Sicily enjoyed a good ribbing (260c–d); Demetrius Poliorcetes was φιλόγελως (261b, 14.614e-615a); Democritus even fast-forwards to the dictator Sulla, quite a comedian (261c; repeated by Ulpian, or 'Athenaeus', at 14.615a). Outstanding here must be King Lysimachus, who is said to have thrown a wooden scorpion into the cloak of his *parasitus* (6.246e); this Lysimachus, best known for killing his own son, was a member of Alexander's bodyguard who became one of Alexander's successor kings in 306 and ruled in Thrace and Macedon. This story opens up a whole world of ancient practical joking, with a small service industry supplying gag props like wooden scorpions: black comedy, considering how these rulers behaved when no longer feeling funny. Lysimachus in another story, when an officer makes a joke about his wife Arsinoe, has him carried around in a cage and fed like a wild animal, before having him killed (14.616b–c; luridly imagined in Sen. *De Ira* 3.17.3–4). Again here, a joke about the queen's body crosses the line: Arsinoe vomits, Biothea farts, and the same Arsinoe, once Lysimachus has died and she has married her brother Ptolemy II, receives his 'poker' in her 'unholy slot'³⁹ – deadly jokes for Stratonicus, Sotades, and the officer of Lysimachus. All part of the story. Twice the story is told of how Philip II, wanting a copy of their jokes, sent a huge sum to the jokers who used to meet in the sanctuary of Heracles in Diomeia (6.260a–b; 14.614d–e) – outside the city wall of Athens, near the Cynosarges gymnasium, a place associated with the Cynics. Mary Beard takes Philip's reported action to be an instance of tyrannical cooptation, one negatively viewed 'in the original Athenian context' (2014, 206–07); but this belongs to a sequence of similar tales, all stories mice tell about cats – indeed, the cats in this sequence are tigers.⁴⁰

---

38 See Tylawsky 2002, 110–11, on the Cynic Crates as hunchback; Winkler 1985, 289–90 on ugly Aesop and the *stupidus* of mime.
39 Trans. Olson 2011, 139.
40 Beard 2014, 206–07. Almost nothing is known about Hegesander, the source of this story, but his estimated date is the 100s BCE (not CE, as at Beard 2014, 275 n. 82), and he certainly belongs to a Hellenistic world no longer centered on Athens.

Kurke argues that Machon's tales champion Athenian civic virtues against the lecherous tyrant Demetrius Poliorcetes, so that when the *aulêtris* Lamia rejects the perfume he offers her, or the *hetaira* Mania offers him her bottom in return for a gift, these women represent Athens, while Demetrius is reduced to self-stimulation; even his ejaculate smells bad. But Machon wrote in Alexandria, for an Alexandrian audience, where gross insults of Demetrius were much safer than they were in Athens; representing Athens as a whore was not really an Athenian position.[41] In any case, Demetrius died in 283 BCE; it seems likely that these stories are protected not only by distance but by time, as in Juvenal's satires. Accordingly, Machon's Ptolemy (still alive) is relatively benign – Gow calls him 'pleasure-loving' (1965, 10). Sotades, in accounts by Hegesander and his own son, jokes about one king in the city of another, until his scabrous verses about jolly Ptolemy and his sister/wife catch up with him in Alexandria. In his checklist of post-Menandrian comic poets, Benjamin Millis emphasizes that, from the 200s onward, comedy 'ought not to be read as a uniformly Athenian product written for an Athenian audience' (2014, 874). The *palliata*, he suggests, may be typical in its local transposition.

Still, Kurke is right to adduce James C. Scott's ideas on the public vs. the hidden transcript as an explanation of why Machon uses prostitutes and comedians to voice his political views, especially when we consider the gross flattery Athenaeus records the Athenians themselves producing as their public face towards Demetrius (2002, 37, 59–62). Kurke's analysis directly addresses Tim Whitmarsh's ideas on the (deipno)sophists, who, after all, referred to the emperor as the βασιλεύς. One of Philip's jokers (here Democritus recaps Theopompus) was a slave, the Thessalian Agathocles, and so successfully did he entertain the king that he was sent to destroy a Thessalian tribe (6.259f–260a): perplexing, until we find out from other sources that this Agathocles was Lysimachus's father. An old slander here becomes an inspirational tale of upward mobility. The anecdote collectors like Lynceus and Machon, even the historians and biographers, served an audience that liked to hear about talking back to kings, about kings who wished they could be funny, about a king who would go out and get a wooden scorpion. Gripus wants to be like his idea of Stratonicus: to travel where he pleases, to be the one trading instead of the one traded, to own land and a house and slaves, to name a city after himself (*Rud.* 930–35a). 'I will be known as a king

---

41 Kurke recognizes that this would be an 'unusual representational strategy' (27), 'a politically sensitive act' (32), a problem (51), and in some cases treats Machon's position as critical of Athens (esp. 51–55); still, she leans hard on the faint suggestion in Athenaeus's wording that Machon spent some time in Athens; but his perspective is much easier to explain as Alexandrian.

among kings', he sings – *apud reges rex* (931). The actor who played Gripus was more like the real Stratonicus, busking for a living, and perhaps it was the actors who kept the kings' names in circulation, far away, in a country that had no βασιλεύς.

The kings of comedy

Comedians and kings, then, belonged together, in the wake of Alexander; *parasitus* was both a stage character and a job description. The *parasiti* in the *palliata*, waiting for a dinner invitation from their *rex*, live on a much humbler level; they talk about dying of hunger, but they run no risk of being forced to drink poison. Whereas Athenaeus's banqueters align *parasitus* and *kolax*, and many of the men named by Athenaeus are clearly courtiers, the *parasitus* in the *palliata* often most closely resembles a slave, just as the actors in the *palliata* were often, apparently, slaves.[42] The circulation of jokes and comedians through the slave trade brought the *parasitus* to central Italy – in Fraenkel's phrase, 'a barbarian island in a sea of teeming Hellenistic life'.[43] Ζεῖ ὁ βασιλιᾶς Ἀλέξανδρος.

Bibliography

Bäbler, B. (1998), *Fleissige Thrakerinnen und wehrhafte Skythen: Nichtgriechen im klassischen Athen und ihre archäologische Hinterlassenschaft*, Stuttgart.
Beard, M. (2014), *Laughter in Ancient Rome: On Joking, Tickling, and Cracking Up*, Berkeley.
Bettini, M. (2012), *Vertere: un'antropologia della traduzione nella cultura antica*, Torino.
Bosher, K. (2014), 'Epicharmus and Early Sicilian Comedy', in: M. Revermann (ed.), *The Cambridge Companion to Greek Comedy*, Cambridge, 79–94.
Burton, P. J. (2011), *Friendship and Empire: Roman Diplomacy and Imperialism in the Middle Republic (353–146 BC)*, Cambridge.
Carney, E. D. (2000), *Women and Monarchy in Macedonia*, Norman, OK.
Christenson, D. M. (ed., comm.) (2000), *Plautus Amphitruo*, Cambridge.
Colvin, S. (2000), 'The Language of Non-Athenians in Old Comedy', in: D. Harvey/J. Wilkins (eds.), *The Rivals of Aristophanes: Studies in Athenian Old Comedy*, London, 285–98.

---

[42] Athenaeus's alignment of *parasitus* and *kolax*: 6.248d; Tylawsky 2002, 60–61.
[43] Fraenkel (2007, 133), insisting that Plautus could certainly have heard of Zeuxis and Apelles without copying their names from a Greek comedy, in fact says this is *not* what Rome was – not at all cut off from current trends; yet in some ways central Italy was, precisely, apart from the south. Cf. Fraenkel's second thoughts about the interrelationship between Athenaeus's parasites and Plautus (2007, 343 n. 100).

Courtney, E. (ed., comm.) (1993), *The Fragmentary Latin Poets*, Oxford.
Dalby, A. (ed., trans.) (1998), *Cato On Farming*, Totnes, UK.
_____ (2000), 'Lynceus and the Anecdotists', in: D. Braund/J. Wilkins (eds.), *Athenaeus and his World: Reading Greek Culture in the Roman Empire*, Exeter, 372–94.
Damon, C. (1997), *The Mask of the Parasite: A Pathology of Roman Patronage*, Ann Arbor.
DuBois, P. (2003), *Slaves and Other Objects*, Chicago.
Fields, D. (in progress), 'King, Tyrant, and Emperor in Imperial Fable'.
Forsdyke, S. (2012), *Slaves Tell Tales and Other Episodes in the Politics of Popular Culture in Ancient Greece*, Princeton.
Fraenkel, E. (2007), *Plautine Elements in Plautus*, T. Drevikovsky/F. Muecke (trans.), Oxford.
Gabba, E. (1981), 'True History and False History in Classical Antiquity', *JRS* 71, 50–62.
Gilula, D. (2000), 'Stratonicus, the Witty Harpist', in: D. Braund/J. Wilkins (eds.), *Athenaeus and his World: Reading Greek Culture in the Roman Empire*, Exeter, 423–33.
Gow, A. S. F. (ed., comm.) (2004), *Machon: The Fragments*, Cambridge.
Hägg, T. (2012), *The Art of Biography in Antiquity*, Cambridge.
Hall, E. (2013), 'The Aesopic in Aristophanes', in: E. Bakola/L. Prauscello/M. Telò (eds.), *Greek Comedy and the Discourse of Genres*, Cambridge, 277–97.
Hansen, W. (ed.) (1998), *Anthology of Ancient Greek Popular Literature*, Bloomington, IN.
Harsh, P. W. (1936), 'Possible Greek Background for the Word *Rex* as Used in Plautus and Terence', *CP* 31, 62–68.
Hartman, L. F./Di Lella, A. A. (eds., trans.) (2005), *The Book of Daniel (Anchor Bible)*, New Haven.
Hawkins, S. (2010), 'Greek and the Languages of Asia Minor to the Classical Period', in: E. J. Bakker (ed.), *A Companion to the Ancient Greek Language*, Oxford, 213–27.
Henderson, J. (2001), *Telling Tales on Caesar: Roman Stories from Phaedrus*, Oxford.
Henry, M. (2000), 'Athenaeus the Ur-Pornographer', in: D. Braund/J. Wilkins (eds.), *Athenaeus and his World: Reading Greek Culture in the Roman Empire*, Exeter, 503–13.
Holzberg, N. (2002), *The Ancient Fable: An Introduction*, Bloomington, IN.
Hunter, R./Rutherford, I. (eds.) (2009), *Wandering Poets in Ancient Greek Culture: Travel, Locality and Pan-Hellenism*, Cambridge.
Janse, M. (2002), 'Aspects of Bilingualism in the History of the Greek Language', in: J. N. Adams/M. Janse/S. Swain (eds.), *Bilingualism in Ancient Society*, Oxford, 332–91.
Jasanoff, J. H./Nussbaum, A. (1996), 'Word Games: The Linguistic Evidence in *Black Athena*', in: M. R. Lefkowitz/G. M. Rogers (eds.), *Black Athena Revisited*, Chapel Hill, 177–205.
Kay, P. (2014), *Rome's Economic Revolution*, Oxford.
Kurke, L. (2002), 'Gender, Politics and Subversion in the *Chreiai* of Machon', *PCPhS* 48, 20–65.
_____ (2011), *Aesopic Conversations: Popular Tradition, Cultural Dialogue, and the Invention of Greek Prose*, Princeton.
Lefèvre, E. (2001), '*Nimium familiariter* – plautinische Sklaven unter sich: *Epidicus* I 1', in: U. Auhaugen (ed.), *Studien zu Plautus' Epidicus*, Tübingen, 105–29.
Lewis, D. (2011), 'Near Eastern Slaves in Classical Attica and the Slave Trade with Persian Territories', *CQ* 61, 91–113.
Lott, E. (1993), *Love and Theft: Blackface Minstrelsy and the American Working Class*, New York.
Ma, J. (2003), 'Kings', in: A. Erskine (ed.), *A Companion to the Hellenistic World*, Oxford, 177–95.
_____ (2013), *Statues and Cities: Honorific Portraits and Civic Identity in the Hellenistic World*, Oxford.

Mann, K. (2015), *The Fabulist in the Fable Book*, PhD diss., UCLA.
Miles, M. (2008), *Art as Plunder: The Ancient Origins of Debate about Cultural Property*, Cambridge.
Millis, B. (2014), 'Post-Menandrian Comic Poets: An Overview of the Evidence and a Checklist', in: M. Fontaine/A. C. Scafuro (eds.), *The Oxford Handbook of Greek and Roman Comedy*, Oxford, 871–84.
Mitakidou, C./Manna, A. L. (2002), *Folktales from Greece: A Treasury of Delights*, Greenwood Village, CO.
Momigliano, A. (1971), *Alien Wisdom: The Limits of Hellenization*, Cambridge.
Morris, S. P. (1989), 'Daidalos and Kadmos: Classicism and "Orientalism"', *Arethusa* special issue, *The Challenge of Black Athena*, 39–54.
_____ (1992), *Daidalos and the Origins of Greek Art*, Princeton.
Olson, S. D. (ed., trans.) (2008), *Athenaeus*: The Learned Banqueters. *Books VI-VII*, Cambridge, MA.
_____ (ed., trans.) (2011), *Athenaeus*: The Learned Banqueters, *Books 13.594b-14*, Cambridge, MA.
_____ (2015), 'Fragmentary Prose Authors in Athenaeus of Naucratis', paper delivered at the Ioannou Centre for Classical and Byzantine Studies, Oxford, April 1, print version forthcoming.
Panayotakis, C. (2014), 'Hellenistic Mime and its Reception in Rome', in: M. Fontaine/A. C. Scafuro (eds.), *The Oxford Handbook of Greek and Roman Comedy*, Oxford, 378–96.
Richlin, A. (2014a), *Arguments with Silence: Writing the History of Roman Women*, Ann Arbor.
_____ (2014b), 'Talking to Slaves in the Plautine Audience', *CA* 33.1, 175–226.
_____ (forthcoming a), *Slave Theater in the Roman Republic*, Cambridge.
_____ (forthcoming b), 'The Traffic in Shtick', in: M. P. Loar/C. MacDonald/D. Padilla Peralta (eds.), *City of Plunder: Appropriation in Roman Culture*.
Robinson, E. G. D. (2004), 'Reception of Comic Theatre Amongst the Indigenous South Italians', *Mediterranean Archaeology* 17, 193–212.
Roselaar, S. T. (2012), 'Mediterranean Trade as a Mechanism of Integration between Romans and Italians', in: S. T. Roselaar (ed.), *Processes of Integration and Identity Formation in the Roman Republic*, Leiden, 141–58.
Rothwell, K. S., Jr. (1995), 'Aristophanes' *Wasps* and the Sociopolitics of Aesop's Fables', *CJ* 90.3, 233–54.
Sells, D. (2013), 'Slaves in the Fragments of Old Comedy', in: B. Akrigg/R. Tordoff (eds.), *Slaves and Slavery in Ancient Greek Comic Drama*, Cambridge, 91–110.
Shaw, B. D. (1998), '"A Wolf by the Ears": M. I. Finley's *Ancient Slavery and Modern Ideology* in Historical Context', in: B. D. Shaw (ed.), M. I. Finley, *Ancient Slavery and Modern Ideology*, expanded edition, Princeton, 3–74.
Stephens, S. (2002), 'Commenting on Fragments', in: R. K. Gibson/C. S. Kraus (eds.), *The Classical Commentary: Histories, Practices, Theory*, Leiden, 67–87.
Tordoff, R. (2013), 'Introduction: Slaves and Slavery in Ancient Greek Comedy', in: B. Akrigg/R. Tordoff (eds.), *Slaves and Slavery in Ancient Greek Comic Drama*, Cambridge, 1–62.
Tylawsky, E. I. (2002), *Saturio's Inheritance: The Greek Ancestry of the Roman Comic Parasite*, New York.
Weinstock, S. (1957), 'Victor and Invictus', *Harvard Theological Review* 50, 211–47.
Welch, K. (2003), 'A New View of the Origins of the Basilica: The Atrium Regium, Graecostasis, and Roman Diplomacy', *Journal of Roman Archaeology* 16, 5–34.

Wessinger, C. (ed.) (2011), *The Oxford Handbook of Millennialism*, Oxford.
West, S. (2003), 'Croesus' Second Reprieve and Other Tales of the Persian Court', *CQ* 53.2, 416–37.
Whitmarsh, T. (2000), 'The Politics and Poetics of Parasitism: Athenaeus on Parasites and Flatterers', in: D. Braund/J. Wilkins (eds.), *Athenaeus and his World: Reading Greek Culture in the Roman Empire*, Exeter, 304–16.
Wilkins, J. (2000a), *The Boastful Chef: The Discourse of Food in Ancient Greek Comedy*, Oxford.
─────── (2000b), 'Dialogue and Comedy: The Structure of the *Deipnosophistae*', in: D. Braund/J. Wilkins (eds.), *Athenaeus and his World: Reading Greek Culture in the Roman Empire*, Exeter, 23–37.
Winkler, J. J. (1985), *Auctor & Actor: A Narratological Reading of Apuleius' Golden Ass*, Berkeley.
Wright, J. (1974), *Dancing in Chains: The Stylistic Unity of the Comoedia Palliata*, Rome.

Alison Sharrock
Genre and Social Class, or Comedy and the Rhetoric of Self-aggrandisement and Self-deprecation

In Ovid *Amores* 3.1, Tragedy and Elegy are pitted against each other as a respectable woman and a prostitute respectively, a hierarchy of class more than it is a hierarchy of morals. Elegy wins. This serves Ovid's own rhetorical purposes, as an introduction to a book of elegies, for it is also a hierarchy of genres. Tragedy represents a dynasty fulfilled and immortality won, whereas Elegy is just right for a quick bash (*Am.* 3.1.68). To adapt the metaphor slightly, Elegy is not the genre with whom one can produce legitimate children. The same poetological structure could apply to comedy. One might expect Comedy to play *scortum* to Elegy's *meretrix*.[1] Could it be that comedy is the genre least susceptible to mixing, despite the fact that miscegenation sounds exactly like the kind of messy, chaotic, badly behaved features that comedy should present?[2]

The question of this paper is how Plautus might use (or indeed be used by) a hierarchy of genres to express his new poetic voice. Its initial motivation was the question of whether the well-known identification in Roman comedy between the playwright and a slave is primarily a matter of politics or poetics.[3] I would like to think that it is a matter of politics, but the short version of the answer is that, unfortunately, I think it is probably poetics. What remains surprising to me is that Plautus' audiences, ancient and modern, have so easily accepted the identification of the poet's voice with a slave: the all-powerful, all-controlling creator *ex nihilo* of the dramatic world with a non-person. This is something for which there is essentially no precedent. The playwright gets away with something so outrageous, I suggest, because it is constructed through a rhetoric of ironic self-aggrandisement which is dependent on and contributes to the low position of comedy within a hierarchy of genres. This social metaphor for the position of comedy, together with the assump-

---

[1] This, despite the fact that there are as many wives as prostitutes in comedy. The metaphor here is about poetics, not the content of comedy. I'm very grateful to the organisers for inviting me to contribute to what was an exceptionally stimulating conference. I am particularly grateful to Stavros Frangoulidis for his generous welcome and his friendly tolerance of a tardy contributor.
[2] Gowers 1993.
[3] This paper takes its starting point from a brief discussion in Sharrock 2009, 131–40. The ur-text for the metatheatrical reading of the slave-role is Slater 2000 (1st edn., 1985).

tion of a slave persona for the poet's voice, creates a rhetoric of self-deprecation which is a generically appropriate *captatio benevolentiae*.

There are two strands of thought which must be pursued before we can enter into the main body of this paper: one to do with poetic tradition and one to do with social realities (or at least the representation of them). I shall first look briefly at the sociopolitical question, before returning to the poetological matter which is key to my argument.

The story of Plautus and social class is an old one. In the early years of modern scholarship, conventional wisdom regarded Plautine comedy as entertainment for the 'unwashed masses', with the playwright a 'professional man of the theatre' who, in accordance with the ancient trope which makes biographical points out of literary critical ones, had himself been a slave. More recently, this view has been challenged from a number of directions. One is the exposition of, and insistence on, the sophisticated and literary nature of republican comedy, which posits an implied audience with, at least in part, effectively an upper-class education. The other is the view that comedy is deeply implicated in the ideology of the ruling class.[4] It is certainly possible for a popular ('debased') literary form to propagate aristocratic values, even by inversion. Indeed, it can be difficult for subversive literary forms to maintain their subversive stance, in that the very act of subverting can be a form of approbation. If X subverts Y, X makes Y into the standard and so has to work very hard to avoid reinforcing the very hierarchies it seeks to undermine. There is no need, however, for the pendulum to swing to the opposite pole so as to deny entirely the lower-class associations of the genre.

In an article published while I was working on the initial draft of this paper, Amy Richlin makes a strong argument that Roman comedy grew up in response to 'endemic warfare and mass enslavement',[5] as a cultural production of slaves and lower class non- or ex-slaves, with only the best troupes being picked out for translation to the elite environment of the official *ludi*. As such, according to Richlin, we can see in the texts traces of slaves' doublespeak, as the plays offer the slaves fantasies of freedom and of getting their own back on their masters, without associated dangers that would apply in real life. In this, she makes use of James Scott's notion of the 'hidden transcript' – the obscured or suppressed defiance of subaltern peoples through the ages.[6] If Richlin is right, then my paper is wrong: politics trumps poetics and the oppressed are set free (at least in fantasy). Unfortunately, I think that there is good reason to believe that any subver-

---

[4] Gruen 1992.
[5] Richlin 2014, 174.
[6] Scott 1990.

sive transcript, hidden or otherwise, in the plays of Plautus is itself always subject to suppression. The poet may be godlike, but he is also entirely at the mercy of the audience, while his characters' bids for freedom, whether real or metaphorical, are subject to a fatal condition: they must not be working for themselves. Slaves on the stage do indeed give slaves in the audience the vicarious pleasure of insulting and cheating their masters, usually without serious punishment. In my view, however, it is surprising how few slaves achieve freedom during the plays, especially how few *architecti* achieve freedom as a reward for their activities. Richlin states that 'twenty-five slaves (plus a chorus) are or become freed in the twenty full texts extant',[7] but that list is made up primarily not of the clever slaves with whom the poet closely identifies but rather of freeborn foundlings and captives who are subject to the comic magic of recognition.[8] The crucial point for me is that successful slaves in comedy are not working for themselves.[9] Epidicus and Trachalio in *Rudens* are freed, but they have not been working for themselves, while many even of those who have been working only for the young master are still not freed, crucially Pseudolus. It is the disinterestedness of the poet-slave that makes his self-aggrandisement acceptable – and ultimately weak. To be fair, Richlin is concerned with all the slaves of comedy, characters and actors, whereas I am concerned only with the 'clever slave' character who is renowned for his metatheatrical power and whom I call the *architectus*. Also, Richlin is concerned with politics, whereas I am concerned with poetics, though neither can wholly escape from the other.

Next comes the poetic strand.

Few people would deny that in Augustan Rome there is a hierarchy of genres, with epic and tragedy at the top, comedy and satire at the bottom. It is reasonably clear, despite the paucity of the fragments, that the metaphor of social hierarchy in genre is active in archaic Latin epic, in which Ennius engaged wholeheartedly in the social elevation of epic,[10] and in republican satire, where Lucilius seems to have made a show of constructing a persona which is dis-

---

7 Richlin 2014, 192 referring also to Rawson 1993.
8 This last might be offering a dream but it also, I suggest, reinforces the idea of inherent freedom and slavery. Of course, there is no requirement for the hidden transcript to be philosophically abolitionist rather than simply reflecting the individual hopes and desires of the speaker.
9 Here, I am in agreement with McCarthy 2000, 160: 'one of the central features of the clever slave, the one that permanently separates him from any society based on the values of the freeborn, is his refusal to act teleologically to bring about his own manumission.'
10 On which see the excellent article of Gildenhard 2003, 109–13.

tanced from (what are probably) the realities of his actual social position.[11] Would differences of genre be seen in such hierarchical terms on the republican stage, and if so how did Plautus use such a hierarchy?[12] I suggest that when Plautus made the controller of his comedy, the image of himself, out of a slave, he did so, with whatever degree of consciousness, drawing on a poetological tradition of generic self-presentation in a way that is more surprising than we are inclined to realise. That is, the tradition offers him reason to identify his voice with a non-aristocratic and even anti-aristocratic character, but not with a slave.

In the poetic self-positioning of many genres, including epic throughout its history, archaic Greek iambic and elegiac poetry, and Aristophanic comedy, it is possible to see a connection between genre and something that can be at least loosely called social class. For epic, the genre is unashamedly aristocratic, while although the poet in persona is not himself usually aristocratic/heroic, he is wholly integrated into that world and takes up a position which endorses it. Notoriously, in archaic Greek iambic that aristocratic-heroic subject-position is undermined, with whatever degree of artfulness and insincerity. The famous case of Archilochus 'throwing away his shield' (fr. 5 W) is not just a personal or political statement of the rejection of heroic values, but also a generic statement about the nature of his poetry.[13]

So the epic voice is closely identified with the aristocracy and heroic values; iambic moves down a level to a position of disillusioned aristocracy, or lower; then Old Comedy makes its hero and poet's voice out of a character who is the opposite of the heroic ideal (although, like most opposites, with marked similarities), but someone who is clearly identified by his connection with the polity, even where, as for example in *Birds*, he seems to reject civic virtues. One might expect that comedy would present itself as coming from the position of the little man, people 'worse

---

[11] It is important to be clear that this strategy, and not only in Lucilius, is probably primarily a matter of rhetorical self-positioning, which may itself have social implications which are by no means straightforward. For example, the rhetoric of aristocratic epic may cause an identification between the poet and those values which is dependent on the poet himself precisely not being himself a member of that class, while the rhetoric of the common man's satire may be a loosely-veiled alternative self-presentation of essentially the same upper-class subject-position. Intellectual self-positioning as working class from a position of privilege is as much a feature of Greek and Roman poetry as it is of certain kinds of contemporary celebrity.
[12] I am leaving Terence aside in this paper, because his poetological rhetoric raises a host of other complexities.
[13] Anderson 2008 offers an amusing reading of the poem in which the reason for the loss of the shield was in fact a call of nature, which 'comically humanises the heroic ideal' (259). This suggestion nicely reinforces the role of poetics in the scene. For other examples in archaic lyric and elegy, see Anderson 2008, 257.

than ourselves', as Aristotle says (*Poetics* 1448a17).[14] Although the Aristophanic voice has often been seen as socially conservative, it would be easy to present that conservativism as the little man against the bosses. It makes no difference how wealthy or otherwise we can make out individual comic heroes to be.[15] For my purposes, what matters is that such a character is lowly but not an outsider.[16]

Menander is undoubtedly very interested in the relationship between rich and poor within the citizen body, but most of his core characters are rich, while he has no clear cipher for the poet. I am not convinced that any particular character or character-type holds the poet's voice in Hellenistic Greek comedy with any consistency sufficient to create the kind of speaking subject-position that I am talking about here.[17] In fact, by contrast, Plautus appears to have little interest in citizen poverty. In most plays of Roman comedy, most of the citizen characters are rich. It is not the case that comedy represents the lives of ordinary people, if by that we mean members of the polity who are not rich. Rather, slaves have taken over the role of the 'ordinary/not-rich'. The romantic lead, in those plays where he features, is a young man of considerable wealth and privilege, but is probably the last character to make a bid for the poet's voice. If any other character contributes to this role, it will be either a cook[18] or parasite, both of them peripheral to Roman society. One might have expected the parasite to function as the poet's voice, as will become the case to some extent in the later Roman satiric tradition, but this is not in fact what we find in Plautine comedy (or indeed Terentian). Plays with parasites generally also have slaves who contend with the former for control – and, I think, often win.[19] Rather, it is the 'clever slave', a detached, ironic observer and the skilled controller of the action, who holds this position. Plautus makes an important innovation here.[20] He uses it to comment on the nature of the comic dramatist's situation, apparently in control but actually at the mercy of his masters.

---

14 But what does he mean by 'ourselves'? The link between Aristotle and modern academics is too easily made.
15 Zumbrunnen 2004.
16 Although it is outside the scope of this paper, it is worth noting how Roman satire draws on both the comic and iambic traditions, with its subject-position of the poor citizen, lowly, but emphatically not an outsider to the polity.
17 In Terence, who has to be ignored here, I think the character who most effectively holds the poet's voice is simply the poet.
18 Gowers 1993.
19 That is part of my argument in Sharrock 2014.
20 That the predominant role of the slave is a Plautine innovation is, of course, hardly news, since it goes back most famously to Fraenkel's analysis of this particularly powerful piece of *Plautinisches*. What I mean, rather, is that Plautus has made an innovation in the tradition of socially-based poets' voices.

This paper concentrates on two plays: *Persa* and *Aulularia*. I use the former as a focus for what I see as the essential weak point in the identity between the playwright and lower-class characters, whether in the play or in the audience, which is that the controlling slave with whom the poet's voice is so closely identified must not work for himself. I use the second play to explore the problem, as it seems to me, of how and why Plautus identifies with slaves and *not* with the citizen poor.

Persa is not one of the most popular of Plautus' plays. Woytek opens the introduction to his edition and commentary on the play by remarking on the rarity of scholarly works devoted to it as an indicator of the value placed on this comedy by the scholarly world. He continues: 'Die Beschäftigung mit einem Stück, dessen *argumentum* schon Camerarius *exile* genannt hatte und in dem fast nur Sklaven agieren, war offensichtlich nur wenig attraktiv.'[21] Although, as far as I am aware, we have no evidence as to the immediate reception of the play, apart from the fact of its survival, the relative unpopularity of the play in the modern world, and particularly the attribution of that unpopularity to the excessive involvement of slaves, gives accidental support to my theory. Apart from Plautine scholarly perennials, plus some interest in the workings of Greek and Roman law, the greatest recent interest in the play is in its metatheatre and morals, particularly those regarding the Virgo,[22] rather than in my focus, which is the *metapoetic* status of the playwright as slave and lover. Both Slater[23] and McCarthy[24] have written very effectively on the sociology and metatheatricality of this play. The point I wish to add is met-

---

[21] Woytek 1982, 9. In addition to Woytek's edition, with extensive introduction and commentary, the play has benefited from the monograph of Chiarini 1979 (2nd edn., with addenda, 1983) in which it is interpreted powerfully as a full-scale piece of farce (meant in the general modern sense of the term, rather than that specific to *comoedia Atellana*), a reading which should be better known than perhaps it is as an important early metatheatrical reading of Plautus. The extensive discussion of the play in McCarthy 2000 is a crucial reading, as is that of Slater 2000, 31–44. Auhagen 2001 is unusual and valuable in her concentration on the 'paradoxical pair of lovers', Toxilus and Lemniselenis. For her also, the play is a kind of 'meta-comedy' (96).
[22] See Chiarini 1979; Lowe 1989; McCarthy 2000; Manuwald 2001; Hardy 2005. I wonder whether part of the reason both that this episode provokes the greatest interest and also that the play is not one of the best loved may come from our anxieties that the behaviour of the citizen-parasite in using his own daughter in the furtherance of the plot seems callous. If this is so, we should note that we are playing into the social norms of Roman society in finding it more offensive that a freeborn and necessarily virginal citizen girl should be used as part of a plot, even though all she has to do is dress up and pretend for a short time, whereas the use of prostitute girls, slaves or ex-slaves, does not offend us in the same way, even when they might have to endure a great deal more than an offence to their sense of propriety. On the other hand, the particular offence here is that the perpetrator is the victim's father, on which see Sherberg 2001.
[23] Slater 2000, 31–44.
[24] McCarthy 2000, 122–66.

apoetic rather than metatheatrical. This paper is little more than an expansion of the comment I made in my 2009 book on Roman comedy, which I take the liberty of quoting here: 'To this [i. e. McCarthy's] sociological reading I would only add a poetico-sociological footnote. This is the play where the ultimately powerless get some sort of a voice, some sort of power: the passive Virgo gets to play tricks *and* state her own objections; the normally useless lover gets to plan his own trick-solution; and the *architectus* gets to work on his own behalf. This might, then, be the most subversive of Plautine plays, in which the poet subliminally expresses his irritation and frustration at always having to work for someone else, to respond to the demands of the master, the convention, the audience, rather than his own desires and wishes. What a shame that it doesn't work.'[25]

My argument, in brief, is that Toxilus is an *architectus*, in the tradition of the greats,[26] throughout the play, but that he fails because he is working for himself. We see him in his role as *architectus* (not just *callidus*) in his stage-managing of the play-within-the-play; his control of the plot for the sake of the play as a whole, rather than just the immediate goal of the plot; and his use of self-aggrandising language.[27] We see his failure in that he does not achieve the comic resolution between slave and master (playwright and audience) which is necessary for ending. His closural *leno periit* is only an attempt to appropriate comic propriety. It cannot work because the *architectus* cannot be allowed to work for himself.

The opening of the play provides a good example of generic positioning, high and low:

> TO. Qui amans egens ingressus est princeps in Amoris uias
> superauit aerumnis suis aerumnas Hercul<e>i.
> nam cum leone, cum excetra, cum ceruo, cum apro Aetolico,
> cum auibus Stymphalicis, cum Antaeo deluctari mauelim
> quam cum Amore: ita fio miser quaerendo argento mutuo   5
> nec quicquam nisi 'non est' sciunt mihi respondere quos rogo.
>
> (Plaut. *Pers.* 1–6)[28]

TOXILUS: He who as a lover and needy has entered first onto the paths of Love has surpassed with his labours the labours of Hercules. For with the lion, with the snake, with the deer, with the Aetolian boar, with the birds of Stymphala, with Antaeus I would prefer to wrestle, rather than with Love. So I am made miserable seeking for a loan and those whom I ask have nothing to say except 'nothing'.

---

25 Sharrock 2009, 137–8.
26 Sharrock 2009, 17; Slater 2000, 31–44.
27 It is worth noting that the idea of Toxilus as playing the role of poet's voice, which is central to my argument, goes back at least as far as Chiarini 1979, for example, 43–5, 194–5, and indeed *passim*.
28 Throughout this paper, I use the text of Lindsay 1904 and 1905. Translations are my own.

The character who emerges onto stage is deeply confusing: he looks like a slave and he speaks with the magnificent excess, heroic overstatement, and generic pretension that we associate with the *architectus*.[29] The trouble is that we soon realise that he is not describing his young master when he uses the programmatically charged description *amans egens* ('in love and in need'), but rather it is he himself who has been made programmatically miserable trying programmatically to get loans from friends (5–6).[30] This is the comic dissonance which is the unique selling point of this play.[31] Alongside these expressions of comic programme, which make him look like a slave and sound like a citizen-lover, however, Toxilus has delusions of epic and tragic grandeur, in the comparison of his situation with the labours of Hercules, which do not belong easily with the language of the citizen-lover. The catalogue of monsters (3–4) which would be preferable to the lover's situation are both comic and the opposite of comic: in content they belong to grand poetry, but in expression to the presumptuous pretensions of the comic slave. The parallels offered by Woytek[32] for mythological comparisons elsewhere in Plautus are all in comic moments and are not statements from their own mouths about the problems of lovers. Pretension to mythic status is generally comic, not romantic.[33] This is because it is part of the ironic

---

[29] The *locus classicus* for the slave's magnificent excess in language and metaphor is the Troy image used by Chrysalus in *Bacchides* for his assault on the paternal money, together with Fraenkel's analysis of it (2007, 46–53 = 1922, 61–72). See Woytek 1982, 43–5 for a good account of Toxilus as *architectus doli*, a term he also uses. Auhagen 2001 also discusses the programmatic nature of this introduction.

[30] McCarthy 2000, 128; Slater 2000, 31; Chiarini 1979, 35–9, including discussion of the question of masks, 38.

[31] For example, McCarthy 2000, 130–1. Although most modern commentators agree on the existence and comic importance of dissonance in this play, I am inclined to think that McCarthy 2000 exaggerates the distinction between what she terms the romantic plot and the revenge plot. See for example McCarthy 2000, 146: 'because the original goal of bringing Lemniselenis has been overtaken by Toxilus' desire for vengeance against Dordalus, the play continues and takes as its new goal the punishment of the *leno*'. That vengeance, according to McCarthy, is not just personal spite but the attempt by Toxilus to appropriate citizen values and to punish Dordalus for failing to live up to them. Together with Chiarini 1979, I see the play as more integrally structured than this implies, in that the plan for the trick with the Persian was instigated before the chance arrival of the money via Sagaristio and continues to be necessary in order to avert immediate disaster. More importantly perhaps, it continues because Toxilus is the poet. Insofar as Toxilus is indeed appropriating citizen values, however, that argument supports my case, especially since he fails to do so effectively. If anyone has sinned against *fides*, it is Toxilus himself, rather than Dordalus.

[32] Woytek 1982, 139.

[33] Such a pretension contributes to the audacity of Terence's excessive young lover in *Eunuchus*, who does use mythological parallels for his erotic role, but he is exceptional. Woytek

self-aggrandisement of comedy. On the other hand, the close linguistic parallel for the programmatic phrase *amans egens* (together with *aerumna*, toil) at the opening of this speech and play is *Curculio* 142: *edepol qui amat, si eget, adficitur misera aerumna* ('by Pollux, anyone who is a lover, if he is needy, is assailed by miserable toil'). The *Curculio* line is, quite properly, spoken by a slave, and one who is playing those parts of the *architectus* role that involve programmatically-knowing irony and commentary, although he shares other parts of the role, including bombast, with a parasite. In that context, it is an expression of the ironic deprecation and down-cutting with which the slave treats his master's pretensions; in our context, at least for the knowing reader, the phrase hints at ironic undermining of Toxilus' erotic and social pretensions.[34] And since he is playing the role of Plautine *architectus*, such undermining applies also to the poet.

In true Plautine style of balance and contrast, a second character enters with a speech that is pure slave/comedy:

SAG. qui ero suo seruire uolt bene seruos seruitutem,
ne illum edepol multa in pectore suo conlocare oportet
quae ero placere censeat praesenti atque apsenti suo.
ego neque lubenter seruio neque sati' sum ero ex sententia,   10
sed quasi lippo oculo me eru' meus manum apstinere hau quit tamen
quin mi imperet, quin me suis negotiis praefulciat.
                                                              (Plaut. *Pers.* 7–12)

SAGARISTIO: He who wants to slavishly slave well as a slave for his master, should indeed by Pollux have in mind what he judges would please his master both when he is present and when he is absent. I neither slave away happily nor am I sufficiently to my master's liking, but my master can't keep his hand away from me like a bad eye but that he gives me orders and loads me up with his business.

Sagaristio's opening words say SLAVE, with comic repetition and *figura etymologica*,[35] also for a moment tricking us with the possibility that he might be a good (stupid) slave (7–9). A particularly interesting parallel mentioned by Woytek is *Aulularia*

1982, 142 shows rightly how Toxilus' song stands in the tradition of lovers' hyperbole. He describes Toxilus as a caricature of the citizen-son in love.

34 It must be admitted that the collocation of *amans* and *egens* is used by the citizen-lover himself at *Pseud.* 273, in the magnificent comic scene between Pseudolus (*seruus*), Calidorus (*adulescens*), and Ballio (*leno*), when Calidorus responds to Ballio's conventional (but of course in the context ironic) greeting, *quid agitur?*, with a remarkably knowing reference to his role, *amatur atque egetur acriter*, using the distancing impersonal passive which Pseudolus will use to such great effect at 453–7.

35 See Woytek 1982, 142 for parallels on the particular sound effect here; for the general principle, see Sharrock 2009, 167–90.

589: *nam qui ero ex sententia seruire seruos postulat* ... ('for he who as a slave plans to serve his master as he would wish ...'). This comes in the programmatic opening speech by the slave of Lyconides, where he presents himself as playing the role of loyal slave. He too emphasises SLAVE, by repetitions in 591–2. The point here is not just that both Sagaristio and the unnamed slave of *Aulularia* are using wordplay that is suited to comic slaves, but also that they are doing so precisely to emphasise their slave status – and to ironise the question of the kind of slave-role they might be playing, and therefore the status of slaves in the comic programme. Sagaristio's pose of servile self-abasement is quickly ironised (10) with a corporeal joke, which starts out sounding more vicious than it is. Just as someone with conjunctivitis can't keep his hands off his sore eye, so Sagaristio's master can't keep his hands off – not from beating the speaker, as we expect, but from entrusting him with business. The implication is that this is despite his previous subversion of his master's orders.

These two balanced opening speeches are followed by an ironic iteration of the standard comic meetings scene (13–15), which is described by Woytek as one of the nicest examples of the Plautine meeting-duet.[36] Before they make any real progress with the plot, there is a diversion consisting of *Plautinisches* between the two slaves, which is of interest to us here because of its class-based elements. Toxilus has opened the play with its essential problem, that he is transgressing the bounds of class by acting both as citizen-lover and play-controlling slave. In this, we should remember that the role of 'play-controlling slave' means that the playwright identifies his voice with the lowest class. It cannot be neutral, therefore, for the language of the two slaves to exhibit such knowing playfulness with social status:

> SAG. negotium edepol – TO. ferreum fortasse? SAG. plusculum annum
> fui praeferratus apud molas tribunus uapularis.
> TO. uetu' iam istaec militiast tua.
>
> (Plaut. *Pers.* 21–3)

> SAGARISTIO: Business matters – TOXILUS: The iron business, perhaps?
> SAGARISTIO: For more than a year I have been in the frontline of that business at the mills, a Tribune of the Vapulariate. TOXILUS: Of old this is your military service.

Sagaristio is in the iron business – not exactly trading, but rather being chained (that is, not a merchant but a slave). Then the interchange morphs from commerce to the military, thus moving from (what is rhetorically positioned as) middle to upper class.

These typical servile jokes are put aside in order for the play to return to its business, a love story with slaves, but improperly with slaves as lovers:

---

[36] Woytek 1982, 145.

> TO. saucius factus sum in Veneris proelio:
> sagitta Cupido cor meum transfixit. SAG. iam serui hic amant?
>
> (Plaut. *Pers.* 24–5)

> TOXILUS: I have been wounded in the battle of Venus. Cupid has transfixed my heart with an arrow. SAGARISTIO: Are slaves lovers around here now?

Here again Toxilus appropriates the language of love and the language of war, both the prerogative of the master class.[37] Woytek describes the phrase *Veneris proelio* as 'auffallend',[38] and gives a number of parallels from elevated and/or upper-class literature, as he does also for *Cupido cor meum transfixit*. Although the use of bombastic language and military metaphors for the action of the *architectus* is one of the hallmarks of Plautine language, the outstanding example being Chrysalus' famous Troy metaphor in *Bacchides*, what we have here is much closer to a direct appropriation by the slave of upper-class language. I would say that when Toxilus says to Sagaristio *uetu' iam istaec militiast tua*, he is speaking in the tradition of Chrysalus and other bombastic slaves, but when Toxilus says *sagitta Cupido cor meum transfixit*, he is daring actually to use the language of his betters without irony.

In answer, Sagaristio puts his finger on the problematic paradox of the play with his response *iam serui hic amant?*. As Chiarini brilliantly noted, *hic* here is metatheatrical, and means 'in this play, in contravention of the norms of New Comedy'.[39] The verb *amare*, in comedy, does not generally have the broad sense of everything from liking hot dinners to having sex, but, at least in programmatic context, has the specific indication that the subject is acting as a citizen-son pursuing either an expensive prostitute for immediate pleasure or a citizen-daughter as a wife – or, in recognition plays, both.[40]

---

37 If, as suggested by Chiarini 1979, 28–9, underneath the servile appropriation of elite discourse there is a trace of the Greek original in which the lover was indeed an elite citizen-son, the outrageousness of Plautus' creation is only enhanced.
38 Woytek 1982, 152.
39 Chiarini 1979, 24–5.
40 The instances of the verb in the plays of Plautus are, of course, legion, the vast majority of them applying to the action of citizen-sons, *adulescentes*, while a few apply to those usurping such a role. I would just like to note the nice class-based rejoinder of Olympio to Lysidamus (it will be remembered that the two are engaged in a complex play around the hierarchical control of sexual access, with the supposedly respectable married citizen-father arranging for his slave to 'marry' a desirable apparent slave girl, so that he himself can enjoy her first night). Olympio says, *tu amas: ego essurio et sitio* ('you love, I am hungry and thirsty', *Cas.* 724). Love belongs to the upper classes, while the language of food, as has been so effectively shown by Gowers 1993, belongs to the lower classes. The additional complexity here, however, is that the language of hunger and still more of thirst can apply metaphorically to sexual desire. It is undoubtedly true that there are instances of the verb in

But Toxilus doesn't see the problem. Rather, he continues in tragic vein, with a statement of *aporia*, followed by what in Augustan poetry we would call *recusatio* of gigantomachy:[41]

> TO. quid ego faciam? disne aduorser? quasi Titani cum is belligerem
> quibu' sat esse non queam?
>
> (Plaut. *Pers.* 26–7)
>
> TOXILUS: What am I to do? Should I oppose myself to the gods? Should I like a Titan fight against them to whom I am not equal?

Sagaristio's response to this appropriation of upper-class discourse is to copy the medium with a suitably servile message warning of physical punishment:

> SAG. uide modo ulmeae catapultae tuom ne transfigant latus.
>
> (Plaut. *Pers.* 28)
>
> SAGARISTIO: Watch out that those elmy catapults don't transfix your side.

In doing so, he is wrenching from his interlocutor the true language of the Plautine *architectus*. Throughout the play, Sagaristio tries to hold up the role of *architectus*, both in language and in plotting, and indeed does have many of the attributes of the *servus callidus*,[42] including the extremely important attribute of not working for himself, but he never quite gains metatheatrical control. He regularly speaks metatheatricality, but his role is more like that of Simia (in *Pseudolus*, where the eponymous hero is distinctly concerned that his helper might become a rival[43]) or Milphidippa (a highly self-conscious actress in *Miles*).[44]

Toxilus' next words pull him back into the slave-role in their medium, though they show his lack of awareness of how the role should be played and claim an impossible prize:

> TO. basilice agito eleutheria.
>
> (Plaut. *Pers.* 29)
>
> TOXILUS: I am acting the festival of freedom royally.

Plautus which do not convey this narrow meaning, such as those describing friendship between women (for example *Cist.* 1–7, Selenium to her friend Gymnasium and the latter's mother), or those referring to familial relationships which could be expected to include respect (for example, ironically, the *senex amator* Demaenetus, expressing his desire to be a good father who will be loved by his son, as his own father was to him …).

41 Strictly, titanomachy, but the point is the same.
42 McCarthy 2000, 133.
43 Gowers 1993, 52–6, 78–9 and esp. 93–107; Slater 2000, 110–14.
44 This connection is noted also by Chiarini 1979, 41.

What perhaps he does not remember is that a claim to be acting *basilice* belongs to the clever slave, the *architectus* who manages the plot for the sake of his young master, whether or (more likely) not it results in freedom for himself.[45] The enjoyment of temporary freedom in the absence of the master is indeed the norm for the slaves and young men of comedy. Such an inversion of normal life is, if we follow the carnivalesque reading of Segal,[46] of the essence of comedy. But Toxilus makes a mistake in thinking that he can drive the plot for his own benefit.

Toxilus and Sagaristio contend for control of the plot. It is Sagaristio who brings along the money which enables the purchase of Lemniselenis.[47] The money is poured into his hands by sheer chance, when, in keeping with his self-introduction in the first scene, his own master gives him the money to go and buy some cattle. It thus arrives to Toxilus also as a bolt from the blue, after he has already set his own plot in motion. The trick about the Persian merchant and the exotic slave who turns out to be a free citizen-daughter could equally well have been used without Sagaristio's money, although it is true that the positive atmosphere created by the first deal between Toxilus and Dordalus paves the way for the deception of Dordalus. I would regard Sagaristio's contribution here as similar to the kind of convenient accident which the *architectus* uses to his own advantage, like the sudden arrival of the messenger Harpax who is tricked into providing the convenient letter for Pseudolus.

Both Sagaristio and Toxilus exult, in the way only *architecti* do, when they achieve plot-moving success. Sagaristio's celebration comes when money has fallen from the sky, as he says (258), which allows him to give it to his friend to buy Lemniselenis' freedom. His celebration, which, although probably lacunose,[48] is nonetheless clear for our purposes, takes the form of a hymn of thanks to Jupiter, the language of which, coming as it does from 'der höchesten poetischen Sphäre',[49] is exactly appropriate to the self-aggrandising, but also self-ironic, kind of celebration which I am suggesting is particularly associated with *architecti*:

---

45 Pseudolus' *statum ... quam basilicum* (*Pseud.* 458) is a fine example. See Fraenkel 2007, 131 = 1922, 194–6. See Chiarini 1979, 40–1 for this piece of self-aggrandisement as a precursor to the servile self-aggrandising celebrations.
46 Segal 1987 = 1968.
47 Lemniselenis is necessarily freed by Dordalus, rather than being purchased from him and then freed (or not) by her lover, because as a slave himself Toxilus would not legally be able to free her.
48 Woytek 1982, 253. The third person plural *danunt* in 256 indicates that there must be some words to the effect of 'and the other gods I give thanks'.
49 Woytek 1982, 251.

> SAG. Ioui opulento, incluto, Ope gnato,
> supremo, ualido, uiripotenti,
> opes, spes bonas, copias commodanti
> * lubens uitulorque merito,
> quia meo amico amiciter hanc commoditatis copiam
> danunt, argenti mutui ut ei egenti opem adferam;
>
> (Plaut. *Pers.* 251–6)

> SAG. To Jupiter the wealthy, famous, son of Wealth, greatest, strong, powerful in might, who provides wealth, good hopes, abundance, gladly and rightly I give a cry of joy, because they give to my friend in a friendly way this abundance of obligingness, so that I can give him in his need the resource of a loan.

Sagaristio, be it noted, is working here for someone else.

Toxilus himself has a much more magnificent celebration once Dordalus has fallen into the trap of the Virgo-trick:

> TO. Hostibu' uictis, ciuibu' saluis, re placida, pacibu' perfectis,
> bello exstincto, re bene gesta, integro exercitu et praesidiis,
> quom bene nos, Iuppiter, iuuisti, dique alii omnes caelipotentes,
> eas uobis gratis habeo atque ago, quia probe sum ultus meum inimicum.
> nunc ob eam rem inter participes diuidam praedam et participabo.
>
> (Plaut. *Pers.* 753–7)

> TOXILUS: With enemies conquered, with citizens saved, with the state calm, with peace achieved, with war put out, with the matter done well, with army and garrison whole, since you have aided us well, Jupiter and all the other gods and heavenly powers, I render you grateful thanks, now that I am thoroughly avenged on my enemy. Now therefore I shall divide the plunder among my confederates and share it out.

His language here recalls the famous Troy image developed so outrageously by Chrysalus in *Bacchides*.[50] All three celebrating slaves are alluding more or less explicitly to the Roman institution of the Triumph.[51] They are thus claiming for themselves a position which is among the highest in the Roman citizen-world, a world in which, as slaves, they have no place. This is undoubtedly self-aggrandising. What makes it ironic is not just the outrageousness of the aggrandisement but also the fact that everyone knows that they themselves gain nothing. This nothingness is what makes the association of himself with the controlling slave by the playwright into an act of self-deprecation.

---

[50] McCarthy 2000, 153, and see above, page 107.
[51] Gruen 1990, 137 suggests that triumphing slaves are intended as parodies of generals fighting over whether they get a formal Triumph or not.

The trouble for Toxilus is that in the comic economy he has no right to this celebration, because his victory is won for his own sake. Slaves may win temporary victories over their masters in the negotiation of comic power, as we will consider further below, but they are not allowed to have had the main goal of the play and plot being to get a girl for themselves. My final and core claim for this play is that Toxilus fails. This may seem like a rash claim, since the play ends with him in enjoyment and apparent possession of the girl, as host of the party, and as successful tormentor of the agelast Dordalus, with no sign of any return of his master. And yet, it seems to me that he loses the sympathy of the audience. I do not even know whether Plautus intends this loss of sympathy, although of course I like to think that he does, but I want to claim that my argument depends even less than usual on authorial intention.

Before we consider the ending of the play, we must pay attention to a brief and very unusual interchange just before the play's closing moments, during the ragging scene which constitutes the finale. Toxilus, Sagaristio, and Lemniselenis, with at least Paegnium in attendance, are enjoying a celebratory party when Dordalus appears from the forum, bemoaning his lot. Toxilus insists that they ironically invite him to join them and that *ludificemus*. Lemniselenis demurs at the idea of mocking Dordalus, and Toxilus turns on her aggressively, has a rant about the ingratitude of freed persons and their desire to display their freedom by opposition to their patron, after which Lemniselenis humbly submits to his wishes:

> TO. agite sultis, hunc ludificemus. LE. nisi si dignust, non opust.
> et me hau par est. TO. credo eo quia non inconciliat, quom te emo.
> LE. at tamen non – tamen – TO. caue ergo sis malo | et sequere me. 835
> te mihi dicto audientem esse addecet, nam hercle apsque me
> foret et meo praesidio, hic faceret te prostibilem propediem.
> sed ita pars libertinorum est: nisi patrono qui aduorsatust,
> nec sati' liber sibi uidetur nec sati' frugi nec sat honestus,
> ni id ecfecit, ni ei male dixit, ni grato ingratus repertust. 840
> LE. pol bene facta tua me hortantur tuo ut imperio pareant.
> TO. ego sum tibi patronus plane qui huic pro te argentum dedi.
> * graphice hunc uolo ludificari. LE. meo ego in loco sedulo curabo.
> (Plaut. *Pers.* 833–43)

TOXILUS: Come on then, let's make fun of him. LEMNISELENIS: Unless he's deserved it, there's no need. And it isn't right for me. TOXILUS: Yeah right, since he didn't stand in the way of me buying you. LEMNISELENIS: But but not – but – TOXILUS: You just watch out for trouble and follow my lead. It's fitting for you to obey my words, for by Hercules if it hadn't been for me and my protection, he would be making a common prostitute of you. But this is the way of freed people: unless such a one has not set himself against his patron, he doesn't seem sufficiently free to himself nor good and honourable enough, unless

> he's done this, unless he's spoken badly to him, unless he's been found ungrateful to his benefactor. LEMNISELENIS: Good gracious, your good deeds certainly do urge me to obey your orders. TOXILUS: I, who gave the money to that man for you, am clearly your patron. I want him to be mocked magnificently. LEMNISELENIS: For my part I'll see to it carefully.

The passage touches on some very sensitive matters regarding slavery and freedom. Here we have Toxilus, a slave, speaking rudely to Lemniselenis, a free(d) person. He accuses her of ingratitude towards her patron, which in Roman terms would be a serious moral offence and one which might in its own terms seem to be likely to win the sympathy of a Roman audience. In doing so, however, he claims the role of patron, despite the fact that strictly speaking he paid money to Dordalus not to buy Lemniselenis as his own slave and then free her (as would be usual for a citizen-son, although it is often not clear whether freedom comes into it), but rather to make Dordalus free her, with the result that she could join Toxilus. That such is the situation is clear from 426, 438–9, and 484–8, in the last of which Dordalus invites Toxilus to go along and check with the praetor in the forum if he is in any doubt. It would indeed be true that from Roman understanding of *gratia* Lemniselenis owes a great deal to Toxilus, so his complaint of ingratitude would resonate to some extent in that way. But the specific claim that she is rejecting her patron, her former master and the man who freed her, in refusing to mock Dordalus has the particular absurdity that her patron, her former master and the man who freed her is in fact Dordalus himself (as must also be implied by 849, when Lemniselenis invites someone she addresses as *patrone mi* to come in to dinner, to which Dordalus makes an unpleasant reply). My interest in this legal problem, however, is limited only to pointing out the extent to which Toxilus is at fault in this interchange.

But the absurdity of Toxilus' rant is not the only damaging aspect of this interchange. When he turns on his beloved, interrupting her, aggressively complaining about her ingratitude, and insisting on her behaving in a way contrary to her feelings and good sense, he acts in a manner which has no parallels among comic lovers. Although slaves often abuse other slaves – and we have had an extended example of that in the long scene between Paegnium and Sophoclidisca – lovers do not abuse the beloveds who have just been granted to them.[52]

---

[52] Woytek 1982, 43–5 and 431–2 notes the oddities at work here. First of all, there is the surprisingly ladylike tact of Lemniselenis, on which he explores the rival suggestions either that 833–51 is a later interpolation or that Lemniselenis' intervention comes from the Greek original, the second of which he favours. If one were so inclined, one might guess that such behaviour would be particularly appropriate in a girl who will turn out to be freeborn and marriageable, as the suggested parallel with *Curc.* 697 implies. Woytek is also disturbed by the unpleasantness of Toxilus, which he describes as 'die Grobheit der Drohung, die man einem Verliebten gar nicht

Woytek suggests[53] that with the words *caue ergo sis malo* (835) Toxilus is actually threatening Lemniselenis with physical punishment, which may indeed be the case, given the frequent meaning of *malum* with regard to slaves and comedy. If so, his behaviour is even further out of line with the treatment both of beloveds by lovers (in comedy, if not in real life) and of the free by the enslaved (in comedy, and in real life). It seems to me that commentators are not sufficiently alive to the implications of a lover who turns on his beloved, because there are so many odd things going on here to do with Roman law and Greek originals.[54]

Ragging scenes belong to slaves. When Pseudolus triumphs over his master, the two of them alone on stage (*Pseud.* 1285–328), or Epidicus over his master and the master's friend, again without wider audience (*Epid.* 675–731), we can enjoy the inversion. In this situation, however, the scene could be held to cause Toxilus to lose his role as lover, in that this is a slave scene, and to lose his role as *architectus*, because he lacks the legitimating framework of his *erus minor*, while his triumph is over someone who is not sufficiently different from himself. Dordalus is an outsider, but there is no insider to give us a clear sense of difference. Moreover, there is one line in the celebratory song that constitutes the first scene of 'act five' which could perhaps hint at an association between Toxilus and Ballio. Toxilus claims that it is his birthday (768),[55] just as Ballio does (*Pseud.* 165) in the magnificently awful scene of tyrannical abuse with which he is introduced in *Pseudolus*. Toxilus, working for himself, becomes a monster, just

---

zutrauen würde' (432). In his introduction (44–5), Woytek offers a good account of the dual roles of Toxilus, and of the strangeness and inappropriateness of the scene we are considering. His explanation of the latter is simply the former – so Toxilus' behaviour is just a trace of the Greek original, in which the role of lover was taken by a citizen-son. Like all such reconstructions, while this may or may not be the case, it is not adequate as an interpretation of our play. For one thing, Plautus could easily have left it out. For a second, although citizen-sons do sometimes behave in a high-handed and magisterial manner, I am not aware of any example of a newly successful lover suddenly turning on his beloved in this manner. See also the discussion of McCarthy 2000, 157–8.

53 Woytek 1982, 44.
54 For example, Chiarini 1979, 201, for whom it is the triumph of paradox, as is central to his argument about metatheatrical farce; Lowe 1995, 27–8, n. 15, where Toxilus' behaviour is described as 'out-of-character' and 'bullying', but explained simply as 'signs of the hand of Plautus'. Auhagen 2001, 105–7 is sympathetic to Lemniselenis, but for my reading she is too attached to the notion of Lemniselenis as a 'good *hetaira*' to have much interest in the negative effect on the reception of Toxilus.
55 McCarthy 2000, 129, n. 15 notes this parallel also.

as women who take vengeance into their own hands become monsters (Philomela, Procne, Hecuba, Medea).[56]

There is nothing in the play to say that Toxilus loses, in that his master does not in fact return within the timeframe of the play, so he does not lose his girl nor suffer the immediate threat of punishment. There are, however, hints at the return of the master.[57] What these hints do, I suggest, is to point to the absence of proper resolution for Toxilus.[58] The standard ending for an *architectus* involves some degree of resolution with the master. In the strange case of *Miles*, this is by absolute escape, but that is exceptional in that the role of 'master' is being taken by the soldier (an outsider to be tricked). Unusual also is the case of *Amphitruo*, where Mercury is a parody of the *architectus* – and is also not working for himself, but for Jupiter![59] Among the other great examples, Epidicus is unusual in achieving freedom, but he does so only after the exposure of his tricks, the near-punishment of binding and the power game of forgiveness, which I would suggest constitutes the real resolution of an *architectus* play. The clever slave is typically exposed, and then wins his immunity from punishment. Although he does win some sort of moral battle over the master, he does so only by returning to the *status quo ante*, while the master also regains his position. The difference for Toxilus is that he has not gained any of this resolution, because he has not really faced the true opponent – the master who will return. This is not a case like the end of *Pseudolus*, when the eponymous hero shrugs off his master's threats of future vengeance:

---

[56] Slater 2000, 44 sees Toxilus as 'virtually the Aristophanic hero reborn' in his ability to do the work and also enjoy the girl. I am much less optimistic about his degree of success.

[57] The first mention of the absent master is at line 29; at 787 and 811, Dordalus reminds Toxilus of the risk he is running in this regard, and thus reminds the audience that they might expect such an outcome. Chiarini 1979, 23 sees the absence of the 'fantomatico padrone di Toxilus, Timarchides, e il non meno fantomatico ... padrone di Sagaristio' as lurking in the background, especially in the incomplete ending, what in Augustan literature we would call 'absent presences'. See also McCarthy 2000, 155.

[58] Chiarini 1979, 23: 'la condizione servile di Toxilus esclude in partenza la possibilità del tradizionale lieto fine, il suo successo come "tessitore d'inganni" è riduardato come autosufficiente, lo stratagemma da lui indeato non funge da strumento del destino, non è asservito da alcuna finalità etica, non porta a nulla di definitivo.' On Chiarini's interpretation, this contributes to making the play farce; on mine, it is (deliberate? programmatic?) failure.

[59] Other plays contain versions of the controlling slave who speaks for the poet, but not in their full glory. Tyndarus in *Captivi* has some elements of the *callidus*, especially in his language, although he does not, I think, make explicit any claim to be the poet – and he is most certainly not working for himself.

> PS. non me deices auidum esse hominem? nam hinc numquam eri' nummo diuitior,
> neque te mei tergi misereret, hoc sei non hodie ecfecissem.
> SIMO. erit ubi te ulciscar, sei uiuo. PS. quid minitare? habeo tergum.
>
> (Plaut. *Pseud.* 1323–5)

> PSEUDOLUS: Will you not say I am a greedy man? You shall never be richer by a penny from this side, nor would you be taking pity on my back, if I had not achieved this today. SIMO: There will come a time when I will have vengeance on you, if I live. PSEUDOLUS: Why are you threatening? I have a back.

Similar to Pseudolus, but very different from Toxilus, is the situation for Tranio:

> TR. quid grauaris? quasi non cras iam commeream aliam noxiam:
> ibi utrumque, et hoc et illud, poteris ulcisci probe.
>
> (Plaut. *Most.* 1178–9)

> TRANIO: What are you making a fuss about? As if tomorrow I won't be committing some other crime: then you can take as much revenge as you like, for this and that.

Chrysalus at the last minute is not only exposed but also loses his controlling role to the Bacchis sisters, who achieve the final victory over the old men. *Curculio* is a case, a bit like *Persa*, where there is only a *leno*, not a master, to overcome (although, as I have suggested, this is not really the case in *Persa*). Here the role of *architectus* is shared between the slave and the parasite. Here the victory really is over the *leno*, but final resolution comes by that magic trick of comedy, anagnorisis. Whether or not a Greek original to *Persa* included a resolution which made Lemniselenis a suitable bride for a version of Toxilus played by a citizen-son,[60] Plautus has chosen not to follow that pattern, including only a parody of comic anagnorisis, in the contrived loss and discovery of the Virgo.

Toxilus ends in self-celebration, triumphing over the pimp, but I'm not sure he gets away with it:

> DO. an me hic parum exercitum hisce
> habent? TO. conuenisse * te Toxilum.
> mei spectatores, bene ualete. leno periit. CATERVA. plaudite.
>
> (Plaut. *Pers.* 856–8)

> DORDALUS: Have these guys done me over too little? TOXILUS: * that you have met with Toxilus. My dear spectators, farewell. The pimp has perished. COMPANY: Applaud.

---

[60] See Chiarini 1979, 26.

The *ecce homo* moment is reminiscent also of that at the end of *Epidicus* (732). Toxilus gets the last word,[61] but we need to remember that his victory over the pimp was only half the battle. Pseudolus had a pimp and an *erus maior* to overcome in order to help his *erus minor*. Toxilus has won only half the battle, and for the wrong purposes.

Scott takes trickster stories as being examples of his subversive unofficial discourse.[62] Speaking specifically about Brer Rabbit stories of slaves, he says: 'at another level they appear to celebrate the cunning wiles and vengeful spirit of the weak as they triumph over the strong.' This may well be true, and it may well be – it is likely – that some subordinate people in some of the audiences of Roman comedy enjoyed the triumph of the slave for precisely that reason, but nonetheless the fact that the slave cannot triumph in his own name seems to me to undermine the capacity of the plays to offer an enabling reading to slaves.

The poet takes on the subject-position of the slave, in order to present his comedy programmatically. He exults in his success, but he also cuts it down to size, by the very fact that it is a non-person who is doing this succeeding and exulting. Hierarchy of genres maps onto social hierarchies. The *architectus*' language of celebration is self-aggrandisement given material form, but the rhetoric which Plautus engages with in identifying his own voice with this character is self-deprecatory – because he makes himself a slave who is working for others.

But what about that other possibility for comic identification, the small citizen? The Aristophanic hero worked for himself, most outrageously perhaps in *Acharnians*, where Dicaeopolis (for goodness' sake!) strikes a private peace treaty with the Spartan enemy and refuses to let his compatriots share in its joys, despite his name. I would love to see an echo of this in Plautus, but I fear it is not to be. The one place where Plautus does show an interest in the relative positions of different citizens is *Aulularia*.[63] *Aulularia* is in part a play about the relationship between rich and poor citizens, and the relationship between a particular indi-

---

61 We cannot know whether he or the company as a whole should be assigned the final *plaudite*. We also do not know what is missing from the penultimate line, but it is likely to be something along the lines of 'you won't forget'. The text I have reproduced above is that of Lindsay 1904–1905, vol. 2. Woytek 1982 prints: Tox: *convenisse te Toxilum me<mineris>/spectatores, bene valete. leno periit. plaudite*, thus giving the call for applause to Toxilus as well as completing the sense of the previous line with the emendation from the 16th century editor Camerarius. See Woytek 1982, 440.
62 Scott 1990, 19.
63 *Trinummus* and *Mostellaria* both play with the possibility of loss of wealth, but from the position of the landed elite. See Rosivach 1986 on this.

vidual and his place in society and citizen interaction.⁶⁴ But where is the generic subject-position? Is it, as in Aristophanes, with the little man? Or does it, as with Menander, stand back from any such identification and reflect philosophically on wealth and class? In brief, I would say that while it does indeed flirt with class-conscious comedy, more importantly it holds back from making a generic association with any citizen class. Instead, it gives a small role to a character who toys with the poet's voice, and tells us how to read the role of that identification.

Much of the interest in *Aulularia* has surrounded the character of Euclio, including the question of whether he was always a miser or whether the discovery of the pot of gold made him so and turned him into a paranoid misanthrope.⁶⁵ Be that as it may, he certainly presents himself as 'a poor man' within the scope of the play. The language of wealth and poverty within the play is such that it would be relatively easy to read it as engaged in a philosophical or political discussion about relative affluence within the citizen body. Versions of *pauper* occur nineteen times in *Aulularia*, out of a total of fifty for the entire Plautine corpus. There is, moreover, the tempting fable of the bull and the ass:

> EVC. uenit hoc mihi, Megadore, in mentem, ted esse hominem diuitem,
> factiosum, me item esse hominem pauperum pauperrumum;
> nunc si filiam locassim meam tibi, in mentem uenit
> te bouem esse et me esse asellum: ubi tecum coniunctus siem,
> ubi onus nequeam ferre pariter, iaceam ego asinus in luto,   230
> tu me bos magis hau respicias gnatus quasi numquam siem.
> et te utar iniquiore et meu' me ordo inrideat,
> neutrubi habeam stabile stabulum, si quid diuorti fuat:
> asini me mordicibus scindant, boues incursent cornibus.
>
> (Plaut. *Aul.* 226–34)

> EUCLIO: It occurs to me, Megadorus, that you are a rich man and powerful, but I am the poorest of the poor; now, if I were to give you my daughter in marriage, it occurs to me that you are a bull and I am a donkey. If I were yoked to you, when I couldn't bear the burden equally, the donkey-me would lie down in the mud, whereas the bull-you would have no more regard for me than if I had never been born. I wouldn't have you as an equal and my own order would mock me, I wouldn't have a stable stable on either side, if there

---

64 See Konstan 1983, 33–46 for an influential and insightful reading of the play in relation to the requirements of civic life. Konstan is particularly effective in reading the social implications of the play, although his concern is more with the relationship between individual and society than it is between different classes of individuals.

65 See Kruschwitz 2002 for the history of reading the play as a character study. His argument is that the play is neither simply about character nor simply a morality tale about money as the 'root of all evils', but rather that it is only so in the wrong hands – that is, any hands other than those of Lyconides. There is a good brief account in Stockert 1983, 18–20.

should be a divorce. The donkeys would bite me to shreds, the bulls would attack me with their horns.

At first sight, this looks like a strong reason to see the play as philosophically concerned with the relationship between different social classes within the polity, especially since Euclio seems to be developing a fable in what might be interesting sociological ways, rather than simply reproducing it.[66] Tempting though this moment is for modern readers, Euclio's position is somewhat undermined by the fact that he is in fact in possession of a sum of money which would allow him to interact with Megadorus on, if not an equal, at least not too discrepant a level – as indeed he does at the end of the play (in whatever form that happened).[67] Likewise, when Megadorus appears to be advocating the marriage between rich men and poor girls without a dowry as beneficial to social stability, his case is undermined by the ensuing tirade against *uxores dotatae*, which shows that his contribution to the harmony of the orders was nothing more than self-interested male chauvinism.[68] If there is any class-based generic rhetoric of comedy in this play, it is working in a different way.

The question, for my metapoetic reading, is as to who does hold the poet's voice in this play. Euclio himself regularly addresses the audience and uses bombastic language, which is a feature of the rhetoric of ironic self-aggrandisement. If we could make a strong case for Euclio as holder of the poet's voice, we would be nearer to seeing an interest in social relations within the citizen body reflected in metapoetic terms. But I suggest that this is not the case. Euclio winks at the audience, or rather Plautus winks at the audience from behind Euclio's mask, but not in the form of a poor man getting one over on a rich man. Rather, it is in the form of an actor laughing at a ridiculous character. And Euclio never controls the action, but rather is controlled by it.

Who else, then?

The Lar, who controls the action and drives it towards a suitably comic resolution, is an external character belonging to a different level of existence and is therefore not a good candidate for the poet's voice.[69] Indeed, he makes a less clear bid for the poet's voice than does, for example, Auxilium in *Cistellaria*, who

---

[66] Stocchi 2009, 76–7 describes the passage as recalling several easily identifiable Aesopic fables, although it is not very close to any. Brind D'Amour 1976 suggests that Plautus is responsible for the move from horse to bull, which is later copied by other Roman authors. Neither scholar, however, is particularly interested in the details of Euclio's concerns.
[67] See Konstan 1983, 40.
[68] See Kruschwitz 2002, 153–6.
[69] Lefèvre 2001, 19–20 sees him as a distinctly badly behaved deity by comparison with anything from Greek.

has just been undermined in his telling of the prologue by the overly talkative and unnamed former prostitute who knows the background. Both these divine personifications, along with Arcturus in *Rudens*, could play a role as kind of ghosts of Hellenistic playwrights with and against whom Plautus (and the Plautine slave) construct/s his play. They do not enter into the rhetoric of self-aggrandisement and self-deprecation. Staphyla might be a candidate, since she talks to the audience in a knowing and informative way, but she is too passive to hold the poet's voice. At the other end of the spectrum, there is Megadorus, although he is the (perfectly sanguine) victim rather than the controller of the plot. He does have his magnificent misogynistic moment (475–535, with a bit of commentary from the observing Euclio), which is addressed directly to the audience and seems to step outside the dramatic illusion of the play in something of the manner of the Aristophanic parabasis. The scene begins with the recommendation for social stability that rich men should marry girls without dowries, and develops into the well-known tirade against *uxores dotatae*. It may well be that the first element is a reflection of Hellenistic interest in relationships within the social structure, but it might also be a parody of such, since Megadorus' philosophy is self-interested, having more to do with the control of women than with the relationship between different classes of men. The second element might well be a piece of pure *Plautinisches*.[70] More importantly for my purposes, however, this is not an act of triumph, not an act of conscious self-aggrandising but one of unconscious assumption of natural superiority. Inevitably, therefore, it cannot involve much opportunity for self-ironisation! For these reasons, I suggest that it has no possibility of aligning Megadorus with the poet's voice.

But while what we have considered so far in *Aulularia* might say something about social class and might say something about genre, I don't think it said anything about the two of them together. In particular, the generic subject-position of comedy here, I suggest, is *not* the poor citizen, not Euclio. It might, however, belong to someone rather minor – the *servus Lyconidis*. This character appears only towards the end of the extant play (and clearly towards the end of the whole play). He lacks a name. Some manuscripts call him Strobilus, others Pythodicus, possibly a corruption of the former, but the idea seems to me preposterous that in Plautus' play he is to be identified with the character of that name who jokes about Euclio earlier in the play.[71] His entrance monologue at 587 is programmatic for the role of the comic slave as helper to the young man in love:

---

[70] See Stockert 1983, 136–7.
[71] One is, I suspect, more likely to call the Slave 'Strobilus' if one is thinking also about the construction of the Greek original. One major difficulty in seeing Plautus' two characters as one and the same

> L. S. Hoc est serui facinus frugi, facere quod ego persequor,
> ne morae molestiaeque imperium erile habeat sibi.
> nam qui ero ex sententia seruire seruos postulat,
> in erum matura, in se sera condecet capessere.   590
> sin dormitet, ita dormitet seruom sese ut cogitet.
> nam qui amanti ero seruitutem seruit, quasi ego seruio,
> si erum uidet superare amorem, hoc serui esse officium reor,
> retinere ad salutem, non enim quo incumbat eo impellere.
>
> (Plaut. *Aul.* 587–94)

> LYCONIDES' SLAVE: This is the action of a well-behaved slave, to do what I'm doing, not to regard his master's command as a waste of time and a nuisance. For a slave who desires to slave according to his master's wishes ought to manage things for his master first, for himself last. Even asleep, he ought to sleep in such a way as to bear in mind that he is a slave. For someone who slaves away for a master in love, as I am now slaving, if he sees love overcoming his master, I think it is the duty of this slave to hold him back towards safety, not to push him in the direction he's falling.

What is less common about it is that this helpful slave, like Trachalio in *Rudens*, does not have an *erus maior* to worry about, since Lyconides' father is clearly dead (779).[72] This means that he can draw at the same time on the 'faithful slave' type, but without having to be stupid, and the 'clever slave' type. The monologue tells us how important it is that a slave remembers his slavery and works tirelessly for his young master's benefit. The speech could almost be a comment on the behaviour of the two slaves who open *Persa*.[73] There, it is Sagaristio who plays on the 'faithful slave' type, likewise pushing it in our faces with alliteration and *figura etymologica* on SLAVE, only to ironise it as we saw above. On the other hand, it is Toxilus who gets into trouble because he is not working for his master, having not learned the lesson of 590. In addition, I would suggest that there must be some double-bluffing self-deprecating irony in Lyconides' Slave's presentation of himself here.[74] The good slave is notoriously stupid, the butt rather than the agent of trickery,[75] and never to be seen as the cipher of the poet, while the helper of the

---

is that the joking Strobilus is clearly familiar with Euclio, whereas the spying Slave only thinks that might be the father of the girl his master loves. See Stockert 1983, 16–8; Lefèvre 2001, 26–8.

[72] If we are meant to understand that Lyconides and his mother live with her brother, then I suppose one could regard Megadorus as *erus maior*, but this seems unlikely to me.

[73] I say this purely as a literary critical comment, not a suggestion of direct allusion or a comment on the relative dating of the plays.

[74] See also Lefèvre 2001, 84–5.

[75] Possibly we should see a hint of this point in his comment about the need to remember one's servile position even while asleep, if we connect it with Slater's 2000 account (142) of the imagery of sleep as deception.

amans is readily positioned as the clever slave, trickster, 'bad', and voice of the poet. The Slave of Lyconides challenges us with the idea that he might come in at this late stage and speak for the poet, from the position of the 'good slave'.

Having placed himself in the appropriate generic position, the slave now sits down to watch, like a highly controlling member of the audience. Eavesdropping is a characteristic of the clever slave, who gains the opportunity thereby for plot-development.[76] Euclio, on cue, comes out of the shrine and conveniently but unknowingly tells the world that there is a pot of gold in there. It is then that the Slave gets his first moment of muted celebration, responding to the turn of luck which – what? It ought to be that it allows him to pursue the love plot for his master:

> L. S. di inmortales, quod ego hunc hominem facinus audiui loqui?
> se aulam onustam auri apstrusisse hic intus in fano Fidi.
> caue tu illi fidelis, quaeso, potius fueris quam mihi.
> atque hic pater est, ut ego opinor, huius erus quam amat <meus>.
> ibo hinc intro, perscrutabor fanum, si inueniam uspiam   620
> aurum, dum hic est occupatus. sed si reppererro, o Fides,
> mulsi congialem plenam faciam tibi fideliam.
> id adeo tibi faciam; uerum ego mihi bibam, ubi id fecero. –
>
> (Plaut. *Aul.* 616–23)

> LYCONIDES' SLAVE: Immortal gods, what deed have I heard this man talking about? That he has hidden a pot laden with gold here inside this temple of Good-Faith. You make sure you're not more faithful to him, please, than to me. But, if I'm not wrong, this guy is the father of the girl whom my master loves. I'll go inside and have a look round the temple, to see if I can find the gold anywhere, while he's busy. But if I find it, o Good-Faith, I'll make you a full six-pint bucket of honeyed wine. I'll make it for you, but I'll drink it myself, when I've done it. –

Stronger is his response to the second hiding-and-finding sequence, in the parallel scene at 677, when Euclio has again accidentally told the slave exactly what he's going to do and where he's going to do it:[77]

> L. S. eugae, eugae, di me saluom et seruatum uolunt.
> iam ego illuc praecurram atque inscendam aliquam in arborem
> indeque opseruabo | aurum ubi apstrudat senex.
> quamquam hic manere me erus sese iusserat;   680
> certum est, malam rem potius quaeram cum lucro. –
>
> (Plaut. *Aul.* 677–81)

---

[76] Indeed, in plays where the role of *architectus* is shared between a slave and parasite, such as *Curculio*, the role of internal audience generally belongs to the slave.

[77] On the doubling of the hiding scenes, see Hunter 1981, 41; Lefèvre 2001, 83; Konstan 1983, 37.

LYCONIDES' SLAVE: Hurray, hurray! The gods want me to be safe and saved. Now I shall run over there and climb up on some tree and from there I shall keep watch to see where the old man hides the gold. Although my master had ordered me to stay here, I'd certainly rather risk some trouble with the loot. –

The slave's full-scale celebration, however, comes out at 701–12, after the intervening scene between Lyconides and his mother Eunomia (682–700), which reminds us of the pregnant girl who is the metaphorical parallel for the pot. Here is the slave:

> L. S. Picis diuitiis, qui aureos montis colunt,
> ego solus supero. nam istos reges ceteros
> memorare nolo, hominum mendicabula:
> ego sum ille rex Philippus. o lepidum diem!
>
> (Plaut. *Aul.* 701–4)

LYCONIDES' SLAVE: I alone surpass in wealth the griffins who dwell in the mountains of gold. I don't want to mention those other kings, mere beggars. I am King Philip himself. Oh happy day!

This is a celebration in the true Plautine *architectus* manner, full of extravagant exaggeration and magnificent self-promotion.

There follows another intervening and balancing scene, this time between Lyconides and Euclio – that magnificent piece of failed communication surrounding the girl and the pot (731–807).[78] When the knot is loosened and Euclio goes into the house to find out whether he has really just become a grandfather, the Slave of Lyconides picks up this rhetoric again at 808:

> L. S. Di inmortales, quibus et quantis me donatis gaudiis!
> quadrilibrem aulam auro onustam habeo. quis me est ditior?
> quis me Athenis nunc magi' quisquam est homo quoi di sint propitii?
>
> (Plaut. *Aul.* 808–10)

LYCONIDES' SLAVE: Immortal gods, with what and what great joys you endow me! I have a four-pound pot stuffed with gold. Who is there richer than me? Who in all Athens is there now to whom the gods are more propitious?

But there is going to be a nasty shock for the Slave. He made the mistake of celebrating the finding of the treasure as if it were for himself.[79] Rather, he needs, like

---

[78] See Konstan 1983, 39–40 on the close parallels between girl and pot.
[79] Lefèvre 2001, 24, and 94, notes that he is doing something very unusual within New Comedy, in that he is pursuing the intrigue against Euclio for his own sake. Although this may seem like a small point within the play, for my argument it is important.

every other comic slave, to use it to buy his master's beloved. Now we can note the oddity, remarked on also by Kruschwitz,[80] that in all his celebrations it is not clear what the Slave wants the money *for*. When he first discovers the existence of the pot of gold, his expression of intention to get his hands on it and hope to bargain with Fides is interwoven with his realisation that the victim of his planned appropriation is the father of his master's beloved, and therefore is central to the very task for which he has been commanded by his master to be here in the first place. He wants the money, but he doesn't tell us why. Instead, we have a sort of programmatic hint at the idea of those sorts of plays where it is necessary to appropriate money from a *senex*, ideally (as in the case of *Pseudolus*) the lover's own father, in order to pursue the young master's erotic goals by purchase. But not quite that, because this *senex* is instead the father of the beloved, so she can't be the sort of beloved whom one gains by straightforward mercantile means. When you need money in order to gain possession of a girl of that sort (i. e., one whom you already know to be a citizen), you need it in order to provide a dowry ...

The Slave's celebrations get more and more magnificently Plautine, without telling us about any direct goal until *after* their last iteration. It is only after he has met his master (after a typical meeting scene in which we are reminded of the clever slave's role as helper of his young master, 815) that the Slave wonders what he should say about the 'plunder' and decides to ask for his freedom. We will return to that decision in a moment, but first we might notice other hints about the Slave's intentions.

When the Slave first hears Euclio entrusting the pot to Fides, he plans to appropriate not only the money but also the goodwill of the goddess, to whom he will in recompense make a faithful offering of wine – which he will drink himself, for himself (*ego mihi bibam*, 623). This is entirely in keeping with the behaviour of controlling slaves. Indeed, alcoholic celebration is far more likely to be their reward than anything more substantial. After his first interaction with the crazy old man (who demanded to see his third hand!, 641) the Slave is now even more determined to get his hands on the money – in order to avenge himself on the *senex*:

L. S. Emortuom ego me mauelim leto malo
quam non ego illi dem hodie insidias seni.

(Plaut. *Aul.* 661–2)

LYCONIDES' SLAVE: I'd rather die a terrible death than fail to lay a trap for that old man today.

---

80 Kruschwitz 2002, 157–8.

This is exactly the attitude of a clever slave, for whom getting one over the old man is a goal in its own right.[81]

To return to the Slave's eventual decision to make a bid for freedom:

> L. S. quin ego illi me inuenisse dico hanc praedam atque eloquor?
> igitur orabo ut manu me emittat. ibo atque eloquar.
> repperi – LY. quid repperisti? L. S. non quod pueri clamitant
> in faba se repperisse.
>
> (Plaut. *Aul.* 816–9)

> LYCONIDES' SLAVE: Why don't I tell him that I have found this plunder and speak out? So I'll beg him to free me. I'll go and speak. I have found – LYCONIDES: What have you found? LYCONIDES' SLAVE: Not what the boys keep shouting that they have found in the bean.

When challenged by Lyconides, at first the Slave can only answer with a joke and has to work his way up to popping the question. This proposal, however, goes down like a lead balloon. Lyconides, who has now reached maturity in his civic role, dismisses the idea so contemptuously that the Slave backtracks quickly and pretends that he was only joking – only joking about asking for his freedom and also only joking about having found a pot of gold:

> LY. quod ego facinus audio ex te?[82] L. S. Euclioni huic seni surrupui.[83]
> LY. ubi id est aurum? L. S. in arca apud me. nunc uolo me emitti manu.
> LY. egone te emittam manu,
> scelerum cumulatissume?   825
> L. S. abi, ere, scio quam rem geras.
> lepide hercle animum tuom temptaui. iam ut eriperes apparabas:
> quid faceres, si repperissem?
>
> (Plaut. *Aul.* 822–8)

> LYCONIDES: What's this crime I hear from you? LYCONIDES' SLAVE: I stole[84] it from this old man Euclio. LYCONIDES: Where is that gold? LYCONIDES' SLAVE: In a box at my place. Now I want you to free me. LYCONIDES: Am I to free you, you heap of wickedness? LYCONIDES' SLAVE: Get away, master, I know what you're up to. By Hercules, I tempted

---

81 Compare, for example, Chrysalus at *Bacch.* 1067–75; Epidicus at *Epid.* 675–8, just before his last great tease of his master; or Pseudolus at (among others) *Pseud.* 1321; also Toxilus at *Pers.* 756.
82 Note that this is what Euclio says to Lyconides, 796, when he learns about the rape.
83 Leo (1885, 125) proposed that Lyconides, rather than the Slave, spoke this sentence, as *Euclioni hic seni subripuit*. I mention this because Stockert 1983 follows Leo. It does not make a major difference to my argument, although the outrage is better in the text printed by Lindsay.
84 See n. 83 above.

your mind nicely there. Just now you were getting ready to snatch it. What would you be doing, if I really had found it?

Lyconides is not impressed. The result is that the Slave must give up the gold and stop all that nonsense about freedom.[85]

What has happened since the Slave of Lyconides entered the stage, then, is that he has presented himself generically as the poet's voice, spouted the rhetoric of self-aggrandisement, made a bid for the reality of such self-aggrandising, but at the last moment realised his mistake and self-deprecatingly ironised his position, remaining forever subordinate to his master. The slave may hold the poet's voice, but if he is to remain comic he must do so for the sake of his masters.

Bibliography

Anderson, C. A. (2008), 'Archilochus, his Lost Shield, and the Heroic Ideal', *Phoenix* 62(3/4), 255–60.
Auhagen, U. (2001), 'Toxilus und Lemniselenis: ein paradoxes Liebespaar', in: S. Faller (ed.), *Studien zu Plautus' Persa* (ScriptOralia 121), Tübingen, 95–111.
Brind D'Amour, P. (1976), 'Des ânes et des boeufs dans l'*Aululaire*: commentaire des vers 226 à 235', *Maia* 28, 25–7.
Chiarini, G. (1979), *La Recita: Plauto, la Farsa, la Festa* (2nd edn., with addenda, 1983), Bologna.
Fraenkel, E. (1922), *Plautinisches im Plautus*, Berlin (English tr. by T. Drevikovsky and F. Muecke, *Plautine Elements in Plautus*, 2007, Oxford).
Gildenhard, I. (2003), 'The "Annalist" Before the Annalists: Ennius and his *Annales*', in: U. Eigler, U. Gotter, N. Luraghi and U. Walter (eds.), *Formen römischer Geschichtsschreibung von den Anfängen bis Livius*, Darmstadt, 93–114.
Gowers, E. (1993), *The Loaded Table: Representations of Food in Roman Literature*, Oxford.
Gruen, E. S. (1990), *Studies in Greek Culture and Roman Policy*, Leiden.
―――― (1992), *Culture and National Identity in Republican Rome*, Cornell, NY.
Hardy, C. S. (2005), 'The Parasite's Daughter: Metatheatrical Costuming in Plautus' *Persa*', *CW* 99, 25–33.
Hunter, R. L. (1981), 'The *Aulularia* of Plautus and its Greek Original', *PCPS* 27, 37–49.
Konstan, D. (1983), *Roman Comedy*, Ithaca, NY.
Kruschwitz, P. (2002), 'Ist Geld die "Wurzel allen Übels"? Zur Interpretation von Plautus' *Aulularia*', *Hermes* 130, 146–63.
Lefèvre, E. (2001), *Plautus Aulularia* (ScriptOralia 122), Tübingen.

---

85 Stockert 1983, 7 believes it likely that the Slave is freed at the end, as does Lefèvre 2001, 25. If we were to discover the lost ending of the play and to find that the slave is in fact granted his freedom, this would not significantly change my argument. He would not be granted his freedom because he had succeeded in using the plot for his own purposes, but rather as free gift from his master, with all the obligations that implies.

Leo, F. (1885), *T. Macci Plauti Comoediae*, vol. 1, Berlin.
Lindsay, W. M. (1904–1905), *T. Macci Plauti Comoediae*, 2 vols., Oxford.
Lowe, J. C. B. (1989), 'The *virgo callida* of Plautus, *Persa*', *CQ* 39, 390–99.
Manuwald, G. (2001), 'Die "Figur" der *virgo* in Plautus' *Persa*', in: S. Faller (ed.), *Studien zu Plautus' Persa* (ScriptOralia 121), Tübingen, 155–76.
─────── (1995), 'Plautus' "Indoor Scenes" and Improvised Drama', in: L. Benz, E. Stärk, and G. Vogt-Spira (eds.), *Plautus und die Tradition des Stegreifspiels*, Tübingen, 23–41.
McCarthy, K. (2000), *Slaves, Masters and the Art of Authority in Plautine Comedy*, Princeton, NJ.
Rawson, E. (1993), 'Freedmen in Roman Comedy', in: R. Scodel (ed.), *Theatre and Society in the Classical World*, Ann Arbor, MI, 215–33.
Richlin, A. (2014), 'Talking to Slaves in the Plautine Audience', *ClAnt* 33, 174–226.
Rosivach, V. J. (1986), 'Love and Leisure in Roman Comedy and the Amatory Poets', *AC* 55, 175–189.
Scott, J. C. (1990), *Domination and the Arts of Resistance: Hidden Transcripts*, New Haven, CT.
Segal, E. (1987), *Roman Laughter: The Comedy of Plautus*, 2nd edn. (1st edn. 1968, Cambridge, MA), Oxford.
Sharrock, A. R. (2009), *Reading Roman Comedy: Poetics and Playfulness in Plautus and Terence*, Cambridge.
─────── (2014), 'Terence, the Corrective Reader and Innovator', in: S. Papaioannou (ed.), *Terence and Interpretation*, Newcastle upon Tyne, 119–42.
Sherberg, B. (2001), 'Das Vater-Tochter-Verhältnis im plautinischen *Persa*. Zur Funktion der ersten Szene des dritten Aktes', in: S. Faller (ed.), *Studien zu Plautus' Persa* (ScriptOralia 121), Tübingen, 139–53.
Slater, N. W. (2000), *Plautus in Performance: The Theatre of the Mind*, 2nd edn. (1st edn. 1985, Princeton, NJ), Amsterdam.
Stocchi, C. (2009), 'Tracce esopiche nella commedia plautina', *BStudLat* 39, 75–90.
Stockert, W. (1982), 'Zur sprachlichen Charakterisierung der Personen in Plautus' *Aulularia*', *Gymnasium* 89, 4–14.
─────── (1983), *T. Maccius Plautus: Aulularia*, Stuttgart.
Woytek, E. (1982), *T. Maccius Plautus, Persa: Einleitung, Text und Kommentar*, Vienna.
Zumbrunnen, J. (2004), 'Elite Domination and the Clever Citizen: Aristophanes' *Archarnians* and *Knights*', *Political Theory* 32(5), 656–77.

Martin T. Dinter
Sententiousness in Roman Comedy – A Moralising Reading

It may well seem that there is nothing much edifying to be learnt from Roman comedy. For the genre parades the young (and sometimes also the old) cavorting with courtesans and slaves tricking their masters without an obvious moral message hidden in this mess.[1] Quintilian's much cited judgment on Roman comedy falls in line with this view. It showcases first and foremost his rhetorical and stylistic judgment and general disappointment with Roman efforts in the genre of comedy. When Quintilian finds someone's style worthy of praise, however, he expressed his disdain for the moral content of Afranius' plays, which he explicitly links to the lack of morals of their author. By this reading practice the plays become mirrors of their author's morals.

> [99] In comoedia maxime claudicamus. Licet Varro Musas, Aeli Stilonis sententia, Plautino dicat sermone locuturas fuisse si Latine loqui vellent, licet Caecilium veteres laudibus ferant, licet Terenti scripta ad Scipionem Africanum referantur (quae tamen sunt in hoc genere elegantissima, et plus adhuc habitura gratiae si intra versus trimetros stetissent): [100] vix levem consequimur umbram, adeo ut mihi sermo ipse Romanus non recipere videatur illam solis concessam Atticis venerem, cum eam ne Graeci quidem in alio genere linguae optinuerint. Togatis excellit Afranius: utinam non inquinasset argumenta puerorum foedis amoribus, mores suos fassus.

> Comedy is our weakest point. Although Varro quotes Aelius Stilo as saying that if the Muses wished to speak Latin, they would use the language of Plautus, although the ancients extol Caecilius, and although Scipio Africanus is credited with the works of Terence (which are the most elegant of their kind, and would be still more graceful if the poet had confined himself to the iambic trimeter), we still scarcely succeed in reproducing even a faint shadow of the charm of Greek comedy. Indeed, it seems to me as though the language of Rome were incapable of reproducing that graceful wit which was granted to Athens alone, and was beyond the reach of other Greek dialects to achieve. Afranius excels in the purely Roman comedy, but it is to be regretted that he revealed his own character by

---

[1] Accordingly scholarly views on that topic vary but on the whole they assert Roman comedy as a conservative and socially cohesive genre reinforcing conventional values. Konstan 1983 seeks to locate an ideology and system of values in Greek New Comedy and its Roman adaptations. Segal 1987 suggests seeing Roman comedy as a Saturnalian space in which established social ideals and rules could (briefly) be overturned. McCarthy 2000 purports that Plautine comedy supports traditional Roman values more than it questions them. According to her we should 'reject the romantic impulse to see subversion where none existed' (McCarthy 2000, 6), for 'Plautine comedy does not really undermine authority in any substantial way' (McCarthy 2000, 17).

defiling his plots with the introduction of indecent paederastic intrigues. (Quint. *Inst.* 10.1.99–100)²

trans. Winterbottom

Despite Quintilian's damning judgement we will see, however, when examining one of the most prominent stylistic features of Roman comedy that there is some moral education to be had from Roman comedy after all. In this brief survey I shall concentrate on the *sententiae* in Roman comedy, a so far underappreciated detail of comic writing. By focussing exclusively on *sententiae* we will be able to challenge comedy's bad moral reputation (and in any case, it is somewhat unlikely that Rome's young men needed to read or watch Roman comedy to find out about courtesans and pederasty). First, however, I should explain what exactly *sententiae* are. We will need to do this in retrospect, looking back over Roman comedy through the eyes of Seneca the Elder and Quintilian. In the writings of the former the word *sententia* designates the format of both gnomic generalisations and penetrating epigrams.³ As we will see, Roman comedy on the whole tends to employ gnomic generalisations. The function of *gnomai*, when defined as generalizing statements about particular human actions or the gods, is akin to that of modern day proverbs.⁴ They 'persuade the listener and move him to correct action by utterance of familiar, unassailable wisdom.'⁵ It comes as no surprise then that the contents of *gnomai* cover all of human experience, as can be seen from an edition of Menander's *gnomai* that is not ordered alphabetically as in the manuscript tradition but instead grouped by themes such as 'virtue', 'wedlock', 'old age', 'women', 'death', 'happiness' and 'modesty'.⁶ The same applies to the collection of alphabetically ordered *sententiae* from the mimes of Publilius Syrus, in which the reader can also make out recurrent *topoi*.⁷ Indeed, some of Publilius' *sententiae* provide variations on the same theme. Below I provide a small selection focused on avarice:

> A 14 avarus ipse miseriae causa est suae (The mean man is the cause of his own misery).
> A 21 avarum facile capias, ubi non sis item (You want to catch a mean man? Just be generous!).
> A 23 Avarus nisi cum moritur, nihil recte facit (The mean man only acts well when he dies).
> A 25 Avarus damno potius quam sapiens dolet (Loss hurts the mean man more than the wise).

---

2 Goldberg 1987, 362–7 explains Quintilian's faint praise of Terence by tracing the Roman preference for tragedy.
3 Sinclair 1995, 120–2 outlines the history of the term '*sententia*'.
4 Boeke 2007, 13.
5 Russo 1997, 57.
6 Cf. Jäkel 1986, 116.
7 Flamerie de Lachapelle 2011, 155–8 provides a useful index of shared topics. Note that Costas Panayotakis is currently preparing a new edition of Publilius' *sententiae*.

A 26 Avaro quid mali optes nisi: vivat diu (You want to curse a mean man? Say: Long may you live!)?
A 35 Avidum oportet esse neminem, minime senem (No one ought to be mean, especially not the old).
A 46 Avaro acerba poena natura est sua (cf. A 14).
A 47 Avaro non est vita, sed mors longior (The mean man does not live, but rather dies slowly).[8]

For fame and afterlife, that contemporary of Caesar now depends solely on a collection of *sententiae* extracted from his plays.[9] Studied as a school text in antiquity and praised by the younger Seneca and Gellius, they were still popular in the nineteenth century as edifying reading.[10]

While Publilius Syrus' mimes have been lost, the remnants of these plays, that is a selection of *sententiae*, clearly show that there is some moral lore handed down in the comic tradition.[11] Indeed all dramatic genres pass on a tradition of *sententiae* down the line from Greek into Latin.[12] We should thus keep in mind that comedies brimming with *sententiae* are not Plautus' or Terence's novel invention but rather constitute part of a development, the foundations of which were already laid centuries earlier in Greek comedy and tragedy.[13] However, Roman comedies also mirror the rhetorical education and practice of the Roman Republic.[14] *Sententiae* in particular can be made to serve as all-convincing arguments and construct authority for the speaker.[15] It is hard to argue against their

---

8 Further examples might be added A55, C37, I5, I7, M1, N10, S30, T3. Panayotakis suggested to me viva voce that Publilius' *sententiae* may owe their universal appeal to the complete lack of the use of the first person.
9 Giancotti 1967, 318–38 suggests various origins for this collection in the first century CE: rhetorical schooltext, grammatical gradus or introduction to ethics and philosophy. Publilius is mentioned by Cicero at *Fam.* 12.18.2 and *Att.* 14.2 and Seneca the Elder at *Con.* 7.3.8, who quotes several of his *sententiae*, as does Gellius 17.14. Trimalchio (at Petr. 55) offers 16 pseudo-Publilian sententiae. Macrobius, *Sat.* 2.7 provides Publilius' biography garnished with a wealth of sententiae.
10 Cf. Benz 2001. Seneca himself quotes one of Publilius Syrus' *sententiae* in *Ep.* 94.43. Knecht 1986, 53–5 points out that the frequent use of paronomasia in *sententiae* (as well as proverbs) made them useful school texts for teaching 'beginners' Latin' in antiquity.
11 Terence's commentator Donatus notices the comedies' sententiousness frequently, cf. Bureau 2011.
12 Cf. Dangel 2011.
13 Mauduit and Paré-Rey 2011 have assembled contributions that showcase this tradition from Greek tragedy onwards.
14 The oeuvre of Seneca the Elder bears witness to the importance of *sententiae* for displaying oratorical skills and education, they are worthy to be recorded and remembered, as well as their role in the social advancement of Seneca's family. Cf. Sussman 1978 and Fairweather 1981.
15 Although dating from a later period, Sen. *Ep.* 94.43 exemplifies the persuasiveness of *sententiae*.

universal appeal. A striking example can be found in Plautus, *Mercator* (374–5), where the son – naturally in a weaker position than his father – throws back at him one of the latter's *sententiae*, so as to produce a disarming excuse and escape further paternal attention.

> saepe ex te audivi pater:
> rei mandatae omnis sapientis primum praevorti decet.
>
> But, Father, I have often heard you say yourself: all sensible men should give a commission their very first attention.

The use of a *sententia* – here apparently wisdom inherited from the young man's father – economises on argumentation and cuts short debate. Unless the father wishes to undermine his own moral credibility – and in Roman comedy that always includes sententiousness – he must let his son go.

One play that thematizes and plays out a father's habit to admonish his son with *sententiae* is Terence's *Adelphoe,* which features a number of scenes in which *sententiae* are essential to the plot.[16] *Adelphoe* presents contrasting paternal approaches to bringing up sons. One father, Micio, is overly forgiving towards his adopted son, while his brother Demea, the biological father of the two sons featuring in this play, is overly strict towards his. Leaving aside for the most part the play's fascinating discourse on nature versus nurture, indulgence versus moral stricture, or as Lape 2004 puts it, 'natural kinship' versus 'social kinship', I shall confine my discussion to just a small selection of scenes.[17]

Firstly, however, I have to point to a delightful scene in which the stern father Demea, after learning that his son Ctesipho (supposedly) criticised his brother's Aeschinus lewd behaviour with the words '*non tu hoc argumentum perdis sed vitam tuam*' ('It's not the money that you are squandering, it's your life', *Adelph*. 410), teaches us the basics of moral instruction, handed down from father to son.

---

16 The limited scope of this chapter does not allow me to do justice to all the prominent instances of sententiousness in Terence's *Adelphoe*. I can but highlight a small selection. For a collection of proverbial *sententiae* from this play cf. Otto 1890 and Häussler's *Nachträge zu Otto* 1968. In addition, I cannot address here the subtle differences in the use of *sententiae* between Plautus, Terence and the other Roman comedians, but shall confine myself to pointing to the larger study on the subject, which I am preparing at present.

17 There is abundant secondary literature on the *Adelphoe*. Particularly useful on the educational father-son context are the commentary of Gratwick 1999 and the articles by Barsby 1985 and Henderson 1999.

DE. Saluos sit spero: est similis maiorum suom. SY. Hui!
DE. Syre, **praeceptorum** plenust istorum ille. SY. Phy!
domi habuit unde disceret. DE. Fit sedulo,
nil praetermitto, consuefacio. denique
inspicere tamquam in speculum in uitas omnium   415
iubeo atque ex aliis sumere exemplum sibi.
hoc facito. SY. Recte sane. DE. Hoc fugito. SY. Callide.
DE. Hoc laudist. SY. Istaec res est. DE. Hoc uitio datur.
SY. Probissume.DE. Porro autem SY. [...]
                               et quod queo
conseruis ad eundem istunc praecipio modum,
hoc salsumst, hoc adustumst, hoc lautumst parum,   425
illud recte: iterum sic memento. sedulo
moneo, quae possum pro mea sapientia.
postremo tamquam in speculum in patinas, Demea,
inspicere iubeo et moneo quid facto usus sit.

(Terence, *Adelphoe* 411–29)

DE. Bless him! He gives me hope. He is a chip of the old block. SY. (pretending to be impressed) Wow! **DE. Syrus, he is full of these maxims. SY. (slyly) He had someone to learn from at home.** DE. One does one's best. I never turn a blind eye. I teach him good habits. Above all I tell him to look into the lives of others as if into a mirror and to take from them an example for himself. 'Do this,' I say. SY. Quite right. DE. 'Avoid that.' SY. Splendid. DE. 'This is praiseworthy.' SY. Just the thing. DE. 'This is wrong.' SY. Excellent. DE. Then again ... [...] SY. As far as I can, I instruct my fellow slaves on the same principles as yours. 'Too salty.' I say. 'A bit burnt. Not clean enough. Just right: be sure to do the same next time.' I do my best to advise them with such wisdom as I have. Above all I tell them to look into the saucepan is if into a mirror, Demea, and I advise them what lessons to learn. (trans. Barsby)

Demea in his speech provides the linguistic foundations of any good morally instructive *sententia*. The slave Syrus then comically fills the generic pontificating of 'Father Demea' with situational instructions from his life in the kitchens where the saucepan must do service as the poor man's mirror of life. Syrus, however, has prompted Demea to enter 'pontification mode' by bringing up (or should we say making up) the *sententia* quoted above (*Adelph.* 410). And even before that Syrus is showing himself as a wily as well as sententious slave when he addresses Demea thus: *o Demea, istuc est sapere, non quod ante pedes modost/videre sed etiam illa quae futura sunt prospicere* ('That's real wisdom, Demea, not merely to see what lies under your feet but to foresee the future' (*Adelph.* 385–86)). In addition Syrus is flattering the old man with *tu quantus quantus nil nisi sapientia's/ill' somnium.* ('You are nothing but wisdom from tip to toe, he's a dreamer' (*Adelph.* 394–95)) thereby enhancing the father's position as fountain of all wisdom (and in our case that means *sententiae*). As becomes clear here, the slave has soaked up the family's sententious wisdom better than any of the actual sons.

What is more, *sententiae* will play a central role in staging the conflict between the two brothers (the older pair, that is). Micio confronts Demea with a proverb (a subcategory of *sententiae*) to justify having meddled with the affairs of both sons: *Nam vetus verbum hoc quidemst, communia esse amicorum inter se omnia* ('There is an old saying that friends share everything in common' (*Adelph.* 803; cf. also Plato, *Laws* 739c, *Phaedrus* 279c and Aristotle, *Ethics* 8.9.1)), which Demea dismisses harshly (and almost uniquely – for proverbs usually work) as 'coming too late'. However, just a few verses later it becomes clear that Demea was actually paying attention to his brother's strategy of argumentation. For not unlike the son in the scene from the *Mercator* cited above, Demea is quoting back at Micio a maxim previously employed by his brother. At the play's very end he thus forces Micio into giving away a larg(ish) plot of land.

Let us look at Micio's version first:

> Solum unum hoc vitium affert senectus hominibus:
> attentiores sumus ad rem omnes quam sat est,
> quod illos sat aetas acuet.

> But there is one fault which old age brings to us. We all become far too worried about money, on which time will sharpen *their* (the sons') attitudes soon enough. (*Adelph.* 833–35)

And then consider Demea's version:

> postremo nunc meum illud uerbum facio, quod tu, Micio,
> bene et sapienter dixti dudum: 'vitium commune omniumst,
> quod nimium ad rem in senecta attenti sumus'.

> When all is said and done, can't I adopt for myself the remark which you made just now, Micio, so wisely and so well? 'It's a common fault of all of us that in old age we are too worried about money', (*Adelph.* 952–4).

With this example of comic intratextuality Demea adopts and adapts the argumentative technique his brother has employed previously. In this case the *sententia's* persuasive force succeeds, for Micio cannot easily undermine a *sententia* he has just employed himself without sabotaging his own moral standing.[18]

---

[18] A further intratextual example that employs a similar comic technique involving *sententiae* can be found in Terence's *Phormio* when the old man Demipho, coming back from overseas and finding his son married, unfavourably ponders the vagaries of life and concludes: *quidquid praeter spem eveniat, omne id deputare esse in lucro* ('then everything better than anticipated he can count as pure gain', *Phorm.* 246). This statement is echoed by the slave Geta who expecting to be sent to the mills, being beaten, fettered and made to work on the farm concludes (with a slight change of

Let us now pretend to be a (Roman) student or teacher of rhetoric on the hunt for *sententiae* eagerly excerpting from Roman comedies. In fact, we will see from a 1529 volume from Vienna entitled *ex Publii Terentii comoediis latinissime colloquiorum formulae, ordine selectae: unacum eiusdem poetae insignioribus sententiis* that there are two traditions of excerption in regard to Terence's comedies.[19] This book presents first a selection of everyday speech formulations in Latin in the order of their appearance in the text as one would encounter them when reading the plays; sentences such as *expecto quid velis* ('I await your wishes') and *in memoria habeo* ('I keep it in mind') are indeed useful tools for everyday Latin conversation.[20] The final part of the book then lists gnomic *sententiae* in the order they appear in Terence's plays. This gives us a good impression of what kind of *sententiae* would have caught the eyes of an (ancient) excerpter on the hunt for a phrase one could recycle.

In what follows I shall provide a few examples from the *sententiae* we find excerpted from Terence's plays. My sourcebook lists Terence's plays in alphabetical order and groups *sententiae* by scene. I shall have a look at all the *sententiae* listed from one single play, the *Andria* (*The Woman from Andros*) to get an idea of the variety of themes on offer. To facilitate locating the *sententiae* in the sourcebook I also cite the act and the scene as employed there.

Andria
Prologue

    faciuntne intellegendo ut nil intellegant? (17, *Andria* prologue)
    By being *thus* knowing, do they not show that they know nothing at all?

    ut quiescant porro moneo et desinant
    male dicere, malefacta ne noscant sua (22–3, *Andria,* prologue)
    Therefore, I advise them to be quiet in future, and to cease to slander; that they may not be made acquainted with their own misdeeds.

Act 1

                  id arbitror
    adprime in vita esse utile, ut nequid nimis (60–1, *Andria*, first act, first scene)
    For this I deem in life to be especially advantageous; that *one do* nothing to excess.

---

tense) that 'everything better than my expectations, I'll count as pure gain' (*quidquid praeter spem eveniet, omne id deputabo esse in lucro* 251).

19 There are various versions of this book available in full on Google Books, some with extensive glossulae and (hand-written) translations into French or German.
20 Dionisotti 1982 samples a family of ancient schoolbooks which features a section of *colloquia*, little dialogue scenes for practicing one's everyday Latin.

          hoc tempore
obsequium amicos, veritas odium parit (67–8, *Andria*, first act, first scene)
For in these days obsequiousness begets friends; sincerity, dislike.

          ingeniumst omnium
hominum ab labore proclive ad lubidinem (77–8, *Andria*, first act, first scene)
The disposition of all mankind has a downward tendency from industry toward pleasure.

        si illum obiurges vitae qui auxilium tulit
quid facias illi qui dederit damnum aut malum? (142–3, *Andria,* first act, first scene)
If you censure him who has assisted to preserve life, what are you to do to him who causes loss or misfortune *to it*?

mala mens, malus animus (164, *Andria* first scene).
Bad heart, bad disposition.

omnes qui amant graviter sibi dari uxorem ferunt. (191, *Andria*, first act, second scene)
A man with a mistress dislikes having a wife given to him.

seni [...] cui verba dare difficilest (211, *Andria*, first act, third scene)
It is difficult to trick an old man.

facta transacta omnia (248, *Andria*, first act, fifth scene)
Everything settled and concluded.

aliquid monstri alunt (250, *Andria*, first act, fifth scene)
They are rearing a monster.

dum in dubiost animus, paullo momento huc vel illuc impellitur (266, *Andria*, first act, fifth scene, end of a speech)
While the mind is in suspense, a slight impulse one way or the other sways it.

Act II

quoniam non potest id fieri quod vis,
id velis quod possit (*Andria* 305–6, second act, first scene)
As what you wish for is impossible, better wish for what is possible.

facile omnes quom valemus recta consilia aegrotis damus. (*Andria* 309, second act, first scene)
When you are well, it is easy to give sound advice to a sick man.

verum illud verbumst, volgo quod dici solet,
omnis sibi malle melius esse quam alteri (*Andria* 426–7, second act, fourth scene)
It is a true saying you hear everywhere that every one sets his own good before his neighbour's.

Act III
fidelem haud ferme mulieri invenias virum (460, *Andria* third act, first scene)
Seldom can you find a man faithful to a woman.

ego in portu navigo (480, *Andria*, third act, first scene)
My ship is in haven.

amantium irae amoris integratiost (555, *Andria*, third act, third scene)
Lovers' quarrels are love's renewal.

Act IV
Hoccinest credibile aut memorabile,
tanta vecordia innata quoiquam ut siet
ut malis gaudeant atque ex incommodis
alterius sua ut comparent commoda? (625–8, *Andria*, fourth act, first scene)
Is it credible, is it conceivable, that any man should be so black-hearted as to gloat over misfortunes and buy his own happiness at the cost of another's misery?

    valeant
qui inter nos discidium volunt (696–7, *Andria*, fourth act, second scene)
Away with those who would part us.

non Apollinis magis verum atque hoc responsumst. (698, *Andria*, fourth act, second scene)
Apollo's oracle is not more true than my words.

mirum vero inpudenter mulier si facit
meretrix! (755–6, *Andria*, fourth act, fourth scene)
It really is a wonder if a woman, who is a courtesan, acts impudently!

    fallacia
alia aliam trudit (778–9, *Andria*, fourth act, fourth scene)
One trick on the heels of another.

paullum interesse censes ex animo omnia,
ut fert natura, facias an de industria? (795–6, *Andria*, fourth act, fourth scene)
Do you think it makes so little difference whether you say things honestly and naturally or after preparation?

[sic]
ut quimus [, aiunt,] quando ut volumus non licet (804–5, *Andria*, fourth act, fifth scene)
[As the saying is] we do as we can since we can't as we would.

Act V
beneficium verbis initum dudum nunc re comprobes (824, *Andria*, fifth act, first scene)
Let the boon promised just now by your lips be ratified by your deeds.

> omnis res est iam in vado (845, *Andria*, fifth act, second scene)
> All is in safe waters now.
>
> pro peccato magno paullum supplici satis est patri (903, *Andria*, fifth act, third scene)
> For a great fault, a little punishment may content a father.
>
> si mihi perget quae volt dicere, ea quae non volt audiet (920, *Andria*, fifth act, fourth scene)
> If he persists in saying just what he likes, he will hear what he won't like.
>
> nodum in scirpo quaeris (941, *Andria*, fifth act, fourth scene)
> You look for knots in a bulrush.
>
> ego d<eo>rum vitam propterea sempiternam esse arbitror
> quod voluptates <eo>rum propriae sunt (959–60, *Andria*, fifth act, fifth scene, word order altered)
> To my mind what makes life in heaven eternal is that pleasures there are lasting.
>
> more hominum evenit ut quod sim nanctus mali
> prius rescisceres tu quam ego illud quod tibi evenit boni (967–8, *Andria*, fith act, fifth scene)
> It's the way of the world for you to hear of my bad fortune, before I hear of your good.
>
> somniat
> ea quae vigilans voluit? (971–2, *Andria*, fifth act, fifth scene)
> Is this a daydream of his wakeful desires?

Even this short run through one single play's *sententiae* (as selected by a 16th-century publication) demonstrates that themes such as love, trickery/honesty and father/son relationships are recurrent topics. In addition we can also see that *sententiae* appear in two different contexts: sometimes a character quotes a *sententia* like a proverb in conversation. Characters usually clearly mark that kind of *sententia* with a preamble such as 'there is an old saying' or similar. These are obvious instances of sententiousness that can be easily recognised and which signal that comedy is already looking back to a gnomic tradition. Other less overt instances occur unmarked but have identical nomothetic qualities as their marked counterparts; they are helping to lay down the moral laws of Roman comedy. To exemplify this let me place together those four *sententiae* that deal with one of Roman comedy's pre-eminent concerns: relationships between men and women.

> omnes qui amant graviter sibi dari uxorem ferunt (191, *Andria*, first act, second scene)
> A man with a mistress dislikes having a wife given to him.
>
> fidelem haud ferme mulieri invenias virum (460, *Andria*, third act, first scene)
> Seldom can you find a man faithful to a woman.
>
> amantium irae amoris integratiost (555, *Andria*, third act, third scene)
> Lovers' quarrels are love's renewal.

mirum vero inpudenter mulier si facit
meretrix! (755–6, *Andria*, fourth act, fourth scene)
It really is a wonder if a woman, who is a courtesan, acts impudently!

Despite constituting a random sample from but one of Terence's plays these four *sententiae* provide us with a good idea about the attitude displayed towards women in Roman comedy. If we were to extend my reading practice to all of Terence's extant plays (and those of Plautus too) we would face the 'morals' of comedy expressed though its sententiousness. In addition – at least according to ancient thought that links an author's *persona* to the *sententiae* in that author's oeuvre – we gain a reflection of Plautus and Terence themselves.[21] This is a reading practice that places the *persona* of the authors within their texts and that we have found exemplified in Quintilian's stylistic but also moral criticism of Roman comedy in the passage cited at the very beginning of this chapter. Mayer, in his work on the literary persona in antiquity, shows how this concept (alien as it might seem to the modern reader, who is used to distinguishing author and literary mask) might work in practice: 'in literary contexts *persona* is used by the Romans to refer both to the 'person' who is imagined as speaking (say, Alfius) and to the writer (say, Horace). However disparate the characters of writer and speaker, nonetheless the Romans tended to believe that they could see through the mask: to parody theological terms, they detected only a distinction of person, not a distinction of being. The commentator Porphyrio, therefore, was sure that the moneylender Alfius in the second *Epode* was really voicing Horace's own opinion: *quod vult intellegi neminem* [n. b.] *nescire quid iucunditatis habeat vita rustica*. [...] Roman readers seem generally reluctant to distinguish sharply between the writer's own character and that of his *personae*'.[22] This tendency to construct the author from his *œuvre* continues well into the Middle Ages and might well have played a subconscious role in the mind of the excerptor whose

---

21 Already Anaximenes, *Ars Rhetorica ad Alexandrum* 11.1 defines *gnomai* as expressions of an author's opinion. See also the etymology provided by Quintilian: *Sententiam veteres quod animo sensissent vocaverant.* ('The ancients used the word *sententia* to mean what they felt in their minds': Quint. *Inst.* 8.5.1).
22 Mayer 2003, 65–6. I am aware that this close association of author and character in ancient readings of literature provides a challenge to the sophisticated modern reader well accustomed to the 'death of the author'. Dramatic literature with its complexity of the voices and focalizations evidently does not make things easier. We should, however, not forget that Terence in particular in his comedies has abandoned expository prologues in flavour of personal prologues. While this (mediated) personal voice had long been seen as disconnected from the plays (Lefèvre 1969), recent studies have shown how the prologues to a certain extent mirror the action of the plays (Gowers 2004).

work we have sampled above. While the Renaissance excerpts from Terence's plays that I have cited are primarily meant for teaching Latin through sound bites and paratactic *sententiae,* they simultaneously unearth and showcase the morals of Roman comedy, linking back to the (not always so) stern fathers, the tutors and the elderly that are voicing their moral opinion, as well as the contemporaneous moral discourse of Republican Rome.

Unlike tragedy, comedy itself, however, seems to harbour few illusions as to the effectiveness of its moral teachings, at least when observed through the eyes of the slave Gripus in Plautus' *Rudens.*

> GRIP. Spectavi ego pridem comicos ad istunc modum
> sapienter dicta dicere atque eis plaudier,
> cum illos sapientis mores monstrabant poplo:
> sed cum inde suam quisque ibant divorsi domum,
> nullus erat illo pacto ut illi iusserant.

> GRIP. At times, I've seen the Comedians, when acting, in this fashion repeat sayings in a wise manner, and be applauded for them, when they pointed out this prudent conduct to the public. But when each person went from the theatre his own way home, there wasn't one after the fashion, which they had recommended. (Plautus, *Rudens* 1249–53).

According to this reading of Roman comedy all moral content showcased in the plays is quickly forgotten once people have staggered home. The genre thus does not provide the cathartic edification that tragedy offers. That might well be a realistic assessment of primary audiences, but one should not forget Plautus and Terence's long career as school texts, with their plays being mined explicitly for grammatical instructions and moral guidance. When looking back to Roman comedy through the eyes of a Roman schoolboy in the 3rd or 4th century AD we may well find an image of Cato the Elder in Roman Comedy. For a spurious collection of 144 hexametric *disticha* called *Dicta/Disticha Catonis*, the authorship of which was traditionally ascribed to Cato the Elder, was in quasi-universal use for basic grammar and reading instruction in Late Antiquity and throughout the Middle Ages.[23] This collection frequently offers moral sayings, the gist of which comes very close to both the moral opinions expressed and the proverbs used by

---

23 Cf. Boas 1952 for a critical text and Duff 1961 for an English translation as well as Wayland Johnson Chase 1922. For the history and transmission of the *Disticha* see Boas 1914 and Sallmann 1997. Bloomer 2011, 139–69 traces the *Disticha*'s use as schooltext.

the characters of Roman comedy.[24] Below I have selected but two of 'Cato's' sayings that reflect concerns also found in comedy.

> 16. Multorum cum facta senex et dicta recenses,
> Fac tibi succurrant, iuvenis quae feceris ipse.
> 16. When you as an old man reprimand another's faults,
> recall that when young you too gave cause for blame.
>
> 29. Quod vile est, carum, quod carum, vile putato:
> Sic tu nec cupidus nec avarus nosceris ulli.
> 29. Despise the dear and value the mean thing;
> So no harm can come to anyone through your greed or lust.

To Roman schoolboys reading Plautus and Terence the *Disticha Catonis* must thus have often seemed like a condensed version of comic morals – and in turn this text must have projected a reflection of Cato the Elder into Roman comedy.

Comic sententiousness as a whole merits a larger study, which I hope to provide in the future. In the space of this paper, however, I have pointed out, using Terence's *Adelphoe*, as my main example how *sententiae* contribute to a play's comic technique. In addition, I have showcased the sententiousness of Terence's *Andria* to exemplify how *sententiae* permeate the whole of one play and provide an overview of the moral positions within it, which are on the whole conservative and not dissimilar from those ascribed to Roman moralists of old.

---

24 Indeed, Grimal 1969, 374 showcases this approach when he poses the question which ethical positions displayed in the (Plautine) *Trinummus* would have found Cato's approval and – looking at comedy through the lens of Plutarch's biography of Cato – draws parallels between the moral predispositions of the father figure of Philton and those of Cato. Again I can but point to a larger discussion surrounding the identification of Cato-figures in Roman comedy. For the *Trinummus* Benz 1990, 58 points to Meganorides' use of an initial *sententia* and Lefèvre 1990, 50–1 to the character's use of *castigare* as possible links to Cato's persona. Note also the agricultural imagery of line 31 that suits a Catonian character. See Leigh 2004, 14–19 for further possible allusions to Cato in Plautine comedy and 160 for a revisionist approach to Cato opposing Greek education. See also Leigh 2004, 161–2 and 172–3 on *Adelphoe* opposing a simple identification of Demea with Cato and Micio with M. Aemilius Paullus as suggested by MacKendrick (1954). Echoes, however, remain.

Bibliography

Barsby, J. (1985), 'Fathers and Sons in Menander and Roman Comedy', in: R. Hankey,/D. Little (eds.), *Essays in Honour of Agathe Thornton*, Dunedin, 103–14.
Benz, L. (1990), 'Megaronides Censorius – Eine anticatonische Konzeption im plautinischen *Trinummus*?', in: J. Blänsdorf (with J.-M. André and N. Frick) (eds.), *Theater und Gesellschaft im Imperium Romanum*, Tübingen, 55–68.
_____ (2001), 'Publilius Syrus', in: C. Hubert/H. Schneider (eds.), *Der Neue Pauly*, Stuttgart, 582.
Bloomer, W. M. (2011), *The School of Rome: Latin Studies and the Origins of Liberal Education*, Berkeley.
Boas, M. (1914), '*De librorum Catonianorum historia atque compositione*', Mnemosyne 42, 17–46.
_____ (1952), (ed.), *Disticha Catonis. Opus post Marci Boas mortem edendum curavit Henricus Johannes Botschuyver*, Amsterdam.
Boeke, H. (2007), *The Value of Victory in Pindar's Odes. Gnomai, Cosmology and the Role of the Poet*, Leiden.
Bureau, B. (2011), 'Térence moralisé: les *sententiae* de Térence selon le commentaire attribué à Donat', in: Ch. Mauduit/P. Paré-Rey (eds.), *Les Maximes théâtrales en Grèce et à Rome: transferts, réécritures, remplois*, Lyon, 157–76.
Dangel, J. (2011), 'Les énoncés gnomiques de la tragédie romaine en flux intertextuel: pour quelle théâtricalité?', in: Ch. Mauduit/P. Paré-Rey (eds.), *Les Maximes théâtrales en Grèce et à Rome: transferts, réécritures, remplois*, Paris, 177–88.
Dionisotti, C. (1982), 'From Ausonius's Schooldays? A Schoolbook and its Relatives', *JRS* 72, 83–125.
Fairweather, J. (1981), *Seneca the Elder*, Cambridge.
Flamerie de Lachapelle, G. (2011), *Publius Syrus. Sentences*, Paris.
Giancotti, F. (1967), *Mimo e gnome, studio su Decimo Laberio e Publilio Siro*. Florence.
Goldberg, S. (1987), 'Quintilian on Comedy', *Traditio* 43, 359–67.
Gowers, E. (2004), 'The Plot Thickens: Hidden Outlines in Terence's Prologues', in: A. J. Boyle (ed.), *Rethinking Terence*, Ramus 33, 150–66.
Gratwick, A. S. (2nd edn. 1999), *Terence: The Brothers*, Warminster.
Grimal, P. (1969), 'Analisi del Trinummus e gli albori della filosofia Romana', *Dioniso* 43, 363–77 = (1986), 'Analyse du *Trinummus* et les débuts de la philosophie à Rome', in: P. Grimal (ed.), *Rome. La littérature et l'histoire 1*, Rome, 363–75.
Häussler, R. (1968), *Nachträge zu A. Otto 'Sprichwörter und Sprichwörtliche Redensarten der Römer'* (reprint), Darmstadt
Henderson, J. (1999), 'Entertaining Arguments: Terence, *Adelphoe*', in: J. Henderson (ed.), *Writing Down Rome: Satire, Comedy and Other Offences in Latin Poetry*, Oxford, 38–66.
Jäkel, S. (1986), *Menander Sentenzen*, Leipzig.
Johnson Chase, W. (1922), *The Distichs of Cato, A Famous Medieval Textbook*, Madison.
Knecht, T. (1986), 'Das römische Sprichwort – Abgrenzungen, Formen, Anwendung', in: P. Neukam (ed.) *Reflexionen antiker Kulturen*, Munich, 47–59.
Konstan, D. (1983), *Roman Comedy*, Ithaca, NY and London.
Lape, S. (2004), 'The Terentian Marriage-Plot: Reproducing Fathers and Sons', in: A. Boyle (ed.), *Rethinking Terence*, Ramus 33, 35–52.

Lefèvre, E. (1969), *Die Expositionstechnik in den Komödien des Terenz*, Darmstadt.
─────── (1990), 'Politik und Gesellschaft in Plautus' *Trinummus*', in: J. Blänsdorf (with J.-M. André/N. Frick) (eds.), *Theater und Gesellschaft im Imperium Romanum*, Tübingen, 45–54 (Reprinted in English in: R. Scodel (1993), (ed.), *Theatre and Society in the Classical World*, Ann Arbor, 177–90).
Leigh, M. (2004), *Comedy and the Rise of Rome*, Oxford.
MacKendrick, P. (1954), 'Demetrius of Phalerum, Cato and the *Adelphoe*', *Rivista di Filologia e Istruzione Classica* 32, 18–35.
Mauduit, C./Paré-Rey, P. (eds.), (2011), *Les maximes théâtrales en Grèce et à Rome: transferts, réécritures, remplois. Actes du colloque organisé les 11–13 juin 2009 par l'Université Lyon 3 et l'ENS de Lyon*, Paris.
Mayer, R. (2003), '*Persona Problems*', *Materiali e Discussioni* 50, 1–26.
McCarthy, K. (2000), *Slaves, Masters and the Art of Authority in Plautine Comedy*, Princeton, NJ.
Otto, A. (1891) *Die Sprichwörter der Römer*, Berlin.
Russo, J. (1997), 'Prose Genres for the Performance of Traditional Wisdom in Ancient Greece: Proverb, Maxim, Apothegm', in: L. Edmunds/R. W. Wallace (eds.), *Poet, Public, and Performance in Ancient Greece*, Baltimore, 49–64.
Sallmann, K. (1997), 'Moralistische Spruchdichtung', in: K. Sallmann et al. (eds.), *Die Literatur des Umbruchs. Von der römischen zur christlichen Literatur. 117–284 n. Chr.*, Munich, 606–12.
Segal, E. (2nd edn. 1987), *Roman Laughter*, New York.
Sinclair, P. (1995), *Tacitus the Sententious Historian: a Sociology of Rhetoric in Annales 1–6*, University Park, Penn.
Sussman, L. A. (1978), *The Elder Seneca*, Leiden.
Wight Duff, J./Duff, A. M. (eds.) (1961), '*Dicta Catonis*', in: *Minor Latin Poets*, London and Cambridge, MA, 583–639.

Ioannis M. Konstantakos
Plautus' *Aulularia* and Popular Narrative Tradition

Tale-type 754 in the standard folktale index of Aarne, Thompson and Uther (sometimes entitled 'Happy Poverty') can be summarized as follows: a poor man lives happily despite his scanty means. His wealthy neighbour is amazed by this apparent contradiction or annoyed by the humble fellow's felicity. He therefore gives a good sum of money to the poor man or secretly leaves a sack of gold coins on his doorstep. As soon as the poor hero comes into possession of the money, he is plagued by anxiety about his new wealth. He is constantly afraid of robbers and cannot sleep. He becomes so gloomy that his neighbours notice the change. In the end, the wealthy man reclaims his money; or the poor fellow gives it back of his own free will, cursing the misery it caused him. He thus recovers his former felicity.[1]

This story was popular in the Middle Ages, especially as a moral *exemplum* in the context of religious preaching. Its earliest Medieval Latin variants come from the sermons of the French canon Jacques de Vitry (ca. 1160–1240) and from the didactic parables of the Dominican friar Étienne de Bourbon (ca. 1180–1261). It is also included in several other compilations of preachers' *exempla* from the 14th to the 17th century; most of them are ultimately dependent on the texts of Jacques or Étienne, although they may abridge the narrative and alter details of the action. From the Renaissance onwards, the tale often found its way into works of entertainment literature: storybooks (H. W. Kirchhof's *Wendunmuth*, the *Arabian Nights*), collections of novellas (e. g. by Bonaventure des Périers and Carlo Casalicchio), or fable corpora (La Fontaine, Florian, Burkard Waldis etc.). In such contexts it was creatively adapted or freely developed with new elements, possibly inspired by a live folk tradition. In modern times, the story has been recorded as an oral folktale among various peoples: chiefly in Eastern Europe, the Islamic East, and the Jewish Diaspora, but also in Greece, the Iberian peninsula, and even as far as China.[2] This rich popular tradition was perhaps occasionally influenced by literary models; but it also testifies to a widespread folk substratum, which

---

1 See Uther 2004, I 409.
2 On the dissemination of this tale in medieval and modern times see Kurz 1862, 178f. (Anmerkungen); Österley 1869, V 82f.; Crane 1890, 162f.; Toldo 1903, 421f.; Tobler 1906; Hassell 1957, 89–103; Schwarzbaum 1968, 95, 163f., 470f.; Nörtersheuser 1987; Uther 2004, I 409 with further references.

may have extended much further back in time and have inspired in its turn the elaborations of the storyline produced by various writers.

The tale-type undoubtedly goes back to antiquity. Xenophon (*Cyr.* 8.3.35–48) modelled on it the life account of Pheraulas, a Persian commoner serving in Cyrus' retinue. Pheraulas came from a poor family and supported himself by hard labour in his small farm. Cyrus, however, gave him great wealth and many slaves. A Saka cavalryman is once entertained by the newly enriched fellow and admires him for his prosperity. But Pheraulas confesses that he is unhappy with his present state: riches have only brought him more cares. He is continuously worrying over his slaves and livestock. When he loses something of his property, he is distressed to the point of sleeplessness. Yet, he is obliged to spend much on cult offerings and hospitality to friends, and these expenses seriously discontent him. The Saka insists that possessing and spending much is a great blessing. Thus, Pheraulas proposes to cede him all his riches: he only demands that the Saka maintain him as a member of his household. In this way, Pheraulas (like the folktale hero) gives away his wealth and is relieved of his troubles, finding again his felicity.

Another Greek example takes the form of an anecdote about Anacreon. Two separate versions of it are included in Stobaeus (4.31.78 and 4.31.91, pp. 759f. and 767 Hense). It is also transmitted in the *Gnomologium Vaticanum* (72), the *Loci communes* of Pseudo-Maximus, and other collections of ancient gnomic material.[3] One of Stobaeus' versions is derived, according to the lemma, ἐκ τῶν Ἀριστοτέλους Χρειῶν (4.31.91, Arist. fr. 783 Gigon). This cannot be a genuine Aristotelian work but probably represents a compilation of *chreiai* prepared in the Hellenistic period.[4] The multiple sources and variant forms of this anecdote attest to its popularity. As the story goes, Anacreon receives a large sum of money (one or five talents) from the tyrant Polycrates. For two nights the poet keeps worrying over it. In the end, he returns it to the donor, stating that the money is not worth the cares it causes, or (in a more lapidary variant): 'I dislike a gift that makes me lose my sleep.'

Horace's account of Volteius Mena (*Epist.* 1.7.46–95) reflects the same storyline, adapting it to Roman social realities of the time. The protagonist, a man of modest means working as auctioneer in the market, lives happily enough and quietly enjoys his leisure. By chance, he attracts the attention of the wealthy lawyer Philippus, who invites him to his country estate. Mena is charmed by the countryside and Philippus offers him a substantial sum of money to buy a little

---

3 See Sternbach 1963, 33; Ihm 2001, 194, 323; Searby 1998, 98, 154f.; Searby 2007, I 227, II 579.
4 See Rose 1863, 611–3; Searby 1998, 77–84.

farm. Thus the former *praeco* becomes a landowner and is soon overcome by worries about his crops and animals. In the end, after many losses and disappointments, the overstrained fellow implores his rich patron: 'Please restore me to my former life!'

These three ancient specimens come from different contexts, genres and periods, indicating that the tale-type enjoyed a wide diffusion in the Graeco-Roman world. It must have circulated in popular tradition, developing several variants, of which one or another was occasionally picked up in literary creations.[5] Its ancient dissemination may have extended beyond the cultures of Greece and Rome. The essential concept (riches only bring anxiety) is often expressed as a maxim in Near-Eastern wisdom compositions. See e.g. *Ecclesiastes* 5.11: 'The sleep of a labouring man is sweet, whether he eat little or much; but the repletion of the rich will not suffer him to sleep' (cf. also ibid. 5.12). It repeatedly occurs in Sumerian proverb collections, on cuneiform tablets from the 18th century B.C.: e. g. 'He who possesses many things is constantly on guard'; or 'Who has much silver may be happy; who has much grain may be happy; but he who has nothing can sleep.'[6] Such Sumerian sayings often represent the condensed form of a fable or parable (and indeed coexist with more expanded narrative specimens within the proverb compilations).[7] If such a brief fable underlay the Mesopotamian proverbs quoted above, then some form of the 'Happy Poverty' story may have been current in the Middle East from exceedingly ancient times; it would constitute one of the earliest attested folktales of humankind.

The same tale offers the basis for a good deal of the plot in Plautus' *Aulularia*. The experiences of the comic protagonist, Euclio, replicate in many respects the poor hero's adventures in the popular story.[8] Like the folktale character, Euclio is a man of small means and meagre living conditions, who chances to come across a considerable amount of gold. This changes his life, causing him constant worries and suspicions. It is useful to attempt a detailed comparison between the scenario of the comedy and the many known variants of the 'Happy

---

5 On the ancient sources of the tale see Crane 1890, 162f.; Tobler 1906, 328–30; Trenkner 1958, 124–6; Nörtersheuser 1987, 1318f., 1321f.

6 For the first saying see Alster 1997, 9. For the second one see Kramer 1959, 122; Kramer 1963, 225 (Alster 1997, 84 provides a different rendering: 'He who has silver is happy, he who has grain feels comfortable, but he who has livestock cannot sleep'). Cf. Schwarzbaum 1968, 163f.

7 See Alster 1997, xiii–xix, xxvii–xxix; cf. Konstantakos 2008, 263–6.

8 The scenario of the *Aulularia* has been briefly correlated with a few particular examples of the 'Happy Poverty' narrative by Pokrowsky 1931, 131–3 and Trenkner 1958, 122–6; cf. Lefèvre 2001, 34 with a couple of earlier references. None of them offers an extensive comparison, nor takes account of the large number of folktale variants and their divergent details.

Poverty' narrative, taking into account not only the ancient specimens but also the medieval and later versions. It will thus transpire that numerous elements of the Plautine play are closely paralleled in the folktale tradition. The use of later narrative material in this comparative study should not be taken as a methodological lapse. As indicated above, the widely varying ancient examples imply a rich oral dissemination of the tale-type in Graeco-Roman culture. Thus, specific similarities between the *Aulularia* and later popular versions may suggest that the corresponding motifs were already present in the folk tradition of the story in antiquity.[9]

Plautus makes it clear that Euclio has suffered a conspicuous change in his behaviour after his discovery of the gold. From the first scene, Euclio's old maid Staphyla wonders to herself: 'What evil fortune, what madness has come over my master? I simply cannot imagine what to say! (...) I don't know what follies have taken hold of this man' (67ff.). Euclio's crazy fits of disquietude (driving Staphyla out of the house many times per day, staying awake for whole nights, not budging from his house for days on end) are clearly a new phenomenon to her. The general impression of outsiders about Euclio's character is largely positive: his neighbour Megadorus has always considered him 'a citizen without a single defect' (215f.), in spite of his poverty and parsimony (171, 206). Megadorus' sister Eunomia agrees that Euclio is 'an honest chap' (*hau malum*, 172). This is not the picture of an obsessed fidget, like the one we see already in the first act. Something has happened to Euclio, although it must be recent enough for his fellow citizens not to have noticed yet.[10] The Lar's prologue has of course informed the audience about the reason for this change: the treasure which the poor man found in his house. As soon as he took possession of the gold, Euclio was thrown into a paroxysm of suspicion and anxiety, like the poor hero of the folktale.

---

9 It is also possible that the *Aulularia* itself has influenced some of the later European examples (especially the literary ones), whose authors may well have been familiar with the Plautine script. However, the 'Happy Poverty' tale-type as a whole differs from the scenario of the *Aulularia* to a substantial extent. Therefore, it cannot have been derived wholesale from Plautus' play. It clearly represents an independent creation, already formed long before Plautus, as indicated by the ancient Greek examples. Nevertheless, later writers adapting the 'Happy Poverty' narrative might have recognized its analogies to the plot of the *Aulularia*; they could thus have borrowed specific motifs from this latter comedy, so as to combine them with the traditional storyline of the tale-type and enrich the plot details of their own fiction. Especially Bonaventure des Périers may have followed this practice; see below, n. 12.
10 On Euclio's change of behaviour see Raffaelli 2000, 62–4; Kruschwitz 2002, 148–51.

The particular symptoms of Euclio's distress find many parallels in the popular narratives. The Plautine protagonist does not sleep at night out of worry (72, fr. iv). Such anxious insomnia is the hallmark of the enriched humble fellow in most versions of the tale-type: already Xenophon's Pheraulas (*Cyr.* 8.3.42) and Anacreon in the Pseudo-Aristotelian *chreia* suffer from it; so also the poor hero of many medieval *exempla*, European fables and novellas, and later folktales. Euclio's main fear is, of course, that someone might steal his gold. This is why he keeps checking again and again whether the treasure is still in its place. He also wants his house to be locked and no stranger to be let into it, lest someone get hold of the precious pot (89–104, 274). A similar fear of thieves plagues the protagonist in numerous literary and folk specimens of 'Happy Poverty'.[11] Because of this anxiety, Euclio keeps moving his pot around. As soon as he sees anyone approaching its hiding-place, he deems the spot unsafe and removes the treasure at the first opportunity, to bury it elsewhere (449ff., 580ff., 667ff.). As he admits in the end, looking back at his madness, he used to dig ditches ten times a day, in order to relocate his golden hoard (fr. iii). The hero of Bonaventure des Périers' novella, the shoemaker Blondeau, displays the same symptom: every hour he leaves his workshop, so as to remove his pot of gold to a different hiding-place.[12]

Euclio's dread of theft is inflated to inordinate proportions. He suspects that everyone he meets has learned about his treasure and is determined to steal it. The same delusion occurs in two medieval versified *exempla*. Their central figure, a poor hermit, has amassed a good sum of money in his purse. He then starts thinking that every man he meets by day must be a robber.[13] However, Euclio's

---

[11] For these two symptoms (sleeplessness and fear of theft, often combined together) see e. g. Lecoy de la Marche 1877, 357, 438 (Étienne de Bourbon); Crane 1890, 27 (Jacques de Vitry); Wright 1842, 63f. and Tobler 1906, 333–6 (various medieval *exempla*); Hervieux 1896, 271 and Hassell 1957, 91–5 (Odo of Cheriton and related fables); Furnivall 1901, 198 (William of Wadington and Robert de Brunne); Österley 1869, II 188 (H. W. Kirchhof, *Wendunmuth*); Jacob 1872, 70 (Bonaventure des Périers); La Fontaine 8.2.41–6; Eschenburg 1800, 92f. (F. von Hagedorn, *Johann der Seifensieder*); Burton 1885, 155f., 189f. (*Arabian Nights*); Wolf 1845, 42f. (German folktale); Megas 1962, 180 (Greek folktale); Schwarzbaum 1968, 163 (Jewish folktale); cf. Burkard Waldis 4.82 (Kurz 1862, 211; Holzinger 2013, 442); Toldo 1903, 421; Moser-Rath 1959, 18f.

[12] Jacob 1872, 70. This particular detail may have been inspired by the *Aulularia*: note that the gold is contained and moved around in a pot, just like Euclio's *aula*. Nonetheless, the pot features in folk variants as well, such as a Hassidic Jewish tale (Schwarzbaum 1968, 163), for which it is difficult to assume influence from the Plautine script. Discovery of a treasure in a buried pot or urn (*hydria*) was a very old piece of popular lore: see Ar. *Av.* 599–602 with ancient Scholium *ad loc.*

[13] See Furnivall 1901, 198 (William of Wadington, *Manuel des pechiez* 5229f.; Robert de Brunne, *Handlyng Synne* 6125–8); Hassell 1957, 94.

obsessive mistrust does not apply only to outsiders, such as the cook Congrio (415–50), the strangers calling on his house (90–105), his fellow citizens greeting him in the street (113–7), or Lyconides' slave (628–60). It also extends to his own household: Euclio suspects that his maid Staphyla is on the watch to discover the hiding-place of his gold and steal it behind his back (60–6). Compare the poor fellow in Étienne de Bourbon, who is afraid lest his own wife steal the money.[14] The Plautine hero is even anxious about his cock, which roams and scrapes all around the hiding-spot of the treasure; for this reason he strikes the poor bird dead with a stick (465–72). Similarly La Fontaine's shoemaker and Hagedorn's soap-worker grow afraid of their household animals. The former, upon hearing a noise in the night, thinks that the cat is stealing his money. The latter is alarmed at the nocturnal patter of his dog and cat, mistaking them for robbers; in the end he throws both pets out of the house.[15]

Even the rich neighbour Megadorus cannot escape from Euclio's suspiciousness. The noble gentleman speaks to Euclio politely and asks for his daughter in marriage; but the poor fellow takes this as a sign that Megadorus is keen on his gold (184–203, 215f., 240, 265–7). The cook hired to prepare the wedding feast is regarded as an accomplice of Megadorus, dispatched to snatch the precious pot (462–4). When invited to a drinking bout, Euclio believes that his prospective son-in-law will try to make him drunk, so as to lay hands on his treasure (569–86). Such fears are absurd, since Megadorus is a wealthy man, who does not need more gold. The poor fisherman in the story of the *Arabian Nights* experiences a comparably irrational anxiety. He thinks that the caliph of Baghdad, Harun al-Rashid himself, will learn of his newly acquired dinars, covet them and send his officers to seize them.[16]

Fear of theft or loss is tied up with other obsessive symptoms. Euclio stays in his house without budging for entire days, zealously guarding his treasure (72f.). He only goes out when it is absolutely imperative, with great reluctance; even then he hastens to return as quickly as possible (105ff., 178–81). Similarly, the poor workman in Étienne de Bourbon and in a Greek folktale shuts himself up in his lodging and is unwilling to leave for his ordinary work.[17] Further, Euclio cautiously keeps his treasure a secret from everyone, even from his maidservant (46–59). He takes meticulous care to behave like a poor man (106–12), loudly proclaiming his lack of means at every opportunity (186, 190–2, 220–40, 255–8,

---

[14] Lecoy de la Marche 1877, 357, 438. Cf. a Greek folktale (Megas 1962, 180f.), in which the poor labourer scolds his wife and children because of his nervous irritation.
[15] La Fontaine 8.2.45f.; Eschenburg 1800, 92f. (Hagedorn).
[16] Burton 1885, 155, 189; Chauvin 1902, 19.
[17] Lecoy de la Marche 1877, 357, 438; Megas 1962, 180.

541–4). Even when questioning persons he suspects as thieves (the cook, Lyconides' slave), he dares not name his gold or its container in concrete terms, but only refers to them by vague expressions (e. g. 634–54). The protagonist in Jacques de Vitry exhibits the same behaviour. When his neighbours notice his change of mood and ask him the cause of his sadness, he does not dare speak to them about the money which has rendered him so careworn.[18]

Akin to this secretiveness is another trait: the hero is reluctant to spend any of his money, whether for his own pleasure or for the benefit of others. Euclio mistrusts Megadorus so much, that he cannot bear to give him the slightest indication about his newly-found gold. For this reason, the old grouch cannot provide any dowry for his daughter's marriage, even though his treasure would enable him to make generous provision for her (190–2, 227, 238–40, 255–60, cf. 265–7). A similar situation occurs when Euclio goes to shop for the wedding feast. His present wealth would afford him ample means to give himself a treat. However, once he has reached the salesmen's stalls, he cannot bring himself to buy anything: all nice and tasty food, from fish and lamb to beef and pork, seems to him too expensive, just as he has deemed it throughout his life. In fact, he has set out for the market without taking a sufficient sum of money with him and has no alternative than to return without provisions, disappointed and angry (371–84). Apparently, his innate stinginess, a vice running in his family (see the Lar's prologue, 9–22), renders him incapable of spending for pleasure. Another factor is the kind of life he has led for all his long years: struggling in meagre conditions, with a constant need to economize, Euclio has been addicted to parsimony.[19] His very stealthiness about his treasure may provide a further motivation. Euclio fears that every man he meets in the street is coveting his gold. He therefore thinks that, if he started buying expensive delicacies, beyond his hitherto usual means and habits, he would reveal his fortune to all and thus invite robbers to steal from him.[20] His complacent sally against the wily market people (*ita illis impuris omnibus adii manum*, 378) may imply as much: Euclio tricked those fellows not only by thwarting their expectations of a good sale, but also by maintaining his pretence of poverty. By vociferously denouncing the high prices and refusing to buy, he deceived them all with regard to his true wealth.

Comparable phenomena also occur to the central characters of several versions of the folktale. Already Xenophon's Pheraulas confesses that he is greatly

---

18 Crane 1890, 28. So also in other medieval exempla: Wright 1842, 64; Tobler 1906, 334–6.
19 See Pokrowsky 1931, 130; Enk 1935, 289; Neumann 1958, 88; Ludwig 1961, 58; García Hernández 2004, 231–4, 239.
20 This is implied also by Pokrowsky 1931, 130 and Kraus 1962, 187.

distressed when he has to spend something of his property; even the smallest loss makes him restless at night (*Cyr.* 8.3.42, 44). The hero in Jacques de Vitry is wary of using his money for buying goods or fine clothes: he fears that people will notice his unusual expenditure and suspect he has procured riches in some illegal manner.[21] Once again, as in the *Aulularia*, the poor man is constrained to uphold his habitual image in the eyes of society, and this prevents him from enjoying his unexpected wealth. The blacksmith in Kirchhof's *Wendunmuth* hesitates to pass even a single day without work and to pay with his newly acquired thalers for his daily sustenance. He is afraid to reduce the sum in any way, lest he be unable to restore it complete, in case the rich man asks for it back. This attitude is not far from the maxim by which Euclio rationalizes his reluctance to spend on his daughter's wedding: 'If you waste something on a holiday, you may find yourself in want on the working-day – unless you economize' (380f.). The *bonhomme* discovering the treasure in Florian's fable declines to give alms to a pauper who begs for a few farthings. He claims to have no cash, feigning pennilessness in face of his social obligations, just like Euclio when confronted with his daughter's dowry.[22] In all these cases, despite the varying motivations, the result is the same. The poor protagonist, just as he is psychologically incapable of handling the troubled emotions arising from his new wealth, is also socially unfit to exploit his riches and practically unable to make use of them in real circumstances.

Another sign of Euclio's fixation is his concrete, physical adhesion to his treasure – a highly entertaining trait in scenic terms. Euclio wants to be in continuous bodily proximity to his pot of gold. He cannot bear to distance himself from it for any amount of time. This is why he refuses to leave his house or hastens to return whenever he is obliged to exit. His soul is at home with the money, as he acknowledges (181), and his body is naturally constrained to follow the soul. But coexistence within the same space is not enough: Euclio feels the urge to regularly sight his treasure at short intervals. As implied by Staphyla's complaints, he uncovers and checks his valuable container ten times per day (70). We observe this kind of behaviour staged before our eyes: at any moment the protagonist is ready to desert his interlocutor in the middle of a conversation, abandon all business, and rush back to inspect his treasure again. During his dialogue with Megadorus he does so twice within 50 lines (200–7, 241–50). He continues the same practice after he has removed the *aula* outside his residence. Even though the ongoing preparations for his daughter's wedding are pressing on him (Euclio must ritually wash and take part in the sacrifice, 612f.), yet he

---

[21] Crane 1890, 27. Similarly in other medieval *exempla*: Wright 1842, 64; Tobler 1906, 334–6.
[22] Österley 1869, II 187f. (Kirchhof); Claris de Florian 1856, 49.

keeps forsaking his duties in order to revisit his cache (624–7, 655ff., 709–11). His ideal aspiration, as he himself admits (449f.), is to carry his pot with himself at all times, wherever he goes. He desires to be in constant physical contact with it, to touch and feel it on his body.[23]

This trait is also common in the folktale characters and manifests itself with various compulsive behaviour patterns. The poor fellow in Étienne de Bourbon hides the money in his bed or under his mattress and lies on it, pretending to be sick.[24] Similarly, the hermit in Odo of Cheriton's Latin fable and its multiple medieval offshoots places his purse under his pillow, so as to sleep on it at night.[25] This is the most extreme form of the incessant physical proximity desired by Euclio: the owner is literally covering his treasure. The fisherman in the *Arabian Nights* opts for another manoeuvre, even closer to Euclio's wishes: he puts all his dinars in a pocket of his collar or in the breast of his gown and thus carries them continually on him.[26]

In Plautus' comedy the gold is not given to Euclio by a rich neighbour, as in most folktale versions. The old man finds it in his house, buried in the hearth, where his avaricious grandfather had hidden it long before. It is the household Lar who inconspicuously leads our hero to that discovery, in order to ensure a dowry for Euclio's pious daughter and set the plot in motion (25–7, cf. 6–8). This scenario conforms to the conventions of New Comedy, in which minor divinities often similarly influence the beginning of the dramatic action.[27] Nonetheless, there are variants of the 'Happy Poverty' tale-type that resemble Plautus' arrangement. In several cases the rich man does not directly offer the money to his poor fellow-citizen but secretly leaves it in or around the latter's house: e.g. he places it on the humble man's threshold (Jacques de Vitry), or hangs it before his door (Étienne de Bourbon), or throws it into his lodging from the window (other Latin *exempla*).[28] Thus the poor fellow finds the money in his own home, as

---

23 For this fixation see Steidle 1975, 350–4; Raffaelli 2000, 49–62; García Hernández 2004, 231.
24 Lecoy de la Marche 1877, 357, 438. So also in other Latin *exempla* (Tobler 1906, 333).
25 Hervieux 1896, 271 (Odo); Furnivall 1901, 198 (William of Wadington, Robert de Brunne); Hassell 1957, 91–5 (Latin and vernacular derivatives).
26 Burton 1885, 156, 190; Chauvin 1902, 19.
27 According to many scholars, in the Greek model of the *Aulularia* the Roman Lar's role was probably played by the goddess Tyche (Hunter 1981, 44f.; Primmer 1992, 98–100, 111, 122f.; Lefèvre 2001, 20–3, 51, 131; Martin 2008, 109–11). Other Greek alternatives, closer to Plautus' household divinity, have also been suggested: e.g. a nameless family god (θεὸς ἐφέστιος or θεὸς πατρῷος) or a home-revered Ἀγαθὸς Δαίμων (Ludwig 1961, 46f.; Kraus 1962, 186).
28 Lecoy de la Marche 1877, 357, 438 (Étienne); Crane 1890, 27 (Jacques); Klapper 1914, 155, 195, 354, 388 and Hassell 1957, 100 (15th-century Latin manuscripts); Wright 1842, 63; Tobler 1906, 333–6; Hilka 1912, 11 (other *exempla*). Cf. generally Nörtersheuser 1987, 1321.

though by chance, without knowing its provenance, more or less like the Plautine *senex*. In other examples the hero discovers the treasure accidentally in an out-of-the-way location. Blondeau in Bonaventure's novella comes upon it in an ancient fortress wall. The *bonhomme* of Florian's fable unearths it at an old tower, where it had been buried underground.[29] In such cases the precious item reaches the man like a boon from heaven, comparable to the Lar's divine bounty. A few divergent variants actually present a superhuman power donating the money to the poor protagonist. In a German folktale Jesus, journeying incognito upon earth, visits the poor shoemaker and grants him a large sum. In the *Arabian Nights* the fisherman fishes up a magical monkey, which brings him great professional luck, so that he soon amasses considerable earnings.[30] These storylines resemble the situation in the *Aulularia*, where the god guides the hero to the treasure.

The *Aulularia* does include a character corresponding to the rich donor of the 'Happy Poverty' narratives: Megadorus, the wealthy *senex* who is a neighbour of the poor protagonist, just like his folktale equivalent. Unlike the latter, Megadorus is not the source of his humble neighbour's newly-acquired gold. Nonetheless, he retains some traces of the rich man's role in the folktale. When Euclio complains of his supposed poverty, Megadorus hastens to reassure him: 'Cheer up! I shall give to you, I shall help you. Tell me if you need anything; I am awaiting your orders!' (192f.). This promise is not fulfilled in the comedy: Megadorus does not give Euclio money at any moment, although he undertakes financial burdens with a view to easing Euclio's scanty circumstances (he accepts Euclio's daughter in marriage without dowry and shoulders the entire expense for the wedding feast). Still, Megadorus' statement recalls the rich donor, who provides the poor man with funds in the popular stories. In some variants, indeed, the wealthy neighbour expressly gives the hero money in order to help him with his meagre finances: the poor man may use this sum as backup if he falls in need, or as capital for a prosperous business, or as a means to live more comfortably.[31] Even Megadorus' comic name can be read as an allusion to the rich man's function in the folktales: the latter is indeed the one who offers the humble hero the μέγα δῶρον of the gold.

Megadorus' overall attitude is also relevant. The wealthy man of the popular narratives is standardly intrigued by the joy and peace of mind displayed by the poor neighbour in spite of his meagre financial means. The rich gentleman's offer

---

[29] Jacob 1872, 69 (Bonaventure); Claris de Florian 1856, 49.
[30] Wolf 1845, 41–3 (German tale); Burton 1885, 145–55, 184–9; Chauvin 1902, 18f. (*Arabian Nights*).
[31] See Österley 1869, II 187 (Kirchhof); La Fontaine 8.2.32f.; Kurz 1862, 211 and Holzinger 2013, 443 (Burkard Waldis); Eschenburg 1800, 92 (Hagedorn); Megas 1962, 180 (Greek tale); Hassell 1957, 102.

of money is often meant as a kind of ethical or anthropological experiment, aiming to prove that wealth is not conductive to happiness but may conversely destroy it by causing worries. Thus, the rich fellow appears preoccupied with the theme of wealth versus equanimity.[32] Megadorus is also given to pondering on a similar issue. As he declares, he does not want a rich wife with a large dowry, because he could never put up with her domineering character and luxurious fussing (166–9, cf. 475ff.).[33] In other words, Megadorus prefers tranquillity in his household to a large dowry; like the rich fellow of the folk stories, he is conscious that wealth may cause trouble, destroying a man's peace of mind. Megadorus' reflections are of course focused on a specific area of financial relations (dowry in marriage), not applied to riches in general, and they are amplified with a good deal of exuberant Plautine satire.[34] Nonetheless, the gist of his contemplations is close to the folktale plutocrat's concern. Megadorus once formulates the core of his thoughts in a lapidary manner, rebutting Euclio's complaints: 'If you have peace of mind, you have enough to live happily' (187). This is precisely the theorem proved by the wealthy neighbour's human experiment in the popular stories.

Evidently, the divine provenance or chance discovery of the gold is incompatible with the rich neighbour donating it. In folktale versions these two motifs cannot coexist. The *Aulularia* employs the former while retaining traces of the latter as well. Possibly the comic playwright knew and combined two distinct variants of the popular story, one with a god as source of the poor man's treasure and another with a wealthy citizen in the same role. This is not surprising, in view of the diffusion enjoyed by the 'Happy Poverty' tale in the ancient world. A

---

32 In the medieval *exempla* the rich character, upon conceiving the plan of enriching his poor neighbour, exclaims: 'I shall make him stop feeling joyful and no longer be in the mood for singing.' Conversely, when he sets out to reclaim his money, he predicts that he will now cure the humble fellow of his newly arisen troubles. See Lecoy de la Marche 1877, 357f., 436–8 (Étienne de Bourbon); Crane 1890, 27f. (Jacques de Vitry); Wright 1842, 63f.; Tobler 1906, 333–6; Hilka 1912, 11; Klapper 1914, 155f., 195, 354f., 388 (other *exempla*). See also Megas 1962, 180 (Greek tale); Moser-Rath 1959, 18f.; Nörtersheuser 1987, 1318, 1322.
33 On this aspect of Megadorus see Kruschwitz 2002, 151–6, 162.
34 Megadorus' satirical tirades against the luxury of women are bound up with Roman social realities and clearly of Plautine provenance. Nonetheless, the core of his sentiment (aversion to large dowries and to the overbearing women bringing them) may have been present in the Greek model as well, as acknowledged even by the hardest of analytical scholars: see Lefèvre 2001, 58–61, 76–8, 146–9. Complaints against well-dowried wives, who oppress and torment their husbands, are common in Greek fourth-century comedy: see Anaxandrides fr. 53.4ff.; Antiphanes fr. 270; Alexis fr. 150; Diodorus fr. 3; Menander fr. 296–8, 802, 804, 805; Arnott 1996, 441–4.

literary adapter of a folk narrative may be aware of different versions of it and amalgamate elements from all of them in his creation.[35]

The finale of the *Aulularia* is lost. Its outline can be reconstructed from the information provided by the ancient metrical *argumenta* to the play and by a handful of fragments. According to the second, acrostic argument (8f.), the young Lyconides returned to Euclio the pot of gold stolen by Lyconides' slave. In the end, Euclio gave Lyconides his daughter in marriage and also bestowed on him the gold, presumably as dowry. Two fragments from the lost scenes probably come from a final speech made by the elderly hero, surveying the tribulations he suffered because of his treasure: 'I used to dig ten ditches a day' (fr. iii – presumably to move around the pot in ever new hiding-places). 'Neither at night nor by day was I ever calm; but now I shall sleep' (fr. iv). Clearly, Euclio found his peace of mind after he had handed his gold over to the young couple. Only when he stopped possessing the precious pot was he definitively relieved from the worries it had been causing him.

The protagonist of the folktale has the same experience at the end. In a few versions, the rich man finally asks for his money back, sometimes threatening to prosecute the poor fellow for misappropriation. Most usually, however, it is the humble hero himself who voluntarily returns the funds to the donor. He openly declares that he is giving the wealth back because it has only brought him troubles. He wishes to be relieved of them and indeed finds again his former mental tranquillity, as soon as he has parted from his precious possession.[36] In the variants without a donating neighbour, the hero finds another way to relinquish the treasure he has amassed or discovered: he throws it in the river, or distributes it to the community, or even willingly cedes it to the thieves.[37] Such variations were already formed in the ancient tradition. Anacreon in the Pseudo-Aristotelian anecdote returns the troublesome talents to their donor, Polycrates; Xenophon's Pheraulas, on the other hand, bestows his property on an acquaintance of his. All this perfectly accords with the ending of the *Aulularia*, as reconstructed

---

35 For example, Bonaventure des Périers had clearly heard or read many different versions of 'Happy Poverty' and mixed together their motifs in his novella. See Hassell 1957, 102f.
36 See Lecoy de la Marche 1877, 357f., 438 (Étienne de Bourbon); Crane 1890, 28 (Jacques de Vitry); Wright 1842, 64; Tobler 1906, 333–6; Hilka 1912, 11; Klapper 1914, 156, 195, 354f., 388 (other *exempla*); Österley 1869, II 187f. (Kirchhof); La Fontaine 8.2.46–9; Kurz 1862, 212 and Holzinger 2013, 443 (Burkard Waldis); Wolf 1845, 43 (German folktale); Megas 1962, 181 (Greek folktale); Schwarzbaum 1968, 163 (Jewish tale).
37 See Claris de Florian 1856, 50; Jacob 1872, 70 (Bonaventure); Hervieux 1896, 271 and Hassell 1957, 91–5 (Odo and related fables); Furnivall 1901, 198f. (William of Wadington and Robert de Brunne).

above. Euclio's *nunc dormiam* (fr. iv) is echoed in the conclusion of some Latin *exempla* and later fables, where the protagonist regains his *somnus* or exasperatedly asks the rich man: 'Give me back my sleep.'[38] It is noteworthy that Lyconides, to whom Euclio finally grants his gold, is the nephew of the rich neighbour Megadorus. Thus, the treasure ends up handed over, if not to the rich man himself, at least to his broader family.

The ending of the popular stories may also help us understand Euclio's motivations for his final donation. Students of the *Aulularia* often wonder how such a miserly man, obsessed about keeping his gold and utterly reluctant to use any part of it, would have been brought to give it away wholesale at the end. Various interpretations have been proposed. Euclio may be moved by Lyconides' honesty and selflessness, when the latter returns him his stolen pot; the old grouch thus experiences a profound change of heart. He understands that his mistrust towards everyone was misguided (cf. Menander's Knemon); he now sees that there are other things in life, transcending the value of money or the dichotomy of rich and poor, such as family ties, friendship and love. Alternatively, he may feel the strong social pressure, which obliges him to give his daughter a dowry, now that his treasure is public knowledge and he can no longer feign lack of means. Or he submits to the laws of *philia*, which demand of him a reciprocal gift to reward Lyconides' generous favour.[39] Any combination of these motives may have been suggested in the lost ending of the play. But the folktale parallels point to another possible explanation, which may have operated collaterally with the aforementioned ones. Like the hero in the popular narratives, Euclio may have given away his treasure in order to shake off the worries he suffered because of it. Indeed, the Plautine *senex* is conscious from early on that his pot of gold is the cause of his numerous solicitudes (65f.: *aurum ... quod me sollicitat plurumis miserum modis*). In the end, after the great shock of the theft, Euclio might have realized that his gold was not worth all those soul-rending agonies. He would thus willingly bestow it on the young couple.[40]

---

38 See Lecoy de la Marche 1877, 358 (Étienne de Bourbon); La Fontaine 8.2.48. Cf. Anacreon's final quote (Stob. 4.31.91, p. 767 Hense, *Gnomol. Vatic.* 72): μισῶ δωρεάν, ἥ τις ἀναγκάζει ἀγρυπνεῖν.
39 On the ending of the *Aulularia* and the motives behind Euclio's gift see most notably Jachmann 1931, 138f.; Minar 1947; Neumann 1958, 89f.; Ludwig 1961, 59f., 250; Kraus 1962, 188; Schäfer 1965, 99f., 103–9; Gaiser 1966, 193; Ludwig 1970, 83; Hofmann 1977, 357f.; Stockert 1983, 6–8; Konstan 1983, 40f.; Arnott 1989, 37; Primmer 1992, 126; Kruschwitz 2002, 160; Braun 2007, 107.
40 Cf. Enk 1935, 289f.; Hofmann 1977, 357f.; Raffaelli 2000, 58f., 64. This might seem simplistic by comparison to the other psychological explanations, or out of character in view of Euclio's

What was the genre of the old tale which inspired the plot of the *Aulularia*? In extant ancient sources the 'Happy Poverty' narrative may take various forms: *chreia* in the gnomic anthologies, historical novelette of the Persian court in Xenophon, moral *exemplum* in Horace. However, its prominent didactic and moralistic character renders it especially akin to fables, like those found in the Aesopic collections. Our story puts forward an emphatic precept: wealth brings no happiness, only troubles. This is also the generic essence of the fable, which is by definition a brief story with a moral: a metaphorical narrative which can be applied to particular circumstances of life in order to teach a lesson about the human condition or behaviour.[41] The fable is often used as an *exemplum* in order to support an argument, illustrate a point of view or criticize a specific situation, just as Horace uses the story of Volteius Mena in his poetic epistle. The *exempla* of medieval preachers, among which the 'Happy Poverty' tale-type regularly features, are also akin to fables: they were used as 'stories of instruction' aiming to illustrate a moral or religious precept within the sermon. Indeed, they amply accommodate animal fables or other moralistic tales comparable to the items of ancient Aesopic corpora. Later, in vernacular European literature, our tale was included in many famous collections of fables (La Fontaine, Florian, Burkard Waldis' *Esopus*, Friedrich von Hagedorn etc.), along with animal stories and other Aesopic lore. In the ancient world as well, the narrative may have circulated as a kind of fable. Such didactic stories with all-human cast and realistic setting are not uncommon in the Aesopic tradition.[42]

The correlation with fables is interesting, because Euclio's personality and adventures have further parallels in ancient Aesopic stories. Euclio presents one prominent difference from the usual hero of 'Happy Poverty' narratives. The latter, though poor, is never described as a stingy or avaricious man; on the contrary, all variants stress his *joie de vivre* and some, sketching his character before the acquisition of the treasure, show him wholeheartedly spending his small earnings on personal enjoyment.[43] Euclio, on the other hand, is a natural-born miser, as explained in the prologue: extreme parsimony runs in his family, bequeathed from father to son (9–22). His thrift is commented upon in various ways

---

miserly nature (cf. Jachmann 1931, 135f.). Nevertheless, it should be borne in mind that ancient comedy is not modern psychological drama (cf. Lefèvre 2001, 145f.).

41 On the definition and nature of the fable see conveniently Perry 1965, xix–xxviii; van Dijk 1997, 3–37 and Holzberg 2002, 11–38 with further references.

42 The Sumerian sayings, which express the same moral in proverbial form, may also represent condensations of a fable-like narrative; see above.

43 See La Fontaine 8.2.16–24; Jacob 1872, 69 (Bonaventure des Périers); Claris de Florian 1856, 48.

by the other personages of the play (e. g. 82–4, 101f., 206, 294–319, 539f.). This innate stinginess greatly influences Euclio's attitudes in the course of the action: it prevents him from spending his gold and augments his fear of theft.[44]

This portrayal of Euclio, unparalleled in the 'Happy Poverty' narratives, can nonetheless be connected with other ancient fables featuring a miser as their central personage. Scholars have repeatedly pointed out the similarities between the Plautine hero and the sketches of miserly temperaments in Theophrastus' *Characters*, especially the μικρολόγος ('Penny-pincher,' 10) and the ἀνελεύθερος ('Illiberal man,' 22).[45] But it has not been noticed how much Euclio's disposition and behaviour owes to the stingy figures satirized in fable. For instance, Aesopic fable 225 Perry (from the Augustana and later Greek collections) tells the story of a φιλάργυρος who cashed all his property to buy a lump of gold. He buried this outside the city wall and kept visiting that spot to inspect his treasure. Thus, a labourer, who was working thereabouts, noticed his comings and goings, set his eyes on the gold and stole it, as soon as the miser had left. Afterwards, the stingy fellow returned and found his hiding-place empty. He then started wailing and pulling off his hair out of despair. Another man, however, observed him and advised him: 'Do not grieve; just take a stone, bury it at the same spot, and think of it as your gold. Even when the gold was there, you made no use of it.'[46]

There are obvious similarities between this little story and the scenario of the *Aulularia*. Like the miser of the fable, Euclio keeps his gold buried underground, whether in his house (467 *defossa*) or in other pits outdoors (709 *effodio aulam*, cf. fr. iii *effodiebam*).[47] The final hiding-place he chooses (and the one from which the gold is eventually stolen) is the grove of Silvanus, which lies outside the city wall (*extra murum*, 674), just like the hiding-spot πρὸ τοῦ τείχους in the fable.

---

44 On Euclio's character as a miser see Jachmann 1931, 129–37; Enk 1935; Minar 1947, 272, 274; Lehmann 1960, 84–6; Ludwig 1961, 55–8; Kraus 1962, 187f.; Marcovich 1977, 197–205, 210f.; Hofmannn 1977; Stockert 1983, 18–20; Bain 1992, 70; Raffaelli 2000, 62–4; Lefèvre 2001, 33–8; Kruschwitz 2002, 147–51; García Hernández 2004.
45 See Jachmann 1931, 131; Enk 1935, 285–7; Neumann 1958, 88f.; Ludwig 1961, 56; Marcovich 1977, 200f.; Hofmann 1977, 353; Bain 1992, 70; Raffaelli 2000, 63.
46 See the oldest Augustana recension (Perry 1952, 408f.): Φιλάργυρός τις τὴν οὐσίαν ἐξαργυρισάμενος βῶλον χρυσοῦν ὠνήσατο καὶ τοῦτον πρὸ τοῦ τείχους κατορύξας διετέλει συνεχῶς ἐρχόμενος καὶ ἐπισκεπτόμενος. τῶν δὲ περὶ τὸν τόπον ἐργατῶν τις παρατηρησάμενος αὐτοῦ τὰς ἀφίξεις καὶ ὑπονοήσας τὸ ἀληθές, ἀπαλλαγέντος αὐτοῦ τὸ χρυσίον ἀνείλετο. ὁ δέ, ὡς ἐπανελθὼν κενὸν εὗρε τὸν τόπον, ἔκλαιέ τε καὶ τὰς τρίχας ἔτιλλεν. ἰδὼν δέ τις αὐτὸν ὑπεραλγοῦντα καὶ μαθὼν τὴν αἰτίαν ἔφη πρὸς αὐτόν· 'μὴ λυποῦ, ἑταῖρε, ἀλλὰ λαβὼν λίθον κατάθες ἐν τῷ αὐτῷ τόπῳ καὶ νόμιζε τὸ χρυσίον κεῖσθαι· οὐδὲ γὰρ ὅτε ἦν ἐχρῶ αὐτῷ.'
47 On the burying motif see Marcovich 1977, 216f.; Hunter 1981, 39; Bain 1992, 68; Martin 2008, 108.

The Aesopic miser's incessant visits and inspections of the treasure recall Euclio's most prominent fixation: he also regularly hastens to his cache, many times in the play. As in the fable, so also in the comedy it is precisely the miser's comings and goings that finally betray the location of his gold to an outsider (respectively the workman and Lyconides' slave, *Aul.* 608ff.), who then proceeds to steal it as soon as the skinflint has retired (701ff.). In both cases, once the owner comes back and discovers the theft, he falls into despair and manifestly laments for his loss: the fable miser's 'wailing and hair-rending' read like a dry abstract of Euclio's long lamentation monody (713–30). In the Aesopic story the third man's ironical remark at the end draws attention to another trait, which also characterizes Euclio's idiosyncrasy: the miser made no use of his gold, just as Euclio is unable to spend it on goods or dowry. Both of them simply let their treasure lie in the earth, drawing no more benefit from it than from a plain stone. It seems as though the main storyline of the *Aulularia* has been pieced together by combining the 'Happy Poverty' narrative with this Aesopic fable of the φιλάργυρος.

In Phaedrus' versified Roman fables the miser's role is assigned to personified beasts displaying human characteristics (as standardly in the Aesopic tradition). Their portrayals are also comparable to Euclio's in some respects. Phaedrus 1.27 is expressly designated as a tale fit for *avari* and men of low birth who want to be wealthy (not unlike humble Euclio who is suddenly enriched). The dog, while digging up bones, discovers a treasure and is seized by avidity for riches. He thus stays on the spot, continuously watching over the gold without even remembering to feed, until he dies of starvation. In Phaedrus 4.21 the same motif is placed in a more fairytale setting. The fox, digging a burrow for his lodging, comes upon the remote cave of the dragon guarding his hoard of treasure. The cunning animal then asks the monster: 'What profit do you derive from all this toil? What great reward induces you to pass thus your life in the dark, going without sleep?' The dragon replies that he gets no reward at all but simply performs his divinely appointed task. He neither takes anything from those treasures for himself nor gives anything to another. The fox then remarks: 'The likes of you are born under the gods' displeasure.' The poet adds in conclusion that this fable is directed against the miser who stingily avoids every expense, even depriving himself of food and groaning at the price of foodstuffs (similarly to Euclio in *Aul.* 371ff.). Both these fable figures display the same compulsive attachment to their treasure as Euclio. They constantly remain in position over the gold hoard, without ever moving away from it, even to their own detriment. This recalls Euclio's need to be bodily close to his pot, rushing to it countless times every day. Additionally, the dragon, like the Plautine hero, is unable to benefit from his wealth or to bestow any part of it on others.

The *Aulularia*, therefore, is essentially a dramatization of a fable or parable belonging to the 'Happy Poverty' tale-type and concerning the possession and effects of wealth. This has been amalgamated with other material from the Aesopic tradition, which has furnished additional elements of the storyline (the theft of the treasure, the hero's lament) and aspects of Euclio's character (stinginess, compulsive attachment to his gold, and reluctance to spend). This fable stuff has been combined with a love plot, according to the standard conventions of New Comedy: rape of a citizen girl, illegitimate birth of the baby and complications arising from it, discovery of the young rapist and final marriage with the violated maiden.[48] The girl was made a daughter of the fable's poor protagonist, her young lover was connected with the wealthy neighbour's *oikos*, and the happy couple became the recipients of the relinquished riches in the end. In this way, the fable material and the love scenario were interwoven.

Who was responsible for the scenic adaptation of the fable, Plautus or the author of the Greek model? In principle, the question can be answered in both ways. It cannot be excluded that the Roman poet, taking extensive liberties with the plot of his Hellenic exemplar, picked up and used the 'Happy Poverty' tale and related Aesopic lore in order to metamorphose the poor miser's storyline and freely reshape his character. Versions of the 'Happy Poverty' narrative must have been circulating in Rome as well, as indicated later by Horace's Volteius Mena. As for Aesopic fables, these were primarily oral material, widespread in popular tradition throughout the Graeco-Roman world. Educated Romans in Plautus' time could also have had access to the fable collection of Demetrius of Phalerum and other Hellenistic compilations of the same kind. In that case, the figure of Euclio and the scenario of the *Aulularia* are very largely Plautus' own product. The Greek model will have been much different, lacking all those characteristic components that are traced back to the 'Happy Poverty' tale and the other fables. It might even have been e. g. a recognition play, like the one dreamed up by Eckard Lefèvre, in which the treasure would be discovered late in the action and only have a peripheral function in the story.[49]

However, it seems more likely that the selection and dramatic treatment of the folk material derive from the Greek playwright. If so, the essence of the plot and the gist of Euclio's idiosyncrasy should be traced back to the New Comedy model, although Plautus undoubtedly made many comic amplifications and

---

[48] The love plot has been rather downplayed in Plautus' comedy. It may have occupied more stage time in the Greek model: see below the bibliography in notes 49–50.
[49] See Lefèvre 2001, especially 11–94, 130–44; cf. Trencsényi-Waldapfel 1965, who argues that the *Aulularia* is a free adaptation of the *Dyskolos*.

alterations of detail.⁵⁰ In Greek comic theatre there was an old tradition of using folktale or fable stuff in order to reflect on the theme of wealth and its distribution. Aristophanes' *Ploutos* is practically a dramatization of a folk parable about riches and their rightful ownership. Other fourth-century comedies also exploited such popular lore for the creation of stingy characters, as is suggested by a Paestan kalyx-krater painted by Asteas around 350 B.C. and illustrating a lively comic scene (see figure 1 at the end of this essay).⁵¹ In the centre an elderly character, labelled Charinos, is lying on a chest and tightly clinging on it, as though to protect it. This old man is presumably a comic miser, stretched on the strongbox in which he keeps his funds. Two young fellows have got hold of his arm and foot and are trying to pull him off his trunk. They are doubtless robbers intending to steal the old miser's valuables; it is they that have brought the strongbox out of the house and now strive to remove the owner, so as to carry it away with them. Here the comic skinflint is literally sprawled over his money, thus exhibiting the strong bodily attachment to his treasure that is also manifested by the stingy figures of fable. Compare Phaedrus' avaricious dog and dragon, who remain in position over their hoard. Even closer is the protagonist of certain 'Happy Poverty' variants, who hides the money in his bed and lies on top of it. Indeed, the mantle spread under Charinos on the chest may imply that the old man has made his bed on his strongbox and is sleeping on his treasure, so as to secure it at night.⁵² The Greek model of the *Aulularia* would be continuing and developing this comic tradition.

The association with fables may offer indirect support to the widely advocated theory that the *Aulularia* was based on a Menandrian play. The Peripatetic school, where Menander reportedly studied, was a centre of flourishing research on Aesopic lore. Aristotle and Theophrastus (Menander's teacher according to tradition, Diog.

---

50 This is the thesis of numerous scholars, even though there is not always agreement in pinpointing Plautus' specific contributions. See most notably Webster 1960, 120–7; Ludwig 1961; Kraus 1962; Arnott 1964; Schäfer 1965, 96–110; Ludwig 1970, 71–84; Hunter 1981; Stockert 1983, 8–16; Arnott 1988; Arnott 1989, 34–7; Bain 1992; Primmer 1992; Stockert 2000, 16–8; Braun 2007.
51 Berlin F 3044; *PhV* ² 76 (Trendall 1967, 50). See Heydemann 1886, 282; Zahn 1931, 70–6; Zahn 1932, 178–89; Webster 1948, 26; Catteruccia 1951, 43–5; Webster 1956, 114–6, 184; Bieber 1961, 139; Gigante 1967, 113f.; Trendall/Webster 1971, 131; Green 2001, 51, 53, 64; Green 2003, 130–2; Schwarzmaier/Scholl/Maischberger 2012, 146–8. As is widely recognized in present-day scholarship, these South Italian vase-paintings usually represent Athenian comedies performed in Magna Graecia during the fourth century (see bibliography in Konstantakos 2015, 188f.). Asteas in particular, before emigrating to Paestum, had learned his trade in Sicily. His comic scenes may thus reflect memories from performances witnessed there (Hughes 2011, 72f.).
52 Cf. Catteruccia 1951, 44.

Laert. 5.36) wrote on fables, especially on their use as *exempla* in rhetoric. The first known collection of Aesopic stories was compiled by Demetrius of Phalerum, another student of Theophrastus, also said to have been a friend of Menander's (Diog. Laert. 5.79).[53] The two men may have been schoolmates in the Peripatos. Demetrius, in any case, ruled Athens during Menander's early career (317–307 B.C.). In that intellectual environment, Menander could easily have become familiar with fable lore and conceived the idea of using it as material for his comedy.

The morality of Aesopic fable is predominantly conformist. A standard idea running through the ancient corpora is that weaker or humbler persons should keep their place and not aspire to imitate their superiors. Otherwise, they will bring ridicule and misfortune on their heads.[54] To recall an emblematic example (fables 188, 358 Perry), the ass should be content with being an ass and not disguise himself as a lion. This is precisely the lesson of the animal fable which Euclio narrates to Megadorus early in the comedy, when the rich neighbour proposes to marry Euclio's daughter (228–35): a poor man associating with the rich would be like a donkey hitched together with an ox; he would end up both cast out by the other donkeys and molested by the oxen. The moral of the scenic fable unfolded in the *Aulularia* is similar. Men like Euclio, born and bred in poverty and accustomed to extreme parsimony throughout their lives, are better off without wealth. They are unable to handle riches, both emotionally and materially: they cannot cope with the worries of a large fortune and do not know how to use it for their own and other persons' benefit. Money should rather belong to people like the honest Lyconides and his bride, the pious Phaedrium: persons who can control wealth (rather than be controlled by it) and are prepared to allocate it honestly or spend it on good causes.[55]

In Hellenistic Athens, under Demetrius' mild dictatorship or Macedonian despotism, this was a palatable message, well serving the prevalent social order. On one hand, it consoled the lower classes for their lack of funds (a perennial function of the 'Happy Poverty' narrative in many cultures).[56] On the other hand, it reminded propertied citizens of their responsibility to use their money for the public good. This latter lesson has yet to be learned by the wealthy elites of our times. The rich must be encouraged to read more New Comedy.

---

53 On the Peripatetics' interest in fables see Konstantakos 2008, 263–6 with further bibliography.
54 See Holzberg 2002, 48f., 60–2, 91f.
55 Cf. Hofmann 1977, 354f.; Kruschwitz 2002, 160–3.
56 See Nörtersheuser 1987, 1322f.

Fig. 1: Berlin F 3044. Paestan kalyx-krater painted by Asteas, ca. 350 B.C. Staatliche Museen zu Berlin, Antikensammlung, photographer: Johannes Laurentius. Reproduced by kind permission of the Staatliche Museen zu Berlin, Antikensammlung.

Acknowledgments

I am grateful to the organizers of the 8th *Trends in Classics* International Conference, in particular Professor Stavros Frangoulidis, who gave me the opportunity to develop and test my ideas about the *Aulularia*. Heartfelt thanks are due to the participants who offered valuable comments on my paper, especially Professors W. Stockert, D. Konstan, T. J. Moore, N. W. Slater, and Mr. G. Vidović. I am also greatly obliged to the Staatliche Museen zu Berlin, Antikensammlung, for their kind permission to reproduce figure 1, photographed by Johannes Laurentius.

Bibliography

Alster, B. (1997), *Proverbs of Ancient Sumer: The World's Earliest Proverb Collections*, vol. I, Bethesda.
Arnott, W. G. (1964), 'A Note on the Parallels Between Menander's *Dyskolos* and Plautus' *Aulularia*', *Phoenix* 18, 232–7.
Arnott, W. G. (1988), 'The Greek Original of Plautus' *Aulularia*', *Wiener Studien* 101, 181–91.
Arnott, W. G. (1989), 'A Study in Relationships: Alexis' *Lebes*, Menander's *Dyskolos*, Plautus' *Aulularia*', *Quaderni Urbinati di Cultura Classica* 33, 27–38.
Arnott, W. G. (1996), *Alexis: The Fragments. A Commentary*, Cambridge.
Bain, D. (1992), 'A Recent Suggestion about the Original of Plautus' *Aulularia*', *Liverpool Classical Monthly* 17, 68–70.
Bieber, M. (1961), *The History of the Greek and Roman Theater*, Princeton.
Braun, L. (2007), 'Zu einer neuen Rekonstruktion des Aulularia-Originals', *Hermes* 135, 107–8.
Burton, R. F. (1885), *The Book of the Thousand Nights and a Night*, vol. VIII, Benares.
Catteruccia, L. M. (1951), *Pitture vascolari italiote di soggetto teatrale comico*, Roma.
Chauvin, V. (1902), *Bibliographie des ouvrages arabes ou relatifs aux Arabes publiés dans l'Europe chrétienne de 1810 à 1885*, vol. VI: *Les Mille et une nuits (Troisième partie)*, Liège/Leipzig.
Claris de Florian, J.-P. (1856), *Fables de Florian, suivies des poèmes de Ruth et de Tobie, et autres poésies*, Paris.
Crane, T. F. (1890), *The Exempla or Illustrative Stories from the Sermones Vulgares of Jacques de Vitry*, London.
Enk, P. J. (1935), 'De Euclionis Plautini moribus', *Mnemosyne*, 3rd ser. 2, 281–90.
Eschenburg, J. J. (1800), *Friedrichs von Hagedorn Poetische Werke*, vol. II: *Fabeln und Erzählungen*, Hamburg.
Furnivall, F. J. (1901), *Robert of Brunne's 'Handlyng Synne', A.D. 1303, with Those Parts of the Anglo-French Treatise on Which it Was Founded, William of Wadington's 'Manuel des pechiez'*, vol. I, London.
García Hernández, B. (2004), 'Euclio (Plaut., *Aul.*) parcus atque avarus', *Emerita* 62, 227–48.
Gigante, M. (1967), 'Teatro greco in Magna Grecia', in: *Letteratura e arte figurata nella Magna Grecia*. Atti del sesto convegno di studi sulla Magna Grecia, Taranto 9–13 ottobre 1966, Napoli, 83–146.
Green, J. R. (2001), 'Comic Cuts: Snippets of Action on the Greek Comic Stage', *Bulletin of the Institute of Classical Studies* 45, 37–64.
Green, J. R. (2003), 'Smart and Stupid: The Evolution of Some Masks and Characters in Fourth-Century Comedy', in: J. Davidson/A. Pomeroy (eds.), *Theatres of Action: Papers for Chris Dearden*, Auckland, 118–32.
Hassell, Jr., J. W. (1957), *Sources and Analogues of the Nouvelles récréations et joyeux devis of Bonaventure des Périers*, Chapel Hill.
Hervieux, L. (1896), *Les fabulistes Latins depuis le siècle d'Auguste jusqu'à la fin du moyen âge*, vol. IV: *Eudes de Cheriton et ses dérivés*, Paris.
Heydemann, H. (1886), 'Die Phlyakendarstellungen auf bemalten Vasen', *Jahrbuch des Deutschen Archäologischen Instituts* 1, 260–313.

Hilka, A. (1912), 'Neue Beiträge zur Erzählungsliteratur des Mittelalters', in: *Neunzigster Jahres-Bericht der Schlesischen Gesellschaft für vaterländische Cultur*, IV.c: *Sektion für neuere Philologie*, Breslau, 1–24.
Hofmann, W. (1977), 'Zur Charaktergestaltung in der *Aulularia* des Plautus', *Klio* 59, 349–58.
Holzberg, N. (2002), *The Ancient Fable: An Introduction*, Bloomington/Indianapolis.
Holzinger, M. (2013), *Burkhard Waldis: Esopus*, Berlin.
Hughes, A. (2011), *Performing Greek Comedy*, Cambridge.
Hunter, R. L. (1981), 'The *Aulularia* of Plautus and its Greek Original', *Proceedings of the Cambridge Philological Society* 27, 37–49.
Ihm, S. (2001), *Ps.-Maximus Confessor: Erste kritische Edition einer Redaktion des sacro-profanen Florilegiums* Loci communes *nebst einer vollständigen Kollation einer zweiten Redaktion und weiterem Material*, Stuttgart.
Jachmann, G. (1931), *Plautinisches und Attisches*, Berlin.
Jacob, P. L. (1872), *Bonaventure des Periers, Contes ou Nouvelles récréations et joyeux devis, suivis du Cymbalum mundi. Nouvelle édition revue et corrigée sur les éditions originales avec des notes et une notice*, Paris.
Klapper, J. (1914), *Erzählungen des Mittelalters in deutscher Übersetzung und lateinischem Urtext*, Breslau.
Konstan, D. (1983), *Roman Comedy*, Ithaca/London.
Konstantakos, I. M. (2008), Ἀκίχαρος: Ἡ Διήγηση τοῦ Ἀχικὰρ στὴν ἀρχαία Ἑλλάδα, vol. II: Ἀπὸ τὸν Δημόκριτο στοὺς Περιπατητικούς, Athens.
Konstantakos, I. M. (2015), 'Tendencies and Variety in Middle Comedy', in: S. Chronopoulos/ C. Orth (eds.), *Fragmente einer Geschichte der griechischen Komödie: Fragmentary History of Greek Comedy*, Heidelberg, 159–98.
Kramer, S. N. (1959), *History Begins at Sumer*, New York.
Kramer, S. N. (1963), *The Sumerians: Their History, Culture, and Character*, Chicago/London.
Kraus, W. (1962), 'Menanders *Dyskolos* und das Original der *Aulularia*', in: R. Muth (ed.), *Serta Philologica Aenipontana*, Innsbruck, 185–90.
Kruschwitz, P. (2002), 'Ist Geld die ›Wurzel allen Übels‹? Zur Interpretation von Plautus' *Aulularia*', *Hermes* 130, 146–63.
Kurz, H. (1862), *Esopus von Burkhard Waldis*, vol. II, Leipzig.
Lecoy de la Marche, A. (1877), *Anecdotes historiques, légendes et apologues tirés du recueil inédit d'Étienne de Bourbon*, Paris.
Lefèvre, E. (2001), *Plautus'* Aulularia, Tübingen.
Lehmann, E. (1960), 'Der Verschwender und der Geizige. (Zur Typologie der griechisch-römischen Komödie)', *Gymnasium* 67, 73–90.
Ludwig, W. (1961), 'Aulularia-Probleme', *Philologus* 105, 44–71, 247–62.
Ludwig, W. (1970), 'Die plautinische *Cistellaria* und das Verhältnis von Gott und Handlung bei Menander', in: E. G. Turner (ed.), *Ménandre*. Fondation Hardt, Entretiens sur l'Antiquité Classique 16, Vandœuvres/Genève, 45–96.
Marcovich, M. (1977), 'Euclio, Cnemon, and the Peripatos', *Illinois Classical Studies* 2, 197–218.
Martin, G. (2008), 'Plautinisches im *Aulularia*-Prolog', *Museum Helveticum* 65, 99–113.
Megas, G. A. (1962), Ἑλληνικὰ παραμύθια, vol. II, Athens.
Minar, Jr., E. L. (1947), 'The Lost Ending of Plautus' *Aulularia*', *Classical Journal* 42, 271–5.
Moser-Rath, E. (1959), 'Erzähler auf der Kanzel: Zu Form und Funktion des barocken Predigtmärleins', *Fabula* 2, 1–26.

Neumann, M. (1958), *Die poetische Gerechtigkeit in der neuen Komödie: Untersuchungen zur Technik des antiken Lustspiels*, Speyer.
Nörtersheuser, H.-W. (1987), 'Glückliche Armut (AaTh 754)', *Enzyklopädie des Märchens* 5, 1318–24.
Österley, H. (1869), *Wendunmuth von Hans Wilhelm Kirchhof*, vol. I–V, Tübingen.
Perry, B. E. (1952), *Aesopica: A Series of Texts Relating to Aesop or Ascribed to him or Closely Connected with the Literary Tradition that Bears his Name*, Urbana.
Perry, B. E. (1965), *Babrius and Phaedrus*, Cambridge MA/London.
Pokrowsky, M. (1931), 'Zur Plautinischen Aulularia', *Wiener Studien* 49, 128–33.
Primmer, A. (1992), 'Der ‚Geizige' bei Menander und Plautus', *Wiener Studien* 105, 69–127.
Raffaelli, R. (2000), 'C'è del comico in quella follia', in: R. Raffaelli/A. Tontini (eds.), *Lecturae Plautinae Sarsinates*, vol. III: *Aulularia*, Urbino, 49–65.
Rose, V. (1863), *Aristoteles Pseudepigraphus*, Leipzig.
Schäfer, A. (1965), *Menanders Dyskolos: Untersuchungen zur dramatischen Technik. Mit einem kritisch-exegetischen Anhang*, Meisenheim am Glan.
Schwarzbaum, H. (1968), *Studies in Jewish and World Folklore*, Berlin.
Schwarzmaier, A./Scholl, A./Maischberger, M. (eds.) (2012), *Staatliche Museen zu Berlin: Die Antikensammlung. Altes Museum, Neues Museum, Pergamonmuseum*, Darmstadt.
Searby, D. M. (1998), *Aristotle in the Greek Gnomological Tradition*, Uppsala.
Searby, D. M. (2007), *The* Corpus Parisinum: *A Critical Edition of the Greek Text with Commentary and English Translation. (A Medieval Anthology of Greek Texts from the Pre-Socratics to the Church Fathers, 600 B.C. – 700 A.D.)*, vol. I–II, Lewiston/Queenston/Lampeter.
Steidle, W. (1975), 'Probleme des Bühnenspiels in der Neuen Komödie', *Grazer Beiträge* 3, 341–86.
Sternbach, L. (1963), *Gnomologium Vaticanum e codice Vaticano Graeco 743*, Berlin.
Stockert, W. (1983), *T. Maccius Plautus: Aulularia*, Stuttgart.
Stockert, W. (2000), 'Sull'originalità di Plauto: Metafore e similitudini nell'*Aulularia*', in: R. Raffaelli/A. Tontini (eds.), *Lecturae Plautinae Sarsinates*, vol. III: *Aulularia*, Urbino, 15–30.
Tobler, R. (1906), 'Der Schuster und der Reiche', *Archiv für das Studium der neueren Sprachen und Literaturen* 117, 328–44.
Toldo, P. (1903), 'Aus alten Novellen und Legenden', *Zeitschrift des Vereins für Volkskunde* 13, 412–26.
Trencsényi-Waldapfel, I. (1965), 'Der griechische und der römische Dyskolos', in: F. Zucker (ed.), *Menanders Dyskolos als Zeugnis seiner Epoche*, Berlin, 185–205.
Trendall, A. D. (1967), *Phlyax Vases*, London.
Trendall, A. D./Webster, T. B. L. (1971), *Illustrations of Greek Drama*, London.
Trenkner, S. (1958), *The Greek Novella in the Classical Period*, Cambridge.
Uther, H.-J. (2004), *The Types of International Folktales: A Classification and Bibliography Based on the System of Antti Aarne and Stith Thompson*, vol. I–III, Helsinki.
van Dijk, G.-J. (1997), *Αἶνοι Λόγοι Μῦθοι: Fables in Archaic, Classical, and Hellenistic Greek Literature. With a Study of the Theory and Terminology of the Genre*, Leiden/New York/Köln.
Webster, T. B. L. (1948), 'South Italian Vases and Attic Drama', *Classical Quarterly* 42, 15–27.
Webster, T. B. L. (1956), *Greek Theatre Production*, London.
Webster, T. B. L. (1960), *Studies in Menander*, Manchester.
Wolf, J. W. (1845), *Deutsche Märchen und Sagen*, Leipzig.

Wright, T. (1842), *A Selection of Latin Stories from Manuscripts of the Thirteenth and Fourteenth Centuries: A Contribution to the History of Fiction during the Middle Ages*, London.

Zahn, R. (1931), 'Vom Maler Asteas und der griechischen Posse Unteritaliens', *Die Antike* 7, 70–95.

Zahn, R. (1932), 'Tafel 150,2: Krater des Asteas in Berlin. Phlyakenszene', in: A. Furtwängler/F. Hauser/K. Reichhold (eds.), *Griechische Vasenmalerei: Auswahl hervorragender Vasenbilder*, vol. III, München, 178–207.

Sophia Papaioannou
Plautus Undoing Himself – What is Funny and What is Plautine in *Stichus* and *Trinummus*?

Introduction

The *Stichus* and *Trinummus* are two of the most unusual, or as I prefer to call them, experimental comedies of Plautus.[1] These comedies are intriguing to study because in them Plautus reverses himself; he either omits or fails to develop his artistry as we know it from his other plays. He entertains his audience not by improvising or elaborating further on his well-established comic patterns, characters and plots, but by dramatising on stage their failure to develop. In producing 'un-Plautine' plays he instructs his audiences across time that success depends foremost on talent, thrives on surprise and welcomes innovation. Through the study of these plays emerges a more diverse, sophisticated and mature aspect of Plautus' comic genius: we are confronted with a dramatist who loved experimenting with new tropes and going against paradigm and tradition – even against the very tradition that he himself established. In this respect it would not be an overstatement to suggest that these Plautine plays (and probably others like them, now lost) may well be considered a precedent, even inspiration for Terence's drama. There are distinct similarities in structure, language, themes and characters between these unconventional Plautine plays, especially the *Trinummus*, and Terence's comedy. I find particularly intriguing and certainly worth exploring the idea of Terence developing further innovative initiatives of dramaturgy introduced already by Plautus. The present study, however, does not proceed thus far. I propose to discuss the controversial character of the *Trinummus* and the *Stichus* as expressed, first, in the deliberate transgression of standard Plautine comic conventions, and, second, through encompassing tropes that are familiar from Terence's dramaturgy.

---

[1] Plautus' text and translation quoted throughout follow De Melo 2011–3; Terence's text and translation are taken from Barsby 2001, with adaptations.

The Plays

The *Trinummus*: the *senex* Charmides has gone abroad on a business trip and has charged his friend, the *senex* Callicles, with supervision over the whereabouts of his prodigal son, Lesbonicus. Further, Callicles is made partaker of a family secret: Charmides has a treasure buried in his house, his daughter's dowry. When Lesbonicus, in desperate need of money, plans to sell the house, Callicles buys the house himself, moves in with his own family and decides to expedite the marriage of Charmides' daughter by hiring an impostor to pretend that he has been sent by Charmides to supply the dowry for the marriage – in this way Callicles will dispense the treasure in the house properly. This is exactly what happens, but the impostor arrives to perform his role at the exact same time as Charmides returns: the two meet and the result is an entertaining scene with the impostor enacting his role of the emissary and Charmides pretending that he is not himself. Still, the resolution to the play is hardly a complicated one, according to *palliata* standards, for the daughter already has a suitor in the young Lysiteles, Lesbonicus' close friend, who does not wish to receive a dowry. Contrary to expectations, the spendthrift Lesbonicus realises that such a marriage would be a disgrace to his family: he not only refuses to marry off his sister without a dowry, but also starts to feel remorse for his previous life. The humour centers on the fact that the marriage plot proper in reality is not complicated at all, because the young Lysiteles has his father's support in his desire to marry the sister of Lesbonicus even without a dowry. Complications arise as a result of the persistence of the impoverished Lesbonicus, who does not have a dowry to offer, to follow the rules of a conventional *palliata* (which in the *Trinummus* are not in effect) and refuse to offer his sister in marriage without a dowry. Next to the inventive treatment of the dowry theme, another prominent divergence of the *Trinummus* from the typical Plautine play is the absence of an actual *servus callidus*. The play has an aspiring wily slave, Stasimus, the slave of Lesbonicus, who nonetheless never meets the standards of the role.

The *Stichus*: two sisters, Panygeris and Pamphila, are married to two brothers who have been abroad for three years to improve their fortunes. The wives have not heard anything from their husbands all this time and are pressured by their father to divorce and remarry, but they steadfastly refuse. Before any complication develops as a result of this refusal, however, the two husbands return as wealthy men, and the remainder of the play – fully the two-thirds of it – is taken up by various celebrations, both at the masters' quarters and at their slaves' own. The persistent yet fruitless effort of a parasite, Gelasimus, to secure an invitation to a free dinner, adds a distinct flavour to the merriment reigning throughout.

Trinummus

The *Trinummus* is the only play of Plautus described repeatedly in the modern era of Plautine criticism as 'boring', by the great Wilamowitz and also Erich Segal, the critic whose *Roman Laughter* in 1968 revolutionised the study of *palliata* in the past half century.[2] What led Wilamowitz and Segal to this characterisation is: a) the fact that the *Trinummus* does not feature stereotypical *palliata* characters, or rather the stage-acting of the characters in this play fails to meet expectations; b) the play does not have a 'wily slave' (or a parallel character, such as a parasite); c) as a result of a) and b), the plot does not follow a typical New Comedy plot pattern: it does not involve any intrigue, its plotline is very thin, it is full of moralising talk and little musical variation (all *recitativa* are trochaic septenarii; and the total number of lines that are not in iambic senarii or trochaic septenarii, is less than one hundred in a 1189-line long play), so as to call to mind Terence's *Heautontimorumenos*, a play qualified as *stataria* (*Heaut.* 39) by the dramatist himself, which nonetheless is much more varied in speed and musicality compared to the *Trinummus*.

Another element that brings the *Trinummus* closer to Terence is the emphasis on morality. The pervasive references to the theme of *mos* throughout the play are uncommon for Plautus and as a result of this the *Trinummus* has been repeatedly called a dull play.[3] From the various moralising clusters of the play,

---

2 Wilamowitz-Moellendorf 1925, 165: (as translated and quoted in English in Lefèvre 1993, 178): '[T]he *Trinummus* is boring, even for a Plautine play, and it is only for its old-fogeyish prudery that the *Trinummus* is given preference ... Thus I read the *Trinummus*, and this play at first spoiled my pleasure in Plautine comedy ... '; also Jachmann 1931, 227; and more recently, Segal 1974, 252: 'For though Plautus wrote both good plays and bad, this is his only boring one'. Prior to the 20th century the *Trinummus* used to be a very popular school text, obviously because of the absence of the explicit sexual element from the language, and the noble-mindedness of the heroes; cf. Lefèvre 1993. This article, too, like all recent studies on the *Trinummus*, observes the custom noted in Hunter 1980, 216, and takes Wilamowitz's statement as the starting point of discussion; this custom has been upheld, and self-consciously so, also in Sharrock 2014, 167; detailed full review of critical assessment of the *Trinummus* prior to (and after) Wilamowitz, in Anderson 1979, 33. The most recent comprehensive study of the *Trinummus* is Riemer 1996, while an extensive discussion of the play primarily with respect to its Greek model is included in Lefèvre 1995, 61–168. Several of the ideas in my paper have been advanced most recently in Sharrock 2014, an essay that was still forthcoming and unknown to me when I originally presented this paper at the Thessaloniki Roman Drama Conference in May/June 2014. I was delighted to discover that my appreciation of the *Trinummus* as a profoundly metaliterary composition on conventional Plautine dramaturgy finds endorsement in Sharrock's analysis.
3 Slater 1987; Segal 1974.

Slater singles out the scene following the running entrance of the slave Stasimus, the character who is supposed to enact the part of the 'cunning slave' but repeatedly fails to do so. In this scene the slave after expressing frustration about the loss of a ring fervently denounces contemporary morals to the *senex* Charmides, in a dialogue where 'forms of *mos* occur no less than fourteen times in twenty-seven lines (1028–54)':[4]

> STAS. Vtinam <u>veteres</u> homin\<um *mor*\>es, <u>veteres</u> parsimoniae
> potius \<in\> maiore <u>honore</u> hic essent quam *mores* mali!
> CHARM. Di immortales, basilica hicquidem facinora inceptat loqui!   1030
> <u>vetera</u> quaerit, <u>vetera</u> amare hunc *more maiorum* scias.
> STAS. Nam nunc *mores* nihili faciunt quod licet nisi quod lubet:
> ambitio iam *more* sancta est, libera est a <u>legibus</u>;
> scuta iacere fugereque hostis *more* habent licentiam:
> petere <u>honorem</u> pro flagitio *more* fit. CHARM. *Morem* improbum!   1035
> STAS. Strenuiores praeterire *more* fit. CHARM. Nequam quidem!
> STAS. *Mores* leges perduxerunt iam in potestatem suam,
> magisque is sunt obnoxiosae quam … parentes liberis.
> eae miserae etiam ad parietem sunt fixae clavis ferreis,
> ubi malos *mores* affigi nimio fuerat aequius   1040
> CHARM. Lubet adire atque appellare hunc; verum ausculto perlubens
> et metuo, si compellabo, ne aliam rem occipiat loqui.
> STAS. Neque istis quicquam <u>lege sanctum est</u>: <u>leges</u> *mori* serviunt,
> *mores* autem rapere properant qua <u>sacrum</u> qua publicum.
> CHARM. Hercle istis malam rem magnam *moribus* dignum est dari.   1045
> (*Trin.* 1028–45)

STAS. I wish people's old customs and their old thriftiness were in greater honor here rather than bad customs.
CHARM. (aside) Immortal gods! He's beginning to talk about matters of state! He's looking for the old ways, you can see that he loves the old ways according to our forefathers' customs.
STAS. Yes, customs nowadays don't care for what's allowed, only for what's pleasurable: bribery is now sanctioned by custom and free from the laws; through custom people think they have the freedom to throw their shields away and flee from the enemy. Through custom, public office is sought as a reward for criminal behavior.
CHARM. (aside) An indecent custom!
STAS. It's become the 'custom' to pass over their betters.
CHARM. (aside) Indeed awful!

---

4 The quotations come from Slater 1987, 267–8 with n. 17; actually, all fourteen occurrences are crowded together in eighteen lines, 1028–45.

STAS. Custom has now brought the laws into their power, and the laws are more under their thumb than ... parents are under that of their children. Those wretched laws are even fastened to the walls with iron nails, where it would have been much fairer to fasten bad customs.
CHARM. (aside) I'd like to go up and address him; but I listen to him with great pleasure and I'm afraid that if I address him, he'll begin talking about something else.
STAS. Nothing is laid down as binding by law for them. The laws are slaves to custom, while customs hurry to carry off everything both sacred and profane.
CHARM. (aside) Those customs really ought to be given a big thrashing.

My present discussion proposes that Plautus consciously and deliberately, and in a serious tone, overstates morality in order to produce the exact opposite effect. He makes a point of overemphasising *mos*, because, for one thing, excessiveness in speech and overacting supposedly become tiresome in the end and elicit ridicule – they turn into a source for laughter. Further, this eulogy of *mos* and propriety is particularly entertaining once it is set against the broader context – which is not the *Trinummus* but Plautus' overall dramatic production. To the experienced audience of *palliatae*, who have attended many plays by Plautus and other playwrights of the same tradition, such a profuse praise of *mores* on Plautus' stage is naturally understood as ironic.[5] The humorous approach to morality is invited as early as the entrance of the *adulescens* Lysiteles at 223. Lysiteles defines love as the opposite of business (230: *amorine me an rei opsequi potius par sit*, 'Should I go in for love affairs or attend to business?') – or, in terms of Roman *mores*, affirms the definition of the *palliata* stage reality which centers on impulse and desire, against the norm of Roman civic orthodoxy which focuses on duty and denounces all individual pleasures, including erotic love (Amor), by calling them a disaster for a man's finances and attractive only to the insane:

numquam Amor quemquam	
nisi cupidum hominem	
postulat se in plagas conicere:	
eos cupit, eos consectatur;	238a
subdole [blanditur] ab re consulit,	
blandiloquentulus, harpago, mendax,	239a

---

5 Both the irony and the ridicule noted above as reactions to an exaggerated conduct are typical examples in support of the so-called incongruity theory of laughter. An application of the incongruity theory of laughter is explained, for instance, in Clark 1987. I disagree with Slater 1987, 267–8, who does not see the humor in overstating the un-comic, not only in this speech but throughout the play, but asserts instead that 'given the prominence of this theme of *mos* (and *fides*, with which it is interwoven) throughout the play, we can hardly take this speech as ironic or parodistic, odd though it may sound in the mouth of a slave. The audience has moreover the enthusiastic asides of the eavesdropping Charmides to guide it in its response – Plautus clearly expects the audience to approve of what is said.'

cuppes, avarus, elegans, despoliator,
latebricolarum hominum corruptor, 240a
[blandus] inops celatum indagator.
nam qui amat quod amat quom extemplo 241a
saviis sagittatis perculsust,
ilico res foras labitur, liquitur.

(*Trin.* 236–43)

Love never demands to ensnare anyone, except a passionate man; those people he desires, those people he follows. He cleverly advises them to their disadvantage, a flattering, rapacious, lying, gluttonous, greedy, luxury-loving thief, ruin of men living in the shadow, destitute and prying into secrets. Yes, as soon as a man who is in love with the object of his love is pierced by arrow-like kisses, his wealth slips away and melts away.

Lysiteles' anti-Amor speech, with which the young man enters the play, apart from marking his un-Plautine ethos (an *adulescens* on Plautus' stage is not supposed to resist and denounce the temptations of erotic love), echoes in reverse the credo of a typical Plautine *adulescens amans*, Phaedromus, the young lover of the *Curculio*, in his own entrance speech. Phaedromus' loyal slave Palinurus pokes fun at his master who has fallen madly in love, and tries to caution him. The following passages are indicative of the surrender of the *adulescens amans* to his beloved to the point of losing his sanity:

PALINURUS Quo ted hoc noctis dicam proficisci foras
cum istoc ornatu cumque hac pompa, Phaedrome?
PHAEDROMUS Quo Venus Cupidoque imperat, suadetque Amor:
si media nox est sive est prima vespera,
si status, condictus cum hoste intercedit dies, 5
tamen est eundum quo imperant ingratiis.
.....
PAL. edepol qui amat, si eget, misera affligitur aerumna. 142
....
PAL. Enim vero nequeo durare quin ego erum accusem meum: 175
nam bonum est pauxillum amare sane, insane non bonum est;
verum totum insanum amare, hoc est ... quod meus erus facit.

(*Curc.* 1–6, 142, 175–8)

PALIN. Where should I say you're going out to at this time of night, with that dress and with this accompaniment, Phaedromus?
PHAED. Where Venus and Cupid command me, and Love urges me to go. If it is midnight or early evening, if a court date firmly settled on with your adversary from outside comes in between, one still has to go where they command despite oneself.
....
PALIN. He who is in love, is struck by miserable sorrow, if he's without money.
....

PALIN. I really can't help complaining about my master: yes, it is good to be a little bit in love sanely, but being insanely in love is not good. But being completely insanely in love, that's ... what my master is.

Judging from content (a commentary on the destructive power of love over a young man's sanity and finances) the thematic proximity between the *Curculio* and the *Trinummus* may well seem only suggestive, for such speeches are expected from young lovers and are often delivered when the young men enter the play for the first time in order to establish their dramatic identity as *adulescentes amantes*. The entrance monody delivered by the young man in love in Plautus' *Mostellaria* at 84–156, for instance, in which he compares himself to a dilapidated house and reveals with marked clarity of judgment all the disasters that his amours have cost him, financially and morally, is a strikingly similar passage. Still, the intertextual discussion between the *Curculio* and the *Trinummus* is affirmed later in the *Trinummus*, in the part that records the explosive entrance, in the pattern of the *servus currens*, of the slave Stasimus at *Trin.* 1008–6 – a passage that evidently has been inspired by the *servus-currens*-like entrance of the parasite Curculio in *Curc.* 280–95.[6] The two passages in question are listed below:

CURC. Date viam mihi, noti [atque] ignoti, dum ego hic officium meum	280
facio: fugite omnes, abite et de via secedite,	
ne quem in cursu capite aut cubito aut pectore offendam aut genu.	
ita nunc subito, propere et celere obiectum est mihi negotium,	
<nusquam> quisquam est tam opulentus, qui mi obsistat in via,	
nec strategus nec tyrannus quisquam nec	285
nec demarchus nec comarchus nec cum tanta gloria,	
quin cadat, quin capite sistat in via de semita.	
tum isti *Graeci palliati*, capite operto qui ambulant,	
qui incedunt suffarcinati cum libris, cum sportulis,	
constant, conferunt sermones inter sese drapetae,	290
opstant, opsistunt, incedunt cum suis sententiis,	
quos semper videas bibentes esse in thermopolio,	
ubi quid surrupuere: operto capitulo calidum bibunt,	
tristes atque ebrioli incedunt: eos ego si offendero,	
ex unoquoque eorum crepitum exciam polentarium.	295
(*Curc.* 280–95)	

CURC. Make way for me, known and unknown, while I'm doing my duty here: flee, all of you, go away and get off my head, my elbow, my chest, or my knee. So suddenly, fast, and quickly has this business now been thrown my way, that there's no one anywhere so rich

---

6 The '*servus currens*' routine is identified in nine of Plautus' surviving plays; basic bibliography on the topic includes Law 1922, 31 n. 6; Duckworth 1936; and Csapo 1987, 1989 and 1993.

that he could afford to block my way, not a general, not a despot, not a market inspector, not a district magistrate, not a village superintendent, not anyone with such great fame: no he'll fall, drop from the sidewalk and stand on his head in the street. Then those Greeks in their cloaks, who wander stuffed with books and food baskets, who stop and palaver among each other, those runaway slaves, who stand in your way and block your path, who prance about with their clever sayings, whom you can always see drinking in the tavern when they've stolen something; with their heads covered they drink mulled wine and prance about with a grave expression and drunk. If I meet them, I'll drive the barley-fed farts out of every single one of them. Then those slaves of the city *bon vivants*, who play ball in the street, I'll put all the throwers and players under the ground. So let them stay at home and avoid a thrashing.

STASIMVS Stasime, fac te propere celerem, recipe te ad dominum domum,
ne subito metus exoriatur scapulis stultitia <tua>.
adde gradum, appropera. iam dudum factum est, cum abiisti domo.   1010
cave sis tibi, ne bubuli in te cottabi crebri crepent,
si aberis ab eri quaestione. ne destiteris currere.
ecce hominem te, Stasime, nihili! satin in thermopolio
condalium es oblitus, postquam thermopotasti gutturem?
recipe te et recurre petere <re> recenti.
CHARM.   Huic, quisquis est,   1015
Curculiost exercitor: is hunc hominem cursuram docet.

(*Trin.* 1008–16)

STAS. Stasimus, make yourself really speedy and return home to your master, so that no fear will suddenly arise for your shoulder blades through your stupidity. Quicken your pace and hurry! It's a long time since you left home. Do make sure that cowhide blows won't clatter on you constantly, if you're absent when your master looks for you. Don't stop running!
Look, Stasimus, you're a useless fellow! Did you really forget your ring in the wineshop after you'd warmed your throat with hot drinks? Return and run back to demand it while the matter is still fresh.
CHARM. (aside) Whoever this fellow is, Curculio is his trainer; he teaches him to run.

Both passages are in trochaic septenarii, a meter particularly suitable for the dancing routine of the entering *servus currens*, and both contain ample references to the running routine of their role: both characters are in a great hurry to return home and report to their masters. More importantly, both share the motif of the stolen ring. This proximity is not fortuitous given that the *Trinummus* and the *Curculio* are the only two plays in the Plautine corpus where the motif of the stolen signet ring, which, further, was stolen during a drinking session in similar circumstances (in a wineshop in the company of men of ill-repute; cf. *Trin.* 1012–4, *Curc.* 292–3), occurs, and is set in running-slave monologues.[7]

---

[7] Gratwick (1981, 335–6) calls this proximity remarkable and the outcome of deliberate effort to connect the two plays.

The many and in all evidence deliberate similarities the two plays share lead naturally to Plautus' explicit acknowledgment (through Charmides), in *Trinummus* 1015–6, that he used the *Curculio* as a model:[8] *Huic, quisquis est, Curculiost exercitor: is hunc hominem cursuram docet*, 'Whoever this fellow is, Curculio is his trainer; he teaches him to run'. The intertextual relationship between the two passages is even tighter, because the content of Stasimus' monologue that continues until line 1058, is the decline of *mores* due to the arrival of *luxuria*, the influx of too much wealth (traditionally attributed to the influence of Greece and the Roman expansion eastwards). This tirade aimed at contemporary corruption could have drawn inspiration from Curculio's denunciation of the *Graeci palliati*, whose physical description supposedly calls to the audience's minds actual Greeks in Rome at the time, and the sumptuary laws against *luxuria* implemented in the Urbs in the aftermath of the conquest of the Greek East (e. g. the *lex Metilia* of 217 BCE, *lex Oppia* of 213 BCE, *lex Orchia* of 181 BCE).[9] Considered in isolation, Stasimus' monologue strikes a serious tone, but in light of the *Curculio* precedent, where the vilification of the Greeks is part of the parasite's explosive entrance and means to cause laughter, it is recontextualised:[10] the serious message is undermined, and Stasimus' performance as the indignant moralist makes him sound ironic and outright humorous.[11]

---

8 *Curculiost* is an emendation proposed by Gratwick (1981, 340–1), and prior to him by Lambino; *gurguliost* (*B*), *gurgiliost* (*C*), *gurgula* (*D¹*), *gurgulast* (*D²*), are the forms transmitted in the manuscripts; Gratwick sensibly argues that *Curculiost* and *gurguliost* are variants, the former being the earlier and original form, for the letter 'g' was thought to have entered the Latin alphabet in the early third century BCE (cf. also *TLL* s.vv.). Gratwick's emendation has won general acceptance, and his argument for it is convincing; it has recently been endorsed by Fontaine's own theory about the etymology of 'curculio' from the Greek '*gorgos*', 'fast and furious man'; cf. Fontaine 2010, 64–6. De Melo ad loc. prints the script of manuscript B, and translates *gurgulio* as 'gullet', likely implying wordplay with *gutterem*, 'throat', two lines earlier, and suggesting, unconvincingly in my view, that Stasimus is drunk and that Charmides' words at line 1016 is a comment on his unstable step on account of drunkenness (De Melo 2011-3, vol. 5, 227 n. 42 'after drinking so much he cannot walk straight').
9 The argument that both '*servus currens*' scenes mean to attack Greek influence and *luxuria* has been raised in Slater 1987, 268–9; Slater calls the Curculio '*servus currens*' entrance, 'one of the most famous of Plautus' passages'. On the Roman sumptuary legislation see most recently Zanda 2011.
10 Sharrock (2014, 172) has summed this intertextual aspect of the particular play's structure as follows: contrary to the great plays of Plautus, such as the *Pseudolus*, that may be appreciated in isolation, the *Trinummus* 'needs the help of a knowledge of other plays, in order that its games may be appreciated'.
11 According to Slater (1987, 264–5), the intertextuality should have been easily recognisable by Plautus' loyal audience who likely retained detailed memory of plays that had been performed in the one or two years immediately prior. The fact that audiences could remember very well plays

Stasimus' conscious recollection of Curculio's act, which indirectly points to a very likely date for the play, one or two years after the production of *Curculio*, reflects Plautus' experimental approach to his own drama – evidenced in the production simultaneously of plays which transgress conventions of the genre and plays which indulge in overdeveloping *palliata* norms. This may explain on the one hand the crafting of the un-Plautine *Trinummus*, *Stichus* and *Truculentus*, and on the other the composition of the *Bacchides* and the overtly Plautine *Pseudolus*, both of which feature not just hyperactive *servi callidi*, repeatedly improvising and continuously self-conscious of their wily status, Chrysalus and Pseudolus, respectively, but several other serious antagonists who are eager to usurp from them the *callidus* part and along with it the control of the plot.[12] Even so, despite their obvious differences, Plautus' famous productions share important motifs with the less popular plays. For example, the plots in the *Pseudolus* and also in the *Curculio*, just like the plot in the *Trinummus*, develop around the performance of an impostor.[13]

Plautus' reversing himself self-consciously occurs throughout his dramatic output, to the extent that self-reversal may be defined as a systematic methodological principle of Plautus' dramaturgy, even a leading source for his ongoing popularity. The effectiveness of this strategy depended upon the audience's anticipation, even expectation of being surprised, and upon their ability to identify the routine that is reversed and assess it in comparison to possible earlier treatments of the same routine. Reversals of stereotypes are present even in the most typically Plautine *palliatae*, such as the *Miles Gloriosus*. In the central section of the *Miles Gloriosus*, the *senex* Periplectomenus becomes the vehicle through which Plautus reverses pivotal comic stereotypes repeatedly. First, in a detailed self-presentation (*Mil.* 596–812) the *senex* portrays himself as contrary to the typical *senex iratus*; as an alternative comic *senex* who sympathises with the *adulescens* and plots together with the wily slave. Contemporary readers have detected in Peripectomenus' self-portrayal an early expression of the *senex lepidus*, a *palliata* character that

---

they had attended in the recent past is ascertained by evidence in Aristophanes. Aristophanes often refers to his earlier plays, and when he does so he almost always refers to a play that he staged the previous year. This parallelism leads Slater to the conclusion that '*Curculio* was produced not more than a year before the *Trinummus*, perhaps at the festival just preceding it' (p. 265).
12 The *Stichus* and the *Pseudolus* are the two firmly dated Plautine plays, the former was first staged in the Plebeian games of 200 BCE, the latter in the Megalensia of 191. The *Truculentus* is also held to be one of Plautus' last plays (according to Cicero, *De Senect.* 50); the *Bacchides* seems to date itself to the mid-eighties by an internal reference to the Bacchanalian affair of 186 BCE. The *Trinummus* should have been performed a year or two after the *Curculio*, according to Slater 1987, 267, more likely in the Megalensia of 192 (Gratwick [1981] argues for a later date for the *Trinummus*, 188/87 BCE).
13 Sharrock 2014, 175.

will reach full development fifty years later in the Micio of Terence's *Adelphoe*.[14] Subsequently, the *senex* expresses his displeasure at the *adulescens* Pleusicles' bashfulness because, as the old man notes, it goes against convention which dictates that an *adulescens amans* exhibit no shame or moral hesitation when he has the chance to satisfy his erotic passion (*Mil.* 617–34).

A little later in the same episode, Periplectomenus advocates the bachelor's life and speaks against the chagrins of marriage, which primarily involve the depletion of one's fortune by a spendthrift and heartless wife. Periplectomenus' hypothetical 'typical' *matrona* is echoed in the young Lysiteles' description of the 'typical' courtesan (*meretrix*). The two relevant passages are listed in sequence below:

> PER. Nam bona uxor suave ductu est, si sit usquam gentium   685
> ubi ea possit inveniri; verum egone eam ducam domum,
> quae mihi numquam hoc dicat: 'eme, mi vir, lanam, und' tibi pallium
> malacum et calidum conficiatur tunicaeque hibernae bonae,
> ne algeas hac hieme?' (hoc numquam verbum ex uxore audias),
> verum prius quam galli cantent quae me e somno suscitet,   690
> dicat: 'da, mi vir, calendis meam qui matrem munerem,
> da qui faciam condimenta, da quod dem quinquatrubus
> praecantrici, coniectrici, hariolae atque haruspicae;
> flagitium est si nil mittetur quae supercilio spicit;
> tum plicatricem clementer non potest quin munerem;   695
> iam pridem, quia nihil apstulerit, suscenset ceriaria;
> tum opstetrix expostulavit mecum, parum missum sibi;
> quid? nutrici non missuru's quicquam quae vernas alit?'
> haec atque huius similia alia damna multa mulierum
> me uxore prohibent, mihi quae huius similis sermones sera[n]t.   700
> (*Mil.* 685–700)

PER. Yes, a good wife is sweet to marry, if there were any place on earth when one could be found; but should I marry one who'd never say to me: 'My dear husband, buy me wool from which a soft and warm cloak can be made for you and good winter tunics, so that you won't feel cold this winter'? This word you'd never hear from a wife; instead, before the cocks crow, she'd stir me from my sleep and say: 'My dear husband, give me something to give to my mother on the first of the month, give me something to make preserves, give me something to give to the sorceress on the festival of Minerva, to the dream interpreter, to the clairvoyant, and to the soothsayer; it's a disgrace if nothing is sent to the woman who uses eyebrows to prophesy; next, there is no way round giving a kind present to the woman who folds the clothes; the woman delivering our food has been angry for a while already for not getting any tips; then the midwife has complained to me that she's

---

14 E.g. Lefèvre 2013, 77–8; Konstan 1983, 50; Leach 1980, 199–200 (n. 29 lists earlier bibliography on the *senex lepidus*).

received too little. What? You're not going to give anything to the nurse feeding the slaves born in the house?' These losses caused by women and many others, similar to these, keep me away from a wife who'd torment me with talk of this sort.

> nam qui amat quod amat quom extemplo 241a
> saviis sagittatis perculsust,
> ilico res foras labitur, liquitur.
> 'da mihi hoc, mel meum, si me amas, si audes'.
> ibi ille cuculus: 'ocelle mi, fiat: 245
> et istuc et si amplius vis dari, dabitur'.
> ibi illa pendentem ferit: iam amplius orat;
> non satis id est mali, ni amplius <sit> etiam,
> quod ecbibit, quod comest, quod facit sumpti.
> nox datur: ducitur familia tota, 250
> vestiplica, unctor, auri custos,
> flabelliferae, sandaligerulae,
> cantrices, cistellatrices,
> nuntii, renuntii, ra-
> ptores panis et peni;
> fit ipse, dum illis comis est, inops amator.
>
> (*Trin.* 241a-54)

Yes, as soon as a man who is in love with the object of his love is pierced by arrowlike kisses, his wealth slips away and melts away. 'Give me this, my honey, if you love me and if you want to'. Then that cuckoo says: 'Yes, apple of my eye; you'll get that and anything else if you want to get it.' In that situation she flogs him while he hangs there: immediately she asks for that she drinks up, eats up, and spends money on. He is granted a night: the whole establishment is hired, the dress-folder, the masseur, the guardian of jewelry, the fan-bearers, the sandal-carriers, the female singers, the maids with treasure boxes, the ones who bring messages and the ones who bring messages back, the thieves of bread and sustenance; while the lover is being generous to them, he himself becomes destitute.

The closeness of the two passages brings a legal spouse and a courtesan side-by-side. Plautus challenges his audience's sympathies, and more importantly, the very notion of typical characterisation, but foremost he entertains them as he suggests that in the topsy-turvy world of the *palliata* Lysiteles' meretricious, passionate love (Amor) might not have been worse than a legal, proper marriage, after all, which in due time transforms shy and invisible young maidens into bossy and authoritarian matrons. The agent that primarily contributes to this transformation is the wife's dowry. A Plautine bossy *matrona* is always an *uxor dotata*. Periplectomenus passes over this important detail, probably because conventionally in a *palliata* the nagging *matrona* is presumed to be an *uxor dotata* as well, but this is not the case with another famous and wealthy Plautine bachelor, Megadorus of the *Aulularia*. That play, too, experiments with the convention of the nagging wealthy *matrona*, and the variation on the routine observed therein likewise recalls themes featured in the *Trinummus*. What makes even closer the thematic kinship between the *Aulularia* and the *Trinummus* is the unorthodox stance on marriage without a dowry.

Megadorus rejects the proposal of his sister to marry a wealthy middle-aged woman (*Aul*. 158–9), and later in a soliloquy defends his rejection by arguing that wealthy wives are stressful to live with because they follow their own minds too often as a result of their rights to make independent financial decisions about their dowries (498–502) – this usually means that they spend too much. To prove his point about the latter he quotes a long list of tradesmen who would hypothetically frequent his house (505–22). This list replicates closely the list of tradesmen Periplectomenus envisions to surround his own hypothetical wife at *Mil.* 685 noted above. Megadorus, however, unlike Periplectomenus, does not rule out marriage altogether – or so he professes. He claims that it is the *uxor-dotata* type of a bossy wife that he detests, and that he would gladly marry a wife without a dowry. This idea he first proposes to his sister at 167–9, and confesses that he finds such a marriage liberating. Later, he revisits this statement and elaborates on it, by arguing that marriages between rich men and women without dowries would strengthen social unity (481), curb the wives' independence and thus make them more obedient to their husbands (483), and less costly to them and the marriage (484).

Megadorus' arguments for a marriage without a dowry are radical simply because such marriages were beyond consideration for serious social reasons. A dowry maintained social status for the wife's family, and the cohesion of the community as a whole. A family who would not give a dowry would be disgraced.[15] Precisely this social rule is explained in detail in the *Trinummus* by Lesbonicus in justification of his decision to reject Lysiteles' proposal to marry his sister without a dowry, even though Lesbonicus is completely ruined financially. Lesbonicus explicitly remarks that if he agrees to such a proposal, people will think that he is betrothing his sister into concubinage (*Trin.* 688–94):

> nolo ego mihi te tam prospicere, qui meam egestatem leves,
> sed ut inops infamis ne sim, ne mi hanc famam differant,
> me germanam meam sororem in concubinatum tibi,   690
> si sine dote <dem>, dedisse magis quam in matrimonium.
> quis me improbior perhibeatur esse? haec famigeratio
> te honestet, me conlutulentet, si sine dote duxeris:
> tibi sit emolumentum honoris, mihi quod obiectent siet.

---

[15] The necessity of the dowry to maintain social cohesion becomes the epicenter around which develops David Konstan's analysis of the *Aulularia* in Konstan 1983, 33–46, esp. 41–3.

> I do not want you to look out so much for something with which to alleviate my poverty, as rather to make sure that I won't have a bad reputation in my poverty, so that people won't spread the rumor against me that I've given my own sister to you into concubinage rather than marriage, if I were to give her to you without dowry. Who would be considered to be more worthless than me? This rumor would bring honor to you and disgrace to me, if you were to marry without dowry. You would have an advantageous position of honor, I would have something they could cast in my teeth.

Lesbonicus' reaction may be assessed from a metaliterary perspective: it is a form of explanation on the part of Plautus (or even of Roman drama in general) on why a probably popular theme of the Greek New Comedy, such as marriages without a dowry (part of the happy ending in Menander's *Dyscolus*) has to be excluded from the Roman comic stage. As a matter of fact, the very utterance of this comment by a character in the *Trinummus*, one of Plautus most transgressive plays in terms of generic convention, may be read as an admission that there are certain boundaries which even the most experimental playwright may not be allowed to cross.

The deliberately unorthodox structure of the *Trinummus* has recently received a thoughtful study by Alison Sharrock who opines that the play in question 'is a cento of Plautine drama, as various Plautine comic devices appear in concentration, although to different, than the usual, effects, thus foreshadowing later Terentian evolution.'[16] The self-conscious transgression of comic convention draws Plautus markedly close to Terence. The literary kinship is made clearer by the fact that the *Trinummus* uses another device of Terentian dramaturgy, the surrendering of the control of the plot to a group of old men and the progressive marginalisation of the 'wily slave'.[17] With the exception of the *Eunuchus* and the highly experimental *Hecyra*, all the other Terentian plays feature *senes auctores*, who actually succeed in seeing their original plan eventually materialise even in revised form. The plan of Simo, the *senex* in the *Andria*, for instance, revolves around his desire to have his son married to the daughter of his neighbour – and this is exactly what happens in the end, even though the daughter his son ultimately marries is not the one originally intended but her long-considered-lost sister. Likewise, in the end of the *Phormio* the *senes* Demipho and Chremes are delighted to find out that Antipho, Demipho's son, without knowing it has married Chremes' illegitimate daughter, the very bride the *senes* intended for the youth all along.

---

16 Sharrock 2014, xx; also p. 171.
17 Sharrock 2009, 117; 2014, 172–3.

In Plautus the *senes auctores* are not amiss but despite their efforts they fail to gain control of the plot, because, according to Sharrock, 'within the Plautine comic economy, old men can't be allowed to form successful intrigues'.[18] For Sharrock, the *Trinummus* belongs among the Plautine plays which feature *senes auctores* who ultimately fail, but in my reading the situation in this play is slightly different. Following an opening scene between Luxuria and Inopia, the *senes* Megaronides and Callicles enter the stage and provide the exposition. Callicles is clearly in control of the plot and takes Megaronides, whom he considers a loyal friend, into his confidence, by revealing to him that the *senex* Charmides had entrusted a treasure buried in his house to Callicles when he left home. Charmides' profligate son, Lesbonicus, has since been forced to put the house up for sale, but Callicles has bought the house in order to save the treasure. Megaronides keeps Callicles' secret and helps him later when they decide to hire a sycophant to justify the production of dowry money (money that would actually come from Callicles himself, or more correctly, from the treasure entrusted to his care) for the marriage of Lesbonicus' sister to young Lysiteles. The *senex* Charmides joins the action two thirds into the play, and because he does not know of the plan of the other two *senes* – which actually has been plotted for Charmides' very own interest – at first he nearly wrecks it, by expelling the sycophant from the play, but before any major damage happens he meets the other two *senes* and is informed of their plan – which, actually, at this point has little reason to continue. A fourth *senex* appears in the *Trinummus*, Philto, the father of Lysiteles, and even though he does not participate in the intrigue, he is a sympathetic character, contrary to the expectations an experienced audience may have for a comic father who consents to the marriage of his son to a bride that brings no dowry. In sum, my reading of the *Trinummus* above actually shows that the *senes* are quite successful at carrying through their plan and meet their original objective,[19] to safeguard the third *senex*'s property. This happens because unlike most of the other Plautine comedies the *Trinummus* lacks a proper 'wily slave'. And this omission enables an alternative examination of the *Trinummus* in light of Terence's dramaturgy, so much so that it has been argued that the Plautine play in question is truly Terence's major source of inspiration.[20]

---

18 Sharrock 2014, 175.
19 Something that Sharrock herself, too, accepts (2014, 177): 'Although Stasimus thinks that he has acted like a suitable Plautine trickster (558, 560), Philto's enigmatic reply to Lesbonicus' question as to what it was all about, that Stasimus is just after his freedom, indicates that the old man has kept control of the situation, so Stasimus' attempts to be a Plautine clever slave have not really worked'.
20 Sharrock 2014, 182: 'Terence became the master of this kind of manipulation of the audience. Indeed, I suggest that *Trinummus* holds a particular place in Terence's intertextual world.

The *Trinummus* opens with a brief (22 lines) dialogue between Luxuria and her daughter Inopia. This conversational prologue seems to belong together with other Plautine expository openings that develop into monologues and are delivered by a minor divinity (the Lar Familiaris in *Aulularia* 1–39, Auxilium in the delayed prologue in *Cistellaria* 149–202, and Arcturus in *Rudens* 1–82). This minor divinity communicates (most of) the necessary background information for the better understanding of the plot. Here, however, the dialogue between Luxuria and Inopia does not offer any expository plot information, but seems, instead, to be preoccupied with the central theme of the play, *mores*, and how gravely they are threatened by … Luxuria herself. What is more, personified Luxuria in a metatheatrical address to the audience asserts that she is not going to deliver an expository speech, but concludes with the information that the two *senes* about to enter the stage will inform the audience about the plot.[21] The last part of Luxuria's speech, lines 16–22, will be duplicated nearly verbatim by Terence at the closing of the prologue of the *Adelphoe*. The two texts run as follows:

> sed de argumento ne exspectetis fabulae:
> senes qui huc venient, ei rem vobis aperient.
> huic Graece nomen est Thesauro fabulae:
> Philemo scripsit, Plautus vortit barbare,
> nomen Trinummo fecit, nunc hoc vos rogat   20
> ut liceat possidere hanc nomen fabulam.
> tantum est. valete, adeste cum silentio. –
>
> (*Trin.* 16–22)

But don't wait for me to tell you the plot of the play: the old men who'll come here will disclose the matter to you. This play is called Thesauros in Greek. Philemon wrote it and Plautus translated it into the barbarian tongue; he gave it the name Three-Dollar Day and now asks you that this play may keep this name. That's all. Farewell, attend quietly.

> Synapothnescontes Diphili comoediast.
> eam Commorientis Plautus fecit fabulam.
> in Graeca adulescens est qui lenoni eripit
> meretricem in prima fabula. eum Plautus locum
> reliquit integrum, eum hic locum sumpsit sibi   10

The argument is that this play had a significant influence on Terence's own poetic development, in that it displays features which are important for the Terentian corpus but exist in the extant Plautine corpus only, or predominantly, in *Trinummus*'.

21 The Luxuria-Inopia scene is discussed from a different perspective in Sharrock 2009, 30–2; and also 2014, 177–8. Earlier readings which also comment on the possible relationship of this scene to the *Aulularia*, and even propose an etymology of the play's title and a possible date for the *Trinummus* as a result, include Muecke 1985, 168 n. 5; Anderson 1993, esp. 36–7; Riemer 1996, 50.

> in Adelphos, verbum de verbo expressum extulit.
> eam nos acturi sumus novam: pernoscite
> futurumne factum existumetis an locum
> reprehensum, qui praeteritus neglegentiast.
> ....
> dehinc ne exspectetis argumentum fabulae:
> senes qui primi uenient, ei partem aperient,
> in agendo partem ostendent. facite aequanimitas
>
> (*Ad.* 6–14; 22–4)

> Synapothnēskontes is a comedy by Diphilus; on this Plautus based his comedy Commorientes [both titles mean: 'Partners in Death']. At the beginning of the Greek version there is a young man who abducts a courtesan from her pimp. Plautus left that scene out; and this author [Terence] has taken it over for his Adelphoe, and squeezed it out [expressum extulit] word for word. We now are presenting this as a brand new play: it is for you to decide whether you assess the work as a theft or as the reclaiming of a scene which had previously been carelessly passed over.
> ...
> After this do not expect an outline of the plot. The old men who will come on first will explain part of it and reveal the other part in the course of the action. See that you give the play a fair hearing ...

In Sharrock's analysis Terence's appropriation of Plautus' words at ll. 22–4 has been commented on with respect to the recurrence of the 'the *ne ex(s)petetis* ... motif, where some character playfully tells the audience that they won't hear what they expect to hear' (p. 189).[22] Much more important than this motif as such, but rather ignored, is the significance of Terence's placing the nearly verbatim repetition of the *Trinummus*[23] model a few lines after he has introduced his theory of model appropriation summarised in the phrase *verbum de verbo expressum extulit*, and confessed, immediately afterwards, his confidence that the audience

---

[22] This is a prominent Plautine motif to be identified later in Terence's text; another prominent common motif is the emphasis on moralising discussed in detail above, and Sharrock (pp. 189–92) compares similarly oriented moralising speeches in the openings of the *Trinummus* (23–7) and the *Heautontimorumenos* (53–60, 75–7); both plays finally include (Sharrock 2014, 192–3) a comic episode where the *callidus* character, who enacts a role in disguise, forgets the name of the person who allegedly has sent him, and tries to overcome his embarrassment on stage. This last motif, however, could come from a larger stock of readily available stereotype stand-up comic gigs, from which both Plautus and Terence have drawn independently.

[23] Deufert impressed by the closeness of the parallelism has argued (2002, 28) that the *Trinummus* passage must be an interpolation based on that from the *Adelphoe*; Sharrock (2014, 190) senses correctly that the verbatim reproduction of Plautus' *Trinummus* discloses an aspect of the complex relationship between Plautus and Terence, but she does not elaborate beyond the general observation that Terence 'is picking up an unusual aspect of Plautus here'.

will be able to appreciate his work properly. The phrase *verbum de verbo expressum extulit* has been much and long discussed. Nowadays critics agree that the poem does not mean that Terence has translated if not literally at least very closely a Greek text[24] but that he has fitted a new meaning in,[25] or squeezed a new meaning out of, an old context, or imprinted a new creation or text onto the old, Greek one, which, after the imprinting has taken place, has lost its original appearance.[26]

The particular passage and the enveloping context have overwhelmingly been used to provide arguments about the complex issue of Terence's relationship with his Greek models. The reference to Plautus in the same passage has received less careful attention; it has been used only to the extent it helps define *contaminatio*: Terence knew Plautus' former treatment of the *Synapothnēskontes* well enough to know also that Plautus had left out a whole scene from the original – a scene that Terence now feels entitled to use. It is striking, at least to me, that Terence, a few lines after he has stated his distancing both from Plautus and from translation word for word, quotes the *Trinummus*, a work by Plautus, nearly word for word. The coincidence is not just deliberate but provocative in a way: Terence addresses his erudite audience, the elite who likely have copies of Plautus' scripts in their possession, and foremost his literary rivals (who obviously existed even if the so-identified accuser Luscius probably was a literary construction invented by the poet himself[27]), who like him had complete control of the tradition and the available Greek models,[28] and tongue-in-cheek admits that he *has* taken sections from Plautus verbatim, probably more often than he has admitted openly. For, when at ll. 8–11 above, he claims that he has 'squeezed out' and reproduced 'word for word', a well-known scene from a Greek play that has already been translated in Latin by Plautus, yet denies that he know Plautus' translation of it, and a few lines below quotes a different play of Plautus verbatim, then he slyly confesses not only that he knows Plautus' *Commorientes* but even that he has quoted it

---

24 A view advanced by Traina who believed that *exprimere* is usually used with reference to literal translations, namely the faithful reproduction of the model; cf. Traina 1970, 58. This is still a commonly accepted interpretation of the phrase: see recently McGill 2012, 137.
25 Thus Goldberg 1986, 98.
26 The last two interpretations have been promoted recently in McElduff 2014, 93.
27 See the excellent discussion on Luscius as literary construction in the pattern of the Callimachean Telchines in Sharrock 2009, 78–83.
28 It is unlikely that Terence expected his illiterate audience to identify the word-for-word transference of the Plautine text more than twenty years after the *Trinummus* performance, unless the *Trinummus* had been staged anew, either repeatedly since its original production or in the general audience's very recent memory.

verbatim deliberately, and has brazenly claimed that this verbatim translation of the Plautine translation is an *expressio* 'word for word' of the Greek original![29]

The appropriation of the *Trinummus* passage by Terence is typical of the ingenuity with which Terence successfully emulated his great predecessor by recontextualising him. Under the influence of Terence's style it is easy to forget how un-Plautine is the placement at the opening of the play of a section similar to the passage in 16–22. On the basis of Plautus' other opening sections (normally lengthy extradiegetic monologues which offer ample background plot information and often even refer briefly to the ending) the brevity of the *Trinummus'* opening is striking. Plautus' audience who are accustomed to expect a detailed exposition of the plot are instructed to wait patiently for the dialogue between the two *senes* following next, only to see their expectations failing to materialise, for, even after the end of this dialogue, we do not have a clear picture of what exactly the plot of this play is, simply because the play does not observe a conventional love plot, and the featured love affair is only peripheral to the narrative.

Stichus

The *Stichus* likewise is an unusual play[30] which enmeshes the humorous with the inventive, and offers an even more advanced form of experimental comic plot-making by defying the norms of the *palliata* genre. Duckworth's 1952 assessment underscores the unusualness of this play: the *Stichus* 'almost defies classification; there is nothing quite like it in Roman comedy.'[31] In the six decades since, the *Stichus* has not won critics over.

Arnott's 1972 *BICS* article, which constitutes the only reading that argues for a special kind of artistry in this play, calls the *Stichus* a 'problem pupil' – a play that across the centuries has amassed only negative criticism. Arnott himself admits that 'the *Stichus* is not Plautus' greatest achievement – nobody will rank it with the *Pseudolus*, *Bacchides* or *Rudens*', but he hurries to point out that the various 'allegations of banal characterization and feeble intention' cast against this play in the past, 'are wholly unjustified, springing as they do from the blindness of critics who have failed to respond to the charms of a problem play.' In Arnott's understanding 'the *Stichus* has some remarkable qualities that deserve detailed examination' for 'Plautus deploys in it some unexpected techniques of

---

29 See detailed discussion in Papaioannou 2014, 37–40.
30 Sharrock 2009, 55, calls the *Stichus* an 'extraordinary' play.
31 Duckworth 1952, 146.

characterization and thematic linkage', so as to redraw the relationship between author and audience, Roman play and Greek model.[32]

Arnott's argument had been inspired by a study of the characters in the *Stichus*, which seem to contradict Plautine dramaturgy because they do not correspond to the *dramatis personae* of a typical Plautine *palliata*. The play has no scheming slave (*servus callidus*), though it features several servants who are funny and sharp. There is no *adulescens amans*, no *senex iratus*, no greedy and wicked pimp, no courtesan, kindhearted or evil, no bossy *matrona*.[33] Stichus, the slave character after whom the *palliata* is named, enters the action well into the second half of the play, and plays no important role in the development of the plot, for the play has no plot, or more accurately, as Harsh had remarked seventy years ago, Stichus 'has less plot than any other Roman comedy'.[34] Still, the unconventional plotline does not seem to have been held against Plautus in antiquity, or hindered future stagings of the play given that the *Stichus* was available, a century and a half later, to M. Terentius Varro, who evidently had enough evidence to include it among the twenty-one plays he considered as genuinely Plautine.

As argued earlier about the *Trinummus*, it is my suggestion that the *Stichus*, too, had proven a successful dramaturgical experiment for Plautus because it offered the audience an alternative play where the comic elements were to be found in yet another set of ways in which dramaturgy may develop *aliter*, by deliberately transgressing the norm. In the *Stichus*, Plautus' defiant dramaturgy excludes from his composition the typical *dramatis personae* of a *palliata*; as a result, the plot brought on stage dramatises an unconventional narrative – a narrative which, once again, strongly reminded later critics of Terence and his 'feeble script'.[35] As in the *Trinummus*, the de-structuring of the *palliata* plot in the

---

32 All quotations come from Arnott 1972, 54.
33 A typical *palliata* features an intrigue that engages the participation of several of the characters in the list of *palliata dramatis personae* put together by Terence in his *Eunuch* prologue ll. 35–40: *quod si personis isdem huic uti non licet:/qui magis licet currentem servom scribere,/bonas matronas facere, meretrices malas,/parasitum edacem, gloriosum militem,/puerum supponi, falli per servom senem,/amare odisse suspicari?* ('But in anycase, if he is not permitted to use the same characters again, how is it any more permissible to design a running slave, to create good wives and evil courtesans, a greedy parasite and a braggart soldier, to substitute a baby furtively, to have an old man deceived by his slave, to love, to hate, to have suspicions?').
34 Harsh 1944, 369.
35 Deliberately or unknowingly, the great 16th c. Classics scholar and commentator of Plautus Joachim Camerarius characterises (cf. Arnott 1972, 54) the *Stichus* a play whose plot is 'light' and 'futile' (*Argumentum huius fabulae est leve atque futile*), in language that evokes the de-

Stichus is balanced through the development of alternative plot mechanisms to sustain the *peripeteia* and so, the audience's much-desired attention. This alternative mechanism of narration here revolves around an artful treatment of the *Odyssey* theme: more specifically, in the *Stichus* narrative coherence and, along with it, a comic end, are established through a series of diverse evocations of the *Odyssey* as an epic of arduous adventures. Several of the play's heroes approach, often knowingly, their personal hardships with the moral attitude of an Odyssean character, and several encounters among them recall episodes of the *Odyssey*. The selection of the *Odyssey* theme as blueprint of the narrative, among other things, ascertains the attainment of the desired happy conclusion to the plot and attests to the popularity of the Odysseus myth at Rome.

In a way this popularity is firmly justified. This may be attributed to the wide appeal of Livius Andronicus' *Odusia*, one of the first pieces of Greek literature to be transferred into Latin, which was not a literary accomplishment more than it was a political and ideological one. It advertised the studied 'transference' from Greek into Latin of an emblematic Greek opus:[36] the employment of *vertere*, the technical Latin term for 'translation' as established by Plautus himself in the prologue of the *Asinaria*, appears in the opening line of *Odusia* 1.1, in the participle *versutus*, 'the turned one', to render the Greek *polytropos*, 'the one of many ways', of *Od*. 1.1, an adjective tied to Odysseus ever since.[37] It also showed the way on how to transpose to Rome and into the Latin language a new cultural/ideological theme – Odysseus/Ulysses and his adventures. Apart from the fact that Odysseus'/Ulysses' journeys at sea have been associated with the colonisation of Italy since the early days of the Italian tradition,[38] the transference of the *Odyssey* into Latin initiates the literary appropriation process as metatheme of Latin literature overall, epic and beyond – a metatheme for which the figure of Odysseus becomes emblematic.

The cultural/ideological significance of the Odysseus/Ulysses theme for the Romans and the formation of Latin literature established the popularity of Odys-

---

scription of Terence's style as recorded in Terence's prologues and allegedly coming from his accusers (*tenui oratione et scriputra levi*; etc).

36 To quote Fantuzzi and Hunter 2004, 467: "[t]ranslation' and its discontents has been a (perhaps *the*) central theme of the Roman engagement with Greek literature from the very beginning'.

37 See Andronicus' metaliterary reading of *Odusia* 1.1, as discussed in Hinds 1998, 58–62 and more recently in Kahane 2012, 39–45; also Suerbaum 1968, 1–12, the first discussion of Andronicus' translation as expression of original literary self-representation.

38 Full discussion of the topic in Malkin 1998 (with Antonaccio 2000); and 1999. Earlier important studies on Odysseus as coloniser of Italy include Gatti 1975; Senior 1978, Chapter 'Odysseus at Sea'. Since Malkin's works, see also Lo Schiavo 2003 (arguing among other things for the Sicilian origin of the *Odyssey*); and Braccesi 2010.

seus' legend in Rome beyond the circles of the erudite elite, but nothing contributed to the fame of Odysseus among the masses more than Greek Comedy. Overall, the *polytropos* Odysseus was a favourite hero of Greek drama, certainly tragedy but especially comedy (including the satyric drama). Tradition since the Epic Cycle emphasises improvisation and deception as the hero's principal traits, qualities greatly appreciated inside, and suited to, the constructed reality of metadramatic performances. In the classical and postclassical Greek tradition, he was the title-character of two tragedies by Sophocles, while an '*Odysseus*' is reported among the fragments of each of the tragedians Sophocles II (*TrGF* 62), Apollodorus (*TrGF* 64) and Chaeremon (*TrGF* 71). Even more popular with the comedians, especially the authors of the mythological comic travesties of the fourth century, the tall-tale-teller and crafty Odysseus is the title-character of comedies by Dinolochus, Cratinus, Theopompus, Eubulus, Anaxandrides and Alexis (two plays), among others – without counting those plays, such as Euripides' *Cyclops* most notably, which feature Odysseus as the leading character but are not titled after him.[39] Still, the earliest comic treatments of Odysseus were in the Sicilian mime of the fifth century, which bespeaks a cultural subtext of the broad geographical expansion of Odysseus' adventures around the Mediterranean in the two centuries that separate the composition of the Homeric poems and the rise of the Athenian comic drama. Epicharmus produced two plays titled Ὀδυσσεύς, and at least four more dramatising some episode from Odysseus' adventures.[40] As a rule, in the hands of the comedians the hero's character is thoroughly humanised, even devalued, for he is portrayed as a glutton while his heroism becomes a display of wit and deception.[41]

---

39 The information is taken from Millis 2001, 153.
40 For Phillips 1959, 58, it was Epicharmus who set the tradition of the comic Odysseus; Cratinus' *Odyssēs* (Ὀδυσσῆς), dated to c. 430, is probably the earliest Athenian comic treatment of the hero (according to the ancient scholiast Platonius, in Koster 1.29–31 (with commentary in Nesselrath 1990, 236–9 and Bertan 1984, 171–8), who compares it distinctly to a Middle Comedy); both Epicharmus and Cratinus exercised strong influence on the development of mythological comedy in the next century, where Odysseus has been a strong favorite (see next note); on Epicharmus' Ὀδυσσεὺς αὐτόμολος, see Willi 2012, 56–75, also surveying earlier bibliography on this play; also, Casolari 2003, 47–55; and Kerkhof 2001, 121–8, on Epicharmus' plays inspired by some part of the *Odyssey* myth. On Cratinus' *Odyssēs*, see Bakola 2010, 236–46. Precisely because the *Odyssēs* exhibit so many features of the *Mesē*, Bakola sets out to show that several of these innovative qualities already exist in plays of Old Comedy. The pioneering study on the *Odyssēs* is Tanner 1915, while the brief discussion in Konstantakos (2014a, 164–5) offers the most recent treatment of the same play.
41 The study of Odysseus' popularity in postclassical Greek comedy has received considerable attention in recent decades; in addition to Bakola (see previous note), notable recent studies include Jouanno 2012 (a diachronic and cross-cultural treatment of the comic Odysseus from Epicharmus to Plautus); Casolari 2003, which devotes a special chapter to the development of

This wily Odysseus who is constantly thinking of food, finds himself at home in the *palliata*, where he is projected onto the mastermind of the plot, the *servus callidus* or the scheming parasite. This is famously acknowledged in the monody of Chrysalus, the wily slave of the *Bacchides*, and one of the most celebrated representatives of the Plautine *architectus doli*, at *Bacch.* 925–78 (and especially at 941–52 where the slave refers in detail to the stratagem of the Trojan horse).[42] Like the Homeric hero, Chrysalus, when the audience first encounters him, has just completed a long journey at sea and is proud for his crafty mind. He forges a letter which he likens to the Trojan horse (341), Odysseus' celebrated stratagem of intelligence,[43] and himself to Odysseus (340: *ego sum Ulixes, quoius consilio haec gerunt*, 'I am Ulysses, according to whose plan they're doing this.'). And a few lines later, at 346, he explicitly compares himself at once to Odysseus and Agamemnon. In the same monologue, Chrysalus elaborates on his Trojan-Horse-like enterprise as he attributes the parts of heroes from the Trojan legend to the other characters in the *Bacchides*, involved in his own plot: thus the *senex* Nicobulus is the city of Troy about to be conquered (945); and the *adulescens* Mnesilochus is assigned the part of Paris-Alexander (947). From this passage but also from the rest of Chrysalus' monody and the details of the Trojan story he mentions, we realise that Plautus and obviously his audience, too, knew the Trojan legend, could identify the integration of mythological metaphors in Plautus' plays, and laugh with the incongruity of the ever-shifting identifications of characters in the *Bacchides* with characters from the Trojan cycle.

In two more comedies there are distinct references to Odysseus as a parallel to the wily slave. On both these occasions the figure of Odysseus embodies what can be termed as 'comic heroism', i. e. the ability of the clever slave to devise and successfully execute deceptive plots.[44] At *Men.* 902, Menaechmus of Epidamnus

---

the comic Odysseus (pp. 197–226), and another one (pp. 61–78) to Cratinus' *Odyssēs*; earlier studies of note on the career of the comic Odysseus include Stanford 1968; Phillips 1959; and Schmidt 1888; especially on the contribution of satyric drama to the de-epicisation of Odysseus and his world, see Mastromarco 1998. The various treatments of Odysseus in the *Mesē* have been discussed individually in the context of the different comic dramatists: the fragments of Anaxandrides' comedy *Odysseus* have been treated in Millis 2001, 153–80; on the two Odyssean comedies of Alexis (Ὀδυσσεὺς ἀπονιζόμενος and Ὀδυσσεὺς ὑφαίνων), see Arnott 1996, 463–74; on Eubulus' Ναυσικάα, see Hunter 1985, 159, discussing briefly Odysseus as comic character; Pellegrino (2000, 127–32 and 2013, 61–70) discusses the *Sirens* by Nicophon. Very brief overview on the Odyssean comedies of the *Mesē* in Konstantakos 2014b, 93–5.
42 Detailed discussion of the simile in Jocelyn 1969.
43 Fraenkel 2007, 45–71 argued that grandiose mythological comparisons such as these are marks of Plautine originality.
44 For the term and its definition see Sharrock 1996, 170–1.

angrily calls Peniculus 'my Ulysses' because he believes that he has been betrayed by his parasite: the latter has informed Menaechmus' wife about her husband's plans to entertain himself with an extramarital adventure. In Menaechmus' mind Odysseus is the model of deception and betrayal. The same appellation occurs in *Pseudolus* 1063: Simo refers to the machinating Simia, the slave who on Simo's advice has supplanted Pseudolus in the plot to deceive the pimp Ballio and take from him the *meretrix* Phoenicium, as '*meus Ulixes*'. Later in the same play Simo must admit that Pseudolus has outdone Odysseus and the trick of the Trojan Horse (*Ps.* 1243–4: *nimis illic mortalis doctus, nimis vorsutus, nimis malus;/superavit dolum Troianum atque Ulixem Pseudolus,* 'He is a very smart, very clever, very wicked fellow; Pseudolus has surpassed the Trojan trick and Ulysses'). The attribute *vorsutus* for Pseudolus likens him directly to Odysseus, for it points to Livius Andronicus' *Odusia* 1.1 and alternative spelling *versutus*. Plautus' Odysseus is as Greek (or Roman) as the hero of Livius' *Odusia*.

As in the *Bacchides*, the employment of the Odysseus-analogy in the *Pseudolus* is accompanied by additional details from the mythology of the great hero. In this way, the Homeric material inscribed into the subtext of the Plautine play becomes more complex and presupposes more than superficial familiarity with the name and the identity of the cunning Odysseus. The likening by Simo of Pseudolus to Odysseus is given in relation to the stealing of the Palladium, the statue of Pallas Athene, from the citadel of Troy. The full text runs as follows: *Viso quid rerum meus Ulixes egerit,/iamne habeat signum ex arce Ballionia* (*Ps.* 1063–4: 'I'm checking what my Ulysses has been up to, whether he already has the statue from the Ballionian citadel'). Simo is unaware that Simia, under Pseudolus' direction, has just fled from 'Ballio's citadel' (a concept anticipated already in 384, where Ballio's household is called a 'city', *oppidum*) after taking Phoenicium with him.[45]

The popularity of Odysseus' legend has inspired the complex treatment of the *Odyssey* theme in the *Stichus* as well. But the lack of obvious humour in this play, normally generated in a *palliata* from the successful implementation of

---

[45] The *Bacchides*' Chrysalus similarly refers to his machinations against his master in terms of stealing of the Palladium (*Bacch.* 958: *ibi signum ex arce iam apstuli*, 'then I stole the statue from the citadel'). Two other plays in Plautus' surviving corpus record distinct references to Odysseus' adventures: the shipwrecks that dominate the plot of the *Rudens* are linked to the adventures of Odysseus at sea; the Odyssean setting is established already by Arcturus in his introduction, and is revisited by the slave Palaestra who has been washed up on a shore that reminds her (at *Rud.* 211–4) of one of those places where uncivilised monsters ignorant of cultivation, just like the Cyclops of the *Odyssey*, inhabit (Sharrock 2009, 212, 216); finally, in *Amphitruo* 331–2 Sosia tries to avoid falling into Mercury's traps by using a trick similar to the 'Nobody' ruse of Odysseus (Sharrock 2009, 113).

plotting by the *callidus servus*, has led to an inventive treatment of Odysseus' story. This treatment emphasises not the hero's cunning but his quest to return home. The long-awaited homecoming of the absent head of the household is compared to the nostos of Odysseus: already in the opening words of the play the audience is confronted with two sisters who try to console each other because they have been deserted by their husbands, and explicitly parallel their situation to that of Penelope's:

(PAN.) Credo ego miseram fuisse Penelopam,	1ᵃ
soror, suo ex animo,	
quae tam diu vidua	2ᵃ
viro suo caruit;	
nam nos eius animum	3ᵃ
de nostris factis noscimus, quarum viri hinc apsunt,	
quorumque nos negotiis apsentem, ita ut aequom est,	5
sollicitae noctes et dies, soror, sumus semper.	
	St. 1–6

I believe that Penelope was wretched in her heart, my sister, as she was desolate through her husband's absence for so long; we can understand her state of mind from our experience, since our husbands are away from here and we are always, day and night, worried about their business in their absence, as is right, my sister.

The two husbands have left their households together (though not to join some military expedition but to seek a better fortune). It has been three years since their departure and no news has been sent back home regarding their whereabouts (*St.* 30–3). Yet, neither of the two sisters or their respective husbands, whose separation and getting back together is the theme of the first half of the *palliata*, play any active role in the development of the plot – as a matter of fact, precisely because no intrigue is provided for the play, there is no plot to develop. The play, however, continues to elaborate on the *Odyssey*-like homecoming theme. Following the explicit opening, the audience learns that the marriages of the two sisters are threatened by their father, Antipho, who wishes to dissolve their unions to their absent husbands and remarry them to other suitors financially better off. Indeed, in the second scene of Act I, the father arrives on stage and after some preliminaries he urges his daughters to divorce their husbands and marry anew (*St.* 128ff.), only to be met with a barrage of arguments by the two sisters, in support of a wife's duty to stay loyal to her husband as long as he is alive, and wait patiently for his return. The fervour with which Antipho's daughters stand by their absentee husbands in all evidence convinces the *senex* to withdraw his original proposal.

This twist of the storyline in the *Stichus* is unexpected: when the audience first encounters Antipho as he enters the stage (at *St.* 60–5), he is a typical *senex iratus* with an explosive temper, who leaves the impression that he proposes to assert his authority over his daughters.

> ANT. vos meministis quotcalendis petere demensum cibum: 60
> qui minus meministis quod opus sit facto facere in aedibus?
> iam quidem in suo quicque loco nisi erit mihi situm supellectilis,
> quom ego revortar, vos monumentis commonefaciam bubulis.
> non homines habitare mecum mi hic videntur, sed sues.
> facite sultis nitidae ut aedes meae sint, quom redeam domum. 65

> You fellows remember to demand your rations of food on the first of every month; why don't you remember to do in the house what needs to be done? Now unless every piece of household equipment is put in its proper place when I return, I'll remind you with reminders of cowhide. Not humans, but pigs seem to live here with me. Do make sure that my house is spick and span when I return home.

And yet, at the end of his visit Antipho promptly yields to his daughters' wish not to remarry; the readiness with which he does so is startling. His failure to uphold his emblematic routine of the *senex iratus* serves the promotion of the *Odyssey* theme, which demands from the two women unquestioned loyalty to their spouses even if this leads them to defy family and societal expectations and custom law. This proud declaration of genuine faith in their marriages dominates the opening section of the play that concludes at line 149 with the departure of the father. The faith of the two sisters soon will be rewarded because 130-odd lines later, at 274, Pinacium, the slave of Panegyris, in an impressive imitation of a *servus currens*, enters the play and triumphantly announces the return of the two (now wealthy) husbands.[46] Less than a hundred lines after this announcement the two pairs of spouses are reunited and immediately plan to celebrate. This concludes the first half of the play and rounds up the first expression of the homecoming theme.

The remainder of the play has little to do with the first half. It is the '*Odyssey*' theme, in an alternative expression, that effectively links the two parts. Odysseus'

---

46 Pinacium's identification as a fisherman may draw inspiration from the comic treatment of the '*Odyssey*' theme: fishermen are at home in the marine world of the *Odyssey*; one of the extant fragments surviving from Anaxandrides' *Odysseus*, fr. 34 K.-A., comes from a speech by somebody who praises the art of the fisherman, who displays skills in eloquence and cooking alike, and evokes distinctly the *mageiros alazon* of Middle Comedy; detailed discussion of the fragment in Millis 2001, 154–67. Notice also that Pinacium's name is etymologically connected to food, for it comes from the Greek term πινάκιον, 'the small plate'.

nostos now underscores the parasite Gelasimus' travails to secure an invitation to dinner and inclusion in the festivities of comedy.[47] The parasite's laboring against Hunger for a full ten years[48] echoes the duration of Odysseus' labours at sea; unlike Homer's hero, however, Gelasimus sees no end in sight to his own suffering:

GELASIMVS Famem ego fuisse suspicor matrem mihi,	155
nam postquam natus sum, satur numquam fui.	
neque quisquam melius referet matri gratiam	
[quam ego meae matri refero ... invitissimus.]	157a
nec rettulit, quam ego refero meae matri Fami.	
nam illaec me in alvo menses gestavit decem,	
at ego illam in alvo gesto plus annos decem.	160
atque illa puerum me gestavit parvolum,	
quo minus laboris cepisse illam existumo:	
ego non pauxillulam in utero gesto famem,	
verum hercle multo maxumam et gravissumam;	
uteri dolores mihi [ob]oriuntur cottidie,	165
sed matrem parere nequeo nec quid agam scio.	
<atque> auditavi saepe hoc volgo dicier	
solere elephantum gravidam perpetuos decem	
esse annos; eius ex semine haec certo est Fames,	
nam iam complures annos utero haeret meo.	170
	(*St.* 155–70)

I suspect that Hunger was my mother: from the time that I was born I've never been full. And no one will repay his mother better [than I am repaying my mother ... completely against my will] or has repaid her better than I repay my mother, Hunger: she carried me in her belly for ten months, whereas I have been carrying her in my belly for over ten years. And she carried me as a tiny baby, which is why I think she had less trouble; I am not carrying a tiny Hunger in my belly, but the greatest and heaviest by far. Every day I get pangs in my stomach, but I can't give birth to my mother and I don't know what to do. And I've often heard the common saying that an elephant is normally pregnant for an entire ten years; that's the breed this Hunger is certainly from: it's been attached to my belly for several years already.

---

47 The most thorough reading of the role of Gelasimus in the play, Owens (2000) fails to see the parody of the '*Odyssey*' theme and, rather, approaches the parasite seriously, as a commentator on the situation of the Roman poor, the dependent Roman *clientes*; Damon (1997, 74) also reads the exchange between Gelasimus and the two brothers in terms of a suspended *patronus/cliens* relationship.
48 The selection of the number 'ten' for the years of suffering Hunger's pangs seems to have been devised in correspondence to the ten months of a woman's pregnancy, but in light of the trail of systematic parallels to the *Odyssey* narrative throughout the *Stichus*, the length of Gelasimus' suffering is drawn next to the ten-year-long homecoming travails of Odysseus.

As the play unravels it becomes increasingly evident that Gelasimus' quest for 'home', defined as 'an invitation to dinner', or realisation on stage of his typical comic role of the parasite, may be understood as the intrigue, so to speak, of the play; for, the *Stichus* may lack a proper intrigue but abounds in celebratory festivities and dinners. And Gelasimus despite his repeated effort to become a parasite is not invited to any of them – he is turned away both by the *senex* Antipho and by his two sons-in-law, all three of whom are planning to host dinner parties in their homes and invite the rest. In each of these attempts, the parasite tries in successive one-to-one encounters, like a witty *alter* Odysseus, to manipulate the words of his interlocutors and make them invite him to dinner, but on every occasion he is met with an interlocutor who has had himself played previously the part of Odysseus. Antipho in his unsuccessful attempt to convince his daughters to denounce their husbands calls to mind the disguised Odysseus in his encounter with Penelope in *Odyssey* 23, in the course of which he tests her fidelity for one last time shortly before he reveals his identity. The two husbands, Epignomus and Pamphilippus, in their quest for wealth, their long absence during which they failed to deliver any news to their wives left behind, and finally in their triumphant return, are twin impersonations of Odysseus.

The other major theme attesting to the *Stichus*' originality – and pointing forward to Terence's dramaturgy – comprises the play's dramatic self-consciousness, which is articulated in two different ways a) by expressing repeatedly the intention to dramatise traditional comic routines; and b) by replacing the intrigue with very elaborate dramatisations of traditional comic routines that contribute practically nothing to the development of the narrative. In the first category belong more prominently, firstly, the brief comedy skit Antipho and Epignomus enact over Antipho's desire to enjoy the services of the flute-girls Epignomus has brought home with the rest of his newly-acquired fortune; and, secondly, Gelasimus' statements that he has either consulted or plans to consult his books (*libros*) in order to find (from the tradition of the *palliata* – from earlier well-received performances of famous parasites) a way to perform his assigned role successfully (400: *ibo intro ad libros et discam de dictis melioribus*, 'I shall go home to my books and master by studying the best expressions appropriate'; 454: *libros inspexi; tam confido quam potis me meum optenturum regem ridiculis meis*, 'I have consulted my books; I am as confident as one could be that I will hold my king with my jokes'). In the second category belongs obviously the detailed dramatisation of the slaves' celebratory dinner. This celebration, usually reserved for the last lines of a *palliata*, here covers the entire fifth Act (641–772). In obvious correspondence to the serial dinner celebrations organised by the masters in Acts III and IV, Plautus transforms the typical closural device of a *palliata* into the very plot of the drama, as enacted first upstairs, then downstairs.

The abandonment of the traditional *palliata* plot in the play takes place already in Act I. From the anxious dialogue between the two sisters and Antipho's enraged entrance the audience gets the impression that they are confronted with a typical *senex iratus* determined to dissolve the marriages of his daughters. Given the two sisters' determination to remain loyal to their marriages Plautus has us believe that the rest of the play will develop along the lines of a conflict between the stubborn father and his daughters, the former's determination to exercise at all cost the authority and rights of a *pater familias*, and the women's recourse to the services and cunning of a wily slave – till the arrival of their husbands, which will procure the expected happy end. Nonetheless, the father quite unexpectedly yields to the desires of his daughters – he leaves their home at the end of Act I stating that he has no intention in the future to force his daughters to divorce and remarry. Thus the development of a traditional *palliata* stops abruptly along with the conclusion of Act I. The audience is entertained by the surprising realisation that the plot about to begin is not going to be launched at all.

Similarly incongruous with traditional dramaturgy is the development of the plot in Terence's *Andria*. The *adulescens* of this play, Pamphilus, has promised eternal fidelity to his beloved Glycerium. In order to convince his father that he can marry Glycerium legally he has invented a *palliata*-like story,[49] that Glycerium is the daughter of an Athenian citizen, the child of an extramarital affair (*An.* 215ff.) – which is exactly what Glycerium turns out to be in the end! And yet, already in Act I the young man has agreed to marry someone else, the bride his father has chosen for him (*An.* 99–102), though against Pamphilus' own desire (*An.* 151–3; 254ff.). As the play unravels Pamphilus continues to remain engaged to his original bride: he is too eager to follow his slave Davus' bad advice (recorded in detail at 383ff.) to keep on pretending that he desires to continue with his original engagement. As the play progresses, however, it becomes known that Glycerium is the half-sister of his bride-to-be, the long lost daughter of her father, Chremes. And so, Pamphilus does marry Chremes' daughter in the end, both satisfying his father's plan (to marry the daughter of Chremes) and fulfilling his own promise (to stay loyal to his engagement to the daughter of Chremes).

The incongruity in the structure of the *Andria* relies on the recycling of the same core theme of the plot – of marrying Chremes' daughter. A comparable recycling of the same plot theme in the context of the same play is observed in the *Stichus*, this time, though, in full awareness of the agent engaged in the recycling (in the *Andria* both Pamphilus and his father ignore the existence of two different daughters of Chremes). The pretext Antipho employs in Act I as an introduction to

---

49 Davus ironically describes it as '*fabulae*' (*An.* 224).

the divorce argument, namely that he has been thinking of getting married himself, becomes the main topic of discussion later in the play, and the main part of Antipho's acting in the rest of the play: in his encounter with Epignomus he sets up a little hypothetical drama about an old man and a lute-girl. Epignomus joins the meta-drama, and the audience enjoys a uniquely extensive skit of two characters consciously acting a two-person mime in-performance, with Antipho gradually unravelling a hypothetical script for himself, that casts him as enjoying the company of a flute-girl – a script which Epignomus tries to 'revise' (*St.* 537–69). The dramaturgy at work in this hypothetical script is underscored by the inventive way Antipho and Epignomus build their hypothetical interaction through quotations – which actually comprise real verses in a script that exists only provisionally! Markedly, Antipho introduces this script at 538ff. with the literary term *apologus*. The literary meaning of the term has been noted already in a 1919 article by Knapp, who translated it as 'allegory' or 'parable', an interpretation he founded on the similar understanding of the term by Aulus Gellius 2.19.1, where it characterises an Aesopic *fabula*.[50] In the context of Plautus' *fabula*, the particular term is aptly selected for the impromptu *fabula* which Plautus via Antipho embeds in his *fabula* proper. By projecting himself onto Antipho, Plautus comments on the deliberately loose and plot-less script of the *Stichus*, which may be read as a statement of the improvisatory foundation of Plautine drama overall. The dramaturgical aspirations of Antipho are acknowledged by Pamphilippus, who affirms the literary meaning of Antipho's *apologus* by describing the *senex* at 570 as *graphicum*, 'a painter' or more broadly, 'an artistic designer': *Graphicum mortalem Antiphonem! Ut apologum fecit quam fabre!*, 'What a remarkable fellow Antipho is! How skilfully he made up his story!'

This impromptu mime is framed by two less emphatic but clearly meta-dramatic dialogues. In these dialogues Gelasimus encounters first Epignomus (III.2 454–504) and then Pamphilippus (IV.2 579–640). The two dialogues mirror each other: on each occasion Gelasimus tries to extract an invitation to dinner and tries to control the speech of his interlocutor, to dictate, that is, his replies and so extract slyly an invitation to dinner. Regrettably for the parasite, both brothers are skilled speech manipulators themselves – as they have just proved, Epignomus in his witty exchange with Antipho, Pamphilippus in his succinct assessment of this exchange – and Gelasimus after failing a second time quits the play.

A final element affirming the controversial, self-conscious dramaturgy of the *Stichus* is the structure of Act V. In this final act, the three slaves, including

---

50 Knapp 1919, 233. Knapp's study is the first systematic effort to identify literary (including several meta-literary) references in Plautus' corpus.

Stichus, the character after whom the play is titled, put together their own dinner party after their masters have exited the play to celebrate. The division of this Act into seven scenes (in less than 150 lines) – admittedly a division initiated by critics, not Plautus himself – is indicative of the compartmentalisation of the stage action which is about to reach closure. This anadiplosis of the celebratory dinner may be read as yet another expression of meta-drama, with the slaves enacting on stage the dinner party their masters opted not to. The reception of the slaves' dinner party as an extension of their masters' is suggested in the description of the latter by the slave Stephanium in V.3 (ll. 673–82), who has just come out of the masters' dinner celebration and is set to join the slaves' own, in a way embodying the spirit of the festivities from the inside to the outside, and, by association, from the stage to the *cavea*, for everybody to enjoy:

STEPHANIVM: Mirum videri nemini vostrum volo, spectatores,	
quid ego hinc, quae illic habito, exeam: faciam vos certiores.	674–5
domo dudum huc arcessita sum, <nam> quoniam nuntiatum est	676
istarum venturos viros, ibi festinamus omnes;	
lectis sternendis studuimus munditiisque apparandis.	
inter illud tamen negotium meis curavi amicis,	
Sticho et conservo Sagarino meo, cena cocta ut esset.	680
Stichus obsonatust, ceterum ego operam do: is adlegavi<t>.	
nunc ibo hinc et amicos meos curabo hic advenientis. –	

I don't want it to seem strange to any of you, spectators, why I, who live over there, am coming out from here; I'll let you know. A while ago I was summoned from home to this place: when it was announced that these women's husbands were going to come, we all bustled about; we were busy spreading the couches and cleaning up. Still, during the business I took care that dinner would be cooked for my boyfriends, Stichus and my fellow-slave Sangarinus. Stichus has brought the food, I'm taking care of the rest; that's what he commissioned. Now I'll go away and look after my boyfriends here on their arrival.

Stephanium offers descriptions of both dinner celebrations, and these descriptions are complementary: she describes how she helped with tidying up the house (of the masters) and cooking the feast (for the slaves). Typically the celebratory feast is a comic skit set as a concluding device in a *palliata*, but receives only brief mention and serves to mark the resolution of the plot. In the *Stichus* it supplants the plot of the play: the noun '*cena*' and the verb '*cenare*' occur forty-three times in a play that is a little over 770 lines long (once every thirteen lines, on average, given that the first occurrence is attested on l. 185 along with the entrance of the parasite in the play) – and this without counting a variety of other terms that refer to eating and feasting (e. g. *potatio, potare, prandium*, etc.) or to their opposite, fasting, such as *fames* or *esurire*, which occur respectively, ten and three times, all in speeches by the parasite Gelasimus or with reference to him, and underline the fact that he is the only character of the play who is excluded altogether from the feasting.

Conclusion

The readings of the *Trinummus* and the *Stichus*, two of the least celebrated Plautine *palliatae*, proposed in this study argue for a studied thematic structure in the composition of two scripts generally considered to have been clumsily put together. The *Trinummus* and the *Stichus* in reality are experimental literary compositions which exemplify the ongoing revision of conventions that distinguish the texture of Roman comic drama. Plautus, like every professional *palliata* demiurge, wrote plays that notwithstanding their innovative aspects aimed primarily at generating laughter and appealing to the audience, since broad popular appeal secured the professional survival of the playwright. Given the absence of any testimony in our sources to any information on Plautine failures or even less favourably received performances, we have no reason to believe that the *Trinummus* and the *Stichus* fared poorly when first staged. Rather, the controversial, self-conscious character of these plays as outlined from the reading proposed in this study, suggests that the Roman audiences were much more receptive to dramatic experiments than generally believed – which in turn should lead to a whole new different philosophy of approaching core themes of Roman drama, such as Plautus' originality or Terence's alleged failure.

Acknowledgments

I would like to thank the organisers of the 'Roman Drama and Its Contexts' for the invitation to present my work at the conference and receive invaluable constructive feedback. Particular thanks are due to Stavros Frangoulidis for his insightful comments on an earlier draft of this paper; and to my colleague at Athens, Ioannis Konstantakos, for bringing to my attention important bibliography.

Bibliography

Anderson, W. S. (1979), 'The Absurdity of Officious Morality', *Traditio* 35, 333–45.
―――― (1993), *Barbarian Play: Plautus' Roman Comedy*, Toronto.
Antonaccio, C. (2000), 'Review of Malkin, *The Returns of Odysseus: Colonization and Ethnicity*. Berkeley: The University of California Press, 1998', *AJP* 121.4, 637–41.

Arnott, W. G. (1972), 'Targets, Techniques and Traditions in Plautus' *Stichus*', *BICS* 19, 54–79.
―――― (1996), *Alexis: The Fragments. A Commentary*, Cambridge.
Bakola, E. (2010), *Cratinus and the Art of Comedy*, Oxford.
Barsby, J. (2001), *Terence, Volumes I-II* (LOEB Classical Library), Cambridge, MA and London.
Braccesi, L. (2010), *Sulle rotte di Ulisse. L'invenzione della geografia omerica*, Rome and Bari.
Casolari, F. (2003), *Die Mythentravestie in der griechischen Komödie*, Münster.
Clark, M. (1987), 'Humor and Incongruity', in: J. Morreall (ed.), *The Philosophy of Laughter and Humor*, Albany, 139–55.
Damon, C. (1997), *The Mask of the Parasite: A Pathology of Latin Patronage*, Ann Arbor.
De Melo, W. (2011–13), (ed. and trans.) Plautus, Volumes I-V (LOEB Classical Library), Cambridge, MA and London.
Deufert, M. (2002), *Textgeschichte und Rezeption der plautinischen Komödien im Altertum*, Berlin.
Duckworth, G. (1952), *The Nature of Roman Comedy*, Princeton.
Fantuzzi, M. and Hunter, R. (2004), *Tradition and Innovation in Hellenistic Poetry*, Cambridge 2004.
Fontaine, M. (2010), *Funny Words in Plautine Comedy*, Oxford.
Fraenkel, E. (2007), *Plautine Elements in Plautus*, transl. of *Plautinisches im Plautus* (1922) by T. Drevikovsky and F. Muecke, Oxford.
Gatti, E. (1975), *Odisseo: Il viaggio coloniale di Ulisse. La scoperta di Skera*, Milan.
Germany, R. (2008), *Mimetic Contagion in Terence's Eunuchus*, PhD diss., University of Chicago.
Goldberg, S. M. (1986), *Understanding Terence*, Princeton.
Gratwick, A. S. (1981), 'Curculio's Last Bow: Plautus, *Trinummus* iv.3', *Mnemosyne* 34, 331–50.
Harsh, P. W. (1944), *A Handbook of Classical Drama*, Stanford.
Hinds, S. (1998), *Allusion and Intertext: Dynamics of Appropriation in Roman Poetry*, Cambridge.
Hunter, R. L. (1985), *Eubulus: The Fragments*, Cambridge.
Jachmann, G. (1931), *Plautinisches und Attisches* (Problemata 3), Berlin.
Jocelyn, H. D. (1969), 'Chrysalus and the Fall of Troy (Plautus, *Bacchides* 925–978)', *HSPh* 73, 135–52.
Jouanno, C. (2012), 'Images comiques d'Ulysse, d'Epicharme à Plaute', *Les Etudes Classiques* 80, 247–282
Kahane, A. (2012), 'The (Dis)continuity of Genres: A Comment on the Romans and the Greeks', in: Th.D. Papanghelis, S. J. Harrison, and S. Frangoulidis (eds.), *Generic Interfaces in Latin Literature: Encounters, Interactions and Transformations*, Berlin, 35–54.
Kerkhof, R. (2001), *Dorische Posse, Epicharm und Attische Komödie*, München and Leipzig.
Knapp, C. (1919), 'References to Literature in Plautus and Terence', *AJP* 40, 231-61.
Konstan, D. (1983), *Roman Comedy*, Ithaca, NY.
Konstantakos, I. M. (2014a), 'Comedy in the Fourth Century I: Mythological Burlesques', in: A. Scafuro & M. Fontaine (eds.), *The Oxford Handbook of Greek and Roman Comedy*, Oxford and New York, 160–80.
―――― (2014b), 'Από τον μύθο στο γέλιο: Θαυμαστά μοτίβα και κωμικές στρατηγικές στη μυθολογική κωμωδία', in: M. Tamiolaki (ed.), *Κωμικός Στέφανος: Νέες τάσεις στην έρευνα της αρχαίας ελληνικής κωμωδίας*, Rethymno, 75–102.
Leach, E. W. (1980), 'The Soldier and Society: Plautus' *Miles Gloriosus* as Popular Drama', *Rivista di Studi Classici* 28, 185–209.

Lefèvre, E. (1993), 'Politics and Society in Plautus' *Trinummus*', in: R. Scodel (ed.), *Theatre and Society in the Classical World*, Ann Arbor, 177–90.
_____ (1995), *Plautus und Philemon*, Tübingen.
_____ (2013), *Terenz' und Menanders Adelphoe* (Zetemata 145), Munich.
Lo Schiavo, R. (2003), *La teoria dell' origine Sicilian dell' Odissea: Il cieco, la giovinetta, il Malconsiglio*, Palermo.
Malkin, I. (1998), *The Returns of Odysseus: Colonization and Ethnicity*, Berkeley and Los Angeles.
_____ (1999), 'Ulysse Protocolonisateur', *Mediterraneo Antico* 2.1, 243–61.
Mastromarco, G. (1998), 'La degradazione del mostro. La maschera del *Ciclope* nella commedia e nel dramma satiresco del quinto secolo a.C.', in: A. M. Belardinelli, O. Imperio, G. Mastromarco, M. Pellegrino & P. Totaro (eds.), *Tessere. Frammenti della commedia greca: studi e commenti*, 9–42.
McElduff, S. (2014), *Roman Theories of Translation: Surpassing the Source*, Routledge.
McGill, S. (2012), *Plagiarism in Latin Literature*, Cambridge.
Millis, B. W. (2001), *A Commentary on the Fragments of Anaxandrides*, PhD diss., University of Illinois at Urbana-Champaign.
Muecke, F. (1985), 'Names and Players: The Sycophant Scene of the *Trinummus* (*Trin.* 4.2)', *TAPhA* 115, 167–86.
Nesselrath, H.-G. (1990), *Die attische Mittlere Komödie. Ihre Stellung in der antiken Literaturkritik und Literaturgeschichte*, Berlin.
Owens, W. M. (2000), 'Plautus' *Stichus* and the Political Crisis of 200 BC', *AJP* 121, 385–407.
Papaioannou, S. (2014), 'The Innovator's Poetic Self-Presentation: Terence's Prologues as Interpretative Texts of Programmatic Poetics', in: S. Papaioannou (ed.), *Terence and Interpretation*, Newcastle, 25–57.
Pellegrino, M. (2000), *Utopie e immagini gastronomiche nei frammenti dell' archaia*, Bologna.
_____ (2013), *Nicofonte: Testimonianze e frammenti*, Mainz.
Phillips, E. D. (1959), 'The Comic Odysseus', *G&R* 28, 58–67.
Riemer, P. (1996), *Das Spiel im Spiel: Studien zum plautinischen Agon in 'Trinummus' und 'Rudens'*, Stuttgart and Leipzig.
Schmidt, O. (1888), 'Ulixes Comicus', *Jahrbuch für Klassische Philologie*, Suppl. 16, 375–403.
Segal, E. (1974), 'The Purpose of the *Trinummus*', *AJP* 95, 252–64.
Senior, M. (1978), *Greece and Its Myths: A Traveller's Guide*, London.
Sharrock, A. R. (1996), 'The Art of Deceit: Pseudolus and the Nature of Reading', *CQ* 46, 152–74.
_____ (2009), *Reading Roman Comedy: Poetics and Playfulness in Plautus and Terence*, Cambridge.
_____ (2014), 'Reading Plautus' *Trinummus*: Who'd Bother?', in: E. Karakasis & I. N. Perysinakis (eds.), *Plautine Trends. Studies in Plautine Comedy and Its Reception*, Berlin, 167–95.
Slater, N. W. (1987), 'The Dates of Plautus' *Curculio* and *Trinummus* Reconsidered', *AJP* 108, 264–9.
Stanford, W. B. (1968), *The Ulysses Theme*, New York.
Stein, J. P. (1970), 'Morality in Plautus' *Trinummus*', *CB* 47, 7–13.
Suerbaum, W. (1968), *Untersuchungen zur Selbstdarstellung älterer römischer Dichter: Livius Andronicus, Naevius, Ennius*, Hildesheim.
Tanner, R. H. (1915), 'The Ὀδυσσῆς of Cratinus and the *Cyclops* of Euripides', *TAPhA* 46, 173–206.
Traina, A. (1970), *Vortit barbare: le traduzioni poetiche da Livio Andronico a Cicerone*, Rome.

v. Wilamowitz-Moellendorf, U. (1925), *Menander, Das Schiedsgericht (Epitrepontes)*, Berlin.
Willi, A. (2012), 'Challenging Authority: Epicharmus between Epic and Rhetoric', in: K. Bosher (ed.), *Theater Outside Athens: Drama in Greek Sicily and South Italy*, Cambridge.
Zanda, E. (2011), *Fighting Hydra-like Luxury: Sumptuary Regulation in the Roman Republic*, London.

Kathleen McCarthy
Prologues between Performance and Fiction

> Starveling: I believe we must leave the killing out, when all is done.
> Bottom: Not a whit: I have a device to make all well. Write me a prologue; and let the prologue seem to say, we will do no harm with our swords, and that Pyramus is not killed indeed; and, for the more better assurance, tell them that I, Pyramus, am not Pyramus, but Bottom the weaver: this will put them out of fear. (*Midsummer Night's Dream*, III.1)

With his peerless theatrical instincts, Bottom has put his finger on the purpose of a prologue. The rude mechanicals fear that the fictional world they create will be so powerful that the violence of the scene will prove too much, especially for the ladies of the audience. Bottom's answer is not to tone down the violence in the script but to preface it with a prologue, which will spell out the nature of dramatic illusion and thus allow the audience both to enjoy the thrills and to feel secure. In the event, the prologue given by Quince [V.2] does no such thing: he starts with a mangled *captatio benevolentiae* and follows that up with a detailed summary of the plot.

These three functions of prologues – demystifying the dramatic illusion, soliciting the good will of the audience and explaining the plot – are well represented within Plautine comedy too.[1] What I want to focus on here is the first of these functions, by exploring the oddly self-contradictory potential of prologues – somehow the ideal prologue both makes the audience conscious of the mechanisms through which the dramatic illusion is produced and yet also allows the audience to experience the fictional world more fully. My goal is to inquire more precisely into how these moments work. Although it's relatively simple to recognize a breach of dramatic illusion when we see it, those acts can be constituted in quite different ways and to quite different effects. What follows is an attempt to put under the microscope a few specific moments when prologues enact such breaches and analyze what is happening in each case.[2]

---

[1] I will focus exclusively on Plautus's prologues, since Terence's prologues obviously take a very different tack; see, e.g., Gowers 2004, Lada-Richards 2004. Fourteen of Plautus' twenty plays have prologues, so we can say that they are a well-established feature of his practice, but a prologue does not seem to be a required element. Some plays may have contained prologues that have now been lost. For an overview of the types of prologues Plautus employs see Marshall 2006, 194–6.

[2] The assumptions I apply to prologues here have been worked out in greater or lesser detail in works such as Raffaelli 1984, Slater 1992, Moore 1998, Henderson 1999 and Sharrock 2009. See esp. Moore 1998, 12–7 and Sharrock 2009, 22–63.

Not only have I chosen to focus here on the prologues' potential to comment on the dramatic illusion, but I would argue that the other two functions, which seem to have more practical ends in view, are also (at least in part) caught up in the task of getting the audience to recognize the peculiar nature of theatrical experience. In the past there was a tendency to think about moments that comment on the dramatic illusion as most closely connected with the play's identity as a text and with the issues (including issues of fictionality) that it has in common with other texts, while thinking of *captatio benevolentiae* and plot summary as more oriented toward the exigencies generated by performance. This tendency, however, has been eroded by a now widely-shared skepticism that questions the notion that prologues are shaped primarily by the need to quiet down rowdy audiences or to explain background necessary for understanding the play. It may be that Plautus' audience was loud and boisterous but even if that is true, the way that the prologues ask for attention has rhetorical and aesthetic consequences as well as practical ones.[3] Similarly, as Sharrock 2009, 31, in particular has emphasized, the conventionality of comic plots makes any detailed exposition unnecessary, an argument supported by the fact that many Plautine plays have no prologues at all and many prologues tell nothing of the plot. Therefore, while these two functions certainly might have some effect in preparing the audience for the opening of the play, it is clear that they also should be read as an integral part of the script, not just as verbal analogues to dimming the lights and raising the curtain.

Given this interest in what we could call the literary texture of pleas for the audience's attention and narrations of the plot, the time seems right to consider as well the ways that references to the dramatic illusion are implicated in the relation between the stage and the *cavea*. We are used to the notion of 'induction' as a blanket term for explaining how the prologue bridges the world of the audience and the world of the characters, but I think it is worth taking apart that notion to see how it works.

What might be the rhetorical or aesthetic effect of prologues' harping on the paradoxical closeness and distance of the fictional world? Rather than positing that prologues naturalize the theatrical experience, i.e., make the play easier to understand or closer to the audience's own real experience, I want to suggest that Plautine prologues are more likely to call attention to the act of representation itself. Far from being hard to interpret, there is a danger that the domestic turmoils of New Comedy will seem too much like real life; in comparison to the fantastic spectacles of tragedy and Old Comedy, these three house fronts, populated by families and pimps and slaves, may mask the fundamental weirdness of dra-

---

3 See, e.g., Christenson 2000, 132–3, Sharrock 2009, 23.

matic representation. Many prologues resist this lulling effect by showing off the special way that dramatic representation galvanizes the energy of the moment to put a world on display for our contemplation. I want to explore here two major ways that prologues perform this demonstration. On the one hand, we have prologues that concentrate emphatically on the dramatic illusion itself – rather than inducting us into the fictive world, they highlight the almost magical property by which this world comes to look both robust and ephemeral, both grounded in reality and arbitrary. My primary example for this kind of prologue will be that of the *Menaechmi*. On the other hand, we have prologues that focus intently on the audience in the theater and the counter-intuitive experience of spectatorship; rather than asking them to forget who they are and where, these prologues remind the audience of their real physical presence in the theater and the norms of their Roman world, even as they also prepare the spectators to become absorbed in a fictive (Greek) world. My primary example here will be the prologue of the *Captivi*.

We can orient ourselves to these two ways of proceeding by juxtaposing two of the most direct comments on the act of representation, taken from the prologues of the *Menaechmi* and *Captivi*.[4]

> ego nusquam dicam nisi ubi factum dicitur. (*Men.* 10)
>
> I will say what happened nowhere except where it is said to have happened.
>
> haec urbs Epidamnus est dum haec agitur fabula:
> quando alia agetur, aliud fiet oppidum;
> sicut familiae quoque solent mutarier:
> modo hic habitat leno, modo adulescens, modo senex,   75
> pauper mendicus rex parasitus hariolus.[5]   (*Men.* 72–6)
>
> This city is Epidamnus while this play is being performed. When another play is performed, it will become another city; just as households often change: at one time a pimp lives here, at another a young man, at another an old man ... a poor man, a beggar, a millionaire, a hanger-on, a soothsayer.
>
> haec res agetur nobis, vobis fabula.   (*Capt.* 52)
>
> This will be reality for us, for you a play.

---

4 All Plautus texts quoted from Lindsay 1904. All translations are my own.
5 Gratwick 1993, de Melo 2011 transpose ll. 72–6 to directly after 10. I believe that the argument I'm making for the effect of these lines is valid whether they appear after l. 10 or in their transmitted place near the end of the prologue.

The examples from the *Menaechmi* are about as explicit as Bottom's projected prologue would be as to the nature of the dramatic illusion. To quote Gratwick's 1993 paraphrase of the two meanings packed into line 10, "'I shall say what-happened, nowhere except where it is said to have happened" means the Prologue is about to perform a miracle and redefine Rome as Epidamnus, conveying us thither: Prol. is a magician. But "I shall say what-happened-nowhere, except where it is said to have happened'" means we are about to hear fiction: Prol. is a liar.' In a similar vein, lines 72–6 focus on the arbitrariness of fictive place – it is whatever the playwright tells us it is and the conventions that govern it are similar to the conventions that govern the roster of stock characters, who form in various combinations all possible plots.

The *Captivi* line operates along a different dimension. Rather than calling attention to the arbitrariness of fiction, it focuses on the odd relation between those on stage and the audience – physically they occupy the same space and time, but the world inhabited by those on stage is of a completely different order from the world of the spectators. I will discuss this further below, but I think *nobis* here could be understood as referring to either the characters or the actors – the fictive world is reality for the characters and the performance of the play is reality for the actors. Where the joke in *Menaechmi* line 10 depended on a verbal quibble (centered on *nusquam … factum*), this line is based on a pun. Lindsay 1900 cites Hallidie 1895 explaining that the pun here depends on the fact that the first clause could be read as, 'so that's the story [*res*] we're going to put on today,' until the second clause (with its implied contrast between *res* and *fabula*) shifts the meaning to 'for us this is reality [*res*].'

In each case these might seem like isolated moments, one-liners that depend on word play for their conceptual energy, and yet when seen in the context of their respective prologues, they take on new levels of meaning. The prologue of the *Menaechmi* has an unusual thematic consistency – most prologues have certain idées fixes but this one is almost a mini-essay on the concept of dramatic space and place.[6] Spoken by an uncharacterized prologue speaker, from its beginning lines this prologue foregrounds (by means of puns) the ambiguous kind of reality that is created through language. In line 3, in an oft-quoted pun the *prologus* boasts that he brings Plautus before us, but through language rather than in body.

---

[6] Sharrock 2009, 41–5 offers a reading that draws attention to many of the points I will draw on here. The difference in our readings is rather one of emphasis: Sharrock is interested in the problem of how plays get started and in the question of how information about the fictional world is relayed in the prologue; I am focusing on the ways that these lines point explicitly to verbal representation as the source of the fictive world.

> adporto vobis Plautum – lingua, non manu. (*Men.* 3)

> I bring you Plautus – verbally, not by the hand.

From this point, this prologue develops more thoroughly than any other prologue the idea that the stage both is and isn't a space in Rome, while it also both is and isn't a city in the Greek world which the playwright has arbitrarily designated as the location of these events. In line 56, the prologue again uses a pun to contrast (but also to align) the realities produced by language with the realities produced by bodies.

> verum illuc redeo unde abii atque uno asto in loco. (*Men.* 56)

> But now I'm going back to that place from which I started and yet also standing in the same place.

He uses *redeo* to mean both that he is backtracking in his exposition and that he is "going back" to Epidamnus (after having teased the audience with a little financial sleight of hand) while standing in the same spot. Although it might be tempting to characterize what the prologue speaker does here as exploding the dramatic illusion, I think it is more accurate to say that he both exposes its mechanisms and revels in the apparent solidity of the fictive world. For example, at lines 22–3 and again at 51–5, we have two instances in which he playfully suggests that he himself inhabits the fictive world and then ambiguously reverses that claim.

> ita forma simili puerei uti mater sua
> non internosse posset quae mammam dabat, 20
> neque adeo mater ipsa quae illos pepererat,
> (ut quidem ille dixit mihi, qui pueros viderat:
> ego illos non vidi, ne quis vostrum censeat). (*Men.* 19–23)

> The boys looked so much alike that their own nurse who suckled them could not tell them apart, nor could the very mother who bore them (as in fact one who saw them told me; I did not see them myself, so don't get the wrong idea).

> si quis quid vestrum Epidamnum curari sibi
> velit, audacter imperato et dicito,
> sed ita ut det unde curari id possit sibi.
> nam nisi qui argentum dederit, nugas egerit;
> qui dederit, magi' maiores nugas egerit. (*Men.* 51–5)

> If any one of you would like something taken care of at Epidamnus, give me the order loud and clear; but make sure you give me the wherewithal to take care of the matter. For if anyone doesn't put down money, he's wasting his time; if anyone does put down money, he's *really* wasting his time.

Note that each of these cases involves an explicit address to the audience. In lines 45–46, where he performs only the first half of this one-two punch – pretending he has direct access to the fictive world, with no backtracking – there is no engagement with the audience.

> propterea illius nomen mihi memini facilius
> quia illum clamore vidi flagitarier.
>
> I remember [the grandfather's] name more easily because I saw him being dunned at great volume.

The prologue speaker of the *Menaechmi* is voluble on the subject of fictive space but relatively reticent about the space that he shares in real time with the audience. It is as if he himself exists *nusquam*, brought into being by the playwright's language and as slippery as his own puns.

The *prologus* of the *Menaechmi* playfully revels in the fictive world, which is both (almost) tangible and (almost) virtual. Can such playfulness also acknowledge the complexities of the theater itself, including the audience's own ambiguous relation to the events depicted? Putting the example from the *Captivi* back into its context will offer us a starting point. This prologue as a whole has two striking features: beyond just acknowledging the audience, it is unusually focused on the distinctions (even oppositions) between actors and audience and, secondly, it is laced through with philosophizing about the limits of human understanding, as one might expect in a comedy about *agnoia*. Where the *Menaechmi* prologue displayed for our admiration the magical feat of representation through language (a fact which we take for granted and yet always has the power to amaze us as well), this prologue highlights a different 'miraculous' aspect of the representational act: the fact that it both does and doesn't take place within the audience's own life. By calling attention to the audience's own civic mentality as well as their physical presence in the theater, this prologue complicates the pure play of language exalted in the *Menaechmi* prologue, but does not abandon that notion.

The key line I started from – *haec res agetur nobis, vobis fabula*, l. 52 – poses in very small scope some very big questions. It draws attention to the practical process of putting on a play (when we read the first half as, 'this is the plot we're going to act out for you'), but it also draws attention to the fact that the actors and audience will be experiencing the same event, but separated by their distinctive perspectives. Timothy Moore has interpreted this line not only as referring to the different functions of actors and audience, but to their differing social statuses as well: he paraphrases this line as 'To you free spectators ... this is only a fiction, but we (the slave actors and previously-mentioned slave spectators) know the reality of slavery.' (1998, 196). In other words, this line (and the prologue's general consciousness of the theatrical event) bring into the play a recognition of the life that goes on in the real (not fictive) world in and out of the theater. While this line expresses the idea perhaps most emphatically, when we catalogue the places where this prologue-speaker describes the audience in terms of Roman civic institutions, it begins to seem that this prologue is more than casually interested in the ways that identities formed outside the theater (for spectators) or outside the moment of performance (for actors) have implications for the theatrical experience.

This prologue emphasizes the experience of actors, not just as inert vehicles through which the fictive world is made visible, but as people who live alongside the audience in their daily lives. From the opening lines, in which the prologue-speaker gestures towards spectators at the back of the *cavea* – visible from the stage but not from the rows of seats – we get a subtle but distinctive focus on the perspective of actors.

> hos quos videtis stare hic captivos duos,
> illi quia astant, hi stant ambo, non sedent;
> hoc vos mihi testes estis me verum loqui. (1–3)

> These two prisoners whom you see standing here are standing, not sitting, because those men [at the back of the audience] are standing. You all are witnesses that I am telling the truth.

These lines accomplish multiple things. First, they strikingly merge the worlds of characters and spectators, calling attention to the fact that they share a single physical space and ignoring the usually constitutive distinctions between stage and *cavea*, between fictional character and audience member. Second, the prologue speaker inserts himself into this situation as the bridge between the two worlds, the single person who can perceive the parallel between the two sets of standing figures; the combination of his special status as the emissary from the fictional world (conventionally granted to prologue-speakers) and his visual perspective into the back rows of the audience allows him to make the link between the two. In the final line, the prologue speaker uses legal terminology to ask the audience to confirm his statement, thus both highlighting his claim to trustworthiness and expressing the audience's authority in terms of the institutions of Roman civic life. One could say that these lines not only set up the prologue-speaker as the bridge between the fictive world and the audience's experience (the effect we would expect), but in a more fine-grained effect they perform that function by specifically calling attention to the physical space of the theater, to the prologue-speaker's visual perspective and to the audience's civic experience.

This opening remark is quickly followed up by one of this prologue's more contentious moments (ll. 11–16), when the prologue-speaker wrangles with an audience member in a scripted interruption. This brief passage both strikingly highlights the prologue-speaker's professional identity (*quando histrionem cogis mendicarier*, l. 13; 'since you're forcing an actor to become a beggar') and identifies the good, well-behaved members of the audience by means of their registration in the census (*vos qui potestis ope vostra censerier*, l.15; 'you who can be counted in the census by your wealth'). It describes both actors and audience, then, by means of their position in the real Roman world that goes on around the moment of dramatic performance. A similar effect comes near the end of the prologue (ll. 61–6), where the prologue-speaker first highlights the practical realities of dramatic performance (ll. 61–2 *nam hoc paene iniquomst, comico choragio/conari desubito agere nos tragoediam*; 'for it is is hardly fair for us suddenly to put on a tragedy with the trappings of a comedy') and then suggests a parallel between fictive battles and those a Roman spectator might find in a courtroom (ll. 63–6). Again we see the prologue pointing to the differences in experience between actors and audience, while also characterizing both groups according to the demands of their ordinary lives, not the fictive world they are about to entertain together.

I suggest that these comments present an unusually robust challenge to the audience, namely to recognize that they and the actors continue to participate in their real lives even while they also immerse themselves in the fictive world as fully as possible. The combination of these two dimensions is parallel to but distinct from the combination of ephemerality and solidity that the *Menaechmi* prologue paraded for its audience. While that prologue focused on the power of language and dramatic representation to hold together two apparently contradictory states, in the *Captivi* the prologue speaker pays little attention to the slipperiness of language and instead focuses on the slipperiness of social identity, i. e. how social cues can place the same person in radically different functions at different times. Even a superficial consideration of the plot of this play will suggest reasons for emphasizing such notions in the prologue.[7]

If the *Captivi*'s prologue is not only more engaged with the audience but more insistent on the co-existence of real and fictive worlds, how does that feature relate to this prologue's other thematic focus, the limits of human understanding? Again, line 52, with its contrast of *res* and *fabula*, can provide a starting point, when we note that this line appears in the context of the prologue's most extensive comment on *agnoia*:

> ... reducemque faciet liberum in patriam ad patrem,
> imprudens: itidem ut saepe iam in multis locis
> plus insciens quis fecit quam prudens boni.   45

---

[7] On the other hand, perhaps the reason why the *Menaechmi* prologue focuses on the ambiguous relation between representation and reality is to be found in the plot of twins, whose identical appearance both is and isn't a reliable index of their identities.

> sed <u>inscientes</u> sua sibi fallacia
> ita compararunt et confinxerunt dolum
> itaque hi commenti de sua sententia
> ut in servitute hic ad suom maneat patrem:
> ita nunc <u>ignorans</u> suo sibi servit patri; 50
> homunculi quanti sunt, quom recogito!
> haec res agetur nobis, vobis fabula. (*Cap.* 43–52)

... [Tyndarus] will bring his brother back as a free man into his homeland and to his father – all unknowingly. Just so, often on many occasions before now someone has done more good unknowingly than knowingly. But unknowingly they have contrived by their cleverness and figured out a trick, and invented it in accordance with their own impulse, in such a way that [Tyndarus] will stay here in servitude at his own father's house; thus, now he is a slave to his own father and doesn't recognize him. What tiny/worthless beings humans are, when I think of it! This is reality for us, for you a play.

This passage chimes with a moment earlier in the prologue:

> hic nunc domi servit suo patri, <u>nec scit</u> pater;
> enim vero di nos quasi pilas homines habent. (*Cap.* 21–22)[8]

Now he is a slave to his own father at home, and the father doesn't know it. Yes, indeed, the gods treat us humans like playthings.

These two passages point to a notion that the play proper will express in large scale: that humans themselves understand but little of their world and their experience is fully meaningful only at a level above their own cognition. (This thought is crystallized in the two single-line gnomic utterances offered in ll. 51 and 22). This idea might be understood to operate in different ways for fictional characters, for actors and for audience members, thus both unifying these three groups and registering the differences among them. Fictional characters, most obviously, have no notion that their troubles are providing a story – entertaining or enlightening – for the audience. Actors and audience members in more complex ways combine their real-time perspective on their own experience with varying degrees of consciousness of how that experience might be meaningful from another, higher perspective. While actors maintain a strong consciousness of the audience, they can never really view the play from that perspective; and while audience members might be conscious of the 'roles' they play in civic institutions and in the broad sweep of human life, again they are unable to access that higher, more integrated level of understanding directly.

---

8 De Melo 2011 transposes these lines to after l. 4.

At one level, the claim that these observations on *agnoia* operate in parallel but somewhat differently for characters, actors and audience is obvious – this is, in fact, what the *gnomai* in lines 51 and 22 are pointing to, as they prompt audience members to apply to their own lives the implications of what the play orchestrates in the lives of the characters. But within the specific context of this prologue, I think this claim can be pushed further. First, especially because this passage ends with the *res/fabula* contrast, it subtly points to the ways that actors' experience is distinct both from that of the characters and from that of the audience; after all, *haec res agetur nobis* would mean one thing applied to the characters ('the fictional world is our reality') and another applied to actors (both 'this is the story we'll perform' and, as Moore suggests, 'we ... slave actors ... know the reality of slavery'), both of which contrast with the *fabula* offered to the audience. And yet this line may not let spectators off easy either, since clearly it aims to shake them out of their complacent assumption that this is all 'just a play.' Second, the emphasis on *agnoia* contributes to the ironies of identity and intention with which this play is thoroughly imbued, but in the context of a prologue that has persistently refused to segregate the moment of performance from other aspects of the audience's life, these ironies cannot so easily be contained within the fictive world. Again, we could say that the prologue is challenging to the audience to admit the limits to their understanding of their own lives and positions rather than just to enjoy their superior view of the characters' toils.

Coming back to the comparison with the *Menaechmi* prologue, we can see that the *Captivi* prologue is equally invested in acknowledging the arbitrariness of the dramatic illusion, but it also attaches greater weight to the images of life produced by this improbably powerful practice. Rather than focusing on language as the mechanism that produces the illusion, the *Captivi* prologue focuses on the practical and substantial process through which plays are brought on stage – a process that includes real human actors, props, costumes, etc. Further, by focusing on these practical aspects of staging a play, the *Captivi* prologue also places much greater emphasis on the physical space of the theater and the fact that the audience and actors are together in real time and that this moment of performance – in spite of its obviously special qualities – is also a part of their ordinary lives. What is significant about this prologue, then, is that it shows how recognition of the dramatic illusion can co-exist with the (cognitively and socially) conservative insistence on taking the play 'seriously,' i.e., applying to one's own life the lessons played out on stage.

Central to this distinctive dramatic regime is the prologue's trick of presenting the actors (especially the *prologus* himself) as ambiguously aligned with and segregated from the audience members. The prologue both carefully enumerates the specificity of the actor's experience in ways that differentiate it from that of the audience and repeatedly reminds the audience of the joint presence and common purpose they share with the actors. The *res/fabula* line (l. 52) is an excellent example of how the experience of actors is both set apart and made parallel to that of the spectators. In fact, when we take account of the theme of *agnoia*, we might say that the prologue is extending to the audience the actors' own position: they know the lines they are to speak, but they can't know how their performance looks to a distant viewer. This perfectly sums up this prologue's strange combination of conservative moralizing (the gods are watching you, as you are watching us), with a playful acknowledgment of the theater's unstable realities.

Bibliography

Christenson, D. (2000), *Plautus: Amphitruo*, Cambridge.
De Melo, W. (2011–13), *Plautus*, vols. 1–5, Cambridge, MA.
Gowers, E. (2004), 'The Plot Thickens: Hidden Outlines in Terence's Prologues', *Ramus* 33, 150–66.
Gratwick, A. S. (1993), *Plautus: Menaechmi*, Cambridge.
Hallidie, A. R. (1895), *The Captivi of T. Maccius Plautus*, London.
Henderson, J. (1999), 'Hanno's Punic Heirs: Der *Poenulus*-Neid des Plautus', in: *Writing Down Rome: Satire, Comedy and Other Offences in Latin Poetry*, Oxford, 3–37.
Lada-Richards, I. (2004), 'Authorial Voice and Theatrical Self-Definition in Terence and Beyond: The 'Hecyra' Prologues in Ancient and Modern Contexts', *G&R* 51, 55–82.
Lindsay, W. M. (1900), *The Captivi of Plautus*, London.
_____ (1904), *T. Macci Plauti Comoediae*, Oxford.
Marshall, C. W. (2006), *The Stagecraft and Performance of Roman Comedy*, Cambridge.
Moore, T. J. (1998), *The Theater of Plautus: Playing to the Audience*, Austin, TX.
Questa, C./R. Raffaelli (1984), *Maschere, prologhi, naufragi nella commedia plautina*, Bari.
Sharrock, A. (2009), *Reading Roman Comedy: Poetics and Playfulness in Plautus and Terence*, Cambridge.
Slater, N. W. (1992), 'Plautine Negotiations: The *Poenulus* Prologue Unpacked', in: F. M. Dunn and T. Cole (eds.), *Beginnings in Classical Literature*: Yale Classical Studies XXIX, New Haven, 131–46.

David Christenson
All's Well That Ends Well? Old Fools, Morality, and Epilogues in Plautus

Epilogues, like prologues, are rhetorically privileged moments in drama. While a prologue gets the first word in about the play to follow, an epilogue is positioned to influence an audience's assessment of that play once its action is finished. An epilogue effects the transition from the fictional world of the play to the everyday world of the play's spectators (and actors),[1] and in Plautus an epilogue is always combined with an appeal for applause. More specifically, epilogues seek to smooth over a play's dramaturgical rough spots, anticipate potential objections to its content, offer projections about the characters' post-play prospects, or they simply may tease the audience. In these and other ways epilogues shape audience members' thoughts and discourse about what they have just seen; as Ennis/Slagle summarizes the function of epilogues in 18th-century English theatre: 'they work in combination with the play ... to complete meaningful aesthetic and ideological work among the theater patrons.'[2]

As the ultimate point of intersection between a play and an audience's reception of it, the epilogue constitutes a playwright's final attempt to control the spectacle, and amounts to his *talking over* the play. In early Roman theater more than a playwright's hurt feelings over a panned play was at stake, as there was the additional factor of state sponsorship looming over a performance and a playwright's hope for future contracts.[3] Epilogues were charged liminal moments for low- or no-status Roman actors,[4] which marked their removal from the exhilarating realm of Plautine comedy in which they became someone else,[5] and their return to dreary reality, including the very real possibility of a beating for failing to deliver a successful performance.[6] It thus is appropriate that in the manuscripts of Plautus some epilogues are assigned to the *grex*,[7] which suggests that

---

[1] As Slater 2000, 55 notes, ' ... the epilogue stands with one foot in the world of the play and one foot in the world of the spectators. A mediator is needed between the two worlds, and as the prologue led us in, so the epilogue leads us out again'.
[2] 2007, 21.
[3] Manuwald 2011, 41–54 provides an overview of the production process.
[4] For the status of actors see Richlin 2014, 210–14 and n. 29 below.
[5] As the prologist of *Poenulus* notes: 126 *alius nunc fieri uolo*.
[6] For actors' vulnerability see Moore 1998, 10–12 and Christenson 2000, 141.
[7] For the problems associated with identifying the speakers of epilogues see Sharrock 2009, 251–58.

the entire troupe or perhaps only those actors already on-stage, now performers stepping out of their roles, embraced strength in numbers by delivering the epilogue together.

Sharrock's recent chapter[8] on comic closure offers rich insights into Plautus' deployment of epilogues. This paper, however, takes issue with the assertion of Sharrock and others that the epilogues of the three Plautine *senex amator* comedies, i. e. *Asinaria, Casina,* and *Mercator*,[9] should be read as ironic codas that diverge from the predominant moral outlook of the plays themselves, which they are said to undermine by promoting a contradictory, amoral spirit of comic license.[10] Instead, I will argue that each of these epilogues mirrors the plays' traditional Roman perspectives on marriage and sexual morality and is largely concerned with the actors' post-comic prospects. Interpretation of the epilogues of the *senex amator* plays is also critical to an appreciation of the role of the *matronae* in these plays. Analysis of the *matrona* in Plautus has suffered from the reductive view, canonized by Segal, that she necessarily serves only as the enemy of her husband's pleasure and represents the un-comic antithesis of Saturnalian liberation: 'Plautine wives are nothing but a parade of untamed shrews.'[11] The *senex amator* plays, in which a *matrona* such as Cleostrata in *Casina* functions 'as guardian of the economic and moral integrity of the household,'[12] suggest scope for a realigned view of the *matrona* as a comic hero. Owing to the decorum attaching to the *matrona*'s status and cultural role, her heroism must be

---

8 2009, 250–89.
9 Plautine *senes* in other plays – Antipho in *Stichus* (539ff.), the father of Alcesimarchus in *Cistellaria* (306ff.), Daemones in *Rudens* (829ff.), Megadorus in *Aulularia* (149ff.) – show amorous interest in young women, but their lust is not a focal point of the plot. The case of *Bacchides* is treated below (pp. 14–15). Simo in *Mostellaria* shows an inclination to escape from the erotic attentions of his rich and ageing wife (690–708), but a younger woman is not explicitly mentioned. For accounts of the *senex amator* see Ryder 1984, Cody 1976, and Maurice 2007, 149–51.
10 Sharrock 2009, 264–5 writes (with reference to the epilogue of *Bac.*): 'The *sententia* has subtly metamorphosed from a claim for the moral value of comedy in exposing vices into an intertextual celebration of the comic spirit' and 'The audience is not expected to learn from the experience, but rather is invited to enjoy the vicarious idea of indulging in such comic license 'ourselves''. Barsby 1986, 189 asserts: 'though some of Plautus' epilogues do adopt a moralizing stance (*Captiui, Miles*), their general tone is very much tongue-in-cheek, especially when discussing the behavior of the *senex amator* (*Asinaria, Casina, Mercator*)'. Cf. Slater 2000, 126: ' ... the remaining four [lines of *Cas.*] (1015–19) promise that the revelry can continue after the play is over – if only the audience will applaud. The world of comic freedom need not be left behind'.
11 1987, 25.
12 Rei 1998, 94.

less boisterous and deceitful than that of the more usual servile Plautine comic hero. But the *matronae* of the *senex amator* plays should not be dismissed as humorless, 'uncomic' figures.[13]

I will begin by reviewing in precisely what ways the old men of *Asinaria*, *Casina*, and *Mercator* are represented as morally culpable. Such a review of the old men's offenses against conventional morality is warranted because, while Plautine scholarship generally acknowledges their moral shortcomings, critics sometimes extend Plautus' geriatric lovers a sly wink.[14] While some audience members might have vicariously identified with the old lechers, the plays come down exceptionally hard on the *senex amator*, whose circumscribed familial and social roles, in addition to his biological age, ultimately preclude him from taking refuge in the Roman version of 'boys will be boys.' The epilogues march in step with universal denunciation of the patriarch in the plays.

There is visceral reaction to the very notion of the *senex amator* among these plays' characters, who roundly mock the old men's passion as inconsistent with his age and stage of mortality. In Roman comedy, the age of sixty seems to serve as the threshold at which a man's erotic desires become unpalatable (*Merc.* 525, 1017).[15] Various characters express disdain for the old man's age-inappropriate behavior, as when in *Mercator* Eutychus censures Demipho for attempting to steal his son's girlfriend (*nam te istac aetate haud aequom filio fuerat tuo/adulescenti amanti amicam eripere emptam argento suo*, 972–3; cf. *Cas.* 240, *Bac.* 1163 and Fr. VI, *Merc.* 983a). In addition to wearing the stock costume and mask of the *senex*, an old man in love is visually – and morally – marked out by other characters by his gray hair.[16] In *Cas.* Lysidamus metacomically mocks what has become a disapproving refrain vis-à-vis the lover's hoary head:[17]

---

13 I hope to treat the figure of the Plautine *matrona* in a separate study, the groundwork for which has been laid by Kraus 2004; see especially her analysis (88–152) of the *matronae* of *As.*, *Cas.*, and *Merc.* as knowing and ironic comic agents.
14 E.g. Tatum 1983, 88–9, who is sensitive to Lysidamus' moral failures in *Casina*, nonetheless writes: 'The effect in performance is that in laughing at Lysidamus we come to feel a wry affection for him, even though we know that Cleostrata is upholding stern Roman (or Greek) virtues by her actions. In short, Cleostrata enjoys her anger and her stern morality, but Lysidamus has much more fun'. Cf. n. 10 above.
15 The concept of what constitutes 'old age' was fluid in the ancient world (as today) and not strictly based on chronological age: see further Parkin 2003, 15–26. For an overview of the role of the old within the Roman family see Dixon 1992, 149–59.
16 For negative perceptions of grayness in the comic and other traditions see Parkin 2003, 75 and 344 n. 78.
17 Cf. *As.* 934, *Bac.* 1208, *Merc.* 305.

> quor amem me castigare, id ponito ad compendium,
> 'cano capite,' 'aetate aliena' eo addito ad compendium,
> 'quoi sit uxor,' id quoque illuc ponito ad compendium. (*Cas.* 517–19)

> And as for lecturing me about my love-life: put it in storage. 'With your gray hair!' 'The age difference!': put that in storage too. To say nothing of 'A married man!' Put it all in storage.

The old man's amorous designs provoke an array of stock insults: he is *decrepitus*, literally 'broken down,' as when Demipho's neighbour Lysimachus tells the audience that the smitten old man is as insignificant as a lover depicted on a wall-painting (*Merc.* 313–14; cf. *As.* 863, *Merc.* 291 and *Cas.* 559). The *senex* is said to be afflicted with debilitatingly foul breath; Lysimachus shows surprising sensitivity to the matter when he considers it from Pasicompsa's perspective:[18]

> iaiunitatis plenus, anima foetida,
> senex hircosus te osculere mulierem?
> utine adueniens uomitum excutias mulieri? (*Merc.* 574–6)

> Running on an empty stomach, with your disgusting breath, goat-like old man that you are – you're going to kiss a woman? Why? So she'll vomit as soon as you get close to her?

Lysidamus and Demipho are serially associated with shaggy, stinking goats and sheep (*Cas.* 535, 550, *Merc.* 230ff.), with the latter suffering figurative castration.[19] The thoroughly hircine Lysidamus stands out from the herd of old lovers for his unbridled, non-discriminatory lust (cf. *Cas.* 452ff.),[20] which carries a moral stench that not even the finest scented hair-gel can disguise (*Cas.* 225–49). On the most immediate physical and visual levels, then, the *senex amator* is represented as an unsympathetic and repulsive character. There is an incongruous and unbridgeable gap between the old man's desire and his advanced age: in the sphere of love he has already lost the unwinnable battle against mortality. However persistent he is, the *senex amator* remains an unpleasant locus of mortality and immorality; Cleostrata cleverly dubs Lysidamus *Accheruntis pabulum* ('death-chow,' *Cas.* 159).[21]

---

18 Cf. *Cas.* 727 *fy fy! foetat tuos mi sermo.*
19 See Augoustakis 2008.
20 Chalinus tells the audience that the old man's lust extends to even his adult male slaves (*barbatos*, 466; cf. the discussion of Williams 2010, 84–6); 'Lysidamus' lust is not human, not a straying within the limits that society and comedy can tolerate, but animalistic, frenzied, Bacchic' (Slater 2000, 75). On the purely physical level, Lysdiamus is made more repulsive by being described as a 'toothless goat' (550 *hirqui ... edentuli*; for the topos cf. Juv. 10.201).
21 Lysidamus' insatiable lust for Casina is mirrored by his age-inappropriate appetite for food and drink; whereas ancient science maintained that the 'coldness' of old age (see Parkin 2003, 84 and 348 n. 108, Cokayne 2003, 38–41) curbed these desires, Lysidamus remains disproportionately

To his further discredit within the conservative Roman context of frugality, each *senex amator* is depicted as financially irresponsible. Demaenetus, the indulgent and impecunious father of *Asinaria*, advises his slave Libanus to cheat himself, his wife or his slave (96–7) in order to aid his son's pursuit of the prostitute he loves. Demaenetus later is caught pledging to steal his wife's *palla* (884–6) to give to his son's inamorata, whom he now commandeers for himself. His wife Artemona concludes that she has been unjustly torturing her female slaves over what probably were her husband's household thefts (888–9). Demaenetus effectively has ceded control of his household to his wife and Saurea, the slave who came with her dowry and is said to have more cash-on-hand than the *paterfamilias* (78–86). Although Demipho in *Mercator* has a history of controlling his finances, once smitten with his son's newly arrived *meretrix*, he spares no expense in hiring a cook and arranging a lavish love-fest (692–7). Demipho's wife does not appear in the play, but Dorippa, the wife of his partner-in-crime Lysimachus, assumes the role of offended *matrona* and champion of the family; she rightfully complains (700–4, 784–6) of what she perceives to be her husband's current and habitual misuse of household funds, which have been bolstered by her large dowry. In *Casina*, we witness a similar pattern of extravagance on Lysidamus' part in connection with the faux-wedding (501 *argento parci nolo, opsonato ampliter*). In the first encounter between the married couple, Cleostrata suggests that her husband's prodigality where food, wine, and brothels are involved is habitual, and she warns him that it poses a threat to their finances (248 *immo age ut lubet bibe, es, disperde rem*). As the pull of his emotions clouds his judgment about expenditures, the *paterfamilias* in each play stands in stark contrast to the *matrona*.

Finally, each *senex amator* is represented as derelict in a potentially public way that compromises not only his authority within the household, but also his reputation among his peers and his standing in his community. As we just observed, Demaenetus' self-described exchange of his patriarchal *imperium* for his wife's dowry (86 *argentum accepi, dote imperium uendidi*) seems to be well known. Artemona suspects that Demaenetus has been neglecting his most important public duties (as well as her) in his pursuit of inappropriate pleasure:

> eum etiam hominem <aut> in senatu dare operam aut cluentibus,
> ibi labore delassatum noctem totam stertere!
> ille opera foris faciendo lassus noctu <ad me> aduenit;
> fundum alienum arat, incultum familiarem deserit.
> is etiam corruptus porro suom corrumpit filium   (*As.* 871–5)

---

ravenous (*Cas.* 245–6, 491–501, 780–7). Cleostrata and her colleagues appropriately starve the *senex* (*Cas.* 149–57, 772–88; for gastronomic imagery in the play see Franko 1999, 5–8).

The very idea of this man devoting himself to his work in the senate[22] or to his clients and, as though utterly exhausted from his efforts there, snoring through the whole night! The man comes home to me exhausted at night from conducting his business elsewhere! He's plowing[23] someone else's farm while he leaves his own untilled. And on top of that, this pervert is perverting his own son!

Lysidamus, likewise an impotent and ineffective head of his household,[24] proudly celebrates his failure as an advocate for a relative in the forum because of his distraction over Casina: *Cas.* 567–8 *dum asto aduocatus quoidam cognate meo;/quem hercle ego litem adeo perdidisse gaudeo*. In the closing *flagitatio* of *Mercator*, Demipho is called out for his reckless behavior by the neighbours' son, the *adulescens* Eutychus, who generalizes:

uacuom esse istac ted aetate his decebat noxiis.
itidem ut tempus anni, aetatem aliam aliud factum condecet;
nam si istuc ius est, senecta aetate scortari senes,
ubi loci est res summa nostra publica?   (*Merc.* 983a-6)

You should be free of these faults at your age! As is true for the seasons, different behavior suits different age groups; but if it's right for old men to whore about in their advanced age, where does this leave our affairs of state?

Clearly, the infatuated old man's neglect of his domestic and public duties in these plays is represented as bearing serious consequences.

Other characters repeatedly deem the *senex amator* 'utterly worthless' (*nequissimus, Cas.* 497, *Merc.* 304; cf. *Bac.* 1207, *Cas.* 863) and the virtual incarnation of shamelessness and disgrace (*flagitium hominis, Cas.* 155, 552; cf. 160, 876, 903, 937, 991, *As.* 853, *Merc.* 784, *Bac.* 1208). What makes Plautus' infatuated old men self-deluded figures of derision rather than comedians or loveable, carnivalesque transgressors who embody comic freedom, then, is the persistent depiction of them as biologically and aesthetically incongruous spendthrifts and failed figures of authority who compete with their sons for the same lover. The childlike Demipho succinctly illustrates how badly the old men have misconstrued conventional morality:

---

[22] For the traditional association of *senes* and the senate see Parkin 2003, 100–29 and Cokayne 2003, 95–103.
[23] For the common euphemism of plowing for sexual activity see Adams 1982, 154.
[24] Cf. *Cas.* 260, where Cleostrata chides her husband for his excessive concern with their household's female slaves: *mirum ecastor te senecta aetate officium tuom non meminisse*.

> breue iam relicuom uitae spatiumst: quin ego
> uoluptate, uino et amore delectauero.
> nam hanc se bene habere aetatem nimiost aequius.
> adulescens quom sis, tum quom est sanguis integer,   550
> rei tuae quaerundae conuenit operam dare;
> demum igitur quom sis iam senex, tum in otium
> te conloces, dum potest ames: id iam lucrumst
> quod uiuis.   (*Merc.* 547–54)

> Just a brief span of my life remains now. And yes, I'll take delight in pleasure, wine and love, since it's much more appropriate for men in my age group to enjoy ourselves. The right time to focus your efforts on making money is when you're young and your blood is fresh; it's only when you become an old man that you should devote yourself to leisure and find some loving while you can: the fact that you're breathing already counts as profit.

However salubrious Demipho's exhortation may sound to retirees today, he here ridiculously turns conventional Roman thinking on its head.[25] Earlier in the play, Demipho had even comically subverted the traditional opposition between duty and desire when he informs his neighbour of his helplessness before the latter force:

> <humanum errare est>, humanum autem ignoscere est:
> humanum amare est atque id ui optingit deum.
> ne sis me obiurga, hoc non uoluntas me impulit.   (*Merc.* 319–21)

> It's human to make mistakes, and it's human to forgive: it's human to be in love, which happens through the power of the gods. Please don't lecture me: it wasn't my own choice that drove me to this.

Such sententious self-delusion makes the *senex amator* an exceptionally easy target for ridicule, which the *matronae* of the plays further promote. It should be stressed that while the wives express feelings of being disrespected by their husbands (e. g. *Cas.* 189–96, *As.* 871–5, quoted on pp. 219–20 above), they are not depicted as jealous of the objects of their husbands' obsessions or distraught over their husbands' infidelity per se; rather, they work toward restoring domestic stability.

---

25 Contrary to Demipho's assertions here, in the Roman moral tradition (as it is mostly represented by the literary tradition) older men ideally are supposed to devote themselves to non-physical pursuits, exercise the wisdom they have gained from experience, and practice self-control. Loss of sexual appetite generally was considered a concomitant of aging. As an index of how far Demipho is off the mark here, Cicero's Cato (*Sen.* 29) claims that licentiousness *in youth* leads to a weakened body in old age. See further Parkin 2003, 60–79, Cokayne 2003, 91–3, 115–21, and cf. Krause 2004, 176–80. At 255–65 Demipho admits to being in love in his youth, but declares that he did not then experience the lover's insanity that overwhelmed him upon glimpsing Pasicompsa at the harbor.

To turn to examination of the epilogues themselves: first, at the onset of each epilogue, the play's comic society has been repaired, however arbitrarily,[26] as a consequence of the humiliating defeat of the *senex amator*. The old men's unpalatable *flagitium* has just been exposed as a serious threat to family finances and to the family dynamic itself, especially the relationship between fathers and sons within the patriarchal nucleus. How then do the epilogues reinforce this strong 'pro-family values' stance at the conclusion of each *senex amator* play?

A cluster of oppositions informs the three epilogues: pleasure ~ punishment, old ~ young, public ~ private, and self-control ~ self-indulgence. Each epilogue also highlights the theme of finance and the post-play prospects of the acting troupe. Interpretation of the *Casina* epilogue faces the immediate challenge of determining who delivers it:

> spectatores, quod futurumst intus, id memorabimus.
> haec Casina huius reperietur filia esse ex proxumo
> eaque nubet Euthynico nostro erili filio.
> nunc uos aequomst manibus meritis meritam mercedem dare: 1015
> qui faxit, clam uxorem ducet semper scortum quod uolet;
> uerum qui non manibus clare quantum poterit plauserit,
> ei pro scorto supponetur hircus unctus nautea.   (1012–18)

> Spectators, we're here to tell you what will happen inside: this Casina will be found out to be the daughter of the next-door neighbour here, and she'll marry our young master, Euthynicus. Now the proper thing for you all to do is to give us the props we deserve and you owe us. Whoever does will hire the whore he's always wanted without his wife's knowledge. But those of you who don't clap loudly with everything you've got will be supplied with a he-goat soaked in sewage instead of that dream whore of yours.

Is Chalinus, the character who speaks last when he farcically complains of his two 'husbands'' neglect (1009–11), also given the comedy's final words?[27] The plural verb (*memorabimus* 1012) could point to the *grex*, but the reference to 'our younger master' (1014) most probably identifies the speaker as a member of Lysidamus' *familia* – if not Chalinus, perhaps Pardalisca, as Schoell conjectured. It is impossible to decide with certainty, but regardless of the attribution, the epilogue remains consistent with the play's moral point of view. The epi-

---

26 Nelson aptly summarizes the lingering mood of *Casina*: 'The play displays no faith in marital harmony: the plot germinates from the notion of a family riven by competing interests and longings ... These farcical elements ... are calculated to 'damage the family' because they show marriage being used as a front for unfamilial, indeed antifamilial activities ... Illicit affairs are a threat because they may drain the family fortune or threaten the harmony between family members' (1990, 56).
27 As the MSS suggest; so Sharrock 2009, 254.

logue begins by summarizing the recognition scene in Diphilus that Plautus has removed from his adaptation and forecasts the legitimate marriage between Casina and Euthynicus. In so doing it also recalls the prologue's indecent proposal regarding the member of the acting troupe who will *not* play Casina in the comedy; *haec Casina ... nubet* in 1014 resumes the prologist's closing banter about the comedy not actually presenting any *stuprum* (82), a word that identifies the sexual offense a successful Lysidamus would have committed, and is all the more pointed now that the audience knows that Casina is the (free) daughter of a citizen.[28] But after the play, the prologist had asserted, the male actor who might have played Casina will eagerly 'marry' (86 *ultro ibit nuptum*) any audience member with the necessary cash.[29]

The epilogue thus playfully, and even sympathetically, alludes to the troupe's status in everyday life, where an actor's prostitution might well be a stark reality.[30] This final invocation of acting and homoeroticism also calls to mind the violent emasculation and virtual enslavement that Lysidamus has just experienced during his faux-nuptials with Chalinus disguised as Casina (937–1006). The closing threat of the substitution of a sewage-drenched he-goat for a *scortum*,[31] here collapsed with the call for applause, serves the same end by reminding us of Lysidamus' (and Olympio's) punishment by the bristly-bearded (929) Chalinus during their 'honeymoon.' The audience members' decision to applaud is cleverly figured as a *quid pro quo* that is owed to the troupe for their performance (1015), in contrast to Lysidamus' extravagant, asymmetrical spending as a *senex amator* (cf. p. 219 above); they have, after all, performed a *stuprum*-free play. Finally, married, male audience members are encouraged to applaud on the grounds that they will be rewarded with the *scortum* of their dreams. The detail that they will successfully hire a prostitute *clam uxorem*, 'without their wife's knowledge' (1016), is wholly in step with Roman sexual mores; the smart

---

28 For *stuprum* as the *vox propria* for illicit sex with a virgin see Treggiari 1991, 263–4 and Fantham 1991.
29 For jokes with the audience about hiring prostitutes see Moore 1998, 141. In 18th-century British theatre, female actors frequently delivered 'bawdy epilogues' (see further Solomon 2007, in: Ennis/Slagle, 155–78), in which they teased audience members vis-à-vis their own presumed sexual availability, as could also be part of the dynamic between the troupe member and audience here.
30 Actors were automatically placed on the same level of *infamia* (with all its legal and civic disabilities) as prostitutes and pimps in Rome. See further Edwards 1993, 123–31 and McGinn 2003, 65–8 and *passim*.
31 The pejorative *scortum* (used of both male and female sex workers in Plautus), in contrast to *meretrix*, points to short-term sexual liaisons without emotional attachment: see further Adams 1983, 321–7.

(i. e. applauding) spectator, the epilogue suggests, can escape his wife's notice in amorous endeavors by not committing acts of *stuprum*, jeopardizing the family's finances, traditional hierarchy and stability, or bringing public shame upon the household, as the play has just shown Lysidamus so recklessly striving to do. In the spirit of the anecdote about Cato the Elder's observing his friend exiting a brothel on multiple occasions,[32] husbands in the audience would be well-advised to pursue only non-entangling liaisons – in moderation – with prostitutes.

The same motifs shape the epilogue of *Asinaria*, delivered by the *grex* (so indicated by the MSS):

> Hic senex si quid clam uxorem suo animo fecit uolup,
> neque nouom neque mirum fecit nec secus quam alii solent;
> nec quisquam est tam ingenio duro nec tam firmo pectore
> quin ubi quicque occasionis sit sibi faciat bene 945
> nunc si uoltis deprecari huic seni ne uapulet,
> remur impetrari posse, plausum si clarum datis. (*As.* 942-7)

> If this old man has somehow pursued his personal pleasures behind his wife's back, he hasn't done anything strange or unusual, and he isn't any different from other men; no one's so disciplined or strong-willed that he wouldn't take advantage of a situation when it's presented to him. Now if it's your wish to prevent this old man from getting beaten, we believe this can be granted if you offer your loud applause.

The pragmatic caution we saw in *Casina* regarding the prudent pursuit of pleasure by married men is repeated here in *clam uxorem* (942). The epilogue's assertion that Demaenetus' failed erotic adventure is unexceptional and reasonably aspired to by other men has been taken as a palliative to the play's stern moralism. Henderson's comment on the ending is representative: 'The *Asinaria* audience, too, can go home, go to their party, dream the dream of having their cake and eating it' (2006, 215).[33] But as was the case for *Casina*, the audience has just witnessed the devastating defeat of the *senex* by his clever wife Artemona. And whereas Lysidamus' lost walking stick and cloak, the symbols of his prerogatives as *paterfamilias*, are returned to him at the end of *Casina* (1009), Demaenetus begrudgingly is led home by his wife in an obvious reversal of marriage ritual (940-1). Artemona's complete comic triumph is signaled by her promise to exact due revenge with

---

[32] Having initially congratulated the man for pursuing a liaison with a prostitute instead of another man's wife, Cato supposedly says, 'I praised you because I thought you were a visitor here, not a resident' (the latter detail is preserved by the scholiast on Hor. *Sat.* 1.2.31-5; cf. the discussion of Williams 2010, 45-6).

[33] Cf. Moore 1998, 19, who describes the epilogues of *As.* and *Bac.* as 'mock defenses of the plays' amoral plots'.

a kiss after the play, a pledge she makes (903 *osculando ego ulciscar potissimum*) after eavesdropping on her husband's claim that he would rather drink sewer water than kiss his wife (894–5). Just before the epilogue, the prostitute Philaenium, to whom Demaenetus proclaims his kissing policy, reminds us of Artemona's pledge to fight halitosis with halitosis when she mocks the now shamed Demaenetus with the insincere offer of one of her own sweet, youthful kisses (940). While the epilogue magnanimously characterizes Demaenetus' behavior as unexceptional (943–5), it fails to undermine the play's persistent moral indictment of him as a *senex amator*, who, in response to his son's obvious discomfort and suggestion that the old man find some other girl than his beloved Philaenium, churlishly insists, *at ego hanc uolo* ('But I want this one,' 846).[34] The issue of due punishment again is collapsed with the call for applause, when the audience is coaxed into believing that only their enthusiastic support of the play can spare the old man from a beating. Given the Plautine trope that portrays servile actors as subject to corporal punishment for a poor performance,[35] is the disgraced character Demaenetus or the actor playing him in line for flogging if the audience deems the play unsuccessful? The final emphasis of the epilogue thus again highlights the threatening realities that the acting troupe faces.

The epilogue of *Mercator* comes in the form of Eutychus' legal parody, a coda on sexual mores that prevents the now publicly disgraced Demipho (972–1001) from marking the play's end simply by skulking into his house:

> DEM. Eamus intro. EVT Immo dicamus senibus legem censeo 1015
> prius quam abeamus, qua se lege teneant contentique sint.
> annos gnatus sexaginta qui erit, si quem scibimus
> si maritum siue hercle adeo caelibem scortarier,
> cum eo nos hac lege agemus: inscitum arbitrabimur,
> et per nos quidem hercle egebit qui suom prodegerit. 1020
> neu quisquam posthac prohibeto adulescentem filium
> quin amet et scortum ducat, quod bono fiat modo;
> siquis prohibuerit, plus perdet clam <qua>si praehibuerit palam.
> haec adeo ut ex hac nocte primum lex teneat senes.
> bene ualete; atque, adulescentes, haec si uobis lex placet, 1025
> ob senum hercle industriam uos aequom est clare plaudere. (*Merc.* 1015–26)

DEM. Let's go inside. EVT No, in my considered opinion we should inform the old men about a law before we leave the stage, a law they should respect and not question. We shall apply this law to any man sixty years old that we see whoring around, whether

---

34 Artemona becomes the play's moral center as she frames Demaenetus' crass behavior as a form of corrupting his son (851–3, 933–4).
35 Cf. n. 6 above.

he's married or not married, damn it! We shall adjudge him to be foolish, and as it lies within our power, the person who has squandered his means damn sure will find himself in poverty. Henceforth let no one prevent his young son from hiring and loving a whore, provided this is done in moderation. If someone does so prevent his son, he shall suffer greater losses in private than if he had openly funded this enterprise. Let this law moreover become binding for old men from this night forward. Farewell! And you, young men, if this law meets with your satisfaction, you damn well better clap loudly as payment for the old men's efforts.

The law is to take effect 'from this night forward' (1024), i. e. in the immediately post-dramatic world. This age-specific (1017) and all-inclusive (its applicability extends to unmarried as well as married old men, 1018) comic law purports to punish any *senex amator* with financial loss, which is to come about not by legal penalty but through the offender's own prodigality (1020). For the good of family unity, and here reinforcing the now resolved conflict between father and son as rivals of the same prostitute, the law goes on to advocate qualified indulgence of sons in their amorous affairs: fathers are to finance their sons' pursuit of prostitutes, provided this is done in moderation (1022). Needless for the law to state explicitly, the demand for fiscal moderation in amorous affairs is all the stronger for old men. Fathers found not to be in compliance with the new law again are fantastically threatened with private financial losses (1023).

And finally, as part of the call for loud applause, the young men in the audience are asked to compensate the old men for their *industria* (1026). At a first reading *senum* here seems to indicate Demipho and Lysimachus, who with his son Eutychus has just castigated Demipho for his bad behavior. But it more pointedly refers to the actors playing the two geriatric neighbours, in that neither *senex* in the play is distinguished by his diligence/industry. Such a closing metacomic flourish does not merge the identities of the characters and actors, but primarily credits the histrionic efforts of the latter in performing their roles.[36] As is the case for *Cas.* and *As.*, the epilogue asks the audience to consider the actors' post-comic experience. Its brilliant mock-legal prescriptions do not celebrate comic and sexual freedom, unless one looks for these in the limited license granted the young men directly addressed (1021–2) in the epilogue's final sentence.[37] The ultimate aim of the proposed law is to

---

[36] This could be made obvious in performance by having the actors playing the old men make an appropriate gesture or even remove their masks, though there is no clear evidence for this in Roman comedy.

[37] Thus Sharrock 2009, 267: 'Eutychus' law amounts to a comic programme. 'So, *adulescentes*, clap if you want more comedies.' No doubt anyone might, at least vicariously, identify as an *adulescens* for the purposes of comic appreciation'. Vóyeurism and vicarious experience prob-

discourage old men like Demipho from participating in sexual contests with their sons.

Bacchides, although it is a doubles comedy featuring a remarkably accomplished slave (Chrysalus), merits consideration here because its epilogue, thought to be delivered by the *grex*,[38] shows generic affinities with those of *As.*, *Cas.*, and *Merc.*:

> Hi senes nisi fuissent nihi ii iam inde ab adulescentia,
> non hodie hoc tantum flagitium facerent canis capitibus;
> neque adeo haec faceremus, ni antehac uidissemus fieri,
> ut apud lenones riuales filiis fierent patres.   1210
> spectatores, uos ualere uolumus et clare applaudere.   (*Bac.* 1207–11)

> If these old men hadn't already been worthless dating all the way back to their younger days, they wouldn't be behaving so disgracefully today as graybeards; and we certainly wouldn't be putting on this play if we hadn't previously seen fathers vying with their sons for the same woman in brothels. Spectators, we wish you well and want you to clap loudly.

Bacchides cannot be categorized as a *senex amator* play, as this theme figures only in the plays' closing lines when the old men Nicobulus and Philoxenus are lured into the two Bacchises' brothel. Employing semiotic shorthand, however, the epilogue alludes to fully articulated *senex amator* plays, such as the three discussed here. It claims that the two graybeards have a history of incurring *flagitium* by vying with their sons for the same prostitutes, here framed as an unremarkable tendency of fathers that keeps comic theater companies busy representing their foolish behavior (1209–10). The sisters are obviously manipulating the old men, whom they characterize as sheep in an extended conceit (1120–48). Regarding the prospect of sex with a *senex*, one Bacchis tells her sister, 'it's hideous to embrace death' (1152); that sister in turn is given the play's last words (i. e. before the epilogue) when she sums up the old men's predicament: 'these very men who sought to entrap their sons have been caught up in our charms' (1206). The implication of the epilogue need not be stated: a *palliata* audience conversant with the grammar of *senex amator* plays knows that this cannot end well for the lusty and deluded old men.[39]

---

lematically exist only in the mind of the beholder, but there is no nod here to encourage men in the audience to emulate the rebuked Demipho.

38 See further Barsby 1986, 188–9.

39 Otherwise Sharrock 2009, 279: 'Some plays, after all, actually show us their parties. In doing so, they not only create the opportunity for a great deal of entertaining horseplay, but also work on us (as the Bacchises work on the *senes*), enticing us – vicariously allowing us – to join in'.

While a *senex amator*'s aspirations may at best be understood as predictable human folly, these epilogues confirm that Plautine comedy unceremoniously faults a dirty old man for trying. As codas to what are among the most conservative of Plautus' plays, the epilogues offer the old men no redemption but in the end support the cause of the *matronae*, whose comic triumphs they affirm. The moral outlook of the epilogues is consistent with that of the plays, with the themes of moderate spending and moderated behavior prevailing. If there is irony in these epilogues, it lies in persistent doubts about the prospects of harmonious relations in a family whose head is a *senex amator*. None of the plays leaves us with a secure sense that all will end well in the post-comic household – nor for the acting troupe.

Bibliography

Adams, J. N. (1982), *The Latin Sexual Vocabulary*, Baltimore.
_____ (1983), 'Words for 'Prostitute' in Latin', *Rheinisches Museum für Philologie* 126, 321–58.
Augoustakis, A. (2008), 'Castrate the He-Goat! Overpowering the *paterfamilias* in Plautus' *Mercator*', *Scholia* n. s. 17, 37–48.
Barsby, J. (1986), *Plautus: Bacchides*, Warminster.
Christenson, D. M. (2000), *Plautus: Amphitruo*, Cambridge.
Cody, J. M. (1976), 'The *Senex Amator* in Plautus' *Casina*', *Hermes* 104, 453–76.
Cokayne, K. (2003), *Experiencing Old Age in Ancient Rome*, London and New York.
Dixon, S. (1992), *The Roman Family*, Baltimore and London.
Edwards, C. (1993), *The Politics of Immorality in Ancient Rome*, Cambridge.
Ennis, D. J./Slagle, J. B. (2007), (eds.), *Prologues, Epilogues, Curtain-Raisers, and Afterpieces: The Rest of the Eighteenth-Century London Stage*, Newark, DE.
Fantham, E. (1991), '*Stuprum*: Public Attitudes and Penalties for Sexual Offences in Republican Rome', *Echos du Monde Classique* n. s. 10, 267–91.
Franko, G. F. (1999), 'Imagery and Names in Plautus' *Casina*', *Classical Journal* 95, 1–17.
Henderson, J. (2006), *Plautus, Asinaria: The One about the Asses*, Madison.
Kraus, A. N. (2004), 'Untaming the Shrew: Marriage, Morality and Plautine Comedy', PhD diss., University of Texas at Austin.
Manuwald, G. (2011), *Roman Republican Theatre*, Cambridge.
Maurice, L. (2007), 'Plautus' Rebellious Sons: the Whole Story?', in: T. Baier (ed.), *Generationenkonflikte auf der Bühne*, Tübingen, 147–60.
McGinn, T. (1998), *Prostitution, Sexuality, and the Law in Ancient Rome*, Oxford and New York.
Moore, T. J. (1998), *The Theater of Plautus: Playing to the Audience*, Austin.
Nelson, T. G. A. (1990), *Comedy: An Introduction to Comedy in Literature, Drama, and Cinema*. Oxford and New York.
Parkin, T. G. (2003), *Old Age in the Roman World: A Cultural and Social History*, Baltimore and London.

Rei, A. (1998), 'Villains, Wives, and Slaves in the Comedies of Plautus', in: S. R. Joshel/
    S. Murnaghan (eds.), *Women and Slaves in Greco-Roman Culture: Differential Equations*,
    London and New York, 92–108.
Richlin, A. (2014), 'Talking to Slaves in the Plautine Audience', *Classical Antiquity* 33, 174–226.
Ryder, K. C. (1984), 'The *Senex Amator* in Plautus', *Greece and Rome* 2nd ser. 31, 181–9.
Segal, E. (1987), *Roman Laughter*, Oxford and New York, 2nd edn.
Sharrock, A. (2009), *Reading Roman Comedy: Poetics and Playfulness in Plautus and Terence*,
    Cambridge.
Slater, N. W. (2000), *Plautus in Performance: The Theatre of the Mind*, Amsterdam.
Solomon, D. (2007), 'Tragic Play, *Bawdy* Epilogue?', in: Ennis/Slagle, 155–78.
Tatum, J. (1983), *Plautus: The Darker Comedies*, Baltimore and London.
Williams, C. A. (2010), *Roman Homosexuality*, Oxford and New York, 2nd edn.

T. H. M. Gellar-Goad
Plautus' *Curculio* and the Case of the Pious Pimp

> it's hard for a pimp
> so I'm prayin' and I'm hopin' to God I don't slip
> – Three 6 Mafia, 'Hard Out There for a Pimp'

The *leno*, the pimp or sex-slaver, is a stock villain in the plays of Plautus. The *leno* is a man of ill will, execrable morals, and exaggerated viciousness. In life, too, pimps were the recipients of Roman hostility.[1] Duckworth describes comic pimps as 'characterized by greed and accused of impiety, perjury, faithlessness, cruelty, and inhumanity ... a conventional type of grotesque comic character who is made the victim of deception and the butt of ridicule.'[2] The *leno* of Plautus' *Curculio*, Cappadox, has generally been understood as conforming to this stock type. Welsh refers to Cappadox as 'the reviled *leno*' and Moore comments that, when his affairs take a turn for the worse, 'il ruffiano è un *periurus* e sta ricevendo ciò che si merita.'[3] Marshall calls him 'a disgustingly bloated, morally reprehensible villain who is vain about his appearance,' Fontaine comments that he is 'somewhat effeminate,' and Perna points out the humor generated from his illness with the expression 'la buffa macchietta del lenone malato e superstizioso.'[4]

'Plautus' pimps stand out as individuals,'[5] however, and scholars have identified two unusual characteristics about Cappadox, in addition to his hypochondria. The pimp displays a marked reluctance to perjure himself in the play.[6] Moreover, he shows a 'soft spot' for Planesium, a girl he holds in slavery as a *meretrix*

---

[1] McGinn remarks that pimps experienced 'a series of civic and legal disabilities whose function was to place practitioners outside the pale of the community of honor' (2003, 341), but Arnold 1998, 73–85, explores the evidence for the supposed *infamia* of pimps in Rome, and points out that 'the legal concept of *infamia* may not formally have been developed by the time of Plautus and Terence' (1998, 76–7). On the difficulty of translating Latin terms for Roman sex-slavery into English, see Arnold 1998, 11–3, and Witzke 2015.
[2] Duckworth 1994 [1952], 262.
[3] Welsh 2005, 308; Moore 2005, 30.
[4] Marshall 2006, 142; Fontaine 2010, 118, and compare the pimp Dordalus in *Persa*, called a *cinaedus* by the play's *seruus callidus* (line 8); and Perna 1955, 105. Costas Panayotakis has suggested to me that Cappadox's malady might be reflected in his dance or gesture. Gratwick 1969, 474 n. 1, sees the illness as an aspect of a sympathetic portrayal of the pimp; see *contra* Arnold 1998, 107 and 214.
[5] Marshall 2006, 140; see *contra* Dumont 2011, 110: 'Le *leno* n'est jamais paradoxal: il personifie le mal ou du moins la luxure, la cupidité et la mauvaise foi.'
[6] Cappadox's hypochondria: Richlin 2005, 60. His reluctance to perjure himself: see, e.g., Fantham 1965, 91.

at the beginning of the play.⁷ Paratore christens Cappadox 'il meno spregevole fra i personaggi della sua categoria che appaiono sulle scene plautine.'⁸

Yet the extent to which Cappadox's character is unusual for a *leno* has not been fully explored, particularly when it comes to his religious activity at the onstage shrine of Aesculapius. Each of the other Plautine pimps can be considered 'a cheat, a perjurer, a rascal, a plague of gods and men,'⁹ even on occasion extremely impious or sacrilegious. Cappadox by contrast is surprisingly pious. And pious sacrifice is a positive characteristic in *comoedia palliata*; characters who are regularly pious receive rewards from the gods.¹⁰ Attention to sacrifice and ritual imagery in the play calls for modification of the conventional view of Cappadox as the standard debased comic villain. In *Curculio*, Plautus presents the audience with a kind of oxymoron within the genre – a pious pimp, a character whose religiosity mitigates his criminal behavior and even makes him a somewhat more sympathetic character than might be suggested by his stock type.

Impious pimps and sacrifice: Labrax and Lycus, Dordalus and Ballio

In the plays of Plautus, there is a modest connection between pimps and sacrificial ritual.¹¹ Labrax in *Rudens*, an archetypal example of an impious pimp, 'is repeatedly referred to throughout the play as *scelestus, impius, legirupa, peiiurus* ... This is of course standard Plautine language for a *leno*.'¹² At the beginning of the play we learn he has made fake plans with the young lover for a post-sacrifice lunch (56–62), when in fact he is making an ill-fated getaway on the sea. Labrax later threatens to burn down the shrine of Venus where the young women he holds captive take refuge. In response, the old man Daemones threatens to set

---

7 See, e. g., Duckworth 1994 [1952], 263. The term 'soft spot' is from Marshall 2006, 141–2. According to Wright 1993, 48, 'Cappadox is a relatively harmless character.'
8 Paratore 2003, 93 = 1958, 13.
9 Duckworth 1994 [1952], 314.
10 For instance, the Lar Familiaris of *Aulularia*, acting as divine prologue, foretells a dowered marriage to the *uirgo* Phaedria in reward for her daily sacrifices to him (23–33); and Palaestra the *uirgo* of *Rudens*, who behaves piously throughout the play, receives aid from Arcturus, the play's moralizing divine prologue (67–9). For the theatrical effects of sacrifice in Plautus and Terence, see Dunsch 2009 and Gellar-Goad 2011/2012 and 2013.
11 Cf. Dumont 2011, 110: 'On taxerait à bon droit les *lenones* d'impiété et pourtant certains parmi eux donnent des signes de religiosité.'
12 Hanson 1959, 94.

Labrax himself on fire, roast him halfway through (*ambustulatum*), and feed him to some large birds (761–70). A combination here of sacrifice-style cooking and traditional epic defilement of a corpse by carrion feeders constitutes an assertion by Daemones of a position of theatrical and social power over the pimp.

Near the end of the play, Labrax calls upon the gods for assistance before entering into a verbal confrontation with Daemones' *seruus* Gripus over the money chest lost in Labrax's shipwreck: 'c'mon, gods, help me out!' (*di, quaeso, subuenite*, 1298). His prayer, if we can call it such, is unadorned, direct, and without any material offering.[13] The gods do not seem to be on Labrax's side, for Gripus does not budge until the pimp has promised him an entire talent (an enormous sum of money in Roman comedy) for the return of the luggage. At the end of this conversation, Gripus makes Labrax swear an oath by the altar of Venus (1343–9). But the pimp then immediately declares in an aside to the audience his intention to perjure himself (1353–5)! Hanson suggests Labrax's behavior 'represent[s] the depths of moral degradation, the extreme of *impietas*,' while Tolliver suggests that Labrax's religious misconduct makes him 'not a comic character.'[14] I argue rather that Labrax is an especially comic, larger than life villain. Not only do his duplicity and open acknowledgement of his wicked intent come out as funny on stage, but also his lack of proper respect for religion serves as another way to turn the audience against him.

The second sacrificing pimp is Lycus of *Poenulus*.[15] He enters the stage with a twofold complaint: first, that he has been unable to make a successful sacrifice, and second that his lack of success has been a misleading omen, because he has not faced any misfortune, and in fact has gained four *minae* since his sacrifice attempt.[16] If he was going to get (not lose) some cash, the shortsighted pimp says, the gods should not have rejected his sacrifice, since doing so generally represents an ominous sign for the future. This experience with unsuccessful sacrifice has soured Lycus towards religious ritual, as evident in the way he expresses his incredulity at the big boasts of the play's *miles gloriosus*:

---

13 It even includes the imperatival intensifier *quaeso*, characteristic of male speech in Roman comedy (cf. Adams 1984, 55–66) that adds a sense of urgency and suggests that Labrax thinks he is on a footing equal or superior to his addressee. Dumont 2011, 113, describes this scene and each subsequent appearance of Labrax as a kind of encore for the pimp's actor.
14 Hanson 1959, 95; Tolliver 1952, 54. By contrast, Dumont 2011, 109, describes the pimp as 'un des vecteurs du comique.'
15 Arnold 1998, 203 n. 166, refers to 'the sacrificial Leitmotif' in *Poenulus*; see also Gratwick 1969, 56 and 67–8.
16 *Poenulus* 449–67, discussed at Tolliver 1952, 53–4.

> si hercle istuc umquam factum est, tum me Iuppiter
> faciat ut semper sacruficem nec umquam litem. (*Poenulus* 488–9)

> Hell, if that crap has ever actually happened, then may
> Jupiter make me always sacrifice ... and never succeed!

Here his impiety is on stark display, as he treats an act of ritual devotion to the gods with cynical, flippant disdain. Implicit in his comments is his awareness of the expense imposed on him by his unsuccessful sacrifices. Sacrifice – the fundamental religious act in Graeco-Roman society – has become for Lycus not only a punchline, but even a kind of Sisyphean punishment, and of course a financial liability.[17]

Lycus expresses his disgust with ritual again later in the play, when he repeats his astonishment that failure at the altar has been followed by success in the world of business:

> suspendant omnes nunciam se haruspices
> quam ego illis posthac quod loquantur creduam,
> qui in re diuina dudum dicebant mihi
> malum damnumque maximum portendier:
> is explicaui meam rem postilla lucro. (*Poenulus* 746–50)

> All *haruspices*[18] can go and hang themselves right this minute!
> Why should I believe what they're saying ever again, when
> they were telling me just now at my sacrifice that something bad
> and a huge loss were in store for me – and yet since then
> I've added to my net worth with a profit from this [cash from another character]!

This execration reflects Lycus' impiety. Likewise, his comments reflect his pimpish preoccupation with money: the interpreters' portents foretold financial loss, and yet Lycus has obtained profit. Since his finances are, for the moment, on the rise, Lycus rejects the credibility of these ritual officials. Indeed, Lycus has even

---

[17] Furthermore, Lycus has previously indicated that he prevented the offering of meat from his prior unsuccessful sacrifice, and even called Venus 'undeserving':

> quoniam litare nequeo, abii illim ilico
> iratus, uotui exta prosicarier;
> neque ea poricere uolui, quoniam non bona
> haruspex dixit: deam esse indignam credidi. (*Poenulus* 455–6b)

> Since I couldn't get a successful sacrifice, I went away right away
> angry as hell, and I prevented the guts from being cut up,
> and I didn't want 'em offered up, 'cause the *haruspex* said
> they weren't good – and I figured the goddess was undeserving.

[18] On *haruspices* in Plautus, see Slater 2000, 160 and n. 29, and Traill 2004, 124–5.

previously dismissed the credibility of the *haruspex* in terms of money, by saying that he is not worth half a drachma (*non homo trioboli*, 463).

Finally, Syncerastus, enslaved to Lycus, comes onstage carrying Lycus' sacrificial vessels and reiterates how Lycus could not obtain an auspicious sacrifice, but the girls held captive as *meretrices* by Lycus did obtain one (847–50, cf. 1174, 1205). Plautus here employs characterization through sacrifice as a theatrical device. The offerings of the girls – who will turn out to be freeborn – are accepted, while those of the corrupt pimp Lycus are not. The moral, innocent characters succeed with their sacrifices, whereas the degenerate, sacrilegious character finds his sacrificial authority denied by the goddess herself. In the end, Lycus loses possession of the girls and is practically hauled to court by their free (Carthaginian) father.

There is thus a pattern in the sacrificial capacity of Plautus' *lenones*. Labrax and Lycus are comic villains *par excellence*, and their villainy is reflected in their troubles with sacrifice. Labrax abandons plans of sharing a sacrificial meal with the young lover and gets shipwrecked, while Lycus' offerings go unaccepted by Venus. In each, we see a characteristically pimp-like approach to religion: Labrax uses Venus as a witness to an oath that he intends to break and threatens to burn down her shrine, while Lycus plans to cheat her out of sacrificial offerings.[19] In the realm of religion as in other areas of life, the *leno* will twist and abuse social practices for his own profit or benefit.

Hartkamp suggests that Dordalus, the pimp of *Persa*, is the subject of 'ritual' mockery as an important theme of the play, and that he only takes on stock vices of a *leno* as a 'ritueller Bestandteil des Spiels.'[20] The only substantial evidence that Hartkamp provides for such a 'ritual' function, however, is a set of creative profanities hurled at the pimp, and I do not believe that anti-pimp rhetoric alone is sufficient basis for associating actual Roman ritual with Dordalus in this play. Nevertheless, although Dordalus neither plays a ritual role nor conducts sacrifice, he does from time to time call upon the gods. His main interest in doing so, though, is usually to ask for misfortune to befall other characters.[21]

Similarly, Ballio the superpimp of *Pseudolus* does not offer sacrifice, but he (jokingly) accepts the young lover's assignation to him of a position of power greater than Jupiter, and tries (unsuccessfully) to outdo the play's eponymous

---

19 *Poenulus* 459–62, translated and discussed below.
20 Hartkamp 2001, 132, cf. 114–5.
21 E.g., *di faciant ut id bibatis quod uos numquam transeat*, 'may the gods grant that you drink something that you'll never ... get out of your system!' (*Persa* 823); *di deaeque et te et geminum fratrem excrucient*, 'may the gods and the goddesses provide both you and your [fake] twin with ... torture!' (831).

seruus callidus in the use of dueling sacrificial imagery (326–35). Ballio even claims that his true *pietas* is profit, and indicates a hypothetical willingness to interrupt a sacrifice that he himself might be conducting in order to make some money (265–8). Ballio embraces his stock type's irreligiousness and makes explicit the readiness of the *leno* to commit sacrilege for profit.

Plautus' characterization of pimps other than Cappadox is uniform when it comes to religion.[22] In *Rudens*, the pimp Labrax is patently and concretely sacrilegious. Lycus in *Poenulus* seems to have undertaken his initial sacrifices with pious intentions; but the fact that he illegally holds freeborn girls as enslaved prostitutes overrides his devout intent, and his sacrifice fails. Dordalus makes malevolent prayers in *Persa*, while Ballio in *Pseudolus* replaces respect for the gods with *pietas* toward monetary gain alone. Pimps, therefore, are characterized as impious and even sacrilegious, because of their use of sacrifice, ritual imagery, and religious language on stage, in addition to their generic stereotype.

Cappadox: a different brand of pimp

Cappadox in *Curculio*, on the other hand, makes a significant break with this stock definition of pimps as sacrilegious; he appears to be pious and to conduct several successful sacrifices. Ill at the beginning of the play, he has been incubating in the shrine of Aesculapius in search of a cure, and he repeatedly undertakes acts of devotion at the onstage shrine.[23] Unlike other Plautine pimps whose first appearances showcase villainous bombast, Cappadox's opening scene centers on the extreme duress and disfigurement caused by his illness – far from supervillain material.[24] Cappadox's multiple consultations and offerings to Aesculapius are noteworthy: 'Cappadox den Tempel nicht zu einer einmaligen Konsultation aufsucht, sondern praktisch in ihm wohnt.'[25]

After successfully selling Planesium, whom he holds in slavery, Cappadox decides to perform a sacrifice (532, *nunc rei diuinae operam dabo*, 'now I'm going

---

22 Dumont 2011, 111, suggests that the other pimps' impiety is incomparable to the extremities of Labrax': 'Aucun des autres *lenones* de la *palliata*, même le terrible Ballion, ne se montre sacrilège avec autant de violence.'
23 On the question of the practice of *incubatio* in the Roman west, see Renberg 2006.
24 On the importance of first appearances, see Arnold 1998, 188: 'the first impressions created by any dramatic figure are particularly programmatic for interpreting the character … Plautus therefore paid particular attention to the impact created by his *lenones* in these initial scenes, which are a reference point for the characterisation of the *leno* in the rest of the play.'
25 Lefèvre 1991, 103–4.

to turn my attention to a sacrifice') and exits into the shrine. When he returns, likely wearing a wreath as a symbol of his ritual activity,[26] Cappadox gives indications that the sacrifice went well: 'I believe that the gods are not angry at those to whom they are favorable/propitious' (*quoi homini di sunt propitii, ei non esse iratos puto*, 557). The meaning here is that the gods indicate their disposition towards individuals by granting successful sacrifices (by being *propitius*) or by refusing them.[27] Cappadox does not say, in connection with this declaration, that he has had an unsuccessful sacrifice, but in fact mentions his completion of the act, an indication for the audience to understand that the rite was successful.[28]

Cappadox's *ancilla* Leaena, too, is associated with sacrifice, and as such her presence in Cappadox's household may enhance the sense of religiosity attached to the pimp in this play. The young lover Phaedromus makes a libation of wine to her (evidently she, in accordance with a stereotypical trait of elderly *ancillae*, is an alcoholic) in order to gain access to his beloved (80–92), and Leaena herself pours a parodically tiny libation to Venus from the libation she has received, though not without complaining about the loss of a few drops of her precious wine rations.[29] Leaena's song is central to the humor of the scene;[30] and the libation bowl as a prop is arguably central to *Curculio* as a whole.[31]

In fact, Ketterer suggests, Leaena essentially becomes a 'priestess' in this scenario.[32] Her monody at *Curculio* 96–109 is likened by Ludwig to 'einer magischen Beschwörung' and to 'hymnischer Preis.'[33] The hymnic praise, when combined with the libation made to Leaena, could hint at a (parodic) apotheosis for

---

26 Arnold 1998, 100, points out that Greek terracotta figurines of pimps frequently depict them in wreaths. For a description of the facial features of the stock mask of the πορνοβοσκός, see Pollux, *Onomastikon* 4.145.
27 *Pace* Wright 1993, 77, who calls this line 'tautological' and 'fatuous.' Compare *Curculio* 531, and *Persa* 470 (*quoi homini di propitii sunt, aliquid obiciunt lucri*, with Arnold 1998, 291 n. 166).
28 'I've made a sacrifice,' *rem diuinam feci*, 558. In Plautus (and Menander), sacrifice should be considered unsuccessful only if it is explicitly described so, as with Lycus' failed sacrifice in *Poenulus*.
29 *Curculio* 125–7: Leaena pours the libation at the altar to Venus directly in front of Cappadox's house, cf. Saunders 1911, 100–1. Frangoulidis 2013 reads this scene as an inversion of the standard Greek paraclausithyron.
30 Marshall 2006, 72.
31 Ketterer 1986, 197–200: 'the wine bowl ... tell[s] us something about the characters by the reactions which [it] elicit[s] from the human actors ... [T]he movement of the wine bowl marks a significant change of alliance' as Leaena goes from Cappadox's trusted doorkeeper to facilitator of Planesium's relationship with Phaedromus.
32 Ketterer 1986, 200.
33 Ludwig 1967, 188 and 189.

her.³⁴ These hints are reinforced by Phaedromus' vow – in the ritual sense of the term – to Leaena, if she helps him:

> tibine ego, si fidem seruas mecum, uineam pro aurea statua statuam
> quae tuo gutturi sit monumentum.   (*Curculio* 139–40)³⁵
>
> If you keep faith with me, I'll sure set up for you a vine-y – not a gold – statue,
> to be a monument to your … gullet!

The young lover mocks the old drunk's wine-madness, but he also puts himself in the position of a human subject making an expensive ritual offering to a divinity. In this way he runs parallel to the young lover of *Asinaria*, who is told by his *serui callidi* to set up a statue and sacrifice to them as the divine embodiment of his Salus/*salus* and Fortuna/*fortuna* (712–6). Leaena, then, is analogous to these *serui callidi*, and through religious imagery this member of the pimp's household takes on a symbolic position of authority that reflects her theatrical power over access to Phaedromus' beloved, who is shut up in Cappadox's house.

Furthermore, Cappadox seeks out a dream consultation, a *coniectura*.³⁶ At the recommendation of the *seruus* Palinurus, the pimp consults (of all people!) the cook³⁷ and describes his dream, wherein Aesculapius shunned him (260–3). The cook responds that all the gods must be, in agreement, dissatisfied with the pimp (263–4), and then cracks a joke that Cappadox should be incubating at the temple of Jupiter, god of oaths (265–7). This recommendation is meant by the cook to be taken 'ironically, since a *leno*, according to comic convention, is always *peiiurus*.'³⁸ But Cappadox does not in fact consider himself *peiiurus*, and his response, likewise a joke, seems directed at other pimps, not himself:

> siquidem incubare uelint qui peiierauerint,
> locu' non praeberi potis est in Capitolio.   (*Curculio* 268–9)
>
> Well if everyone who's committed perjury wanted to incubate,
> they couldn't all fit on the Capitoline.

---

34 *Pace* Moore 2005, 13–9, who argues that the doors of Cappadox's household, not Leaena, are the subject of deification. For a humorous deification of the title character of Plautus' *Epidicus*, see Gellar-Goad 2011/2012. Schiesaro (pp. 25–41) suggests that Leaena is a bacchant of sorts, with her use of words such as *Liber*, *euax*, and *persequar*; see also Dutsch 2008, 151.
35 Numbered 140–140b by Lanciotti 2008; discussed at Moore 2005, 25–6.
36 *Curculio* 246–73, with Traill 2004, 123–4. Harris 2009, 166, notes that 'Plautus' characters assume that anyone can learn to interpret dreams, and also that dreams are commonly nonsense.'
37 On the role of the cook in this play, see, e. g., Lowe 1985, 95–9.
38 Wright 1993, 63.

With this stock-type punchline Cappadox dismisses the cook-oneirologist's initial, mocking suggestion.³⁹ I suggest that Cappadox does so here, and does not object to anti-pimp rhetoric elsewhere in the play, because of his own clear conscience when it comes to perjury. Since the pimp does not admit to being *peiiurus*, an act of ritual devotion to the oathkeeper god Jupiter is unnecessary.

After this banter, the cook offers his real solution to the dream's portent:

> pacem ab Aesculapio
> petas, ne forte tibi eueniat magnum malum,
> quod in quiete tibi portentumst.   (*Curculio* 270–2)

> You should make peace with Aesculapius
> so as to avoid the chance of the great evil
> portended in your sleep.

Making peace with Aesculapius will entail sacrifice, an offering of appeasement such as the pimp Lycus has unsuccessfully endeavored to make at the beginning of *Poenulus*. Cappadox immediately responds with both gratitude (*bene facis*, 'you're doing right by me,' 272) and acceptance of his task (*ibo atque orabo*, 'I'll go and beseech him,' 273). The pimp heads into the shrine of Aesculapius forthwith, to perform his propitiation of the god.⁴⁰

---

39 The reference to the Capitoline also, we should note, calls attention to the Roman-ness of the matter at hand, the *coniectura*, despite the ostensible Greek setting and Greek god (cf. the Roman Forum-focused monologue of the Choragus at *Curculio* 462–86, with Moore 1991 and Zwierlein 1990, 260–5). On the stock humor here, cf. Arnold 1998, 214: 'these insults are best regarded as being aimed at the 'stereotype' of the *leno*, of which Cappadox is an (admittedly mild) example.'
40 Harris 2009, 178, calls the dream 'clearly a bad sign' for Cappadox (a character 'due for discomfiture at the end of the play').

An anonymous reader adduces Theophrastus' portrayal of the 'superstitious man' (ὁ δεισιδαίμων, *Characters* 16): 'whenever he has a dream he heads to the dream-interpreters, to the prophets, to the bird-watchers, to ask to which of the gods or goddesses he must pray' (ὅταν ἐνύπνιον ἴδῃ, πορεύεσθαι πρὸς τοὺς ὀνειρκρίτας, πρὸς τοὺς μάντεις, πρὸς τοὺς ὀρνιθοσκόπους, ἐρωτήσων τίνι θεῶν ἢ θεᾷ προσεύχεσθαι δεῖ). This stereotype is indeed one element of the humor in Cappadox's character, but the parallel is not perfect, since the pimp already knows which god he is to pray to and is seeking specific directives on another clearly meaningful, divinely inspired dream (nor does he undertake any of the gamut of other preposterous activities of Theophrastus' δεισιδαίμων). Moreover, Cappadox's interest in the meaning of dreams is in fact an integral component of the process of incubation at the shrine of Aesculapius. What actually is most ridiculous about this scene is Cappadox's credulity in the cook's ability to undertake a dream-interpretation, and the cook's readiness to do so.

Cappadox exhibits the most religious activity of any character in *Curculio*, and although his first incubation at the shrine does not succeed in alleviating his liver problem (216–22), he gives no indication either of ritual failure or of hepatic discomfort upon his next appearance onstage after the *coniectura*. Instead he greets the banker Lyco with a friendly and common religious salutation (*di te ament*, 455). His post-*coniectura* round of sacrifice, I suggest, has been successful, and his ailment has been eased; perhaps the character's costuming has been adjusted to reflect a reduction in his midsection's swelling, so that he is no longer a 'disgustingly bloated' figure. Cappadox's status is remarkable: he is a Plautine pimp who has both piously and properly performed religious ritual – and that ritual has met with acceptance by the god.

Cappadox and perjury

Cappadox's piety informs two other unusual aspects of his character, namely his position on perjury and his rapport with the girl he holds in slavery, Planesium. First, Cappadox seems concerned during most of the play with fulfilling not only duties to the gods, but also duties towards men, in the form of his oaths.[41] When the banker tells the pimp to keep his mind on his money and sell Planesium to the buyer at hand (*argentum accipias, cum illo mittas uirginem*, 'take the money, send the girl away with him,' 457), Cappadox brings up his contractual obligation to another buyer, the soldier: 'what about the fact that I've taken an oath?' (458, *quid quod iuratus sum?*). Likewise, in later conversation with the soldier, Cappadox indicates that he believes that he has fulfilled his oathbound duty: 'I've done what I swore to.'[42] Cappadox acknowledges his agreements to Curculio and the banker (492–4). Furthermore, his deal with the banker, to return the sale price of Planesium if someone successfully claims that she is freeborn,[43] suggests that Cappadox holds a certain respect for the laws of the land – even if he only agrees to this stipulation because he is certain it does not in this case apply to him.

---

41 Fantham 1965, 92, describes him as 'considerably less ruthless than most pimps in Roman comedy' and points out his 'scruples about perjuring himself.'
42 *Curculio* 566: *quod fui iuratus feci*, although at this point Cappadox does appear, in the soldier's eyes, to be committing perjury by cheating him out of his rightful purchase of Planesium, on which see Zwierlein 1990, 259.
43 'If any person should declare this woman free for reasons of freeborn status, all of the money is to be returned to me' (*si quisquam hanc liberali / caussa manu adsereret, mihi omne argentum redditum eiri*, 490–1 ≈ 709–10).

Unlike other pimps, when Cappadox is alone onstage – information provided in a soliloquy is by convention truthful, even factual – he does not boast about perjury or swindling. Instead, though mostly focused on his profit, he actually proclaims his desire to follow up on a well-conducted business transaction with a sacrificial ritual: 'since I've done a good job managing the business, I want to make a supplication in the shrine here,' *quando bene gessi rem, uolo hic in fano supplicare* (527). Moore reads this line as 'straordinariamente ironico,'[44] but most extraordinary here are the honest intentions of a religiously devout character, a stark contrast with the religious contents of soliloquies by other Plautine pimps.

Ballio of *Pseudolus* uses his time alone onstage to say that he would rather commit myriad acts of perjury than once fall prey to the *seruus callidus* (1057–8). Labrax tells the audience of his plans to forswear an oath made to Venus (1353–5). Most remarkably, in *Poenulus*, Lycus calls down a curse upon any pimp who hereafter sacrifices to Venus:

> di illum infelicent omnes qui post hunc diem
> leno ullam Veneri umquam immolarit hostiam
> quiue ullum turis granum sacruficauerit. (*Poenulus* 449–51)

> May all the gods curse any pimp who after today
> ever offers any victim to Venus
> or even sacrifices a single grain of incense!

Lycus' explanation for this bold statement is that Venus was not content with his sacrifices (458). So the pimp feels justified in ignoring proper ritual procedures – namely, attempting renewed offerings until a successful sacrifice is achieved, or else giving up the business for which successful sacrifice cannot be obtained – and even trying to form a boycott of Venus' religious rites. As Lycus says about his own ritual activity:

> ego pausam feci. sic ago, sic me decet.
> ego faxo posthac di deaeque ceteri
> contentiores mage erunt atque auidi minus,
> quom scibunt, Veneri ut adierit leno manum. (*Poenulus* 459–62)

> I've put a stop to it. That's how I act, that's what's right for me.
> I'll make sure that from now on all the other gods and goddesses'll
> be more content and less greedy,
> once they know how a pimp put one over on Venus.

---

44 Moore 2005, 30.

Lycus' soliloquy is one of both impiety and arrogance. Furthermore, a commercial perspective perhaps informs this passage: Lycus is of the opinion that sacrificial offerings are to the gods what cash and slaves are to a pimp. Whereas Cappadox in *Curculio* discusses his continued attempts at ritual incubation in the temple of Aesculapius without rancor, and even with continued commitment to success, Lycus takes his failure as a personal slight that requires vengeance – and, fittingly for his stock type, he intends to do so by 'swindling' the goddess out of her due, just as comic pimps try to cheat their clients out of cash.

In fact, the primary perjurer of *Curculio* is evidently played not by the pimp Cappadox, but rather by the banker Lyco. In the interchange with Cappadox discussed above, Lyco's response to the pimp's objections of being oathbound is crass and mercenary: 'what does that matter to you, as long as you get the cash?' (458–9, *quid id refert tua, | dum argentum accipias?*). Lyco's *modus operandi*, we discover, is to abuse the law for his own fiscal benefit, by perjury or by frivolous (i. e., perjurious) lawsuits (375–6). Indeed Cappadox relates to the audience in (again truthful) soliloquy that Lyco, when unable in the past to repay the pimp immediately, took him to court:

> uelut decem minas dum soluit, omnis mensas transiit.
> postquam nil fit, clamore hominem posco: ille in ius me uocat;
> pessume metui ne mihi hodie apud praetorem solueret. (*Curculio* 682–4)
>
> Well how about this: while he was on the hook for ten minae, he
> Went around to all the bankers' tables. After nothing came of it,
> I sought the guy out with a shout – and he took me to court!
> I've been terribly afraid that he'd settle up with me in front of the praetor today.[45]

Now, Cappadox tries to use this very same tactic against the soldier near the end of the play (722). But he does not get far and quickly gives up when the soldier threatens to beat him up.[46]

Cappadox's attempt at perjury here is merely perfunctory, a half-hearted last-ditch attempt to do the thing pimps do when they find themselves in a sticky situation. Everything before this one moment indicates that Cappadox is not a perjurer by practice, whereas Lyco is exactly that, and hyperbolically so. Lyco and Cappadox are not a dynamic duo of defraudation, but rather the behaviors to

---

45 Wright 1993, 67 and 82–3, suggests that *soluere* here, *sufferre* at line 376, and *soluere* again at line 722 refer to a habit Lyco has of declaring bankruptcy to avoid paying his creditors. Dumont 2011, 111, finds verbal parallels between Cappadox's attempt at perjury at *Curculio* 705–6 and Labrax' at *Rudens* 1374.
46 *Pace* Arnold 1998, 35, who lumps Cappadox into a generalization that 'Plautine *lenones* remain hostile to the last, an attitude which frequently leads to their continued discomfiture.'

be expected of Cappadox are instead mostly transferred to Lyco. By shifting the characteristically pimpish trait of perjury onto a supporting cast member, the cash-hungry banker, Plautus draws attention to the fact that, in *Curculio* as nowhere else in extant Plautine comedy, the play's pimp is relatively honest and mostly observes *pietas* towards humans as well as gods.

Cappadox and Planesium

Another major way in which Cappadox, the pious pimp, behaves unusually for his stock type is in his treatment of Planesium, the girl whom he holds enslaved, and who is eventually recognized as a freeborn citizen. Cappadox in fact demonstrates surprising compassion for her. When Cappadox sells Planesium to her lover Phaedromus via Curculio, he asks the parasite to take good care of her since, as he puts it, 'I raised her well and modestly in my house' (*bene ego istam eduxi meae domi et pudice*, 518).

The audience knows this claim, or at least the *pudice* part of it, to be true, for two reasons. First, the dictates of the genre require that a *uirgo* be *intacta* up until her recognition and the establishment of citizen marriage. Second, her lover himself informs us that Cappadox has kept Planesium away from his own trade, when he tells his *seruus* Palinurus that 'she's chaste and hasn't yet gone to bed with men' (*illa est pudica neque dum cubitat cum uiris*, 57). Palinurus' response fits the generic stereotype of the pimp: 'I'd buy it – if any pimp could have a sense of shame' (*credam, pudor si quoiquam lenoni siet*, 58). At this early point in the play, his words will come off as a typical joke, and may affect audience perceptions of Cappadox (though no more, I think, than would preconceived notions of what comic pimps are like). Yet, contrary to Palinurus' one-liner, Planesium must in fact be *pudica*, and thus there actually is a pimp who actually has *pudor*. That pimp is Cappadox, who shows a degree of *pudor* in respect to both gods and the law. By the point near the end of the play when Cappadox himself tells Curculio that he has preserved Planesium's own *pudicitia* (518), the audience is well positioned to believe him.

But Curculio's response to Cappadox – 'well are you going to pay for her to be all right?' (*ecquid das qui bene sit?* 519) – displays the crass venality normally expected of pimps, not of the play's clever protagonists. Curculio in this play is filling the role of the *callidus*, but unlike many *serui callidi*,[47] he does not use sacrificial terminology to mock and assert theatrical authority over other characters. Nor does

---

[47] E.g., Sosia at *Amphitruo* 738, Libanus and Leonida at *Asinaria* 712–6, and the title character at *Pseudolus* 334.

he, like the clever *meretrices* of *Miles Gloriosus* (411) and *Truculentus* (476), employ sacrifice, faked or genuine, to further a deception plot. Instead, it is the pimp who is associated with ritual activity, while the clever protagonist shows no concern for the enslaved girl, beyond the possibility of using her to drag more money out of his adversary. This unexpected role reversal between comic villain and comic hero thwarts the standard identifications of moral standing based on stock type and reveals a connection between religious behaviors and sympathetic portrayal. Cappadox is linked with sacrifice and with kind treatment of Planesium. He is therefore to be seen as much less detestable than the standard pimp of Roman comedy – and not much more detestable, perhaps, than the low-status parasite Curculio himself.

Hearing Curculio's brusque words in response to Cappadox, Planesium bursts into tears (520). Perhaps she anticipates much harsher conditions under her new captor than she faced in Cappadox's house. The pimp's response, 'don't be afraid, I've done a damn good job selling you,'[48] does not in context mean merely that he has made a good profit out of her, but rather that he also believes he is transferring her to a household where she will not be mistreated. Planesium herself later directly echoes Cappadox's claim of treating her well, when she pleads with her brother the soldier to unhand the pimp: 'he kept me well and chastely at home' (*bene et pudice me domi habuit*, 698).

A former slave, previously destined for prostitution, intercedes on behalf of her past pimp slaveholder, on the grounds of his merit! And in so doing, Planesium uses the same words that Cappadox himself did at line 518. This moment is unique in extant Graeco-Roman comedy.[49] It underscores emphatically the mutual, human compassion between Cappadox and Planesium, despite their generically opposed social statuses and theatrical roles. Plautus moves his dramaturgy beyond stock type to create subtle, nuanced character portraits – not unlike the more-complex characterization of Terence.

The soldier's response to Planesium's request is disingenuous, since he himself has previously paid money to be the one to end her chastity:

> hau uoluntate id sua:
> Aesculapio huic habeto, quom pudica es, gratiam;
> nam si is ualuisset, iam pridem quoquo posset mitteret. (*Curculio* 698–700)

---

[48] 520: *ne time, bene hercle uendidi ego te*. Collart 1962, on lines 520–1, suggests that Planesium may be crying either sincerely or to trick him.

[49] The closest parallel, the intervention of the newly-free Lemniselenis on behalf of her former sex-slaver Dordalus at the end of Plautus' *Persa*, lacks the key features of the girl's gratitude (Lemniselenis merely feels pity) and her success in shielding the pimp from further manhandling (in fact, Lemniselenis is compelled by the play's protagonist to participate in continued violence against Dordalus).

> Not because he wanted to! Give thanks for your chastity
> to Aesculapius here, 'cause if the pimp had been healthy,
> he'd have sent you wherever he could a long time ago.

The soldier tries to generate an alternate backstory to the play's events. In his new version, Aesculapius acts as the protector-divinity of the *uirgo* and so has a function akin to the divine prologues who attend to the citizen girl's well-being elsewhere in comedy (the Lar Familiaris in *Aulularia*, Arcturus in *Rudens*, Pan in Menander's *Dyskolos*, and Agnoia in *Aspis*). The soldier's version, however, does not stand up to scrutiny, for if Cappadox were not so pious, he would have gone about his business without first trying to appease the god. It is Cappadox's devotion to incubating at the shrine of Aesculapius, in fact, that prevented him from handing Planesium over to the soldier as a sex-slave before their recognition as brother and sister – not the rush to sale characteristic of other Plautine pimps, as the soldier alleges. And Planesium's brother does accede to her request to leave Cappadox alone.

Finally, earlier in the play, Cappadox shows us, once more in soliloquy, that he did not knowingly purchase Planesium unfairly or illegally, and that he has no reason to believe that she is of citizen birth:

> nam illam minis olim decem puellam paruolam emi,
> sed eum qui mihi illam uendidit numquam postilla uidi;
> periisse credo.   (*Curculio* 528–30)

> 'Cause I bought her as a little girl for ten minae a long time ago,
> but I've never since seen the guy who sold her to me.
> I think he's dead by now.

Without an omniscient prologue to detail the plot and background of *Curculio* for the audience,[50] theatrical convention suggests that we accept Cappadox's statement in soliloquy as the truth.[51] His claim here fits his characterization throughout the play – generally respectful of laws both human and divine. (Pious or not, if he had known for sure at the time of the transaction that she was a citizen girl, he would never have agreed to the banker's condition that he would have to repay the money if she turned out so.) Even Phaedromus, whose beloved Planesium is enslaved by Cappadox, does not charge the pimp with trafficking in free

---

[50] Marshall 2006, 218, suggests that the dialogue of the play's final scene indicates that the crucial *anagnorisis* – of Planesium and her brother the soldier – 'has not been anticipated … in a prologue that is now lost.'
[51] An anonymous reader contrasts Labrax in *Rudens*, who knowingly conceals the tokens that would prove Palaestra, whom Labrax holds enslaved, to be a citizen girl.

women, but rather hurls that accusation against the soldier: 'you who know how to buy kidnapped freeborn maidens, get yourself to the courthouse!' (*qui scis mercari furtiuas atque ingenuas uirgines,* | *ambula in ius,* 620–1). The call to court here forms a striking connection with the conclusion of *Poenulus,* where it is in fact the pimp who is told to get himself to the courthouse (*in ius* at 1342, 1343, 1349, 1360). Again, as with the transference of perjury from the pimp to the banker, Plautus has shifted a main line of anti-pimp rhetoric away from Cappadox and onto a secondary character, and thus has highlighted how the pimp in this play behaves better than his more-stereotyped counterparts.

Pimps and sacrifice: theatrical effects

Three effects result from Plautus' linking pimps with sacrifice. First, in Plautine comedy, sacrifice functions as In his essay on John Singer Sargent, Henry James comments ona marker or theatrical 'label' of citizen status.[52] Pimps, whose status as slaveholders is in Plautus always central to their theatrical roles, are always free and sometimes are local citizens.[53] Yet they often hold one or more citizens in a state of unlawful slavery, or try to purchase them, whether those citizens' true status is known or not (e. g., Labrax in *Rudens,* Lycus in *Poenulus,* Dordalus in *Persa*).

In all of Plautine comedy, enslaved characters almost never sacrifice. In fact, no enslaved character does sacrifice beyond the anomalous libation of Leaena in *Curculio* and the successful animal sacrifices of the enslaved should-be-citizen *meretrices* of *Poenulus.*[54] The latter case is the exception that proves the rule, for their success in sacrificing not only reinforces the failure of the pimp's own sacrifices and aligns audience identification with them, but also serves as a marker of their true freeborn status. Plautus' theatrical decision not to show enslaved characters sacrificing does not cohere with Roman reality, for slaves could and did offer and officiate over sacrifice, whether as individuals or as ritual officials in *collegia.*[55] For Plautus to depict pimps sacrificing (successfully or unsuccessfully)

---

[52] The term 'label' is from Ketterer 1986, 208.
[53] E.g., Dordalus, an immigrant from Megara: *Persa* 137–8 with McCarthy 2000, 136–7. Cappadox's name suggests a non-Epidaurian ethnic background, and is not elsewhere attested as a proper name, cf. Arnold 1998, 66. See Arnold 1998, 63–74, for itinerant πορνοβοσκοί.
[54] Both instances are discussed above. The *seruus* Strobilus in *Aulularia* vows a libation to the goddess Fides if she will help him find the titular pot of gold (622–3), but when he actually does find the gold later in the play, he simply hands it over to the young male protagonist.
[55] As individuals: Bömer 1981, 184–5, and Noy 2000, 185. In *collegia*: Bömer 1981, 17–29, and Rives 2007, 125–7.

while suppressing the real-life sacrificial capacity of enslaved persons draws out the stark contrast, in Roman comedy and in Roman life, between the pimp's own status and his abrogation of another's. The slaveholder takes advantage of a social prerogative that the people he has enslaved cannot, in Plautine comedy, themselves undertake. His use of this privilege may highlight for the audience that he is denying the same privilege to another who rightfully should have it.

In *Curculio*, however, the contrast stands instead between the pimp, a pious citizen who does not knowingly buy and sell citizens (even though he is engaged in a repellent and morally reprehensible trade), and the parasite, a stock type whose standing as a free man is less important to him than the opportunity to stuff himself.[56] Curculio's role as the clever schemer of this play can lend considerable weight to the audience's interest in and identification with him. Cappadox should not be seen as the protagonist of the play, or even as an unambiguously likeable figure. But his characterization through ritual and sacrifice does constitute a challenge to the audience's understanding of what standard comic pimps value and how they behave.

The second effect of the connection in Plautus between pimps and sacrifice is an apparent contradiction between character traits and characters' actions. Tolliver proposes that, through their archetypal impiousness, Plautus is 'increasing the repulsiveness of his pimps by putting them as completely as possible at variance with the conventions of society.'[57] Such a notion finds support in non-sacrificing, openly irreligious characters like Ballio in *Pseudolus*. Yet in *Curculio*, *Poenulus*, and *Rudens*, these archetypically impious pimps are each to some degree associated with the basic practices and social conventions of Graeco-Roman religion. Thus there is the potential for humor in the dissonance between a pimp's reputation (not to mention his morally repugnant business) and his nominally pious actions – as evidenced by the seemingly inverted exchange between Cappadox and Curculio over Planesium's fate at *Curculio* 518–9. Could viewers react to this back-and-forth with laughter, as if Plautus had mixed up his line assignments for the two stock types? Or perhaps they can find funny the notion of a sentimental, sanctimonious pimp gone devotion-mad: a born-again *leno*.

Third, the failed or misconducted sacrifices of Lycus and Labrax amount to a kind of double determination. These two pimps seem to forswear gleefully and without any expectation of punishment from the gods. In the end, however, they are proven wrong. They lose out and take their punishment, both because they have acted unlawfully in kidnapping or purchasing freeborn girls and because they did

---

[56] On the stock type of the parasite, see Damon 1997 and Tylawsky 2001, especially 107–24.
[57] Tolliver 1952, 54.

not successfully propitiate the gods. In Middle Comedy, '[b]eing true to one's oath is a characteristic of the righteous man,' but at the same time, '[f]orswearing, while disapproved, is portrayed as being widely practiced, without any thought of divine retribution.'[58] The perjurious in Plautus, unlike their counterparts in Middle Comedy, do get their just deserts. The dictates of the genre – that the *leno* be a villain who must meet and endure his fully merited comeuppance at the end of the play – coincide neatly with the religious imagery that Plautus sprinkles through the comedy.

Conclusion

Cappadox of *Curculio* is unusual for a Plautine pimp. The other pimps, particularly Labrax of *Rudens* and Lycus of *Poenulus*, are portrayed as opposed to the gods or hated by them. But Plautus marks Cappadox as pious through his successive visits to the shrine of Aesculapius near his house and the religious activity associated with him. With his piety is connected his reticence to commit perjury, the importance he places on oaths, the moderate degree of respect he shows for the law (he does not try to keep Planesium enslaved after her free status is confirmed), and his care for Planesium. Perhaps the illness from which he suffers at the play's beginning is enough of a punishment for his unknowing traffic in freeborn girls, and his escape from severe punishment at the play's end reflects his kind treatment of Planesium.[59]

With the end of *Curculio* comes the establishment of an improved, healthy, comedic society, as Planesium is recognized as a citizen, reunited with her brother, and certain to marry Phaedromus. It bears consideration at this point to what extent Cappadox is integrated into this comedic society. He is not invited to Phaedromus' celebratory wedding feast along with the soldier; Phaedromus makes this fact clear when he says 'you, soldier, will dine at my house' (*tu, miles, apud me cenabis*, 728). In this respect, he differs both from Labrax, who is explicitly invited by Daemones to a sacrifice and feast in celebration of Daemones' reunion with his daughter,[60] and from Dordalus, who is encouraged to participate in the banquet festivities hosted by the *seruus callidus* Toxilus (*Persa* 791–2, 801–2, 849).

---

58 Werner 1962, 101 and 140.
59 Comments from Alison Sharrock and Goran Vidovic prompted my thinking on this point.
60 Labrax: 'have dinner here today, pimp,' *hic hodie cenato, leno* (*Rudens* 1417); Delcourt 1964, 235, sees this as reflecting negatively on the character of Daemones, sharing dinner with 'l'esclave qu'il avait spolié et l'homme qui livrait sa fille à la prostitution,' while Dumont 2011, 117, believes that this line is delivered out of character, as the leader of the acting troupe invites all its members to a post-performance meal. Daemones has, from one perspective, stolen the *meretrix* Ampelisca away from Labrax, and thus may feel some manner of obligation to com-

Yet Cappadox is not completely outcast from the social unit, for Planesium intervenes in the play's final scene (as we have seen) in order to prevent her brother the soldier from manhandling him. This intercession is analogous to the final scene of *Poenulus* (1372–422), where the two citizen girls are, more explicitly, 'supremely efficient in bringing the play to a harmonious close' and in convincing their father to abandon his plans of suing Lycus the pimp.[61] In neither instance do we see a concrete act of social reintegration of the pimp such as with Daemones' sacrifice in *Rudens*, but in *Poenulus* and *Curculio* alike a harmonious close supports the notion that all characters are essentially reconciled – in contrast to *Persa*, for instance, where at the end Dordalus has kept himself apart from the feast[62] and is violently treated by the character of lowest social status in the play, at the encouragement of the event's host.[63] Furthermore, though Cappadox is not invited to dinner at Phaedromus' house, the pimp's own ritual activity could have itself generated a sacrificial feast. His devotions at the shrine of Aesculapius could replace participation in a feast for this structural element of the play's resolution.

Finally, I turn to some ramifications of this new understanding of the character of Cappadox for Plautus' audience itself. Roman comedy is a genre of stock characters and stock plots, and so most of Plautus' viewership would have a general set of expectations for the traits and tendencies of the people they would see on stage. Many would pick up easily on differences in stock type. Some would allow the stereotype to overwhelm the particulars of any play's pimp, but others, especially those familiar with Greek New Comedy, would be attentive to the interplay between stereotyped expectations and the specifics of the play before them.[64] Pimps are especially good candidates for this kind of attention, since the πορνοβοσκός is much less prominent in surviving Greek comedy.[65]

The Choragus at *Curculio* 462–86 transfers the deception and corruption of the play's nominally Greek setting concretely to the Rome that surrounds Plau-

---

pensate the pimp for his loss. An anonymous reader comments: 'Daemones compensates the pimp because he is just.'

61 Franko 2004, 54.

62 E.g., 'I don't want things to be okay with me,' *nolo mihi bene esse* (*Persa* 851); though Lemniselenis, until recently enslaved to Dordalus, does try (unsuccessfully) to intercede to prevent the violence against Dordalus, as Planesium does successfully for Cappadox.

63 *Persa* 804–58 *passim*. We might also note that, in *Pseudolus*, the *senex* Simo not only lives next door to Ballio, but also seems to be on relatively friendly, even collaborative terms with the pimp.

64 As attested by, among others, Slater 2000 and McCarthy 2000.

65 At Terence, *Adelphoe* 155–96, the pimp Sannio breaks the stereotype: as with Cappadox, Sannio's first appearance centers not on pimpish villainy but on his physical distress (having been unfairly beaten up by an out-of-control young lover); Sannio, too, is humanized.

tus' audience, in a speech 'as disconcerting as it was amusing'; the greed of Cappadox, and the perjurious avarice of Lyco the banker, is present in and around the Roman Forum – as are pimps and loan-sharks themselves.[66] I propose a further connection between Greek scene and Roman society in the figure of Cappadox. He is the most human of Plautine pimps, and despite the repulsiveness and moral turpitude of his profession (to Plautus' contemporaries as to us), a Roman audience saw him undertaking the same religious procedures that they or their family and friends might enact, in a visit to Epidaurus or Athens, or in rites to Aesculapius at home in Rome. Contemporary Rome had its share of openly active pimps, who took part in Roman rituals and thus could be as integrated into the socioreligious life of their city as Cappadox, a participant in the civic rites of Epidaurus, is into that of his own community.[67]

In Cappadox, Plautus has created a humanized figure,[68] more reflective of the everyday realities of Roman life than other pimp characters are. And in Cappadox there is a suggestion that the comedic caricature of the pimp is insufficient for understanding the established, entrenched social roles of pimps in the city of Rome in the time of Plautus, pimps with whom Romans shared their city, their forum, and their sacrifices.[69] *Curculio* is not 'Pimp Appreciation Day.' But rather it is a play that gently, uniquely[70] pushes viewers to acknowledge the unpleasant reality that in Rome – unlike in most Roman comedy – the pimps are present, are doing their disgusting business, are ritually and civically active, and cannot simply be tricked or beaten into irrelevance.

---

[66] Moore 1991, 362.
[67] According to McGinn 2003, 24, pimps 'are not known to have played any explicit role in public cult.' But this precludes neither personal religious activity like Cappadox's nor involvement in interfamilial rites like the sacrificial banquet to which Daemones invites Labrax in *Rudens*. Indeed most of the characters we see in comedy would not play an explicit part in public rituals, but could participate nonetheless (as the title character of Terence's *Heycra* is said to do, 592–3). See further Arnold 1998, 27 n. 89: 'the *leno* is an inescapable feature of a society in which prostitution takes place; as putative members of this society we accommodate this discomforting fact by ... construing him as an outsider and an undesirable and stereotyping him along these lines.'
[68] Paratore 1957, 313, sees in *Curculio* an attempt by Plautus to make New Comedy's stereotyped characters more human. Franko 1996 shows the unusual, pious, humanized characterization of the Carthaginian in *Poenulus*.
[69] Cf. Arnold 1998, 36–7, on the continuities between comedic stereotypes and real-life marginalization.
[70] Lefèvre 1991 argues that no specific Greek original lies behind *Curculio*.

Acknowledgments

Latin text of Plautus is from Lindsay 1910; translations mine. I owe thanks on this project to Sharon L. James, Antonios Augoustakis, Serena S. Witzke, Jarrett Welsh, Stavros Frangoulidis, and audiences at the 8th annual *Trends in Classics Conference* in Thessaloniki, the Wake Forest University Philosophy Club, and the University of North Carolina at Chapel Hill Eta Sigma Phi Undergraduate Research Conference.

Bibliography

Adams, J. N. (1984), 'Female Speech in Latin Comedy', *Antichthon* 18, 43–77.
Arnold, P. J. (1998), 'The Πορνοβοσκός and *Leno* in Greek and Roman Comedy', PhD diss., University of Oxford.
Bömer, F. (1981), *Untersuchungen über die Religion der Sklaven in Griechenland und Rom*, vol. 1 (*Die wichtigsten Kulte und Religionen in Rom und im lateinischen Westen*), 2nd ed., Wiesbaden.
Collart, J. (1962), *T. Maccius Plautus Curculio. Plaute, Charançon*, Paris.
Delcourt, M. (1964), *Plaute et l'impartialité comique*, Brussels.
Duckworth, G. E (1994), *The Nature of Roman Comedy: A Study in Popular Entertainment*, 2nd ed. [1st ed. 1952], Norman.
Dumont, J. C. (2011), 'Labrax', in: B. Delignon, S. Luciani, and P. Paré-Rey (eds.), *Une journée à Cyrène: lecture du Rudens de Plaute*, Montpellier, 109–17.
Dunsch, B. (2009), 'Religion in der römischen Komödie. Einige programmatische Überlegungen', in: J. Rüpke et al. (eds.), *Römische Religion im historischen Wandel*, Stuttgart, 17–56.
Dutsch, D. (2008), *Feminine Discourse in Roman Comedy: On Echoes and Voices*, Oxford.
Fantham, E. (1965), 'The *Curculio* of Plautus: An Illustration of Plautine Methods of Adaptation', *CQ* 15.1, 84–100.
Fontaine, M. (2010), *Funny Words in Plautine Comedy*, Oxford.
Frangoulidis, S. (2013) 'Transformations of Paraclausithyron in Plautus' *Curculio*', in: Th. D. Papanghelis, S. J. Harrison, and S. Frangoulidis (eds.), *Generic Interfaces in Latin Literature: Encounters, Interactions and Transformations*, Berlin, 267–81.
Franko, G. F. (1996), 'The Characterization of Hanno in Plautus' *Poenulus*', *AJP* 117.3, 425–52.
⸻ (2004), 'Ensemble Scenes in Plautus', *AJP* 125.1, 27–59.
Gellar-Goad, T. H. M. (2011/2012), 'The *Seruus Callidus* and Ritual Imagery in Plautus' *Epidicus*', *CJ* 107.2, 149–64.
⸻ (2013), 'Religious Ritual and Family Dynamics in Terence', in: A. Augoustakis and A. Traill (eds.), *A Companion to Terence*, Malden (Massachusetts), 156–74.
Gratwick, A. S. (1969), 'The *Poenulus* of Plautus and Its Attic Original', PhD diss., University of Oxford.
Hanson, J. A. (1959), 'Plautus as a Source Book for Roman Religion', *TAPA* 90, 48–101.

Harris, W. V. (2009), *Dreams and Experience in Classical Antiquity*, Cambridge (Mass.).
Hartkamp, R. (2001) '*leno periit* – Die Rolle des Kupplers Dordalus zwischen Ritual und Realität', in: S. Faller (ed.), *Studien zu Plautus' Persa*, Tübingen, 113–38.
Jonkers, E. J. (1949), '*Macte virtute esto*', *Mnemosyne* 2.1, 63–7.
Ketterer, R. C. (1986), 'Stage Properties in Plautine Comedy I', *Semiotica* 58, 193–216.
Lanciotti, S. (2008), *Titus Maccius Plautus. Curculio*, Urbino.
Lefèvre, E. (1991), '*Curculio* oder Der Triumph der Edazität', in: E. Lefèvre, E. Stärk, and G. Vogt-Spira (eds.), *Plautus barbarus: Sechs Kapitel zur Originalität des Plautus*, Tübingen, 71–105.
Lindsay, W. M. (1910), *Plautus: Comoediae*, 2 vols., 2nd ed., Oxford.
Lowe, J. C. B. (1985), 'Cooks in Plautus', *CA* 4.1, 72–102.
Ludwig, W. (1967), 'Ein plautinisches Canticum: *Curculio*, 96–157', *Philologus* 111.3/4, 186–97.
Marshall, C. W. (2006), *The Stagecraft and Performance of Roman Comedy*, Cambridge.
McCarthy, K. (2000), *Slaves, Masters, and the Art of Authority in Plautine Comedy*, Princeton.
McGinn, T. A. J. (2003), *Prostitution, Sexuality, and the Law in Ancient Rome*, New York.
Moore, T. J. (1991), '*Palliata Togata*: Plautus, *Curculio* 462–86', *AJP* 112.3, 343–62.
⸺ (2005), '*Pessuli, heus pessuli*: la porta nel *Curculio*', in: R. Raffaelli and A. Tontini (eds.), *Lecturae Plautinae Sarsinates VIII: Curculio (Sarsina, 25 settembre 2004)*, Urbino, 11–36.
Noy, D. (2000), *Foreigners at Rome: Citizens and Strangers*, Swansea.
Paratore, E. (1957), *Il teatro di Plauto, con particulare riferimento al Curculio*, Rome.
⸺ (1958), *Plauto: Curculio (Il Gorgoglione)*, Florence.
⸺ (2003), *Anatomie Plautine: Amphitruo, Casina, Curculio, Miles Gloriosus*, in: R. M. Danese and C. Questa (eds.), Urbino. [pp. 85–102 = Paratore 1958, 5–22]
Perna, R. (1955), *L'originalità di Plauto*, Bari.
Renberg, G. (2006), 'Was Incubation Practiced in the Latin West?', *Archiv für Religionsgeschichte* 8, 105–46.
Richlin, A. (2005), *Rome and the Mysterious Orient: Three Plays by Plautus*, Berkeley.
Rives, J. B. (2007), *Religion in the Roman Empire*, Oxford.
Saunders, C. (1911), 'Altars on the Roman Comic Stage', *TAPA* 42, 91–103.
Slater, N. W. (2000), *Plautus in Performance: The Theatre of the Mind*, 2nd ed., Amsterdam.
Tolliver, H. M. (1952), 'Plautus and the State Gods of Rome', *CJ* 48.2, 49–57, 62, 77.
Traill, A. (2004), 'A Haruspicy Joke in Plautus', *CQ* 54.1, 117–27.
Welsh, J. T. (2005), 'The Splenetic *Leno*: Plautus, *Curculio* 216–45', *CQ* 55.1, 306–9.
Werner, J. R. (1962), 'Religion in Attic Middle Comedy', PhD diss., University of Pennsylvania.
Witzke, S. S. (2015), 'Harlots, Tarts, and Hussies? A Problem of Terminology for Sex Labor in Roman Comedy', *Helios* 42.1, 7–27.
Wright, J. (1993), *Plautus: Curculio*, rev. ed. [1st ed. 1981], Norman (Oklahoma).
Zwierlein, O. (1990), *Zur Kritik und Exegese des Plautus I. Poenulus und Curculio*, Stuttgart.

C. W. Marshall
The Young Man in Plautus' *Asinaria* 127–248

In Plautus' *Asinaria*, two young men, Argyrippus and Diabolus, seek the attentions of the *meretrix* Philaenium.[1] Though they eventually decide to share her with a joint short-term lease (847–48, 915–18), earlier in the play the audience is presented with rival lovers. Argyrippus, whose romantic and financial concerns motivate the plot, is onstage at lines 585–745 and 828–942; Diabolus his rival is onstage at 746–827. Which of these two is the young man earlier in the play, at lines 127–248, is the subject of controversy. Despite the testimony of the manuscripts that this is Argyrippus, it has become increasingly common to claim with Havet that the first young man is Diabolus:[2] Fontaine calls this proposition 'the single greatest advance in the history of editing the *Asinaria*.'[3] The increasing prominence of this suggestion, especially in the Sarsina and Loeb texts,[4] elevates it to a position of unwarranted authority.

Havet's theory is mistaken. I am not the first to resist this trend, and the arguments here build on those offered by Lowe, Hurka, and others in support of the manuscript assignment of these lines to Argyrippus.[5] The issue is central to any examination of character in Plautus and to the interpretation of the play.[6] Lowe's arguments should have put the matter to rest, but additional arguments can be mustered.

To be clear, the question of line attribution is not simply an understanding of the manuscript tradition: mistakes can be made,[7] and the unanimity of the Palatine manuscripts (with the silence of the Ambrosian palimpsest) that the young man is Argyrippus does not grant certainty. The approach I am taking privileges instead how meaning is created during performance. Who is the first young man that the audience sees? Framed this way, the problem is not one of textual con-

---

1 I am grateful to John Porter for fruitful conversation on this topic, though his conclusions differ from mine, to Jim Tatum for encouragement, and for the valuable feedback at the *Trends in Classics* conference in Thessaloniki, May 2014.
2 Havet 1905, 94–5 and 1925; see also Bertini 1968, Danese 1999, 59–66 and 76–78, Danese 2004, Hartkamp 2004, 256–60, Henderson 2006, 137–40 and 223–4, de Melo 2011, 136, Porter 2013, and those sources listed at Lowe 1992, 159 n. 36
3 Fontaine 2005.
4 Danese 2004, de Melo 2011.
5 Lowe 1992, 158–63 and 1999, 14–17, Hurka 2010, 46–9; see Webster 1953, 235–6, for an earlier attempt to grapple with the problem.
6 Konstan 1983, 55 n. 7 accepts Havet, notes there may be interpolation (cf. 1978, 220 n. 4). Scafuro 2003/04, 13–4, notes that the play has many inconsistencies, and the identity of the lover is only one.
7 Andrieu 1953, 165–7, esp. 166 where it is argued that similar errors have to occur twice in the text of *Asinaria* for Havet's suggestion to be correct (and see 276). For other cases of misattribution, see Bertini 1968, 295.

servatism or being led astray by (post-Plautine) scene headings. What survives as a question of line attribution originates in practical terms as a question of mask, costume, and actor deployment, and of the interpretability of the theatrical *mise-en-scène* by an audience in Rome.

Meaning must be able to emerge from the performed reality: in adopting this approach, it is possible to circumvent some non-arguments that have been offered. It is not sufficient to claim that the manuscript reading presents narrative inconsistencies, since there are inconsistencies in *Asinaria* under both readings of the play:

(a) If the young man is Argyrippus, he does not obey instructions well: the *lena* Clearata suggests he write a contract (238), and Argyrippus does not do this, though Diabolus does.[8]
(b) If the young man is Diabolus, there are financial inconsistencies that are not explained: 'The lover ... has no money now ... [but] Diabolus appears to have no lack of funds.'[9] The audience must assume that there has been a substantial change in Diabolus' fortunes off-stage during the course of the play that is not mentioned.

Given that at least one of these inconsistencies must exist in the play, neither argument can stand on its own.

Stage movement is also not a determinative variable for this question. One could also point to the fact that the young man exits to the market (245 *ad forum*) along a wing, and Argyrippus' next entrance is from within the house of Philaenium at 585. Though such a move is paralleled elsewhere (Tranio exits along a wing at *Most.* 932 and enters through the house at 1044), there is the appearance of a greater consistency of movement if it is Diabolus who goes to market at 248 and returns with a contract and a parasite at 746. Appearances can deceive, of course. The presence of two empty stages following the initial departure of the *adulescens* (*Asin.* 503/4, 544/5) means that there exists no narrative/cognitive dissonance when Argyrippus appears from within the house. The audience sees a recapitulation of the earlier scene, with Argyrippus' different behavior arising from the woman to whom he speaks (the *lena* Clearata at 153–242, Philaenium at 582–745). Further, regardless of who the initial young man was, the audience must assume that Argyrippus has entered the house unseen, a move that is easily

---

8 De Melo 2011, 136.
9 Lowe 1992, 160.

assumed to have happened at one of the empty stages (504, 545).[10] This is easier, I contend, if the audience has some previous visual familiarity with the character making the unexpected entrance, but the matter is not determined in either case.

Characterization is similarly open-ended. I am suspicious of an argument that suggests that the anger expressed by the young man is somehow inconsistent for the character of Argyrippus.[11] Diabolus' cold and mechanical treatment of his relationship when he is dealing with the contract is no less inconsistent than if it the earlier discussion comes from an emotional, desperate Argyrippus (quite the opposite, in fact). Beneath this line of argumentation lies an assumption that characterization in Plautus is somehow predictable or simplistic. The *adulescentes* in Plautus are not all nice men, and they do not behave identically. There is much to be gained by comparing Argyrippus with Charinus in *Mercator* and Diniarchus in *Truculentus*, neither of whom are the morally upstanding ineffectual naïf that Havet and others would have Argyrippus be. As a result, I would even resist the concession granted by Lowe, that 'Plautine rewriting has in these scenes depicted Argyrippus' relationship with Philaenium in a way that is inconsistent with what is implied elsewhere in the play.'[12] Subsequent Latin literature presents the locked-out lover vacillating between anger and heartfelt passion, and that must be seen as a viable possibility here. Characterization only emerges from the play and the directorial choices made in staging it: presumptions of how a character should act cannot determine the shape of a play. Similarly irrelevant are arguments concerning contamination, source criticism, and interpolation, which have beset the play since the 19th century, and to which Havet was originally responding.

Any play must be interpretable by an audience in performance: I contend that structural and performance-based factors argue in favor of Argyrippus as the first young man, and one such factor is the use of music. In the play's only polymetric *canticum*, the young man sings as an *exclusus amator* (*Asin*. 127–52). As I argued in 2006, Plautus' metrical and musical practices elsewhere demonstrate that this should be the sympathetic *adulescens* Argyrippus.[13] *Asinaria* contains one of the longest musical passages in Plautus, with continuous accompaniment from the

---

10 For the *angiportum* as a narrative device that allows a run from a wing to behind the stage building, see Marshall 2006, 54–5 and 107–8. For the stage setting generally, see Rosivach 1970, 446–9.
11 E.g. de Melo 2011, 136: 'the angry outbursts seem more in keeping with Diabolus' character, whereas Argyrippus is presented as a man more prone to tears.' Porter 2013: 'Argyrippus is both the naively devoted lover and (as reported by Leonida at 267–71) the young rake, who mocks his father in the final scene before retiring to enjoy the delights of his courtesan paramour.' It is over-interpreting 270 *pariter scortari solent* to take this to refer to spending time with any courtesans except on the terms that (I argue) we have already seen in the play at 127–248.
12 Lowe 1992, 163.
13 Marshall 2006, 205–6, and see Moore 1998, 250.

tibicen from lines 127–745 (66.4% of the total length of the play), with the second musical section from 830–947 (constituting another 12.5% of the play). The only time music is not playing once it begins is in the scene between Diabolus and the parasite. In the later scene, Diabolus' presence on stage stops musical accompaniment. Music starts again when Argyrippus returns to the stage. Moore's work on characterization by means of musical accompaniment makes it clear that the locked-out lover in the first scene should be the character elsewhere associated with music, and that is Argyrippus, who even describes himself as having been shut out (596 *exclusus*).[14]

Another structural measure involves how an audience identifies a dramatic character. Because characters are for the most part costumed and masked in stereotypical ways, their identities become fixed for an audience in performance through naming and through the explicit identification of relationships. This is in fact true of any theatrical character: the audience must continually negotiate identity through observation of the *mise-en-scène*. Following a short prologue (1–15), there is an iambic scene between the *senex* Demaenetus and his slave Libanus that establishes both the focus on Demaenetus's son and the ways that this plot differs from other similar plots the audience might have seen in other plays. The scene's first line identifies *tuom ... unicum gnatum* (16, 'your only son'), and subsequent discussion states the problem (49–57, the son is in love but has no money; 67–83, yet his father is uncharacteristically willing to help) and names Argyrippus (74–6):

> nam me hodie orauit Argyrippus filius
> uti sibi amanti facerem argenti copiam;
> et id ego percupio opsequi gnato meo.
>
> Today my son Argyrippus has asked me to supply him with money for his affair. And I'm very keen to oblige my son in this.[15]

The problem is restated with specifics: *uiginti iam usust filio argenti minis* (89, 'My son needs twenty silver minas at once'). Then follows the twist that distinguishes this plot form other *palliatae*: Demaenetus challenges Libanus to cheat him of the money his son will need (90–117). This is similar to the challenge in *Pseudolus* (484–556), as Pseudolus reveals to his master Simo that he will trick Simo out of the money Calidorus needs to purchase Phoenicium. This provides exciting variation on an expected narrative pattern.[16]

---

[14] For the musical structure of *Asinaria*, see Moore 1998, 249–50.
[15] I use the text and translation of de Melo 2011 throughout, so as not to stilt my argument.
[16] Of course, this later proves to be a false clue, when it is revealed Demaenetus is in fact angling for his own sexual gratification (734–6), re-asserting the father-son rivalry seen, e.g., in *Casina* and

Following the young man's scene, Argyrippus is again named when Libanus fears he is going to be corporally punished *ni hodie Argyrippo argenti essent uiginti minae* (364, 'unless Argyrippus had twenty silver minas today'). This use of proper names becomes a frame around the young man's scene, and should be conclusive for determining the visible character's identity.[17] The fact that the basic economic demand is also repeated within the scene allows for each spectator to maintain the connection when Clearata names her price: *tene? uiginti minas; / atque ea lege: si alius ad me prius attulerit, tu uale* (230–1, 'For you? Twenty minas. And on these terms: if anyone else brings it to me earlier, it's good-bye to you'). If this is addressed to Argyrippus, spectators recognize that Clearata is repeating information she has given him before; the reference to another (231 *alius*) constitutes the initial pointer to the existence of an unspecified rival, urging him to act quickly. This situation offers no interpretative difficulties. If however this is addressed to Diabolus, spectators perceive that Clearata is here repeating the same deal that Argyrippus' father knew had been offered to someone else; since Diabolus is unnamed at this point, we must also assume that an audience when hearing *alius* makes the association with the young man who has been named. Of these two possibilities, the case favouring Argyrippus requires the audience to extrapolate less information.

Diabolus is not mentioned by name until much later in the play (633–5):

argenti uiginti minae med ad mortem appulerunt,
quas hodie adulescens Diabolus ipsi daturus dixit,
ut hanc ne quoquam mitteret nisi ad se hunc annum totum.

Twenty silver minas has driven me to my death; young Diabolus said he'd give it to her today so that she wouldn't send her anywhere except to him for a whole year.

He appears at 746 and is again named right away, when the parasite begins reading the proposed contract (751 *Diabolus Glauci filius* ...). This makes the stage figure's identity unambiguous right away, in a scene that demonstrates his relationship to Philaenium. For a spectator making sense of the play in performance, spectators must assume that Argyrippus was told of the rival by name during his time with Philaenium inside (545–84). This is the case regardless of who the initial young man was, and as a narrative inconsistency, this is relatively minor. More striking is the fact that only Argyrippus is named in the discussion between

---

Mercator. It is not impossible that the rival lover be brought onstage first: that happens, e. g., in *Miles Gloriosus*. The contrast between these two scenes is striking, however, Pyrgopolynices appears onstage with his parasite Artotrogus, before the prologue, in a scene that names both characters.
17 Andrieu 1953, 275–7.

Clearata and Philaenium (504–44, cf. 522 *Argyrippum filium Demaeneti*). The absence of any mention of Diabolus when the two women are alone on stage and free to discuss all suitors again suggests that Diabolus has had no stage presence before line 504: at this point of the play Diabolus does not exist.

Naming is important, because it provides a crucial marker that a spectator can use to identify a character with certainty. This is the central obstacle to Havet's theory: if the first *adulescens* is Diabolus, then Plautus deliberately creates confusion among his audience. Having spoken about Argyrippus (16–126) and introduced a young man (127–248), the audience has no resource to understand that it has not been Argyrippus for some time. The confusion persists throughout the exchange between Libanus, Leonida, and the Merchant (249–503), and the exchange between Clearata and Philaenium (504–44). Argyrippus has been mentioned by name in both scenes (364, 522), and the natural assumption for every audience member is that the character being named is the infatuated young man that they have seen. Further, if we have not seen Argyrippus before the mother-daughter exchange, the stakes of that scene are greatly reduced: Philaenium is pining for an abstraction that may not even appear as a character in the play.[18] It is of course possible that costume or skin tone on the mask could be used to discourage the identification (e.g. if the young man wore exotic, foreign clothing that suggested that he was not related to Demaenetus),[19] but even with the assistance of costuming, the use of proper names means that there will always be part of the audience who will be confused.

For those in the audience who make the association between Argyrippus and the young man they have seen regardless, there is nothing in the play that would challenge this impression until 585–6. Henderson, who follows Havet, is explicit that this is Plautus' intention: 'I am sure Plautus does fool with his audience here: it's no great feat to trick spectators in this theatre ...'.[20] When Argyrippus

---

[18] In *Casina*, neither the title character nor the lover Euthynicus appear on stage; the possibility of withholding the appearance of a character must be considered by an audience, even if it is a rare event.

[19] Porter 2013 suggests, 'it is possible that the actor's attire helped to identify him from the start as the dissolute impoverished lover [by which he means Diabolus] rather than the lovelorn son.'

[20] Henderson 2006, 137. He continues, '... in fact it's a built-in option because (say it out loud), *in the absence of names, a mask for a part such as the* adulescens amator *specifies the role, not the individual*.' This is, no matter how loudly spoken, not true. During performance, any stock mask represents an individual within the world of the play, and (as we've seen) there in fact is a name that any intelligent spectator might reasonably attribute to the character. If fooling the audience is part of Plautus' intention, this must be so. Henderson continues in his footnote uninterested in engaging with opposite views: seeing Diabolus in the first scene as 'vital to any

appears, he is named immediately (585–6), but this is also the beginning of a split-focus (eavesdropping) scene (585–618), which becomes the extended *ludificatio* (619–745).[21] If Havet were correct, audience members who have been successfully confused must suddenly reconfigure what they think they know about Argyrippus in the light of new evidence at this point and interpret it on the fly, during a split-focus scene. Confirmation of this realignment of identities does not come until Argyrippus makes reference to a rival named Diabolus at 633–5.

Only at these lines would the identity of the initial young man be unambiguously clarified, as they then anticipate Diabolus' return to the stage at line 746. They also recall the earlier discussion between the young man and Clearata at 230–5, where the price and duration of the contract are outlined.

Havet's theory therefore requires Plautus to mislead part of his audience at least from line 127 until 586 (460 lines; almost exactly half the play), with the likelihood of some residual confusion until line 635 (509 lines; 54%). For modern readers, who know the play's outcome and have access to a cast list, this is possible, but still a challenge to follow. In its original performance context, the play becomes simply uninterpretable. The ambiguity created, where spectators are misled about the identity of an on-stage character when the other stage characters are not so misled through the deliberate contrivance of the playwright, is without parallel in ancient theatre practice (and, I think, ancient narrative practice generally). Elsewhere, we see Plautus at pains to ensure that the audience has the resources to interpret his play: compare the care with which he warns the audience that apparent twins (*Miles Gloriosus* 72–4) will in fact be the same woman pretending to be twins, or the opening of *Captivi* (1–68), where actors are brought onstage to model the unusual narrative features of the plot described by the prologue.

The scene with Diabolus, introducing the new rival late in the play, is crucial to the play's overall structure, because it is only through Diabolus that the play's true blocking figure, Demaenetus, will be overcome. Diabolus's intended contract becomes a plot device: because of the contract, Argyrippus can exclude his father whose sudden revelation as the blocking figure, despite his initial boasts, means that he must be defeated. Argyrippus' victory is accomplished through the deal with Diabolus, who has arrived just in time. This narrative arc makes most sense if Diabolus has not been previously seen, and appears as a fulfillment of the unspeci-

---

reading of the play which is *not* after analyst dismantling' (224 n. 5) is – as I hope to have demonstrated in this study – also not true. Henderson's note misleadingly suggests the last voice sounded against Havet was Phillimore 1926.

21 Lowe 1992, 169–70, traces the so-called Plautine expansion in this scene; see also Marshall 1999, 114–15.

fied other (231 *alius*). Two young men sharing a non-citizen *meretrix* is not objectionable; and given her uncharacteristically high price it might even be seen as a practical solution. Neither is under the illusion that this is a permanent relationship: that is never the case with free prostitutes in Roman comedy. Their deal is better than the alternatives seen in *Cistellaria* and *Truculentus*, even if it is not quite exclusive.

Seldom does uncertain line assignment change the narrative and emotional shape of the play as drastically as does the identity of the *adulescens* at 127–248. If this were Diabolus, then necessarily Plautus misleads his audience for over 450 lines (*Asin.* 127–586). Such uncertainty is unparalleled for unnamed characters in Roman comedy, and it actively limits audience interpretation of the play. As Argyrippus, the *adulescens* becomes more emotionally complex and dramatically polarized against the legalistic Diabolus who arrives unexpectedly only at line 746 and threatens to undermine Argyrippus' faltering sexual pursuit of Philaenium, preparing for the surprise revelation that the true opponent to Argyrippus's relationship is his father.

Preference has to be given to the solution that entails the least confusion for the audience. This also allows Argyrippus to emerge as a more nuanced character. My case against the devil's advocates assumes that any playwright will want his play to be interpretable by an audience in performance. Arguments about the nature of dramatic arias and the practices of identifying new characters in comedy can be added to the more analytical (but still persuasive) arguments of Lowe.[22] *Asinaria* is a challenging play, but it should not be a confusing one. At its most elemental level, part of the play's communication with its audience resides in

---

[22] One final argument can perhaps be mustered. According the online database of the Archive of Performances of Greek and Roman Drama, there have been five productions of the play since Havet's idea was first presented:
1. University of Sydney (1964);
2. Westminster School, England (1976);
3. University of Victoria, Canada (1997), directed by myself;
4. Ancient Theatre of Segobrigo, Spain (1997); and
5. Teatro del Semenario Diocesano, Spain (2003; these last two part of the Festival Juvenil peo de Teatro).

See <http://www.apgrd.ox.ac.uk/productions/canonical-plays/asinaria-the-comedy-of-asses/130>. While I have not been able to confirm details about the Spanish productions, I have anecdotal or first-hand knowledge that the other three productions had Argyrippus appear as the first young man. I can find no evidence that any modern director has attempted to stage the play with the young man as anyone other than Argyrippus. I do not think it is possible to make such a dramatic choice coherent in performance without aggressively heavy-handed intervention from the director.

characters appearing and being named at moments when failing to do so would result in identity confusion and a loss of dramatic coherence. Roman comedy is not averse to complexity, but it does not dupe the audience into believing something is the case that every character on stage knows not to be the case. That is how we know that Argyrippus is the young man in *Asinaria* 127–248.

Bibliography

Andrieu, J. (1954), *Le Dialogue Antique: Structure et Présentation*, Paris.
Bertini, F. (1968), *Plauti Asinaria cum commentario exegetico*, 2 vol., Genoa.
Danese, R. M. (1999), 'I meccanismi scenici dell'Asinaria', in: R. Raffaelli and A. Tontini (eds.), *Lecturae Plautinae Sarsinates II. Asinaria*, Urbino, 49–95.
―――― (2004), *Titus Maccius Plautus: Asinaria*, Sarsina and Urbino.
de Melo, W. (2011), *Plautus I*, Cambridge, MA.
Fontaine, M. (2005), Review of Danese 2004, *BMCR* 2005.7.39.
Gomme, A. W. and F. H. Sandbach (1973), *Menander: A Commentary*, Oxford.
Hartkamp, R. F. (2004), 'Mutter und Kupplerin? – Zur Darstellung, Entwicklung und Funktion der plautinischen *lenae* in *Cistellaria* und *Asinaria*', in: R. Hartkamp and F. Hurka (eds.), *Studien zu Plautus' Cistellaria*, Tübingen, 247–266.
Havet, L. (1905), 'Études sur Plaute. Asinaria I: La seconde et la troisième scènes et la composition générale', *Revue de Philologie* 29, 94–103.
―――― (1925), *Pseudo-Plaute, Le prix des ânes (Asinaria)*, Paris.
Henderson, J. (2006), *Asinaria: The One about the Asses*, Madison, WI.
Hurka, F. (2010), *Die Asinaria des Plautus: Einleitung und Kommentar*, Munich.
Konstan, D. (1978), 'Plot and Theme in Plautus' *Asinaria*', *CJ* 73, 215–21.
―――― (1983), *Roman Comedy*, Ithaca.
Lowe, J. C. B. (1992), 'Aspects of Plautus' Originality in the *Asinaria*', *CQ* 42, 152–75.
―――― (1999), 'L'Asinaria e il suo modello greco', in: R. Raffaelli and A. Tontini (eds.), *Lecturae Plautinae Sarsinates II. Asinaria*, Urbino, 13–24.
Marshall, C. W. (2006), *The Stagecraft and Performance of Roman Comedy*, Cambridge.
Moore, T. J. (1998), 'Music and Structure in Roman Comedy', *AJP* 119, 245–73.
Porter, John (2013), '*Asinaria*', *The Literary Encyclopedia* [http://litencyc.com/php/sworks.php?rec=true&UID=34718, accessed 3 December 2015].
Rosivach, V. J. (1970), 'Plautine Stage Settings (*Asin., Aul., Men., Trin.*)', *TAPA* 101, 445–61.
Scafuro, A. C. (2003/04), 'The Rigmarole of the Parasite's Contract for a Prostitute in *Asinaria*: Legal Documents in Plautus and his Predecessors', *LICS* 3.4.
Webster, T. B. L. (1953), *Studies in Later Greek Comedy*, Manchester.

Robert Germany
Civic Reassignment of Space in the *Truculentus*

The prologue of the *Menaechmi* contains a famously metatheatrical reference to the civic fungibility of the stage's 'here.' Usually it's Athens, he says, but this time it's Epidamnus, just like the characters who live onstage and who alternate from play to play but are always drawn from a fixed pool of stock types (7–10; 72–6). There is a similar, if less well-known, instance of this kind of play in the prologue of the *Truculentus*, which opens with a plosive paroemion and an offer too good to be refused (1–13).

>   Perparvam partem postulat Plautus loci
>   de vostris magnis atque amoenis moenibus,
>   Athenas quo sine architectis conferat.
>   quid nunc? daturin estis an non? adnuont.
>   fateor quid de urbe[1] me ablaturum sine mora;   5
>   quid si de vostro quippiam orem? abnuont.
>   eu hercle! in vobis resident mores pristini,
>   ad denegandum ut celeri lingua utamini.
>   sed hoc agamus qua huc ventumst gratia.
>   Athenis mutabo[2] ita ut hoc est proscaenium   10
>   tantisper dum transigimus hanc comoediam.
>   hic habitat mulier, nomen quoi est Phronesium
>   haec huiius saecli mores in se possidet:

>   The smallest smidgen of space is all Plautus asks,
>   Loaned from your large and lovely burgh,
>   Where he'll bring in Athens without engineers.
>   Well? What say you? The motion is carried!
>   Apparently I can make off with public property, no problem.
>   And if I hit you up for private property? The motion fails!

---

1 I follow Enk's conjecture for the first four words of this line. The MSS have *melior me quidem vobis*, which is obviously wrong. Other suggestions are similar enough to Enk's: *scio rem quidem urbis* (Leo), *meliorem urbis quidem* (Lindsay), *sciunt quid de urbe* (Kruse). Lindsay's *meliorem urbis* (without *partem*) seems strained, whereas Leo's and Kruse's conjectures are both good Latin, but Enk's *fateor* may be marginally easier to square with the transmitted text. Except where otherwise noted, I have followed Lindsay's OCT; translations are all my own.
2 *mutabo* is Leo's emendation of the MSS' *tracto*. Other suggestions have been *instructo* (Lindsay), *traicio* (Schöll 1900, 495), and *traveho* (Enk, Kruse). For a defense of *tracto*, see Fontaine 2010, 21 n. 30. Antony Augoustakis has pointed out to me that if Schöll's *traicio* is right, the passage offers yet another interesting parallel to the fetial ritual discussed below.

> Well done. I see you've kept alive the old time wont
> Of saying your nay without delay.
> But to come to the point, the reason we came here:
> I shall change this stage, just as it is, to be – at Athens!
> At least for as long as the comedy is on.
> A woman lives here, named Phronesium.
> She's got the character of this age.

Plautus is the punchline of an absurdly alliterative string (*Perparvam partem postulat Plautus*), an effect picked up in the final words of the following line describing Rome (*amoenis moenibus*). If the city enclosure is doubled in sound it will soon be doubled in civic identity, as the allotted space of the stage is dubbed a tiny piece of Athens.[3] This can, however, only happen (so the conceit runs) if the audience, acting as a public assembly, votes to cede the stage to Plautus' temporary civic reassignment. The Prologue then pretends to go further and ask for something from the audience themselves, a mock appeal scripted to be denied. Of course we should understand this second request primarily as a flirtatious plea for money, not space, but the Latin is quite ambiguous, and the generality of the second request puts it in close tension with the first. He asks for something from the city and gets it; he asks for something from themselves (*de vostro quippiam*, 6) and is denied. The audience is happy to loan this tiny tract of real estate for the play, but the encroachment of make-believe Athens on their world stops where the stage ends. The fiction that the audience has granted the first request enables theatrical transmigration of space, but the equally fictional refusal of the second request means that the audience themselves will remain as they were, intact and at Rome. The invisible 'fourth wall' separating the stage from the audience becomes here a boundary between the space of public largesse and that reserved for private frugality, and also between temporary Athens and permanent Rome.

It is not my intention to argue here that there are allusions to specific public practices and rituals in these lines, but rather that there are structural similarities between their rhetoric and the logic of two peculiarly Roman traditions: public

---

[3] Apuleius quotes these opening three lines entire in the context of the wondrous mutability of dramatic setting and the importance of believing that the stage's *hic* is wherever it's supposed to be, even if it is a matter of civic substitution. Today he will not be asking his audience to credit substitution of a far away, overseas city, but merely of the senate house or library right here in Carthage: quapropter, ut poetae solent hic ibidem varias civitates substituere, ut ille tragicus, qui in theatro dici facit: '*Liber, qui augusta haec loca Cithaeronis colis,*' item ille comicus: '*perparvam partim postulat Plautus loci/de vostris magnis atque amoenis moenibus,/Athenas quo sin\<e\> architectis conferat,*' non secus et mihi liceat nullam longinquam et transmarinam civitatem hic, sed enim ipsius Karthaginis vel curiam vel bybliothecam substituere (*Flor.* 18.15–24 Helm).

assemblies and the procedure for declaring war. Such homologies would not necessarily be legible by the audience as ritual citations, but both the way the prologue constructs the audience as a voting body and the way it articulates and fictionalizes alien civic space are reminiscent of practices the audience would know from other contexts. It goes without saying, perhaps, that such echoes of Roman ritual and public custom, however subtle, would be *Plautinisches im Plautus*, but apart from being an obviously non-Greek element of the play, they would also serve as a reminder that Plautine comedy sits within a matrix of local usage and performative practice.

The general similarity of this scenario in the *Truculentus* to a public assembly is obvious, but it may resonate with pointedly Roman practices in ways that are not immediately clear for us.[4] Early Roman assemblies do not seem to have relied on individual voting, but on a group vote expressed by shouting or rattling of arms. As Lily Ross Taylor pointed out, this same primitive method of polling is familiar enough from Homer and classical Sparta, but of course it is quite different from Athenian practice, where votes were taken by show of hands (*cheirotonia*) or secret ballot (*psephos*).[5] The *contiones* of Plautus' Rome may generally have relied on just this kind of *clamor* or *succlamatio* to determine the group will, but of course there were also *comitia*, with a more formal voting procedure.[6] When proposals were made in such assemblies, it seems the standard positive response was *uti rogas* ('as you ask'), and the standard negative was *antiquo* ('I'm for the old way').[7] Late in the 2nd century BCE Roman assemblies would adopt the use of written ballots with these standard options, but in Plautus' day the procedure for *suffragium* still involved spoken response to a *rogator*'s prompt.[8] The Roman practice of oral voting, whether as a group or individually, thus differs markedly from the two silent options known at Athens, so when the Prologue praises the audience for using a swift tongue (*celeri lingua*, 8) in refusal, he is framing their action as a distinctively Roman form of civic participation. Of course, they were just as swift (at least within the fiction of the Prologue's performance) in granting the space for the stage as they were in refusing the additional request, but it is telling that he only praises their *mores pristini* (7) in the latter, for if the standard response for 'nay' was *antiquo*, then there was indeed a close notional connection between voting down a proposal and hewing to the old ways. In fact the verb

---

4 For example, Hofmann (2001, 131) notes that *hoc agamus* in line 9 are 'Formen der Amts- und Sakralsprache.'
5 Taylor 1966, 2.
6 On *suffragium* < *fragor* (=*armorum sonitus*), see Vaahtera 1993.
7 Lintott 1999, 47.
8 On Cicero's treatment of these reforms and their political consequences, see Vishnia 2008.

antiquare seems to be a technical term, used for no other context than legislative assemblies, and when later lexicographers have to define this archaic word, they do so in language strikingly similar to Plautus': *antiquare est in morem pristinum reducere* (Paul. *Fest.* 24 L.).

The mock assembly conducted in the opening lines of the *Truculentus* establishes a strong spatial dichotomy between *hic* and *istic*, here onstage and there where you, the audience, are.[9] By the audience's leave, the stage is allowed to be Athens, but the foreign encroachment of the play and its world is limited by the same means. The audience will remain in a Roman space because they have voted to do so in a pointedly Roman fashion.[10] By itself the *huc* in line 9 might just be the stage and not Athens, but the next two lines will clarify what the first three lines of the prologue meant and what these proximal demonstratives mean: *this* stage and *this* comedy will be at Athens. When the Prologue then immediately goes on to say here (*hic*) lives a woman, he stands firmly in a fictional Athenian reference space. But the difference between the stage and the audience is not merely one of notional location; it also has a moral dimension. *This* Athenian prostitute has the character of *this* age (*haec huiis saecli mores in se possidet*, 13), in pointed contrast to the audience whose *mores pristini* drew a line that kept themselves outside its incursion.

The battle for hearts, minds, and wallets is, of course, only just begun, and these prostitutes will be steadily applying themselves to the corruption of one man after another, including even the sternly disapproving Truculentus.[11] In case the censorious titular hero does not already obviously enough figure the naysaying Roman audience of the prologue, Phronesium herself will get a crack at them in the play's closing lines (964–8).[12]

---

9 Dessen 1977, 148: 'This minor *captatio benevolentiae* invites the audience to compare themselves favorably with the prodigals onstage.'
10 The Greekness of this play's Athens may be limited in other ways as well. Lefèvre 1991 claims that the *Truculentus* probably has no Greek original and that its generic debt to Italian folk theater is far greater than to Greek New Comedy. Satire may technically begin with Lucilius, but as Dessen 1977 argues there is a qualitative difference between the satirical elements occasionally seen in other New Comedy and the sustained (proto-)satire of the *Truculentus*. The generic space of this play is thus twisted from the notionally Greek *fabula palliata* towards Roman satire. As Konstan (1983, 162) puts it, 'To understand the plot of the *Truculentus*, we must see it as a comedy *sous rature*, a kind of canceled presence, metamorphosed by the pressure of a different genre.'
11 Hofmann 2001, 132: 'Das Thema des Lustspiels, das wichtiger ist als die Handlung.' On Truculentus' ethical reversal as emblematic of this play's non-conventional structure and flouting of genre norms, see Papaioannou 2008, 138–9.
12 Phronesium = 'Miss Sensible'? Perhaps that should be Phrynesium = 'Mini-Phryne'; see Fontaine 2010, 21–30. Phryne was, as Fontaine calls her (24), 'the Marilyn Monroe of fourth-

lepide ecastor aucupavi atque ex mea sententia,
meamque ut rem video bene gestam, vostram rusum bene geram:
rem, amabo, siquis¹³ animatust facere, faciat ut sciam.
Veneris causa adplaudite: eius haec in tutelast fabula.
spectatores, bene valete, plaudite atque exsurgite.

Fine catch I've made, just to my taste,
And as I see I've handled my business well, I'll handle yours too:
If anyone wants to do a little business, just let me know.
Clap, for Venus' sake. This play's in her department.
That's all, folks. Get up and make some noise!

The Prologue's bid for a little something of the audience's (*de vostro quippiam*, 6), beyond what they have already granted Plautus for the stage, fell on resistant ears, but perhaps now that they have seen Phronesium at work, they will find her invitation into her world (*vostram rusum bene geram*, 965) harder to turn down.

Plautus' request for a miniscule and temporary territorial secession to create a fictional Athens in Rome may sound utterly fanciful to us, and it is a comical conceit, to be sure, but it has an interesting corollary in the Roman practice of declaring war. Early on Rome's enemies were her neighbours, and fetial law developed on the presumption of geographical contiguity.¹⁴ The chief of the college (*pater patratus*) would proceed to Rome's border with the hostile territory, where he would pronounce a prepared list of grievances and demands. This formulaic ultimatum would be repeated once he had stepped over the border, again to the first person he met,

---

century-BC Athens,' so just as the stage is a miniature Athens built on a *perparvam partem* of Rome, perhaps 'Mini-Phryne' contributes to the play's Athenian local color.

13 This is Ernout's emendation, followed also by Paratore, Kruse, and Hofmann. The MSS have *romabo si quid*, emended by Spengel to *intro abeo si quid* and by Enk to *si quis quid ob amorem*.

14 I follow Livy's account here more or less uncritically; in most respects it conforms to those of Cincius (= Gell. 16.4.1) and Dionysius of Halicarnassus (2.72 and 15.9). Most scholars believe the fetial ritual was discontinued at some point and then revived by Octavian in 32 BCE. Although there is great uncertainty as to when exactly this obsolescence is to have occurred, *termini ante* from the end of the 3rd century or the first half of the 2nd century are most common. A few have gone further and suggested that Octavian's 'revival' was an invention out of whole cloth and that there was no early *indictio* ritual involving a spear toss (see Wiedemann 1986, 482–3; Rüpke 1990, 106–7). More recently, however, a number of scholars have argued that the fetial priesthood was never discontinued and that the archaic spear ritual was no Augustan fictionalization (see, for example, Broughton 1987, 60; Blaive 1993, 192; Ferrary 1995, 421; Santangelo 2008, 87; Zollschan 2011). I find these recent arguments in favor of continuity persuasive, and it seems likely that some version of the *indictio* ritual persisted through the 2nd century. But even if it was suspended at some point, it was very likely either after Plautus' time altogether or within living memory of his audience.

again at the enemy's city gate, and a fifth and final time in their forum (Livy 1.32.12). Then he would return home and after 33 days, assuming the Romans' demands had not been satisfied, he would proceed to the border again, attended by at least three witnesses, pronounce the formula of *indictio* and cast a blood-dipped spear literally into the hostile territory. This enactment of sacralized aggression across the liminal space of the border was the final step in *rerum repetitio,* a process apparently designed to create transparency in Rome's dealings with her enemies and secure the support of the gods for a just war. But this fetial act also had the effect of articulating with particular clarity the notional boundary of Roman territory and of scripting foreign space into the ritual drama of Rome's self-definition.

Such a practice could work beautifully as long as Rome's enemies were her Latin neighbours and, with some hedging, could be extended for other Italian foes as well, but once her opponents hailed from overseas, the ritual would obviously need to be reformed. Thus it was precisely in her contest with Pyrrhus (280–275 BCE) that the fictional construction of Roman and enemy space in the *indictio belli* assumed the form it would have for centuries to come.[15] A captive soldier from Pyrrhus' army was forced to 'buy' a tiny plot of land in the Circus Flaminius, just in front of the Temple of Bellona. This patch of earth, now a foreign pied-à-terre, was declared sovereign territory of Rome's enemy, so the traditional requirements of *indictio* could be fulfilled there, including the spear cast from Roman into hostile terrain. It was on this spot that the Romans erected the *columna bellica,* a diminutive pillar, which would subsequently serve as alien soil *ad libitum,* a tiny incursion of the generalized enemy's polity into the heart of Rome. It is unclear just when the Romans stopped declaring war this way, but

---

15 Servius ad Verg. Aen. 9.52: PRINCIPIUM PUGNAE *hoc de Romana sollemnitate tractum est. cum enim volebant bellum indicere, pater patratus, hoc est princeps fetialium, proficiscebatur ad hostium fines, et praefatus quaedam sollemnia, clara voce dicebat se bellum indicere propter certas causas, aut quia socios laeserant, aut quia nec abrepta animalia nec obnoxios redderent. et haec clarigatio dicebatur a claritate vocis. post quam clarigationem hasta in eorum fines missa indicabatur iam pugnae principium. post tertium autem et tricesimum diem quam res repetissent ab hostibus, fetiales hastam mittebant. denique cum Pyrrhi temporibus adversum transmarinum hostem bellum Romani gesturi essent nec invenirent locum, ubi hanc sollemnitatem per fetiales indicendi belli celebrarent, dederunt operam, ut unus de Pyrrhi militibus caperetur, quem fecerunt in circo Flaminio locum emere, ut quasi in hostili loco ius belli indicendi implerent. denique in eo loco ante aedem Bellonae consecrata est columna. Varro in Caleno ita ait 'duces cum primum hostilem agrum introituri erant, ominis causa prius hastam in eum agrum mittebant, ut castris locum caperent.' ergo bene hoc poeta de more Romano tractum Turno utpote duci dedit. sed in hac consuetudine fetialis, qui bellum indicebat, antequam hastam iaceret, etiam terram hostium contestabatur: unde quidam volunt Aenean scientem quod bellum gesturus esset, sicut a sibylla cognoverat, ubi ad Italiae partem debitam venit, primum adorasse terram, ut 'geniumque loci primamque deorum Tellurem.'*

the ease with which the fungible column could be reassigned to any hostile power meant that the ritual could be reused indefinitely. Down at least as late as Marcus Aurelius the Romans would gather at this spot to declare war and cast the ceremonial spear over the offending column.[16]

It seems interesting that it would be, of all things, a column. The pre-Pyrrhus version of the ritual involved the *pater patratus* marching from the border to the enemy's gate and forum a month before the final declaration and the spear cast, so the full ritual included an encounter not just with enemy soil but with their city. The *columna bellica* neatly recaptures this urban contact in the abridged post-Pyrrhus version, but it also seems to suggest that the wrinkle in space that ritually folds enemy land into Rome penetrates all the way to the built cityscape of the enemy's capital. The architectural function of columns is to support larger structures, but this single column by itself could support nothing except the weight of signification attached to it. As Ovid (*Fasti* 6.206) says, 'a slight column of no slight import' (*non parvae parva columna notae*). Precisely because of its obvious architectural uselessness, the miniature *columella*, as Festus (30 L.) calls it, is a perfect metonymy of the urban other, Rome's favorite enemy.

Another interesting feature of a single column is that, unlike most buildings, it has radial symmetry, i. e. it does not present a clear directional orientation, but looks the same from any angle. In the earlier version of the ritual, spatial orientation was variable, as the fetial and his attendants must face the enemy's territory whichever direction it lay. But after the early 3rd-century BCE reform the symbolic stamp of hostile terrain was surrounded by Rome on all sides, so it could be faced down from any direction or always from the same direction, regardless of where the real lands of the current enemy were. Both the telescoping of distance implied by its miniature urban synecdoche and the arbitrary treatment of orientation implied by its radial symmetry make the *columna bellica* a perfect icon of the logic of the ritual's fictionalization of space.

---

16 For this event in 178, see Dio 72.33.3. Whether this was simply continuity of inherited practice or Marcus was self-consciously reviving an antiquarian form of *indictio belli* we can only guess, though there is no indication that it was the latter, and perhaps Dio's use of the article (τὸ δόρυ τὸ αἱματῶδες ... ἀκοντίσας) suggests that this was a recognizably usual procedure, made somewhat remarkable only by the Emperor himself casting the spear. Likewise it remains unclear how long this ritual persisted after the 2nd century. In 359, when Grumbates, king of the Chionitae, initiated hostilities against the Romans by throwing a blood stained spear, Ammianus Marcellinus notes that this was 'by ancestral rite and the custom of our fetial' (*ritu patrio nostrique more ... fetialis*, 19.2.6). This was far from the Temple of Bellona, of course, but Ammianus' point is the coincidence of traditional practice in Transoxiana and the way things are done at Rome, and there is no indication that he regards this *mos fetialis* as obsolete.

If the column could be regarded from all sides equally, it was however only attacked from one: the Temple of Bellona, immediately to the north, seems to have been the spot from which the fetial would launch the spear. Servius describes the location of the column as *ante aedem Bellonae*, but he does not give it the epithet it has elsewhere, *bellica*. The onomastic similarity between the *columna bellica* and the Temple of Bellona highlights their thematic and physical proximity, and when later grammarians gloss one they do so in terms of the other. So Luctatius Placidus 14 (Deuerling): *bellica columna ante aedem Bellonae, quae Pyrri temporibus constituta dicitur, ut exeuntes ad bellum superiacerent eam hasta, veluti conspecto hoste issent* ('The *bellica columna* in front of the Temple of Bellona, said to have been founded in the days of Pyrrhus, so those departing for war could throw the spear over it, as if they had come within sight of the enemy'). And Festus 30 L.: *Bellona dicebatur dea bellorum, ante cuius templum erat columella, quae bellica vocabatur, super quam hastam iacebant, quum bellum indicebatur* ('Bellona they called the goddess of war, before whose temple was a little column, which was called *bellica*, over which they threw the spear upon declaring war'). The Circus Flaminius was a fairly crowded space, and there might have been any number of other reference points, but these two structures are consistently described in relation to each other and to the ritual that linked them.

Inscriptional evidence indicates that the Latin goddess of war had been worshipped in some fashion since at least the 5th century (*CIL* I² 441), but this temple in the Circus Flaminius was vowed by Appius Claudius Caecus, who invoked the goddess in a particularly harrowing moment in 296 BCE and promised her a temple in return for her military aid against the Samnites (Livy 10.19.17).[17] It was only a few years later that this same Appius Claudius was pushing for war against Pyrrhus (Plut. *Pyrrh.* 18–9), so the construction of the Temple of Bellona and the relocation of the *indictio* ceremony to this very spot are both events of the early 3rd century and both connected with the influence of Appius Claudius. Ovid neatly connects these strands of history and ritual with the June 3rd anniversary of the temple's consecration (*Fasti* 6.199–208).

> Mane ubi bis fuerit Phoebusque iteraverit ortus
>   factaque erit posito rore bis uda seges,   200
> hac sacrata die Tusco Bellona duello
>   dicitur, et Latio prospera semper adest.
> Appius est auctor, Pyrrho qui pace negata
>   multum animo vidit, lumine captus erat.

---

[17] Ziolkowski 1992, 18.

> prospicit a templo summum brevis area Circum: 205
> est ibi non parvae parva columna notae;
> hinc solet hasta manu, belli praenuntia, mitti,
> in regem et gentes cum placet arma capi.
>
> When day has dawned and Phoebus has risen twice
> And the fields are twice wet with the falling of dew,
> On this day, they say, in a Tuscan war, Bellona
> Was consecrated, always ready with help for Latium.
> Appius the founder, when there could be no peace with Pyrrhus –
> He saw so much with his mind, though blind at the eyes.
> From the temple a small open space looks out
> Onto the heights of the Circus where stands
> A slight column of no slight import.
> From here a spear, the herald of war, is cast by hand
> When the decision is made to attack a king and nation.

If we did not know from other sources that the spear was thrown over the column, rather than from it, we might be tempted to construe Ovid's *hinc* (207) as referring to the previous line's *ibi*, but the theme of the day's poem is the Temple of Bellona, and the focalization of lines 205–6 is from the temple precinct looking out onto the Circus Flaminius, so the *hinc* must be understood as referring to this *brevis area*.

To be clear, I do not wish to claim that there is a direct allusion to fetial procedure in the prologue of the *Truculentus*. My contention is rather that there is a suggestive homology more generally between the way space is fictionalized in Roman theater and in the practice of *indictio belli*, a homology that becomes especially clear in the *Truculentus'* play with its audience. A foreign cityscape is ritually incorporated into Rome for a time, to be watched, thought with, and then obliterated. The spatial synapse and directional disorientation required for this incorporation is part of what seems to fascinate the audience, as is the urban alterity of this similar, yet by definition alien, place. In dramatizing this civic stand-off between the world of the audience and the world of the play, the prologue of the *Truculentus* recapitulates a spatial poetics Romans will know from another context. The fact that the audience sits, in all likelihood, on the steps of a temple makes this homology all the more acute. We cannot know in which *ludi* the *Truculentus* was performed, but it is tempting to speculate that it may have been at the *ludi Apollinares*, in which case the audience would be sitting on the steps of the Temple of Apollo Medicus, exactly next to and parallel with the Temple of Bellona, with the stage set up literally beside the *columna bellica*.[18]

---

18 On the staging of *ludi scaenici* in front of the Temple of Apollo Medicus, see Marshall 2006, 37–8.

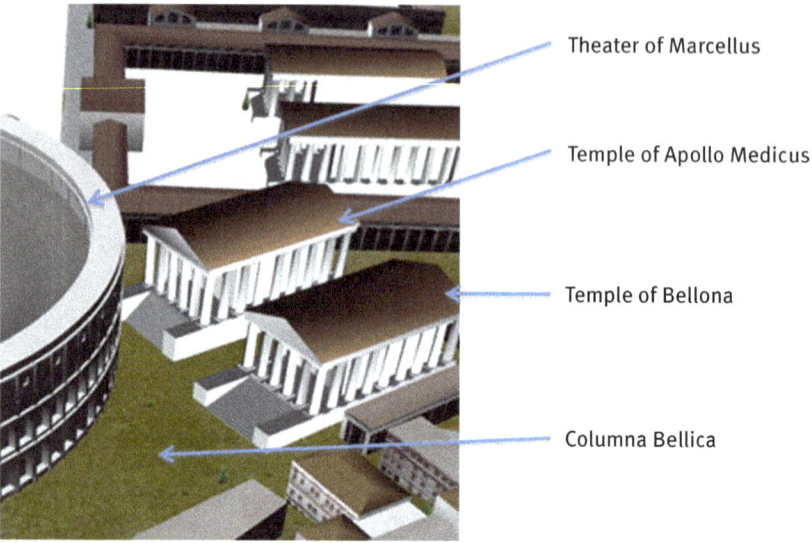

Fig. 1: Image source: http://romereborn.frischerconsulting.com/ge/TS-017.html (modified).

For any other *ludi* the echo would not be quite as obvious, though I think it would be clear enough whenever the same basic configuration of stage and temple obtained, as was the case in the Megalensia and very likely in others as well. When the prologue of the *Truculentus* praised the audience's *mores pristini* in defending their own space against his incursion with a ready tongue (*celeri lingua*), this sounds remarkably like the fetial's shouted declaration just before the spear cast, which, as Servius explains, was called *clarigatio* from the loudness of the voice (*haec clarigatio dicebatur a claritate vocis*, ad Verg. Aen. 9.52).

Quite apart from the *Truculentus*, the theatricality of the *indictio belli* and the similarity of its spatial grammar to that of the Roman stage may have suggested comparison with drama, especially because of the placement of the stage for the *ludi Apollinares* literally next door. Ovid may be alluding to the collocation of the Temple of Apollo Medicus with the Bellona-*columna* complex when he mentions Phoebus rising in the opening line of the poem. He certainly emphasizes the visual aspect of the relationship between these structures, as he personifies the *brevis area* itself 'watching' (*prospicit*) the column, just as the audience might watch the stage from the Temple of Apollo. Luctatius Placidus also describes the spear cast as involving a kind of imaginary vision of the enemy (*veluti conspecto hoste*). Most telling of all, Julius Caesar cleared a space for his planned monumental theater just south of the temples of Apollo and Bellona, a project completed by Augustus in 13 BCE as the Theater of Marcellus. Sander Goldberg has noted the aptness of this location for its contiguity to the site of the old temporary stages set up in front of the Temple of Apollo every summer since the late 3rd century.[19] But it seems relevant too that the Theater of Marcellus was equally just south of the Temple of Bellona, only a few meters away from the *columna bellica*, and that just like both temples it also faced south.[20]

One of the great open questions, at least to my mind – and one we cannot hope to address here adequately – is how the Romans of the 1st century BCE did eventually manage to look past their earlier qualms about building a permanent stone theater, but the Theater of Marcellus may give a partial clue. Augustus provided a monumental and permanent venue for watching plays, but he may have wanted to emphasize continuity with older Roman practices that were so persuasive at articulating the temporal and spatial limits of such incorporation. For all the grandeur and luxury of his theater, he had every reason to want to frame it as a seamless extension of earlier authorized habits. The temples of Apollo and Bellona supplied side-by-side platforms for two different, yet oddly similar, ways of spectating fictionally alien space and overcoming a temporary incursion of a foreign city in Rome. The theatrical audience of Augustus' *Ludi Saeculares* sat just in front of this twin platform looking the same direction, spectating their stage with these ancestors, as it were, watching over their shoulders. By now, of course, we are far from the world of Plautus and the Middle Republican stage, but the strategy for managing this later audience's experience of practically the same space may help us understand the tradition of spatial practice that was already informing the rhetoric of the *Truculentus* some two centuries before.

Bibliography

Blaive, F. (1993), '*Indictio belli*: recherches sur l'origine du droit fécial romain', *RIDA* 40, 185–207.
Broughton, T. R. S. (1987), 'Mistreatment of Foreign Legates and the Fetial Priests: Three Roman Cases', *Phoenix* 41, 50–62.
Dessen, C. S. (1977), 'Plautus' Satiric Comedy: The *Truculentus*', *Philol. Q.* 56, 145–68.
Enk, P. J. (1953), *Plauti Truculentus*, Leiden.
Ferrary, J.-L. (1995), '*Ius fetiale* et diplomatie', in: E. Frézouls and A. Jacquemin (eds.), *Les Relations internationales: actes du colloque de Strasbourg, 15–17 juin 1993*, Paris, 411–32.
Fontaine, M. (2010), *Funny Words in Plautine Comedy*, Oxford.
Goldberg, S. (1998), 'Plautus on the Palatine', *JRS* 88, 1–20.

---

19 Goldberg 1998, 10.
20 On the archaeological remains of all these structures, see now Vitti 2010.

Hofmann, W. (2001), *Plautus: Truculentus*, Darmstadt.
Konstan, D. (1983), '*Truculentus*: Satiric Comedy', in: *Roman Comedy*, Ithaca, 142–64.
Kruse, K. H. (1974), *Kommentar zu Plautus Truculentus*, PhD diss., Heidelberg.
Lefèvre, E. (1991), 'Truculentus oder Der Triumph der Weisheit', in: E. Lefèvre, E. Stärk, G. Vogt-Spira (eds.), *Plautus barbarus: sechs Kapitel zur Originalität des Plautus*, Tübingen, 175–200.
Lintott, A. (1999), *The Constitution of the Roman Republic*, Oxford.
Marshall, C. W. (2006), *The Stagecraft and Performance of Roman Comedy*, Cambridge.
Papaioannou, S. (2008), 'The Undoing of Comedy and the Role of Cyamus in Plautus' *Truculentus*', *Ordia Prima* 7, 119–23.
Rüpke, J. (1990), *Domi militiae: Die religiöse Konstruktion des Krieges in Rom*, Stuttgart.
Santangelo, F. (2008), 'The Fetials and their *ius*', *BICS* 51, 1–49.
Schöll, F. (1900), 'Zu Ciceros Ligariana', *RhM*. 55, 489–500.
Spengel, A. (1868), *T. Macci Plauti Truculentus*, Göttingen.
Taylor, L. R. (1966), *Roman Voting Assemblies: From the Hannibalic War to the Dictatorship of Caesar*, Ann Arbor, MI.
Vaahtera, J. (1993), 'The Origin of Latin *suffragium*', *Glotta* 71, 66–80.
Vishnia, R. F. (2008), 'Written Ballot, Secret Ballot and the *iudicia publica*. A Note on the *leges tabellariae* (Cicero *De legibus* 3.33–39)', *Klio* 90, 334–46.
Vitti, M. (2010), 'Note di topografia sull'area del Teatro di Marcello', *MEFRA* 122/2, 549–84.
Wiedemann, T. (1986), 'The *Fetiales*: A Reconsideration', *CQ* 36, 478–90.
Ziolkowski, A. (1992), *The Temples of Mid-Republican Rome and their Historical and Topographical Context*, Rome.
Zollschan, L. (2011), 'The Longevity of the Fetial College', in: O. Tellegen-Couperus (ed.), *Law and Religion in the Roman Republic*, Leiden, 119–44.

Catherine Connors
Nothing to do with *Fides*? The Speaker of the Prologue and the Reproduction of Citizenship in Plautus' *Casina*

Saluere iubeo, spectatores optumos
Most excellent members of the audience, I bid you be well.

So begins the prologue of Plautus' *Casina*, the play in which the enslaved young woman Casina is revealed at the end to be an Athenian citizen, and thus eligible to transmit Athenian citizenship to legitimate children. But who speaks the prologue? More than a century ago Skutsch suggested that the speaker of the prologue is the goddess Fides.[1] MacCary and Willcock are cautious, remarking that it 'is not at all clear what this divinity has to do with the present play.'[2] The broad array of social and familial responsibilities embodied in the quality of *fides* are important in several of Plautus' other plays including the *Aulularia*, the *Pseudolus*, and the *Captivi*.[3] In terms of its literary context, the *Casina*'s prologue is closely comparable to the divine prologues in other plays by Plautus. In terms of its context within Roman culture, the *Casina* also may play on a topographical awareness of the worship of Fides as a physical presence within the city of Rome and a social and civic awareness of Fides' connection to the reproduction of citizenship. These contexts, I will argue, suggest that Fides might well have something to do with the *Casina*.

Divine prologues and the reproduction of citizenship

As it happens, I recently had to make a decision about who speaks the *Casina*'s prologue with the particular urgency that comes with performance. Since I had agreed to play the speaker of the prologue in a production undertaken by one of my students, I had to decide whether to appear as an unnamed male Prologus or

---
[1] Skutsch 1900. Those who have welcomed this suggestion include Mattingly and Robinson 1932, 52 and Pansiéri 1997, 37, 600.
[2] MacCary and Willcock 1976, 98. Cf. Hunter 1987, 298 (= 2008, 641) for the idea that the god who speaks a prologue typically does have some kind of relationship to the actions of the play.
[3] Jeppesen 2014, 101–53 (*Aulularia*), Feeney 2010 (*Pseudolus*), Franko 1995 (*Captivi*), Burton 2004, 220–3 (*Captivi*). On *Fides/fides* in Roman society, see Heinze 1928, Freyburger 1986.

as the goddess Fides.⁴ I decided on Fides mainly because of the obvious way that speaking as Fides sharpened the metatheatrical joking in the first few lines:

> saluere iubeo spectatores optumos,
> Fidem qui facitis maximi – et vos Fides.
> si verum dixi, signum clarum date mihi,
> ut vos mi esse aequos iam inde a principio sciam. (*Casina* 1–4)⁵
>
> Most excellent members of the audience, I bid you be well – you who consider Fides most important – and Fides considers you likewise. If I have spoken the truth, give me a clear sign, so that I may know already from the beginning that you are fair to me.

Beyond the immediate context of that joke though, it makes sense to ask how comparable a prologue spoken by Fides would be to Plautus' other divine prologues. Mercury speaks the prologue of the *Amphitruo*, the Lar speaks the prologue of the *Aulularia* (1–39), Auxilium speaks a delayed prologue in the *Cistellaria* (149–202), Arcturus speaks the prologue of the *Rudens* (1–82). In each case, a child is at risk of being alienated from a citizen household. Amphitruo's suspicion of Alcmena's marital fidelity puts at risk the children she is about to give birth to: impersonating Amphitruo, Jupiter as he departs specifically tells Alcmena 'see to it that you raise the child that will be born' (*quod erit natum tollito*, *Amph.* 501). In the *Aulularia*, the miser's daughter Phaedrium is pregnant and unmarried; the Lar has brought the pot of gold to the surface to provide the family with the funds for a dowry for her (*Aul.* 25–7). In the *Cistellaria*, Selenium's citizen status has been obscured, as the god Auxilium explains: she was abandoned as a baby by Phanostrata because she was conceived outside of marriage in a rape by Demipho. In the *Rudens*, a shipwreck has separated a kidnapped and enslaved Athenian citizen girl from the tokens that prove her citizenship; the god Arcturus says 'I have brought the girl help' *tetuli ei auxilium* (68). Might *Casina*, in which Casina's citizen status is put in jeopardy when she is abandoned by Myrrhina, and protected when she is raised by Cleostrata, belong in a list of Plautus' plays with divine prologues?

Of course, the abandoned child is a common feature of comedy.⁶ Plautus associates the child at risk very closely with the divine prologue, in part because the omniscient perspective of the divinity allows the authentication of the identity of the child. When there are people who remember what happened to a cap-

---

4 Dudley 2013.
5 The text of Plautus is cited from De Melo 2011. Translations are my own.
6 See Traill 2008, 72–3 on the motif of the exposed child as a version of what she calls the 'lost-daughter plot' in Menander and New Comedy, and cf. Ar. *Nu.* 530–3.

tured child – as there are in the *Menaechmi*, the *Captivi*, and the *Epidicus* – perhaps a divine prologue was felt to be less necessary.⁷ Because of the *Casina*'s similarity to other plays that use a divine prologue to authenticate the identity of a child, it could make sense to suppose that this play too had a divine prologue. Each of the other divine prologues announces his name, and it does not seem impossible that the mention of Fides in *Casina*'s second line could serve to signal the prologue's identity in a comparable, if less straightforward, way.⁸

The prologue gives quite a lot of detail about how the baby was abandoned:

> is seruos – sed abhinc annos factum est sedecim
> quom conspicatust primulo crepusculo   40
> puellam exponi. adit extemplo ad mulierem
> quae illam exponebat, orat ut eam det sibi;
> exorat, aufert, detulit recta domum,
> dat erae suae, orat ut eam curet, educet.
> era fecit, educauit magna industria,   45
> quasi si esset ex se nata, non multo secus.

This slave – it was sixteen years ago, when he caught sight at first light of a girl being exposed. He went right up to the woman who was exposing her. He asked that she give the infant to him. He got what he wanted, he took her away, he brought her straight home. He gave her to his mistress, and asked that she take care of the baby, and raise her. The mistress did it, raised her with great care, as if she was her own child, not much different (*Cas.* 39–46).

Casina's narrative of abandonment, rescue and recognition is closest to that of the *Cistellaria*. It is made explicit in the *Cistellaria* that women work together to

---

7 The brief prologue of the *Trinummus* parodies a wedding procession when the divine Luxuria escorts her daughter Inopia (Want) to enter a house to live with the young man, Lesbonicus (*Trin.* 15). The *Truculentus* has a very short prologue (Leo marks a lacuna after line 20) that does not indicate who is speaking. The play's final lines suggest the idea that Venus has been involved in the protection of the identity of the abandoned child in terms that replicate the ways in which Roman families protected the interests of their own children. Children whose fathers have died are placed in the *tutela* (guardianship) of a guardian to protect their interests. This play, it turns out in the closing lines, has been in the protection (*tutela*) of Venus: *Veneris causa adplaudite: eius haec in tutelast fabula* ('Applaud, for the sake of Venus: this plot is in her protection,' *Truc.* 967). It seems at least possible that the speaker of the prologue of the *Truculentus* was Venus.

8 *Amph.* 19: *nomen Mercurio est mihi*; *Aul.* 2: *ego Lar sum familiaris ex hac familia*; *Cist.* 154: *nam mi est Auxilio nomen*; *Rud.* 8: *nomen Arcturo est mihi*; *mihi Plautus nomen Luxuriae indidit*; *Trin.* 8. In the *Truculentus*, when Dinarchus enters after the prologue, the first thing he says is that not even Venus herself (*eapse ... Venus*) will be able to count all the ways that a lover is tricked (*quot amans exemplis ludificetur, Truc.* 24–6); the humor would be especially sharp here if Venus was the speaker of the prologue.

preserve the citizen producing capacity of an exposed baby girl.[9] The prominence of female networking in that play is clear in the mosaics from Pompeiii, Mytilene, Antioch, and Zeugma that depict Menander's *Women who lunch together* (*Synaristosai*), which is the source of Plautus' play.[10] In the backstory of Plautus' play, produced in the late 200s BCE (De Melo 2011, 130), a man from Lemnos named Demipho attends a Dionysiac festival in Sicyon and rapes a woman named Phanostrata. Realizing he deserves punishment, he flees back to Lemnos, marries, and produces a daughter. Phanostrata meanwhile gives birth to a baby girl. As she is unmarried, she is put in the difficult position of deciding whether or not to raise the child. To protect her status as a marriageable woman who can be trusted to transmit citizenship to legitimate children 'she gives the girl to a slave to be exposed to death' (*dat eam puellam ei servo exponendam ad necem*, 166). Some seventeen years later, Demipho, his wife having died, has returned to Sicyon, reacquainted himself with Phanostrata, and they have married. They now are searching for the exposed girl, with the help of the slave who did the actual deed. This slave, Lampadio, knows that the baby was picked up by a *lena* and is on the alert to track her down. Meanwhile though, Phanostrata's child had been given by the *lena* to her friend Melainis, also a sex worker. It suited Melainis to tell her lover from abroad that she had given birth, so that he would send more funds for her housekeeping. Melainis has now allowed Selenium (Phanostrata's child) to move in to the house next door with Alcesimarchus, the young man who loves her and whom she loves. Selenium pressed her foster mother for this because, as she says, 'I do not want to be called a prostitute' (*quia ego nolo me meretricem dicier*, *Cist.* 83). Meanwhile, Alcesimarchus' father has arranged that Alcesimarchus, who has been out in the country, is to marry Demipho's daughter from his first wife. As the play begins, Selenium has invited the unnamed *lena* and the *lena*'s daughter Glycerium for a morning meal. She tells them how upset she is that Alcesimarchus is to marry another, and asks Glycerium to stay in Alcesimarchus' rented house while she (Selenium) heeds her foster-mother's decision that she return home. This scene was the source of the title in Plautus' model, Menander's *Synaristosai*, and the meal embodies and performs the female

---

9 See Fantham 2011, 157–75, building on her discussion of issues of reproduction, citizenship and status in Fantham 1975, Raccanelli 1998, 179–84, and cf. Konstan 1987 on Menander's *Perikeiromene*, and Feltovich 2011. On the broader context of rape narratives in Menander see Lape 2001.
10 Fraenkel 1932, Süss 1935, 1938; on the visual evidence see Nervegna 2013, 135–45. Pompeiii: Naples Museo Archeologico 9987; Mytilene: House of Menander, cf. Charitonidis, Kahil, and Ginouvès 1970, 41–4; Antioch (Daphne): cf. Gutzwiller and Çelik 2012, 597–606; Zeugma: cf. Abadie-Reynal et al. 2003.

networking that is central to the plot. The backstory is explained in two delayed prologues, one by Syra, who picked up the exposed child (*Cist.* 120–48) and the other by the god (*deus*) Auxilium (*Cist.* 149–202).[11] Auxilium's narrative concludes by exhorting the audience in lines that are very similar to lines that close the *Casina*'s prologue:

> bene valete et vincite
> virtute vera, quod fecistis antidac

Do well, and prevail by true excellence, which you did before this (*Cist.* 197–8, cf. *Cas.* 87–8).

Selenium thus occupies a kind of middle ground between concubinage or slavery and full recognition of her ability to transmit citizenship to legitimate children. Since Selenium was exposed with tokens, there is from the beginning the possibility that she may eventually be recognized and welcomed back into a citizen household. In any event, Melainis cannot afford to keep Selenium at home forever, and once Alcesimarchus sees Selenium at a festival of Dionysus and starts wooing her with gifts, the canny and strategic Melainis consents to their setting up housekeeping in rented accommodation. But, unwilling to let Selenium be seen as coming second to a legitimately married citizen wife, Melainis summons Selenium home immediately when news breaks that Alcesimarchus is to marry someone else.

In both the *Casina* and the *Cistellaria*, prologues with an omniscient perspective explain that an abandoned child's identity has been concealed without being fully eradicated. The raising of the abandoned girl is described in terms that align her experience with that of citizen girls. In the *Casina* we are told by the prologue that Cleostrata, upon taking in the child, *educavit magna industria/quasi si esset ex se nata, non multo secus* ('raised her with great care, as if she was her own child, not much different,' 45–6). In the *Cistellaria* Auxilium says that 'She raised the baby [Selenium] well and chastely, as her own daughter' (*eaque educavit eam sibi pro filia/bene ac pudice*, *Cist.* 172–3). Attributing this chaste child-raising to the *meretrix* Melainis would no doubt provoke a laugh from Plautus' audience at the same time as it guarantees Selenium's eligibility for eventual citizen marriage to Alcesimarchus.

In the *Casina*, the prologue may hint at conscious safeguarding of Casina's capacity to enter into citizenship. In Rei's reading of the play, Cleostrata knows that Casina is a citizen from the very beginning: 'being well aware of the found-

---

11 On the role of Auxilium in the *Cistellaria* and Boethia in the *Synaristosae*, see Ludwig 1970, 67–71; for detailed discussion of Auxilium's prologue see Stockert 2012 *ad loc.*

ling's free status, she [Cleostrata] supports her son's wish to marry the young woman.'¹² Cleostrata's knowledge of Casina's origins makes sense as a reading of Cleostrata's actions since it draws on a common feature of New Comedy, which, as Traill notes, 'is full of women who secretly rescue illegitimate or unwanted babies.'¹³ How exactly does Cleostrata know that the baby's origins are free? No tokens are mentioned at any point in the play. The slave who brought the baby to Cleostrata saw the person who was exposing her (*Cas.* 40–2). Pardalisca brings a close to the day's proceedings by stating that Casina is the daughter 'from next door' (*ex proxumo, Cas.* 1013), that is of Cleostrata's neighbours Alcesimus and Myrrhina. With this in mind, it makes sense to suppose that the slave not just saw but also recognized the woman from the neighbouring house doing the exposing. If the prologue's assertion that Casina was raised 'as if she were [Cleostrata's] own daughter, not much different' implies that Cleostrata knows already from the very beginning the truth of Casina's origins, then it is striking to notice that the very idea of knowing something consequential 'already from the very beginning' is already in play when the speaker of the prologue asks the audience to give a clear sign (*signum clarum*) so that the speaker may know that the audience is favorable *iam inde a principio* (*Cas.* 3–4).

In this play that thematizes the idea of restaging a play that some in the audience remember (*Cas.* 13–4), it becomes tempting to reconsider – or re-watch, in the mind's eye – Cleostrata's conversations with Myrrhina in light of the possibility that Cleostrata has known all along that Casina is her neighbour's child. In this context, Cleostrata's urgency at the beginning of the play comes not only from the urge to get the better of Lysidamus, but also from the desire to protect Casina's potential to have a free life, to live under the protection of a citizen household, and to produce citizen children. The two women are close:¹⁴ Myrrhina says *nam quod tibi est aegre, idem mi est dividiae*, 'for what is painful for you is upsetting to me' (*Cas.* 180–1). Cleostrata responds affectionately: *credo, ecastor, nam vicinam neminem amo merito magis quam te/ne qua in plura sunt/mi quae ego velim*, 'I believe it, by Castor, for I rightly love no neighbour more than you, and there is no woman in whom there are more qualities I would wish for myself,' (*Cas.* 182–3). Myrrhina does not yet know the whole story because, when Cleostrata complains about Lysidamus' designs on Casina, Myrrhina says, *sine amet, sine quod lubet id faciat/quando tibi nil domi delicuom est*, 'let him love, let him do as he pleases,

---

12 Rei 1998, 99.
13 Traill 2008, 87–8 citing Menander's *Phasma, Perikeiromene*, and possibly the *Heros*, along with Plaut. *Cist.* 123–4, *Truc.* 407–9, and Ter. *Heaut.* 629–30, 636.
14 Raccanelli 1998, 177–9.

since nothing is lacking for you at home' (206–7). Cleostrata rebukes her: *satin sana es? nam tu quidem advorsus/tuam istaec rem loquere*, 'Are you in your right mind? You are speaking in opposition to your own interests' (208–9). These lines are typically understood as Plautus' strategy for contrasting the two structures of Roman marriage: *cum manu* when the wife goes fully into the *potestas* of her husband (which corresponds to Myrrhina's understanding of her marriage), and *sine manu* when the wife's family retains more control of her assets (which corresponds to Cleostrata's view of marriage).[15] But if Cleostrata already knows who Casina is, perhaps in saying 'you are speaking against your own interests', she also means to send Myrrhina some kind of hint or *signum clarum* about Casina. Myrrhina's subsequent gleeful participation in the plan to trick Lysidamus, with her mention that *numquam ecastor ullo die risi adaeque* 'never on any day by Castor have I laughed so much' (857) may show a glimpse of her relief after years of suffering the loss of her daughter. To be sure, the *Casina* is a raucous play, full of boisterous and bawdy scenes. But paying attention to the implications of what the prologue says and hints about the serious side of the reproduction of citizenship gives an additional dimension to Cleostrata's character. Her plot, perhaps, is not just a one-day wonder to thwart and ridicule her husband, but a sixteen-year strategy to help her neighbour and her neighbour's child.

Casina and the Topography of Fides

It has become increasingly clear that Plautus could make references to Roman sites and practices even in the midst of plays set in Greek cities.[16] Especially crucial in the discussion of Roman topographical references in Roman drama is Moore's discussion of *Curculio* 462 ff. when the *choragos* (producer) character comes on stage during the *Curculio* – set in Epidauros – and suddenly starts describing all kinds of shifty behavior in spaces that are easily matched up with places in the Roman forum: 'To an audience with even the slightest perceptiveness, the speech must have been as disconcerting as it was amusing, for it suggests in a far from subtle way that the separation the Romans liked to assume between themselves and the "Greeks" they laughed at in comedies was in fact

---

15 Rei 1998, 97–100, Moore 1998, 170, Treggiari 1991, 28–36.
16 Marshall 2006, 36–48; Manuwald 2011, 298, and Germany, this volume. Jeppesen 2013 offers spatially contextualized readings of religious parody in the *Aulularia*, *Rudens*, and *Poenulus* that demonstrate how productive this approach can be: see esp. 62–78, 120–3, 146, 216–40, 256–7.

non-existent, and that even with respect to the all-important Roman quality of *fides*, many in the very presence of the audience were no different from the *Graeculi* on stage.'[17] As Moore acknowledges, it is not simply a matter of Plautus' laying one city plan over another. Rather, in sketching this perfidious topography of deceit in the Roman forum, Plautus gets to the very heart of – or jokes about – what it means to be Roman. Livy (1.21.4), Dionysius of Halicarnassus (2.75) and Plutarch (*Num.* 16.1) report as part of Rome's foundation narrative that Numa devised the worship of *Fides* and linked it to the establishment of trustworthy oaths that made Roman civilization's rule of law possible and enduring.

The temple of Fides, built in 250 or 254 by A. Atilius Calatinus (Cic. *de nat. Deor.* 2.61), occupied a commanding position in Rome just by the temple of Jupiter Optimus Maximus on the Capitoline.[18] Several recent scholars have argued for a topographical reading of literary references to Fides. Corbeill has made an attractive argument that Propertius 1.16 'portrays the door of the Temple of Fides lamenting her mistress's recent moral decline', and he makes a comparison between this poem and Euclio's prayer to Fides.[19] Jeppesen has recently proposed a topographical reading of the shrine of Fides in the *Aulularia*. That is, he argues, one of the spaces at Rome where the *Aulularia* could have been performed was in the Circus Flaminius, perhaps near where the theater of Marcellus now stands. The audience of an *Aulularia* performed in that vicinity could look up toward the Capitoline and see or be aware of the temple of Fides in the background. Jeppesen argues for a powerful parodic effect in Euclio's address to Fides as he hides the pot of gold in her *fanum* (shrine) on the stage. The lofty political maneuvering that sought to celebrate Fides as a distinctively Roman virtue would thus be pointedly contrasted with Euclio's miserly mission to hide the gold.[20]

I would like to bring the idea of Fides in the *Casina* into this conversation about Plautus' use of a topography of Fides. I do this in the spirit of Anna Clark's recent study *Divine Qualities*: she argues that references in drama may connect with the ways that individual Romans might think about and interact with divine personifications including Pietas, Virtus, Salus and Fides.[21] A general might build a temple that celebrates his military successes, a working man might wish for better days to come. I would like to extend this notion of varied ways of thinking about Fides by thinking specifically about Fides' possible connections with reproduction

---

17 Moore 1991, 362.
18 Reusser 1995; Coarelli 2007, 28, 35, cf. Cato at Cic. *de off*. 3.104.
19 Corbeill 2005, 94, 88–9.
20 Jeppesen 2013, 125–47, 2014. On Plautus' handling of the shrine of Fides see also Hunter 1981 (= Hunter 2008, 612–26).
21 Clark 2007, 73–116.

and citizenship in the *Casina*. After all, what is at stake in the *Aulularia* when Euclio ducks into the shrine of Fides with his pot of gold is not merely Euclio's money. His daughter has been impregnated by their neighbour who is afraid to proceed with arrangements to marry her since she has no dowry. By denying her a dowry from the newly discovered pot of gold, and instead hiding it in the shrine of Fides, Euclio is, precisely, putting his daughter's capacity to reproduce citizenship in jeopardy. And, as Jeppesen argues, if Euclio carries the pot of gold hidden under his clothes, he probably looks like the pregnant Phaedria looks at the beginning of the play.[22] In discussing the concept of Fides during the Augustan period, Galinsky stresses the responsibilities of those with power to embody *fides* toward their dependents: *fides* 'is not so much the faithfulness of the conquered subjects to their masters, but the fiduciary obligation of the powerful to all those entrusted to them.'[23] It is this kind of responsibility that Euclio is trying to escape when he hides the gold in the shrine of Fides.

It is worth noting too that in addition to Fides being associated by the historians with oaths in general, other factors can contribute to a perception that Fides has a special interest in the reproduction of citizenship. On the level of legal and social regulations, treaties were kept at the temple of Fides. Romans established treaties with its Latin allies that granted them rights including the *ius commercii*, the right to own property and enter into contracts as a Roman citizen, and *ius conubii*, the right to contract legitimate marriage with a Roman citizen. After 52 CE the temple of Fides is used as a repository for bronze tablets inscribed with documents granting soldiers rights to marry and thus transmit Roman citizenship to children. Discharged soldiers carried their own folded and sealed copies of these – their diplomas. Thus the Capitoline temple of Fides for centuries has in part to do with regulating the transmission of citizenship at the level of the state.[24]

The Temple of Fides on the Capitoline may have had a line of sight down to the *forum holitorium*, where it was later said that "the *lactaria* (milk) column in the *forum holitorium* was a place where people brought infants who needed to be fed" (*lactaria columna in foro olitorio dicta, quod ibi infantes lacte alendos deferebant*, Festus p. 105 L (118 M)). It is probably true that this would be the place to go to hire a wet nurse for an infant.[25] But that does not exclude the possibility

---

22 Jeppesen 2013, 130–1.
23 Galinsky 1996, 61.
24 On the treaties, see Baronowski 1988 and the useful discussion of Colognesi 2014, 92–103; on *conubium* and the transmission of citizenship see Treggiari 1991, 43–9. On the keeping of treaties at the Temple of Fides on the Capitoline see Coarelli 2007, 35; Dio 45.17.3 and Obsequens 68 record the destruction of many tablets in a storm in 43 BCE. On diplomas, see Phang 2001, 53, 55.
25 So Corbier 2001, 62–3.

that infants were set down – abandoned – here because they could not be cared for by the mother who bore them.[26] Is it possible that the idea of Fides watching over the scene might be part of a Roman topography of abandonment and possible rescue? If so, that would be another reason why it would be attractive to have the goddess Fides speak the prologue of the *Casina*: the goddess can describe what happened to the baby all those years ago because in comedy's Roman world, she was in a position to see that kind of thing herself.[27]

Casina and the Halcyon days

The speaker of the *Casina*'s prologue tells the audience that they should cast away all thoughts of being required to pay back debts since during the festival 'the bankers are on holiday' (*ludus datus est argentariis, Cas.* 25). This reference to credit and banking is one more reason to understand Fides as the speaker of the prologue, for *fides* is the institution that makes banking and commerce function effectively.[28] To describe the quietness of the business world during the festival, the speaker of the prologue says *Alcydonia circum forum*, 'it is the Halcyon days all around the forum' (*Cas.* 26). The Halcyon days fell in the calendar in December, during the week before and the week after the winter solstice. It may be that Plautus' Greek model, Diphilus' *Kleroumenoi*, contained a reference to Halcyon days since they would fall during the month of Poseideon near the time of the Rural Dionysia festival in Athens, at which comedies might be performed.[29] Yet the mere presence of a reference to Halcyon days in the Greek model would not suffice to explain why Plautus chose to include a reference to Halcyon days in his adaptation. Plautus' prologue is speaking metaphorically here because there were no regularly scheduled *Ludi*

---

26 Boswell 1988, 51–137 emphasizes narratives of the rescue of abandoned children in the Roman evidence. For wide-ranging discussion of the evidence for the exposure of infants in Greece and Rome see Evans Grubbs 2013, with further references, and Rawson 2003, 114–19.
27 The *Cistellaria*'s story that Selenium was taken up 'from the racetrack' *ab hippodromo* (549, 552), may also map its descriptions of actions at Sicyon onto a Roman topography of foundlings in the Circus Flaminius and the adjacent *forum holitorium*. On the structures of the Circus Flaminius see Humphreys 1986, 540–5 with Wiseman 1974 and 1976. Evidence for racing in the Circus Flaminius: Plut. *Quaest. Rom.* 66, Varro *LL* 5.154, Val. Max. 1.7.4, although it is not clear exactly what kind of horse races were held there. On the possibility that the *Truculentus* may engage with its audiences' topographical awareness of the *columna bellica* in the Circus Flaminius (cf. Servius on Verg. *Aen.* 9.52) see Germany in this volume.
28 Skutsch 1900, 273; cf. Gell. *NA* 20.1.41.
29 Skutsch 1900, 281.

during December in Rome. The metaphor usefully conveys the holiday quality of the comic festival. Discourse about the natural history of the Halcyon days and their mythical origins may also contribute to the *Casina*'s overall engagement with the theme of the risky business of reproducing citizenship. According to Aristotle, Simonides had referred to quiet days in winter when the *halcyon* (kingfisher) cares for her young (Arist. *HA* 542b; *PMG* 508); Aristotle endorses this idea of quiet days during the week before and the week after the winter solstice, and the account is repeated by Ovid, Pliny (*Nat*. 10.47) and Isidore.[30] The miraculous aspects of halcyon reproduction are clear in Ovid, who writes of the transformed Ceyx and Alcyone, who is the daughter of the wind god Aeolus:

> tum quoque mansit amor, nec coniugiale solutum est
> foedus in alitibus; coeunt fiuntque parentes,
> perque dies placidos hiberno tempore septem   745
> incubat Alcyone pendentibus aequore nidis.
> tum iacet unda maris, ventos custodit et arcet
> Aeolos egressu praestatque nepotibus aequor.   Ovid, *Met*. 11.743–8[31]

... then still their love persisted, nor was the marital treaty dissolved in their bird shapes; they join together and become parents, and during those seven calm days in wintertime Alcyone sits on the nests that are suspended on the sea. At that time the wave of the sea lies still and Aeolus keeps custody of the winds and keeps them from setting out and provides a calm sea for his grandsons.

Isidore too makes explicit the extraordinary life-saving things that have to take place for the halcyon to reproduce (Isidore, *Etym*. 12.7.25):

> Alcyon pelagi volucris dicta, quasi ales oceanea, eo quod hieme in stagnis oceani nidos facit pullosque educit: qua excubante fertur extento aequore pelagus silentibus ventis continua septem dierum tranquillitate mitescere, et eius fetibus educandis obsequium ipsa rerum natura praebere.

The Alcyon is called a bird of the sea, as though *ales oceana*, because in the winter it makes nests in the still waters of the ocean and raises (*educit*) its young. It is said that while it nests, the sea remains calm for seven days in continuous tranquility, the surface of the sea level and the winds silent, and that the very nature of the world furnishes aid to the nurture of its young.

---

30 On the myths of the halcyon see Gresseth 1964 and Levaniouk 2011, 287–318; on Plutarch's discussion of the halcyon as an exemplar of marital virtue (*Mor*. 982f–3e), see Jazdzewska 2013 and cf. Gutzwiller 1992.
31 On Ovid's creative handling of his sources for the Alcyone and Ceyx myth see Fantham 1979.

Thus, Halcyon days are not only days of calm weather at sea, and metaphorical calm times in the forum, but they are also the time when young born into a risky situation can be brought up safely. The enslaved man who alertly noticed the baby being exposed, who brought the baby to Cleostrata and asked that she be taken in and raised, and Cleostrata herself, who acceded to that request, are the forces in the larger world who worked together to make possible that baby's ultimate emergence into citizenship. The prologue's description of the play as taking place during the Halcyon days aligns the tale of a citizen Casina rescued with mythical and natural historical accounts of miraculously safe birth and nurturing.

There are thus several answers to the question of what *Casina* might have to do with Fides. The *Casina*'s plot is suitable for a divine prologue. Fides' varied connections to the reproduction of citizenship, and the possibility that Roman audiences might have an idea of a topography of abandonment within sight from the temple of Fides offer social and cultural contexts for seeing preservation of Casina's citizen identity as something that could have to do with Fides.[32] Of course, it is possible that the goddess Agnoia, Misconception, is presiding (as she does in Menander's *Perikeiromene, The Girl who was Shorn*) over my reading of what *Casina*'s drama of citizenship lost and restored might have to do with Fides.[33] If so, my hope is that she will advance the plot so that I am set straight before too long.[34]

Bibliography

Abadie-Reynal, C., Darmon, J.-P. (2003), 'La Maison et la mosaïque des Synaristôsai: (les Femmes au déjeuner de Ménandre)', in: R. Early et al. (eds.), *Zeugma: Interim Reports, Rescue Excavations (Packard Humanities Institute), Inscriptions of Antiochus I, Bronze Statue of Mars, House and Mosaic of the Synaristôsai, and Recent work on the Roman Army at Zeugma, JRA Supplement* 51, 79–99.

Baronowski, D. W. (1988), 'Roman Treaties with Communities of Citizens', *CQ* 38.1, 172–8.

---

[32] Such ideas about the relation of Fides to the reproduction of citizenship would make it even more sharply pointed that in the *Aulularia* Euclio tries to hide the pot of gold in the shrine of Fides, for in the shrine of Fides he is hiding the gold in just the kind of place where others might try to entrust a baby to a different life. There may even be some jokes about *fides* and citizenship in the way the *Epidicus* represents a *fidicina* – a cithara player – and organizes its plot around the idea that the *fidicina* can be mistaken for a long-lost citizen girl.

[33] P. Oxy. 2652, Turner 1967, 180.

[34] I thank Sophia Pappaioannou, Seth Jeppesen, Ashli Baker, and Lauren Dudley for their contributions to this project. It is also pleasure to acknowledge the support of a *Modern Language Quarterly* Faculty Travel Grant.

Boswell, J. (1988), *The Kindness of Strangers: The Abandonment of Children in Western Europe from Late Antiquity to the Renaissance*, Chicago.
Burton, P. J. (2004), '*Amicitia* in Plautus: A Study of Roman Friendship Processes', *AJP* 125.2, 209–43.
Charitonidis, S., Kahil, L., and Ginouvès, R. (1970), *Les Mosaïques de la maison du Ménandre à Mytilène*, AntK-BH 6, Bern.
Clark, A. J. (2007), *Divine Qualities: Cult and Community in Republican Rome*, Oxford.
Coarelli, F. (2007), *Rome and Environs: An Archaeological Guide*. Trans. J. J. Clauss and D. P. Harmon, illustrations adapted by J. A. Clauss and P. A. MacKay, Berkeley.
Colognesi, L. C. (2014), *Law and Power in the Making of the Roman Commonwealth*, Cambridge.
Corbeill, A. (2005), 'The topography of Fides in Propertius 1.16', in: W. W. Batstone and G. Tissol (eds.), *Defining Genre and Gender in Latin Literature*, New York, 79–96.
Corbier, M. (2001), 'Child Exposure and Abandonment', in: S. Dixon (ed.), *Childhood, Class and Kin in the Roman World*, London, 52–73.
De Melo, W. (2011), (ed. and trans.), *Plautus: Casina, The Casket Comedy, Curculio, Epidicus, The Two Menaechmuses*, Cambridge, MA and London.
Dudley, L. (2013), *Casina: What the Women Knew*. Adapted and produced by Lauren Dudley. http://www.youtube.com/watch?v=AsWW0ywTerE
Evans Grubbs, J. (2013), 'Infant Exposure and Infanticide', in: J. Evans Grubbs and T. Parkin (eds.), *The Oxford Handbook of Childhood and Education in the Classical World*, Oxford, 83–107.
Fantham, E. (1975), 'Sex, Status and Survival in Hellenistic Athens: A Study of Women in New Comedy', *Phoenix* 29, 44–74.
——— (1979), 'Ovid's Ceyx and Alcyone: The Metamorphoses of a Myth', *Phoenix* 33.4, 330–45.
——— (2011), *Roman Readings: Roman Responses to Greek Literature from Plautus to Statius and Quintilian*, Berlin and New York.
Fraenkel, E. (1932), 'Das Original der *Cistellaria* des Plautus', *Ph* 87, 117–20.
Feeney, D. (2010), 'Crediting Pseudolus: Trust, Belief and the Credit Crunch in Plautus' *Pseudolus*', *CP* 105.3, 281–300.
Feltovich, A. C. (2011), *Women's Social Bonds in Greek and Roman Comedy*. PhD diss., University of Cincinnati.
Franko, G. (1995), '*Fides*, Aetolia, and Plautus' *Captivi*', *TAPA*, 125, 155–176.
Freyburger, G. (1986), *Fides: Étude sémantique et réligieuse depuis les origines jusqu' à l'époque augustéenne. Collection d'Études Anciennes*, Paris.
Galinsky, K. (1996), *Augustan Culture*, Princeton.
Gresseth, G. K. (1964), 'The Myth of Alcyone', *TAPA* 95, 88–98.
Gutzwiller, K./Çelik, Ö. (2012), 'New Menander Mosaics from Antioch', *AJA* 116, 573–623.
Gutzwiller, K. (1992), 'The Nautilus, the Halcyon, and Selenaia: Callimachus' 'Epigram' 5 Pf. = 14 G. P.', *CA* 11.2, 194–209.
Heinze, R. (1928), 'Fides', *Hermes* 64.1, 140–66.
Humphreys, J. (1986), *Roman Circuses: Arenas for Chariot Racing*, Berkeley and Los Angeles.
Hunter, R. L. (1981), 'The *Aulularia* of Plautus and its Greek Original', *PCPS* 27, 37–49.
——— (1987), 'Middle Comedy and the *Amphitruo* of Plautus', *Dioniso* 57, 281–98.
——— (2008), *On Coming After: Studies in Post-Classical Greek Literature and its Reception, Part 2: Comedy and Performance, Greek Poetry of the Roman Empire, The Ancient Novel. Trends in Classics Supplementary Volume 3/2*, Berlin and New York.

Jazdzewska, K. (2013), 'The Husband-Loving Kingfisher: Plutarch on Marriage, Marital Virtues, and Animals', in: *144th APA Annual Meeting Abstracts*, 76.
Jeppesen, S. (2013), *Performing Religious Parody in Plautine Comedy*. PhD diss., UC Santa Barbara.
_____ (2014), 'Plautine *Fides*: Parody of Cults to Divine Qualities', Lecture at Hendrix College, March 6, 2014, http://www.youtube.com/watch?v=wXgf281ivWs
Konstan, D. (1987), 'Between Courtesan and Wife: Menander's *Perikeiromene*', *Phoenix* 41.2, 122–39.
Lape, S. (2001), 'Democratic Ideology and the Poetics of Rape in Menandrian Comedy', *CA* 20.1, 79–119.
Levaniouk, O. (2011), *Eve of the Festival: Making Myth in Odyssey 19*, Hellenic Studies 46, Washington, D.C.
Ludwig, W. (1970), 'Die plautinische *Cistellaria* und das Verhältnis von Gott und Handlung bei Menander', in: *Entretiens sur l'Antiquité Classique* 16, 43–96.
MacCary, W. T./Willcock, M. M. (1976), *Plautus Casina*, Cambridge.
Manuwald, G. (2011), *Roman Republican Theatre*, Cambridge.
Marshall, C. W. (2006), *The Stagecraft and Performance of Roman Comedy*, Cambridge.
Mattingly, H./Robinson, E. S. G. (1932), 'The Prologue to the *Casina* of Plautus', *CR* 47.2, 52–4.
Moore, T. J. (1991), 'Palliata Togata: Plautus, *Curculio* 462–86', *AJP* 112.3, 343–62.
_____ (1998), *The Theater of Plautus: Playing to the Audience*, Austin.
Nervegna, S. (2013), *Menander in Antiquity: The Contexts of Reception*, Cambridge.
Pansiéri, C. (1997), *Plaute et Rome ou les ambiguïtés d' un marginal*. Collection Latomus 236, Brussels.
Phang, S. (2001), *The Marriage of Roman Soldiers (13 BC- AD 235): Law and Family in the Imperial Army*, Leiden.
Raccanelli, R. (1998), *L'amicitia nelle commedie di Plauto: Un' indagine antropologica*, Bari.
Rawson, B. (2003), *Children and Childhood in Roman Italy*, Oxford.
Rei, A. (1998), 'Villains, wives, and slaves in the comedies of Plautus', in: S. R. Joshel and S. Murnaghan (eds.), *Women and Slaves in Greco-Roman Culture: Differential Equations*, London and New York, 92–108.
Reusser, C. (1995), 'Fides populi Romani/Publica', in: Steinby, E. M., ed., *Lexicon Topographicum Urbis Romae*, Roma, vol. 2, 249–52.
Skutsch, F. (1900), 'Ein Prolog des Diphilos und eine Komödie des Plautus', *RhM* 55, 272–85.
Stockert, W. (2012), *T. Maccius Plautus Cistellaria. Einleitung, Text, und Kommentar*. Zetemata 143, München.
Süss, W. (1935), 'Zur *Cistellaria* des Plautus', *RhM* 84, 161–87.
_____ (1938), 'Nochmals zur *Cistellaria* des Plautus', *RhM* 87, 97–141.
Traill, A. (2008), *Women and the Comic Plot in Menander*, Cambridge.
Treggiari, S. (1991), *Roman Marriage: Iusti Coniuges from the Time of Cicero to the time of Ulpian*, Oxford.
Turner, E. G. (1967), 'Ink Drawing', *The Oxyrhynchus Papyri* 32, 180–1, no. 2652.
Wiseman, T. P. (1974), 'The Circus Flaminius', *PBSR* 42, 3–25.
_____ (1976), 'Two Questions on the Circus Flaminius', *PBSR* 44, 44–7.

Katerina Philippides
Symmetrical Recognitions in Plautus' *Epidicus*

Epidicus is an extremely short play of 733 lines. It has attracted scholarly interest on account of the concise and often elliptical representation of its plot details, particularly with regard to its 'prehistory'. In the past, a few scholars have noticed flaws in the plot and made the assumption that such inconsistencies were absent from the Greek model[1], though the latter has not been recovered or even identified. Goldberg has questioned the existence of a specific Greek model; he also argues for a 'coherent structure' in this particular Roman comedy, based upon comparison of the beginning and end, and parallels in the manner that the identity of the two girls, Telestis and Acropolistis, is revealed.[2]

I shall corroborate this interpretation and further show that the second half of the comedy consists not of two recognitions but six, which are symmetrically distributed and constitute opposing pairs. I shall first briefly examine the lines that precede the recognitions and pave the way for these scenes to be enacted. The recognitions are related to disclosure of the cunning slave's intrigues, whereas the lines preceding them are linked to their fabrication. The first part of the play is also symmetrically composed. The existence of symmetries reveals the meticulous construction of the comedy, a fact which permits us to appreciate Plautus' artistry.

My approach to *Epidicus*' text is based on the comedy's stage arrangement and action as well as on its thematic correspondences;[3] Moore reaches a similar conclusion about the play's artistic value by examining its metrical and musical structure.[4]

---

[1] On a survey of the earlier bibliography regarding these issues see Duckworth 1979, 97–98. More recently Fantham 1981, 1–10 has claimed that the sometimes elliptical representation of extra-dramatic facts is due to the absence of a Hellenistic-type prologue. Lowe 2001, 57 notices the elliptical plot and peculiarities in its construction. On the other hand, Manuwald 2001, 133–61 states that all the necessary information is disclosed to the audience, whereas that which is withheld contributes to the suspense.
[2] Goldberg 1978, 81–91.
[3] In terms of approach, this paper forms a triptych with two preceding papers on *Mostellaria* (*Drama*, 1999) and *Captivi* (*Plautine Trends*, 2014).
[4] Moore 2001, 313–33. Moore 2001, 323–32 brilliantly points out a very important element of *Epidicus*, its "frenetic pace".

A summary of the plot is here in order. In place of the typical prologue, the comedy begins with a conversation between two protatic characters, both slaves: Epidicus, who lends the play its name, and Thesprio, who acts out the role of a *servus currens* (1–80). From their dialogue the audience learns that the *adulescens* Stratippocles, newly returned to Athens from a campaign, was until recently in love with a *meretrix* named Acropolistis. For the young man's sake, Epidicus devised a scheme to buy the girl from her pimp. This he did by tricking Periphanes, the father of Stratippocles, into believing that Acropolistis was his illegitimate daughter, born of a rape committed long ago in a far-off city. With this lie Epidicus succeeded in extracting the necessary money from the old man; Acropolistis has been freed and is now at the house of Periphanes, acting out her part in the slave's trick. However, Thesprio informs Epidicus that his young master has had a change of heart and has turned his affections to Telestis, a young prisoner, whom he has liberated by borrowing money. Epidicus realizes to his dissatisfaction that he must devise a new plan to convince the old man to give him yet more cash, this time to pay off Stratippocles' loan to release Telestis.[5]

This second scheme is hatched in a later scene (166–305), which Sharrock has characterized as a second prologue.[6] Epidicus overhears Periphanes confiding to his friend Apoecides that he intends to find a bride for his son Stratippocles. Exploiting this information, Epidicus assumes the role of a *servus currens*[7] to suggest that Periphanes purchase the freedom of an imaginary prostitute with whom Stratippocles is purportedly infatuated, so as to get her out of the picture and arrange the young man's marriage more easily. The money will in fact be paid to the moneylender who made the loan used for Telestis. A music-girl impersonating the fictional harlot will be ensconced in Periphanes' house for the purpose; in the end it will turn out that Telestis is the old man's daughter.

Several pairs of characters appear in the play: the two old men, Periphanes and Apoecides, who are friends; the two young men, Stratippocles and Chaeribulus, also friends; and the two girls who are the object of Stratippocles' affections, Acropolistis and Telestis. The stage represents two Athenian houses, the one belonging to Periphanes and the other to Chaeribulus.

---

5 It should be noted that this play, which is so abundant with recognitions, starts with one more quasi-recognition: the two slaves recognize and greet each other at the very beginning of the play; see Slater 2001, 191–92.
6 Sharrock 2009, 124 and n. 64.
7 Cf. Ergasilus, the parasite in *Captivi*, who assumes the role of a *servus currens* when throwing his cloak around his neck (779).

The first part of the play: Symmetrical encounters

The first part of the play is characterized by parallel stage action. The introductory dialogue is followed by a sequence of symmetrical scenes: Epidicus utters a monologue, then two characters appear and engage in a dialogue. Having approached and conversed with them, Epidicus is left alone on stage to soliloquize once more.[8] The two conversing characters are either old or young; the cunning slave either bemoans the predicament he finds himself in or brags about the success of his sly scheme. The diagram presented below makes this quite spectacular symmetry clear:

Epidicus' first monologue	(vv. 81–103)
Dialogue between Stratippocles, Chaeribulus and Epidicus	(vv. 104–58)
Epidicus' second monologue	(vv. 158–65)
Dialogue between Apoecides, Periphanes and Epidicus	(vv. 166–305)
Epidicus' third monologue	(vv. 306–19)
Dialogue between Stratippocles and Chaeribulus	(vv. 320–36)
Epidicus' fourth monologue	(vv. 337–45)
Dialogue between Chaeribulus, Stratippocles and Epidicus	(vv. 346–81)

As the play unfolds, the symmetry is disrupted: in the next scene the old men converse with each other and a slave other than Epidicus, while the music-girl escorts them in silence. It is obvious that Epidicus advances the threads of the plot after coming to an agreement with two pairs of characters who differ in age. Thus, conforming to the comic role of *servus callidus,* he conspires with the young to fool the old.

The symmetry in the first part of the play is not simply limited to the distribution of characters on stage or their action. It is also observable in its thematics, given that all dialogues revolve around the love affairs of youth. Stratippocles discloses to his friend the shame he feels (*pudet*, 107) at buying a prisoner secretly from his father. An analogous feeling is shared by Periphanes[9]: as a widower he wishes to marry Philippa, the woman he raped in the past. The *senex* feels embarrassed to talk about such a delicate issue with his son, who is ignorant of his father's reckless behavior. Both Apoecides and Chaeribulus try to console their friends.

Consequently, it is legitimate to say that the first part of the play presents a coherence achieved through action paralleled by similarity or contrast (*similitudo*

---

8 Sharrock 2009, 122–23 and n. 63 speaks of "two parallel movements".
9 For the sense of shame felt by both Stratippocles and Periphanes see Lowe 2001, 62.

per contrarium). The parallelism of the preceding dialogues as well as of the recognitions discussed below, is reinforced by the fact that there is usually a limited number of actors on stage.[10]

Although I leave out of my diagram the first scene of the comedy, it is worth to note that even there, as Moore observes, the parallelism is achieved by symmetrical metrical patterns: vv. 1–24 correspond to vv. 25–47.[11]

The second part of the play: symmetrical recognitions

I shall now come to the core theme of my paper. In this short play, an unusually long section (one third of the play, to be precise) is taken up by a series of recognition scenes, totaling six in all and forming three pairs. Each pair comprises a positive and a negative recognition. I define 'negative recognition' as a situation where no connection is established between the characters: that is, those seeking a lost family member or acquaintance are presented to entire strangers. In the case of 'positive recognition', the characters involved used to know each other in the past, but were separated and are now reunited.[12]

The first quasi-recognition, 437–71 (positive)

The first quasi-recognition is positive. A soldier is looking for the house of Periphanes. The *senex* is already on stage and approaches the person seeking him, who is escorted by a mute character, a slave. Although this is not the usual type of recognition encountered in the genre (as we shall see, the characters involved were not acquainted in the past, and this is the first time they have ever met), there are nonetheless elements indicating that this case does resemble a recognition scene. Periphanes reveals to his interlocutor that he too was a *miles gloriosus*, Periphanes from the region of Plothea. The old man's name leads the

---

10 I owe this observation to Costas Panayotakis.
11 Moore 2001, 317.
12 Willock 1995, 27 succinctly and without elaborating, comments on the four more apparent recognitions: "Now that the situation has been developed, we have two successive scenes unmasking the two girls in the house, which are interwoven with two identifying the other two women".

soldier to recall rumors of his feats: *nemp' quem in adulescentia/memorant apud reges armis, arte duellica/diuitias magnas indeptum*? (You mean the one who people say acquired great wealth in his youth in the service of kings for his arms and art of war?) (449–51).[13] At the same time, as soon as the soldier asks to see a prostitute named Acropolistis, Periphanes recognizes him as the soldier: *nunc demum scio ego hunc qui sit: quem dudum Epidicus/mihi praedicauit militem* (Now at last I know who he is: the soldier Epidicus was telling me about a while ago) (458–59).

The disclosure of a name and the memories it evokes are decisive elements in the realization of traditional recognitions. Moreover, this scene is the first of six similar repeated scenes. What we have here is a pattern that contributes to audience perception of the relevant scene as a recognition, even if only in retrospect.[14] It should be noted that Epidicus plays his part in this quasi-recognition since Periphanes was confident that he was telling the truth about the soldier's identity. Epidicus is not always a reliable witness, as will be shown below.

Second recognition, 472–525 (negative)

In this scene Periphanes orders a slave to ask the girl bought by Epidicus to appear. Epidicus has replaced Acropolistis, lover of both Stratippocles and the soldier, with a music-girl impersonating her. To his great surprise, the soldier finds himself face to face with an unknown character. Repetition of the deictic pronoun *haec* (477, 480, 481, 482, 484), used by both male characters when they address the girl, stresses their astonishment and disagreement over her identity. Seeing things objectively from the outside, the soldier tells the *senex* that he has been duped by his slave. He eventually exits disappointed and empty-handed, while Periphanes is left alone with the girl, whom he promptly questions to establish her true identity. She responds that she was simply hired to provide an accompaniment on the lyre for a sacrifice taking place in the house. She also informs the old man that the real Acropolistis has been freed by his son, having assured him in irony that she knows her as well as she knows herself. Periphanes then angrily drives the music-girl away from his house. It should be noted that

---

13 For the Latin text I use Lindsay (Oxford, 1904); all English translations are quoted from de Melo (2011).
14 At this point we might recall Taplin 1978, 123; when discussing his theory of mirror scenes in Greek tragedy, he argues that the audience watches a doublet of scenes and reconsiders and reevaluates the first of them. In this case the scenes do not reverse each other, but repeat each other.

during this failed recognition scene, the name of the person of interest, Acropolistis, is heard twice (479, 503) to no avail: the soldier does not connect it with the girl presented to him, and after his exit the music-girl recalls the real Acropolistis, who is however not present. Thus, the precondition for a successful recognition does not function as expected.

It has been argued in previous studies that in the case of Periphanes, the exploitation of the braggart warrior motif is irrelevant to the plot.[15] Yet setting aside the emphasis this play accords to recognitions, the recollection of war achievements emphasizes Periphanes' general recall of the past. In an earlier scene, he speaks of his own youthful escapades in order to justify the actions of his son. In addition, the military side to Periphanes' personality serves a further function: as soon as Epidicus' schemes are exposed, the *senex* realizes that he has been defeated by a far better warrior. Like every cunning slave in Plautine comedy, Epidicus and his exploits are portrayed by frequent reference to military jargon.[16]

Third recognition, 526–69 (positive)

In the third, positive recognition, Telestis' mother Philippa enters looking for the house of Periphanes, clearly in a state of distress over the imprisonment of her daughter. The *senex* is again alone on stage and approaches her. The names Periphanes and Epidaurus (the place where the rape occurred) and the recollection of past events contribute to the recognition. In a moving scene involving the use of symmetrical lines, the characters gradually come to recognize each other

---

15 Lowe 2001, 67. Arnott 2001, 87–88 claims that what is to his mind the unexpected transformation of the *senex* Periphanes into a former *miles gloriosus* is the most solid evidence indicating that *Epidicus* follows a Greek model.

16 Cf. *bellum* (160), *oppugnare* (163), *uirtute* (381), *pugnasti* (493), *tragulam* (690). According to the soldier Epidicus cut his master to pieces limb by limb (*articulatim concidit*, 488); *concido* means 'cut to pieces in war' (see Lewis & Short s. v. B2). De Melo 2011, 384 thinks differently that this phrase alludes to the myth of the dismemberment of Pelias by his daughters as a result of Medea's trick. Epidicus also displays political skills, since he convenes a session of the senate in his heart (159) to befool the *senes*, the pillars of the senate (189) or Periphanes in particular, the proponent of important decrees (517) and Apoecides who understands *iura ... et leges* (292). Epidicus also has *consilia* (152). Even his name derives from the Greek verb ἐπιδικάζειν, used when officials adjudicate matters of inheritance; see De Melo 2011, 333. Cf. also Thesprio's comic presentation of Epidicus as *praetor* (25–28a). For a general examination of the slave in Plautus as military and political leader see Segal 1987, 128–36. Fraenkel 2000, 231–50 has argued that Plautus has expanded the role of slave by adding legal and military metaphors to it, quite apart from increasing the number of slave monologues.

as victim and repentant perpetrator. Periphanes reassures Philippa that their daughter is safe in his house, wrongly assuming that Acropolistis is his daughter Telestis. For a second time he orders a slave to fetch the girl, on this occasion to be reunited with her supposed mother.[17] Despite the exposure of Epidicus' first scheme regarding the music-girl, the old man continues to trust him.

Fourth recognition, 570–606 (negative)

In the fourth (negative) recognition, Acropolistis enters instead of Telestis, as a consequence of Epidicus' plotting. As before, the deictic pronoun *haec* is repeatedly exploited (574, 575, 576), this time to shows the parents' perplexity over the unknown girl. Philippa strongly denies that she knows this girl or has ever set eyes on her before (*ego hanc quae siet/neque scio neque noui neque ego hanc oculis uidi ante hunc/diem*, 576–77). The recognition has failed. Albeit frustrated, Philippa does not exit like the soldier earlier, but remains on stage until the real identity of the mystery girl is revealed. Instead of the name Telestis, kinship terms are heard: father, mother, daughter, but for comic effect. The *senex* yet again interrogates a young woman, on this occasion an insolent character who admits to having called him *pater* although he was not her father, because he himself called her *filia*. Slater has examined these words as an allusion to incest, which makes Periphanes furious the moment he perceives it; he consequently demands that the girl stop calling him father.[18]

Philippa directs attention to a fake recognition which took place in the 'prehistory' of the play. She asks Periphanes which signs (*signis*, 597) he used to recognize the girl as his daughter. The old man admits that he saw no signs but took Epidicus' word on the matter, since he himself had only seen his daughter once. The tokens will later play a significant role in the recognition of the real daughter. Philippa finally withdraws into Periphanes' house along with Acropolistis. The presence of both women there is required by the plot.

It might be useful to stress Periphanes' comic role, or rather its reversal. At first, in the cases of both girls, he appears as a respectable old man who acts as a guarantor or a go-between. Both the soldier and Philippa count on him to reunite them with their beloved. Yet Periphanes' sanity is called into question by both characters (475, 575), when he insists on defending the false identities of the two girls. More importantly, the *senex* turns out to have been duped by his slave. He

---

17 See Goldberg 1978, 87.
18 Slater 2001, 199–202.

has twice given money to buy girls who so far seem to be entirely unrelated to his family. His frustration is therefore understandable when he states that he has turned into a pimp (*ego lenocinium facio*, 581), i.e. he has assumed a dishonest and inappropriate role for a decent *senex*. Periphanes' comic role is further exaggerated in the finale. Instead of restoring some power and dignity to the deceived old man, as he does in *Mostellaria*, for example, here Plautus literally gives the first and the last word to the cunning slave, who not only is excused by his master but also in reverse makes Periphanes beg that he be forgiven.

Fifth recognition, 634–45 (positive)

In the fifth brief (positive) recognition, the leading part is played by Periphanes' daughter Telestis, the girl whom the audience has been anxiously waiting to see from the very outset. In this scene it is Epidicus and Telestis who mutually recognize each other in the presence of the money-lender. The slave remembers her as a child, from the time he brought her presents for her birthday. This is the most traditional recognition scene in the play, since names are heard (Telestis, Periphanes' daughter, born of Philippa in Thebes, conceived in Epidaurus), signs are mentioned (the little golden moon and ring), and memories from the past are shared. It is unusual that the tokens are not brought onto the stage, as Ketterer notices, but are described to the audience.[19]

It is also rather unusual that instead of a family member recognizing Philippa, the process is led by a slave. Epidicus substitutes for the girl's parents, since their reunion with her will occur off-stage. Thus, the more traditional recognition will be not witnessed by the spectators.[20]

The sixth recognition, 646–59 (negative)

In the sixth similarly brief recognition the *adulescens* Stratippocles enters with the cash he intends to give the money-lender, only to learn from both Telestis and Epidicus that the girl is in fact his sister. Here instead of first names, kinship

---

[19] Ketterer 1986, 99.
[20] Cf. the analogous off-stage recognition of Selenium by her father in *Cistellaria*. Telestis' recognition pertains essentially to her father, who only once set eyes on her in the remote past. Philippa has only briefly been parted from her daughter. Telestis will of course be reunited with her brother on stage.

terms (brother and sister) are employed to comic effect. Finding it very hard to believe that the girl he loves is a blood relative, Stratippocles wonders whether Telestis is in her right mind (*sanan haec est?*, 649). The accusation of madness recalls the equivalent allegations made by the soldier and Philippa against Periphanes, and indicates the unusual repetitive mixing of characters and identities. In common with Philippa, and above all the soldier, Stratippocles is disappointed to discover that he cannot be with the person he cherishes. Yet Epidicus has a solution: he consoles the young man that Acropolistis is available and waiting for him in his house.

A diagram of the recognition scenes makes more apparent the symmetries in both dramatic and thematic articulation:

> First quasi-recognition (positive), 437–71: *Miles* and *senex* Periphanes
> Second recognition (negative), 472–525: *Miles*, Periphanes and a girl (lyre-player)
> Third recognition (positive), 526–69: Periphanes and *domina* Philippa
> Fourth recognition (negative), 570–606: Periphanes, Philippa and *meretrix* Acropolistis
> Fifth recognition (positive), 634–45: *servus* Epidicus and the girl Telestis
> Sixth recognition (negative), 646–59: *adulescens* Stratippocles, Telestis and Epidicus

★★

I shall close my paper with a few brief observations regarding the series of recognitions. Firstly, each case involves either two or three characters. Periphanes participates in the first four such scenes, whereas Epidicus is absent, despite being largely responsible for the whole mess.[21] His absence is imperative for his plotting to be exposed and for the *senex* to be ridiculed, thus increasing audience enjoyment of the play. When Epidicus is absent he cannot resolve the entanglement he has created; but he must be present during the last two recognitions, when the situation has reached such an impasse that he is the only one who can save the day and escape punishment. Thus, apart from restoring Telestis to her family, the purpose of the two last recognitions is to absolve the slave of blame. Epidicus manages to reunite Telestis with her parents and Acropolistis with Stratippocles. Thus, paradoxically he has used Periphanes' money wisely to free both daughter and lover.

We might expect a play with consecutive recognition scenes to have a loose plot. Yet the symmetrical, repeated scenes lend cohesion to *Epidicus*, in the sense that the spectators perceive and anticipate a recurring pattern involving pairs of

---

21 See Goldberg 1978, 87.

positive and negative recognitions. Bearing in mind the similarly symmetrical first part of the play, it is I think legitimate to say that *Epidicus* is a coherent comedy, artfully constructed by a master playwright.

Acknowledgments

I would like to thank both Stavros Frangoulidis and Niall W. Slater for their continuous encouragement and comments.

Bibliography

Arnott, W. G. (2001), 'Plautus' *Epidicus* and Greek Comedy', in: U. Auhagen (ed.), *Studien zu Plautus' Epidicus*, Tübingen, 71–90.
Duckworth, G. E. (1979), *T. Macci Plauti Epidicus. Edited with Critical Apparatus and Commentary*, New York (^{1}1940, Princeton).
Fantham, E. (1981), 'Plautus in Miniature: Compression and Distortion in the *Epidicus*', *PLLS* 3, 1–28.
Fraenkel, E. (1922/2000 rpt.), *Plautinisches im Plautus*, Berlin.
Goldberg, S. M. (1978), 'Plautus' *Epidicus* and the Case of the Missing Original', *TAPA* 108, 81–91.
Ketterer, R. C. (1986), 'Stage Properties in Plautine Comedy II', *Semiotica* 59, 93–135.
Lowe, J. C. B. (2001), 'Greek and Roman Elements in *Epidicus*' Intrigue', in: U. Auhagen (ed.), *Studien zu Plautus' Epidicus*, Tübingen, 57–70.
Manuwald, G. (2001), 'Informationsvergabe und Spannungsverteilung in Plautus' *Epidicus*', in: U. Auhagen (ed.), *Studien zu Plautus' Epidicus*, Tübingen, 133–61.
De Melo, W. (2011), *Plautus: Casina, The Casket Comedy, Curculio, Epidicus, The Two Menaechmuses*, Cambridge, Mass. & London.
Moore, T. J. (2001), 'Music in *Epidicus*', in: U. Auhagen (ed.), *Studien zu Plautus' Epidicus*, Tübingen, 313–34.
Segal, E. (1987), *Roman Laughter: The Comedy of Plautus*, Cambridge, Mass. (^{1}1968).
Sharrock, A. (2009), *Reading Roman Comedy: Poetics and Playfulness in Plautus and Terence*, Cambridge.
Slater, N. W. (2001), 'Appearance, Reality, and the Spectre of Incest in *Epidicus*', in: U. Auhagen (ed.), *Studien zu Plautus' Epidicus*, Tübingen, 191–203.
Taplin, O. (1978), *Greek Tragedy in Action*, Berkeley.
Willcock, M. (1995), 'Plautus and the *Epidicus*', *PLILS* 8, 19–29.

Mario Telò
Basket Case: Material Girl and Animate Object in Plautus's *Cistellaria*

In his essay on John Singer Sargent, Henry James comments on the American artist's most iconic painting, *The Daughters of Edward D. Boit* (1882; Fig. 1) – a remake of Velasquez's *Las meninas*:

> Two of the sisters stand hand in hand at the back, in the delightful, the *almost equal, company* of a pair of immensely tall emblazoned jars, which overtop them and seem also to *partake of the life of the picture*; the splendid porcelain and the aprons of the children *shine together*, while a mirror in the brown depth behind them catches the light.[1]

This passage eloquently captures the symbiotic, 'almost equal' relationship between human and non-human presences in the picture. Leaning against one of the Japanese jars, the only daughter portrayed in profile seems to establish a physical, intimate connection with the 'immensely tall emblazoned' objects. Such a connection engenders an exchange of personhood and thingness, of the girls' physicality and the vases' materiality. In this 'portrait of vases' or 'still-life of girls,' the blurring of human and non-human 'discloses how children, dolled-up, can be loved as material treasures, and how treasures can become objects of something like parental affection.'[2] As Bill Brown has shown, this dynamic also shapes the narrative output of Henry James – particularly, the *Golden Bowl* whose title announces a distinctive fusion of characters with objects; a materialization of human bodies, feelings and relations; and a transformation of items into entities charged with vital energy.[3]

In this paper, I explore the convergence between a 'material treasure' and a child in Plautus's *Cistellaria* – a play that capitalizes on the punning resonance between the *cistella* ('basket, box') and the *puella* ('girl'), abandoned and re-found, around whom the plot revolves. My interest is in the eponymous object's mediation between *puella* and play, in the interconnected ways the *cistella* becomes a surrogate of the girl and, at the same time, reifies the play onstage as an animated presence.[4] As I hope to show, the transference of vitality from person to thing, from *puella* to *cistella*, exposes the characters to affective experiences,

---

[1] James 1956 (1893), 222. The emphasis is mine.
[2] The quotations are from Brown 2003, 140, who strongly influenced this discussion.
[3] Cf. Brown 2003, 135–76.
[4] Relying on Veltrusky 1964, Ketterer 1986, 33 notes that in *Cistellaria*, when we do not see the *puella*, 'the prop ... replaces her as a presence on stage.' This chapter investigates the implications of this replacement by connecting the titular object's materiality with the play's self-reflexivity.

seen onstage or called forth from the past.[5] Actions such as dropping the *cistella*, lamenting its loss and searching provide moments for the play to reflect on itself both as a theatrical artifact and a narrative construct.

Fig. 1: John Singer Sargent, *Daughters of Edward D. Boit* (1882), Museum of Fine Arts, Boston.

My reading centers on the third and fourth acts, in which the *cistella*'s appearance weaves together an array of intratexts, as well as the plot's prehistory. I begin by examining two scenes, corresponding to the third act, in which the *cistella* makes

---

5 Recent studies on theatrical objects, informed by phenomenology and the so-called New Materialism, have emphasized 'the affective impact of props' as a complement to their semiotic and symbolic valences: see Sofer 1997, 2003, esp. 11–6. On props as time machines, turning the past into a presence felt onstage, cf. Sofer 1998 and 2003; for a wide-ranging discussion of the props of Greek tragedy and their intertextual past, see Mueller 2015.

its entrance and, in a climactic moment – a unique coup de théâtre in the corpus of Roman comedy – is dropped and left alone onstage. I suggest that the actions leading to the *cistella*'s solitary presence dramatize the entanglements of the prop, the *puella*, the play, and its Menandrean model. I then examine the *cistella*'s stage life after the return of human actors in the fourth act. I show how, amid the interlocking misunderstandings that usher in the customary happy ending, multiple intimations of narrative regression invest the *cistella* with a quasi-human vibrancy similar to that of Sargent's animated urns. The emotional intensities triggered by the *cistella*'s movement from character to character cause a synchronic re-creation of the events that followed the original exposure of the *puella*. Its woven texture gives tangible shape to the drama's temporal stratification, in which prop and *puella* operate interchangeably.

Before focusing on the epiphany of the *cistella* in the third act, I will consider two related issues: the object's material configuration and the self-reflexive ways in which the play's Greek model, Menander's *Synaristosai* ('Women lunching together'), is inscribed in the text.[6] This discussion will help us interpret the presence of the *cistella*, in a scene that, like the Menandrian title, presents three female characters acting together.

Though we cannot be certain of the object used in the original performance of *Cistellaria*, in a play about the exposure and recognition of children the term *cistella* (diminutive of *cista*; Gr. κίστη) clearly evokes the wicker containers (baskets, boxes, chests) employed in the Graeco-Roman literary imaginary as vessels for abandoned babies. The *TLL* defines *cista* as *corbis, arculae genus viminae* ('basket, a kind of wicker box').[7] Isidore's paretymology emphasizes the object's woven texture (20.9.8): *cistella a costis ex canna vel ligno, quibus contexitur, nominata* ('the *cistella* is so called from the 'ribs' of reed or wood with which it is woven'). The verb *contexo* also appears in Columella's description of the container (12.56.2): *solide ... crassis viminibus contexta* ('tightly woven with thick wicker'). In *Rudens*, the only other Plautine play with a *cistella*, the adjective *caudea* (1109, 1133) clarifies that the object, similarly implicated in the recognition of a *puella*, is woven with rushes.[8] Hesychius (κ 2799 L.) glosses κίστη as ἀγγεῖον πλεκτόν ('a woven container') in keeping with the Euripidean sketches of the 'woven container' in which Ion was exposed (*Ion* 37 πλεκτὸν ... κύτος; 39–40 κύτος/ἑλικτόν), a replica of the vessel in which

---

6 On the relationship of Menander's *Synaristosai* with *Cistellaria*, cf. Stockert 2012, 22–9 and, with specific reference to the use of the *cistella*, Manuwald 2004 and Riemer 2004. Though I am not concerned here with *Quellenforschung*, I will consider loci in the Plautine comedy that playfully signpost its incorporation of *Synaristosai*.
7 Theoph. *HP* 3.10, 3.13, 5.7 describes κίσται as made from a lime tree or willow.
8 We find another *cistella* containing recognition tokens at Ter. *Eun.* 753.

Athena shut Erichthonius at birth.⁹ Ovid in turn describes that vessel as 'a basket woven with wicker' (*cista texta de vimine*, *Met.* 2.554). Other abandoned babies – Oedipus, as well as Romulus and Remus – are associated with plaited containers.¹⁰ From the action of *Cistellaria*, we infer that the *cistella* involved in the recognition of the *puella*, Selenium, is not the container in which she was abandoned but a box employed by her foster mother, Melaenis, to store and transport the tokens (*crepundia*) hung around the baby's neck at the time of exposure.¹¹ Still, the essential role of the *cistella* in the recognition imbues it with strong evocative power, turning it into a stand-in for the 'original' hollow object in which the *puella* must have been found – one that the narrative, mythological density of *cista* invites ancient and modern audiences to identify with a plaited container. In sum, a woven box is the primary candidate for visualizing *Cistellaria*'s titular prop. But even if we opt for an object of solid material (like the famous 'Ficoroni *cista*'), the layering of associations with the play's prehistory and other similar stories of exposure makes a woven texture a resonant element in spectators' or readers' perceptions.¹²

A Menandrean antecedent of Plautus's *cistella* appears in the most recently discovered mosaic of *Synaristosai*, a depiction of the women's banquet that gives the play its title and has conditioned its ancient reception. The largest panel of a third-century CE mosaic from the Antioch region portrays 'six figures, three masked – an old woman sitting on a chair and two younger women sitting on a couch,' as well as 'three unmasked (mute) female slaves,' of whom one is preparing wine, one is pouring it, and a third is displaying an open ornamental box.'¹³ As indicated by the label συναριστωσων με(ρος) α' ('first act of *Women Lunching Together*'), the three masked figures are participants in the eponymous scene, which in all likelihood opened the play: Philaenis (an old procuress), her daugh-

---

9 Cf. Young 1941, 140 and Huys 1995, 201. Ion's basket is referred to as ἄγγος in ll. 1337, 1398, 1412; on its ideological symbolism, see Mueller 2010 and 2015.
10 For the tradition of Oedipus's exposure in a basket, see the relief on a second-century BCE bowl from Tanagra discussed by Huys 1995, 183–4, 227. According to Liv. 1.4 and Ov. *Fast.* 2.407, 409, Romulus and Remus were abandoned in an *alveus* – a woven, layered vessel, as confirmed by the word's additional meanings of 'hull of a ship' and 'beehive.' A σκάφη, the Greek equivalent of *alveus*, appeared in Sophocles' *Tyro* (cf. Arist. *Poet.* 1454b25).
11 Differently from *Ion*, in which the reunion with Creusa is triggered by her sight of the basket (cf. ll. 1398–9), in *Cistellaria* the contents of the *cistella* – the *crepundia* – lead Selenium's mother to recognize her lost daughter (cf. ll. 636, 660–5, 745–6). On the practice of hanging tokens around babies' necks, see *Mil.* 1399.
12 Vessels of solid metal could be employed for babies exposed on water. The usual word for such vessels is λάρναξ: cf. Simon. *PMG* 543, A.R. 1.622, D.S. 5.62. As we learn from one of the prologues of *Cistellaria*, Selenium was abandoned in an alley (cf. ll. 123–4). Baskets were customary for exposure on land: see Huys 1995, 200–2.
13 The quotations are from Gutzwiller/Çelik 2012, 597.

ter Pythias (a courtesan), and Plangon, the young hostess. In *Cistellaria*'s presentation of the iconic Menandrean scene, these characters correspond, respectively, to an unnamed *lena* ('procuress'), her daughter Gymnasium, and Selenium – the *puella*, raised by the courtesan Melaenis, who will ultimately be reunited with her biological parents. The visualization of *Synaristosai*'s opening meal in another three mosaics – ranging from the late second century BCE to the fourth century CE – suggests a consistent assimilation of the play to its title scene and to the image of female unity.[14] What sets the Antioch mosaic apart is the bronze box held open by one of the maids of Plangon/Selenium, probably to show the guests the hostess's engagements gifts (Fig. 2).[15] We do not know the plot of Menander's play, but in light of the Plautine remake, we can imagine, as Gutzwiller and Çelik have proposed, that this box coincided with or at least foreshadowed the container of Plangon/Selenium's recognition tokens.[16]

Fig. 2: Detail from *Synaristosai* mosaic, from Antakya, Turkey. Photo by Ö. Çelik.

Though the Antioch mosaic is unique in its use of a box, it shares with the others another significant non-human actor. In the other mosaics, which conform to a unified iconographic model (Fig. 3a–c), the characters are seated around a three-legged circular table. A ring-like arrangement, most pronounced in the second-

---

14 On the consistency of this tradition, see Blanchard 2004, 11 and Nervegna 2013, 151–3. For discussions of the three mosaics – from the House of Cicero in Pompeii (second century BCE), from Zeugma (Gaziantep), in modern Turkey (third century CE), and from the House of Menander in Mytilene (fourth century CE) – all placed in dining areas, see esp. Charitonidis/Kahil/Ginouvès 1970, 41–4, Csapo 1997, 172–3, Arnott 2004, Gutzwiller/Çelik 2012, 598–600, Slater 2014.
15 I follow the reconstruction of Gutzwiller/Çelik 2012, 605.
16 Cf. Gutzwiller/Çelik 2012, 606.

century BCE Dioscurides mosaic, originally from the House of Cicero in Pompeii, closely matches the group to the table.[17] No mere prop, the table activates the physical, emotional and social unity signaled by the title while itself serving as a material expression of the fusion of human actors.[18] I want to suggest that the Plautine rendition of the signature scene of *Synaristosai* intimates a similar reflection of Menander's iconic thematics of female cohesion in the materiality of an object – that is, in the woven texture of the titular *cistella*.

Plautus's version of Menander's female meeting unfolds as a retrospective conversation, which figures *Cistellaria*'s own backward glance to its Greek model. What launches *Cistellaria* is not the gathering in the mosaics, but its aftermath. While Menander probably staged the opening meal, Plautus looks in on the trio of women – Selenium, Gymnasium, and the *lena* – after the *convivium* has just taken place.[19] Their confab yields glimpses of the meeting, during which Selenium obtained a promise of help. Thus, at the beginning of *Cistellaria*, the lunch becomes an offstage event, an element of the play's past, which the characters turn into narrative. This temporal recasting makes the initial scene an emblem of the Plautine play as a whole: both the scene and the play look back on an archived performance (the dining together and the Menandrean comedy).

Plautus's postprandial conversation articulates notions of companionship and social alliance that are reflected in its linguistic texture. The polysyndetic structure of the play's first three lines, delivered by Selenium, interweaves personal pronouns, underscoring the integration of the three women into a group: ***ego*** *antidhac* **te** *amavi* **et** *mi amicam esse crevi,/mea Gymnasium,* **et** ***matrem tuam****, tum id mihi hodie/aperuistis,* **tu** **atque** **haec** ('Even before today I loved you and thought, my dear Gymnasium, that you were my friend, and also your mother, but today you and she have shown it'). In a way, this syntax acts out the definition of friendship as social cohesion and mutuality supplied by the *lena* a few lines later (26): *amicitiam ... iunctam bene habent inter se*, 'they (= *matronae*, 'upper-class women') keep their friendship well tightened between themselves.'[20]

---

17 As remarked by Csapo 2010, 160, a similar annular effect is visible in another iconographic interpretation of the Menandrean scene that Seeberg 2003, 45–6 has detected in an ivory consular diptych of the year 517 CE (Cabinet des Médailles et Antiques, Paris).
18 Another sign of blending between the women's bodies and the table is supplied by the Mytilene mosaic (Fig. 3c), in which the legs of Philaenis are covered – and, in a sense, replaced – by those of the object: cf. Charitonidis/Kahil/Ginouvès 1970, 42.
19 On the staging of the Menandrean lunch as an indoor scene, cf. Slater 2004, 268.
20 On the *lena*'s vision of courtesan unity as a purely Saturnalian *adynaton* or a potentially serious bid for social change – cf., respectively, Raccanelli 1998, 183–4 and Fantham 2004, 232–7. The preposition *inter* appears at another point in the *lena*'s speech (22–3): *decet ... /hunc esse ordinem benevolentis inter se.*

Fig. 3: (a) *Synaristosai* mosaic, by Dioscurides of Samos, Villa of Cicero, Pompeii. National Archaeological Museum of Naples. (b) *Synaristosai* mosaic, from the House of Zosimos, Zeugma. Gaziantep Museum of Archaeology. Photo by A.-M. Manière-Lévêque, with the permission of J.-P. Darmon. (c) *Synaristosai* mosaic panel, from the House of Menander, Mytilene. New Archaeological Museum of Mytilene. Photo reproduced by permission of the Hellenic Ministry of Culture, Education and Religious Affairs and the Ephorate of Antiquities of Lesbos.

In this scene, wordplay on the preposition/prefix *cum* spotlights the connection between the agency of 'women dining together' in Menander's *Synaristosai* and the object-centered orientation of *vimina* ('osier, wicker') woven together in *Cistellaria*. The ideology of companionship influences the construction of the relationship between Selenium and her lover, Alcesimarchus, who, in accordance with the typical script of New Comedy, has been forced by his family to marry another woman. The *lena* refers to Selenium's romance with the verb *consuesco*, 'to have an intimate companionship' (86); Selenium uses the cognate term *consuetudo* to characterize the beginnings of her amorous attachment to Alcesimarchus (94); and another *cum* compound describes his commitment to marrying her (*conceptis ... verbis* 98).[21] A concentration of *cum* phrases and compounds appears in Selenium's account of her first encounter with Alcesimarchus, one of the few passages in the play that can be identified as translations from Menander's *Synaristosai* (89–93):[22]

> per Dionysia
> mater pompam me spectatum duxit. dum redeo domum,   90
> conspicillo consecutust clanculum me usque ad fores.
> inde in amicitiam insinuavit cum matre et mecum simul
> blanditiis, muneribus, donis.
>
> During the Dionysia my mother took me to see the procession. While I was coming back home, he [=Alcesimarchus] spied on me and pursued me secretly all the way to the door. Then he came to be close with my mother and me at the same time through sweet talk, services, gifts.

These lines almost introduce Alcesimarchus into the circuit of friendship that binds together the three characters onstage. But, more importantly, the recurrence of *cum* – in explicit or encrypted form (**conspicillo consecutust clanculum** 91; **cum matre et mecum** 92) – within two lines punningly inscribes the title of Menander's play (Συναριστῶσαι) in the Plautine alliterative, translation.[23] This preposition, elevated to a refrain, expresses a 'binding' relevant to its Roman adaptation's title prop, which is made of osier plaited together, **con***texta*, as Columella and Isidore describe it.[24] Toying with the language and thematics of human connection, this initial scene draws attention to the play's programmatic association with a tightly bound composite object. Not just the shift in Menander's temporal coordinates, but

---

21 See also l. 245, where Alcesimarchus describes Selenium as *quae mihi esset **com**mendata et meae fide **con**credita*. Alcesimarchus is an unusual Plautine lover, as he acts independently and his interest in Selenium seems to be anchored, from the beginning, in a marital framework: cf. esp. Zagagi 2004, 177–84. On the legal conundrums of Alcesimarchus's cohabitation with Selenium, see Brown 2005.
22 Cf. Men. fr. 337 KA Διονυσίων <˘> ἦν/πομπή ... /ὁ δ' ἐπηκολούθησεν μέχρι τοῦ πρὸς τὴν θύραν·/ἔπειτα φοιτῶν καὶ κολακεύων <ἐμέ τε καὶ>/τὴν μητέρ' ἔγνω μ'. Both Traina 1974, 163 n. 1 and Fontaine 2014, 410–1 underscore Plautus's transformation of Menandrean diction through alliteration and semantic amplification.
23 For Plautus's punning on titles, see e.g. Copley 1970 and Fontaine 2010, 20 on the Greek title of *Poenulus* and Henderson 2006, 172 and Gowers, *forthcoming* on *Asinaria*.
24 On the metapoetic implications of 'plaiting together' (*texo* and compounds) in Columella, see Gowers 2000, 134. The placement of *cum* and its variants in ll. 91–2 – at the beginning and end – creates a ring-composition resembling the bending back of wicker in a basket.

also the binding together embedded in the linguistic texture makes this opening, like the *cistella* itself, synechdochal for the Plautine comedy. The wordplay signposting Plautus's translation of Menander, then, in its binding of people, suggests a further binding of person and thing, female and feminine object, that transforms *Synaristosai* into *Cistellaria*. As we will now see, this connection of person and object is central to the third act, which brings the *cistella* onstage just when the female alliance of the opening scene sparks into action.

The appearance of the *cistella* in the first scene of the third act triggers a scenario like the one in Sargent's painting – an exchange of *puella* and *cistella* that objectifies the former and animates the latter. After learning that Selenium's biological parents are on her tracks, Melaenis resolves to help them (627–9). Her resolution, which closes the second act (630), unravels in the next one, in which she returns carrying the *cistella*, accompanied by Selenium and the servant Halisca. Bringing the basket with Selenium's recognition tokens to her parents' door, a task assigned to Halisca, would amount to restoring (*reducere*) her to them. The boundaries of personhood and thingness collapse in Melaenis's words, as she seems to construe parenthood as ownership, while Selenium, who showed agency in the initial scene, is like a mute extra or even a stage prop (632): 'follow me this way, Selenium, so that you may belong to those who you should belong to (*eorum quoiam esse oportet te*) instead of me.'[25] In turn, while handing the *cistella* over to Halisca, Melaenis intratextually endows it with human vitality. The expression *accipe hanc cistellam* (637 'receive this basket') brings to mind Melaenis's original acceptance of the *puella* from the *lena*, who refers to the transfer in one of the play's two prologues: *postquam eam puellam a me accepit* (139 'after she [=Melaenis] received the girl from me'); *illa quae a me accepit* (146 'the woman who received [the girl] from me'). Melaenis explicitly evokes this moment just before placing the *cistella* in Halisca's hands, pointing to the basket and addressing Selenium: *hic crepundia insunt, quibuscum te illa olim ad me detulit,/quae mihi dedit* (635–6 'inside here are the objects with which that woman who gave you to me brought you to me'). As the feminine object makes its entrance onstage, it almost becomes a female character, duplicating but also gradually eclipsing the *puella* – a process that climaxes at the end of the third act.

The second part of the third act features a generic crisis – Alcesimarchus's threat of suicide by sword – solved by a precipitate happy ending, in which female solidarity and the *cistella* are allied forces of comic restoration. Alcesimar-

---

[25] This is the only time in the Plautine corpus that *quoius, quoia, quoium*, commonly applied to non-human and human 'property' (objects, land, slaves, and courtesans), designates a parental relationship. For Selenium's agency in the initial scene, see for example ll. 83–5, in which she prides herself on having refused to become a courtesan like her foster mother.

chus suddenly bursts on stage lamenting the separation from Selenium, whom Melaenis has kept away from his house, outraged by his new marriage plans. Carrying a sword, he threatens to take his life in the manner of Ajax, but Selenium averts this (para-)tragic danger.[26] Seeing her rush toward him with Melaenis and Halisca, who is holding the *cistella*, Alcesimarchus salutes her as his *salus* ('deliverance' 644), presumably throws away the sword, and departs with her. Clearly, a clash of props – the intrusive icon of a tragic script and a customary accoutrement of New Comedy – reifies a conflict of generic drives: death vs. (re)birth, inertia vs. movement, and isolation vs. community, as the trio of women re-enacts the programmatic female solidarity that opened the play.[27] The re-creation of the initial scene, while re-energizing the plot, dramatizes a coming together of womanly alliance and woven object.[28] It is as though, in fighting to redirect a plot momentarily led astray, the three women, together with the plaited prop, are invested in preserving the play's comic quality. The composite object and the coterie of women stand *up* – and *in* – for the comic play, almost realizing a confederation of its Menandrean and Plautine versions (*Synaristosai* and *Cistellaria*). Thus, the generic crisis provoked by Alcesimarchus brings out the self-reflexive potential of womanly cooperation and the *cistella*. These human and nonhuman aggregations materialize the play onstage, keeping it together, as it were.

The removal of Alcesimarchus's generically disruptive prop coincides with an accident – the fall of the *cistella* – that furthers the convergence of object and *puella*. Alcesimarchus addresses Selenium (644b–5) just after she enlists the aid of Melaenis and Halisca (643b–4a), obscuring the stage business following the women's intervention, but as we discover later, Halisca lets the basket fall in the midst of the turmoil.[29] Alcesimarchus's last speech before he and Selenium make their final exit touches on the forgotten *cistella*, albeit indirectly and unwittingly (647b–50):

> hanc ut habeo certum est non amittere;
> nam hercle iam ad me agglutinandam totam decretum est dare.
> ubi estis, servi? occludite aedis pessulis, repagulis
> ilico. hanc ego tetulero intra limen.   650

---

[26] On Alcesimarchus's evocation of Ajax, see Ketterer 1986, 32 and Stockert 2012, 237–8.
[27] In comedy, a sword conjures tragedy: see Revermann 2013. While minimizing Alcesimarchus's danger, Melaenis's use of *severum* (probably meaning 'serious') at l. 646 signposts the transgeneric potential of his conduct. Her last line before departing equally suggests the potential for a cisgeneric shift back to comedy: *si possum tranquillum facere ex irato* ('if I can change him from angry to calm,' 652).
[28] In the surviving fragmentary text of *Cistellaria*, only this scene and the initial one present three women onstage at the same time, acting as a group.
[29] For a reconstruction of the staging, cf. Marshall 2006, 165.

Now that I have this girl, it is my intention not to let her go; for indeed I have decided to glue her entirely onto me. Where are you, slaves? Lock the house with bolts and door bars immediately. I will bring this girl inside the threshold.

To both spectator and reader, the demonstrative *hanc*, the direct object of *amittere* (l. 647), may sound ambiguous, referring to Selenium – as Alcesimarchus intends – but also to the *cistella*, which has just been dropped (*amissa*). *Amittere* conjures up the original abandonment of the *puella*, which, in turn, evokes baskets, boxes and similar protective vessels. Thus, in proclaiming his eternal attachment to Selenium, the young lover inadvertently alludes to Halisca's mishap through a subliminal, negatively expressed stage direction, which renders *puella* and *cistella* as complementary presences: when the former is refound, reunited with her beloved, brought inside, the latter is lost, separated from its owners, taken and left outside.

The consequence of this complementarity is the sense of a material encounter – a reconnection – of the comic plot's originating moment, prior to the play's beginning, and its ending. Declaring 'it is my intention not to let her [= Selenium] go (*amittere*),' Alcesimarchus indicates that the circle has been closed. He has found Selenium again, as her mother will (in a fashion) in the following act. However, Alcesimarchus's embrace with Selenium is the only dramatized reunion, since Phanostrata, her mother, will recognize the *crepundia* in the absence of the *puella* – an utterly unconventional circumstance.[30] What safeguards against the tragic destabilization of a suicide is, paradoxically, the premature 'death' of the play triggered by the rushed reunion. The verb *agglutino* ('to glue on'), which for Alcesimarchus marks the re-establishment of his bond with Selenium (648), clearly signals narrative binding, closure.[31] So does his order to lock the doors of the house with bolts and bars (649–50a). The closural force of romantic bliss seems even to defer the resolution of a crucial narrative node – the recognition of Selenium – to an offstage, postdramatic future.[32] Conversely, for all its connotations of negligence and chaos, the *cistella*'s fall takes on a constructive, regenerative force. Planted on the stage, the prop, in its expression of generic rescue, anchors the rest of the plot, stabilizing it and precluding possible detours. Furthermore, as an image of exposure, the *cistella* revives onstage the

---

30 Cf. Zagagi 2004, 174.
31 On binding as a condition for narrative ending, see Brooks 1984, 101, 121.
32 Both Süss 1938, 134 and Ludwig 1970, 65–6 consider the reunion of Alcesimarchus and Selenium purely formal and insufficient because it takes place without the sanction of parental consent; for a critique of their readings, cf. Konstan 1983, 104–14. I am not concerned here with legal realism, but with theatrical effects and their reflection of the plot's movement.

abandonment, excluded from the plot's temporal span, that set the story in motion. Thus, the commotion set off by Alcesimarchus's (para)tragic antics serendipitously reunites not only the two lovers, but also the narrative edges of the play. The last time we hear Selenium's voice is when, to save her lover, she asks her female allies for help. Joyfully addressed by Alcesimarchus, she remains silent. As she is led inside by him, uttering not even a farewell to Melaenis, she almost becomes an inert prop brought back into the actors' quarters after a performance. On the contrary, the dropped *cistella* corresponds to the breathing body of a wailing baby, the birth of a comic plot.

In the transition from the third to the fourth act, the *cistella*'s solo appearance hints at the idea of the prop as a textual object. The exit of all actors after the pre-matrimonial reunion of the two lovers resembles an exodos, the moment that, by definition, permanently restores the stage to its initial emptiness.[33] At the same time, the replacement of human agents with the titular prop means the exodos is not complete. As with an exodos, spectators are led back to the very beginning of the show, before the actors' arrival, when the play was an inert name waiting to be enacted. But in this case the play is present as an object. As the source of the title, the desolate prop almost becomes an image of the textual object prior to performance, an object that, in occupying center stage and holding the audience's focus, seems to be about to perform itself.

This textual object, represented by the *cistella*, reflects the narrative complexity of the play, comprehending its various temporal dimensions. Appearing onstage with the *cistella* in hand, Melaenis began the third act with these words, addressed to Selenium (631): **rem** elocuta sum tibi omnem ('I've told you the whole thing'). Referring back to an offstage conversation, *res* collects various events (in and outside the plot) into a narrative whole: most likely, the abandonment of Selenium, her rescue by the *lena*, Melaenis's acceptance of the baby as her own child, and earlier in the play, the search by the slave Lampadio for the lost *puella* on behalf of her biological parents – which induced Melaenis to reunite her foster daughter with her family. This narrative *res* is materialized by the *res* that Melaenis is holding, as some of its elements (first and foremost the exposure) are symbolically stored in the *cistella*, ready to be brought out in the open through the *crepundia* it contains.[34] Melaenis's reference to a *res* while she carries a *res* calls attention to the temporal capaciousness of both: the *cistella* reifies the

---

[33] In a Roman context, Alcesimarchus's bringing Selenium inside (*intra limen*) connotes matrimony: cf. Süss 1938, 134, Konstan 1983, 107 n. 16, Ketterer 1986, 33.
[34] Containers can be conceptualized as dramatic repositories: cf. esp. Mueller 2015 (on the urn of Sophocles' *Electra*). For other material and spatial figures of narrative containment, cf. Razzall 2006 (on Henry Fielding's pockets).

whole narrative span of the play – not only its buried 'secrets' (the backstory), but also the more recent and not entirely concluded performative past. In the rest of the play – the solitary *cistella* seems to announce – the temporally stratified textual object reminiscent of the abandoned *puella* will effectively become the dramatic focus, and its different narrative layers (before and after the exposure) will haunt the characters' actions.

The action following the pseudo-exodos turns the plot back to Selenium's rescue by the *lena*. At the beginning of the fourth act, Lampadio arrives onstage, frustrated with his failure to find the *puella*, the daughter of his mistress Phanostrata (653–4). His soliloquy is interrupted by his awareness of two separate (but closely related) presences – Phanostrata and the forgotten *cistella* (655–9):

> LAM.   sed eccam eram video. sed quid hoc est, haec quod cistella hic iacet   655
>   cum crepundiis? nec quemquam conspicor alium in via.
>   faciundum est puerile officium: conquiniscam ad cistulam.
> PHAN. quid agis, Lampadio?
> LAM.   haec cistella numnam hinc ab nobis domo est?
>   nam hinc ab ostio iacentem sustuli.

> *Lampadio* But look, I see my mistress here. But what's this? This basket is lying here with the tokens. And I don't spot anyone else in the street. Now I have to do a boy's service: I'll bend over to the basket. *Phanostrata* What are you doing, Lampadio? *Lampadio* The basket isn't from here, from our home, is it? I picked it up from here, by the door, where it lay.

In this passage, the recurrence of the preposition/prefix *cum* and its phonic approximations (**cum** *crepundiis* 656; **con***spicor* 656; *offi***cium** 657; **con***quiniscam* 657) seems to bring us back to the initial tableau of feminine conversation and collaboration. But, in bending over to the basket, Lampadio triggers a deeper regression – to the position assumed, in the play's prehistory, by the *lena*, a participant in the women's gathering.[35] This regression is an effect of the intratextual density of *sustuli* (659), since the *lena*, the only other character to use that form of the verb *tollo*, does so while referring in one of the play's two prologues to her collection of the baby Selenium (123–4): *nam ego illanc olim ... parvolam/puellam proiectam ex angiportu sustuli* ('a long time ago I picked up that girl, when she

---

[35] This connection between Lampadio and the *lena* is undoubtedly sexual. As the slave observes, his bending forward to fetch the *cistella* resembles the position for a *puerile officium* (657), a passive erotic role that further assimilates him to the old prostitute responsible for rescuing Selenium. Cf. Fontaine 2010, 83 on the sexual meaning of *conquiniscam* and Slater 2004 on other cases of gender reversal in the play. What interest me here are the metanarrative implications: though Lampadio is physically bending forward, he is figuratively bending *back* – toward the past represented by the basket.

was a baby, from the alleyway where she had been abandoned'). The perfect of *tollo* univocally refers to the same event in the second prologue, delivered by the god Auxilium, and in all the other narrative flashbacks interspersed throughout the play.[36] Lampadio's encounter with the *cistella* does not just point toward the plot's official closure through recognition (the reunion of daughter and parents), but causes the play to circle back on itself, incorporating suggestions of its prehistory within its dramatic compass.

Halisca's arrival expands the affective inventory of the *cistella*, restoring to felt presence abandoned maternal emotions. Melaenis's maid enters without noticing Lampadio and Phanostrata, who is firmly holding the *cistella*. Unable to locate the object, she wanders, breaching the dramatic illusion to ask the spectators for help (675–79), and launches into melodramatic despair (686–90):

> nulla est, neque ego sum usquam. perdita perdidit me.
> sed pergam ut coepi tamen, quaeritabo.
> nam et intus paveo et foris formido,
> ita nunc utrubique metus me agitat,   688ᵃ
> ...
> ille nunc laetus est, quisquis est, qui illam habet   690

> The *cistella* ['she'] is nowhere, and I am nowhere too. Having been lost, it ['she'] lost me. But still I'll continue as I began. I'll search, for inside I'm afraid and outside I'm scared. That's how much fear now drives me crazy in both places ... Whoever he is, the man who has it ['her'] now is happy.

The double translations '*cistella*/she' and 'it/her' render the indeterminacy of feminine adjectives, pronouns and participles in this passage. Is the subject of *perdidit* the *puella* or the *cistella*? Translators are divided, but choosing one over the other kills the way the monologue plays on the intersecting destinies of the object and its human counterpart. In the last line, *illam* would suit the *puella*, who, in fact, as we know from the previous act, is making Alcesimarchus – 'the man who has her' – happy (*laetus*).[37] But the following relative clause (691) shifts the game in favor of the *cistella*.[38] This grammatical ambiguity reflects a conver-

---

36 Cf. ll. 167, 183–4 (from Auxilium's prologue), 424, 548, 550, 564, 618. A prologic quality can be detected in ll. 616–22, where Lampadio echoes Auxilium's account and, as noted by Sharrock 2009, 171, seems to grow 'exasperated at the failures of his interlocutors to understand the background to the plot.'
37 The clause *quis eam abstulerit quisu' sustulerit*, which Halisca employs at l. 679, strengthens the connection of the 'lucky man' with Alcesimarchus. At the end of the third act, Melaenis comments on his 'theft' of Selenium in similar terms: *abiit, apstulit/mulierem* (650–1).
38 *quae neque illa illi quicquam usui et mi [esse] potest*.

gence of emotional responses to lost children and objects, as we can infer from a comparison with another entrance monologue, sung, in *Epidicus*, by Philippa – a mother looking for her daughter (526–32): 'Multiple toils are keeping me agitated (*multiplex <me> aerumna exercitam habet*), poverty and fear are frightening my soul ... my daughter has been captured by the enemy, and I don't know where she is (*neque ea nunc ubi sit scio*).' In Halisca's melodramatic voice, we can perceive the strains of maternal anxiety and lamentation. The complex of emotions unleashed by the loss of the *cistella* does not just define Halisca's present, but also provides a belated disclosure of Phanostrata's past – her distress when forced to abandon her daughter.

The shared emotions of Halisca and Phanostrata juxtapose present and absent characters – Phanostrata and Melaenis, Phanostrata now and her younger self. The temporal poles in Phanostrata's life – her separation from the *puella* and the impending reunion – are visualized as synchronic. The present Phanostrata, about to reconnect with her daughter, also resembles Melaenis, who previously held both *cistella* and *puella*. The scene's spatial configuration – Halisca and Phanostrata are physically close, but their interaction is delayed – recalls the relationship (or the lack thereof) between the young Phanostrata and Melaenis: the unhappy mother deprived of her daughter and the happy (foster) mother, clinging to the *puella*, who never meet despite their proximity. It is as though Halisca's moaning brings the play back in time, opening the neighbouring houses and revealing the opposing maternal conditions. Together with the scene's staging, the affective force of the *cistella/puella* realizes impossible synchronies of time and space, coexisting tableaux.

The *servus callidus* Lampadio haunts Halisca's monologue as much as his mistress does, adding another retrospective element to the temporal spectrum. Shifting from emotion to reason, Halisca embarks on a search for the forgotten object (693–4): *Halisca, hoc age, ad terram aspice et despice,/oculis investiges, astute augura* ('Halisca, come on, look down at the ground, search with your eyes, cleverly take auspices'). In Halisca's search (693–703), we see a constellation of words (*investiges, astute, vestigium, persequar*) typical of clever-slave problem solving.[39] Halisca's quest for the *cistella* is clearly a miniature of Lampadio's for the *puella*, which began before the play.[40] Lampadio and Phanostrata are internal spectators of Halisca's *canticum* and search. In watching her perform

---

39 Cf. esp. *Mil.* 260–9. As a synonym of *callidus*, *astutus* is frequently applied to clever slaves: see e. g. *Amph.* 268 and *Pseud.* 385.
40 Cf. ll. 184–7 (from Auxilium's prologue).

their past emotions and actions – dramatized in the play or not – they are like the audience, which sees the plot continually regressing while approaching the end.

There is more than one way that the exchange of thingness and personhood matches *Cistellaria*'s shape with the materiality of the *cistella*: a serial conjunction of ending and beginning but also an interaction of temporal and affective elements conceivable as either forming or contained by the basket. In the finale, as we have seen, every action – dropping the *cistella*, picking it up, searching – touches a counterpart in the recent or more distant past. Beginning and ending are reconnected in the manner of wicker or a reed bent back on itself in a basket or a box. This aggregate of circular temporal threads can be seen as a weave of emotional layers or a repository of affective contents – images that equally bring to mind plaited boxes and baskets. The past moments evoked in the ending (the birth of Selenium, her collection after exposure, the search for her) come imbued with their original psychic textures (distress, surprise, anxiety, sorrow); they survive, in other words, as traces of felt experiences reanimated onstage. The combination of these experiences conveys an entanglement of affective fibers, an intricate pattern of bygone yet vibrant emotions.[41] But such emotions can also be seen as deposited in the recesses of a container.[42] As soon as the *cistella* appears, the play's main actions (both past and present) come into view, as though pulled out of a vessel; the play keeps all its temporal and affective elements always in storage, so to speak, making past experiences as accessible – and lively – as the present.

Acknowledgments

This chapter is adapted from a book in progress on Plautine plays with object-based titles (including *Aulularia*, *Rudens*, and *Vidularia*). Warm thanks are due to Stavros Frangoulidis, Stephen Harrison, and Richard Hunter for inviting me to the Thessaloniki conference; to Stavros and Gesine Manuwald for their editorial care; and to Emily Gowers, Melissa Mueller, Alex Press, Alex Purves, Amy Richlin, and the anonymous referees for much help, guidance, and encouragement.

---

[41] On the relations between affect, temporality and woven materiality, the theoretical considerations of Bruno 2014, 33–43 are particularly illuminating.
[42] On emotions in chests or drawers, see Hancock 2010, discussing Virginia Woolf's objects.

Bibliography

Arnott, W. G. (2004), 'A New Mosaic of Menander's *Synaristosai*', in: R. Hartkamp/F. Hurka (eds.), *Studien zu Plautus' Cistellaria*, Tübingen, 399–405.
Blanchard, A. (2004), 'Les *Synaristosai* et la constitution du choix de Ménandre', in: R. Hartkamp/F. Hurka (eds.), *Studien zu Plautus' Cistellaria*, Tübingen, 11–19.
Brooks, P. (1984), *Reading for the Plot: Design and Intention in Narrative*, Cambridge, MA/London.
Brown, B. (2003), *A Sense of Things: The Object Matter of American Literature*, Chicago.
―――― (2005), 'The Legal and Social Framework of Plautus's *Cistellaria*', *PLLS* 12, 53–70.
Bruno, G. (2014), *Surface: Matters of Aesthetics, Materiality, and Media*, Chicago.
Charitonidis, S./Kahil, L./Ginouvès, R. (1970), *Les mosaïques de la Maison du Ménandre à Mytilène*, Bern.
Copley, F. O. (1970), 'Plautus, *Poenulus* 53–55', *AJP* 91, 77–8.
Csapo, E. (1997), 'Mise en scène théâtrale, scène de théâtre artisanale: les mosaïques de Ménandre à Mytilène, leur contexte social et leur tradition iconographique', *Pallas* 47, 165–82.
―――― (2010), *Actors and Icons of the Ancient Theater*, Malden, MA/Oxford.
Fantham, E. (2004), 'Women of the *Demi-monde* and Sisterly Solidarity in the *Cistellaria*', in: R. Hartkamp/F. Hurka (eds.), *Studien zu Plautus' Cistellaria*, Tübingen, 221–38.
Fontaine, M. (2010), *Funny Words in Plautine Comedy*, Oxford.
―――― (2014), 'The Reception of Greek Comedy in Rome', in: M. Revermann (ed.), *The Cambridge Companion to Greek Comedy*, Cambridge, 404–23.
Gowers, E. (2000), 'Vegetable Love: Virgil, Columella, and Garden Poetry', *Ramus* 29, 127–48.
―――― forthcoming, 'Pun-Fried Concoctions: Word-Blending in the Roman Kitchen'.
Gutzwiller, K./Çelik, O. (2012), 'New Menander Mosaics from Antioch', *AJA* 116, 573–623.
Hancock, N. (2010), 'Virginia Woolf's Glasses: Material Encounters in the Literary/Artistic House Museum', in: S. H. Dudley (ed.), *Museum Materialities: Objects, Engagements, Interpretations*, London/New York, 114–27.
Henderson, J. (2006), *Asinaria: The One About the Asses*, Madison, WI.
Huys, M. (1995), *The Tale of the Hero who Was Exposed at Birth in Euripidean Tragedy: A Study of Motifs*, Leuven.
James, H. (1956) [1893], 'John S. Sargent', in: J. L. Sweeney (ed.), *The Painter's Eye: Notes and Essays on the Pictorial Arts by Henry James*, Cambridge, MA, 216–28.
Ketterer, R. C. (1986), 'Stage Properties in Plautine Comedy iii', *Semiotica* 60, 29–72.
Konstan, D. (1983), *Roman Comedy*, Ithaca/London.
Ludwig, W. (1970), 'Die plautinische *Cistellaria* und das Verhältnis von Gott und Handlung bei Menander', in: E. Turner (ed.), *Ménandre*, Vandoeuvres/Genève, 43–110.
Manuwald, G. (2004), 'Das verlorene Kästchen – Die gefährdete Anagnorisis in Plautus' *Cistellaria*', in: R. Hartkamp/F. Hurka (eds.), *Studien zu Plautus' Cistellaria*, Tübingen, 137–48.
Marshall, C. W. (2006), *The Stagecraft and Performance of Roman Comedy*, Cambridge.
Mueller, M. (2010), 'Athens in a Basket: Naming, Objects, and Identity in Euripides' *Ion*', *Arethusa* 43, 365–402.
―――― (2015), *Objects as Actors: Props and the Poetics of Performance in Greek Tragedy*, Chicago.
Nervegna, S. (2013), *Menander in Antiquity: The Contexts of Reception*, Cambridge.
Raccanelli, R. (1998), *L'amicitia nelle commedie di Plauto*, Bari.

Razzall, L. (2006), 'The Pockets of Henry Fielding's Writing', *Cambridge Quarterly* 35, 361–77.
Revermann, M. (2013), 'Generalizing About Props: Greek Drama, Comparator Traditions, and the Analysis of Stage Objects', in: G. W. M. Harrison/V. Lapis (eds.), *Performance in Greek and Roman Theater*, Leiden/Boston, 77–88.
Riemer, P. (2004), 'Das *cistella*-Spiel der *Cistellaria*: Menander oder Plautus?', in: R. Hartkamp/F. Hurka (eds.), *Studien zu Plautus' Cistellaria*, Tübingen, 107–16.
Seeberg, A. (2003), 'Tragedy and Archaeology, Forty Years After', *BICS* 46, 43–75.
Sharrock, A. (2009), *Reading Roman Comedy: Poetics and Playfulness in Plautus and Terence*, Cambridge.
Slater, N. W. (2004), 'Men are from Lemnos, Women are from Sicyon: Space and Gender in the *Cistellaria*', in: R. Hartkamp/F. Hurka (eds.), *Studien zu Plautus' Cistellaria*, Tübingen, 267–79.
―――― (2014), 'The Evidence of the Zeugma *Synaristosai* Mosaic for Imperial Performance of Menander', in: S. D. Olson (ed.), *Ancient Comedy and Reception: Essays in Honor of Jeffrey Henderson*, Berlin/Boston, 366–74.
Sofer, A. (1997), 'Felt Absences: The Stage Properties of *Othello*'s Handkerchief', *Comparative Drama* 31, 367–93.
―――― (1998), 'No Ideas but in Things: Beckett's Uncanny Props', *Text and Presentation* 19, 123–9.
―――― (2003), *The Stage Life of Props*, Ann Arbor.
Stockert, W. (2012), *T. Maccius Plautus: Cistellaria*, München.
Süss, W. (1938), 'Nochmals zur *Cistellaria* des Plautus', *RhM* 87, 97–141.
Traina, A. (1974), *Vortit barbare: le traduzioni poetiche da Livio Andronico a Cicerone*, Rome.
Veltrusky, J. (1964), 'Man and Object in the Theater', in: P. L. Garvin (ed.), *A Prague School Reader on Aesthetics, Literary Structure, and Style*, Washington, DC, 83–91.
Young, R. S. (1941), 'ΑΝΤΙΠΗΞ: A Note on the *Ion* of Euripides', *Hesperia* 10, 138–42.
Zagagi, N. (2004), 'Tradition and Originality in *Cistellaria*: The Characterization of Selenium and Alcesimarchus as Comic Lovers', in: R. Hartkamp/F. Hurka, eds., *Studien zu Plautus' Cistellaria*, Tübingen, 167–86.

Bernhard Zimmermann
Elements of Pantomime in Plautus' Comedies

Translation by Katharina Epstein

Look at that, will you, how he's positioned himself, worrying and thinking with an earnest countenance. He's tapping his chest with his fingers, I think he's going to call out his heart. Look, he's turned away; he has his left hand leaning on his left thigh, with his right hand he's making calculations on his fingers, beating his right thigh. He's beating so strongly, he can hardly think of anything to do. He's snapped his fingers: he's anxious, he's frequently changing positions. But look, he's shaking his head: he doesn't like what he's found. Whatever it is, he won't produce it half-baked, he'll give it done to a turn. But look, he's building something: he's supporting his chin with a pillar. Away with that, I don't like that sort of building work at all:
[...]
Hurray! He's set himself up in a graceful position, right for a slave and a comedy. He'll never rest today until he's finished what he's seeking. He's got it, I think.[1]

illuc sis vide	200
quem ad modum astitit, severo fronte curans, cogitans.	
pectus digitis pultat, cor credo evocaturust foras;	
ecce avortit: nixus laevo in femine habet laevam manum,	
dextera digitis rationem computat, ferit femur	
dexterum. ita *vehemter icit*: quod agat aegre suppetit.	205
concrepuit digitis: laborat; crebro commutat status.	
eccere autem *capite nutat*: non placet quod repperit.	
quidquid est, incoctum non expromet, bene coctum dabit.	
ecce autem aedificat: columnam mento suffigit suo.	
apage, non placet profecto mihi illaec aedificatio;	210
[...]	
eugae! euscheme hercle astitit et dulice et comoedice;	
numquam hodie quiescet priu' quam id quod petit perfecerit.	
habet opinor.	215

With these words in trochaic septenarii, Periplectomenus describes the slave Palaestrio's thought process in Plautus' *Miles Gloriosus* (200–15). Not only does he draw attention to individual gestures and movements the slave makes, he also explains their meaning.

---

1 Translation by De Melo 2011; Latin Text according to the edition of Lindsay 1904–05. Elements drawn from pantomime are indicated by italics.

This short scene is the oldest literary testimony[2] to the presence of pantomime[3] on the Roman stage. Pantomime was a subliterary genre which was firmly established in Rome by Bathyllus and Pylades in the Augustan period[4] and, along with mime, went on to become the most popular dramatic genre of the imperial period. While the scene features the most important formal elements typical of pantomime after its 'standardization' by Pylades and Bathyllus, Periplectomenus' explanatory comments indicate that pantomime was still at an early stage without canonical form.[5]

We are well informed about the history and structure of pantomime through Lucian's essay *De saltatione*, 'On Pantomime Dancing'.[6] Pantomime was usually performed by a single dancer who took on all necessary roles. The text used to be recited in the background by a chorus or a singer and accompanied by music, but became dispensable in later times because the dancer was able to communicate everything through expressive dancing, most of all through the use of the hands (χειρονομία).[7] After Bathyllus and Pylades, there must have been a fixed canon of movements for conveying certain contents, especially emotions.[8] It is of particular interest for our line of discussion that Lucian stresses the fact that drama was always open to mimetic dancing (26 ff.). Xenophon's *Symposium*

---

2 On placing this comedy among Plautus' early works (206/5 BC), see Brix – Niemeyer – Köhler ⁴1916, 20; Blänsdorf 1978, 152 n. 20; cf. also Slater 2000, 132.

3 It must be noted, of course, that the use of the technical term 'pantomime' is anachronistic in this context because it is probably not until after this form had been standardized by Bathyllus and Pylades that we can speak of 'pantomime' as an established form. I use the term in reference to Plautine comedy with the intention of highlighting the genetic relationship between these early forms and the later canonical form of the genre. Also, one needs to be aware that the corresponding technical terms in Greek are ὄρχησις and ὀρχεῖσθαι, which appear in the earliest dramatic record of an instance of pantomimic parody in Aristoph. *Vesp.* 1474 ff. (repeatedly); see also Herodotus VI 129, 2 (see below n. 10).

4 Cf. Hall 2008, 10 f. ('Introduction').

5 See the study by Rotolo 1957. In the last few years the pantomime has moved more and more in the centre of interest, cf. Csapo – Slater 1994, 369–89 (discussion of ancient sources); Hall – Wyles 2008, with a collection of *testimonia* (p. 378–419); Webb 2005, 3–11; Del Giudice – Van Deusen 2008; Macintosh 2010.

6 On dating Lucian's essay to 163/164 A.D. and on its position in literary history, see Jones 1986, 68 ff. Lucian himself refers to a multitude of other authors who wrote about pantomime before he did and from whom he wishes to dissociate himself. Surely Lucian relied on handbooks as sources, perhaps the book about pantomime written by Pylades; for testimonies see Rotolo 1957, 23 f.

7 Cf. Sittl 1890, 242; Rotolo 1957, 34.

8 See the anonymous epigram *De pantomimo* (Anth. Lat. 111 Riese), 4: *sollerti spondet prodere verba manu.*

gives an idea of what these pantomime performances, a form of popular entertainment, were like: A group of actors and jugglers from Syracuse (c. 2), consisting of a director, a female flute player, a female dancer and a male dancer who also played the kithara, begins by performing acrobatic dances (c. 2,7 ff.) before dancing a mythological pantomime scene such as 'Dionysus and Ariadne', to which the director, doubling as a kind of prologue-speaker, has given a brief introduction in advance (c. 9,2).[9] It thus appears that a kind of theater subculture had emerged towards the end of the fifth and the beginning of the fourth century B.C. It was represented by groups of actors with a repertoire of mythological scenes and mere vaudeville acts (θεάματα or θαῦμα). Such performances seem to have had their place primarily at the symposia of the wealthy,[10] as also indicated by Philocleon's grotesque pantomime dance in the exodus of Aristophanes' *Wasps* (1474–537).[11]

The scene from Plautus' *Miles gloriosus* cited above is an actual pantomime scene:[12] an actor comments on dance moves (201 *quem ad modum astitit*; 206 *crebro commutat status*); and the expression *euscheme* in line 213 is an explicit reference to dancing, since the Greek word σχῆμα is the technical term for 'dance move';[13] most of all, however, Palaestrio's χειρονομία, which is typical of pantomime dancing, is emphasized.

What sets this pantomime scene apart is that Periplectomenus adds a scenic commentary on the individual figures and moves Palaestrio makes and interprets them, thus enhancing the scene's comic effect (the 'column' of thought Palaestrio 'builds', for example).[14]

---

9 The prologue-speaker of Plautus' *Captivi* introduces the audience to the action in a similar way, albeit in greater detail (cf. 1: *Hos quos videtis stare hic captivos duos*).
10 This is confirmed by the unfortunate performance of Hippoclides at the symposium of the tyrant Cleisthenes of Sicyon (Herodotus VI 129, 2 f.): 'As they sat late drinking, Hippoclides [...] bade the flute-player play him music, and when the flute-player so did, he began to dance; [...] Hippoclides bade a table be brought; when it came he danced on it Laconian first (σχημάτια) and then Attic figures; last of all he rested his head on the table and made gestures with his legs in the air' (τοῖς σκέλεσι ἐχειρονόμησε). English translation by Godley 1971. Herodotus is therefore already familiar with the technical term χειρονομία in the context of sympotic dancing; cf. also Corbato 1982, 65–76.
11 Cf. especially Rossi 1978, 1149–70; Zimmermann, Vol. II, 1985, 82 f.
12 Ter. *Heaut.* 674 ff., referred to by Brix – Niemeyer – Köhler ⁴1916, 51, does not provide a perfect comparison, because what the scene lacks is precisely a description of the movements expressing a thought process.
13 Cf. *LSJ* s. v. σχῆμα 7. It even appears to be the case that σχῆμα is used especially for comic dance moves; cf. Roos 1951, 92.
14 A comic effect of a similar kind is produced in the exodus of Aristophanes' *Wasps* (1474 ff.), when Philocleon, an old man, makes indecent comments about his tragic dance.

Another pantomime scene is featured in *Persa* (757 ff.). Toxilus calls Paegnium and other slaves out into the street to make preparations for a banquet. We must visualize all slaves as executing the orders – which are sung to them in a *canticum* in Cretan rhythms – in a kind of mimetic dance.[15] *Poenulus* (504 ff.) contains a similar scene: Agorastocles tries to hurry along his lazy witnesses and angrily rants about their slow, sluggish walk in trochees (506 f. *homines spissigradissumos,/tardiores quam corbitae sunt in tranquillo mari;* 510 *loripedes, tardissumos;* 532 *podagrosi estis ac vicistis cocleam tarditudine*).[16] I would also like to mention *Pseudolus* I 2 (133 ff.), where Ballio drives his lazy slaves from the house using trochaic long verse like Agorastocles in *Poenulus* (133 *exite, agite exite, ignavi, male habiti et male conciliati*); he describes their laziness and underlines his words with whip lashes (154 f.). It is even more obvious that we are dealing with a pantomime scene because Plautus marked it as such by having Calidorus and Pseudolus attend as spectators who are even threatening to disturb the 'show' (193–5; 207–9).[17]

Finally, I would like to add *Stichus* (769 ff. in iambic septenarii and octonarii with inserted reiziana, 772 ff.), which will lead us to a second type of inserted pantomime scene. Like Aristophanes' *Wasps*, *Stichus* ends with a burlesque dance performance accompanied by the flute.[18] Sangarinus and Stichus give a challenging description of the pirouettes and jumps they are executing. Since Stichus is referring to a professional dancer when he says *Ionicus aut cinaedus* (769),[19] they must be imitating or parodying the kind of ballet show a professional dance troop would put on.[20] The *Stichus*' finale and its culmination in a pantomime dance is prepared in detail in advance; Stichus already asks Sangarinus

---

15 It is a noteworthy fact that this dance scene is composed in Cretan rhythms. In Aristophanes, *Ecclessiazusae* 1165, the female chorus leader asks Blepyrus to join in the dancing in the Cretan way (Κρητικῶς), and the exodus of the *Eccl.* (1163 ff.) leads to a banquet as well.

16 Cf. the parodoi of Aristophanes' *Knights* (242 ff.) and *Peace* (299 ff.), where trochees are also used to order the choruses to move quickly. On the character trochaic meter has in this context, cf. Zimmermann, vol. I, ²1985, 63.

17 For the *loci classici* of eavesdropping, cf. Sophocles, *Electra* 77 ff. and Aristophanes, *Frogs* 315 ff. In Plautus' scene, however, the crucial point is that the two are eavesdropping on a pantomime performance embedded in a comic performance, in a metatheatrical scene, as it were, similar to the way Xanthias and Dionysus in Aristophanes' *Frogs* (316 ff.) are spectators of a hieratic scene within the comic action. Cf. Slater 2000, 133–6.

18 Cf. Vogt-Spira 1991, 172 f.

19 Cf. Wille 1967, 176 f. For *cinaedus*, see Nonius, p. 5: *cinaedi dicti sunt apud veteres saltatores vel pantomimi*, ἀπὸ τοῦ κινεῖν τὸ σῶμα, cf. ThLL s. v. *cinaedus*. For *Ionicus* cf. Hor. C. 3.6.21–4 (*motus doceri gaudet Ionicos*).

20 Cf. Sittl 1890, 238.

if he would like to call Stephanium outside for a dance (735 *vin amicam huc evocemus? ea saltabit*), and final preparations for the pantomime scene are made in V 5, when the flute player who is supposed to accompany the dance is introduced (754–61)[21] before they gather for a *komos* (762 ff.).

The mocking of Dordalus in the exodos of *Persa* (especially 824 ff. in trochaic septenarii and octonarii) is very similar to the finale of *Stichus*. The dancers, Toxilus and Sagaristio, also comment on the steps and moves they are dancing (824–6).[22] Even before that passage, but still within the context of mocking Dordalos, another reference to a pantomime dance is made in lines 804 ff., where Paegnium's movements are described in cretici as *basilice et facete*.

These two exodoi have led us to a second group of pantomime scenes, which are particularly typical of the early phase of the genre. In his historical overview over pantomime (c. 30), Lucian emphasizes the fact that dancer and singer used to be one and the same person, and that these two roles were redistributed later to a silent dancer and a singer or a chorus for reasons of performance practice.

When studying Plautus' comedies under the aspect of such performances of pantomime dancing, the *cantica* immediately emerge as scenes in which a singer unmistakably demonstrates that he is dancing and singing at the same time.[23] I would like to begin with a scene of particular importance. The last act of *Pseudolus* (1246 ff.) is opened by a long solo performance by the protagonist in the context of a typical *komos* scene, as is also featured in the finales of *Stichus* and *Mostellaria*. Pseudolus arrives drunk from a symposium and narrates his experiences in a messenger report. As he launches into a polymetric description of his dance at the feast (1272 ff.), he begins to reenact his unsuccessful performance. Deictic

---

21 STI. *ita me di ament, numquam enim fiet hodie haec quin saltet tamen./age, mulsa mea suauitudo, salta: saltabo enim simul./*SA. *numquam edepol med istoc vinces quin ego ibidem pruriam./*STE. *siquidem mihi saltandum est, tum vos date bibat tibicini./*STI. *et quidem nobis.* SA. *tene, tibicen, primum; postidea loci/si hoc eduxeris, proinde ut consuetu's antehac, celeriter/lepidam et suavem cantionem aliquam occupito cinaedicam,/ubi perpruriscamus usque ex unguiculis. inde huc aquam.* On the erotic effect of 'Ionian' singing cf. Aristophanes, *Thesmophoriazusae* 130–3: Mnesilochus reacts to Agathon's feminine singing (i.e. probably in falsetto voice) in Ionian rhythms with the following words: 'How sweet the song, venerable Genetyllides, how feminine and like a French kiss, how wanton – while listening to it, I feel a tickling sensation creep up my very behind' (Translation by Katharina Epstein). On the ethos of Ionian rhythm in Greek drama, cf. Zimmermann 1987, 124–32 and Zimmermann 1988, 199–204.

22 SAG. *nequeo, leno, quin tibi saltem staticulum olim quem Hegea/faciebat. vide vero, si tibi sati' placet.* TO. *me quoque volo/reddere Diodorus quem olim faciebat in Ionia.* For an interpretation of the scene, see Chiarini 1979, 197 ff.; also Santelia 1991, 79 f.

23 I do not wish to enter into a discussion of the origins of *cantica* here; see Fraenkel 1922, 321 ff.; Wille 1967, 175 ff.; Gentili 1979, 37 ff.

pronouns and technical terms indicate that he is acting out the messenger report of his ill-fated bout of dancing (1272–8):

> But after I got up, they asked me to dance. I struck a pose for them like this (*demonstrates*), in good form and very much in the correct style, since I learned the Ionian dance well. But dressed in a mantle I merrily strutted these steps like this. (*demonstrates again*) They clapped and shouted 'encore' at me so that I'd return. I began again, in this way (*demonstrates again*), yet I didn't want to. I was showing off to my girlfriend so that she'd love me; when I was doing a pirouette, I fell: that was the unhappy end of my performance.[24]

>   sed post
> quam exsurrexi, orant med ut *saltem*.
> *ad hunc* me *modum intuli* illis sati' facete
> nimis ex disciplina, quippe ego qui
> probe *Ionica* perdidici, sed palliolatim[25] amictus
> sic haec incessi ludibundus.
> plaudunt, 'parum' clamitant mi uti revortar.
> occepi denuo, *hoc modo*: nolui:
> idem amicae dabam me meae,
> ut me amaret: ubi *circumvortor*, cado:
> id fuit naenia ludo.

The second group of pantomime scenes in which singer and dancer are identical is represented by passages like *Cistellaria* (671 ff.), where Halisca is singing while searching for the box and trying to make sense of the footprints she has found (cf. 693 f.; 698 ff.). The beginning of the alcoholic bawd's aria in *Curculio* (96–8) is similar.[26] In *Mostellaria* (313 ff.) a drunken Callidamates staggers across the stage. His duet with Delphium must have been accompanied by a grotesque dance, which probably showcased the young man's drunkenness and his lover's efforts to keep him on his feet. *Menaechmi* (753 ff.) begins with a *canticum* by a father-in-law complaining about old age because it does not allow him to come running as fast as he used to. A rhythm made up of bacchiacs and molossi complements the old man's slow pace.

This survey of Plautus' oeuvre has presented us with scenes which can be considered to be strongly influenced by pantomime dancing. We can distinguish two forms of pantomime scenes:

---

24 Translation by De Melo 2012. Elements drawn from pantomime are indicated by italics.
25 This must mean that Pseudolus is wearing a short Greek cloak (cf. 1279) during his performance. This can be taken as a reference to Greek pantomime.
26 Similar investigations of footprints are featured in Greek drama, cf. Aeschylus, *Eumenides* 254 ff.; Sophocles, *Ichneutai* 91 ff. Radt; Aristophanes, *Acharnians* 204 ff. In *Rudens* (458 ff.), the actor engaged in a search speaks his text and does not sing, so there is no dancing in that scene either.

1. The dance figures and steps, and most of all the gestures of a dancing actor or a group of actors, are described by another actor in long verse, i. e. in recitative style.
2. In the second form, which is featured in some *cantica*, there is no distinction between dancer and singer. The singer himself comments on the steps he dances. It is worth noting that this form often occurs in the context of symposia or *komoi*.

What conclusions can we draw from these findings? The ancient tradition[27] connects the introduction of pantomime in Rome with the names of Pylades and Bathyllus and dates it to 22 B.C. This does not, however, conflict with my argument for the presence of pantomime scenes in Plautus' comedies long before that date, for, to be precise, the innovations made by Pylades and Bathyllus actually consisted in, firstly, systematizing[28] the popular, formerly free form of pantomime dancing;[29] secondly, introducing a tragic and a comic variant of pantomime and establishing the genre in theaters; and thirdly, making a strict distinction between singer and dancer.[30] There is another ancient tradition based on Zosimus and the *Suda*, which completely denies the existence of pantomime before Pylades and Bathyllus.[31] Both texts make use of the topos of a πρῶτος εὑρετής, that is to say, they link the invention of a genre to an actual historical person; however, within the context of this topos, 'invention' or 'introduction' often merely means that a particular person gave a genre the form it was to have in its prime. Therefore, an argument against the existence of pantomime or pantomime dancing before Pylades and Bathyllus cannot be based on these two testimonies.[32]

The pantomime scenes in Plautus' comedies exhibit the characteristics of a form that had not yet been canonically fixed. Its dance figures and sign language still require explanation, and singer and dancer are often identical. It is striking that we find pantomime scenes either in passages composed in long verse or in the *cantica*, for this means that we have to study them with the notion in mind

---

27 Cf. the discussion of testimonies in Rotolo 1957, 23 ff.
28 Pylades is even supposed to have written a book about pantomime. It is a popular *topos* of ancient (especially Peripatetic) literary history to ascribe to the πρῶτοι εὑρεταί of a genre a treatise about it.
29 Hor. *Sat.* 1.5.51 ff. gives a glimpse of this popular type of performance. See also Brink 1982, 347f.
30 On Hieronymus' testimony, see Rotolo 1957, 23.
31 Opelt follows this tradition without taking Greek pantomime into consideration; see Opelt 1978, 452: 'Der Pantomimus ist eine Schöpfung des Jahres 22 vor Christus.'
32 We are faced with a similar problem in the case of the history of the dithyramb, whose 'inventor' is generally assumed to be Arion, although Archilochus already refers to the dithyramb as a genre two generations earlier; see Zimmermann 2008 (a), 21–5.

that Plautus made substantial changes in these passages. Such changes are probable in the case of long verse, and beyond doubt in the case of the *cantica*. If we take further into account that Plautus must have been familiar with groups of actors from *Magna Graecia* with pantomime dances in their repertoire (like the group from Syracuse described in Xenophon's *Symposion*), the idea that Plautus was inspired by this kind of popular performance turns out to be very likely.[33] We also know from the prologue of the second presentation of Terence's *Hecyra* that acrobatic shows were part of the entertainment schedules for official celebrations (4 f. *ita populu' studio stupidus in funambulo/animum occuparat*).

A much-discussed passage in Livy's history proves that pantomime scenes in drama were a phenomenon that was typical of Roman drama (7.2.8–11):[34]

> Livius was the first, some years later, to abandon *saturae* and compose a play with a plot. Like everyone else in those days, he acted his own pieces; and the story goes that when his voice, owing to the frequent demands made upon it, had lost its freshness, he asked and obtained the indulgence to let a boy stand before the flautist to sing the monody, while he acted himself, with a vivacity of gesture that gained considerably from his not having to use his voice. From that time on actors began to use singers to accompany their gesticulation, reserving only the dialogue parts for their own delivery.

> Livius post aliquot annis, qui ab saturis ausus est primus argumento fabulam serere, idem scilicet – id quod omnes tum erant – suorum carminum actor, dicitur, cum saepius revocatus vocem obtudisset, *venia petita puerum ad canendum ante tibicinem cum statuisset, canticum egisse aliquanto magis vigente motu quia nihil vocis usus impediebat*. Inde *ad manum cantari* histrionibus coeptum diverbiaque tantum ipsorum voci relicta.

In a kind of aetiological explanation, Livy attributes pantomime or rather pantomime scenes in Roman plays to the father of Roman drama, Livius Andronicus. The question of whether or not Livy is transposing his own theater experience into a time when Roman drama was first emerging cannot be assessed. What is essential is that he links pantomime dancing to drama, and in doing so increases its prestige, as Lucian will do later, by granting it a spot in the history of Roman drama.[35] This is also made clear by the Greek tradition of literary history, where

---

[33] On theater culture in *Magna Graecia*, see Taplin 1993, e.g. 41 about an Oscan vase. On theater culture in the Roman provinces, see especially Fugmann 2013; Bosher 2012.

[34] Translation by Foster 1924, 363. Cf. Gentili 1979, 46 f. and, with a detailed discussion of the current status of research, Schmidt 1989, 77–133.

[35] Pantomime later holds the same spot in Seneca's tragedies; cf. Zimmermann 2008 (b), 218–26. I argue that Seneca and Plautus integrate elements of pantomime with the same intention: on the one hand, these playwrights have realized how attractive the subliterary genre of pantomime is and try to use this to the advantage of their plays; on the other hand, they are elevating a subliterary genre by incorporating it into an already established literary genre.

comic pantomime is called Ἰταλικὴ ὄρχησις (Athenaius I 20 d-e, Suda s. v. Πυλάδης).[36]

For Plautus, we can venture the hypothesis that he draws on elements of the native, subliterary form of pantomime to make his plays more attractive and able to compete with forms of mere popular entertainment, similar to the way Seneca employs elements of pantomime in his tragedies.[37] Pantomime dances and scenes in Plautus' plays allow us to take a brief but thorough look at the way Plautus worked by conveniently illustrating how Plautus integrated subliterary elements from a native tradition into his writings. As observed in the scene from *Miles gloriosus* reviewed above, he uses elements of pantomime to enhance the action with mimetic details and to visualize emotions and other processes which would otherwise remain unseen. According to Lucian (c. 67), the *mimesis* of emotions through dancing is precisely the aim of pantomime.[38] When interpreting Plautus' *cantica*, and their origins in particular, one should entertain the possibility, I think, that they may have their roots in mimetic dancing.[39] At the same time, studying Plautus' comedies sheds some light on the early phase of pantomime, when it was still a form of actual popular entertainment without established norms or a canonical form, and when its movements had not yet turned into a subtly coded language of their own. Finally, the existence of pantomime dances in Plautus' comedies clearly demonstrates that when searching for the origins of Plautine comedy, the cultural environment of *Magna Graecia* and its native popular forms of drama should not be disregarded.[40]

---

36 Cf. Sittl 1890, 246 n. 7.
37 Cf. Zimmermann 2008 (b), 218–26.
38 In the same context, Lucian stresses in *De saltatione* 64 (as does Libanius in *Pro saltatione* 112) that words are basically no longer relevant in pantomime, because the dancer can adequately communicate everything to the audience through his movements. See also the anonymous epigram *De pantomimo* (Anth. Lat. 111 Riese), in particular 9 f.: *Tot linguae quot membra viro. mirabilis ars est,/quae facit articulos ore silente loqui*. This fits in perfectly with the multiple layers of Plautus' (and also Aristophanes') comedy, which allow him to cater to both the educated and the uneducated spectator.
39 Gellius, too, notes this in his comparison of Menander's *Plokion* and Caecilius' *Plocium* when he writes (2.23.11): (Caecilius) [...] *et alia nescio qua mimica inculcavit*. On this famous comparison of a model and its adaptation, see Riedweg 1993, 133–59 with a detailed discussion of literature; see also Gentili 1979, 50 for an explanation of *mimica*.
40 With regard to the 'Plautine question', it needs to be taken into account that *Magna Graecia* in particular was home to performance forms containing original elements of higher-class culture which had 'sunken down'. This may mean that when trying to reconstruct the road from a Greek model to one of Plautus' comedies, we need to assume that there were several subliterary stops in between.

Bibliography

Blänsdorf, J. (1978), 'Plautus', in: E. Lefèvre (ed.), *Das römische Drama*, Darmstadt, 135–219.
Bosher, K. (2012), (ed.), *Theater outside Athens. Drama in Greek Sicily and South Italy*, Cambridge.
Brink, C. O. (1982), *Horace on Poetry. Epistles Book II*, Cambridge.
Brix, J. Niemeyer, M., Köhler, O. ([4]1916), *Ausgewählte Komödien des T. Maccius Plautus*, Bd. 4: *Miles gloriosus*, Leipzig/Berlin.
Chiarini, G. (1979), *La recita. Plauto, la farsa, la festa*, Bologna.
Corbato, C. (1982), 'Symposium e teatro: dati e problemi', in: *Spettacoli conviviali dall'antichità classica alle corti del' 400*, Viterbo, 65–76.
Csapo, E., Slater, W. J. (1994), *The Context of Ancient Drama*, Ann Arbor.
Del Giudice, L., van Deusen, N. (2005), (eds.), *Performing Ecstasies: Music, Dance, and Ritual in the Mediterranean*, Ottawa, 3–11.
_____ (2008), (eds.), *Demons and Dancers: Performance in Late Antiquity*, Cambridge, MA.
De Melo, W. (2011), (ed., tr.), *Plautus. The Merchant, The Braggart Soldier, The Ghost, The Persian*, Cambridge, Mass./London.
_____ (2012), (ed., tr.), *Plautus, The Little Carthaginian, Pseudolus, The Rope*, Cambridge, Mass./London.
Foster, B. O. (1924), (ed., tr.), *Livy*, Vol. III, London/Cambridge, Mass.
Fraenkel, E. (1922), *Plautinisches im Plautus*, Berlin.
Fugmann, J. (2013), *Römisches Theater in der Provinz*, Freiburg i. Br./Berlin/Wien.
Gentili, B. (1979), *Theatrical Performances in the Ancient World*, Amsterdam.
Godley, A. D. (1971), (ed., tr.), *Herodotus in four volumes*, Vol. 3, Books V-VII, Cambridge, MA./London.
Hall, E. (2008), 'Introduction', in: E. Hall, R. Wiles (eds.), *New Directions in Ancient Pantomime*, Oxford, 1–40.
Jones, C. P. (1986), *Culture and Society in Lucian*, Cambridge, MA/London.
Lindsay, W. M. T. (1904–05), (ed.), *Macci Plauti Comoediae*, 2 vols., Oxford.
Macintosh, F. (2010), (ed.), *The Ancient Dancer in the Modern World: Responses to Greek and Roman Dance*, Oxford.
Opelt, I. (1978), 'Das Drama der Kaiserzeit', in: E. Lefèvre (ed.), *Das römische Drama*, Darmstadt, 427–57.
Riedweg, Ch. (1993), 'Menander in Rom – Beobachtungen zu Caecilius Statius *Plocium* fr. 1', in: N. W. Slater, B. Zimmermann (eds.), *Intertextualität in der griechisch-römischen Komödie*, Drama 2, 133–59.
Roos, E. (1951), *Die tragische Orchestik im Zerrbild der altattischen Komödie*, Lund.
Rossi, L. E. (1978), 'Mimica e danza sulla scena comica greca', *RCCM* 20, 1149–70.
Rotolo, V. (1957), *Il pantomimo*, Palermo.
Santelia, S. (1991), *Charition liberata*, Bari.
Schmidt, P. L. (1989), '*Postquam ludus in artem paulatim verterat*. Varro und die Frühgeschichte des römischen Theaters', in: G. Vogt-Spira (ed.), *Studien zur vorliterarischen Periode im frühen Rom*, Tübingen, 77–133.
Sittl, G. (1980), *Die Gebärden der Griechen und Römer*, Leipzig.
Slater, N. W. (2000), *Plautus in Performance. The Theatre of the Mind*, Amsterdam.

Taplin, O. (1993), *Comic Angels and Other Approaches to Greek Drama through Vase-Paintings*, Oxford.
Vogt-Spira, G. (1991), '*Stichus* oder Ein Parasit wird Hauptperson', in: E. Lefèvre/E. Stärk/ G. Vogt-Spira (eds.), *Plautus barbarus. Sechs Kapitel zur Originalität des Plautus*, Tübingen, 163–74.
Webb, R. (2005), 'The Protean Performer: Mimesis and Identity in Late Antique Discussions of the Theatre', in: L. Del Giudice, N. van Deusen (eds.), *Performing Ecstasies: Music, Dance, and Ritual in the Mediterranean*, Ottawa, 3–11.
Wille, G. (1967), *Musica Romana*, Amsterdam.
Zimmermann, B. (^{2}1985), *Untersuchungen zur Form und dramatischen Technik der Aristophanischen Komödien*, Vols. I–II, Königstein.
——— (1987), 'Ioniker in den Komödien des Aristophanes. Prolegomena zu einer interpretativen Metrik', *Prometheus* 13, 124–32.
——— (1988), 'Critica ed imitazione. La nuova musica nelle commedie di Aristofane', in: B. Gentili, R. Pretagostini (eds.), *La musica in Grecia*, Roma/Bari, 199–204.
——— (2008 a), *Dithyrambos. Geschichte einer Gattung*, Berlin.
——— (2008 b), 'Seneca and Pantomime', in: E. Hall, R. Wyles (eds.), *New Directions in Ancient Pantomime*, Oxford, 218–26.

Part II: **Roman Tragedy**

Gesine Manuwald
History and Philosophy in Roman Republican Drama and Beyond

When Roman writers started to develop a formal literature in Latin by adapting Greek literature to the Roman world from around 240 BCE onwards, they were confronted with a variety of options of what to select and how to transfer it. The pieces transposed introduced recipients in Rome to a range of literary genres and of ideas new to them; these included performances of dramas in Latin on the model of Greek plays. While it is obvious that Roman poets took over the plots of Greek plays chosen for adaptation, there was no need for them to include some of the social, moral and intellectual issues, i.e. 'philosophy' in a broad sense, found in many Greek dramas. Interestingly, however, Roman poets did so, and they also presented Roman historical events in plays, thereby using drama as a vehicle beyond narrating entertaining stories.

A telling example is a line from the tragedy *Chryses* by Ennius' nephew Pacuvius (c. 220–130 BCE): this play, which, like many Republican dramas, only survives in fragments, seems to have featured a section on 'natural philosophy', looking forward to Lucretius' didactic poem on Epicurean philosophy in the first century BCE.[1] If a number of fragments dealing with aspects of 'natural philosophy' are correctly attributed to *Chryses*, the play contained a discussion of *aether*.

Apparently in this context a character says: 'this, which I mention, our people call 'sky', the Greeks 'aether' ' (Pac. *Trag.* 89 R.$^{2-3}$ = 110–11 W. = 79 S.). As the interlocutor in Cicero's dialogue, where this line is transmitted (Cic. *Nat. D.* 2.91), notes, the comment disrupts the dramatic illusion: for, although the character speaks in Latin, he is supposed to be a Greek, and therefore the audience is meant to assume that he is speaking Greek. The linguistic form seems even to have been commented on in dramas since Cicero's interlocutor goes on to remark that Pacuvius has a character remark elsewhere: 'a Greek by birth: the speech itself reveals that about him' (Pac. *Trag.* 364 R.$^{2-3}$ = *Trag. inc.* 14 W. = *Trag.* 266 S.).[2] While these observa-

---

1 References for all major editions of fragments will be given (for details and key to abbreviations see bibliography). English translations are the author's own unless otherwise indicated.
2 Cicero, *Nat. D.* 2.91: *principio enim terra sita in media parte mundi circumfusa undique est hac animali spirabilique natura cui nomen est aer – Graecum illud quidem sed perceptum iam tamen usu a nostris; tritum est enim pro Latino. hunc rursus amplectitur inmensus aether, qui constat ex altissimis ignibus (mutuemur hoc quoque verbum, dicaturque tam aether Latine quam dicitur aer, etsi interpretatur Pacuvius: 'hoc, quod memoro, nostri caelum, Grai perhibent aethera' – quasi vero non Graius hoc dicat. 'at Latine loquitur.' si quidem nos non quasi Graece loquentem audiamus;*

tions are true, the appearance of such a statement on vocabulary in drama indicates that the drive to discuss scientific issues and to make the terminology clear to audiences was apparently stronger than maintaining the dramatic illusion.[3] It is remarkable that such notions, which pose a challenge for the poet to integrate, are presented to the public in early Rome, when drama and literature more broadly are only just emerging, there is hardly any tradition of literary theatre and philosophical discussions, and a Latin literary language has not yet been established.

In the light of this, scholars have suggested that, prior to the evolution of literary forms for specific topics, such as philosophical treatises in prose, drama was an important pathway for introducing the Roman public to philosophical ideas derived from the Greeks and perhaps even the earliest vehicle for this in Rome. Since drama was a public genre, this would explain how philosophy might have become known in Rome, but it does not give a reason why Roman writers felt prompted to address such issues in drama. A key figure in this process seems to have been the poet Ennius (239–169 BCE),[4] who not only wrote dramas and an epic, like his predecessors Livius Andronicus (c. 280/70–200 BCE) and Naevius (c. 280/60–200 BCE), but also satires, epigrams and philosophical works. This expansion may have to do with Ennius' personal interests, but could also have been fuelled or supported by general interests at the time, at least

---

docet idem alio loco: 'Graiugena: de isto aperit ista oratio'). – 'To begin with, the earth, set at the mid-point of the universe, is surrounded on all sides by that living element which we breathe. The name it bears is *aer* (air), a Greek term but one which our compatriots have adopted in everyday use, for it commonly passes for Latin. In turn, the air is encompassed by the boundless aether, which is composed of fires lying at the furthest height; we Romans can borrow this word 'aether' as well, and express it as Latin just as we do *aer*, though Pacuvius translates it: 'Greeks call it aether, but we speak of heaven above.' The joke is that a Greek speaks this line! You will retort: But he is speaking in Latin. True, but we are to imagine him saying it in Greek, for he says elsewhere: 'My words declare that I'm a native Greek'.' [trans. P. G. Walsh]. – Varro (*Ling.* 5.17) quotes pieces from Pacuvius partly overlapping with the first quotation in the Cicero passage, but with a different wording (*id quod nostri caelum memorant*). Scholars have often assumed that both authors refer to the same passage and that one of them, probably Cicero, does not quote verbatim; on this basis the two quotations have been combined (see Schierl 2006 *ad loc.*). In any case Latin and Greek terms were juxtaposed in Pacuvius, and Cicero comments on the use of *nostri* with reference to the Romans in the mouth of a Greek dramatic figure.

3 All fragments surviving for Pacuvius are likely to come from dramas since this is the only genre he is certain to have been active in. Some ancient sources report that Pacuvius wrote satires (Porph. on Hor. *Sat.* 1.10.46; Diom. *Ars* 3, *Gramm. Lat.* 1, p. 485.32–4); but no traces remain, and it is unclear whether this information can be trusted.

4 On Ennius' life and works (with bibliography) see Suerbaum 2002, § 117; for a bibliographical survey see Suerbaum 2003.

among the educated elite. All these literary forms were continued after Ennius, but never again all represented by the same writer.

In what follows, connections between drama and issues associated with other forms of formal writing (and attested in other literary genres) will be discussed with reference to philosophy and history as well as with respect to the linguistic form, to indicate the role of drama in the literary and intellectual history of early Rome.[5]

In view of the example from Pacuvius' *Chryses*, which provides an explanation of Greek terminology, fragments from works by Ennius in non-dramatic literary genres indicate that the discussion of such issues was not restricted to drama. A couple of lines from Ennius' *Annales* read: 'and an eagle came flying with thick wings, battling with the wind, which the Greek nation calls in its tongue 'aer' ' (Enn. *Ann.* 147–8 V.^{2} = 151–2 W. = 139–40 Sk.).[6] Here a Latin and a Greek term for a natural phenomenon are juxtaposed; in an epic it is possible that a narrator introduces such explanations, which would not disrupt the flow and the narrative setting too much. That Ennius was not only concerned with the terminology for 'air', but also with the position of this natural phenomenon within the mythical world could be suggested by the following line, which also survives for Ennius: 'that is this Jupiter, whom I mean, whom the Greeks call 'aer' ' (Enn. *Var.* [*Epicharm.*] 54–8 V.^{2} = *Epicharm.* 10–4 W. = *Trag.* 356–60 J. = F 39* [*Epicharm.*] *FPL*^{4} = 206 *TrRF*).[7] Since the quotation of this extract (Varro, *Ling.* 5.65) does not indicate the context, scholars have attributed the fragment

---

5 Since this paper focuses on the literary context, aspects such as the historical, political or sociological background of Roman Republican drama will be disregarded. – 'History' here refers to the explicit presentation of historical events rather than to potential allusions to the contemporary situation. – On pilosophical themes in early Roman literature see now Dutsch 2014.
6 Ennius, *Ann.* 147–8 V.^{2} = 151–2 W. = 139–40 Sk.: *et densis aquila pennis obnixa volabat | vento quam perhibent Graium genus aera lingua.* – For other equations of terms in *Annales*, though without explicit mention of Greek as the point of reference, see Ennius, *Ann.* 2, 218, 409 V.^{2} = *Spur.* 43, *Ann.* 229, 387 W. = *Ann.* 487, 211, 399–400 Sk.
7 Ennius, *Var.* 54–8 (*Epicharm.*) V.^{2} = *Epicharm.* 10–4 W. = *Trag.* 356–60 J. = F 39* (*Epicharm.*) *FPL*^{4} = 206 *TrRF*: *istic est is Iup<p>iter quem dico, quem Graeci vocant | aerem, qui ventus est et nubes, imber postea, | atque ex imbre frigus, ventus post fit, aer denuo. | † haec propter † Iuppiter sunt ista quae dico tibi | † qua † mortalis atque urbes beluasque omnis iuvat.* – 'That is this Jupiter, whom I mean, whom the Greeks call 'aer', who is wind and clouds, later rain, and cold from rain, then becomes wind, 'aer' again. Therefore (?) these things that I mention to you are Jupiter because he (?) strengthens all mortals and cities and animals.' – On the possible philosophical sources of this fragment see Kessissoglu 1990, 77–80.

opened by this line to Ennius' tragedies, as it recalls passages in Euripides,[8] or to his philosophical piece *Epicharmus*, or have placed it among the *incerta*.[9]

The precise nature and specific sources of Ennius' *Epicharmus* are uncertain, but it seems to have consisted of a collection of philosophical doctrines derived from the writings of the Greek comic writer Epicharmus (c. 540–450 BCE) or those ascribed to him (*Pseudepicharmeia*).[10] Epicharmus' dramas included philosophical sayings and comments on philosophers; philosophical works later circulated under his name. Wherever the contents of Ennius' *Epicharmus* ultimately derive from, the Latin work does not seem to be a drama, but rather a narrative of the poet's (alleged) experiences; at least it included a mention of a dream of the poet (Cic. *Ac*. 2.51).[11] Moreover, since the fragment on *aer* sounds rather didactic, including explicit backward references and a summative tone, its attribution to *Epicharmus* is plausible. The speaker would be a character giving a philosophical exposition.

At any rate in this fragment Greek *aer* is not translated, but Jupiter is identified with air. In other fragments, clearly assigned to *Epicharmus*, the mind is linked to the Sun (Enn. *Var*. 51, 52–3 [*Epicharm*.] V.^{2} = *Epicharmus* 7, 8–9 W. = F [*Epicharm*.] 39, 37 C. = F 37*, 38* [*Epicharm*.] *FPL*^{4}).[12] Ennian fragments evidently

---

[8] On references to the divine nature of 'aether' in Euripides see Egli 2003, 80–94.

[9] For a collection of Ennian fragments with a possible philosophical background see Gabarino 1973, 126–38, 167–73 (F 232–79, 399–426), with discussion (pp. 259–312).

[10] Remains of Epicharmus in Kaibel, *CGF*, vol. I, 88–147; *PCG*, vol. I, 8–173 K.-A. (including fragments from the comedies and *Pseudepicharmeia* as well as Ennius' version); 'philosophical works' in DK 23; for discussion of *Pseudepicharmeia* see e. g. Kerkhof 2001, 79–115. – On Ennius' *Epicharmus* see e. g. Brink 1972, esp. 562–4; Garbarino 1973, 276–89; Bettini 1979, 31–42; Kessissoglu 1990, 75–80.

[11] Cicero, *Ac*. 2.51 (Ennius, *Var*. 45 [*Epicharm*.] V.^{2} = *Epicharm*. 1 W. = F 35* [*Epicharm*.] *FPL*^{4}): *eadem ratio est somniorum. num censes Ennium cum in hortis Servio Galba vicino suo ambulavisset dixisse 'visus sum mihi cum Galba ambulare'? at cum somniavit, ita narravit: 'visus Homerus adesse poeta'* [Ennius, *Ann*. 6 V.^{2} = 5 W. = 3 Sk.], *idemque in Epicharmo: 'nam videbar somniare med ego esse mortuum'. itaque simul ut experrecti sumus, visa illa contemnimus*. – 'The same argument applies to dreams. Or do you think that when Ennius had been walking in the garden with his neighbour Servius Galba, he said, 'It seemed to me I walked with Galba'? Yet when he had a dream, he related it thus: 'The poet Homer seemed to be present.' Likewise in the *Epicharmus*: 'I seemed to dream that I was dead.' We make light of such impressions as soon as we have woken up, since we don't consider them on a par with what we have done in the forum.' [trans. C. Brittain].

[12] Ennius, *Var*. 51, 52–3 (*Epicharm*.) V.^{2} = *Epicharmus* 7, 8–9 W. = F (*Epicharm*.) 39, 37 C. = F 37*, 38* (*Epicharm*.) *FPL*^{4}: *terra corpus est at mentis ignis est | istic* [i. e. *mens*] *est de sole sumptus ignis | isque* [i. e. *sol*] *totus mentis est* – 'the body is earth, but the mind is fire' | 'this is fire taken from the sun' | 'and this is entirely mind'.

coming from tragedies establish a close connection between Jupiter and the Sun (Enn. *Trag.* 302, 237–9 R.$^{2-3}$ = 351, 291–3 W. = 301, 234–6 J. = 134, 95 *TrRF*).[13] Such aspects treated in dramas indicate that Roman poets did not just take over the plot from Greek models and allow the conclusion that Ennius assumed that recipients of his works were interested in these questions.

The engagement with philosophical ideas can itself become the object of a comment by a dramatic character: Ennius' Neoptolemus makes the famous statement that one should not philosophize too much (Enn. *Trag.* 340 R.$^{2-3}$ = 400 W. = 95 J. = 147 *TrRF*).[14] This may be caused by his particular situation in the (unknown) play; still, the speaker acknowledges some level of involvement with philosophy. 'Philosophy' and philosophical attitudes must have quickly become a common concept, with the result that they also appear in light dramatic genres. When Pseudolus says in Plautus' homonymous comedy that there has been enough doing philosophy (Plaut. *Pseud.* 687), the word seems to be used in a more 'colloquial' sense and to refer to general reflections rather than 'philosophy' in a strict sense (also Plaut. *Merc.* 147).[15] In Terence's *Eunuchus* the parasite Gnatho reports how he has instructed someone else in the principles of the best way of being a parasite (Ter. *Eun.* 232–64) and concludes (Ter. *Eun.* 262–4): 'I told him to enrol as my pupil, in the hope that, just as philosophical schools take their names from their founders, so parasites may be called Gnathonists.'[16] This is mockery of the establishment of philosophical schools and (for the audience) of the character of Gnatho; at the same time it shows a familiarity with the concept of philosophical schools. In Atellane plays such as Pomponius' (*fl.* 89 BCE) *Philosophia* and Novius' (*fl. c.* 85 BCE) *Mortis et vitae iudicium* philosophical issues are likely to have played a major role. That 'philosophy' at least on the level of *sententiae* was relatively common is indicated by the metadramatic mockery of

---

13 Ennius, *Trag.* 302 R.$^{2-3}$ = 351 W. = 301 J. = 134 *TrRF*: *aspice hoc sublime candens, quem vocant omne Iovem* – 'look at this shining in a lofty position, whom all call 'Jupiter' '; 237–9 R.$^{2-3}$ = 291–3 W. = 234–6 J. = 95 *TrRF*: *Iuppiter tuque adeo summe Sol qui res omnis inspicis | quique lumine tuo mare terram caelum contines | inspice hoc facinus, prius quam fi<a>t, prohibessis scelus.* – 'Jupiter and indeed you, greatest Sun, who see all things and who surround sea, earth and sky with your light, look at this deed before it happens: you may prevent a crime.'
14 Ennius, *Trag.* 340 Ri.$^{2-3}$ = 400 W. = 95 J. = 147 *TrRF*: *philosophandum est, paucis; nam omnino haud placet* – 'one must do philosophy, but in moderation; for entirely it does not please'.
15 Plautus, *Pseud.* 687: *sed iam satis est philosophatum.* – 'But there has now been enough doing philosophy.'; *Merc.* 147: *nescio ego istaec: philosophari numquam didici neque scio.* – 'I do not understand this: I have never learned to do philosophy, and I do not know how to do it.'
16 Ter. *Eun.* 262–4: *sectari iussi, | si potis est, tamquam philosophorum habent disciplinae ex ipsis | vocabula, parasiti ita ut Gnathonici vocentur.* [trans. J. Barsby].

these in Plautus, suggesting their limited usefulness for the lives of members of the audience (Plaut. *Rud.* 1249–53).[17]

Altogether these pieces of evidence show that, from Ennius' time onwards, aspects of philosophical discussions appear in early Roman literature across the board and that comments on philosophical themes in a broad sense were deemed worthwhile and relevant to audiences, for whom a certain familiarity with such issues was soon assumed. Insofar as content can still be discovered, there seems to have been a focus on explaining the natural world and linking traditional religious concepts with natural phenomena, even though such rationalistic interpretations of gods possibly contrasted with Roman state religion. That across Ennius' works various perspectives are being proposed might be due to the fact that they are presented by individual speakers who put forward different views and whose opinions need not be those supported by the poet and/or that the ideas in *Epicharmus* derive from Greek writings under Epicharmus' name and those in the tragedies come from different backgrounds.[18] In the kind of questions addressed there is little difference between dramatic and non-dramatic literary genres. It may just be the case that the phrases from drama tend to be less technical, shorter and more apt to display religious veneration or light-hearted ridicule (depending on genre); yet the limited number of examples and the brevity of many of the excerpts may distort the picture.

That there was a tendency in drama to address major topics even beyond the plot can also be seen with respect to history. As regards philosophical ideas in drama, Roman poets were able to take over a selection of concepts from Greek literature, presumably those that they believed to be of interest to contemporary audiences, and integrated this material into their presentation of the plots adapted from existing Greek plays. For the dramatic representation of topics from Roman history, however, Roman poets were not in a position to fall back on Greek models for the content, though they could use dramatic forms established by Greek writers and adopted in Rome (mainly pieces on Greek myths, but also

---

[17] Plaut. *Rud.* 1249–53: *spectavi ego pridem comicos ad istunc modum | sapienter dicta dicere atque eis plaudier, | cum illos sapientis mores monstrabant poplo: | sed cum inde suam quisque ibant divorsi domum, | nullus erat illo pacto ut illi iusserant.* – 'I have often seen comic poets pronounce statements of this kind in a wise way before and they being applauded, when they showed those wise ways of life to the people: but when each went back into their own home afterwards, nobody behaved in that way in which those had ordered them.'

[18] On the different philosophical views found in Ennius' works see also Garbarino 1973, 287–8, 302. – Dutsch (2014) notes that early Roman dramatists allude to an eclectic mix of philosophical doctrines (and use a variety of different intertexts), with greater interest in the matters as such than in specific philosophical schools.

individual examples of dramas on events from Greek history). Therefore it is noteworthy that Roman writers employed drama to present such topics and even developed a specific dramatic genre for this, the *fabula praetexta*. Just like philosophy, history appears across literary genres at the time when the *praetexta* emerges in the late third century BCE.

Ennius, for instance, wrote a *praetexta* entitled *Sabinae*, which dramatizes the rape of the Sabine women after the foundation of Rome. Owing to the dramatic presentation, the Sabine women appear as speaking characters (Enn. *Praet.* 5 R.^{2} = 5–6 R.^{3} = *Trag.* 379–80 W.).[19] Fragments show that this story was also included in the chronological treatment of Roman history in Ennius' epic *Annales* (Enn. *Ann.* 101 V.^{2} = 108 W. = 98 Sk.)[20] and was narrated in the historiographical work of his elder contemporary Fabius Pictor (c. 270–200 BCE), who produced *Annales* in Greek prose (Plut. *Rom.* 14.1: F 6 *FRHist* = 9 *FRH* = 7 Peter = 5 Jacoby).[21] Since the surviving individual fragments refer to different stages of the incident, it is difficult to determine differences in presentation.

The situation is similar for the *praetexta* entitled *Romulus/Lupus* by Ennius' predecessor Naevius: it features the early stages of the story of Rome's founder,[22] a section also covered in Ennius' epic *Annales* (Enn. *Ann.* 68, 70–2 V.^{2} = 71, 72–4, W. = 65, 66–8 Sk.) and the historiographical work of Fabius Pictor (Fabius Pictor, F 4a, 4b, 4c, 29, 4d, 4e *FRHist* = F 7a–f *FRH* = 5a, 5b, 4 Lat., 2 Lat., 3 Lat. Peter = 4a, 4b, 30b, 30a, 31, 32 Jacoby), apparently with a similar version of the story.

Even if details cannot be established, these overlaps show that, with respect to topics from the Roman past, plots for dramas could be taken from the shared cultural memory and were treated in different literary genres, emerging at roughly the same time, which again suggests a widespread interest. Since these events from what might be called mythical prehistory according to modern categories appear not only in drama, but also in historiographical narratives, they are evidently seen as part of Roman history, rather than 'fictional' material. All these

---

19 Ennius, *Praet.* 5 R.^{2} = 5–6 R.^{3} = *Trag.* 379–80 W.: *cum spolia generi<s> detraxeritis, quam <, patres,> | inscriptionem dabitis?* – 'when you have dragged us as spoils from your sons-in-law, <fathers,> what inscription will you give?' – On this praetexta see Manuwald 2001, 172–9 (with further references).
20 Ennius, *Ann.* 101 V.^{2} = 108 W. = 98 Sk.: † *virgines nam sibi quisque domi Romanus habet sas* – 'maidens (?); for each Roman has theirs at home for themselves'.
21 Plutarch, *Rom.* 14.1: F 9 *FRH* = 7 Peter = 5 Jacoby: τετάρτῳ δὲ μηνὶ μετὰ τὴν κτίσιν, ὡς Φάβιος ἱστορεῖ, τὸ περὶ τὴν ἁρπαγὴν ἐτολμήθη τῶν γυναικῶν. – 'In the fourth month after the founding [i. e. of the city of Rome], as Fabius reports, the activity around the abduction of the women was dared.'
22 On this praetexta see Manuwald 2001, 141–61 (with further references).

literary genres, historiography, historical epic and historical drama, equally addressed events from the recent past, such as contemporary victories (as presented in Naevius' *Clastidium* or Ennius' *Ambracia*), which were relevant to audiences at the time.

Contemporary events may be shown in further literary genres: the literary form of Ennius' piece entitled *Scipio* has been debated, but it seems clear that it is not a drama or an epic, but rather a self-contained poem about a Roman politician and general (P. Cornelius Scipio Africanus, c. 235–183 BCE).[23] Valerius Maximus confirms that Ennius praised Scipio, although he does not identify the work, and he notes that the writing was not as polished as Homer's (Val. Max. 8.14.1).[24] According to the *Suda* (*Suda*, s. v. Ennios) the poem was written in praise of Scipio. When Ennius is said to have claimed in this context (in mock-modesty) that 'only Homer composes praises worthy of Scipio', he implicitly compares his own activity to that of Homer; this establishes a connection to epic or to Homer as the paradigm for all types of poetry.[25] For *Annales* too a link to Homer is created by the poet's dream appearance as narrated in the proem to book 1;[26] and, obviously, *Annales* 9 includes a narrative of the battle of Zama between Scipio and Hannibal in 202 BCE.

Just as Scipio's activities were described in works of different literary genres (*Scipio* and *Annales*), M. Fulvius Nobilior featured in *Annales* 15 and the *praetex-*

---

[23] For a recent overview of the issue see Russo 2007, 195–207.
[24] Valerius Maximus 8.14.1: *Superior Africanus Ennii poetae effigiem in monumentis Corneliae gentis collocari voluit, quod ingenio eius opera sua illustrata iudicaret, non quidem ignarus quam diu Romanum imperium floreret, et Africa Italiae pedibus esset subiecta, totiusque terrarum orbis summum columen arx Capitolina possideret, eorum exstingui memoriam non posse, si tamen litterarum quoque illis lumen accessisset, magni aestimans, vir Homerico quam rudi atque impolito praeconio dignior.* – 'The elder Africanus wanted the portrait of the poet Ennius placed among the monuments of the Cornelian clan because he judged that by Ennius' genius his own performances had been illuminated. He was not ignorant that as long as Roman empire flourished and Africa lay subject at Italy's feet and the citadel of the Capitol possessed the topmost pinnacle of the globe their memory could not be extinguished, but he thought it of great moment that the light of letters too should accrue to them. A man worthy to be celebrated by Homer rather than in rude, unpolished strains.' [trans. D. R. Shackleton Bailey].
[25] *Suda*, s. v. Ἔννιος (*II*, p. 285 Adler, E 1348): Ἔ ν ν ι ο ς, Ῥωμαῖος ποιητής· ὃν Αἰλιανὸς ἐπαινεῖν ἄξιόν φησι. Σκιπίωνα γὰρ ᾄδων καὶ ἐπὶ μέγα τὸν ἄνδρα ἐξᾶραι βουλόμενός φησι μόνον ἂν Ὅμηρον ἐπαξίους ἐπαίνους εἰπεῖν Σκιπίωνος. – 'Ennius, a Roman poet; of him Aelianus [a sophist of the 2nd cent. CE] says that he is worthy of bestowing praise. For, singing about Scipio and wishing to exalt the man to something great, he says that only Homer composes praises worthy of Scipio.'
[26] Suerbaum (1968, 103–4) sees a substantial difference between the presentation of Homer and Ennius' relationship to him in *Annales* and in *Scipio*.

ta Ambracia, named after the city in Aetolia conquered by him in 189 BCE (Liv. 38.3.9–11.9; Polyb. 21.25–30).[27] Even if the *praetexta* was performed in connection with Fulvius Nobilior's fulfilling a vow made in case of victory in the war (Liv. 39.5.7–10; 39.22.1–2), due to the public presentation, it was probably not as obviously glorifying as an individual poem, though the idea to celebrate outstanding generals and their achievements for the Roman republic will have been similar. Contemporary Roman politicians could obviously be portrayed in a variety of literary genres in Rome, ultimately developed from Greek models.

The fluidity and cross-fertilization between tragedy, Roman history plays and other equally elevated literary genres extends to the area of diction (while the language of comedy is closer to colloquial, spoken discourse).[28]

Ennius' tragedy *Hectoris lytra* includes the phrase 'the Scamander, I believe, has come to a standstill; the trees are free from wind' (Enn. *Trag.* 151 R.$^{2-3}$ = 197 W. = 159 J. = 64 *TrRF*).[29] It is unclear what Ennius' line refers to, since there is no parallel in the Homeric narrative, on which the drama's plot seems to be based; but this certainly is a character's description of a particular incident in a specific location. The verb *vacant* is, admittedly, an old emendation for *vagant* (by Columna), but generally accepted.

In *Scipio*[30] there is a line 'the ever-flowing rivers stood still, the trees were free from wind' (Enn. *Var.* 9–12 [*Scipio*] V.^{2} = *Scipio* 1–4 W. = F 31* [*Scipio*] *FPL*^{4}).[31] With the emendation in *Hectoris lytra* accepted, exactly the same phrase can be found in Ennius' tragedy and in his *Scipio*, where it forms part of a description of the stillness of the world, including heaven, sea, sun, rivers and trees. It sounds like an authorial sketch of the reaction to something awe-inspiring. Whether the portrayal of stillness in the tragedy included other elements beyond river and trees cannot be ascertained. At any rate, owing to the insertion of *credo*, it is a subjective description of a situation, whereas the passage in *Scipio* looks like a poetic portrait, where the sun and the sea are identified metonymically and the

---

27 On this praetexta see Manuwald 2001, 162–72 (with further references).
28 On the language of Roman comedy see e. g. Karakasis 2005; Dutsch 2008.
29 Ennius, *Trag.* 151 R.$^{2-3}$ = 197 W. = 159 J. = 64 *TrRF*: *constitit, credo, Scamander; arbores vento vacant* [Columna : *vagant* codd.].
30 On *Scipio* e. g. Suerbaum 1968, 239–48; Bettini 1979, 161–7; Scholz 1984. Suerbaum believes that *Scipio* is identical with the third book of Ennius' *Satires*. Scholz regards *Scipio* as a poem in trochaics composed around 200 BCE, which had some success in its time, but was not of lasting literary value.
31 Ennius, *Var.* 9–12 (*Scipio*) V.^{2} = *Scipio* 1–4 W. = F 31 (*Scipio*) C. = F 31* (*Scipio*) *FPL*^{4}: *mundus caeli vastus constitit silentio | et Neptunus saevus undis asperis pausam dedit, | sol equis iter repressit ungulis volantibus, | constitere amnes perennes, arbores vento vacant.*

silence is indicated by actions of Neptune and the Sun. Even the stillness of the rivers is more comprehensive since it affects more than one river, and they are described as *perennes*.

This fragment from *Scipio* survives because the late-antique author Macrobius (6.2.26) transmits it as a model for a passage in Virgil's *Aeneid* (10.100–3),[32] although he claims elsewhere that the Virgilian passage was modelled on a Homeric precedent.[33] In line with the parameters of the section in Macrobius, this is not an instance of Virgil picking up verses of earlier poets verbatim, but rather an example of the use of a similar motif: Virgil describes the great stillness in the world when Jupiter begins to speak. This is certainly not the context in Ennius' tragedy, while it may be the case in Ennius' *Scipio*. The appearance of the motif in yet another literary genre shows that the conceit and the phrasing are not specific to tragedy, but may be used in various literary genres, adapted to individual contexts. This indicates that the Latin literary language, emerging alongside the adaptation of Greek literature, was developing similarly in comparable

---

[32] Virgil, *Aen.* 10.96–103: *talibus orabat Iuno, cunctique fremebant | caelicolae adsensu vario, ceu flamina prima | cum deprensa fremunt silvis et caeca volutant | murmura venturos nautis prodentia ventos. | tum pater omnipotens, rerum cui prima potestas, | infit (eo dicente deum domus alta silescit | et tremefacta solo tellus, silet arduus aether, | tum zephyri posuere, premit placida aequora pontus).* – 'So argued Juno, and all the celestial company murmured diverse assent, just as when rising blasts, caught in the forest, murmur, and roll their unseen moanings, betraying to sailors the coming of the gale. Then the Father Almighty, prime potentate of the world, begins; as he speaks, the high house of the gods grows silent and earth trembles from her base; silent is high heaven; then the Zephyrs are hushed; Ocean stills his waters to rest.' [trans. H. Rushton Fairclough/G. P. Goold].

[33] Macrobius, *Sat.* 5.13.37–8: *vultis aliam fruendi aviditatem videre? loci cuius supra meminimus fulgore correptus ἦ καὶ κυανέῃσιν ἐπ' ὀφρύσι νεῦσε Κρονίων, | ἀμβρόσιαι δ' ἄρα χαῖται ἐπερρώσαντο ἄνακτος | κρατὸς ἀπ' ἀθανάτοιο· μέγαν δ' ἐλέλιξεν Ὄλυμπον* [Hom. *Il.* 1.528-30] *sero voluit loquenti Iovi adsignare parem reverentiam. nam cum et in primo volumine et in quarto et in nono loquatur quaedam Iuppiter sine tumultu, denique post Iunonis et Veneris iurgium, 'infit (eo dicente deum domus alta silescit | et tremefacta solo tellus, silet arduus aether, | tum Zephyri posuere, premit placida aequora pontus)'* [Virg. *Aen.* 10.101–3] *tamquam non idem sit qui locutus sit paulo ante sine ullo mundi totius obsequio.* – 'Would you like to consider another example of the greedy pleasure Virgil takes in Homer? He was ravished by the brilliance of the passage I quoted earlier "The son of Kronos spoke and with his dark brow nodded, | and his divine locks swept down from the lord's | immortal head: he made great Olympus tremble" and he wanted to show equal, if belated, respect for the speech of Jupiter. For though he has Jupiter speaking in Books 1, 4, and 9 without making a fuss about it, at long last, after the quarrel of Juno and Venus, "He speaks: and as he speaks the gods' lofty house is hushed, | the earth is shaken to its foundation, high heaven is silent, | then the west winds fall, the sea holds its calm surface in check" as though it wasn't the same person who spoke just a little earlier without the whole world paying dutiful obeisance.' [trans. R. A. Kaster].

literary genres, which may have been supported by similarities in content, such as in the area of history and philosophy.

Elsewhere Macrobius (6.4.6) quotes Ennius' use of *horreo* in *Scipio* (Enn. *Var.* 14 [*Scipio*] V.^{2} = *Scipio* 6 W. = F 33* [*Scipio*] *FPL*^{4}) alongside occurrences of *horresco* in the epic *Annales* (Enn. *Ann.* 393 V.^{2} = 380 W. = 384 Sk.) and the tragedy *Erectheus* (Enn. *Trag.* 131 R.$^{2-3}$ = 145–6 W. = 143 J. = 51 *TrRF*); the notion and the wording are different in each case, yet the basic idea is similar.[34] Again it is the presentation of the idea in *Scipio* that Virgil picks up in the *Aeneid* (11.601–2) according to Macrobius; both Macrobius and Servius comment on the unusual use of the verb in Virgil. The line in *Scipio*, where the phrasing is most audacious, since the bristling is not attributed to the weapons, but to the area affected by the weapons, was ridiculed by the Republican satirist Lucilius (fr. 1190 M. = 413 W.),[35] just as he comments on epic and tragedy elsewhere. Virgil may have taken account of this criticism when he adopts Ennius' bold image, but distributes the two verbs over two phrases, which makes the expression more straightforward.[36] Obviously, the diction chosen by early Roman poets was closely watched by other writers, who engaged with it, though irrespective of literary genre, since on this level drama was apparently not identified with a distinctive linguistic shape.

In the light of the issues covered by Republican drama, it is perhaps not a surprise that in the mid first century BCE Cicero assigns to the poet and the stage a position as influential as that of a parent or a teacher (Cic. *Leg.* 1.47).[37] Cicero also claims that the exhortations of characters in dramas are written for 'us' rather than the interlocutors, presumably with reference to moral and ethical ad-

---

[34] Macrobius, *Sat.* 6.4.6: 'tum ... ferreus hastis | horret ager'. 'horret' mire se habet, sed et Ennius in quarto decimo: 'horrescit telis exercitus asper utrimque', et in Erectheo: 'arma arrigunt, horrescunt tela', et in Scipione: 'sparsis hastis longis campus splendet et horret'. sed et ante omnes Homerus: ἔφριξεν δὲ μάχη φθισίμβροτος ἐγχείῃσιν [Hom. *Il.* 13.339]. – ' 'Then ... the iron field bristles with lances.' 'Bristles' [*horret*] is a remarkable usage, but Ennius has it, too, in Book 14: 'On both sides the fierce host bristles with lances', and in *Erectheus*: 'Their arms are raised, their missiles bristle', and in *Scipio*: 'When the long lances have been broadcast, the plain gleams and bristles'. But Homer has it, too, before all others: 'The man-destroying battle bristled with lances'.' [trans. R. A. Kaster].

[35] Servius ad Virg. *Aen.* 11.602: Lucilius 1190 M. = 413 W.: 'horret ager', terribilis est. est autem versus Ennianus, vituperatus a Lucilio dicente per inrisionem debuisse eum dicere 'horret et alget'. – 'The field bristles' is terrible. And it is an Ennian verse, criticized by Lucilius, saying in mockery that he [i. e. Ennius] ought to have said 'bristles and shivers'.'

[36] On this Ennian line and Lucilius' reaction see e. g. Mariotti 1963; Russo 2007, 239–42.

[37] Cicero, *Leg.* 1.47: nam sensus nostros non parens, non nutrix, non magister, non poeta, non scena depravat, non multitudinis consensus abducit – 'our senses are not distorted by a parent, a nurse, a teacher, a poet, or the stage; the agreement of the multitude does not lead them from the truth' [trans. J. E. G. Zetzel].

vice (Cic. *Planc.* 59; cf. also Cic. *Rab. Post.* 29). Since Roman dramas of all kinds might not only present stories that can be enjoyed as such and may have a didactic element, but also convey information about Roman history or philosophical doctrines, it is understandable that they were not just appreciated as poetry, but could also be regarded as fulfilling a practical function. Roman drama initially seems to have been a comprehensive genre covering a variety of aspects later to be discussed in works of specified literary genres. It stands out because of the public nature of its presentation and thus its potentially wide audience appeal, which brings such issues to the attention of larger sections of the populace.

This role of drama has to be seen against a background in which, in the introductions to his philosophical works, Cicero feels obliged to comment on the views of people who disapprove of the study of philosophy (Cic. *Fin.* 1.1–3). This view of philosophy in Rome is perhaps one reason why Cicero claims that before him only one person (C. Amafinius) wrote philosophical works in (bad) Latin (Cic. *Tusc.* 1.6; 4.6). Cicero obviously feels empowered to change the situation, and he acknowledges that drama plays a part in philosophical and moral education. Still, he does not seem to regard dramas or Ennius' other writings as equivalent to what he sees as a philosophical work.

Even though Roman drama started as a kind of comprehensive genre, already in the early period there was an awareness of generic differences (which may lead to nuanced treatment of the same issues): for instance, the comic poet Plautus (*c.* 250–184 BCE) speaks of and plays with differences between comedy and tragedy (e. g. Plaut. *Capt.* 61–2; *Pseud.* 707), and the late-Republican tragic writer Accius (170–*c.* 80 BCE) distinguishes *genera poematorum*.[38] Cicero later recognizes five types of writers: orators, philosophers, sophists, historians and poets (Cic. *Orat.* 61–8). The early dramatists, however, also blurred boundaries in a variety of directions: elements of rhetoric can be identified in Roman Republican drama, most obviously in Terence's prologues;[39] and it is acknowledged that specific contemporary forms of speech, such as edicts, oaths and prayers, have left their marks in dramatic texts, often in the shape of parodies.[40]

Early Roman dramatists evidently were not content with mechanically following Greek models, but rather modified them according to Roman needs and developed them creatively in line with an apparent interest in new material. The

---

38 Accius, *Did.* 14–15 W. = *Gram.* 12–13 D. = F 13 (*Did.*) *FPL*⁴: *nam quam varia sint genera poematorum, Baebi, quamque longe distincta alia ab aliis nosce.* – 'Then learn, dear Baebius, if you please, how varied the sorts of poems are, and how by far they differ from one another.' [trans. E. H. Warmington].
39 See e. g. Manuwald 2013 (with further references).
40 See e. g. Cèbe 1966, 77–102 (and 103–17 with reference to literary texts).

achievement of the early Roman dramatists finds its place in the context of the development of a Latin literary language, which was shared by all emerging literary genres; the poets did not just provide entertainment, but also adopted stylistic features and major themes from the existing literary genres in Greece. The *praetexta* as a genuine Roman dramatic genre, but also Plautus in *palliata* comedies, rework various components of drama in novel ways, and this shows most obviously that Roman dramatists consciously engaged with Greek models. Philosophical aspects too were not only included in isolated remarks: such issues were equally shown by the plots themselves and recognized by Roman audiences, as Cicero demonstrates by his comments on an ethically intriguing dramatic scene in which both Orestes and Pylades claim to be Orestes, so as to die in place of the other (Cic. *Fin.* 5.63; 2.79; *Amic.* 24).

After Roman 'literature' had emerged within a relatively brief period, an educated Roman like Cicero noticed that Ennius had a dramatic character make an explicit statement, which breaks the dramatic illusion; the content shows to what extent Roman drama was integrated into the development of the contemporary literary and intellectual culture in Rome: it offered one way of presenting topical issues and is likely to have been special because of the dramatic form and the public display rather than because of the topics addressed.

Bibliography

Bettini, M. (1979), *Studi e note su Ennio*, Pisa.
Blänsdorf, J. [*FPL⁴*] (2011), (ed.), *Fragmenta poetarum Latinorum epicorum et lyricorum praeter Enni Annales et Ciceronis Germanicique Aratea, post W. Morel et K. Büchner editionem quartam auctam curavit*, Berlin/New York.
Brink, C. O. (1972), 'Ennius and the Hellenistic Worship of Homer', *AJP* 93, 547–67.
Cèbe, J.-P. (1966), *La caricature et la parodie, dans le monde romain antique des origines à Juvénal*, Paris.
Courtney, E. [C.] (1993), (ed.), *The Fragmentary Latin Poets. Edited with Commentary*, Oxford [repr. with add. 2003].
Dutsch, D. M. (2008), *Feminine Discourse in Roman Comedy. On Echoes and Voices*, Oxford.
―――― (2014), 'The Beginnings: Philosophy in Roman Literature Before 155 B.C.', in: M. Garani, D. Konstan (eds.), *The Philosophizing Muse: The Influence of Greek Philosophy on Roman Poetry*, Newcastle upon Tyne, 1–25.
Egli, F. (2003), *Euripides im Kontext zeitgenössischer intellektueller Strömungen. Analyse der Funktion philosophischer Themen in den Tragödien und Fragmenten*, München.
Garbarino, G. (1973), *Roma e la filosofia greca dalle origini alla fine del II secolo a. C. Raccolta di testi con introduzione e commento, 2 vols.*, Torino/Milano/Genova/Padova/Bologna/Firenze/Pescara/Roma/Napoli/Bari/Palermo.

Jocelyn, H. D. [J.] (1967), (ed.), *The Tragedies of Ennius. The Fragments edited with an Introduction and Commentary*, Cambridge [repr. with corr. 1969].

Karakasis, E. (2005), *Terence and the Language of Roman Comedy*, Cambridge.

Kerkhof, R. (2001), *Dorische Posse, Epicharm und Attische Komödie*, München/Leipzig.

Kessissoglu, A. (1990), '*Enniana*', *RhM* 133, 70–80.

Manuwald, G. (2001), *Fabulae praetextae. Spuren einer literarischen Gattung der Römer*, München.

――――― (2012), (ed.), *Tragicorum Romanorum Fragmenta (TrRF). Volumen II. Ennius*, Göttingen.

――――― (2013), 'Oratory on the Stage in Republican Rome', in: C. Kremmydas, K. Tempest (eds.), *Hellenistic Oratory. Continuity and Change*, Oxford, 277–94.

Mariotti, I. (1963), '*Horret et alget*', in: *Lanx satura. Nicolao Terzaghi oblata. Miscellanea philologica*, Genova, 249–60.

Marx, F. [M.] (1904–5), (ed.), *C. Lucilii carminum reliquiae. Vol. I–II*, Leipzig [repr. Amsterdam 1963].

Ribbeck, O. [R.²] (1871), (ed.), *Scaenicae Romanorum poesis fragmenta. Vol. I. Tragicorum Romanorum fragmenta, secundis curis recensuit*, Leipzig [repr. Hildesheim 1962].

――――― [R.³] (1897), (ed.), *Scaenicae Romanorum poesis fragmenta. Vol. I. Tragicorum Romanorum fragmenta, tertiis curis recognovit*, Leipzig.

Russo, A. (2007), (ed.), *Quinto Ennio. Le opere minori. Introduzione, edizione critica dei frammenti e commento. Vol. I*, Pisa.

Schierl, P. [S.] (2006), *Die Tragödien des Pacuvius. Ein Kommentar zu den Fragmenten mit Einleitung, Text und Übersetzung*, Berlin/New York.

Scholz, U. W. (1984), 'Der "Scipio" des Ennius', *Hermes* 112, 183–99.

Skutsch, O. [Sk.] (1985), (ed.), *The Annals of Q. Ennius. Edited with Introduction and Commentary*, Oxford.

Suerbaum, W. (1968), *Untersuchungen zur Selbstdarstellung älterer römischer Dichter. Livius Andronicus, Naevius, Ennius*, Hildesheim.

――――― (2002), (ed.), *Handbuch der Lateinischen Literatur der Antike. Erster Band. Die Archaische Literatur. Von den Anfängen bis Sullas Tod. Die vorliterarische Periode und die Zeit von 240 bis 78 v. Chr. (HLL 1)*, München.

――――― (2003), *Ennius in der Forschung des 20. Jahrhunderts. Eine kommentierte Bibliographie für 1900–1999 mit systematischen Hinweisen nebst einer Kurzdarstellung des Q. Ennius (239–169 v. Chr.)*, Hildesheim/Zürich/New York.

Vahlen, I. [V.²] (1903), (ed.), *Ennianae poesis reliquiae*, iteratis curis recensuit, Leipzig [= Leipzig ³1928, Amsterdam 1963, 1967].

Warmington, E. H. [W.] (1935), (ed. and tr.) *Remains of Old Latin. Newly ed. and trans. Vol. I. Ennius and Caecilius*, Cambridge (MA)/London (LCL 294) [rev. and repr. 1967, several repr.].

――――― (1936), (ed. and tr.), *Remains of Old Latin. Newly ed. and trans. Vol. II. Livius Andronicus, Naevius, Pacuvius and Accius*, Cambridge (MA)/London (LCL 314) [repr. 1957, with minor bibliographical additions, several repr.].

――――― (1938), (ed. and tr.), *Remains of Old Latin. Newly ed. and transl. Vol. III. Lucilius, The Twelve Tables*, Cambridge (MA)/London (LCL 329) [rev. and repr. 1979].

Timothy J. Moore
Music in Roman Tragedy

Any attempt to understand and appreciate the music of Roman theater faces many challenges. No melodies survive from Roman plays, and most evidence for singing and instrumental accompaniment is late and difficult to interpret. The challenges multiply when we consider specifically Roman tragedy. Only the tragedies attributed to Seneca survive complete, and controversy remains as to whether those plays were meant to be 'performed' in our sense at all.[1] An examination of the testimonia for and fragments of Roman tragedy, however, reveals that, at least in the Republican period, tragedy was a profoundly musical genre. A closer look into what can be known about Roman tragedy's music, therefore, is well worth the effort. In what follows I review briefly our evidence for the importance and mechanics of music in Republican tragedy, then consider how the tragedians' use of music might have compared to that of Plautus and Terence and how tragic music appears to have changed over time. I conclude with some preliminary thoughts on possible music in the plays attributed to Seneca.

Importance and Mechanics

Of the importance of music in Republican tragedy there can be little doubt. Cicero refers to connoisseurs, *qui primo inflatu tibicinis Antiopam esse aiunt aut Andromacham*, ('who can say at the first sound from the *tibicen* that they are hearing Antiope or Andromache,' *Luc.* 20). *Antiopa* and *Andromacha* are tragedies of Pacuvius and Ennius, respectively. Whether Cicero's interlocutor refers to overtures played before full performances of those plays or to solo performances of arias excerpted from the plays is not clear.[2] What is clear is the strong association between the *tibicen* and tragic performance. Elsewhere Cicero writes of an actor performing in Pacuvius' *Iliona, tam bonos septenarios fundat ad tibiam* ('he pours forth such fine septenarii to the accompaniment of the *tibia*,' *Tusc.* 1.107). Interlocutors in Cicero's *De oratore* discuss cooperation between the tragic actor Aesopus and the *tibicen* in performances of Ennius' *Andromacha* (3.102) and claim that if Aesopus is even a bit hoarse, he is hissed off the stage (*Aesopum, si paulum irrauserit, explodi*, 1.259).

---

[1] For a review of the question, see Fitch 2000.
[2] Moore 2012, 19–21.

In spite of the lack of both melodies and extant texts, much can be said about this important music. First, we know a good deal about the accompanying *tibia* and the kinds of sounds it could produce: piercing, probably rasping, but flexible in both volume and tone, playing heterophonically (different notes and rhythms on each pipe, but without modern polyphony or harmony).[3] Second, we can make good guesses about the nature of Roman actors' singing: loud, nasal, high, probably harsh to modern Western ears, but again flexible and highly expressive.[4] Most important, we can be confident that metrical variation in the tragic fragments meant musical variation in performance. Evidence from the plays and manuscripts of Plautus and from later authors establishes that in Roman comedy iambic senarii were virtually always performed without accompaniment, other meters with accompaniment.[5] There is no reason to assume that the relationship between meter and music was any different in tragedy: Livius Andronicus, Naevius, and Ennius, after all, wrote both comedies and tragedies, and the two genres in the Republic share numerous features of style, meter, and prosody.[6] We are therefore justified in assuming that fragments of Republican tragedy in meters other than iambic senarii were performed to the accompaniment of the *tibicen*.

What exactly the actors did during accompanied scenes is less certain. A significant majority of the accompanied verses of Roman drama are trochaic septenarii. Trochaic septenarii share prosodic and metrical features with iambic senarii and other iambo-trochaic meters (most notably trochaic octonarii, iambic octonarii, and iambic septenarii) not found – or at least less frequent – in most non-iambo-trochaic meters.[7] These similarities suggest that accompanied iambo-trochaic meters may have been delivered in a way less distinct from iambic senarii than were non-iambo-trochaic meters. Within the iambo-trochaic sections, there may also have been a distinction in vocal performance between stichic and polymetric passages.[8] Many modern scholars thus use terms like 'chant' or 'speak' for the actors' delivery of stichic passages of trochaic septenarii and similar verses, in contrast to 'sing,' used to describe performance of lyric verses and polymetric passages. Ancient authors do not explicitly distinguish between the vocal performance of accompanied iambo-trochaic meters and non-iambo-

---

3 Moore 2012, 35–63.
4 Moore 2012, 80–92.
5 Moore 2008.
6 Cf. Manuwald 2014, 580–1.
7 See especially Soubiran 1988, passim, Questa 2007, 128, 327, 370–413.
8 In stichic passages the meter remains the same from verse to verse; in polymetric passages it changes.

trochaic meters or between stichic and polymetric passages, however, except to suggest that the melody, like the meter, remained largely the same from verse to verse during passages in stichic meters but changed frequently in polymetric passages. We should therefore acknowledge a possible difference between the vocal performance of accompanied stichic passages in iambo-trochaic meters and passages where the meter changes frequently and/or where non-iambo-trochaic meters occur; but the difference between what the actors did in all these forms and what they did while speaking iambic senarii was probably much more significant.[9] In what follows, therefore, I will use the words 'sing' and 'song' to describe all accompanied portions of the plays. Passages in trochaic septenarii, like those in other accompanied meters, were performed musically and no doubt sometimes offered impressive musical moments.

We can also take for granted a close association between Roman tragedy's meters and the rhythm of its music. Correspondence between the length of syllables and sung rhythms was never exact, and the practice of consistently singing a long syllable at twice the length of a short syllable appears to have become less and less the norm in the Greek world at least from the fifth-century BCE onward. Our evidence nevertheless suggests that in Rome of the second century BCE meter still formed the foundation of sung rhythm.[10]

Tragedy and Comedy

Rome's tragedies, like her comedies, thus featured alternation between passages in iambic senarii and those in other meters: that is, between musical and non-musical passages. Within the musical passages, in tragedy as in comedy, playwrights could vary meters to encourage musical variation. The tragic fragments suggest that tragic playwrights shared with Plautus and Terence ways of using this alternation and variation to produce various effects.

The comic writers repeatedly used music to contribute to characterization, primarily in two ways: they created metrical (and therefore musical) contrasts between characters, and they allowed characters to demonstrate their power by controlling the music.[11] Given the fragmentary nature of our evidence, we can say nothing for certain about such matters, but reasonable attribution of fragments in several plays suggests that these same phenomena occurred in tragedy.

---

9 Cf. Moore 2012, 92–103, 136–7.
10 Moore 2012, 144–6.
11 Moore 1999; 2012, 88–9, 176, 258, 353–4 and *passim*.

The plot of Accius' *Armorum Iudicium* appears to have included the contest for Achilles' arms followed by Ajax's madness, then events largely corresponding to Sophocles' *Ajax*: Ajax's response to his madness and suicide and the debate surrounding his burial.[12] Four fragments can with some assurance be assigned to Ajax and Ulysses defending their claims to the arms during the first part of the play:

> quid est cur componere ausis mihi te aut me tibi? (164, ia6)[13]
>
> How is it that you would dare to compare yourself to me or me to you?
>
> huius me dividia cogit plus quam est par loqui. (165, ia6)
>
> My disgust for him makes me say more than I should.
>
> ... nam tropaeum ferre me a forti viro
> pulcrum est; si autem vincar, vinci a tali nullum <mi> est probrum. (166–7, tr7)
>
> For it is a fine thing for me to win a trophy from a brave man; but if I should be defeated, there is no shame to me in being defeated by such a man.
>
> inter quos saepe et multo inbutus sanguine (168, ia6)
>
> Among whom stained often and with a lot of blood.

Ajax almost certainly speaks the first, second, and fourth of these fragments, all of them in iambic senarii: he expresses disgust at and disdain for Ulysses (164–5), reveals his characteristic reluctance to speak many words (165), and boasts of his prowess in battle, where he slaughtered many of the enemy (168).[14] The third fragment, however, is almost certainly delivered by Ulysses the subtle orator: he professes modesty in a *captatio benevolentiae* (166–7). A metrical contrast between Ajax and Ulysses in the scene or scenes surrounding the contest appears likely.

---

[12] Cf. Dangel 2002, 300.

[13] The tragic fragments are cited according to the following editions: Livius, Naevius, Minor Tragic Poets, and *Adespota*: Schauer 2012; Ennius: Manuwald 2012; Pacuvius: Schierl 2006; Accius: Dangel 2002. Numbers in the text after citations from Schauer, Manuwald, and Schierl are fragment numbers; those after citations from Dangel are verse numbers. Numbers in citations of all these works in the notes refer to page numbers unless otherwise noted.

[14] Dangel 2002, 304 attributes verse 168 to another character describing Ajax's madness later in the play. *saepe*, however, suggests description of recurring events rather than the slaughter of the sheep on one occasion. Cf. Warmington 1936, 363. Warmington also assigns three additional fragments, also in iambic senarii, to Ajax in this part of the play (1936, his verses 103–8, 109–14, 115–7); but these are cited without author and may be from Pacuvius' *Armorum Iudicium* or another play.

Comedy does not lead us to expect that such a contrast would be rigidly kept throughout the play: very few major characters in Plautus and Terence deliver only accompanied or unaccompanied verses. Hence it is no surprise that Ajax appears to deliver iambic senarii when he addresses his son Eurysaces after his madness (*virtuti sis par, dispar fortunis patris*, 'may you be like your father in *virtus*, unlike him in your fortune,' 171) but trochaic septenarii as he praises Tecmessa and feels a twinge of his madness recurring (*bene facis: sed nunc quid subiti mihi febris civit mali?*[15] 'You do well. But what sudden evil has the fever excited in me now?' 169).

The fragments also offer us some evidence for a single character controlling a play's music. Accius' *Philoctetes* appears to have begun, unusually, in sung anapaests, as the chorus addresses Ulysses and describes the play's Lemnian setting (195–211). The meter changes to iambic senarii as someone describes the situation of Philoctetes (214–223) and warns Ulysses of the danger Philoctetes presents (224–226), and Ulysses says that he must approach Philoctetes cautiously (227). The meters have changed to iambic octonarii and cretics, however, in passages in which, it seems, Philoctetes greets someone (228), describes his lot (229), and begs that his illness not drive away his interlocutor (230). It looks very much as if Philoctetes brought music with his entrance.[16]

Another pattern evident in comedy is a switch to iambic senarii, and hence a stop in the music, for significant moments and important statements.[17] The phenomenon is especially conspicuous in recognition scenes. In Plautus' *Curculio*, for example, the meter switches to iambic senarii as Therapontigonus begins to explain where he got his ring: his story will confirm that he is Planesium's brother (635, cf. Plaut. *Cist.* 747). The following fragments of Pacuvius' *Atalanta* suggest that the same pattern occurred in tragedy:

habeo ego, istam qui distinguam inter vos geminitudinem.	(45, tr7)
I know a way I can tell you apart, even though you are like twins.	
... is vestrorum uter sit, cui signum datum est, cette ...	(46, ia6)
Tell me which one of you it is, who received the token.	
suspensum in laevo brachio ostendo ungulum.	(47, ia6)
I show the ring held up on my left arm.	

---

15 I follow here the text of Ribbeck 1897, 180.
16 Contrast Sophocles' *Philoctetes*, in which Philoctetes delivers iambic trimeters as he enters (219ff.).
17 Moore 2012, 175, 255.

> mi gnate, ut vereor! <pro>loqui porcet pudor. (48, ia6)
>
> My son, how I am afraid! Shame stops me from speaking.

It is probable that in the first passage, an accompanied trochaic septenarius (45), Atalanta has realized that she can use the ring her abandoned infant received to learn whether Parthenopaeus or Telephus is her long-lost son. In the second fragment, in iambic senarii (46), she uses that knowledge and asks the youths which of them received the ring. Parthenopaeus shows her the ring in the third fragment (47), and in the fourth she responds to the recognition (48). It appears that the music stopped when Atalanta turned from pondering how to bring about the *anagnorisis* to actually bringing it about, and spoken unaccompanied dialogue continued as the *anagnorisis* occurred.

The fragments of Pacuvius' *Medus* suggest a pattern in which a character's power over music combined with a musical break for an important moment. The fragments and Hyginus' account of the myth (*fab*. 27) suggest that this play included the return of Medea to Colchis. Several fragments appear to be from a messenger speech reporting the arrival of Medea in a chariot drawn by winged serpents (168–172, and perhaps 173[18]). Schierl places a fragment in trochaic septenarius next:

> caelitum camilla, expectata advenis: salve hospita! (174)
>
> Servant of the heavenly gods, you arrive waited for: hail, guest!

This is almost certainly a joyful greeting to Medea upon her arrival. It appears very likely that Pacuvius' Medea, like Accius' Philoctetes, brought music with her entrance. In a second trochaic septenarius fragment someone describes a famine:

> postquam calamitas <com>plures annos arvas calvitur (175)[19]
>
> After the disaster has made our fields bald for many years.

Hyginus tells us that there was a famine in Colchis when Medea arrived, and that she promised to end it. Here someone appears to be explaining the dire situation

---

18 173, *mulier egregissima/forma*, is either iambic senarii or trochaic septenarii. I think it is probably the former and is part of the messenger speech.

19 I think Schierl, following D'Anna 1967, 122, is right in attributing this fragment to *Medus*. The fragment's source, Nonius (283L) does not name the play, though, and Lindsay reads *Periboea* for *postquam*. Ribbeck 1897, 150 left the fragment among Pacuvius' *incertae fabulae*.

in Colchis to the newly arrived Medea. Schierl's next fragment is an iambic senarius:

> possum ego istam capite cladem averruncassere. (176)
>
> I am able to drive away that disaster from your head.

Here we almost certainly have Medea promising to end the famine. A scene change between the description of the famine and Medea's promise to end it is unlikely. If Schierl's arrangement of the fragments is correct, therefore, Medea appears to have stopped the music with her promise to end the famine.

When we move from the musical dichotomy between accompanied and unaccompanied verses to rhythmic patterns within the accompanied verses, we also find in the tragic fragments patterns similar to what we find in comedy. Although Republican tragedy's meager remains do not show us the same *numeri innumeri* for which Plautus was famous, we do see a wide variety of meters, and, with one exception, meters similar to what comedy uses in its polymetric passages.[20] That one exception is significant: dactylic meters do not occur in comedy, except perhaps in one verse of Terence's *Andria* (625). Several tragic fragments, however, include dactylic verses, surely a reflection of tragedy's closer relationship to epic and hymns.

Tragedy not only used the same meters as comedy for its polymetric passages, but it also used those meters in similar ways. Several scholars have pointed to the use of cretics in laments such as those of Ennius' Andromache (23) or Melanippe (104) as parallels to, or indeed precedents for, cretic laments such as those of Palaestra in Plautus' *Rudens* (199ff., 664ff.).[21] Bacchiacs present another similarity. With their short syllable followed by two long syllables, bacchiacs are the slowest of meters. They therefore find themselves in comedy associated with lugubrious laments, attempts to stop motion, and references to slow movement.[22] These same uses for bacchiacs occur in the surviving fragments of tragedy. In a passage from Ennius' *Alexander*, probably in bacchiacs, Cassandra appears to prophesy mournfully the death of Hector (21).[23] A character in Pacuvius' *Iliona* demands in bacchiacs that another character stop (147). Characters in unidentified plays command in bacchiacs that they not be approached (*Adespota* 56) and ask why another character is reluctant to draw near (*Adespota* 22).

---

20 On lyric meters and polymetry in the tragic fragments, see Hurka 2008.
21 E.g., Jocelyn 1967, 243, Hurka 2008, 796, Moore 2012, 195.
22 Moore 2012, 197–9.
23 On the meter here see Jocelyn 1967, 231–2.

In Ennius' *Thyestes* a character, uncertain who another character is, refers in bacchiacs to the slowness of his old age:

> quemnam te esse dicam, qui tarda in senectute ... (133)
>
> Who should I say it is, who in his late old age ...

Bacchiacs also seem to accompany a reference to the slowness of old age in a passage from Pacuvius' *Teucer*. Telamon probably sings of what he will do in spite of his old age:

> quamquam annisque et aetate et hoc corpus putret (249)[24]
>
> Although this body is rotten with its years and its age.

The last two passages are close parallels to the bacchiacs that reinforce the slowness of the *Senex* as he enters in Plautus' *Menaechmi* (753ff.). I suspect we have not tragic parody here, but rather a common musical language associating a slow rhythm with the physically lugubrious.

A pattern that occurs often in comedy, especially in Terence, is the long string of trochaic feet expressed by one or more trochaic octonarii followed by trochaic septenarii. The pattern suggests that additional emotional intensity on the part of the singer delays the expected catalexis.[25] It appears to have occurred in a number of tragic scenes preserved partially in our fragments. Most surviving examples are from Ennius: someone praying (59) and Priam begging Achilles' guards to pity him in *Hectoris lytra* (66), Achilles railing against Calchas in *Iphigenia* (82), and Thyestes cursing Atreus (132). The pattern also seems to occur when Althaea raves and then decides to bring about her son's death in Accius' *Meleager* (517–518).

In the case of trochaic septenarii following trochaic octonarii, I suspect that at least sometimes we do have tragic parody in the comedies. Among the characters who use the pattern the most are Terentian lovers lamenting their lot (*An.* 245ff., 301ff., 607ff., *Hec.* 281ff., *Ph.* 153ff., 465ff.). We have tended to take these Terentian youths more seriously than their Plautine counterparts. Awareness that they are parodying their tragic cousins helps us to appreciate that they, too, are subjects of laughter.

The most common non-iambo-trochaic meter in Roman tragedy, as in Plautus, is anapaests. Like Plautus,[26] the tragedians used anapaests for a wide range

---

24 The verse may be an iambic senarius with its first syllable missing (Schierl 2006, 508).
25 Moore 2012, 211–4.
26 Cf. Moore 2012, 201–2.

of scenes, often in moments of special emotional intensity, like the laments of Accius' Philoctetes noted above (237–240), of the wounded Ulysses in Pacuvius' *Niptra* (199), of someone discussing exile in Accius' *Eurysaces* (335–338), and of someone wishing for death in Ennius' *Hecuba* (80).

It appears, then, that in Republican Rome tragedy and comedy used basically the same musical language. There is nevertheless one significant way in which the two genres appear to have differed musically: tragic characters seem to have been much more likely than their comic counterparts to sing rather than speak when they were relaying important information. There are no hard and fast rules around this in comedy, but there is a very strong tendency for passages where characters share important information either to the audience or to other characters to be in iambic senarii; enough so that when, for example, Pamphilus in Terence's *Hecyra* reports in trochaic septenarii important events he has just observed off stage, the exception would be striking (361ff.).[27]

In fact, Pamphilus' monody in trochaic septenarii would bring thoughts of tragedy. Tragic characters regularly sing trochaic septenarii, and sometimes other meters as well, even when it is clear that presentation of information is their primary goal. For example, the tragedians use trochaic septenarii for a significant number of speeches delivered by anonymous messengers or by named characters acting like messengers. Characters use trochaic septenarii to report actions of bacchants in Naevius' *Lycurgus* (22), Perseus killing the sea monster in Ennius' *Andromeda* (40), and storms in Pacuvius' *Teucer* (238–41) and Accius' *Clytaemnestra* (291–3). Some passages that look like messenger speeches, such as a report of a storm in Ennius' *Andromacha* (33, an4?) and a battle report in Accius' *Aeneadae* (676–7, an4), even include other accompanied meters. It is no surprise, therefore, that Sosia sings a variety of accompanied meters when he parodies a tragic messenger in Plautus' *Amphitruo* (203ff.).

Beyond messenger speeches we repeatedly find other information-heavy tragic fragments in trochaic septenarii and other sung meters: Bacchus' announcement that he will punish Lycurgus in Accius' *Stasiastae* (403), for example, the call of a herald in Pacuvius' *Armorum Iudicium* (21), and Naevius' Danae describing how she was raped by Jupiter (12). Oaths in comedy are nearly always unaccompanied, but a character sings as he seems to deliver an oath in Ennius' *Achilles* (2). Reports of dreams are likewise in iambic senarii in extant comedy. In Accius' *Brutus*, in a passage where we can see most clearly change from spoken to sung verse, Tarquinius Superbus tells his dream to a seer in iambic senarii, but

---

27 Cf. Moore 1998, 253.

the seer's response, surely more important in terms of the information it relays, is in trochaic septenarii (651–72).[28]

This penchant of tragedy for presenting information in sung form should cause us to rethink the unaccompanied information of comedy. It is tempting to associate comedy's informational iambic senarii with the need for audibility: audience members could understand better what was spoken without accompaniment. The plethora of sung information in tragedy, however, much of it clearly essential to the audience's comprehension, suggests that Republican playwrights were not worried about music interfering with spectators' understanding of actors' words. Other factors, such as structural aims, character contrast, and emotional tone determined what was and was not to be sung. In comedy, for example, informational passages are often moments of calm. That is much less true in tragedy, where those who relay information tend to be emotionally involved in what they report.

This high tolerance in tragedy for sung information has bearing especially on three types of passages. One is the formal agon. The fragments of these, from Jason responding to Medea in Ennius' *Medea* (92) to the trial scenes in Ennius' *Eumenides* (52, 55) and Accius' *Erigona* (320–3), are almost all in trochaic septenarii. Closely related is the persuasive speech, where again trochaic septenarii dominate, whether Teucer is defending his father in Accius' *Eurysaces* (360–6) or Brutus recounts the crimes of Tarquinius Superbus in the same author's *Brutus* (674). Finally, the many scenes of philosophizing that so impressed Cicero and others (see Manuwald in this volume) seem to have been primarily in trochaic septenarii, including such famous passages as the discourse on *otium* by the chorus of Ennius' *Iphigenia* (84) and the skeptical response to *haruspices* in Pacuvius' *Chryses* (78–81). All these scenes, which we might expect to be unaccompanied because of their emphasis on information and argumentation, appear to have become musical set pieces in the hands of the Roman tragedians.

Musical Change

Thus far, I have treated Republican tragedy as a monolith in terms of its music. This, of course, is not the case. Cicero shows an awareness of musical differences between individual plays when he claims that tragic actors chose plays based on

---

[28] Tarquinius' explanation and the seer's response are quoted separately in a single passage of Cicero's *De divinatione* (43–45). As Manuwald 2001, 225–6 points out, Cicero's second quotation need not have followed immediately upon his first in Accius' play. That scenario does seem most likely, however.

their strengths: those who trusted most in their voices liked to perform in Accius' *Epigoni* or Pacuvius' *Medus*, those who were most proud of their gestures preferred Ennius' *Melanippa* or Accius' *Clytaemnestra* (*off*. 1.114). Much gesturing in Roman theater appears to have been a kind of dance to music.[29] Both the plays where actors could show off their voices, therefore, and those where they showed off their gestures are likely to have been highly musical.

What of musical changes between playwrights and over time? Jocelyn has charted the percentage of surviving verses dedicated to iambic senarii in the major Republican tragedians: Livius, 40%; Naevius, 35%; Ennius, 30%; Pacuvius, 45%; Accius, 55%.[30] As Jocelyn points out, the value of these statistics is limited because of the small corpora of the authors and the large number of verses whose meter cannot be determined. Nevertheless, they allow us to construct a tentative history of Roman tragedy's musicality.

Our sources tell us that Roman theater started as musical performance: dancers – Livy says they were from Etruria – performed to the accompaniment of the *tibicen* (Livy 7.2.3–8, Val. Max. 2.4.4). Livius first introduced plots to the musical miscellanies that preceded him on the Roman stage. As he adapted Greek plots Livius made a point of mixing with traditional Roman musical forms the Greek iambic trimeter and its unaccompanied performance.[31] It has been cogently suggested that Naevius 'Romanized' Roman drama in numerous ways.[32] One of those ways, I suggest, was to make a larger proportion of his verses musical. Ennius represents the musical peak of Roman tragedy just as Plautus represents the musical peak of Roman comedy. Pacuvius, then Accius, like Terence, each moved closer to the patterns of their Greek predecessors, in which iambic trimeters dominated.[33]

Though the fragments of the tragedians between Accius and Seneca are exceedingly sparse, every indication is that they continued the trend towards more 'Greek-like' musical patterns, just as they made their iambo-trochaic meters more Greek-like.[34] Indeed, Horace, when he describes his contemporary Pollio's tragedies, writes:

> Pollio regum
> facta canit pede ter percusso (*S*. 1.10.42)
>
> Pollio sings the deeds of kings in iambic trimeters.

---

[29] Moore 2012, 114–9.
[30] Jocelyn 1967, 30, n. 1.
[31] Cf. Blänsdorf 2000, 149.
[32] E.g., Boyle 2006, 37.
[33] On Pacuvius' music cf. Manuwald 2003, 123–5.
[34] On the development of the Latin iambic senarius/trimeter and trochaic septenarius/tetrameter, see Soubiran 1988.

By the Augustan age, it could be taken for granted that Roman tragedy, like Greek, was primarily written in iambic trimeters/senarii, with only occasional musical interruptions.

We should not assume, however, that tragedies of the late Republic and early Empire lacked impressive musical moments. Cicero suggests changes in dramatic music over time when he compares the *severitas iucunda* of Livius and Naevius with the elaborate melodies of his own day:

> illud quidem video, quae solebant quondam conpleri severitate iucunda Livianis et Naevianis modis, nunc ut eadem exultent et cervices oculosque pariter cum modorum flexionibus torqueant. (*Leg.* 2.39)

> I see that the audience, which once was satisfied with the pleasant severity in the tunes of Livius Andronicus and Naevius, now rejoice and twist their necks and eyes together with the bendings of tunes.

We must always be suspicious of Roman authors talking about the 'good old days,' and Cicero's conception of change in Roman music is certainly influenced here by objections on the part of Plato and others to Greek 'New Music.' Nevertheless, the passage would not make sense to Cicero's contemporaries if they did not have experience with elaborate melodies on the stages of their own day. Horace likewise writes of 'numerisque modisque licentia maior' ('greater license in both rhythms and melodies') in the years between Rome's earliest days and his own (*Ars* 211).[35] Cicero's *flexiones* may refer specifically to modulation between keys, or it may describe ornamentation of the melody or similar features. Either way, it refers to complexity of melody, not rhythm. It is quite possible, therefore, that what Cicero describes would not be reflected in greater metrical complexity in the texts.

This leads us back to anapaests, which, as was noted above, are the most common non-iambo-trochaic meters in Roman tragedy. Of the three fragments of Livius' tragedies that Schauer thinks are probably in non-iambo-trochaic meters, one might be in anapaests (25).[36] The fragments of Naevius's tragedies include no non-iambo-trochaic meters, according to Schauer. Manuwald concludes that twenty fragments of Ennius are likely to include non-iambo-trochaic meters. Twelve of those (60%) appear to include anapaests. According to Schierl, twelve fragments of Pacuvius are in non-iambo-trochaic meters. Of those, nine (75%) include anapaests. Dangel's text of Accius includes twenty-nine fragments in non-iambo-trochaic meters. Twenty-three (79%) of them of them are anapaests.

---

35 Cf. Manuwald 2011, 329–30.
36 Cf. Spaltenstein 2008, 146–7.

Eight fragments of tragic authors after Accius appear to be in non-iambo-trochaic meters: five (Varius 2–3, Gracchus 2, Ovid 2, Scaevus Memor 1: 63%) appear to be anapaests, two dactylic (Pomponius 2–3), and one a variation on sapphics (Scaevus Memor 2[37]).

Though we would be unwise to make too much of statistics based on such a small sample that includes verses of uncertain attribution, text, and meter, a plausible scenario presents itself. Anapaestic meters, present in the earliest tragedies, became more and more the non-iambo-trochaic meter of choice for Roman tragedians from Ennius on. This is a striking contrast to Terence, who used a tiny amount of other non-iambo-trochaic meters but abandoned anapaests completely.

Compared to lyric meters such as cretics, aeolics, and bacchiacs, anapaests bring rhythmic simplicity. Unlike every other meter used in Republican drama except dactylics, anapaests have a basic rhythmic unit – the foot – that never varies in its length. Assuming that long syllables last twice as long as short syllables, every anapaestic foot has four time units: two long syllables, a long syllable and two short syllables, or four short syllables. In addition, anapaestic feet, unlike the feet of most other Latin meters except dactyls, are always divisible into two units of equal duration: two short syllables or one long syllable. This rhythmic consistency would make it easier for singers and *tibicines* to produce melodic complexity.

Anapaests also stretch further than any other archaic Latin meter the rules of *brevis brevians*, in which concern for metrical rhythm appears to 'trump' standard syllabic length.[38] Such prosodic liberty suggests a form in which, more than in other meters, music takes precedence over words. The increasing dominance of anapaests is thus conducive to – and probably reflects – greater melodic complexity.

The fragments of post-Accian tragedy leave us some hints of elaborate anapaestic arias and choruses. Note the moving anapaests of Ovid's *Medea*:

> feror huc illuc ut plena deo   (2, an4)

> I am carried here and there like one full of the god.

On stage, this is likely to have been part of a great monody. In a fragment of Varius, probably from his famous *Thyestes*, a chorus describes in anapaests the music of the spheres:

---

37 On the meter of this verse, see Strzelecki 1952/53, 117.
38 Questa 2007, 445.

> primum huic
> nervis septem est intenta fides
> variique apti vocum moduli,
> ...
> ad quos mundi resonat canor in
> vestigia se sua volventis.   (2)[39]

> First for this the lyre was tuned with seven strings and the various tones of the voices were fixed, ... to which the song of the universe, turning itself upon its own tracks, resounds.

Aphthonius/Marius Victorinus quotes this passage in the context of a chorus imitating those celestial movements with varied dance steps.[40] We can easily envision a lively and elaborate dance on stage here.

Seneca

Finally, what of music in Seneca?[41] With the possible exception of some mime performances, theater in Rome meant musical theater. If, therefore, Seneca's tragedies were performed on stage, those performances almost certainly included music. Furthermore, several scholars have observed the likely analogies between Senecan performance and pantomime, the most popular theatrical genre of Seneca's day.[42] As discussions such as Lucian's and visual portrayals make clear, pantomime was an emphatically musical genre.[43]

We cannot know for sure how strong the dichotomy between unaccompanied iambic trimeters/senarii and accompanied other meters remained in the Empire. Papyrus finds include passages where iambic trimeters are put to music; but these are probably drawn from individual solo performances rather than from performances of whole plays.[44] The metrical-musical dichotomy plays a strong enough role throughout the history of Greek and Roman theater that use of meters other than iambic trimeters/senarii probably would have encouraged, if not demanded,

---

39 The exact meter of this fragment is uncertain, but it is certainly anapaestic. See Lefèvre 1976, 10–1.
40 Keil 1874, 60.
41 For a review of the meters of Seneca's tragedies, with some discussion of their possible musical effects, see Dangel 2001. On Seneca's references to and attitudes towards music, see Luque Moreno 1997.
42 Eg., Zimmermann 1990, Slaney 2013, Zanobi 2014.
43 Wille 1967, 180–3, Hall 2008, 25–8.
44 Gentili 1979, 28–30, Moore 2008, 12.

musical performance in the first century CE as well. If so, Seneca's meters too can give us a sense of his plays' musicality. Just over 27% of the verses in the corpus of plays attributed to Seneca are in meters other than iambic trimeters. The fragmentary *Phoenissae* consists entirely of iambic trimeters, but in no other play do meters other than iambic trimeters make up fewer than 22% of all the verses. *Medea* is almost 34% meters other than iambic trimeters, *Octavia* 39%.[45]

A complete review of how music might have contributed to each of Seneca's plays must wait for another work. In conclusion, however, I offer a scene from the (potentially) very musical *Medea* as an example. Through most of *Medea*, Seneca follows the standard pattern he had inherited from his Greek predecessors: iambic trimeters for monologues and dialogues of characters, other meters for the chorus. At verse 740, however, when Medea has prepared her potion against Creusa and Creon, she enters and calls upon beings of the underworld in trochaic tetrameters, the more Greek-like form of trochaic septenarii. This meter, so pervasive in earlier Roman drama, is used only two other times in the Senecan corpus (*Oedipus* 223–32, *Phaedra* 1201–12).[46] After twelve verses, Medea switches back to iambic trimeters as she boasts of her power as a sorceress (752–70). She then dedicates various objects to Hecate, and the meter changes again, first to iambic trimeters alternating with iambic dimeters (771–86), then to anapaests as she sees a vision of Hecate and dedicates herself to vengeance (787–842). The ritual of dedication completed, she returns to iambic trimeters when she summons her sons and sends them off with the poisoned gifts (843–8).

These changes of meter could, of course, be effective if the words were spoken without accompaniment, even as part of a recitation rather than an on-stage performance. Their potential becomes much greater, however, when we see them as reflections of musical phenomena.[47] After only speaking throughout most of the play, Medea sings when she has begun to put her vengeance in motion, recalling rhythmically the songs of countless tragic characters before her (740–51). She stops singing for a description of what she has accomplished (752–70). Whether she sings or speaks the next verses, in which the usually unaccompanied iambic trimeters alternate with shorter iambic verses, is unclear (771–86). Her vision of Hecate leads Medea to anapaests, the meter most conducive to

---

45 Statistics for the other plays are as follows: *Thyestes*: 31%, *Oedipus* and *Agamemnon*: 30%, *Hercules Oetaeus*: 29%, *Phaedra*: 26%, *Hercules Furens* and *Troades*: 22%. These statistics rely on the *conspectus metrorum* of Zwierlein 1986, 464–6. Cf. Dangel 2001, 292.
46 Costa 1973, 137 notes that all three trochaic tetrameter passages share 'a somewhat similar tone of frenzied or sinister excitement.'
47 Cf. Boyle 2014, 314.

melodic exuberance, and she concludes with a great aria (787–842). The song concludes, and she reinforces that it is time for action by speaking the words:

> peracta vis est omnis. huc natos vota (843)

All my violence has been accomplished. Call my sons here.[48]

Much work remains to be done on just what it means to acknowledge that Rome's tragedy, like its comedy, was profoundly musical. Of one thing, however, we can be certain. If Seneca's plays were performed musically, they continued a long tradition of extensive and elaborate musical performance that extended from the proto-tragedies sung in Rome before Livius Andronicus all the way through the tragedians of the early empire.

Bibliography

Blänsdorf, J. (2000), 'Livius Andronicus und die Anverwandlung des hellenistischen Dramas in Rom', in: G. Manuwald (ed.), *Identität und Alterität in der frührömischen Tragödie*, Würzburg, 145–56.
Boyle, A. (2006), *An Introduction to Roman Tragedy*, London.
_____ (2014), *Seneca: Medea*, Oxford.
Costa, C. (1973), *Seneca: Medea*, Oxford.
Dangel, J. (2001), 'Sénèque, *poeta fabricator*: Lyrique chorale et évidence tragique', in: J. Dangel (ed.), *Le poète architecte: Arts métriques et art poétique latins*, Louvain, 185–292.
_____ (2002), *Accius: Oeuvres: Fragments*, Paris.
D'Anna G. (1967), *M. Pacuvii fragmenta*, Rome.
Fitch, J. (2000), 'Playing Seneca?', in: G. Harrison (ed.), *Seneca in Performance*, London, 1–12.
Gentili, B. (1979), *Theatrical Performances in the Ancient World: Hellenistic and Early Roman Theatre*, Amsterdam.
Hall, E. (2008), 'Introduction: Pantomime, a Lost Chord of Ancient Culture', in: E. Hall and R. Wyles (eds.), *New Directions in Ancient Pantomime*, Oxford, 1–40.
Hurka, F. (2008), 'Entwicklungslinien in der Liedkomposition der republikanischen Tragödie', in: L. Castagna and C. Riboldi (eds.), *Amicitiae templa serena: Studi in onore di Giuseppe Aricò*, vol. 2, Milan, 789–811.
Jocelyn, H. (1967), *The Tragedies of Ennius*, Cambridge.
Keil, H. (1874), *Grammatici Latini*, vol. 6, Leipzig.
Lefèvre, E. (1976), *Der Thyestes des Lucius Varius Rufus: Zehn Überlegungen zu seiner Rekonstruktion*, Mainz.

---

48 On the effect of this passage, cf. Dangel 2001, 287–9.

Luque Moreno, J. (1997), 'Seneca musicus', in: M. Rodríguez-Pantoja (ed.), *Séneca, dos mil años después: Actas del congreso internacional conmemorativo del bimelenario de su nacimiento (Córdoba, 24 a 27 de Septiembre de 1996)*, 77–115.
Manuwald, G. (2001), *Fabulae praetextae: Spuren einer literarischen Gattung der Römer*, Munich.
_____ (2003), *Pacuvius: Summus Tragicus Poeta*, Munich.
_____ (2011), *Roman Republican Theatre*, Cambridge.
_____ (2012), *Tragicorum Romanorum Fragmenta II: Ennius*, Göttingen.
_____ (2014), 'Tragedy, Paratragedy, and Roman Comedy', in: M. Fontaine and A. Scafuro (eds.), *The Oxford Handbook of Greek and Roman Comedy*, Oxford, 580–98.
Moore, T. (1998), 'Music and Structure in Roman Comedy', *AJP* 119, 245–73.
_____ (1999), 'Facing the Music: Character and Musical Accompaniment in Roman Comedy', *Syllecta Classica* 19, 130–53.
_____ (2008), 'When Did the *Tibicen* Play? Meter and Musical Accompaniment in Roman Comedy', *TAPA* 138, 3–46.
_____ (2012), *Music in Roman Comedy*, Cambridge.
Questa, C. (2007), *La metrica di Plauto e di Terenzio*, Urbino.
Ribbeck, O. (1897), *Tragicorum Romanorum Fragmenta*, 3rd ed., Leipzig.
Schauer, M. (2012), *Tragicorum Romanorum Fragmenta I: Livius Andronicus, Naevius, Tragici Minores, Fragmenta Adespota*, Göttingen.
Schierl, P. (2006), *Die Tragödien des Pacuvius*, Berlin.
Slaney, H. (2013), 'Seneca's Chorus of One', in: J. Billings, F. Budelmann, and F. Macintosh (eds.), *Choruses, Ancient and Modern*, Oxford, 99–116.
Soubiran, J. (1988), *Essai sur la versification dramatique des Romains: Sénaire iambique et septénaire trochaïque*, Paris.
Spaltenstein, F. (2008), *Commentaire des fragments dramatiques de Livius Andronicus*, Brussels.
Strzelecki, W. (1952/53), 'Quaestiones tragicae', *Eos* 46, 107–19.
Warmington, E. (1936), *Remains of Old Latin II: Livius Andronicus, Naevius, Pacuvius and Accius*, Cambridge, MA.
Wille, G. (1967), *Musica Romana: Die Bedeutung der Musik im Leben der Römer*, Amsterdam.
Zanobi, A. (2014), *Seneca's Tragedies and the Aesthetics of Pantomime*, London.
Zimmermann, B. (1990), 'Seneca und der Pantomimus', in: G. Vogt-Spira (ed.), *Strukturen der Mündlichkeit in der römischen Literatur*, Tübingen, 161–7.
Zwierlein, O. (1986), *L. Annaei Senecae Tragoediae*, Oxford.

Cedric Littlewood
Seneca, Horace and the Poetics of Transgression

Seneca's tragic poetics are typically characterized by an impulse towards amplification and transgression. Its actions are hyped as not only bigger but also badder than any previously witnessed or conceived. At the beginning of her tragedy Medea dismisses as trivial the acts of her youth and plots greater crimes worthy of her maturity (*Med.* 48–50). Fury, the guiding spirit of *Thyestes*, aims at a re-enactment of the Thracian crime, but with greater numbers (*Thy.* 56–7). Before Atreus conceives this particular model of revenge he is resolved somehow to surpass the boundaries of the conventional (*Thy.* 267–8). Convention is established by the mythological record and Seneca's literary predecessors, such as, in this case, the crimes of Tereus and Procne as narrated in Ovid's *Metamorphoses* 6.424–674.[1] The agonistic spirit of Senecan tragedy is expressed primarily through engagement with the Augustan poetry which, largely through such engagement, Neronian writers established as canonical. For Seneca in lyric mode, Horace's odes are the single most important point of reference.[2]

Augustan poetry is as important for shaping the discourse of transgression as it is for constituting the conventional: Fury is recognizable as Virgil's Allecto; the trajectory of Medea's maturation is already traced by Ovid, *Heroides* 12.[3] Central in discussions of Medea's transcendence is a crossing of generic boundaries as the heroine moves from elegy to tragedy. One cannot discuss how forcefully the acted horror of Seneca's *Medea* surpasses the ironies of the elegiac epistle without acknowledging the role of Ovid's poem in defining excess. Seneca's tragic Medea is terrible in and of herself, but also because we recognize her as the character which *Heroides* 12 anticipated, but could not openly express. We receive her as inconceivable, unspeakable and transgressive in part because we pick up her story in Seneca where *Heroides* 12 had imposed a boundary and fallen silent – and not just her story.[4] Finding echoes of the close of *Heroides* 12 not

---

1 Seidensticker 1985 on the *maius*-motif, Agapitos 1998, 247–8, Schiesaro 2003, 34 and *passim*.
2 See Mayer 1982 on the Neronian making of the Augustan canon generally and 313–4 on Horace particularly. For a collection of imitations of Horatian lyric in Senecan tragedy see Spika 1890.
3 See Schiesaro 2003, 32–6 on Juno and Allecto, Trinacty 2007 on Seneca's *Medea* as 'a hypothetical projection of her Ovidian self' (76) and Hinds 2011, 22–8 on Ovid's Medeas as programming or coding their successors.
4 Seneca's *Medea* tragedy and Ovid's own would have been rival sequels of *Heroides* 12. Though the rivalry cannot be discussed the common transition from elegy to tragedy can.

just in *Medea*, but in the words of protagonists of other plays (including Atreus at *Thy.* 266–70), Stephen Hinds writes that 'in intertextual terms they are in a sense *all* becoming Medeas' (2011, 26). The detail I wish to emphasize is the generic boundary. Protagonists like Medea and Atreus recall the inchoate and oblique *nescioquid maius* at the very limit of *Heroides* 12 (12.212) so as then to move beyond it into open expression and enactment of tragic crime.

Alessandro Schiesaro has argued for a different Augustan pattern behind Atreus' tragic inspiration: the 'densely programmatic Horatian ode, 3.25, where the poet explicitly connects the force of Bacchus' inspiration with his transportation into uncharted perilous territories'.[5] There can be no transgression without boundaries, and lyric, so very concerned to remain within proper limits, offers a rhetoric of moderation to be broken and surpassed.[6] The uncharted territory into which Bacchic ecstasy transports Horace is a grand style which the poet typically disavows.[7] Locating the genesis of Atreus' tragic madness at Horace's point of departure creates a similar effect to that achieved by the reminiscence of the close of *Heroides* 12. The lower genre in each case creates a boundary to be transgressed and thereby stages an 'ascent' into sublime horror.[8]

In the discussion that follows I consider first the role of the first chorus in Seneca, *Thyestes* 122–75 and argue that Tantalid *nefas* is unspeakable most particularly for a lyric voice. Seneca inherits from Horace, and Pindar before him, a rhetoric of lyric piety which marks its boundaries. In Section 2 I address Horace's accommodation of Augustan imperialism within his lyric poetry. His odes do not simply elevate and extend their register to celebrate a world ruler; lyric order within fixed boundaries offers a figurative expression of imperial control. It is a neat trick, a delicate balance, and one which does not survive translation to a polarized Senecan environment in which kings know no limits and only a sage exercises true power. In the final section of this essay I turn from *Thyestes* to the first Argonautic Ode of *Medea* 301–79 in which Virgilian prophecies of global dominion are remembered through the critical lens of Horace, *Odes* 1.3.

---

5 Schiesaro 2003, 51 on *Thy.* 260–62 and *C.* 3.25.1–3 and see also Trinacty 2014, 202–4 on the same text inspiring Cassandra at *Ag.* 720–5.
6 On Horatian lyric space, a middle ground between the opposing poles of elegy and epic, see Lowrie 1997, 77–93. Epic, tragedy and history all lie beyond lyric's upper limit. While there are of course distinctions to be made between them, they represent collectively also a continuum of grand writing in their relation to Horatian lyric. See e. g. Lowrie 1997, 181 on *C.* 2.1, 'Although history and tragedy are first differentiated as two sides of Pollio's literary career, they collapse when it comes to Horace's self-definition.'
7 So Davis 1991, 107–14 on Horace, *C.* 2.19 and 3.25 and more generally Mazzoli 1996, 33–6.
8 On generic ascent see Harrison 2007, 8–10.

Lyric Piety and the Unspeakable Tragedy of the Tantalids

Before addressing the rhetoric of transgression in Horatian lyric and its relevance to Senecan tragedy, I shall consider briefly and more generally the relationship between the first choral ode of *Thyestes* and the material that surrounds it. The first two acts of the play stage and restage the victory of passion over the reservations of first Tantalus and then Atreus. The ghost of Tantalus seeks to escape to his infernal prison (68–83) and the spirit of Atreus recoils when the image of slaughter appears before his eyes (281–4). Essentially the same event is portrayed twice.[9] Between these enactments of the triumph of passion a chorus sings of Pisa, famous for its Olympic games, and describes the river's cool waters and the cycle of the seasons (122–31). It prays that the cycle of nature not be replaced by the cycle of unnatural Tantalid crimes which occupy the rest of the song. The song is undermined in various ways by what has preceded it. Because the games have their origin in crime and treachery the chorus' characterization of Pisa as beloved by the gods and famed sounds 'an ironic note' (Tarrant 1985, 107). Only a few lines before the chorus sings of the cool waters of the river Alpheus Fury had described the Argolid as a desert and the royal palace as shuddering at the touch of Tantalus (*Thy.* 101–21).[10] Indeed, the chorus of this drama is persistently a victim of dramatic irony, painfully and problematically unaware of the tragic plot.[11] Commenting on the chorus' curious failure to comprehend the sun's banishment at *Thy.* 789–884 Richard Tarrant (1985, 204) adds a crucial refinement in mapping the dramatic irony onto a distinction of genre rather than character: 'It is almost as if the chorus that took part in the previous scene is a different entity from the lyric voice of the ode.'[12]

If we compare Pindar's with Seneca's treatment of the Tantalid material, we see in *Olympians* 1 that Pindar attributes the story of the cannibal banquet to the envious and banishes it from his own lyric. It is spoken only to be formally and

---

9 So Shelton 1975 and Cf. Owen 1970 on a similar technique in *Troades*.
10 A similar effect is created in *Oedipus* where a hymn's closing celebrations of cosmic order and the cycles of nature 'seem dramatically designed to contrast starkly with the reality of their inversion by the Theban plague' (Boyle 2011, 228), as vividly portrayed in the preceding act. See further Davis 1993, 202–7 on this 'ironic commentary on recent events in Thebes.'
11 Hill 2000, 574–80.
12 Cf. Brecht, 'When an actor sings he undergoes a change of function. Nothing is more revolting than when the actor pretends not to notice that he has left the level of plain speech and started to sing' (Willett 1964, 44).

programmatically unspoken.[13] To make gluttons and cannibals of the gods in the words of his poem would be to recreate Tantalus' crime, to challenge the order of the world and to stray beyond the proprieties of the genre – and Pindar isn't going there: ἀφίσταμαι (*Ol.* 1.52).[14] The banquet survives in the imagery of Pindar's alternative account of the mythological history of the house of Tantalus, for example in the description of Tantalus unable to 'digest' (καταπέψαι, 55) his great blessings, but not in naked, literal truth.[15] I do not suggest that Seneca is responding in any immediate way to Pindar, *Olympians* 1 in the first ode of *Thyestes*,[16] but that one way of approaching the poetics of transgression and the 'dialectic between repression and its removal' (Schiesaro 2003, 42) in this tragedy is through and against the constraints of specifically lyric piety. Pindar represents for Horace and Quintilian the grandest form of lyric, but even at this upper end of the lyric spectrum there are limits.[17]

Pushed to and even beyond such limits by Bacchic possession and the god's heavy thyrsus (*gravi ... thyrso* 2.19.8) in *C.* 2.19, Horatian lyric insists that this material too may be spoken: *Fas ... est mihi ... cantare ... fas et ... tectaque Penthei/disiecta non leni ruina/Thracis et exitium Lycurgi* (I am allowed to sing ... I am allowed to sing ... how the palace of Pentheus was blasted apart and collapsed in devastation, and how the Thracian Lycurgus was destroyed, *C.* 2.19.9–16). The pious concern over betraying the god's secrets tropes a poetic concern about poetic boundaries. Or, to put it another way, the tearing apart of Pentheus and his house is marked as tragic, as dangerously sublime poetry, precisely by the suggestion of religious reticence. The expectation is that this is something that lyric should not say and the repeated *fas est* indicates an extension of the genre to incorporate this new material. After a description of gigantomachy and an impious assault on the heavens (21–2) the poem is wrestled down to something more pedestrian in its final stanza.

---

13 'One of the envious neighbours immediately said in secret that into water boiling rapidly on the fire they cut up your limbs with a knife, and for the final course distributed your flesh around the tables and ate it. But for my part, I cannot call any of the blessed gods a glutton – I stand back.' (*O.* 1.48–52)
14 On Pindar, the limits of lyric, and 'the precarious pursuit of a *kleos* that is not *dusphamon*' see Goldhill 1991, 138–44 (quote 143).
15 See Nagy 1986, 84–6 on the imagery of the cauldron '*ostentatiously retained*' (his emphasis, 86).
16 Cf. Tarrant 1985, 204 on the play's fourth ode and *Paeans* 9, 'Direct imitation of Pindar by Seneca would be surprising.'
17 Davis 1991, 133–43 on Horace, *C.* 4.2, and Quintilian's judgment: *longe Pindarus princeps spiritus magnificentia* (Pindar is by far the greatest in the grandeur of his inspiration, 10.1.61).

> te vidit insons Cerberus aureo
> cornu decorum, leniter atterens
>   caudam, et recedentis trilingui
>   ore pedes tetigitque crura. (Hor. C. 2.19.29–32)

When Cerberus caught sight of you, arrayed in all your beauty with golden horns, he did you no harm, but meekly brushed his tail against you; and as you went away he licked your feet and legs with the tongues of his three muzzles

With *insons ... decorum ...* and *leniter atterens* Horace leaves tragic violence behind to return within the more familiar boundaries of lyric decorum. The house of Pentheus torn apart by no gentle ruin is exchanged for a tame Cerberus gently rubbing his tail against the god's legs.[18] The generic opposition is perhaps reinforced by reminiscence of *Georgics* 4.483 (*tenuitque inhians tria Cerberus ora*). Stephen Harrison (2013, 383) sees here at the poem's close the taming not just of Cerberus, but of the violence of the *Georgics*: 'Once again the Horatian passage defuses the tragedy of the original'. The ethics and aesthetics of containment is a subject to which we shall return shortly.

In the opening stanza of *C.* 3.1 Horace authorizes a departure into uncharted territory with a statement of religious purity:

> Odi profanum vulgus et arceo;
> favete linguis. carmina non prius
>   audita Musarum sacerdos
>   virginibus puerisque canto. (Hor. C. 3.1.1–4)

I shun the uninitiated crowd and keep it at a distance. Pray silence! As priest of the Muses I am singing to girls and boys songs never heard before.

But at the ode's end, the valley is preferred to the heights, humble seclusion to envy and novelty:

> cur invidendis postibus et novo
> sublime ritu moliar atrium?
>   cur valle permutem Sabina
>   divitiosas operosiores? (Hor. C. 3.1.45–8)

... why should I struggle to build a towering hall in the modern style with a doorway that arouses envy? Why should I change my Sabine valley for riches that will bring an increase only of trouble?

---

18 Stevens 1999, 293 argues for Cerberus as humorously and Orphically vegetarian – hence 'innocent' - Cf. Nisbet and Hubbard 1978, 330 for a creature that merely does no harm.

The boundaries of lyric – Horace's as Pindar's – are policed by a rhetoric of piety that determines what may and may not appropriately be said, as much aesthetically as ethically.[19] Commonly in his more elevated poems Horace makes a point of stepping back from these boundaries as a closural and genre-defining gesture.[20] If at the poem's opening Horace looks down from Olympian heights on the kings of the earth, the poem ends with what is in some sense a rejection of the sublime.[21] The ethical paradox, that quiet retirement affords a magnificent invulnerability, is expressed through shifts in poetic register and, typically, a descent from the heroic ambitions of high poetry.

Imperialism and the Aesthetics of Containment in Seneca's *Thyestes*

Ellen Oliensis writes (1998, 107), 'Horatian lyric matches the aesthetics of containment with an ethics of contentment that would seem to leave little room for imperial ambitions.' And this one might take as the antithesis of the old passion for power (*vetus regni furor*, 302) that possesses the Atrides. A crime beyond limits is Atreus' and Fury's elusive goal: in the tragedy's tortured logic, 'the crime is characterized as "enough" only because it is "too much" and at times even this too much is not enough': *nescioquid animo maius et solito amplius/supraque fines moris humani tumet* (Something greater, larger than usual, beyond normal human limits is swelling in my spirit, *Thy.* 267–8).[22] The crossing of borders (*fines*) is not an incidental but an essential feature of imperial ambition: it is impossible to gain an empire without crossing borders of some kind. As Atreus' determination to

---

19 Contrast Davis 1991, 101 on *C*. 3.4.6 '*pius*, as so often in the *Odes*, is not so much a moral as a literary badge of competence,' with Nisbet and Rudd 2004, 7 on *C*.3.1.1, 'But here the religious metaphor refers primarily to content rather than literary style.' On piety in the Roman odes particularly see Oliensis 1998, 124. On the subjugation of Cerberus by Bacchus at the close of *C*. 2.19 as a triumph of *pietas* see Stevens 1999, 292.
20 See Oliensis 1998, 131–3 and representatively, 'In *Odes* 3.2, *Virtus* ascends to heaven … on "fugitive wing" … , but the ode returns to earth, ending … with the "limping foot" (*pede … claudo*, 32) of Punishment, a humbler and more mundane means of poetic locomotion' (132).
21 See Hardie 2009, 181 on *sublimis* in Horace generally as 'at times hinting at a poetics of the sublime' and 192–3 on the shift in poetic elevation and the closing rejection of the *sublime atrium* in *C*. 3.1 particularly. Hardie's discussion of sublimity in Virgil and Horace is a discussion of engagement with Lucretius. See also Harrison 2013, 373–4 on the Lucretian inspiration of the Bacchic ecstasy of *C*. 2.19. On Lucretius as *sublimis* see Ovid *Am*. 1.15.23 with Mazzoli 1996, 28.
22 Curley 1986, 166 and 161–68 more fully on 'the "modus" theme' (161).

surpass a limit is the echo and fulfilment of Fury's earlier command,[23] so the chorus' prayer echoes Tantalus' programmatic stand against Fury at the very beginning of the play: *advertat placidum numen et **arceat*** (let his kindly power be with us and forbid, 132) picks up ... *stabo et **arcebo** scelus* (I shall stand and block the crime, 95); *poena **decentior*** (apter penalty, 151) picks up *me pati poenas **decet*** (my proper role is to suffer punishments, 86).[24] In this lyric space at least, crime is contained by appropriate punishment. Tantalus drinks deep from a raging torrent in the last lines of the ode before the word *pulverem* cuts his mad desire short: *hic bibit/altum de rapido gurgite pulverem* (He drinks the deeps left from the whirling flood: deep dust, 174–5). The raging torrent is so common an image of expansive speech in ancient literary criticism, that one may read here also the abrupt curtailment of poetic as well as political ambition.[25] Pervasive though the image of a river in flood is, its pollution with mud or dust recalls particularly the Callimachean critique deployed in passages such as this:

> eo fit
> plenior ut si quos delectet copia iusto,
> cum ripa simul avolsos ferat Aufidus acer.
> at qui tantuli eget quanto est eget quanto est opus, is neque limo
> turbatam haurit aquam, neque vitam amittit in undis.   (Hor. S. 1.1.56–60)

> So it comes about that when any find pleasure in undue abundance, raging Aufidus sweeps them away, bank and all; while the man who craves only so much as he needs, neither draws water thick mud, nor loses his life in the floods

The pun on *tantuli* is underlined a few lines later (*Tantulus a labris sitiens fugientia captat/flumina*, Tantalus, thirsty soul, catches at the streams that fly from his lips, S. 1.1.68). The criticism is more immediately ethical here as the criticism of Lucilius' muddy eloquence is more immediately aesthetic at Hor. S. 1.4.11, but life and speech are inextricably connected.[26] Outside the boundaries of Seneca's ode the spirit of Tantalus roams unchecked. The description of the parching of the Argolid is modelled on Ovid's epic account of the world burned by Phaethon's fatal chariot ride.[27] As important as the imagery of the chariot in the characteriza-

---

23 *FU: Ne sit irarum **modus*** (Let there be no limit to their anger, 26) Cf. *AT: nil quod doloris capiat assueti **modus*** (Nothing conforming to the limits of ordinary bitterness, 255).
24 Tarrant 1985, 108 connects *arceat* with *arcebo*.
25 See Freudenburg 1993, 158–62 with bibliography.
26 Gowers 2012, 74 *ad loc.* and Cf. Graver 2014, 282–4 on Sen. Ep.114.3.
27 Tarrant 1985, 104 on *ripae vacent* (rivers are empty, *Thy.* 108) Cf. *ostia septem/pulverulenta vacant* (The seven mouths lie empty, filled with dust, *Met.* 2.255–56), Jakobi 1988, 156 on *en*

tion of power in this play is the generic opposition between the decorum of lyric containment and a sublime, Phaethonic over-reaching, which transgresses human limits so far as to set the whole world ablaze.[28]

Though the relation seems more general than particular, one may take up also Tarrant's detection of 'an inverted allusion to Horace's snow-covered Soracte' (1985, 105): *et Cithaeronis iuga/stant parte nulla cana deposita nive* (Cithaeron's ridges stand nowhere white, their snow sloughed off, Sen. *Thy.* 117–8) Cf. *vides ut alta stet nive candidum/Soracte* (Do you see how Soracte stands there shining with its blankets of deep snow, Hor. *C.* 1.9.1–2). *Dissolve frigus* (Thaw the cold, *C.* 1.9.5), advises Horace, but this means piling wood on the domestic hearth, not global-warming on a Senecan scale. *C.* 1.9 is founded morally on an acceptance of the separate spheres of human and divine activity[29] and poetically, as the culmination of a sequence of poems beginning with *C.* 1.4, on the demarcation of lyric from heroic epic.[30] If indeed Seneca offers an inverted allusion to Horace in these lines it is to transgress this particular Horatian boundary.[31]

A similar approach may be taken in the play's second ode in which true Stoic kingship within the confines of the soul is opposed to the illusory attractions of tyrannical power. At its close the chorus prefers peaceful contentment and a life unspoken, to death lying heavy on those too well known (391–403). Horace has influenced this anachronistically Roman ode.[32] If its references to the unstable favour of the restless mob and the desire to secure all of Libya's harvests picks up the opening of *C.* 1.1,[33] then this is an allusion reinforced by Thyestes' entrance at the end of the ode where he looks on the Cyclopean masonry of Argos and its famous racetrack (*Thy.* 407–10). Olympic competition which promises only dust is the very first illustration in the *Odes* of the world that lyric Horace renounces (*C.* 1.1.3–6). Seneca's chorus does not simply assume a Horatian persona, however. Tarrant comments on *Thy.* 369–79 and the gathering of foreign kings, 'While echoing Horace's phrases [from *C.* 4.15.21–4], Seneca pointedly alters their application: in Horace Roman power … guarantees the *otium* of peoples, whereas for Seneca that security belongs exclusively to the isolated *sapiens*.' (1985, 143). In Seneca the

---

ipse Titan dubitat (See, even the Titan hesitates, *Thy.* 120) and *Atlas en ipse laborat* (See, Atlas himself is troubled, *Met.* 2.296) and Littlewood 2004, 130–3.
28 See Barchiesi 2005, 263 on Ov. *Met.* 2.326–8.
29 *Permitte divis cetera* (Leave the rest to the gods, *C.* 1.9.9) and Davis 1991, 150–5.
30 So Santirocco 1986, 32–41.
31 Cf. also Sen. *Med.* 587–90, where Haemus is melted into gore and Hor. *C.* 1.12.5–8 where Haemus remains cool as Orpheus practises his art.
32 Tarrant 1985, 137–8 for detail.
33 Sen. *Thy.* 351–7 Cf. Hor. *C.* 1.1.7–10 with Tarrant 1985, 141.

Dahae and the Sarmatians and others engage in the endless and pointless struggle for political power – they are not docile elements in an orderly Roman cosmos.

This correction of Horace strikes at a very familiar tension – namely the degree to which his lyric can simultaneously distance itself from epic ambition and yet provide a model for Augustan imperialism.[34] Lyric order within fixed boundaries offers a figurative expression of empire in a different mode from that offered by the madness of epic. If empire is won by epic ambition and, dare one say it, cross-border aggression, might it not be maintained through lyric restraint – not least the restraint of those who would challenge its harmonious order?[35] In Don Fowler's happy *sententia*, 'Augustus will make good Callimacheans of the Geloni if it kills them' (1995, 257 on *C.* 2.9). Seneca's Stoic lyric has no time for so ingenious an accommodation of imperialism. To elaborate the significance of his 'pointed alteration of Horace' we might say that, as so typically, the Neronian text probes at a point of Augustan sensitivity. This is the play, after all, in which the palace of Latinus offers a pattern for the palace of Atreus, and whose impulse to civil war finds its inspiration in the *Aeneid*.[36]

At the heart of the royal palace is a sacred grove where Atreus sings his lethal poem (692). The palace looms over the city, oppressing it, and the sacred grove is a space separated from and unknown to the people.

> post ista vulgo nota, quae populi colunt,
> in multa dives spatia discedit domus.
> arcana in imo regio secessu iacet,   650
> alta vetustum valle compescens nemus,
> penetrale regni   (*Thy.* 648–52)

> Behind these public rooms, where whole peoples pay court, the wealthy house goes back a great distance. At the farthest and lowest remove there lies a secret area that confines an age-old woodland in a deep vale – the inner sanctum of the realm

If the massivity of Seneca's palace and the infernal powers that inhabit the grove point to a tragic aesthetic, its exclusivity points to another: *me gelidum nemus/nympharum leves cum Satyris chori/secernunt a populo* (the cool grove and the light-footed bands of Nymphs and Satyrs set me apart from the crowd, *C.*1.1.30–2); *Odi profanum vulgus et arceo* (I shun the uninitiated crowd and keep it at a distance, *C.*3.1.1). Both of these programmatic statements in Horace have

---

34 Oliensis 1998, 112–4.
35 Cf. Hardie 2009, 153 and 175–6 on Lucretius 1.951–83 on sublime ambition and the philosophical mind's limitless empire.
36 Schiesaro 1992, 61.

been interpreted as expressions of Callimachean exclusivity and for just that reason problematic.[37] David Coffta writes that any grand poetic endeavour 'is necessarily at odds with the Callimachean programme' (2001, 95). That view has been challenged by Schiesaro, who sees a fusion, an alliance, established at the end of *Odes* 2 and carrying over into *Odes* 3, of Pindaric loftiness and Callimachean originality (2009, 72). But a tension remains in such Bacchic poetics.[38] If it didn't, Horace wouldn't claim novelty and an elevated position in the first stanza of *C*. 3.1 only to reject it in the last.

Seneca revisits this point of Augustan tension. The passion to rule in *Thyestes* is uncontrolled and insatiable, and it shatters the cosmos. It is impious and transgressive. The Horatian project of aligning the ethics and aesthetics of lyric with those of imperial order is challenged and rebuked by the reminiscence of *Odes* 4.15 with pointedly different application.[39] When we read Atreus' proud boast, *Aequalis astris gradior et cunctos super/altum superbo vertice attingens polum* (Peer of the stars I stride, out-topping all, my proud head reaching to the lofty sky, *Thy*. 885–6), surely it would be inappropriate to recall *sublimi feriam sidera vertice* (I shall soar aloft and strike the stars with my head, *C*. 1.1.36), but this is precisely what Tarrant recommends we do (1985, 217). On 'topics … that Horace tried to keep separate' (1995, 260), Fowler writes, 'I would not deny that Horace is trying to keep us off that tack, but it is not necessarily the critic's job to reproduce bad faith: sometimes we should expose it' (1995, 261).[40] Seneca, I suggest, can help with that.

---

37 Coffta 2001, 70–2, 93–5
38 See Schiesaro 2009, and Batinski 1991 on Horace's rehabilitation of Bacchus more generally.
39 Cf. Curley 1986, 156–57, arguing that the reminiscence of *otium* (Verg. *Ecl.* 1.6) at *Thy*. 560–1 is striking because it collapses an expected dichotomy between passion and tranquillity: 'it implies that peace is … in some ways like war' (157). The ethical argument could be extended to the collapsing of an expected generic opposition between pastoral and the high genres of epic and tragedy.
40 Fowler 1995, 260–4 underlies much of this argument and would have improved an earlier draft of these ideas at Littlewood 2004, 140–8.

Augustan Ambition: Seneca's *Medea* and Horace *Odes* 1.3

I turn finally to *Medea* and its Argonautic odes. As noted by Giuseppe Biondi and many others, Seneca's ode on an audacious first voyage owes something to Horace, *Odes* 1.3. *Audax nimium* with which it opens takes it cue from the repeated *audax* in the seventh stanza of the Horatian ode. In both poems a fragile craft is entrusted to the savagery of the sea (*C.* 1.3.9–12), challenging the divinely-ordained boundaries of the world.[41] *Odes* 1.3 offers, if one follows Hans Peter Syndikus (1972, 67), the theme of transgression or, if one follows Steele Commager (1962, 119), 'paradigms of heroic freedom'. The nature of this heroic transgression is closely tied to Virgil and to the *Aeneid* in particular. For Matthew Santirocco (1986, 25–9) *Odes* 1.3 is the culmination of a sequence of poems tracing Virgil's career. Horace's anxious propemptikon as he parts from Virgil demarcates the boundary separating lyric from heroic epic.[42] The contrast between the fragility of the craft and the savagery of the sea, 'virtually enacts the Callimachean contrast between the two kinds of poetry' sketched at the beginning of the *Aetia* (Santirocco 1986, 27). Virgil's exploit is initially dangerous, and, in the generalizing second half of Horace's poem, criminal. Ocean-voyaging ships are impious (*impiae*, 1.3.23). The human race boldly rushes into forbidden sacrilege (*per vetitum nefas*, 1.3.26). Bold Prometheus brought fire to mortals by an act of criminal deception (*fraude mala*, 1.3.28).

In Seneca's ode it is natural to attribute excessive daring to the Argonauts, and to Jason as a type of 'marine Phaethon' (Henderson 1983, 100). However, the goal and prize of their voyage is Medea (361–3) and one may argue equally that, as the punishment that fits the crime, she embodies Argonautic transgression. In the act preceding the ode it is Medea who is accused of *audacia* (267)[43] and *fraus* (290). The phrase *palluit audax*, used of the Argonaut Tiphys later in the ode (347) is borrowed from *C.* 3.27.28 where it is used of Europa, who unwisely betrayed her father and was carried off by her lover. It is a characterization that fits Medea much better than an Argonaut. The larger point is Medea's own from her argument with Creon: why distinguish between two guilty parties (*cur sontes duos distinguis?* 275–6)? The Argo brings Medea, the stereotypical outsider, to the

---

41 See Biondi 1984, 87–141 for the fullest commentary.
42 On the generic opposition see Farrell 1991, 333–4, Pucci 1992 and Cf. other genre-distinguishing propemptika like Propertius 1.8 and Juvenal 12.
43 Medea also inspired the impious wickedness dared by the daughters of Pelias (*piae sorores impium auderent nefas*, 261).

heart of civilization, and in such a way as to confuse the very category and conception of 'other'.[44]

Medea is very much implicated in the transgressive poetics of the Argonautic odes. If we follow Santirocco in reading the fragility of the boat stylistically in *Odes* 1.3, then we might reasonably consider the development of that theme in the Senecan imitation – in phrases such as *tenui ... ligno* (thin wooden planks, 306) and *gracili limite* (slender margin, 308). Opposed to these fragile boundaries is the dangerously novel form of writing[45] in which Tiphys engages as he spreads his canvas on the vastness of the sea and stretches the ropes as the sails fill out:

> Ausus Tiphys
> pandere vasto carbasa ponto,
> legesque novas scribere ventis,
> nunc lina sinu tendere toto ...   (*Med.* 318–21)
>
> Tiphys dared to spread his canvas on the vast waste sea and write new laws for the winds: now to strain the ropes with sails full-bellied ...

One may compare Juvenal's programme for satire on the grand scale: *utere velis/totos pande sinus* (Up with your sails and shake out every stitch of canvas, 1.149–50).[46]

An early hazard in the Argo's voyage are the Symplegades (340–5). Wickedly (*improba*, 340) the boat breaks through the barriers of the deep (*claustra profundi*, 342). There is a groan as if from heaven, and the citadels or the stars, depending on what text you read,[47] are spattered with salt spray. Tiphys pales and Orpheus falls silent. The passage is significant in combining the criminality of the voyage with the rhetoric of sublimity, particularly as defined by Lucretius at

---

44 See further Segal 1983, 238, 'Medea herself embodies the two extremes of culture and nature. She is identified with both the dominated natural world and the magical arts that exercise dominion,' and Benton 2003, 281–84: '(B)ringing the periphery to the center also changes the nature of the center' (281).
45 On poetic innovation Cf. Boyle 2014, 352 on *nuptias specto novas* (I am watching a new kind of wedding, *Med.* 894).
46 See Bramble (1974, 166–8) on 'an exhortation to aspire to ὕψος' (168).
47 Defending MS A's *astra* see Fitch 1987, 36–7 and Boyle (2014), though I prefer *arces* with Zwierlein (1986) and Hine (2000). Such a reading would avoid the anti-climax of moving from stars to mere clouds and intensify the epic heroism of the ascent. Compare Hor. C. 3.3.9–10 *hac arte Pollux et vagus Hercules/enisus arces attigit igneas* (It was through this quality that Pollux and roving Hercules/after a long struggle reached the fiery heights).

1.62–79.⁴⁸ Breaking the barriers of nature to surge impiously beyond the stars or the divine citadels, and beyond the limits of fear, is the language of Lucretian daring and the first flight of the human mind. Whereas the achievement of Epicurus entails, paradoxically, an understanding of the deep-set boundaries of the universe and the limits of power (Lucr. 1.76–7), the achievement of the Argo's voyage is a world in which all boundaries are removed and nature becomes penetrable (*pervius*, *Med.* 372) by anyone.⁴⁹ The anachronistically Roman close of the ode alludes to the impossible fantasy of East meeting West in *Eclogues* 1, Caesar's imperial destiny in *Georgics* 1 and to Jupiter's prophecy which reassures Venus after Aeneas' stormy voyage in *Aeneid* 1.⁵⁰

Rome's victory in the *Aeneid*, like Epicurus' in *De Rerum Natura*, is characterized by a mixture of boundary-breaking and limitation: Caesar, who bounds his fame with the stars, rules an empire without end or limits.⁵¹ For Biondi (1984, 136) the lack of any such balance or paradox in Seneca, the unqualified surpassing of boundaries, puts the tragedy ideologically at odds with Virgil's epic. This divergence from Virgil derives in part from the influence of Horace's ode. *Odes* 1.3 described the removal of boundaries and the transformation of the world. Herculean labour broke through Acheron and the result is an age in which nothing is too high to scale (*C.* 1.3.36–7). If the comparable freedom of every little boat to sail wherever it chooses sounds a triumphant note in Seneca's ode and time (*quaelibet altum cumba pererrat*, 368),⁵² the punishment which closes Horace's ode undermines it. For Victoria Rimell the destruction of all boundaries is anti-Horatian: 'Gone is the world of Horatian lyric, with its (in part, convincing) drive to create secure nooks within insecure empire' (2012, 229). The Senecan ode remembers the *Aeneid*'s vi-

---

48 See Hardie 2009, 153–60 on Lucretius, and 204 on *C.* 1.3 where, 'Horace offers a remythologized version of the Epicurean flight' and the assault on Olympus.
49 See Hardie 2009, 158 on this aspect of the Lucretian triumph.
50 With e. g. Trinacty 2014, 160–4: *Indus gelidum potat Araxen,/Albin Persae Rhenumque bibunt* (The Indian drinks the cold Araxes,/Persians the Albis and the Rhine, *Med.* 373–4) Cf. *aut Ararim Parthus bibet aut Germania Tigrim*, (or the Parthian shall drink the Arar, and Germany the Tigris, *Ecl.* 1.62), *venient annis saecula seris* (There will come an epoch late in time, *Med.* 375) Cf. *veniet lustris labentibus aetas* (There shall come a day, as the sacred seasons glide past, *A.*1.283), and *Tethysque novos detegat orbes/nec sit terris ultima Thule* (Tethys will disclose new worlds and Thule not be the farthest of lands, *Med.* 379–80) Cf. *tibi serviat ultima Thule,/teque sibi generum Tethys emat* (farthest Thule owns thy lordship and Tethys … buys thee to wed her daughter, *G.* 1.30–1).
51 Cf. Hardie 1986, 197 who contrasts the Virgilian and Lucretian passages though noting the paradox in the *Aeneid* that 'the infinitude [of Rome's *imperium*] is achieved through enclosure'.
52 Cf. Nussbaum 1994, 465 for whom the ode's close is a 'bitter reflection' lacking any admiration for human ingenuity.

sion of imperial boundaries coextensive with those of the cosmos, but via a lyric whose primary source, *Odes* 1.3, recoils from such aspirations.

The third ode of *Medea* is a prayer for deliverance and an end of punishment for sacrilege. It ends, *arsit angustas vagus inter undas. Iam satis, divi, mare vindicastis* ([Pelias] seethed while wandering in narrow waters./Enough reparations, you gods, for the sea, *Med.* 667–8). *Iam satis* are the first words of the *Odes* 1.2. If the punishment exacted from the author of the Argo's voyage – wandering Pelias, boiled in a cauldron – does not specifically recall that of the wandering Tiber in Horace's poem (*C.* 1.2.17–20),[53] it is generically an expression of a very lyric containment of human presumption.[54] Seneca's two Argonautic odes are closely related thematically,[55] and both look back to Horace. The relationship between Horace *Odes* 1.2 and 1.3 is relevant for Seneca. Santirocco (1986, 25) argues that Horace's first three odes retrace Virgil's poetic ascent, with the second and third poems recalling the *Georgics* and the *Aeneid* respectively, but that at the same time there is a countervailing trajectory with the divine punishment looming at the end of *Odes* 1.3 casting the reader back to the beginning of *Odes* 1.2. 'Enough already' are the first words of *Odes* 1.2 but they have their origin in the prayer at the end of *Georgics* 1 (*G.* 1.501). If the first Argonautic ode at its close alluded to the prospect of an imperial peace imposed on the world and to the taming of *furor* and Junonian anger (*A.* 1.278–96), the second ode at its close recalls only violence unloosed on the world, perjury not yet expiated and a chariot hurtling wildly off course.[56] Seneca rereads these Virgilian moments – the one decisively answering the other and with their chronology reversed – through the frame of Horatian lyric.

Lyric's concern with boundaries, its recoiling from poetic audacity and sublimity, is fundamental to Seneca's reception of the genre in his tragedies. Often, as in the first ode of *Thyestes*, the chorus offers a foil for the criminal poetics of Seneca's protagonists. More complex effects are created where Seneca recalls his predecessor in such a way as to shake up Horace's accommodations: between sublime yearnings and lyric control, empire's ambition and its restraint. The fundamental generic opposition between lyric and the higher genres of epic and tragedy is a formal basis for a collision of perspectives. Horace's *Odes* afford many examples of

---

53 Cf. also *vagus errat* (586) of the Danube compared to raging Medea at the ode's opening.
54 See Rimell 2012, 232 on Augustan inspiration for 'Medea's/Seneca's perverse, high imperial cramming' and Cf. with Nisbet and Hubbard 1970, 320-2 the containment of the 'far-ranging physicist' (322) Archytas in *C.* 1.28.1–4.
55 See Biondi 1986, 174 for a table of correspondences.
56 *Georgics* 1 closes with the chariot out of control (511–4). Cf. *Med.* 599–602 (Phaethon) and 866 (Medea). See also Gowers 2012, 83 on the reuse of the image – and a poem and acquisitive appetites threatening to get out of control – at the end of Hor. *S.* 1 (114–6).

'enrichment', the genre expanding to incorporate material from beyond its borders.[57] The catastrophe of Seneca's *Medea*, the tragedy of 'a huge bullion heist',[58] sends us back to reevaluate borders, enrichment and Augustan ambitions.

Bibliography

Agapitos, P. A. (1998), 'Seneca's *Thyestes* and the Poetics of Multiple Transgression', *Hellenika* 48, 231–53.
Barchiesi, A. (2005), *Ovidio Metamorfosi Volume I (Libri I-II)*, Milan.
Batinski, E. (1991), 'Horace's Rehabilitation of Bacchus', *CW* 84, 361–74.
Benton, C. (2003), 'Bringing the Other to Center Stage: Seneca's *Medea* and the Anxieties of Imperialism', *Arethusa* 36, 271–86.
Biondi, C. G. (1984), *Il Nefas Argonautico: Mythos e Logos nella Medea di Seneca*, Bologna.
Boyle, A. J. (2011), *Seneca, Oedipus*, Oxford.
―――― (2014), *Seneca, Medea*, Oxford.
Bramble, J. C. (1974), *Persius and the Programmatic Satire*, Cambridge.
Coffta, D. J. (2001), *The Influences of Callimachean Aesthetics on the Satires and Odes of Horace*, Lewiston.
Commager, S. (1962), *The Odes of Horace: A Critical Study*, New Haven.
Curley, T. F. (1986), *The Nature of Senecan Drama*, Rome.
Davis, G. (1991), *Polyhymnia. The Rhetoric of Horatian Lyric Discourse*, Berkeley.
Davis, P. J. (1993), *Shifting Song: The Chorus in Seneca's Tragedies*, Hildesheim.
Farrell, J. (1991), *Virgil's Georgics and the Traditions of Ancient Epic*, Oxford.
Fitch, J. G. (1987), *Seneca's Anapaests. Metre, Colometry, Text and Artistry in the Anapaests of Seneca's Tragedies*, Atlanta.
Fowler, D. P. (1995), 'Horace and the Aesthetics of Politics', in: S. J. Harrison (ed.), *Homage to Horace: A Bimillenary Celebration*, Oxford, 248–66.
Freudenburg, K. (1993), *The Walking Muse: Horace on the Theory of Satire*, Princeton.
Goldhill, S. (1991), *The Poet's Voice. Essays on Poetics and Greek Literature*, Cambridge.
Gowers, E. (1993), *The Loaded Table*, Oxford.
―――― (2012), *Horace, Satires Book I*, Cambridge.
Graver, M. (2014), 'Honeybee Reading and Self-Scripting: *Epistulae Morales* 84', in: J. Wildberger, M. L. Colish (eds.), *Seneca Philosophus*, Berlin, 269–93.
Hardie, P. R. (1986), *Virgil's Aeneid: Cosmos and Imperium*, Oxford.
―――― (2009), *Lucretian Receptions*, Cambridge.
Harrison, S. J. (2007), *Generic Enrichment in Vergil and Horace*, Oxford.
―――― (2013), 'Didactic and Lyric in Horace *Odes* 2: Lucretius and Virgil', in: T. D. Papanghelis, S. J. Harrison, S. Frangoulidis (eds.), *Generic Interfaces in Latin Literature: Encounters, Interactions and Transformations*, Berlin, 367–74.

---

[57] Harrison 2007 especially 198–206, and in similar spirit Hutchinson 2013, 29 on Horace as more wide-ranging (and particularly more Pindaric) than his lyric persona claims.
[58] Henderson 1995, 115 on Sen. *Medea* as anticipating Juv. 1.10–11.

Henderson, J. (1983), 'Poetic Technique and Rhetorical Amplification: Seneca, *Medea* 579–669', in: A. J. Boyle (ed.), *Seneca Tragicus*, Berwick, 229–51.

―――― (1995), 'Pump up the Volume: Juvenal, *Satires* 1.1–21', *PCPS* 41, 101–37.

Hill, D. E. (2000), 'Seneca's Choruses', *Mnemosyne* 53, 561–87.

Hinds, S. (2011), 'Seneca's Ovidian *Loci*', *SIFC* 9, 5–63.

Hine, H. M. (2000), *Seneca: Medea*, Warminster.

Hutchinson, G. (2013), 'Genre and Super-Genre', in: T. D. Papanghelis, S. J. Harrison, S. Frangoulidis (eds.), *Generic Interfaces in Latin Literature: Encounters, Interactions and Transformations*, Berlin, 19–34.

Jakobi, R. (1988), *Der Einfluß Ovids auf den tragiker Seneca*, Berlin.

Littlewood, C. A. J. (2004), *Self-Representation and Illusion in Seneca's Tragedy*, Oxford.

Lowrie, M. (1997), *Horace's Narrative Odes*, Oxford.

Mayer, R. (1982), 'Neronian Classicism', *AJP* 103, 305–18.

Mazzoli, G. (1996), 'Orazio e il sublime', in: P. V. Cova (ed.), *Doctus Horatius, Atti del Convegno di Studi per Virginio Cremona (Brescia 9–10 febbraio 1995)*, Milan, 21–40.

Nagy, G. (1986), 'Pindar's *Olympian* 1 and the Aetiology of the Olympic Games', *TAPA* 116, 71–88.

Nisbet, R. G. M. and Hubbard, M. (1970), *A Commentary on Horace Odes, Book I*, Oxford.

―――― (1978), *A Commentary on Horace Odes, Book II*, Oxford.

Nisbet, R. G. M. and Rudd, N. (2004), *A Commentary on Horace Odes, Book III*, Oxford.

Nussbaum, M. (1994), 'Serpents in the Soul: A Reading of Seneca's *Medea*', in: *The Therapy of Desire: Theory and Practice in Hellenistic Ethics*, Princeton, 439–83.

Oliensis, E. (1988), *Horace and the Rhetoric of Authority*, Cambridge.

Owen, W. H. (1970), 'Time and Event in Seneca's *Troades*', *WS* 4, 118–37.

Pucci, J. (1992), 'Horace and Virgilian Mimesis: A Re-reading of *Odes* 1.3', *CW* 85, 659–73.

Rimell, V. (2012), 'The Labour of Empire: Womb and World in Seneca's *Medea*', *SIFC* 10, 211–38.

Santirocco, M. S. (1986), *Unity and Design in Horace's Odes*, Chapel Hill.

Schiesaro, A. (1992), 'Forms of Senecan Intertextuality', *Vergilius* 38, 56–63.

―――― (2003), *The Passions in Play. Thyestes and the Dynamics of Senecan Drama*, Cambridge.

―――― (2009), 'Horace's Bacchic Poetics', in: L. B. T. Houghton and M. Wyke (eds.), *Perceptions of Horace: a Roman Poet and his Readers*, Cambridge, 61–79.

Segal, C. (1983), 'Dissonant Sympathy: Song, Orpheus and the Golden Age in Seneca's Tragedies', in: A. J. Boyle (ed.), *Seneca Tragicus*, Berwick, 229–51.

Seidensticker, B. (1985), '*Maius solito*: Senecas Thyestes und die *tragoedia rhetorica*', *AA* 31, 116–36.

Shelton, J. A. (1975), 'Problems of Time in Seneca's *Hercules Furens* and *Thyestes*', *CA* 8, 257–69.

Spika, J. (1890), *De imitatione Horatiana in Senecae canticis chori*, Vienna.

Stevens, J. A. (1999), 'Seneca and Horace: Allegorical Technique in Two Odes to Bacchus (Hor. "Carm." 2.19 and Sen. "Oed." 403–508', *Phoenix* 53, 281–307.

Syndikus, H. P. (1972), *Die Lyrik des Horaz: eine Interpretation der Oden*, Darmstadt.

Tarrant, R. J. (1985), *Seneca's Thyestes*. Atlanta.

Trinacty, C. V. (2007), 'Seneca's *Heroides*: Elegy in Seneca's *Medea*', *CJ* 103, 63–78.

―――― (2014), *Senecan Tragedy and the Reception of Augustan Poetry*, Oxford.

Willett, J. (1964) *Brecht on Theatre: The Development of an Aesthetic*, New York.

Zwierlein, O. (1986), *Senecae, Tragoediae*, Oxford.

Christopher Trinacty
Tragic *Translatio*: *Epistle* 107 and Senecan Tragedy

'Translations are inevitably partial: meaning in a text is always overdetermined, and the information in a source text is therefore always more extensive than translation can convey. Conversely, the receptor language and culture entail obligatory features that shape the possible interpretations of the translation, as well as extending the meanings of the translation in directions other than those inherent in the source text.'[1]

Introduction

In spite of his protests that he writes letters off-the-cuff (*inlaboratus et facilis*, *Ep.* 75.1), Seneca's epistles are well-crafted compositions exhibiting a variety of rhetorical techniques and discriminating erudition.[2] Their epistolarity stresses their place within the tradition of letters in antiquity, whether Ciceronian or Epicurean,[3] and highlights their textual nature, as Wilson comments:

> Seneca's adoption of the epistle form relocated philosophical language from an ostensibly oral into an unambiguously textual condition. Texts can be reread, criticized and interpreted more closely and in more leisurely circumstances than oral performances ... Consequently the manner of expression becomes elevated in significance as a permanent marker of the philosopher's quality of mind and character and as a constituent of meaning.[4]

In this paper I argue that *Epistle* 107 acts as a paradigmatic example not only of Seneca's epistolary technique, but also of his tragic compositions. This epistle features an original Latin translation of a hymn of Cleanthes, which stresses the importance of living one's life according to fate. Placed near the conclusion of the letter in a position of prominence, this poem acts as the final summation of Seneca's philosophical argument, and also reflects upon itself as an act of translation. When translating Cleanthes' poem, Seneca follows the tragic meter of the original (iambic trimeter), includes phrases that resemble those of his tragedies,

---

[1] Tymoczko and Gentzler 2002, xviii.
[2] Cf. Currie 1966; Coleman 1974; Henderson 2004; Edwards 2005, 277–9; Wilson 2001, 2007; Wilcox 2012.
[3] Cf. *Ep.* 21.4, 117.3–5, 108.30–34, 118 (and *Ep.* 107 below) for mentions of Cicero in the *Epistulae*; as emulations of earlier philosophers, cf. Inwood 2007.
[4] Wilson 2007, 436.

provides additional layers of meaning through the use of intertextuality, and ties the poem into the fabric of the letter as a whole through intratextual repetitions. These repetitions indicate the importance of the new context for the source material and guide the reader to an interpretation of Cleanthes' poem. A similar hermeneutic of translation is found throughout his tragedies when Seneca actively translates Greek material, and reveals a shared compositional style between his tragedies and his prose works. While I do not believe that Seneca composed his tragedies with the Greek originals cluttering his desk, I do believe that certain moments of the tragedies come about from direct consultation of a Greek model.[5] After considering *Epistle* 107, I will turn to two examples from his tragedies in which Seneca practices a similar methodology in his translation of Greek poetry. These translations are marked, much like the translation of *Ep*. 107, as moments in which Seneca displays a rich bilingual *contaminatio* that both engages in metaliterary play and reinforces themes of the works.

Epistle 107 in its Epistolary Contexts

Epistle 107 acts as a *consolatio* to Lucilius, who is grieving because a certain number of his slaves have fled while he was attending to business elsewhere. Seneca contends that such a loss is an everyday occurrence (*nihil horum insolitum, nihil inexpectatum est, Ep*. 107.2) and certainly nothing to distress the would-be Stoic philosopher. Through linguistic repetition, Seneca also ties this loss into the *Epistulae Morales* as a whole. Earlier in the collection, Seneca commended Lucilius for treating his slaves as friends, writing that such an action befitted his 'prudence and erudition' (*hoc prudentiam tuam, hoc eruditionem decet, Ep*. 47.1). Thus his initial 'where is that prudence of yours?' (*ubi illa prudentia tua?, Ep*. 107.1) denotes a continuation of Lucilius' character from an earlier epistolary time.[6] In addition, Lucilius' 'subtlety in examination' (*in dispiciendis rebus subtilitas, Ep*. 107.1) is likewise strongly connected to the previous letter, where Seneca imagines Lucilius' disapproving words about the discussion at hand (the corporeality of the Good): 'we're playing games here. Subtlety is being worn away in pointless unessentials. These questions do not produce good people, merely learned ones' (*latrunculis ludimus. In supervacuis subtilitas teritur;*

---

[5] Tarrant 1978 offers the most succinct expression of Seneca's independence from the fifth century Attic tragedians. A glance at recent commentaries (e. g. Boyle 2014), however, reinforces the importance of the Greek originals for certain imagery, scenes, and *sententiae*.
[6] These are the only two times *prudentia* is modified with *tua* in all of Seneca's letters.

non faciunt bonos ista, sed doctos, *Ep.* 106.11).[7] These examples of intratextual repetition within the corpus of *Epistulae Morales* indicate that Seneca is interested in placing his letters in a dialogue with one another to create thematic and philosophical connections.

Seneca goes on to describe life's journey as a harsh business (*non est delicata res vivere*, *Ep.* 107.2) and encourages Lucilius to rehearse the sort of hardships that may occur by practicing a *praemeditatio malorum futurorum* (*Ep.* 107.3–4).[8] In doing so, one should recall the lessons Vergil offers; Seneca quotes from the *Aeneid*, describing the denizens of the underworld that will meet us at our death:

luctus et ultrices posuere cubilia curae
pallentesque habitant morbi tristisque senectus. (*Ep.* 107.3 = *Aen.* 6.274–5)

Grief and avenging Cares have settled there,
Pale sickness and grievous old age reside as well.

Epistle 107 is the centerpiece of three letters (*Ep.* 106–108) that consider, in part, the works of philosophical poets (like Cleanthes) and the application of other literature (Vergil, especially) for philosophical ends.[9] As a hinge between *Epistle* 106 and 108, this recollection is important because at the conclusion of *Ep.* 106 Lucilius was presented as wondering if we waste our time in our obsessive study of literature (*litterarum ... intemperantia*, *Ep.* 106.12) because it does not help us develop 'a good mind' (*ad mentem bonam uti litteris*, *Ep.* 106.12). In contrast, Seneca will go on in the subsequent letter to talk about the philosophical benefits of Vergil's poetry, culminating in a discussion of this very line of the *Aeneid* (*Ep.* 108.24–9)![10] There (*Ep.* 108.29) he mentions that it should not be odd that different readers (philosophers, philologists, grammarians) extract different information from a single text – after all, Seneca explains, the same field will provide grass for cows, lizards for storks, and rabbits for dogs to consume.[11] So great

---

[7] Cf. Inwood 2007 for this translation (modified) and discussion of this letter. Note how *subtilitas* is an issue that has both positive and negative connotations in the *Epistulae Morales* (*Ep.* 82.24, 88.43, 95.61, 113.1 – in connection with *prudentia*, 113.4).
[8] For more on this practice, cf. Armisen-Marchetti 1986.
[9] Seneca places these letters in dialogue with one another by recalling similar passages, themes, and authors. Cleanthes and Vergil appear in both *Ep.* 107 and *Ep.* 108, and certain elements of *Ep.* 106, such as the corporeality of bodies, may derive from Cleanthes (*Ep.* 106.4, cf. *SVF* I 518). Note that, in *Ep.* 33, Cleanthes becomes an important foil for Lucilius' own philosophical progress.
[10] Seneca quotes Cleanthes on the effectiveness of poetry for philosophical *sententiae* at *Ep.* 108.10.
[11] This acts as a further way to instill in Lucilius the correct way to read these lines – as if to say to him, 'you should know how to interpret this line, if you properly read the previous letter!'

works of literature can support multiple interpretations; a passage from the *Aeneid*, Seneca suggests in this letter, can be used within the Stoic activity of *praemeditatio*, and, if done correctly, 'you will not be a mere schoolboy in the face of such evil' (*hoc cogitatio adsidua praestabit, ut nulli sis malo tiro, Ep.* 107.4).[12]

Seneca infuses the latter half of this letter with language that both foreshadows and reflects the philosophical content of Cleanthes' hymn, while also musing on the art of translation. The incorporation of language from his Latin version in the larger context of the letter is a technique that Seneca practices elsewhere in his prose and poetic works, and thus is an important aspect of Seneca's reception of his Greek (and Roman) predecessors.[13] Seneca introduces his translation of Cleanthes with a humorous jab at Cicero and his role as a translator of Greek philosophy into Latin (*Ep.* 107.10–12):[14]

> et sic adloquamur Iovem, cuius gubernaculo moles ista derigitur, quemadmodum Cleanthes noster versibus disertissimis adloquitur, quos mihi in nostrum sermonem <u>mutare</u> permittitur Ciceronis, disertissimi viri[15], exemplo. Si <u>placuerint</u>, <u>boni</u> consules;[16] si displicuerint, scies me in hoc <u>secutum</u> Ciceronis exemplum:
>
> Duc, o parens celsique dominator poli,
> quocumque <u>placuit</u>: nulla parendi mora est;
> adsum inpiger. Fac nolle, comitabor gemens
> <u>malusque patiar</u> facere quod licuit <u>bono</u>.
> Ducunt volentem fata, nolentem trahunt.[17]
>
> Sic vivamus, sic loquamur; paratos nos inveniat atque <u>inpigros</u> fatum. Hic est magnus animus qui se ei tradidit: at contra ille <u>pusillus</u> et degener, qui obluctatur et de ordine mundi male existimat et <u>emendare</u> mavult deos quam se. Vale.

---

12 Thus connecting this examination of and musing on literature with the negative conclusion of *Ep.* 106, where it appears that we learn merely for the sake of learning (*non vitae sed scholae discimus, Ep.* 106.12).
13 Cf. Trinacty 2014, 26–61, for further examples.
14 McElduff 2013, 162, finds *Ep.* 58 particularly indicative of 'Seneca's textual and philosophical struggles with Cicero' in the realm of translation. Additional translations of Greek material in his letters are not prefaced with such care (cf. *Ep.* 49.12, 115.14).
15 At *Ep.* 118.1 Seneca likewise styles Cicero a 'most learned man,' only to criticize his epistolary topics. Does this jab at Cicero ultimately stem from Catullus, *Carm.* 49.1 (<u>Disertissime Romuli nepotum</u>)?
16 Cf. *De Beneficiis* 5.17.1ff. with the use of *boni consules* to help explicate a line of Vergil's *Aeneid*.
17 Epictetus quotes Cleanthes' original (*Ench.* 53.1): ἄγου δέ μ', ὦ Ζεῦ, καὶ σύ γ' ἡ Πεπρωμένη,/ὅποι ποθ' ὑμῖν εἰμι διατεταγμένος:/ὡς ἕψομαί γ' ἄοκνος· ἢν δέ γε μὴ θέλω,/κακὸς γενόμενος, οὐδὲν ἧττον ἕψομαι. Setaioli 2014, 283–4 n. 55, believes Seneca's expanded version is due, in part, to mixing details taken from a commentary on Cleanthes' hymn.

And so let us address Jove, by whose governance the entirety of the universe is guided, how our Cleanthes addresses him in most learned verses, which is it permitted for me to change into our language by the example of Cicero, a most learned man. If they please you, you are a good judge; if not, know that I am only following Cicero's example:

Lead, O father and ruler of high heaven,
Wherever it pleases you: there is no delay to my obedience;
I am present without delay. Like it or not, I will follow
Groaning, I, an evil man, suffer to do what a good man chooses.
Fate leads the willing, but drags the unwilling.

Let us live thus, and speak thus; let fate find us prepared and enthusiastic. This man has a great spirit, who handed himself over to fate: but that man is wretched and feeble, who struggles and reckons wrongly the order of the world and prefers to change the gods, rather than himself. Farewell!

Dahlmann has pointed out a number of the similarities/differences between the original and Seneca's version, stressing that Seneca has highlighted the poetic license he applies to his production (*quos mihi in nostrum sermonem mutare permittitur*).[18] Seneca often uses the term *mutare* to indicate the process of translation and relates this to the larger philosophical concept of the letter: namely to pay attention to what one is able to change and what one must accept (*Ep.*107.7–8).[19] Additional metaliterary language dealing with the very act of translation comes in the form of *sequor*, a verb embedded in the Cleanthes poem itself (a literal translation of the final two lines would read 'indeed I will follow [you] without delay; but even if I am unwilling/being evil, nevertheless I will follow').[20] While Seneca cautiously avoids using forms of *sequor* to translate ἕψομαι, he does use this verb in each of the previous four paragraphs, leading one to believe that he may be play-

---

18 Dahlmann 1977, 350. Setaioli 2014, 283–5, determines that 'Seneca's translation shows that for him the choice between following or not, between being good or bad, is in our power.'
19 Cf. *Ep.* 58.7: *magis damnabis angustias Romanas, si scieris unam syllabam esse, quam mutare non possum* ('you will rail against Roman limits all the more, if you know there is a word of one syllable which I am unable to translate'). For more on the terms of translation, cf. McElduff 2013, 189–96. Setaioli 2014, 278 remarks on the power of philosophy to influence moral progress and self-transformation, 'to which one can turn regardless of whether one believes in fate, providence, or mere chance.'
20 Seneca makes use of similar language when discussing his philosophical progress at *Ep.* 80.1: *non ergo sequor priores? Facio, sed permitto mihi et invenire aliquid et mutare et relinquere* ('Therefore, do I not follow my predecessors? I do, but I allow myself to discover something new, to change, and to renounce'). Additional metaliterary language in this letter includes *composuerat* (*Ep.* 107.4), *quo auctore* (*Ep.* 107.9), *intextum* (107.10, cf. *Ep.* 94.27) and *derigitur* (*Ep.* 107.10) – a verb used by Cicero when discussing his translations of Demosthenes and Aeschines (*Opt. Gen.* 23).

ing with his avoidance of it in his translation.[21] For example, in the previous section, Seneca writes, 'it is best to attend god without complaint; he is a bad soldier who follows his commander with groans' (*optimum est ... deum ... sine murmuratione comitari; malus miles est qui imperatorem gemens sequitur*, *Ep.* 107.9). Seneca is priming the reader for his translation of Cleanthes' poem by using language at this point of the letter that he will reclaim in the translation (note his choice to use *comitabor* there). In doing so, Seneca shows how the translation fits in with the general thrust and push of the ethical teaching at hand and that the act of translation can be a metaphor for the ethical changes that Lucilius must undergo. Terms such as *patior, impiger* and *emendare* also appear numerous times in the previous four paragraphs, including the phrase 'it is best to endure what you are unable to change' (*optimum est pati, quod emendare non possis*, *Ep.* 107.9). This stresses that Seneca believes that literary 'emendation' will occur just as well as ethical 'emendation' in the course of this epistle. *Emendare* then appears at the conclusion of the letter as a way of summing up the faulty view of the individual who has not trusted himself to fate, 'that man is wretched and feeble (*pusillus*), who struggles and reckons wrongly the order of the world and prefers to change (*emendare*) the gods, rather than himself.'[22] The use of *emendare* here as earlier reveals the slippage this term from moral reform to textual reform, just the sort of reform that Seneca has practised in his translation.[23]

Seneca's translation must not be viewed within a vacuum, but rather as part of this carefully constructed letter. It aims to illuminate the themes that Seneca has been working on through the latter half of the letter and works as a final

---

[21] *Sequor* can also be seen as a signpost of *imitatio* and *aemulatio*, such as, famously, Lucretius 3.3 or Statius *Thebaid* 12.817. Cf. Peirano 2009, 161 n. 41 for more on this use of *sequor*. But also see Quint., *I.O.* 10.1.122, where it is used in a context of rhetorical *imitatio* and *aemulatio* and Horace, *Ars* 119 (*famam sequere*). Quintilian believes that 'the grammatical paradigm for translation is essentially grounded in the terms of rhetorical imitation' (Copeland 1991, 25).

[22] This also recalls the opening of the letter, where Seneca writes of the meager (*pusilla*) issue now tormenting Lucilius (*Ep.* 107.1). If you allow such miniscule things to affect you, you show yourself to be a 'weakling' (*pusillus*). *Emendare* had also been used to indicate Seneca's moral progress at *Ep.* 6.1. Note how speaking and living are equated so the 'textuality' of the individual is encouraged (thus foreshadowing *Ep.* 114 and the motto, *talis hominibus fuit oratio qualis vita*, *Ep.* 114.1).

[23] Cf. Too 1994, 216–19, on *emendare* in the corpus of Seneca's letters and the *compositio* of the soul (cf. *Ep.* 4.1 and *Ep.* 107.4). Staley 2010, 144 n. 15 disagrees with some of Too's more radical ideas, 'While I agree with Too that Seneca's language of moral reform would have had literary overtones for a Roman audience, I emphasize that for Seneca the moral meaning of *emendare* is always primary.'

poetic call-to-arms. It is clear that Seneca views Cleanthes as another example of a poet-philosopher, much like Seneca himself.

Epistle 107 in its Literary Contexts

A closer look at the translation itself indicates that Seneca is interested in rendering the Greek material through the Latin literary and rhetorical tradition:

> Duc, o parens celsique dominator poli,
> quocumque placuit: nulla parendi mora est;
> adsum inpiger. Fac nolle, comitabor gemens
> malusque patiar facere quod licuit bono.
> Ducunt volentem fata, nolentem trahunt.

This is *not* the word-for-word translation that Cicero and Horace find so problematic,²⁴ but it has been updated to Seneca's own time and is replete with his rhetorical and literary tricks-of-the-trade. Summers points out that the first three lines find parallels in Seneca's tragedies, so the diction is undoubtedly Senecan.²⁵ The meter (following the original) likewise matches Seneca's iambic trimeters, and the final line certainly is a *sententia* worthy of Seneca and may indicate his own interpretation of Cleanthes' original four-line hymn (of course, as we have just seen, the intratexts hint that this sort of elaboration is part of the act of translation). In fact, this final line takes up language found in the work of Seneca the Elder, both in one of the headings to a *controversia* ('A father tries to stop his son who has acted heroically three times and wants to go to fight a fourth time, he disinherits his son who refuses him' *ter fortem pater in aciem quarto volentem exire retinet; nolentem abdicat*, 1.8)²⁶ and in a line from another *controversia* ('she was not led but dragged the whole way', *et toto*

---

24 Cic. *Opt. Gen.* 14, Hor. *Ars* 131–5. For more on the general theory of translation in antiquity, cf. Kytzler 1989 and McElduff 2013.
25 Summers 1905, *ad loc.* An additional intertext may be found in Seneca's *Troades*, when Hecuba follows Ulysses; *Tro.* 993–4: *Duc, duc, Ulixe, nil moror, dominum sequor;/me mea sequentur fata* ('Lead, lead, Ulysses, I do not delay, I follow my master;/my fate will follow me').
26 This may evoke some of the military imagery found at *Ep.* 107.9–10. In his *De Beneficiis*, Seneca is fond of juxtaposing these words: *quod volens acceperis, nolenti reddere* (4.40.4), *quod a nolente accepi, volens reddam?* (6.10.1). Note that the practice of repeating wording found in the theme at some point, usually the conclusion, of one's declamation occurred often enough that Cestius gave it a term 'echo' and would humorously comment on other declaimers' use of this *figura* (*Contr.* 7.7.19).

itinere non ducitur sed trahitur, 2.5.3).[27] In addition, a fragment of the Elder's work cited in Quintilian features the line 'Lead me, I follow, take this old hand of mine and direct it where you will' (*duc, sequor: accipe hanc senilem manum et quocumque vis inprime ... I.O.* 9.2.42). With help from his father's language, Seneca hones his rhetorical edge, compact *sententiae*, and vivid descriptions; so vivid, in fact, that Quintilian comments on that fragmentary line of the Elder's work, 'this figure is too dramatic: for the story seems to be acted, not narrated' (*habet haec figura manifestius aliquid; non enim narrari res, sed agi videtur, I.O.* 9.2.44). Once a dramatist, always a dramatist?

Seneca's own tragedies furnish intertexts that help to clarify his philosophical point. The *Phaedra* (composed before this letter)[28] features a choral ode beginning 'O nature, great mother of the gods' (*O magna parens, natura, deum*, 959). This ode focuses especially on the order of *natura* in comparison with human disorder, and the letter previously mentions the way *natura* should be viewed as an *exemplum* of the proper attitude towards the hurdles of life (and, of course, as a good Stoic, one should 'follow Nature as a guide').[29] In addition, Vergil's *Aeneid* also lurks behind some of Seneca's wording; when Anchises recognizes a sign from heaven as indicative of Jupiter's will and claims, 'Now, now there is no delay and I follow, and where you lead, there I am, gods of the fatherland!' (*iam iam nulla mora est; sequor et qua ducitis adsum,/di patrii, Aen.* 2.701–2).[30] This recollection models the way one should respond to the decrees of fate or the gods, and advocates the willing acceptance of what must be done. As in his allusive tragedies, so in his translations of Greek material Seneca supplements his poetry with intertextual traces that reinforce his message.

These intratextual and intertextual connections reveal how Seneca will often make reference to Latin poetry, philosophy, and rhetoric in the very act of translating from the Greek. This letter foregrounds the very act of translation, and Seneca incorporates and emphasizes metaliterary language about translation and

---

[27] Cf. *Dial.* 1.5.6.7 *fata nos ducunt* ... In the context of this letter, one may wonder about the etymology of 'fate' as something said before (*fari*) and the possible literary antecedents to this phrase. Cf. Bettini 2008, 315–17 and Setaioli 2014, 294 n. 130 claims 'the very etymology of *fatum* encouraged a Roman Stoic to conceive of fate as a series of uttered propositions.'

[28] According to most scholars, cf. Fitch 1981; Coffey and Mayer 1990, 3–5; Marshall 2014, 37–41.

[29] Cf. *Ep.* 107.7–8 for *natura* as exemplum and the language there repeated in the translation (*mutare, bono, patiamur, mutationibus*). For more on 'following nature' cf. Setaioli 2014, 397 n. 161. Boyle 1987, *ad* 959 for more on the connections between the *Phaedra* and this translation of Cleanthes.

[30] Cf. *Aen.* 12.11 (*nulla mora in Turno est*), a line Seneca quotes in his *de Beneficiis* 6.41.2 with supplementary discussion and application in the context of gift-giving.

adaptation in order to call attention to his own abilities and tendencies as a translator.[31] His translations thus act as marked moments in Seneca's works in which he illustrates his own distinctive abilities as a poet and interpreter of the past.

Tragic Translatio

Can we see a similar contextualization of translated material in the tragedies? The primary example of a moment in which Seneca translates Greek material is found in his *Hercules Furens* – namely the opening ode's strong connections to Euripides' *Phaethon*. Diggle, expressing the party line of previous critics of Senecan tragedy, finds that Seneca exploits Euripides' brief and incisive illustration 'to tedious excess' while recognizing 'That the one ode was written with full knowledge of the other is beyond dispute'.[32] While Seneca follows Euripides' topics for the most part, he also elaborates certain sections such as his opening twelve lines on the constellations in order to keep with 'the general emphasis in this play on the heavens and their phenomena'.[33] In fact, Seneca will often find ways to contextualize the Greek material within his own tragic context, and supplement that material with additional Latin intertexts. In regards to the *Hercules Furens*, Fitch, Jakobi, and Littlewood have recognized the way that Seneca cleverly includes allusions to Ovid's version of the Phaethon myth to endorse his own reading of Ovid's version as dependent in some sense on Euripides' (Fitch notes, 'clearly Seneca associated Ovid's version with Euripides' play').[34] One can note additional connections that merge the Greek and Latin sources in a fruitful manner – for instance, the description of the nightingale in Seneca's song both looks back to the Euripidean original, and is also rife with connections to Ovid's description of the myth of Procne and Philomela as well as intratextually linked to

---

31 By incorporating such references to translation, Seneca is making apparent a general truth of translation, as Benjamin posits, 'But translation, unlike an original work, does not see itself as within the forest depths of language but rather outside it, facing it; without itself entering those depths, it calls the original inside, at that one point where, at a given moment, the echo in the translator's language can resound to the work in the foreign language' (Benjamin 1968, 88).
32 Diggle 1970, 96.
33 Fitch 1987, 159.
34 Fitch 1987, 159; Jakobi 1988, 7; Littlewood 2004, 107–27, for an in-depth investigation of the importance of Phaethon for the characterization of both Hercules and Juno as well as for the Senecan sublime. The cross-pollination of Ovid and Euripides is also found in the examples below and is representative of Seneca's translation technique in the tragedies.

the *Hercules Furens*.³⁵ Seneca's identification of the nightingale as *Thracia paelex* (149) clearly responds to Ovid *Met.* 6.537: *omnia turbasti; paelex ego facta sororis*, which may add dark implications to Seneca's *turba* (150, of nestlings), and also recalls Juno's opening comments of the play, as she fulminates against Jove's *paelices* (3, 4). Intratextual repetitions include the sounds of the nightingale (*stridula*, 146; *sonat*, 150), which reappear during Hercules' murderous rampage, describing the whistle of an arrow (*stridet*, 993) and the fracturing of a skull (*sonuit*, 1007). Fitting, considering the nightingale's song is one of lament (as stressed in Euripides), and also suitable to Seneca's tragic context.

Continuing the theme of lament, the *Troades*' first choral passage involves an antiphonal song between the Trojan women and Hecuba in which they mourn Hector and Priam in a call-and-response structure similar to the *kommos* of Euripides' *Troades* (153ff.). Seneca's chorus highlights the ritual language of mourning and allows Seneca to muse upon the position of Hecuba and the Trojan women, once again grieving and seemingly used to it – the chorus' first words are 'You order no inexperienced crowd unused to tears to mourn' (*non rude vulgus lacrimisque novum/lugere iubes*, 67–8).³⁶ Their repeated actions (and the very theme of repetition) can be highlighted by one moment in this choral exchange when the chorus describes Echo as 'dwelling in hollow caves' (*habitansque cavis montibus Echo*, 109).³⁷ This repeats the words of Euripides' Agamemnon in his *Hecuba* (1109–13):³⁸

> Οὐ γὰρ ἥσυχος
> πέτρας ὀρείας παῖς λέλακ' ἀνὰ στρατὸν 1110
> Ἠχὼ διδοῦσα θόρυβον: εἰ δὲ μὴ Φρυγῶν
> πύργους πεσόντας ᾖσμεν Ἑλλήνων δορί,
> φόβον παρέσχεν οὐ μέσως ὅδε κτύπος.

> For in no quiet tones did
> Echo, child of the rocky cliff, raise a cry throughout the
> host. If we did not know that Troy's towers had fallen to
> the Greek spear, this noise would have caused us alarm
> in no small degree! (trans. Kovacs)

---

35 The dawn-song of *Phaethon* was notable in part because of its self-referentiality and its use as a pre-wedding song for the play. In Seneca's *Hercules Furens* additional language may be metapoetically referring to the very act of translation (*tradere*, 147; *murmure mixto*, 151), especially poignant as the nightingale's song in Euripides was described in a way that may recall Callimachean poetics (λεπτάν ... ἁρμονίαν), but now muddled and confused (*confusa*)?
36 Boyle 1997, 119 finds that Hecuba 'trains the chorus of Trojan women to play their prescribed roles.'
37 Schiesaro 2003, 190–202, on repetition in *Troades*. This is the most emphatic personification of Echo in all of Euripides, so it may have motivated Seneca's use in this instance.
38 Calder 1970 points out the elaboration of Euripides, although he believes that the *Hecuba* should not be thought of as a source for Seneca's *Troades* as a whole.

Agamemnon's rationale is interesting here: the sound of Polymestor's mourning and his cries for help are so great that Agamemnon would have thought that the Trojans were attacking. For a reader who thinks about the way such echoes can resound through the literary accounts and the mythological timeline, one can see that the sequel to the suffering of Seneca's chorus and Hecuba will be Polymestor's own lamentation (in a sense, the final attack of the Trojans on a Greek ally).[39] Of course, Echo is ultimately more identified with Roman mythology and Ovid's *Metamorphoses*, and Seneca enriches his account with a quotation from Ovid's epic. Ovid delimits Echo's ability as follows, 'as is permitted, that one [Echo] is prepared to await the sound, to which she may send back her own words' (*quod sinit, illa parata est/exspectare sonos, ad quos sua verba remittat*, 3.377–8).[40] Seneca cleverly quotes Ovid's exact words in his chorus (108–13):

> *Rhoetea* sonent *litora* planctu,
> habitansque cavis montibus Echo
> non, ut solita est, extrema brevis
>   verba remittat: 110
> totos reddat Troiae *gemitus*,
> *audiat* omnis *pontus* et aether.

> Let the Rhoetean shores resound with mourning,
> Let Echo, who dwells in mountain caves, not
> Send back briefly the final words, as expected:
> Let her give back all the groans of Troy,
> For the sea and sky to hear.

In the spirit of allusive *aemulatio*, Ovid's Echo is quoted only to be surpassed (*non, ut solita est*).[41] Seneca's chorus blends the representation of Echo from Ovid's *Metamorphoses* as well as the mention of Echo from Euripides' *Hecuba*, but hopes

---

39 Is Seneca indicating allusively that his version will combine the murderous actions of the *Hecuba* with the *Troades*, as Ovid had done (cf. *Met.* 13.408–571 and Curley 2013, 102–15)? Surprisingly Seneca will join the sacrifices of Polyxena and Astyanax, 'there seems to be no precedent in the tragic tradition for combining in this manner the fates of the two Trojan youths' (Schiesaro 2003, 193).
40 Jakobi 1988, 21 points out additional recollections from Ovid's account. This formulation bookends Echo's relationship with Narcissus – his final words are repeated *remisit/verba locus* (*Met.* 3.500–1).
41 For Fantham 1982, *ad loc.* this is a 'frigid conceit.' Cf. Hinds 1998, 5–8, for Echo 'as the trope of mannered repetition, within texts and between texts.' Following Hinds' lead, one may find Hecuba's recognition of the Trojan women (*agnosco Troada turbam*, 95) may also be a version of 'allusion troped as recognition' (Hinds 1998, 9) and indicate the long textual tradition of mourning Trojan women.

to outdo them in part through the further repetition of this antiphonal lament. Seneca provides a panorama of the sufferings of the Trojan women that linguistically stresses repetition: for instance the final two lines of this choral section respond to the final two lines of Hecuba's beginning: *solitum flendi vincite morem./Hectora flemus* (*Tro.* 97–98) ~ *non sum solito contenta sono./Hectora flemus* (*Tro.* 115–16).[42] The larger call for the Rhoetean shores to ring with mourning will be repeated at the conclusion of the play because Achilles' tomb borders Rhoeteum's shallows (*Rhoetea ... vada*, 1122) where both Trojans and Greeks mourn Polyxena's death, 'both sides weep: but the Phrygians emit a timid sob while the victorious side groans more loudly' (*uterque flevit coetus; at timidum Phryges/misere gemitum, clarius victor gemit*, 1160–1). In addition, the use of Echo may encourage the reader to look for additional 'echoes' in these lines, and this is rewarded by finding recollections of Catullus 65 and Ovid's *Ibis* which resound in this tragic context.[43]

When Seneca writes of the death of Hippolytus, he relies primarily on Ovid's *Metamorphoses* 15, but also appears to translate certain sections of Euripides' *Hippolytus*. For instance, when the messenger tells of the size of the wave in Euripides' play, he claims (1207–9):

> ὥστ' ἀφῃρέθη
> Σκίρωνος ἀκτὰς ὄμμα τοὐμὸν εἰσορᾶν,
> ἔκρυπτε δ' Ἰσθμὸν καὶ πέτραν Ἀσκληπιοῦ
>
> My eye lost sight of Sciron's ridge,
> And the Isthmus and Asclepius' cliffs were hidden.[44]

This description is missing from Ovid's account, but Seneca's messenger includes it (1022–4):

---

42 Additional repetitions include *felix primus* (145, 157, 161) – it is likewise a recollection of both Ovid (*Met.* 13.520, 521) and Euripides' *Hecuba* (620–1), cf. Curley 2013, 155–6.
43 *Rhoeteo ... litore* also appears at Cat. 65.7, when he writes about the death of his brother at Troy. Ov. *Ibis* 29: *audiat hoc Pontus ...* may be another apposite intertext, especially as he is writing from exile on the shores of the Black Sea and the chorus is contemplating exile from their homeland.
44 Both Euripides and Seneca name Sciron's cliff as a mark of Theseus' heroic deeds, for Euripides it is a way for Theseus to justify his banishment of Hippolytus 'For if I am to be bested by you when you have done this to me, Isthmian Sinis shall no longer attest that I killed him but say it was an idle boast, and the Skironian rocks near the sea shall deny that I am a scourge to evildoers!' (976–80, trans. Kovacs). For Seneca a possible *exemplum* of suicide: 'Should the top of pine forced to the ground split me in two as it shoots to heaven, or should I drop headlong from Sciron's cliff?' (1223–5).

<u>latuere</u> rupes numine Epidauri dei
et scelere petrae nobiles Scironides
et quae duobus terra comprimitur fretis.

The cliffs sacred to Epidaurus' god were hidden,
And the rocks of Sciron, famous for his crime,
And the land that is hemmed in by two straits.

On first glance, it seems like a straightforward translation of the Euripidean lines (note how the two verbs occur in the same initial position, occupying three-quarters of the iambic metron), but Seneca makes sure that while his language recalls Euripides' terms, it also fits in with the verbal matrix of the *Phaedra*. If Euripides' wave hid (ἔκρυπτε) the Isthmus and Asclepius' ridge, this shows the importance of this verb of concealment for the play as a whole: whether it is Phaedra bidding the nurse to hide her head because of her shame (243, 245), her desire to hide her malady (279, 394), the Nurse wondering how to hide her ill-advised revelation to Hippolytus (674), Hippolytus telling Theseus not to hide what's on his mind (915), or Hippolytus' final request of Theseus to hide his face in death (1458). One can trace a thematic arc within the play through this verb that such suppression and repression builds up until its eventual tragic explosion.[45] Seneca's own reading of Euripides' *Hippolytus* picked up on the thematic use of this verb. One can find Seneca pursuing a similar arc with his use of *latere*, which the Nurse marshals against Phaedra repeatedly when trying to dissuade her from her passion (151, 158) and which Phaedra uses of the fiery passion 'hiding' in her breast (643). But Seneca also enriches this *imitatio* by intertextually including pertinent information from Ovid's telling of the tale. At the conclusion of Hippolytus/Virbius' story in the *Metamorphoses*, we read (*Met.* 15.543–6):

'qui' que 'fuisti
Hippolytus,' dixit 'nunc idem Virbius esto!'
hoc nemus inde colo de disque minoribus unus   545
numine sub dominae <u>lateo</u> atque accenseor illi

She said, 'You who once
Were Hippolytus, now will be Virbius!'
From that time I live in this grove and, as one of the lesser gods,
I hide under the divinity of my mistress and am assigned to her.

---

45 Each is consistent with his use of this verb in the play (192, 243, 245, 250, 279, 394, 674, 915, 1209, 1222, 1247, 1290, 1458).

By inscribing this nod to Ovid (and one can find additional moments in which he alludes to the survival of Virbius – an issue of some debate among Augustan poets),[46] Seneca indicates how he can combine the Euripidean and Ovidian motifs in his own translation and how such *contaminatio* acts to bridge the Greek and Latin traditions in an wholly Senecan manner.[47] Greek and Latin, Euripides and Ovid come together in this allusive *aemulatio* that shows how Seneca places these previous renditions in dialogue with one another and may give the reader some hope at this moment that Hippolytus may live on, hidden in another land and under an assumed name (although the final transformation into *disiecta membra*[48] of bloody meat probably crushes any such hope ...).

Conclusion

In looking at these examples of Seneca's translation technique, we can observe how Seneca employs these moments to reflect on his compositions and contemplate the two worlds (Greek and Roman) that he mediates in his translations. The source text is modified in its new context, whether moral epistle or Roman tragedy and its integration into that particular context and genre is facilitated and enhanced by intratextual and intertextual connections. Seneca's writings are incredibly self-conscious of their position as texts, and these translations touch upon metaliterary language and figures of thought to help celebrate the diversity of influences that shaped his own consciousness. The works of his father, the Augustan poets, and Greek poets and philosophers are blended together with an eye to expressing his own particular take on the subject at hand, whether ethical encouragement or tragic suffering. Seneca suggests that texts and characters (even the self) are constructs that can be emended, improved upon, or torn to pieces.

---

46 Cf. *Aen.* 7.761–82, Ov., *Fast.* 3.261–6, 6.733–62, and Hor., *Carm.* 4.7.25–8 in addition to Ov., *Met.* 15. *Phd.* 820–4 can be compared to *Met.* 15.538–40 and *Phd.* 847–8 to *Met.* 15.531–2.
47 Directly after these three lines, he launches into another Ovidian adaptation, cf. Jakobi 1988, *ad loc.*
48 Cf. *Phd.* 1256. The Horatian intertext here likewise figures the body as text (*Serm.* 1.4.62), cf. Most 1992 for more on the rhetoric of dismemberment in Seneca.

Bibliography

Armisen-Marchetti, M. (1986), 'Imagination et méditation chez Sénèque: L'exemple de la 'praemeditatio'', *REL* 64, 185–95.
Benjamin, W. (1968), 'The Task of the Translator', (trans. J. Hynd and E. M. Valk), *Delos* 2, 76–96.
Bettini, M. (2008), 'Weighty Words, Suspect Speech: *Fari* in Roman Culture', *Arethusa* 41, 313–75.
Boyle, A. J. (1987), *Seneca's Phaedra*, Leeds.
―――― (1997), *Tragic Seneca: An Essay in the Theatrical Tradition*, London and New York.
―――― (2014), *Seneca: Medea*, Oxford.
Calder, W. M. (1970), 'Originality in Seneca's *Troades*', *CP* 65, 75–82.
Coffey, M. and R. Mayer (1990), (eds.), *Seneca: Phaedra*, Cambridge.
Coleman, R. (1974), 'The Artful Moralist: A Study of Seneca's Epistolary Style', *CQ* 24, 276–89.
Copeland, R. (1991), *Rhetoric, Hermeneutics, and Translation in the Middle Ages*, Cambridge.
Curley, D. (2013), *Tragedy in Ovid: Theater, Metatheater, and the Transformation of a Genre*, Cambridge.
Currie, H. MacL. (1966), 'The Younger Seneca's Style: Some Observations', *Bulletin of the Institute of Classical Studies* 13, 76–87.
Dahlmann, H. (1977), 'Nochmals 'Ducunt volentem fata, nolentem trahunt'', *Hermes* 105, 342–51.
Diggle, J. (1970), *Euripides: Phaethon*, Cambridge.
Dominik, W./J. Hall (2007), (eds.), *A Companion to Roman Rhetoric*, Oxford.
Edwards, C. (2005), 'Epistolography', in: S. Harrison (ed.), *A Companion to Latin Literature*, Oxford, 270–84.
Fantham, E. (1982), *Seneca's Troades*, Princeton.
Fitch, J. G. (1981), 'Sense-Pauses and Relative Dating in Seneca, Sophocles, and Shakespeare', *AJP* 102, 289–307.
―――― (1987), *Seneca's Hercules Furens*, Ithaca.
Harrison, S. J. (2001), (ed.), *Texts, Ideas and the Classics: Scholarship, Theory, and Classical Literature*, Oxford.
Henderson, J. (2004), *Morals and Villas in Seneca's Letters: Places to Dwell*, Cambridge.
Hinds, S. (1998), *Allusion and Intertext: Dynamics of Appropriation in Roman Poetry*, Cambridge.
Inwood, B. (2007), 'The Importance of Form in Seneca', in: R. Morello and A. D. Morrison (eds.), *Ancient Letters: Classical and Late Antique Epistolography*, Oxford, 133–48.
Jakobi, R. (1988), *Der Einfluß Ovids auf den Tragiker Seneca*, Berlin.
Kytzler, B. (1989) ''Fidus Interpres': The Theory and Practice of Translation in Classical Antiquity', *Antichthon* 23, 42–50.
Littlewood, C. (2004), *Self-Representation and Illusion in Senecan Tragedy*, Oxford.
Marshall, C. W. (2014), 'The Works of Seneca the Younger and Their Dates', in: G. Damschen and A. Heil (eds.), *Brill's Companion to Seneca: Philosopher and Dramatist*, Leiden, 33–44.
McElduff, S. (2013), *Roman Theories of Translation: Surpassing the Source*, London.

Most, G. W. (1992), '*Disiecti membra poetae:* The Rhetoric of Dismemberment in Neronian Poetry', in: R. Hexter and D. Selden (eds.), *Innovations of Antiquity*, New York and London, 391–419.
Peirano, I. (2009), '*Mutati Artus*: Scylla, Philomela and the end of Silenus' Song in Virgil Eclogue 6', *CQ* 59, 154–62.
Schiesaro, A. (2003), *The Passions in Play:* Thyestes *and the Dynamics of Senecan Drama*, Cambridge.
Setaioli, A. (2014), 'Ethics III: Free Will and Autonomy', in: G. Damschen and A. Heil (eds.), *Brill's Companion to Seneca: Philosopher and Dramatist*, Leiden, 277–99.
Staley, G. A. (2010), *Seneca and the Idea of Tragedy*, Oxford.
Tarrant, R. J. (1978), 'Senecan Drama and its Antecedents', *HSCP* 82, 213–63.
Too, Y. L. (1994), 'Educating Nero: A Reading of Seneca's *Moral Epistles*', in: J. Elsner and J. Masters (eds.), *Reflections of Nero: Culture, History, and Representation*, Chapel Hill, 211–24.
Trinacty, C. (2014), *Senecan Tragedy and the Reception of Augustan Poetry*, Oxford.
Tymoczko, M./E. Gentzler (2002), (eds.), *Translation and Power*, Amherst and Boston.
Wilcox, A. (2012), *The Gift of Correspondence in Classical Rome*, Madison.
Wilson, M. (2001), 'Seneca's *Epistles* Reclassified,' in: S. Harrison (ed.), *Texts, Ideas and the Classics: Scholarship, Theory, and Classical Literature*, Oxford, 164–87.
─────── (2007), 'Rhetoric and the Younger Seneca', in: W. Dominik and J. Hall (eds.), *A Companion to Roman Rhetoric*, Oxford, 425–38.

Stavros Frangoulidis
Seneca's *Agamemnon*: Mycenaean Becoming Trojan

Introduction

Seneca's *Agamemnon* dramatizes the murder of the play's eponymous hero by his wife Clytemnestra and her lover Aegisthus, following the king's victorious return from Troy.[1] Clytemnestra is thus seen to exact revenge on her husband for murdering Iphigenia and leading an adulterous life with Cassandra, among other offences, whereas Aegisthus punishes his uncle Atreus for the Thyestean feast by murdering his son. Although Clytemnestra and Aegisthus' plot appears as a private act of revenge, motivated by personal grievances, it has clear political implications as well, for it leads to a change in the public sphere with the shift of power in Argos at the play's end. The play can thus be seen as a revenge drama, designed to render justice for wrongs done in the *domus*.

Perhaps most importantly, the fact that Seneca chooses to include Cassandra in his retelling of the myth advances an original view of the deeds taking place inside the palace at Mycenae, according to which Agamemnon's murder and the destruction of the fleet are to be viewed as a re-enactment of Priam's death and the fall of Troy. As king of Argos, Agamemnon stands as an embodiment of the entire city. In fact, Cassandra goes so far as to claim that the defeated Trojans have won a military victory over their captors at Mycenae, in revenge for Greek atrocities at Troy (869b-71). Such an interpretation of the murder turns what initially appears to be an act of individual vengeance with undoubted political impact into an event of historical and cosmic proportions.

The differing Mycenaean and Trojan perspectives on events run through the play. Though the poet cannot alter the core plot, he can add new elements to it.[2] By merging two different viewpoints, Seneca brings Agamemnon's guilt all the more to the fore, rendering his death a suitable outcome.

Scholars have read the Argive king's death as a re-enactment of the fall of Troy, as featured in parts of the play. Thus A. J. Boyle points out several analo-

---

[1] The text of Seneca is from Zwierlein (1986). English translations of *Agamemnon* are by Fitch (2004), whereas Vergil's rendering in English follows Fairclough and Goold (2006).
[2] Motto and Clark (1988, 166) see a structural division in the play: the first one focuses on the familial theme, whereas the second on the Greek/Trojan connections and the ending thereof.

gies in the play between Troy and Argos, which lead to a sense of history repeating itself.[3] In a short but brilliant analysis, Alessandro Schiesaro notes how by looking backwards to Troy, Cassandra is able to see the breaking down of historical progression, and to foretell that it is now the Greeks who will suffer.[4] In a more recent and comprehensive study, Schiesaro addresses the issue of the play's dramatic structure and also discusses the analogies between Argos and Troy.[5] While exploring various Augustan literary antecedents, most recently Christopher Trinacty has seen Cassandra as a surrogate poet and has further drawn attention to a number of analogies between Argos and Troy.[6]

This paper concentrates on a hitherto overlooked aspect of Seneca's *Agamemnon*: the continual interaction between two diverse viewpoints concerning the protagonist's death, one Mycenaean and the other Trojan. From the Mycenaean perspective, Clytemnestra and Aegisthus understand Agamemnon's murder as the result of their desire to avenge the king's ill-treatment of the royal *domus*. Cassandra, on the other hand, offers the Trojan standpoint: she views Agamemnon's murder and the earlier damage to the Argive fleet as re-enacting Priam's death and the destruction of Troy; the conquered Trojans are thus given the opportunity to triumph over their captors. This innovative retelling of past events adds a noteworthy Roman touch to the plot and, what is more, crucially underscores Seneca's originality in dealing with a traditional myth.

The dramatic tradition before Seneca

Let us start with an overview of the few instances prior to Seneca where Cassandra hints at the theme of Agamemnon's death as punishment for Greek atrocities against Troy. In Aeschylus' *Agamemnon*, Cassandra foretells the king's death and assuages fears about her own demise by reflecting that Agamemnon will meet a fortune similar to that of the Trojans (1287). Similarly, in a conversation between Cassandra and her mother in Euripides' *Troades*, the future 'queen' views herself as an instrument of revenge, claiming that her marriage will lead to the king's death and the destruction of the palace; she further asserts that she will descend

---

[3] Boyle 1983, 200–02. On the cyclical construction of history see also Tola (2009) 92–94.
[4] Schiesaro 2003, 202–04.
[5] Schiesaro 2014, 182–84; 186–88.
[6] Trinacty 2014, 204–13, *passim*.

victorious into the realm of the dead.[7] However, in the Euripidean play Cassandra reads events from the *oikos* perspective: she makes these remarks while still at Troy, and furthermore views herself as a means of avenging the death of her father and brothers. We have a few further fragments from earlier Roman plays, including *Aegisthus* by Livius Andronicus and *Clytemestra* by Accius. The paucity of evidence makes it difficult to determine the perspective adopted in these plays. If this is not due to the poor transmission of such early plays, then one may conclude that Seneca is innovating in adding Roman coloring to the original plot, because the Romans viewed themselves as descendants of the Trojans.[8]

The play

Seneca's play opens with the appearance of Thyestes' ghost from the Underworld. The ghost familiarizes the audience with past family grievances and foretells future action (1–56). The ghost perceives events from a Mycenaean perspective, insofar as Thyestes assesses them from an intrafamilial point of view, unrelated to events at Troy.

The sight of Atreus' palace with its dining hall brings to mind the hideous memory of having been tricked into eating his children (5–6).[9] The intensity of Thyestes' horror becomes clear from his desire to return to the nether world and see the mythic sinners. Reference to Orcus' palace prompts his comparison with the sinners of the lower world, considering himself as surpassing all of them for two reasons: (1) he has eaten his children's flesh and (2) he has carried out Fortuna's order to sleep with his daughter and produce Aegisthus, so as to exact revenge on his brother (22–36). Thyestes' consciousness of his criminal nature is meant to trigger audience expectations about the nature of the revenge drama to be acted out. In relation to dramatic time, the fact that Fortuna's prophecy can only be fulfilled now, following Agamemnon's ten-year absence overseas, explains why the ghost of Thyestes now rises from the lower world to open the play. What is more, at this point the Argive king is at the height of his glory, while Clytemnestra and Aegisthus are in love with each other.

---

[7] Eur. *Tro.* 353–54, 356–64, 403–05, 445–47, 456–81. See Liedloof 1902, 16; Ntina Gakopoulou (*per literas*) reads Cassandra in the *Troades* as a means of Troy to avenge itself.
[8] As Henderson (2009, 34) puts it: "In the national legent, Troy was the origin of Rome, through diaspora of refugees."
[9] See Braund 2013, 427.

As a figure coming from the other world, and therefore endowed with prophetic vision, the ghost announces Agamemnon's victorious return from Troy, and refers to the circumstances of his death, which is to occur in a festive setting, involving deceit. The fact that he goes on to urge his wavering son to participate in the murder, as the conditions of his birth have now been met, may hint at a meta-dramatic departure from the Aeschylean model, in which Aegisthus shies away from carrying out the deed (*Ag.* 1635), yet claims to be the brains behind it (*Ag.* 1604, also 1627).[10] Having illuminated past and future action, the ghost descends into the lower world.

All of Act II dramatizes the efforts made by both Clytemnestra and Aegisthus to assume a meta-dramatic role as makers of fiction to exact revenge on Agamemnon for intrafamilial grievances. Whereas Clytemnestra and Aegisthus view their act as merely private vengeance, the political implications of the regicide for Argos are also apparent, if one takes into account that Agamemnon is head of state.

First, Clytemnestra appears on stage and exhorts herself to devise a trick to take revenge on her husband. The meta-dramatic dimension of her endeavor is stressed by her desire to follow in the footsteps of figures of tragedy, such as Stheneboea, Phaedra and Medea. On the other hand, the nurse recommends self-restraint and spousal loyalty, which could be read as an attempt to prevent the plot from moving forward.[11] However, Clytemnestra indicates four reasons why she must go ahead with the ruse: (1) the sacrifice of Iphigenia (162–73); (2) Agamemnon's infidelities (174–88a); (3) jealousy of Cassandra (188b-91); and (4) fear that Agamemnon will kill her first for her marital infidelity (192–94).

In a similar vein, when Aegisthus appears on stage, he encourages himself to cast aside his fears and avenge himself on his cousin for the Thyestean feast, and further calls on Clytemnestra to act as an accomplice to the murder (226–38). In the presence of Aegisthus, Clytemnestra expresses a desire to secure her marital bliss, perhaps because of the influence earlier exerted on her by the nurse; however, Aegisthus, whose plot presupposes the involvement of the queen, eventually succeeds in persuading her to return to her initial resolve. Clytemnestra's subsequent exhortation to her lover to head indoors, where they can make common cause in plotting their revenge, points to their both assuming the role of poets within the play, that is, fabricators of the central plot structure (308–09).[12] What is

---

[10] In Aeschylus' *Agamemnon*, Clytemnestra is the contriver of the trick and Aegisthus (most likely) simply encourages her: 1379, 1406.
[11] A near similar exchange between the nurse, who advises restraint, and her mistress is seen in Seneca's *Medea*. On this see Boyle 2014, 165.
[12] Clytemnestra and Aegisthus act as savvy slaves do in Plautus, self-consciously mounting a plot within the larger drama.

more, later, at 983, Electra identifies Aegisthus as *sceleris ... artifex*, possibly for his role in persuading her mother to change her mind and co-operate with him.

Enacted as a meta-play, the ruse involves using a cloak to murder the king during the festivities for his return (402–03; 583–85; 778b-81; 791; 881–83a).[13] Clytemnestra impersonates the faithful wife; as Clytemnestra's lover, Aegisthus can only join her in the murder at the point when Agamemnon puts on the cloak, allegedly woven by his loyal wife, and is therefore no longer able to resist. The act of revenge, preceded by a plot, is in accord with the sequence of events as seen, e. g., in Seneca's *Thyestes*: Atreus first devises the trick in which he feigns reconciliation with his brother and then murders his children. In a similar vein, in Seneca's *Medea*, Medea initially comes up with a ruse to kill Creusa and Creon through bridal gifts, poisoned by Medea's magic arts, and then murders her children. This regicidal ruse is consistent with Seneca's approach in other plays and therefore generally the tragic *genus*, capitalizing on disasters befalling a royal *domus*.

The meta-dramatic performance begins in Act III. Eurybates, messenger of Agamemnon, enters the stage announcing his master's victorious return (402–03). The messenger reflects the Mycenaean perspective of events, viewing the Greeks as victorious. Upon learning of the messenger's report, Clytemnestra declares festivities to mark the occasion, as befits her role as actor in the meta-dramatic plot. The queen's concern over the fortune of Menelaus and her sister shifts the focus of the messenger's report from Agamemnon's return to the near-total destruction of the Argive fleet, which he explains as divine retribution for the Greek atrocities at Troy (577). Yet, in spite of the heavy damage befalling the fleet, Eurybates considers Agamemnon as having achieved a great victory over Troy, in accordance with the mythical plot. After expressing uncertainty as to whether to rejoice or lament, Clytemnestra restates her intention to declare celebrations, lending new impetus to the ruse.

Despite being motivated by intrafamilial grievances, the revenge plot gradually acquires a completely different dimension: politics renders it an act of historical significance of universal proportions. This is a new and original interpretation of the mythical plot, which takes into account the status of Agamemnon as a king; in his capacity as a sovereign, he appears as an incarnation of the city as a whole. An almost similar shift of focus from familial sin to issues of dynastic politics appears in Seneca's *Oedipus*.[14] In the latter, as David Konstan compellingly argues, Seneca superimposes on the Sophoclean account of fate and pollution a tale of forcible

---

[13] For the meta-dramatic dimension of plots, devised by trickster slaves, in Plautine plays, see Slater 2000. Also Schiesaro 2003, 56.
[14] Konstan 1994, 11–14.

usurpation of power which demands revenge: "[w]hile Laius reproaches Oedipus with parricide and incest, his anger is motivated by an attack upon himself as king of Thebes and it is this insult to his dignity and position that he wishes to avenge".[15]

The recasting of events begins in Act IV, when Cassandra pulls off her sacred diadems (693–94), since she does not see any further sense in carrying on her cultural role as Troy's *vates*. This behavior may be related to resentment over the loss of her homeland and the death of her entire family (693–709). Furthermore, as Agamemnon's mistress Cassandra can no longer be a prophet. Yet, Cassandra soon falls into a manic frenzy, thus indicating the special role reserved for her as *vates* even after the fall of Troy, a fact that she is unable to comprehend at this stage.

In her subsequent prophecy, Cassandra presents the situation in Mycenae in terms of and as parallel to past events at Troy. In a vision, she sees two suns, a double Argos and two palaces (726–40). One of these two sets refers to the final day at Troy and Priam's palace, events and places that Cassandra has recently experienced. The other refers to the present: the day of Agamemnon's return, the city of Argos and the Mycenaean palace. This doubling allows Cassandra to present Mycenae in terms of Troy: she sees Mount Ida and Paris, meaning Aegisthus.[16] The vision establishes a parallel between the two cities. As a *vates*, Cassandra is able to prophesy future events that the audience onstage is unable to know: Agamemnon will die at the hands of Clytemnestra and Aegisthus. These events do *not* find their analogue at Troy: Priam was killed by Pyrrhus at the altar of Hercean Jupiter (Verg. *Aen.* 2.550b; 2.557b-58). However, Cassandra equates the fortunes of two kings on the basis of parallelisms between Troy and Mycenae. Cassandra escaped the death in the first Troy, but in the second she foretells her own demise: she sees her own relatives, who are calling her from the realm of the dead, and assures them of her readiness to join them.

Recently, Trinacty has observed the connection between Cassandra, narrating her vision of Agamemnon's death, and Thyestes, who rises up from the other world to foretell his vision of Agamemnon's death, and has further observed that "for Cassandra, Agamemnon's killing is in recompense for the Greek actions at Troy, not familial bloodshed".[17]

---

15 Konstan 1994, 12. In the same article Konstan (p. 23), cites Cicero, *Phil.* 2.13.31 and observes that under an autocracy an offense against blood is subordinate to a crime against the supreme authority.
16 Boyle (1983, 201) observes the analogy between Agamemnon and Priam (514, 794, 879f.), between Argos and Troy (644f., 728f., 971f., 875f.) and between the Argive chorus and the deluded Trojan *pubes* and *festae matres* (310ff. and 638ff.).
17 Trinacty 2014, 209.

In terms of the present analysis, one may also argue that in both instances the speaker addresses his or her respective audience onstage: Thyestes calls upon his son Aegisthus (47b-52), whereas Cassandra invites all Trojan souls, her relatives included, to turn their eyes to Mycenae and watch the action unfolding (756–58). Yet, Cassandra clearly views events from a broader historical perspective, in accord with her status as a princess, insofar as she views Argos in terms of Troy.[18] On the other hand, Thyestes assesses the events as an act of private revenge inside the *domus*. The political motives of the act are also apparent for the audience as Agamemnon is king of Argos. Moreover, Aegisthus does not respond to his father's plea, perhaps in order to suggest his wavering over meeting the condition of his birth, whereas the souls in the underworld interact with Cassandra. What is more, the dramatic conflict between Argives and Trojans onstage is transferred to the lower world: Tantalus is in sorrow over the imminent death of his grandchild (769–72), whereas Dardanus is joyful at the prospect of his opponent being punished (773–74).

The representation of current events at Argos from a wider historical perspective, in terms of Troy and the past, continues to be seen in the ensuing stichomythia between Agamemnon and Cassandra, who is still in a state of frenzy. The king orders Cassandra to recover her senses, and invites her to make offerings to the altars and pray to Jupiter, as the day is festive (791–99):[19]

> [Ag.] festus dies est. [Ca.] Festus et Troiae fuit.
> [Ag.] Veneremur aras. [Ca.] Cecidit ante aras pater.
> [Ag.] Iouem precemur pariter. [Ca.] Herceum Iouem?
> [Ag.] Credis uidere te Ilium? [Ca.] Et Priamum simul.
> [Ag.] Hic Troia non est. [Ca.] Vbi Helena est, Troiam puta.   795
> [Ag.] Ne metue dominam famula. [Ca.] Libertas adest.
> [Ag.] Secura uiue. [Ca.] Mihi mori est securitas.
> [Ag.] Nullum est periclum tibimet. [Ca.] At magnum tibi.
> [Ag.] Victor timere quid potest? [Ca.] Quod non timet.

---

18 Cassandra seems to recall the Vergilian Sybil, who sees the Trojan 'wars renewed' in Italy, so she specifically defined Aeneas' mission as retaliation for the Trojan disaster (Verg., *Aen.* 6.86b-94).
19 See Boyle 1983, 201. Schiesaro 2003, 202–04; also Shelton 1983, 174. Shelton further points out the contrast with Agamemnon in the *Troades* (263–73) who is a more perceptive person: he acknowledges that Priam makes him proud but also fearful because of the instability of fortune. Furthermore, Calder (1976, 31) observes that: "The Senecan king enters at 781 and exits at 807 (twenty-six verses later). His function is to elicit from Cassandra in tight epigrammatic *antilabai* the information that establishes him as the deutero-Priam, the *semper idem* motif (31) that we have already noted in the Tantalus-Thyestes equation of Thyestes." Lohikoski (1966, 63–70) examines the presence of the motif of Mycenae-Troy in the exchange between Agamemnon and Clytemnestra as well as in the entire play.

[Ag.] This is a festive day! [Ca.] It was festive too at Troy.
[Ag.] Let us do reverence at the altar. [Ca.] Father fell before an altar.
[Ag.] Let us pray to Jove together. [Ca.] Hercean Jove?
[Ag.] You think you see Ilium? [Ca.] Yes, and Priam as well.
[Ag.] Here is not Troy. [Ca.] Where Helen is, I think it Troy.
[Ag.] Do not fear your mistress, though a slave. [Ca.] Freedom is close.
[Ag.] Live in security! [Ca.] For me death is security.
[Ag.] There is no danger for you. [Ca.] But great danger for you.
[Ag.] What can a conqueror fear? [Ca.] What he does not fear.

Here Agamemnon views events at Argos from a narrower perspective, with reference to the present, which he knows. On the other hand, Cassandra makes meaning of the present through reference to the Trojan past she has experienced. She identifies Argos as another Troy, for reasons very similar to those mentioned by the king: (a) the festive day; and (b) the presence of the altars at which her father lost his life. Representation of Argos as another Troy allows Cassandra to prophesy that Agamemnon will have a fate similar to that of Priam, especially considering that Cassandra identifies Clytemnestra with Helen, the cause of the Trojan War. This reading seems to have been anticipated by Clytemnestra, who at 190 identifies Agamemnon as Priam's son-in-law: *Priami gener*. In meta-theatrical terms, Cassandra exposes the illusion of the plot within the larger drama. However, Agamemnon, being a native of Argos, who knows both the location and its inhabitants, dismisses any such association between Troy and Mycenae. What is more, he assures Cassandra of her safety and views himself as invincible, ironically failing to perceive Cassandra's insinuation that his very intrepidity as conqueror will lead to his death. His ensuing prayers and offerings to Jupiter and later to Juno recall the Chorus' earlier reference to the offerings made at the altars of Troy, when the horse was being dragged into the city, increasing the sense of foreboding in the play (644–45).

This wider interpretation of individual revenge for grievances inside the royal *domus*, itself an act of political significance, is clearly seen at the beginning of Act V, where Cassandra narrates Agamemnon's murder.

In her new vision, Cassandra is able to detail offstage action, occurring inside the palace (867–909). She thus appears in a position analogous to that of a tragic messenger, in the sense that she is not an eyewitness to the events she narrates.[20] Cassandra interprets the event taking place indoors as a re-enactment of Priam's death and the fall of Troy.[21] This recasting of the king's murder in terms of the

---

[20] Trinacty (2014, 214) observes the double function of Cassandra as *vates* and messenger.
[21] Zanobi (2014, 121–23) has read Cassandra's vision of Agamemnon's killing, as narrated by Cassandra, from the perspective of pantomimic performances.

Trojan past allows Cassandra to claim that Troy has been metaphorically reborn, enabling the defeated Trojans to win a military victory over their captors, comparable to that of their opponents (869b): *vicimus victi Phryges* ('we have conquered Phrygians!'). As king, Agamemnon serves as an incarnation of the city as a whole; thus, his murder leads to the rebirth of Troy and its vengeance on her captors. So too, at *Aeneid* 4.670–71, Vergil likens the suicide of the abandoned queen Dido to the capture and devastation of Carthage or Tyre by an enemy attack: *non aliter quam si immissis ruat hostibus omnis/Karthago aut antiqua Tyros.*

There are at least three ways, in which Cassandra clearly turns what is essentially a private act – revenge inside the palace – into an event of world-historical dimensions, re-enacting the situation at Troy. First, the lavish dinner indoors is likened to the last feast of the Trojans (876).[22] Secondly, there is abundant purple and the cup of Assaracus, which were looted from Troy (878).[23] Third, as a mark of identity the Argive king dons Priam's royal attire (881–83a).[24] This garment prompts Clytemnestra to ask her husband to wear a cloak woven by her, thus preserving the illusion that she is a loving wife. The cloak suggests the climax of the ruse; the wearing of it terminates the illusion of the inset play. Here one could argue for a remote parallel with the Trojan Horse, when the door of its belly is opened and the Achaeans come out, leading to Priam's death and the fall of his city.[25] What is more, as the Trojans receive warnings not to trust the offering of the Greeks, so Agamemnon is admonished by Cassandra regarding his imminent death.

As an intruder into the palace, Aegisthus can make his entrance and deal the first blows only when the king is unable to move his hands, in compliance with both the meta-dramatic ruse and the order of events, outlined by Thyestes' ghost at the opening of the play. Agamemnon eventually faces the harsh reality as he tries to disentangle himself from the cloak. It is at this point that the Argive king finally perceives the irony of his previous exchange with Cassandra: the one thing he was incapable of contemplating was that the conqueror could become the vanquished, even if, as Schiesaro notes, the opposite does not apply to the Trojans.[26]

The portrayal of the king falling dead near the altars, likened to a boar slaughtered in a sacrifice, brings to mind Priam, who met his death at the altar of

---

22 Schiesaro 2014, 184.
23 Schiesaro 2014, 184.
24 Shelton 1983, 175; and Trinacty 2014, 213 and n. 82.
25 A near similar parallel is found in Seneca's *Medea*. In that play Medea destroys Jason's new bride and her father through gifts, poisoned by Medea's magic arts. This testifies to the regal greediness as far as gift donations are concerned.
26 Schiesaro 2003, 203.

Hercean Jupiter (Verg. *Aen.* 2.550b-53).[27] The ensuing cutting of the king's body into pieces by the regicides may recall the Vergilian image of Priam's decapitation, when he is turned into a *truncus*, perhaps as a symbolic act, given the fact that Priam is 'the ruler of Asia' (*Aen.* 2.557b-58). The horror of the crime is only to be anticipated since Cassandra identifies Aegisthus as the offspring of Thyestes on the one hand, and Clytemnestra as Helen's sister on the other (907). Aegisthus was conceived with the sole purpose of exacting revenge. By getting involved with him, Clytemnestra became responsible for the 'war' at Mycenae, just as her sister's involvement with Paris was the cause of the Trojan War.

This interpretation of revenge for intrafamilial grievances and the resulting shift of power in the palace, finally appears at the play's end, from an entirely original perspective, as an event of significant historical proportions. Clytemnestra is determined to put her rival Cassandra to death for taking her husband away from her, ironically failing to take into consideration that Cassandra was the spoil of war, whereas she has had an affair with Aegisthus for many years. Cassandra eagerly embraces death, so as to convey to the Trojan souls the news of the destruction of the Argive fleet, the capture of Mycenae and the death of the king as retribution for Greek atrocities overseas (1004b-09):

> repletum ratibus euersis mare,
> captas Mycenas, mille ductorem ducum,   1005
> ut paria fata Troicis lueret malis,
> perisse dono, feminae stupro, dolo.

> How the sea was filled with capsized ships,
> how Mycenae was taken, how the leader of
> a thousand leaders – to meet a fate, commensurate
> with Troy's sufferings – perished by a gift,
> by a woman's lust, by a trick.

Here Cassandra advances an all-embracing reading of the play's events both at sea and Argos from a broader perspective. The damage befalling the Argive fleet, incurred on the return journey, is seen as paralleling the destruction that took place at Troy, while the murder of the Argive king via the ruse appears as a reenactment of Priam's death and the fall of Troy through the trickery of the horse. The Trojan *vates* is able to read the various separate incidents at sea and Argos as

---

[27] Cf. Shelton, who reads Agamemnon falling dead near the altars as a re-enactment of the death of Iphigenia. See also Seidensticker (134, n. 170), who makes a comparison with the Thyestean banquet. However, one must point out that there is no eating involved, as happens in the Thyestean feast.

a whole, and, by extension, as parallel to Troy, because Agamemnon is both commander of the fleet and king of Mycenae. This reading of the play's events in their entirety from a wider perspective enables Cassandra to view the events both at sea and Argos as retribution of the Trojans, avenging themselves on their opponents for their atrocities overseas.

Cassandra's Trojan view is set in direct opposition to the Mycenaean perspective, adopted by both Agamemnon's messenger and the regicides. Eurybates views Agamemnon as having achieved a great military victory over Troy and justifies the heavy damage befalling the Greek fleet, later incurred on the return journey, as divine retribution for Greek atrocities overseas. In a similar vein, the regicides perceive the murder of Agamemnon through the meta-dramatic ruse, as revenge for private grievances, occurring inside the *domus* of Atreus.

On exiting the stage and therefore departing from life, Cassandra's expression of joy at her opponents' defeat suggests that she has at last reached an understanding of her cultural role as a *vates* of Troy, once the city is lost.

Cassandra's descent into the lower world to convey to the Trojan souls her innovative reading of Agamemnon's murder as the destruction of Argos and a Trojan military victory at the play's end (1003–06a) reverses the pattern of Thyestes rising from the realm of the dead at the outset of the play to announce Agamemnon's death upon his victorious return from Troy (39–49a). The parallelism becomes stronger, given the fact that both Thyestes and Cassandra are endowed with prophetic vision. Yet, the ghost perceives Agamemnon's murder merely as private vengeance, whereas Cassandra views the same incident from a broader perspective as an event of historic significance. Thus, the ghost and Cassandra introduce the two different standpoints, one Mycenaean and the other Trojan, interacting through the play.

This constant interplay between the two differing Argive and Trojan perspectives on events enhances Agamemnon's guilt and makes his punishment a fitting retribution for all his crimes within the play's horizon. First, it offers Clytemnestra the chance to exact perfect vengeance on her husband for her own grievances, which include the sacrifice of Iphigenia. Second, it serves as atonement for the Thyestean banquet. These crimes mark a personal vengeance for wrongs committed in the *domus*. The shift of power at Mycenae following the king's murder in the final act also underlines the political impact of the revenge, though Clytemnestra and Aegisthus themselves seem to see their act as merely private vengeance. However, Cassandra reassesses the same event in a new light, as a matter of major importance: a military victory finally scored by a spirit of

Troy over its captors at Argos, as retribution for Greek atrocities overseas.[28] What is more, Cassandra develops her point of view in the enemy territory of Argos where Trojans are also present, albeit as war captives.

Roman coloring

Representation of the revenge on Agamemnon as a military victory in reaction to Priam's death and the fall of his city underscores the work's Roman character, lending the myth a universal and diachronic impact: the myth of Troy is employed, in Roman terms, to illuminate events, occurring some time later at Argos. This is made possible through the extended and dominant presence of a Trojan *vates* in the play, when compared with her more subordinate role in the Aeschylean version. This considerable emphasis placed on the wider dimension of the king's murder adds a noteworthy Roman touch to the mythical plot, enriched with Trojan resonances. What is more, it underscores Seneca's originality in handling the plot, when compared to other treatments of the same event, which place considerably less emphasis on the Trojan element of the traditional myth.

Political resonances

In Roman political terms, the horror aroused by Cassandra, when narrating the slaying of the Argive king and, ultimately that of Priam, could also be read as having contemporary resonances: it may invite the audience to reflect upon the political conditions in which Seneca lived and authored his plays.[29] In imperial Rome, frequent attempts against the lives of emperors were taking place, in the context of dynastic strife or even as an attack against the *princeps*, although many were unsuccessful. For example, there is Cassius Chaerea and Cornelius Sabinus' plot to murder Caligula in fear for their lives (Suet. *Calig.* 58.1–3); more importantly for the case in question, the scheming empress Agrippina the younger purportedly had her husband Claudius killed with poisoned mush-

---

28 The Augustan *topos* of *Troia renascens/resurgens* mainly refers to the building of Troy's kingdom in Latium and strictly speaking does not relate to Seneca's treatment of the myth (Ovid, *Fasti* 1.523–26).
29 Tarrant (1976, 7) considers the play as a youthful production and claims that it might be regarded as Claudian, Gaian or even Tiberean. In all likelihood the play must be one of Seneca's earliest plays.

rooms, so that her son Nero could inherit the throne under her influence (Suet. *Claud.* 44.2). Thus, the plot of regicide could be contextualized within the historical evolution of the late Julio-Claudian period.[30]

Conclusion

Seneca's *Agamemnon* artfully interweaves two themes: a) the revenge of Clytemnestra on her husband for the sacrifice of Iphigenia, among other offences; and b) Aegisthus' revenge for the Thyestean feast. This linkage in turn explains why both Clytemnestra and Aegisthus appear as fabricators of the meta-dramatic ruse to murder the king upon his victorious return from Troy, unlike the Aeschylean model, in which Clytemnestra alone acts out the plot, and Aegisthus only claims to be the brains behind it. However, Cassandra offers a radically new reappraisal of Agamemnon's demise as an event of historical and universal proportions. In this reading, the defeated Trojans are offered the chance to triumph over her captors at Argos. This constant interplay of alternative perspectives, running through the play, makes Agamemnon's death all the more inevitable. Such a treatment of the Argive king's death may also disclose the originality of the Roman tragedian: it makes private vengeance serve a public cause, unlike other treatments, which place considerably less emphasis on the historical dimension of the mythical plot. This proposed reading depends on the assumption that no comparable treatment of the myth appears in the models available to the playwright.

Acknowledgments

I wish to thank David Konstan for his invaluable comments; and Katerina Philippides, Eleni Manolaraki, Stephen Harrison and Gesine Manuwald for their helpful observations.

---

30 For an opposite view see Tarrant 1976, 7.

Bibliography

Audano S. (1998), 'Apollo nel secondo coro dell'Agamennone (vv. 322–339)', *Paedeia* 53, 3–8.
Baerschi, A. M. (2010), 'Drama and Epic Narrative. The Test Case of Messenger Speech in Seneca's *Agamemnon*', in: Ingo Gildenhard and Martin Revermann (eds.), *Beyond the Fifth Century: Interactions with Greek Tragedy from the Fourth Century BCE to the Middle Ages*, Berlin, 249–267.
Bartsch, S. and A. Schiesaro (eds.) (2015), *The Cambridge Companion to Seneca*, Cambridge.
Boyle, A. J. (ed., tr., comm.) (2014), *Seneca: Medea*, Oxford.
_____ (2006), *Roman Tragedy*, London.
_____ (1997), *Tragic Seneca: An Essay in the Theatrical Tradition*, London.
_____ (1987), 'Senecan Tragedy: Twelve Propositions', *Ramus* 16, 78–101.
_____ (1983), '*Hic epulis locus*: The Tragic World of Seneca's *Agamemnon* and *Thyestes*', *Ramus* 12, 199–228.
Braund, S. (2013), 'The Ghost of Seneca in Renaissance Drama', in: Emma Buckley and Martin T. Dinter (eds.), *A Companion to the Neronian Age*, Malden, MA, 425–443.
Calder, W. M. III (1976), 'Seneca's *Agamemnon*', *CP* 71.1: 27–36.
Calder, W. M. (1975), 'The Size of the Chorus in Seneca's *Agamemnon*', *CP* 70, 32–35.
Davis, P. (1993), *Shifting Song: The Chorus in Seneca's Tragedies*, Hildesheim.
Fairclough R. H. and G. P. Goold (eds., tr.) (2006). *Virgil: Eclogues, Georgics, Aeneid I-VI*, Loeb, Cambridge, MA & London.
Fantham, E. (1981–1982), 'Seneca's *Troades* and *Agamemnon*: Continuity and Sequence', *CJ* 77.2, 118–129
Fitch, J. G. (ed., tr.) (2004), *Seneca: Oedipus, Agamemnon, Thyestes, [Seneca]: Hercules on Oeta, Octavia*, Loeb, Cambridge, MA & London.
Fletcher, G. B. A. (1990), 'On Seneca's *Agamemnon*, *Thyestes* and *Hercules*', *LCM* 15, 69–72.
Henderson, J. (2009), *A Plautus Reader: Selections from Eleven Plays*. Mundelein, IL.
Hendry, M. (2000), 'A Beastly Love Triangle? Seneca, *Agamemnon* 737–40', *CQ* 50.1, 317–320.
Henry, D. and B. Walker (1963), 'Seneca and the *Agamemnon*: Some Thoughts on Tragic Doom', *CP* 58.1, 1–10.
Johnston, P. A. (trns.) (2012), *The Aeneid of Vergil*, Norman, OK.
Kirichenko, A. (2013), *Lehrreiche Trugbilder. Senecas Tragödien und die Rhetoric des Sehens*, Heidelberg.
Konstan, D. (1994), 'Oedipus and his Parents: The Biological Family from Sophocles to Dryden', *Scholia* 3, 3–23.
Kugelmeier, C. (2013), 'Agamemnon', in: Gregor Damschen and Andreas Heil (eds.), *Brill's Companion to Seneca: Philosopher and Dramatist*, Leiden, 493–500.
Lavery, J. (2004), 'Some Aeschylean Influences on Seneca's *Agamemnon*', *MD* 53, 183–194.
Liedloff, K. (1902), Die Benutzung griechischer und römischer Muster *in* Seneca's *Troades* und *Agamemnon*, Fürsten- und Landesschule Grimma, 599, 1–18.
Lohikoski, K. K. (1966), 'Der Parallelismus Mykene-Troja in Senecas *Agamemnon*', *Arctos* 4, 63–70.
Mader, G. (1988), '*Fluctibus variis agor*. An Aspect of Seneca's Clytemnestra Portrait', *Acta Classica* 31, 51–70.
Motto A. L. and J. R. Clark (1988), *Senecan Tragedy*, Amsterdam.

Motto A. L. and J. R. Clark (1985), 'Seneca's *Agamemnon*: Tragedy without a Hero', *Athenaeum* 63, 136–144.
Paschalis, M. (2010), 'Cassandra and the Passionate Lucidity of *furor* in Seneca's *Agamemnon*', in: Stavros Tsitsiridis (ed.), *Parachoregema: Studies on Ancient Theatre in Honour of Professor Gregory M. Sifakis*, Heraklion, 209–228.
Philippides, K. (2013), 'On the Fourth Choral Song in Seneca's *Agamemnon*', *Logeion* 3, 120–131.
Schenkeveld, D. M. (1976), 'Aegisthus in Seneca's "Agamemnon"', in: J. M. Bremer, S. L. Radt and C. J. Ruijgh (eds.), Miscellanea tragica *in honorem J. C. Kamerbeek*, Amsterdam, 397–403.
Schiesaro, A. (2014), 'Seneca's *Agamemnon*: The Entropy of Tragedy', *Pallas* 94, 179–191.
_____ (2003), *The Passions in Play. Thyestes and the Dynamics of Senecan Drama*, Cambridge.
Seidensticker, B. (1969), *Die Gesprächsverdichtun in den Tragödien Senecas*, Heidelberg.
Shelton, J. A. (1983), 'Revenge or Resignation: Seneca's *Agamemnon*', *Ramus* 12, 159–183.
Slater, N. W. (2000), *Plautus in Performance. The Theatre of the Mind*, Amsterdam.
Tietze, V. (1987), 'The Psychology of Uncertainty in Senecan Tragedy', *ICS* 12, 135–141.
Tola, E. (2009), 'Una lectura del *Agamemnon* de Séneca: Nefas trágico e imaginario poético', *Auster* 14, 85–99.
Trinacty, C. (2014), *Senecan Tragedy and the Reception of Augustan Poetry*, Oxford.
Watt, W. S. (1985), 'Notes on Seneca, *Agamemnon*', *Phoenix* 39, 162.
Zanobi, A. (2014), *Seneca's Tragedies and the Aesthetics of Pantomime*, London.
Zwierlein, O. (ed.) (1986), *L. Annaei Senecae Tragoediae*, OCT, Oxford.
Θεοδωράκης, Ά. (2001), *Αισχύλου Αγαμέμνων, Σενέκα Αγαμέμνων: σύγκριση δύο τραγωδιών*, Αθήνα.

David Konstan
When Reason Surrenders its Authority: Thyestes' Approach to Atreus' Palace

Seneca's *Thyestes* begins with the complaint of Tantalus' ghost: "Who has dragged me from the baleful abode of those below, where I pursued the food that fled my eager mouth?" (1–2).[1] The Fury that drew him forth tells him a little later in the prologue: "You'll be a guest at a crime not new to you; we have granted you a day off and suspended your hunger for this banquet: sate your starving, let blood mixed with wine be drunk while you look on. I have discovered a feast that you yourself would flee" (62–7). Tantalus would prefer to return to his torture of perpetually frustrated appetite, and threatens to stand his ground and keep clear of the crime. But the Fury has a means of dominating his will: "Why," Tantalus exclaims, "do you terrify my eyes with whips and threaten writhing snakes in your savagery? Why do you rouse the hunger fixed in my deepest marrow? A fire burns my heart, seared with thirst, and flares in my scorched entrails. I follow [*sequor*]" (96–100); to which the Fury replies: "Spread this, this rage throughout the house."

The theme of Tantalus' punishment by thirst and hunger is pronounced. But the torture resides not only in his frustration, but in the fact that he reaches out for the fruit and water even though he knows that they will recede before he can eat or drink of them. The increment in physical need or appetite overpowers his resolution. This is just what happens with his submission to the Fury's demands: as his need is intensified, it overcomes his ability to reason and he pursues what he knows to be vain.

The madness that the Fury sows in the house of Atreus finds expression, no doubt, in the implacable anger of Atreus and his fanatical desire for revenge. But Atreus' depravity is not modelled on Tantalus' behavior. Atreus is perfectly clear-headed about his wishes, and there is no tension between his better judgment and deeper urges that overcome it. Rather, as some scholars have observed, there is a better fit with the behavior of Thyestes in the play. To be sure, Thyestes is nothing like his vicious brother; although he committed a terrible offense against Atreus in the past in seducing his wife and seizing the kingship, and he fully recognizes and accepts his guilt, he has been humbled by his years in exile and acquired what seems like a philosophical or Stoic contentment that does not depend on external possessions – which does not mean that he must reject them,

---

[1] Translations are my own.

only that he does not need them. His comportment in the play has led some to conclude that he is an exemplar of Stoic wisdom, or, if he is not a fully realized sage, then at least a *proficiens*, on the way to understanding. For example, the author of a fine article on Seneca's philosophy and poetry writes: "Atreus' perception of his brother's character is fundamentally one-sided. In the following scene, Seneca introduces Thyestes, who, altered by his years of exile, is nothing like the out-and-out villain Atreus described earlier on … . His analysis is wrong," and the audience will soon "become aware of the complete change that has taken place in Thyestes, and realise that he no longer corresponds to Atreus' image of him; he has been reformed by exile" (Wiener 2014, 200, 208–9).

Now, this conception of a deep transformation has been not so much challenged as nuanced by other scholars. Alessandro Schiesaro, for example, even as he recognizes that a "long-standing tradition … has chosen to recognize in Thyestes a Stoic sage," observes: "The 'moral' aspirations of Thyestes and the chorus … are criticized even as they are apparently endorsed" (Schiesaro 2003, 147–8). Peter Davis, in turn, remarks that Thyestes "is not as indifferent [sc., to power] as he makes himself out to be," and concludes: "There is a discrepancy between Thyestes' professed and his actual values" (Davis 2003, 46–7).

The issue hangs, of course, on Thyestes' hesitations about returning to Argos at Atreus' invitation: though he accepts it as a gesture made in good faith, he feels a deep reluctance: "Seek rather your woodland refuge and the dense groves and a life among and like that of beasts" (412–4); what looked rough was a place where he was bold and happy, whereas now he is in fear: "my mind halts and wishes to turn my body back, I'm taking unwilling steps" (419–20). His son Tantalus is baffled by his father's hesitation, and Thyestes too is confused: "I wish to advance, but my legs totter on sluggish knees, and I am drawn in a direction other than that toward which I'm struggling" (436–7). The young Tantalus praises power, but Thyestes claims it is worthless if you desire nothing; yet he finally yields to his son's persuasion, with the excuse "I follow [*sequor*] you, I do not lead" (489).

Scholars have observed the analogy between Thyestes' acquiescence to his son and the elder Tantalus' submission to the Fury; thus Peter Davis comments: "where Thyestes assigns responsibility for his actions to Tantalus, his son, we might assign responsibility to Tantalus, his grandfather" (2003, 48). Richard Tarrant (1985, 160 ad v. 489) speaks of Thyestes' "pathetic attempt to salve his conscience, which convicts him of failure to fulfill a parent's role as guide and model. Thyestes' willingness to 'follow' links him with Tantalus as seen in the prologue, cf. 100 *sequor* (Tantalus' last word)." Alessandro Schiesaro too notes the echo of the word *sequor* (2003, 149), but he questions the comparison: "The analogy highlights the difference. Tantalus was tortured and in fact has no means of escape from an overwhelming supernatural entity. Thyestes has been engaged in a dialectic exchange with his son which would easily leave room for retreating. The tragic-sounding acceptance of what appears to be an inevitable destiny is totally disproportionate to the situation."[2]

I am inclined to think, however, that the analogy between Tantalus and Thyestes may shed some light on the question of Stoic motivation. What is it that draws a person forward when one simultaneously wants to retreat? It is true, as Schiesaro says, that the Fury brandishes whips before Tantalus' eyes, but she also augments his hunger and thirst, his appetites; why should this influence his judgment and cause him to yield? Is it simply pain that he cannot withstand? And does Thyestes' appetite for power, if that is what it is, lure him on in a similar way, like a hunger that he knows cannot be appeased and yet, as he approaches the palace, nevertheless overcomes his will and induces him to follow, as he yields to the immature judgment of another Tantalus?

The Stoics tended to investigate irrational judgments in connection with the emotions. According to Seneca, the first stage in the formation of an emotion is an impression (*species*, rendering the Greek *phantasia*; *De ira* 2.1.3). Now, impressions can be fairly complex – they are not reducible to mere sensations, such as a color or a taste. Thus, the impression that initiates the emotion of anger is not simply pain, but an *iniuria*, an unjust harm or injury. Nevertheless, the impression of an *iniuria* alone is insufficient to produce the emotion. Rather, as Seneca explains, for the emotion of anger to arise, the mind must assent to two propositions: that we ought not to have been harmed in this way and that it is legitimate to seek revenge, and these judgments require the deliberate exercise of the will or *voluntas*. If the emotion did not involve assent but were simply an automatic reaction, it could not submit to reason and thus could never be mastered. Seneca gives a number of examples of such reflexes, which constitute at first sight a rather puzzling set: shivering when splashed with cold water, recoiling from certain kinds of touch, hair standing on end on account of bad news or blushing at indecent language, vertigo upon looking down from a height. As Seneca says, everyone, even the sage, is subject to such responses, which he dubs the initial preliminaries to emotion (*principia proludentia adfectibus*, 2.2.6). He goes on to say that the initial reaction to the impression of a wrong also falls

---

2 *Sequor* suggests active obedience, but often under pressure; e.g. the slave Lydus to his master in Plautus, *Bacchides* 499 (cf. 525 *sequimini*); Cleanthes *Hymn to Zeus hepsomai* (bis); Seneca, *Ep.* 107 *malus miles est qui imperatorem gemens sequitur*, and the famous *ducunt volentem fata, nolentem trahunt*; the word appears often in Seneca's *Phaedra*, and cf. also Quintilian 9.3.42 (*duc, sequor*); Virgil, *Aen.* 2.701–2 (*sequor et qua ducitis adsum*). I am grateful to Christopher Trinacty for calling my attention to these passages as well as for other helpful comments.

in this latter category. As he observes, we respond this way upon seeing a play or reading about past events, yet clearly this response is not genuine anger (2.2.6).[3]

In Seneca's tragedy, Tantalus and Thyestes are not moved by emotion. As we have seen, Tantalus obeys the Fury because of intense pangs of hunger and thirst and the instinctive shock he experiences at the sight of a whip brandished before his eyes. It is true that Tantalus acknowledges his submission to the Fury's will with word *sequor*. But is this tantamount to voluntary assent, or is it more like those initial preliminaries to emotions, which are ineluctable and independent of reason?

Michael Frede, in his Sather lectures published under the title, *Free Will: The Origins of the Notion in Ancient Thought* (Frede 2011), thinks the response is voluntary. He writes: "In the same way in which the Stoics treat a fear, they also treat an appetite, the supposedly natural desire of the non-rational part of the soul. In truth it is nothing but a belief of a certain kind, a belief generated by assent to a highly agreeable impression to the effect that something one conceives of as a good is coming or might come one's way" (40). As Frede explains, "any human desire (*orexis*) is a desire of reason. Thus any desire of a grown-up human being is a willing, a *boulêsis*" (42). Frede observes: "If a carnivorous animal like a lion feels depleted or hungry, and it has the agreeable impression of a nice piece of meat in reach, this impression in itself will suffice to make it go after the meat … . It is these impressions which constitute the desire of an animal or a child to get something or to avoid something" (36). The association of animals with children is not casual, of course; as Frede puts it: "According to the Stoics, there is this much continuity between being a child and being a mature human being – that as grown-up human beings we continue to have impulsive impressions. The discontinuity lies in the twofold fact that these impulsive impressions now have a completely different character and that in themselves they no longer constitute an impulse sufficient to impel us to do something. To move us they require an assent of, or acceptance by, reason" (36).

On Frede's description, Tantalus would stand convicted of behaving contrary to reason in reaching out for food and drink in the underworld, since he knows it is unobtainable, and equally for submitting to the will of the Fury under the stress of intense hunger and thirst. But the situation may not be quite so straightforward. John Stevens, in a paper entitled "Preliminary Impulse in Stoic Psychology," writes: "A case can be made that some impulse was conceived as preceding assent, even in the most orthodox fragments of Chrysippus," and he adds: "Behind all of the evidence for preliminary impulse lies the problem of how Stoic

---

[3] For Seneca's theory of the emotions, see Graver 2007; Konstan 2015.

psychology accounts for 'temptation'" (Stevens 2000, 139). As Stevens goes on to note, "Chrysippus' statement that *phantasiai* are persuasive' does not explain why they affect us, nor what one should or should not feel when thirsty. It does not explain 'temptation' unless as a full-blown passion" (141). The details of the Stoic position, assuming it was uniform from Zeno to Seneca, are the subject of much debate, but nowhere do the Stoics seem to take account of the intensity of our needs (as opposed to our moral disposition) as a factor in explaining why we yield to certain kinds of temptations or assent to propositions even though our reason counsels otherwise. It is one thing to see food that is tasty and reject it, knowing that it may be fattening; it is another thing to be at the point of starvation and yet refuse to assent to the idea that one should extend one's hand to grasp food that looks delicious and is within easy reach – even if each time in the past it has retreated. Under the lash of such stimuli, can anyone be said to be wholly responsible for such acts?[4]

If one could perhaps excuse Tantalus' behavior, as Schiesaro suggests, what about Thyestes as he hesitantly approaches the palace of Atreus? We may exonerate the younger Tantalus, who is not yet of an age to apply reason and so is simply attracted to what seems pleasant, as a lion is to its prey. As Frede puts it, such impressions "constitute the desire of an animal or a child to get something or to avoid something." The case is different with the adult Thyestes, for whom "these impulsive impressions ... no longer constitute an impulse sufficient to impel us to do something." Like the senior Tantalus, Thyestes has experienced the false attractions of power and learned to judge them properly as things indifferent – not necessarily to be spurned, but not having value in themselves. Yet the appetite for a comfortable life, after years in hiding in remote and inhospitable surroundings, is not wholly unlike the desire for food: ease too is a natural pleasure, even a need; indeed, the very attraction it exerts on the young Tantalus is a sign that it is in and of itself a positive thing, of a sort to draw to itself rather than repel those in whom reason is not yet developed. As Frede notes, adults, like children, "continue to have impulsive impressions," even though they are now subject to rational assent. But is the rupture really so absolute? Even a sage, according to Zeno, retains a scar in the soul, and, as Seneca puts it, "will feel a

---

[4] Tantalus' punishment in Hades is an infinitely repeated version of his submission to the Fury on earth and also, in another register, of Thyestes' inability to resist succumbing to the temptation of comfort and well-being. Lucretius had already observed (3.978–1023) that the torments of Hades are in fact allegories or projections of the frustrations of this life, which result from unnatural and hence insatiable desires. Seneca would readily enough have seen, or rather constructed, the analogy between Thyestes' behavior and Tantalus' ordeal in the afterlife. I am grateful to Stavros Frangoulidis for steering me toward this observation.

kind of light and thin motion …; he will feel certain hints and shadows of the emotions but will lack emotions themselves" (*sentiet itaque suspiciones quasdam et umbras adfectuum, ipsis quidem carebit, De ira* 1.16.7).

The essence of Stoic tragedy is to place people in situations that test the limits of Stoic rationalism. That there should be so radical a breach between the child and the adult, and that desires even for the things most necessary to life, such as food, drink, and physical comfort, should be predicated on a wholly voluntary assent and leave no room for excusable equivocation, are just the places where Stoic doctrine is at its most rigorous and uncompromising. I expect that in planting the analogy between Thyestes' behavior and that of the elder Tantalus, Seneca meant us to feel, even as he calls in question, our instinctive sympathy with both.

Bibliography

Davis, P. J. (2003), *Seneca: Thyestes*, London.
Frede, Michael (2011), *A Free Will: The Origins of the Notion in Ancient Thought*, edited by A. A. Long, Berkeley.
Graver, M. (2007), *Stoicism and Emotion*, Chicago.
Konstan, D. (2015), 'Senecan Emotions', in: S. Bartsch and A. Schiesaro (eds.), *The Cambridge Companion to Seneca*, Cambridge, 174–84.
Schiesaro, A. (2003), *The Passions in Play: Thyestes and the Dynamics of Senecan Drama*, Cambridge.
Stevens, J. A. (2000), 'Preliminary Impulse in Stoic Psychology', *Ancient Philosophy* 20, 139–68.
Tarrant, R. J. (ed.) (1985), *Seneca's Thyestes*, Atlanta.
Wiener, C. (2014), "'Stoic Tragedy': A Contradiction in Terms?', in: M. Garani and D. Konstan (eds.), *The Philosophizing Muse: The Influence of Greek Philosophy on Roman Poetry*, Cambridge.

Lauren Donovan Ginsberg
History as Intertext and Intertext as History in the *Octavia*

The *Octavia* is one of the puzzles of Latin literature. We do not know who wrote it, or precisely when.[1] Nor are we entirely sure of its relationship to the lively but almost entirely lost Republican genre of *fabula praetexta*.[2] As a play that dramatizes the recent past of Neronian Rome and the political strife surrounding Nero's divorce from and execution of his erstwhile wife, the *Octavia* has often seemed to sit uncomfortably on the threshold between poetry and history, somehow never satisfying scholars in either field. Its intertextuality in particular has come under negative scrutiny as an index of the play's wider lack of artistry.[3] On the one hand, its allusive echoes seem too blunt, taken almost verbatim from earlier poets without the creative modification associated with learned poetry. On the other, the play simultaneously seems to borrow phrasing haphazardly from too many disparate sources to constitute the sort of meta-literary program that we see, for example, in authentic Senecan drama. In fact, the resurgence of interest in Senecan poetics has paradoxically reinforced the *Octavia*'s status as a marginal, less sophisticated exemplar of imperial drama through the long history of viewing the play primarily as a piece of Senecan reception rather than as a work of historical drama with its own independent aims. As Sander Goldberg has noted, "in the case of the *Octavia*, the urge to put a face to a text has meant giving the Senecan presence ... a surrogate author-function. The authority we vest in the argument of the *de Clementia* or the value we place on the conventions of Sene-

---

1 For the history of speculation on the *Octavia*'s authorship and its pitfalls, see Goldberg 2003. Scholars overwhelmingly agree that it dates to soon after Nero's fall; some prefer Galba's brief reign (Barnes 1982; Kragelund 1982, 1988, 2005; Wiseman 2001; Flower 2006), others the early years of Vespasian (Junge 1999; Smith 2008; Boyle 2008), though see Ferri (2003, 5–30) on the possibility of a Domitianic date. While my interpretation of the play does not depend on so precise a dating, I follow the majority in viewing it as a product of the early post-Neronian/post-Julio-Claudian period.
2 Questions of the *Octavia*'s genre are inevitably bound up with our attempts to reconstruct the genre of Republican historical drama. On the *Octavia*'s resemblance to Republican *praetextae*, see Manuwald 2001; Kragelund 2002; Wiseman 2005. For arguments against generic continuity within Roman historical drama between Republic and empire, see Dupont 1985; Schmidt 1985; Flower 1995.
3 For a general introduction to the *Octavia*, its intertextuality, and its critical reception, see the complementary recent commentaries of Ferri 2003 and Boyle 2008 as well as Wilson 2003a. Boyle 2008 in particular has laid important groundwork for reconsidering the *Octavia*'s allusivity.

can tragedy becomes the standard for judging the effectiveness of this play's arguments."⁴ And yet, I suggest, a more fruitful model for interpreting the *Octavia*'s intertextuality comes not from the field of Senecan studies but from recent work on the allusive practices of Roman historiography.

Over the past decade scholars have paid increasing attention to the role that intertextuality plays in works dedicated to commemorating the lived historical past.⁵ They suggest that, while poets incorporate echoes of their predecessors for a wide variety of effects, the peculiar nature of historical genres causes historians to use intertextuality to serve historical aims, especially when a historian alludes to the histories of his predecessors and/or to historical events that lay outside his focus. Ellen O'Gorman in particular has argued that an important function of the device in historiography is to collapse time, to create a *synkrisis* between past and present in order to show history's cyclic nature and the way that the past bears upon those making decisions in the present.⁶ So too Cynthia Damon has seen historical and literary allusion working in tandem with the result that individual points of contact (e. g. the reuse of a particular phrase or narrative structure) can serve to create wider allusive patterns through which one historical period evokes another.⁷ Moreover, as Rhiannon Ash, Cynthia Damon, and David Levene have suggested, historiographical characters are often written as keen observers of the past and self-consciously keen readers of the literature of that past for whom, like historians, historical literature offers interpretive keys to the present and *exempla* for action.⁸ Thus intertextual moments in historiography are fundamentally meta-historical moments in which a text's historical actors ask the reader to interpret the present through various representations of the past. In doing so, intertextuality becomes a fundamental tool for commenting on the process of making and commemorating history.

Although this recent work has often assumed *a priori* a privileged position for historical prose, I suggest that the principles outlined above apply equally to works

---

4 Goldberg 2003, 27. I do not dispute the significance of Senecan allusions, but I am inclined to agree with Harrison that "the number of near quotations from [Seneca] ... is too sizable to be accidental and too often remarked in scholarly literature to bear repeating here" (Harrison 2003, 116). Rather, I wish to build on that history of interpretation to showcase other texts looming in the background that contribute to the play's interpretation of Neronian history. For this reason, discussion of Senecan intertexts will largely be kept to the notes. For Senecan echoes, see especially Ladek 1909; Runchina 1964; Whitman 1978; Calder 1983, 193–5; Zwierlein 1984, 224–33; Poe 1989; Williams 1994, 191; Manuwald 2002 and 2003; Wilson 2003b; Ferri 2003 *passim*; Boyle 2008 *passim*.
5 See especially O'Gorman 2007 and 2009; Damon 2010; Levene 2010; Marincola 2010; Chaplin 2012.
6 O'Gorman 2007.
7 Damon 2010. The title of this paper itself alludes to her article.
8 Ash 2007, 200; Damon 2010, 385; Levene 2010, 117.

of historical poetry, and especially to works of historical drama like the *Octavia*. Thus in this paper I offer a case study for investigating how literary allusion serves one playwright's historical interpretation as he shapes how Nero's Rome would be remembered. I focus on the representation of the popular revolution that preceded Octavia's execution in 62 CE and consider two important perspectives on this revolt: that of Nero in dialogue with two interlocutors (Seneca at *Oct.* 440–532; an anonymous prefect at *Oct.* 844–76) as well as the perspective of an anonymous messenger in dialogue with a chorus of Roman citizens (*Oct.* 780–805). Throughout these scenes, I argue, the playwright alludes to two key texts of Julio-Claudian literature to suggest important historical parallels between the popular riots of 62 CE and the civil strife of the late Republic: Vergil's *Aeneid* and Lucan's *Bellum Civile*.[9] As the *Octavia*'s characters attempt to understand the crisis that threatens their imperial present, their language asks us to read that present in light of the Republic's bloody past.

Nero and Seneca: *populus et furor*

Nero first appears on stage in a boiling rage, ordering the deaths of his relatives, Plautus and Sulla, in front of a horrified Seneca on the grounds that these men along with his sister-wife Octavia foment popular *seditio* against him (*Oct.* 462–9):[10]

> An patiar ultra sanguinem nostrum peti,
> inultus et contemptus ut subito opprimar?
> exilia non fregere summotos procul
> Plautum atque Sullam, pertinax quorum <u>furor</u>
> <u>armat</u> <u>ministros</u> sceleris in caedem meam,
> absentium cum maneat etiam ingens favor
> in urbe nostra, qui fovet spes exulum.
> tollantur hostes ense suspecti mihi.[11]

---

9 I use the term "Julio-Claudian" to refer to the entirety of the period in which Augustus and his heirs ruled Rome. While many handbooks of Latin literature differentiate between the Augustan period (in which Vergil would be categorized) and the subsequent Julio-Claudian Period, the *Octavia*, in my view, responds retrospectively to the dynasty Augustus founded and its cultural monuments as a coherent system of political and cultural importance.
10 The play builds to the crescendo of Octavia's execution by including in its purview the other Julio-Claudians who died as part of Nero's dynastic purge of 62 CE and the popular revolts that arose as a result.
11 The text used throughout is Zwierlein 1986 unless otherwise noted. All translations are my own.

> Should I then keep allowing my own blood to be sought such that I am suddenly overwhelmed unavenged and despised? Exile did not break Plautus and Sulla though they have been far removed; madness for them keeps arming agents of crime for my murder, since even in their absence a large faction remains for them in my city which fosters the ambition of the exiles. Let my enemies, once suspected, fall by the sword.

While some would see Nero's role here as little more than that of an irrational stage tyrant, the intertextual weight of his language lends a historicizing weight to his reasoning.[12] For as he presents his case for execution, he borrows language from the famous *seditio* simile of *Aeneid* 1 (Verg. *A*.1.148–56):

> Ac veluti magno in populo cum saepe coorta est
> seditio saevitque animis ignobile vulgus,
> iamque faces et saxa volant, furor arma ministrat;
> tum, pietate gravem ac meritis si forte virum quem
> conspexere, silent, arrectisque auribus astant;
> ille regit dictis animos et pectora mulcet.[13]

> And just as when civil strife has arisen in a great people, which often happens, and the base crowd rages in their minds, and now already torches and rocks fly, their madness supplies their weapons; then if by chance they have seen a man marked by piety and merit, they fall silent, and they stand with their ears ready to listen; he rules their minds with his words and soothes their breasts.

Although Plautus and Sulla are nowhere near Rome itself, Nero views them as an ever-present catalyst for sedition within his capital city (*maneat etiam ingens favor/in urbe nostra*, *Oct.* 467–8), just as such catalysts appear omnipresent in Vergil's Rome. In Vergil's simile, sedition first takes hold of the people's minds and then spurs them to take up arms against the state's authority (*furor arma ministrat*, Verg. *A*.1.150). It is this very language that the playwright has Nero borrow when he describes the *furor* that Plautus and Sulla awaken in the people and the threat against the emperor that this *furor* engenders (*furor/armat ministros sceleris in caedem meam*, *Oct*. 465–6).[14] Thus in some senses Nero offers

---

12 For Nero as voicing the typical concerns of tyrants, see Marti 1952; Giancotti 1954; Whitman 1978; Sullivan 1985, 64; Poe 1989, 450–1; Manuwald 2003, 48–52; Wilson 2003b, 86–7. For the significance of the tyrants of Senecan drama to the intertextual fabric of this scene, see Boyle 2008 ad loc.
13 The text of Vergil is Mynors 1969.
14 Though logic dictates that allusive language stems from the poet, rather than his dramatic characters, the historical actors which the *Octavia* commemorates would have been exceedingly familiar with the works of Vergil and Lucan. Thus I suggest that the poet allows for the interpretive possibility that his characters are aware of the intertextual and historical dimensions of

proof of Vergil's introductory assertion that such sedition often arises even in a great people (*ac veluti magno in populo cum saepe coorta est/seditio*, Verg. *A*.1.148–9) as Neronian Rome becomes one more iteration of the cycle Vergil's simile of Republican strife imagines. Nero's redeployment of Vergil's programmatic language of *seditio* also reinforces the significance of the threat that his Julio-Claudian rivals pose as figureheads for revolution; under the empire, Julio-Claudian blood is enough to reawaken the passions of civil strife.[15]

Vergil's first simile has long been considered programmatic for his epic project, its system of morals, and its political allegories.[16] By taking its analogy from the Republic's recent civil wars and political strife in the Forum, it also becomes the first explicit point of contact between Vergil's world of myth and events within the living memory of Vergil's Roman audience; here Vergil lays bare for his audience the historical allegories that lie behind his narrative and, in doing so, illuminates a strategy of reading to be applied to the epic as a whole. For all these reasons, this simile becomes a *locus classicus* for subsequent Roman civil-war narrative, both in terms of its themes and its vocabulary of strife.[17]

Nero's intertext, therefore, does more than filter Neronian Rome generally through Vergil's *Aeneid*. Rather, it brings Neronian Rome into dialogue with the *Aeneid*'s meditations on the strife of the Republic and the role of "great men" in quelling the *furor* that drives a state to war against itself. As Vergil uses this simile to ask us to read his epic as reflective of the turbulence of the 1st c. BCE, so Nero's Vergilian language asks us to read the strife that threatens Neronian Rome as an iteration of the *seditiones* witnessed at the Republic's end.

These echoes would encourage the *Octavia*'s audience to hunt for further reminiscences as the drama of 62 CE unfolds.[18] Towards the end of Nero's debate with Seneca and after an extended digression on Augustan history (*Oct.* 472–

---

their allusive language, much as historiographical characters are often imagined to be (see, e. g., Batstone 2010, 48 and Levene 2010, 117). See also Edmunds 2001, 74–5.

15 Nero goes on to lament the *ingens favor* (*Oct.* 467) that drives men to the side of his rivals. If one reads *ingens* as a pun on the idea of "within or against a *gens*", as I have argued in Ginsberg 2011, it becomes even more clear that the men themselves are less of an issue than the catalyst for strife that their bloodlines foster.

16 On this simile and its thematic importance, see Pöschl 1962, 13–24; Putnam 1965, 8ff; Hardie 1986, 90–110; Harrison 1988.

17 For the programmatic influence of Vergil's simile on the poetics of civil strife in later literature, see, for example, Hershkowitz 1998, 200–3 on Lucan's *Bellum Civile* and Lovatt 2005, 299–301 on Statius' *Thebaid*.

18 For a discussion of the ways in which an audience is encouraged by more obvious and obviously intended echoes to actively hunt for less obvious and less obviously intended echoes, see Edmunds 2001, 153–5 who quotes a now frequently cited email from Joseph Farrell.

532), the two return to the nature of the relationship between ruler and ruled in contemporary Rome. Here too more subtle echoes of the same passage of Vergil reappear (*Oct.* 575–79):

> Se. Maiora populus semper a summo exigit.
> Ne. Libet experiri, viribus fractus meis
> an cedat animis temere conceptus furor.
> Se Obsequere potius civibus placidus tuis.
> Ne. Male imperatur, cum regit vulgus duces.

> Sen. The people always demand greater things from one on high.
> Ne. It pleases me to test whether the madness rashly conceived in their minds will yield once it has been broken by my power.
> Sen. You should calmly instead obey your citizens.
> Ne. That is a badly run government, when the crowd rules their leaders.

Seneca suggests that Nero bend his will to that of his people and thereby set a good example of imperial authority. Nero, however, replies that doing so would be an inversion of the natural hierarchy between ruler and ruled, leading to chaos rather than peace. To underscore this point, his language recalls the words with which Vergil characterizes the seeds of sedition prior to the eruption of violence and civil strife (*ac veluti magno in populo cum saepe coorta est/seditio, saevitque animis ignobile vulgus/iamque faces et saxa volant, furor arma ministrat*, Verg. *A*.1.149–50). Similar madness, according to Nero, first seizes the minds of his people (*animis temere conceptus furor*, *Oct.* 577), and thus the emperor fears that soon this mental madness will erupt into physical violence.[19] Moreover, when Seneca urges that Nero yield (*obsequere*) to the will of his people, Nero responds that only bad government is characterized by a crowd which rules its leader (*male imperatur, cum regit vulgus duces*).[20] This language too Nero draws from Vergil's simile, for the image of the ideal statesman that Vergil creates flatly contradicts Seneca's advice. According to Vergil, when the base rabble rages savagely in their minds, it is the statesman's job to rule *them* (*saevitque animis ignobile vulgus … ille regit dictis animos*, Verg. *A*.1.149–53). Nero's lan-

---

19 *A* reads *favor* for *furor* here, but I follow Zwierlein 1986 and Ferri 2003 in adopting the conjecture of Avantius. The intratextual parallel with *concepta rabies* at 784, the frequency of forms of *concipio* with *furor* (see Ferri ad loc), and the intertextual force of *furor* all lend weight to the reading.

20 While Kragelund (1988, 504–6) makes much of the distinction between Nero's terminology for the Roman people (*vulgus, turba*: cf. 455, 579, 835, 851) and that of Seneca and the anonymous Prefect (*populus*), Vergil's simile uses both terms as *furor* turns a *magnus populus* into an *ignobile vulgus*.

guage supports his opinion that the Roman people cannot be trusted to make sound decisions lest their pre-existing *furor* plunge Rome once more into civil war.

By activating Vergil's simile at the beginning and end of his dialogue with Seneca, Nero betrays that he views his Principate as a breeding ground for passions that at any time could erupt into the strife out of which his dynasty came to power during the fall of the Republic. The question remains, however, whether Nero – a man who believes only in the power of political exile and execution – can achieve the success of the Vergilian statesman in quelling the *furor* that will soon seize the minds of his people.

The seeds of sedition: *quis furor*?

A few scenes later, a messenger runs on stage with an urgent message for Nero about a revolution that threatens to overtake the city. On his way to the *princeps*, however, he briefly converses with a different group of Roman citizens about the scale of the threat and the motives of the rebels (Oct. 778–88):[21]

> CH. Sed quis gressu ruit attonito
> aut quid portat pectore anhelo?
> CH. Quicumque tectis excubat miles ducis,
> defendat aulam, cui <u>furor</u> populi <u>imminet</u>.
> trepidi cohortes ecce praefecti trahunt
> praesidia ad urbis, victa nec cedit metu
> concepta <u>rabies</u> temere, sed vires capit.
> CH. <u>Quis</u> iste mentes agitat attonitus <u>furor</u>?
> NUN. Octaviae favore percussa agmina
> et efferata per nefas ingens ruunt.
> CH. Quid ausa facere quove consilio <u>doce</u>.

> CH. But who rushes with thunderstruck step, or what news does he bear with breathless chest?
> NUN. Whatever soldier keeps watch in the house of the emperor must defend the palace – the madness of the people threatens it. Look, the fearful Prefects drag the cohorts out to

---

[21] The existence of two choruses in the *Octavia* has caused considerable debate over the identity of this second group. I follow Manuwald (2001, 292–6) and Smith (2003, 419) in seeing in the two choruses two groups of Roman citizens of equal import. For a wider history of the debate and other possible identities for the second chorus (i. e. courtiers, praetorians), see Ferri 2003 and Boyle 2008 *ad loc*.

protect the city, nor does the frenzy that is conceived rashly in their minds yield, to fear, but rather gains strength.
CH: What insane madness has so struck their minds?
NUN: Columns driven by frenzy for Octavia rush uncontrollably into great crime.
CH: Tell us what they dare to do or what plan they have!

He urges them to watch (*ecce*) as prefects rouse their cohorts to defend a city under siege by its own citizens. As the messenger speaks, we and the chorus of Roman people come to understand that this is no minor struggle, but that Rome's people are actively waging war against the city itself.

This sudden influx of military imagery disrupts the festive atmosphere of Nero's wedding to Poppaea. So too does the Lucanian backdrop of the messenger's language and the way in which he brings current events into dialogue with those of Lucan's *Bellum Civile*. In Lucan's text, *furor* and *rabies* often function in tandem as programmatic synonyms for the madness that drives Roman to wage war against Roman.[22] The wider architecture of this scene, however, and the messenger's language recall a particular moment from the end of *Bellum Civile* 1 where Nigidius Figulus prophesies for Rome a bleak future filled with civil war whose only benefit is to hold off the age of empire for a few more years (*inminet armorum rabies, ferrique potestas/confundet ius omne manu, scelerique nefando/nomen erit virtus, multosque exibit in annos/hic furor*, Luc. 1.666–9).[23] Figulus appears as the second of three vatic figures in a carefully designed sequence to end Lucan's first book.[24] This overabundance of vatic activity, in turn, becomes a programmatic and metapoetic moment through which Lucan reduplicates his poetic voice to anticipate and authorize his vision of Rome's catastrophic future.

The *Octavia*'s messenger borrows Figulus' language, switching the syntactical position of *furor* and *rabies*, while keeping the language of looming military conflict and the close pairing of the two near-synonyms (*furor populi imminet ... victa nec cedit metu/concepta rabies temere*). In doing so, the messenger aligns himself with one of Lucan's most significant poet-figures and messengers of strife while aligning his narrative of the riots of 62 CE with Lucan's civil war. His is a tale of the beginnings of revolution that Rome has seen before: through an

---

[22] For Lucan's use of *rabies* and *furor* in tandem, see e.g. 1.8, 1.68, 1.666, 1.669, 1.680, 7.51, 7.245, 7.474.
[23] The text of Lucan is Housman 1927.
[24] For Nigidius Figulus as one of Lucan's prophet-poet figures, see Dick 1963, esp. 38–41; Masters 1992, 65, 146, 185, 252. For *vates* figures in Lucan generally, see O'Higgins 1988; Masters 1992, 138–9 and 205–6; Casali 2011. Roche 2009 ad Luc. 1.2 notes that the proem of the epic is later echoed by Figulus, creating a ring-composition that binds the first book together.

intertextually-driven *synkrisis*, the strife of the past has become one with the Neronian present.

The messenger's audience is primed for such historical and literary allusions. Their language picks up on and expands the messenger's Lucanian frame by appealing in their response to the next and final vatic figure from the end of Lucan's first book. Following Nigidius Figulus, the final *vates* of *Bellum Civile* 1 is a matron inspired to a frenzied vision of the civil wars by Apollo (Luc. 1. 676–95). Amidst other insistent questions, she asks Apollo to teach her the nature of the madness that drives Rome's citizens to arms against each other (*quis furor hic, o Phoebe, doce, quo tela manusque/Romanae miscent acies bellumque sine hoste est*, Luc. 1. 681–2). Through these questions and her visions of future civil wars across time and space, the *matrona* articulates not only the subject matter of Lucan's narrative, but also the sequel to those events outside the bounds of Lucan's poem (*vidi iam, Phoebe, Philippos*, Luc. 1. 694). The *Octavia*'s chorus borrows both the *matrona*'s language (*quis furor*) and also her rhetorical stance (*doce*) as one who seeks from an authoritative power (Phoebus versus the messenger) the knowledge through which to make sense of a chaotic situation.[25] While the messenger is aligned with Figulus as one who is able to see Roman strife through his own observations,[26] the chorus follows the Lucanian *matrona* in seeking a dialogic relationship with a more secure source of knowledge.

And yet the chorus is no passive recipient of another's vision; instead, like Lucan's *matrona*, it plays an active role in shaping our response to the information the messenger provides. As critics have been quick to point out, Lucan's *matrona* echoes Lucan's own proem (*quis furor, o cives, quae tanta licentia ferri?*, Luc. 1.8), further uniting poet and prophet in a metapoetic ring that surrounds the message of endless doom in the epic's inaugural book.[27] When Lucan's

---

[25] Ferri 2003 ad 788 notes that "there are no parallels in Senecan tragedy for this use of the imperative of *docere* when a chorus or speaking character interrogates a messenger ... this mode of expression has parallels, however, in epic. Cf. Luc. *Bell.Civ.*1.681–2 (a matron prophesying the horror of the civil wars)."

[26] For the messenger's authority over the account he gives and its metapoetic aspects, see de Jong 1991, 12–30; Barrett 2002, xvi; Baertschi 2010, 250–1.

[27] Lucan borrows this phrase from earlier contexts of strife (cf. Verg. *A.*2.42; Verg. *A.*5.670–2; Tib. 1.10.33). Cf. especially Ovid's Pentheus (*quis furor, anguigenae, proles Mavortia, vestras/attonuit mentes*? Ov. *Met.* 3.531–2) and Sen. *Phoen.* 557, both in the context of Theban civil strife. The phrase also appears in Petronius' parody of civil-war poetry (*quis furor, exclamat, pacem convertit in arma?* Pet. *Sat.*108.14), itself perhaps a parody of Lucan. While the wider engagement with the finale of *Bellum Civile* 1 suggests that the Lucan is the *Octavia*'s primary model here, the widespread use of *quis furor* for Roman strife opens the *Octavia*'s reference to

matrona asks Phoebus to teach her what passions drive civil war, she echoes a programmatic and insistent question that Lucan repeatedly asks his fellow Roman citizens, both those waging war within the poem and those reading about that war in Neronian Rome.[28] When the *Octavia*'s chorus borrows this same language, it aligns itself not only with one of three vatic figures through which Lucan inaugurates his tale of Republican disaster, but with the chief *vates* of the epic as a whole: Lucan himself. Like Lucan, the chorus is horrified at the actions of its fellow citizens, and like Lucan it seeks to understand the precise nature of the madness which could drive citizen to attack citizen. Moreover, by importing Lucan's poetic voice into their own reaction to the messenger's pronouncement, the chorus suggests that it too views the crisis through a Lucanian lens and encourages us to do the same.

As the Roman people's *furor* once more threatens to return the city to the bloodshed and chaos of the late Republic, both the anonymous messenger and the chorus interpret the riots of 62 CE as but a further instantiation of the civil wars that Lucan immortalized. In doing so, they mimic Nero in creating an important *synkrisis* between past and present, Republican *bellum civile* and imperial *furor*. At the same time, however, they eschew Vergil's teleological epic in preference for Lucan's epic of chaos and civil strife without end.

Pietas in Neronian Rome

Nevertheless, despite this gloomy Lucanian vision, Rome may not be completely bereft of the hope Vergil's simile provided for a man endowed with the ability to calm this *furor*. Just as Rome seems poised to inaugurate *bellum civile* once more, such a man does appear on stage (*Oct.* 844–57):

> NE. Sed adesse cerno rara quem pietas virum
> fidesque castris nota praeposuit meis.
> PRF. Populi furorem caede paucorum, diu
> qui restiterunt temere, compressum affero.
> NE. Et hoc sat est? sic miles audisti ducem?

---

include wide swaths of history. On the inseparability of specific intertexts and more general *topoi*, see Hinds 1988, 29–47.

28 The larger metapoetic aspects of *furor* in post-Vergilian literature are well studied. For its use in this sense in epic, see Dick 1963, 37–49; Masters 1992, 142–9; Hardie 1993, 107ff; Hershkowitz 1998, 95–124. For Senecan drama see, for example, Littlewood 2004, 10–11 and more extensively Schiesaro 2003, 26–36 and 85ff.

compescis? haec vindicta debetur mihi?
PRF. Cecidere motus impii ferro duces ...
PRF. Poenam dolor constituet in cives tuos?
NE. Constituet, aetas nulla quam famae eximat
PRF. Tua temperet nos ira, non noster timor ...
NE. Parere dubitas? P. Cur meam damnas fidem?
NE. Quod parcis hosti. P. Femina hoc nomen capit?
NE. Si scelera cepit. P. Estne qui sontem arguat?
NE. Populi <u>furor</u>. P. Quis <u>regere</u> de<u>mentes</u> valet?
NE. Qui concitare potuit.

NE: But I see a man whom rare piety and notable loyalty put in charge of my guard.
PRF: I bring back news that, by the slaughter of a few who rashly resisted for some time, the frenzy of the people has been suppressed.
NE: Is this enough? Thus, soldier, you obey your leader? You subdued? This is the punishment owed me?
PRF: The impious revolution's leaders died by the sword ...
PRF: Will grief impose a punishment on your citizens?
NE: It will impose one which no age will remove from my reputation.
PRF: Your anger tempers us, not our fear ...
NE: Do you hesitate to obey? PRF: You doubt my loyalty?
NE: Because you spare the enemy. PRF: A woman takes this title?
NE: If she takes up crimes. PRF: Is there someone who would call her guilty?
NE: The frenzy of the people. PRF: Who is able to rule their crazy minds?
NE: The one who was able to rouse them.

As Nero reaches a fever pitch in his narrative of the siege, he sees in the distance one of his Prefects approaching and stops for a moment, eager to listen to the man's words (*sed adesse <u>cerno</u> rara <u>quem</u> <u>pietas</u> <u>virum</u>* Oct. 844). While this language is certainly a convenient transition from Nero's monologue to his dialogue with the Prefect, it is also one of the few unproblematized appearances of *pietas* in the play and its sudden effect on Nero is striking.[29] Nero's language also recalls once more Vergil's description of the great statesman (*tum <u>pietate</u> gravem ac meritis si forte <u>virum</u> <u>quem</u>/<u>conspexere</u>* Verg. A.1.151–2). As Vergil's mob had paused in their frenzy at the sight of such a man, so too does Nero.

As has often been noted, the Prefect in this scene forms a doublet for Seneca as each man debates with Nero the utility of imperial violence.[30] At the same time, however, the Prefect shows himself to be much more in tune with the political realities of strife-ridden Rome than his philosophical counterpart and as

---

29 On the "intrusion from the ethical world of the *Octavia* poet" in this moment, see Ferri 2003 *ad loc*.
30 See Ferri 2003 and Boyle 2008 *ad loc*. See also Sutton 1983 and Kragelund 1988.

such forms a more apt doublet for Vergil's simile. He attempts to soothe Nero's anger with words, and to restore order to the chaos of Rome. As he wonders aloud what type of person could rule the maddened crowd (*quis regere dementes valet*, *Oct.* 866), his language reminds us of the very skills that characterize his Vergilian model (*ille regit dictis animos*, Verg. *A*.1.153). The repetition of the verb *regere* is further reinforced by the substitution of the substantive "crazy" (*dementes*) or, more literally, "out of their mind" for the original Vergilian *animos* which were infected with *furor* and *ira*. Thus this nameless Prefect brings the *Octavia* once more into dialogue with Vergil's great statesman at a point in the play at which the *seditio* Vergil imagined threatens to swallow Nero's city. As history replays itself, Nero hardly seems a leader capable of quelling *ira* and *furor* – either the people's or his own. Only the Prefect recognizes the proper course of action which could bring Rome back from chaos.

What prevents such a man from carrying out the actions that Vergil's *Aeneid* declares him capable of and from saving the state from plunging further into civil strife? Nero and, more broadly, the Julio-Claudian system. The Prefect has no freedom to respond to the crisis as he sees fit, but instead loyally (*nota ... fides*, *Oct.* 845; cf. 854) carries out Nero's vengeful orders. In a world ruled by the Julio-Claudian dynasty where bloodlines, not statesmanship, entitle a man to supreme power, there is no room for the statesman of *Aeneid* 1. The Principate, at least in its Julio-Claudian incarnation, has rendered him obsolete. Instead Rome seems doomed to wage internal wars without end. Nevertheless, the existence of a man of the Prefect's qualities in Neronian Rome should perhaps provide hope that in the future a man of Vergilian character might gain power and bring Rome back from the brink of civil war once again. The world will not have long to wait, for the year 69 CE looms just offstage.

Conclusion

This paper proposes a strategy of reading the *Octavia*'s intertextuality that foregrounds the drama's status as a work of drama with historical as well as literary aims. In doing so, I borrow a mode of interpretation drawn from historiographical scholarship – a mode well articulated by Damon in her work on history and intertext in Tacitus: "even where the textuality of an allusion seems the strongest ... its actual target may be bigger than the text alluded to."[31] In other words,

---

[31] See Damon 2010, 377 on Tacitus' similar use of literary allusion to bring 69 CE into dialogue with the civil wars of the Republic.

when an historian borrows language from an historical predecessor, his aims are often wider than any one individual point of textual contact; rather, individual echoes contribute to wider patterns of historical allusivity through which the author asks his audience to consider an event in light of previous events and previous commemorations of those events. In doing so, he creates a *synkrisis* between disparate historical periods that furthers the interpretive aims of his historical project.

Throughout his account of 62 CE, the *Octavia* poet creates a series of pointed echoes of purple passages from the first books of Vergil's *Aeneid* and Lucan's *Bellum Civile*, from authors who were themselves deeply concerned with the process of making and commemorating history under the rule of Rome's first imperial family. In doing so, I argue, the playwright suggests wider parallels between the political *furor* that led to the collapse of the Republic and the *furor* that drives popular rebellions in Neronian Rome. Moreover, by using two epics of programmatic significance to the Julio-Claudian dynasty – texts which Nero and his contemporaries would have known exceedingly well – the *Octavia* poet makes his characters complicit in creating this intertextually generated *synkrisis*. Nero's dialogues with Seneca and the Prefect are simultaneously debates about political strife and about Vergil's representation of that strife; so too, the anonymous messenger and chorus of Roman citizens both use Lucan's *Bellum Civile* as a means of articulating the seriousness of the threat posed by what might otherwise seem to be a minor popular insurrection. Historical and literary allusion work together to bring Neronian *seditio* into dialogue with Republican *furor* as the *Octavia* stages for Rome the final years of Julio-Claudian rule.

This historiographically-oriented mode of interpretation, moreover, need not apply only to the *Octavia*. Though we have precious few remains of its Republican counterparts, what evidence we have suggests that the *Octavia* was not alone in using intertextuality to create historical connections. As has been well noted, the fragments of Accius' *Brutus* as preserved in Cicero's *De Divinatione* (1.43–5) demonstrate the playwright's sophisticated adaptation of Aeschylus' *Persae*.[32] In this way, Accius suggests that the downfall of the Tarquins was a moment of constitutive significance to Roman cultural memory as significant as Greece's destruction of their eastern, tyrannical enemy was to Athens. So too when Ennius' Sabine women borrow language from Euripides' Jocasta, Ennius suggests that Rome's early history of civil strife was of a piece with Thebes' legendary past.[33]

---

[32] See especially Manuwald 2001, 232 and Erasmo 2004, 59–63.
[33] Enn. *Sab.* frag. 1 Ribbeck with Eur. *Phoen.* 571–6. For interpretations, see Joceyln 1972, 82–8; La Penna 2000, 246–9; Manuwald 2001, 172–79; Boyle 2006, 86–7.

While it is impossible to say more from the state of the fragments left to us, the evidence remaining suggests that the *Octavia* might be part of a lively generic tradition in which historical and literary memory had long been working to complementary ends to bring individual points of Rome's past into dialogue with the wider cycles of history.

Acknowledgments

This paper has benefited much from the comments and questions of the lively participants of the 8th *Trends in Classics* conference, from the thoughtful feedback of the readers and editors for this volume, and from the subsequent incisive readings of Neil Bernstein, Caroline Bishop, Liz Gloyn, Isabel Köster, and Christopher Trinacty. Any remaining faults are entirely my own.

Bibliography

Ash, R. (2007), *Tacitus Histories II*, Cambridge.
Baertschi, A. (2010), 'Drama and Epic Narrative: The Test Case of Messenger Speech in Seneca's *Agamemnon*', in: I. Gildenhard and M. Revermann (eds.), *Beyond the Fifth Century. Interactions with Greek Tragedy from the Fourth Century BCE to the Middle Ages*, Berlin, 243–63.
Batstone, W. (2010), 'Word at War: The Prequel', in: B. Breed, C. Damon, and A. Rossi (eds.), *Citizens of Discord: Roma and its Civil Wars*, Oxford, 45–72.
Barrett, J. (2002), *Staged Narrative: Poetics and the Messenger in Greek Tragedy*, Berkeley.
Boyle, A. J. (2006), *An Introduction to Roman Tragedy*, New York.
_____ (2008), *Octavia: Attributed to Seneca*, Oxford.
Calder, W. M. (1983), '*Secreti loquimur*: An Interpretation of Seneca's *Thysestes*', in: A. J. Boyle (ed.), *Seneca Tragicus: An Essay in the Theatrical Tradition*, Berwick, 184–98.
Casali, S. (2011), 'The *Bellum Civile* as Anti-*Aeneid*', in: P. Asso (ed.), *Brill's Companion to Lucan*, Leiden, 81–109.
Damon, C. (2010), 'Déjà vu or déjà lu? History as Intertext', *PLLS* 14, 375–88.
De Jong, I. (1991), *Narrative in Drama: The Art of the Euripidean Messenger-Speech*, Leiden.
Dick, B. F. (1963), 'The Technique of Prophecy in Lucan', *TAPA* 94, 37–49.
Dupont, F. (1985), *L'acteur-roi: le théatre à Rome*, Paris.
Edmunds, L. (2001), *Intertextuality and the Reading of Roman Poetry*, Baltimore.
Erasmo, M. (2004), *Roman Tragedy: Theatre to Theatricality*, Austin.
Ferri, R. ed. (2003), *Octavia: A Play Attributed to Seneca*, Cambridge.
Flower, H. I. (1995), '*Praetextae* in Context: When Were Plays on Contemporary Subjects Performed in Republican Rome?', *CQ* 45, 170–90.
_____ (2006), *The Art of Forgetting: Disgrace and Oblivion in Roman Political Culture*, Chapel Hill.

Giancotti, F. (1954), *L' Ottavia attribuita a Seneca*, Torino.
Ginsberg, L. D. (2011), '*Ingens* as an Etymological Pun in the *Octavia*', *CP* 106.4, 357–60.
Goldberg, S. (2003), 'Authorizing *Octavia*', in: M. Wilson (ed.), *The Tragedy of Nero's Wife: Studies on the Octavia Praetexta*, Auckland, 13–36.
Hardie, P. (1986), *Vergil's Aeneid: Cosmos and imperium*, Oxford.
_____ (1993), *The Epic Successors of Virgil: A Study in the Dynamics of a Tradition*, Cambridge.
Harrison, G. M. W. (2003), 'Forms of Intertextuality in the *Octavia*', in: M. Wilson (ed.), *The Tragedy of Nero's Wife: Studies on the Octavia Praetexta*, Auckland, 112–25.
Harrison, S. J. (1988), 'Vergil on Kingship: The First Simile of the *Aeneid*', *PCPhS* 34, 55–9.
Hershkowitz, D. (1998), *The Madness of Epic: Reading Insanity from Homer to Statius*, Oxford.
Hinds, S. (1998), *Allusion and Intertext: Dynamics of Appropriation in Roman Poetry*, Cambridge.
Housman, A. E. (1927), *M. Annaei Lucani Belli Civilis Libri Decem*, Oxford.
Jocelyn, H. D. (1967), *The Tragedies of Ennius*, Cambridge.
_____ (1972), 'Ennius as Dramatic Poet', in: O. Skutsch (ed.), *Ennius: Sept Exposés Suivis de Discussions (Fondation Hardt Entretiens* 17), Geneva, 41–95.
Junge, R. (1999), *Nicholas Trevet und die Octavia Praetexta*, Paderborn.
Kragelund, P. (1988), 'The Perfect's Dilemma and the Date of the *Octavia*', *CQ* 38, 492–508.
Kragelund, P. (1982), *Prophecy, Populism and Propaganda in the Octavia*, Copenhagen.
_____ (1988), 'The Perfect's Dilemma and the Date of the *Octavia*', *CQ* 38, 492–508.
_____ (2005), 'History, Sex and Scenography in the *Octavia*', *SO* 80, 68–114.
La Penna, A. (2000), 'Le *Sabinae* di Ennio e il tema della *concordia* nella tragedia arcaica latina', in: G. Manuwald (ed.), *Identität und Alterität in der frührömischen Tragödie*, Würzburg, 241–54.
Ladek, F. (1909), 'Die römische Tragödie *Octavia* und die *Elektra* des Sophokles', Wiener Eranos, 189–99.
Levene, D. S. (2010), *Livy on the Hannibalic War*, Oxford.
Littlewood, A. J. (2004), *Self-Representation and Illusion in Senecan Tragedy*, Oxford.
Lovatt, H. (2005), *Statius and Epic Games: Sport, Politics, and Poetics in the Thebaid*, Cambridge.
Manuwald, G. (2001), *Fabulae pretextae: Spuren einer literarischen Gattung der Römer*, Munich.
_____ (2002), 'Der Fürstenspiegel in Senecas *De Clementia* und in der *Octavia*', *MH* 59, 107–26.
_____ (2003), 'Tyranny in *Thyestes* and in *Octavia*', *Prudentia* 35, 37–59.
Marti, B. M. (1952), 'Seneca's *Apocolocyntosis* and *Octavia*: a Diptych', *AJP* 63, 24–36.
Masters, J. (1992), *Poetry and Civil War in Lucan's Bellum Civile*, Cambridge.
Mynors, R. A. B. (1969), *P. Vergili Maronis Opera*, Oxford.
O'Gorman, E. (2007), 'Intertextuality, Time and Historical Understanding', in: A. Macfie (ed.), *The Philosophy of History*, Palgrave Macmillan, 102–117.
_____ (2009), 'Intertextuality and Historiography', in: A. Feldherr (ed.), *The Cambridge Companion to the Roman Historians*, Cambridge, 231–42.
O'Higgins, D. (1988), 'Lucan as *Vates*', *ClAnt* 7, 208–26.
Poe, J. P. (1989), '*Octavia Praetexta* and its Senecan Model', *AJP* 110, 434–59.
Pöschl, V. (1962), *The Art of Vergil: Image and Symbol in the Aeneid*, Ann Arbor.
Putnam, M. C. J. P. (1965), *The Poetry of the Aeneid: Four Studies in Imaginative Unity and Design*, Cambridge, MA.
Roche, P. (2009), *Lucan: De Bello Civili Book 1*, Oxford.
Runchina, G. (1964), 'Sulla pretesta *Octavia* e le tragedie di Seneca', *RCCM* 6, 47–63.

Schiesaro, A. (2007), *The Passions in Play: Thyestes and the Dynamics of Senecan Drama*, Cambridge.
Schmidt, P. L. (1985), 'Die Poetisierung und Mythisierung der Geschichte in der Tragödie *Octavia*', *ANRW* II.32.2, 1421–53.
Smith, J. A. (2003), 'Flavian Drama: Looking Back with *Octavia*', in: A. J. Boyle and W. J. Dominik (eds.), *Flavian Rome: Culture, Image, Text*, Leiden, 391–430.
Sullivan, J. P. (1985), *Literature and Politics in the Age of Nero*, Ithaca.
Sutton, D. (1983), *The Dramaturgy of the Octavia*, Beitr. zur klass. Philol. CXLIX.
Williams, G. (1994), 'Nero, Seneca and Stoicism in the *Octavia*', in: *Nero* J. Elsner and J. Masters (eds.), *Reflections of Nero*, London, 178–96.
Wilson, M. (2003a), 'Introduction: The Importance of *Octavia*', in: M. Wilson (ed.), *The Tragedy of Nero's Wife: Studies on the Octavia Praetexta*, Auckland, 1–12.
―――― (2003b), 'Allegory and Apotheosis in the *Octavia*', in: M. Wilson (ed.), *The Tragedy of Nero's Wife: Studies on the Octavia Praetexta*, Auckland, 60–88.
Wiseman, T. P. (2001), *The Principal Thing* (Presidential Address to the Classical Association), Sherborne.
―――― (2005), *Myths of Rome*, Exeter.
Whitman, L. Y. (1978), *The Octavia: Introduction, Text and Commentary*, Stuttgart.
Zwierlein, O. (1986), *Lucii Annaei Senecae tragoediae. Incertorum auctorum Hercules [Oetaeus], Octavia*, Oxford.

Part III: Reception of Comedy and Tragedy

Ruth Rothaus Caston
Terence and Satire

Terence and Lucilius are rarely discussed together, despite the fact that they lived within a generation of each other.[1] There seem to be persuasive reasons to keep them apart. Horace, an important if sometimes misleading source for the lineage of Roman satire, offers an account that puts Terence and Lucilius in opposite camps. While his own satires derive their gentle approach from New Comedy, Horace tells us, those of Lucilius descend from the more spiteful Old Comedy.[2] The two poets also come from vastly different social worlds. Terence was brought to Rome as a slave from Carthage, while Lucilius was an *eques* and wealthy landowner from Suessa Aurunca.[3] While scholars once believed in a 'Scipionic Circle' to which both poets would have belonged (though at different times), this idea is widely discounted today, giving us even less reason to view Terence and Lucilius as part of the same milieu.[4]

Whatever the differences between Terence and Lucilius, however, the fact remains that comedy and satire have a lot in common. Both are performative genres, whose speakers adopt a persona or role. They both address human flaws like greed, hypocrisy, excessive desire and ambition, and do so with wit and humor. Our earliest examples of satire use dramatic meters, though later the dactylic hexameter would become the rule. There is so much in common that it would be surprising if Terence and Lucilius really were as different as Horace, and later scholars, have

---
[1] Terence's last play, the *Adelphoe*, was performed in 160 BCE, while Lucilius' first books were published 131 BCE. For the dating of Lucilius' first five books, see Raschke 1979, and on the problems associated with dating Lucilius more generally, Gruen 1992, 274–7. There are a few treatments of the relationship between the fragments of Lucilius and Terence's plays: see Fiske 1920, 183, 393–8; Petersmann 1999, 296–310; Goldberg 2005, 159, 173–4; Muecke 2005, 45–6; Auhagen 2001, 13–9; and most recently Ferriss-Hill 2015, 128–38. Donatus frequently turns to Lucilius to explain something in Terence, but the points are for the most part linguistic rather than thematic (see e. g., at *Andr.* 324 (= W 412), *Andr.* 914 (= W 698), *Phorm.* 183 (= W 503).
[2] See Hor. *Sat.* I.4 1.10, and II.1. This lineage should not be taken at face value, but forms part of Horace's own self-construction: on this, see the excellent introductions to I.4 and I.10 in Gowers 2012. Indeed, a few recent studies focus on Lucilius and New Comedy (Auhagen 2001), and on Terence's prologues and Old Comedy (Sharrock 2009, Ferriss-Hill 2015).
[3] The question of status is of course important to Horace himself, son of a freedman: see *libertino patre natum*, *Sat.* I.6.6, 45, and Gowers 2012 *ad* I.6.6. It is possible that some of our emphasis today on Lucilius' status is due to the way Horace himself highlights the issue, though as Goldberg points out (2005, 165–6), Horace does not say anything about Lucilius' status in his *Satires*.
[4] For doubts about the existence of a Scipionic circle, see Goldberg 1986, 8–15, Hanley 2013, and cf. Umbrico 2010.

made them out to be.⁵ This is all the more so when we consider Ennius' satires. Like Lucilius' earliest books, they, too, incorporated comic meters and themes, showing that the two genres were engaged with each other even before Terence began to compose his plays.⁶ We should be asking not only about Lucilius' relationship to comedy, but about Terence's relationship to satire, though of course the fragmentary state of both Ennius and Lucilius makes these questions especially challenging.

Studies of the relationship between Lucilius and Roman comedy have tended to focus on one of two areas: either Lucilius' early books with their dramatic meters and obvious comic themes, or Terence's prologues, whose defensive posture and literary critique have been compared to a select group of Lucilian fragments.⁷ In what follows, I suggest some other areas where we may find common ground. My aim in juxtaposing their work is not to argue for any direct influence, but rather to re-evaluate the relationship between comedy and satire in the Republican period as well as to point to some Roman dimensions of Terence's plays. Before turning to the parallels, however, I begin with a methodological issue that, like Horace's characterization of Terence and Lucilius in terms of Old and New Comedy, has tended to drive a wedge between these writers.

Status and *libertas*

The status of Lucilius and Terence could not be more different, the one a wealthy landowner, the other a freed slave. Even though the 'biographical fallacy' has been debunked in the field as a whole, social status has often been used to explain aspects of Terence and Lucilius' poetry, in particular their tone and *libertas*: Lucilius' security meant that he could say what he pleased about anyone, no matter how important they might be, while Terence's dependence on aristocratic friends required more delicacy. Despite this apparent difference, however, the

---

5 See Muecke 2005, 45 on Lucilius 'Whereas relatively few direct verbal borrowings from Plautus, Caecilius, and Terence have been identified – and perhaps they should not be expected – the stylistic influence is pervasive, both in the creation of a racy colloquialism and in the use of comic coinages, vulgarisms, and other devices of popular comedy.'
6 Ennius was of course himself a dramatist. On the relationship of Ennius' satires to comedy, see Muecke 2005, esp. 37. Ennius is often discounted in modern studies of satire (see e. g., Freudenburg 2005, 2–3), no doubt because Horace (and later Quintilian) call Lucilius the *inventor* of the genre. Yet even the small number of lines from Ennius that have survived (see Russo 2007) display the topics and tone we associate with later satire. For an echo of Ennius' satires in Terence's plays, see *Phorm.* 338–42 and the discussions in Damon 1997, 98 and 105–7 and Petersmann 1999, 295.
7 See n. 1 above.

context in which these assessments arise is the same: did these poets compromise their poetic independence?[8]

I begin with Terence, whose prologues, as is well known, provide a picture of the embattled playwright, defending himself from charges about his use of Greek sources and help from unnamed *nobiles*.[9] These charges, which were later incorporated into Suetonius' *Vita*, implied Terence's dependence on others and had a serious effect on scholarship on the plays, which tended to attribute any successful feature of Terence's play to Greek originals, even if none was extant. Today it is more common to interpret the accusations not as autobiographical details, but as a carefully scripted *captatio benevolentiae* and boast about the playwright's influential friends.[10] Nonetheless, even studies that credit Terence with crafting this picture to his own advantage still mention his close dependence on aristocratic support. A recent book on plagiarism in Roman literature, for example, describes Terence's references to the aristocracy as 'advertising his good relationship with the *homines nobiles*,' but then goes on to characterize the relationship as one of dependence and gratitude:

> Indeed, by conveying that he appreciated how generously the nobles behaved toward him, Terence would appear, in part, to be thanking Scipio (as well as Fabius) for selecting his comedy ... I am inclined to connect Terence's remarks on the *nobiles* back to the plagiarism charge. By relating that he greatly values his relationship with the aristocrats who were said to have aided in the composition of his plays, Terence makes it evident that he would do nothing to endanger his standing with them.[11]

However much Terence had apparently seized the upper hand, in the end he still had to cater to élite support. The implication is that the plays defend certain values and perspectives.

Lucilius, too, was the victim of suspicions concerning his relationship to the élite. Among other things, Horace's description of Lucilius' close intimacy with Scipio gave rise to suspicions that satires like those attacking Metellus and Lupus were designed to protect Scipio's interests.[12] Gruen demonstrates how thin the evidence is for such a view and argues that we should read Lucilius' critiques as signs of his *libertas*, not partisanship.[13] Yet even though Gruen himself argues

---

8 Ennius was suspected on the same grounds: see Goldberg 1995, Ch. 5, Gruen 1990, 121, and Breed and Rossi 2006, 405–8.
9 On the latter, my focus here, see *Heaut.* 22–4 and *Ad.* 15–21.
10 See e. g. Sharrock 2009, 68–87 and Ferriss-Hill 2015, 128–38.
11 McGill 2012, 142.
12 Hor. *Sat.* 2.1.62–74.
13 Gruen 1992, ch. 7, an outstanding treatment of the issues.

against a biographical fallacy, that of using Lucilius' relationship to Scipio as the basis for interpreting some of the satires, he and others still take Lucilius' wealth to be key to understanding Lucilius' position. The contrast with Terence is obvious: unlike the playwright who needed help from the élite, the wealthy Lucilius never needed any support. One had his hands tied, while the other was free to say whatever he wished. The quotation below about Lucilius and Ennius, again from a recent book, could just as easily have been directed at Lucilius and Terence:

> Lucilius' self-assertion and polemical stance, which transformed the mode of comic realism he took up from Ennius, must be linked to his higher social position. If Ennius acquired a certain status from his writing, he remained in modest circumstances, socially dependent upon the politically powerful figures who were his patrons.[14]

Yet Lucilius' financial independence does not preclude his having a patron. As Goldberg points out, patronage was a complex relationship that did not necessarily involve a difference in status or 'a rigid set of social rules or the expectation of specific favors bestowed and received.'[15] Nor does Lucilius seem entirely unconcerned with what other people might think about his relationship to his aristocratic supporters, at least to judge from the following fragment (W 632–4):

> <ab indoctissimis>
> nec doctissimis <legi me>; Man<ium Manil>ium
> Persiumve haec legere nolo, Iunium Congum volo.

> ... I don't want to be read either by the very unlearned or by the very learned; I don't want Manius Manilius or Persius to read these things, but I do want Junius Congus to do so.

By stating that he prefers a reader somewhere between uneducated and educated, Lucilius may be trying, however playfully, to preempt any accusations that his poetry caters to the élite.[16]

Although the evidence may never allow us to settle the truth about any of these charges, the issue is surely too complex to reduce to one of social status

---

[14] Muecke 2005, 42. See also Goldberg 2005, 170–1: 'Nor, as a pioneer in a new style of writing, did he have to concern himself with the expectations of that audience or with any complex of generic conventions: subjects, meters, tone, diction could be of his own choosing, as their variety makes clear. Lucilius' social status thus vastly enhanced his creative license'; and also Reinhardt 2013, 529: 'Unlike Terence who, if we can trust his biographer Suetonius, came to Rome as a slave from Carthage, Lucilius ... came from a senatorial family and commented in his satires on the foibles of his class with the ease and self-confidence of someone who was writing about his peers.'
[15] Goldberg 1995, 120.
[16] Ferriss-Hill 2015, 139–40 compares this and other Lucilian lines about his readership to similar remarks about audience in Old Comedy, Callimachus and Terence.

alone. Perhaps we should attribute these charges to patronage and the ways in which suspicions were naturally aroused by the support of the leading class, no matter who the poet was. Or they may be due to the poets' success and rise in popularity.[17] Consider the difference between how Terence responds to the plagiarism charges in the prologue to the *Heauton Timoroumenos*, his second play, and the *Adelphoe*, his sixth. In the former, he simply asks his audience not to be biased against him and to give him a fair hearing (25–30). In the *Adelphoe*, by contrast, he moves the discussion from the accusation that he received help, to the approval this would signal, to the high opinion everyone has of these *nobiles* (15–21). The focus shifts from prejudice to achievement, from an isolated 'I' to a broad 'we' (see *vobis univorsis* and *populo, Ad.* 19). There may be other factors generating these suspicions as well, several of which could even be operating at the same time. We should not be reductive or biographical, then, in evaluating Terence and Lucilius, but should base our judgment of their relationship on the poetry itself.

Beyond love and courtesans

Despite the fact that Horace describes Lucilius as drawing on Old rather than New Comedy, Lucilius was clearly invested in the themes and language of New Comedy. Books 26–30 of Lucilius' satires – his earliest compositions – not only use dramatic meters, but are full of vignettes drawn from New Comedy, including the loss of love (e. g., W 742), an attack on a lover's house (W 793–803) and the aftermath of a fight (W 737).[18] But we do not need to limit ourselves to erotic themes in order to find connections with New Comedy. In what follows, I look briefly at three other topics – secrecy and revelation, urban decadence, and the representation of anger – in order to suggest a wider range of correspondences between Lucilius and Terence.

I begin with secrecy and disclosure, a subject close to the heart of satire, which delights in unveiling the flaws we hide from ourselves and others. A number of fragments from Lucilius address this issue, though the first is perhaps the most often cited (W 670–1, 672–3, 696–7, 699):[19]

---

17 See McGill 2012, 121.
18 For discussions of these and other erotic themes from Lucilius' earliest books, see Fiske 1920, 183, 393–8; Petersmann 1999, 296–310; Goldberg 2005, 159; and Auhagen 2001, 13–9.
19 All quotations of Lucilius are from Warmington's 1938 Loeb edition. Warmington prints this group of fragments in Book XXVI, Lucilius' first book, suggesting their programmatic nature.

> Ego ubi quem ex praecordiis
> Ecfero versum,

When I bring forth some line from my heart

> At enim dicis 'clandestino tibi quod conmisum foret,
> neu muttires quidquam neu mysteria ecferres foras.'

But you say, 'What was entrusted to you in secret,
Don't reveal any of it or spread its mysteries abroad.'

> Mihi necesse est eloqui,
> nam scio Amyclas tacendo periise.

I must speak out, for I know that Amyclae perished because of keeping quiet.

> Evadat saltem aliquid aliqua quod conatus sum.

May what I tried to do come out in some way at least.

All but one of these fragments use first-person verbs to refer to speaking out (*ecfero, dicis, eloqui*), while a single example with second-person verbs emphasizes keeping things to oneself (*neu muttiris, neu ecferres*). Although we cannot be sure who the speakers of these lines are, they seem to support Lucilius' reputation for frank speech and a confessional style (see Hor. *Sat.* 2.1.30–4). These fragments are not, however, actual examples of any candid appraisal or critique, but are instead references to the act of disclosure itself. They appear therefore to be programmatic reflections on the satirist's job, and indications of the necessity, even urgency, for the speaker to reveal what he knows.[20]

It may seem surprising to find something similar at work in Terence. Of course secrets are an integral part of the comic plot, where they play an important role in creating conflict and suspense. Typically a son's love affair has been kept hidden from his father; only when something causes it to come out can the play move forwards towards reconciliation and resolution.[21] Yet not all secrets are tied so closely to the plot, and as in the fragments from Lucilius examined above, the question of how to handle privileged information may itself become a topic of conversation.

---

[20] Horace makes himself out to be a master of discretion: see e. g., *Sat.* I.6.56–61 and I.9, where in the first case he says little about himself, in the second, little about Maecenas.

[21] The *Hecyra* is the exception, in that the secrets concern not the love affair, but the marriage. The play is unusual in a number of ways, on which see Goldberg 2014, 21–5.

In the beginning of the *Eunuchus,* for example, as Thais prepares to reveal her family story, the slave Parmeno tells her that his discretion depends upon the truth of her account (*Eun.* 103–4):[22]

> quae vera audivi taceo et contineo optume;
> sin falsum aut vanum aut finctumst, continuo palamst:
>
> When I've heard something true, I keep quiet and I hold it in. But if on the other hand it's false or groundless or made up, it's out in the open immediately:

Given Parmeno's low opinion of courtesans, we may suspect that he has already made up his mind not to believe her.[23] But he threatens her with the possibility that he could go either way and articulates the terms on which he will decide. Given that Thais' tale bears some resemblance to a typical plot of New Comedy, Parmeno's threat to make it a subject of his own story assimilates his role to that of the playwright.[24] But this is not a metatheatrical point, or not just: Parmeno also sounds like a satirist here, one who feels a pressing need to reveal dishonesty and pretense.

In the *Hecyra*, Pamphilus also asserts control over the circulation of a secret, in this case his own. Towards the end of the play, he discovers that everything will work out for the best in what has been a troubled relationship with his wife. But he does not want his past mistakes to be revealed to everyone. He asks his courtesan Bacchis to keep to herself the humiliating things she knows about him, even if it means breaking the comic convention of telling everything at the play's end (*Hec.* 865–7):

> Neque opus est
> adeo muttito. placet non fieri hoc itidem ut in comoediis
> omnia omnes ubi resciscunt.
>
> Then there's no need to talk about this. It's better if this doesn't turn out the way it does in comedies when everyone ends up knowing everything.

Like Parmeno, Pamphilus believes he can control what gets communicated and how much damage is done, though of course Pamphilus represents the opposite

---

[22] All quotations from Terence are from Kauer and Lindsay's 1926 OCT.
[23] See line 121: *utrumque hoc falsumst: effluet*. The play is full of negative stereotypes about courtesans: see lines 50–69, 79–80, 382–5. Thais is well aware of this prejudice and hopes she will not be unfairly judged as a result: see *Eun.* 197–8.
[24] See Sharrock 2009, 154 on both Parmeno as playwright and the similarity of Thais' story to a plot of New Comedy.

perspective in wanting to keep things hushed up. He, too, is a playwright within the play, this time trying to direct the ending of the play. Shame is his motivation, however, not artistry, and Terence seems to critique this desire to suppress speech and bad behavior.[25] Passages like these from the *Eunuchus* and the *Hecyra* allow us to see Terence's interest in the ethics of frank speech, a central dimension of Roman satire.[26]

A second area on which we can compare both writers is their depiction of the decadent life in the city, whether Rome or Athens. In an unassigned fragment, Lucilius describes the frantic pace at Rome, where everyone is intent upon personal gain (W 1145–51):[27]

> Nunc vero a mani ad noctem festo atque profesto
> totus item pariterque die populusque patresque
> iactare indu foro se omnes, decedere nusquam;
> uni se atque eidem studio omnes dedere et arti –
> verba dare ut caute possint, pugnare dolose,
> blanditia certare, bonum simulare virum se,
> insidias facere ut si hostes sint omnibus omnes.

> Now from morning till night, on holidays and workdays, all the people and senators alike rush into the Forum and never leave. All them devote themselves to one and the same pursuit and art, to deceive as warily as possible, to contend with cunning, to strive by means of flattery, to affect being a good man, and to lay plots as though enemies of all men.

The forum draws everyone in, not for hard work and business, but for opportunities to swindle and cheat. It does not matter whether you are a common man or a senator: both are equally interested in deception and pretense (*verba dare* and *bonum simulare virum se*).[28]

Terence, too, depicts the city as a place of opportunism and fraud, even if it is not Rome that is being described, at least not overtly. The most obvious example of the decadence of city life is of course the *Adelphoe*, where the indulgent ways of the urban Micio are contrasted with the simple values of the farmer Demea, though the play emphasizes luxury and money more than corruption.[29] Other plays take up fraud and deception in the city more pointedly.

---

[25] See Goldberg 2014, *ad loc.*: 'It certainly has a serious implication: by avoiding a full recognition, Pamphilus escapes its full consequences.'
[26] On *parrhesia* in Roman satire, see e. g., Hunter 1985, Braund 2004, and Rosen 2013.
[27] See Goldberg 2005, 156 for a stylistic analysis of this fragment.
[28] Note that Muecke 2005, 45–6 compares this fragment to Plautus's *Curculio* and comments that 'Terence retreated from Plautus' satiric involvement with Roman social and political issues.'
[29] On luxury and excess in Lucilius, perhaps as part of a contrast between city and country life, see W 159–71 (city) and W 149–58 (country).

In the *Eunuchus*, for example, the parasite Gnatho encounters a former acquaintance in the forum who has fallen on hard times. Gnatho repeats for us the lessons he gave this man about how to become a successful parasite (255–8). His teaching centers on playing up to someone else's desires through flattery and submission. It is a deceptive performance in which one pretends to be someone other than who one really is, and all for personal gain. While it is a parasite who behaves this way in Terence, not the *populus* or *patres* we hear about in the Lucilian excerpt, both passages are similarly about debasement and a devotion to flattery and pretense.

In a last pair of examples, I consider Terence and Lucilius' representation of anger and violence. In a satire about a gladiatorial fight, Lucilius has the speaker, Pacideianus, describe how he plans to attack his opponent (W 176–81):

> 'Occidam illum equidem et vincam, si id quaeritis,'
> > inquit.
> 'verum illud credo fore: in os prius accipiam ipse,
> quam gladium in stomacho surdi ac pulmonibus sisto.
> Odi hominem, iratus pugno, nec longius quicquam
> nobis, quam dextrae gladium dum accommodet alter;
> usque adeo studio atque odio illius ecferor ira.'

> I'll kill him and I'll win, if that's what you're asking,' he said. 'For this is surely how it will turn out. First I myself will take a blow on the face, then I'll plant one in that moron's belly and chest. I hate the man, I'm burning for the fight. We won't delay any longer than it takes him to put the sword in his right hand. I'm completely carried away with anger by my eagerness to fight and my hatred for him.

He is confident about his strength (*accipiam, sisto*) and his eventual victory in the contest (*occidam, accipiam*). He even maps the fight out for us, predicting where the blows will fall and in what order. But the gladiator not only reveals his physical prowess. He also describes the emotion that fuels his violence: the repetition of anger and hatred (*odi, iratus, odio, ira*) together with *ecferor* give a sense of how much antagonism he feels. So clear a statement is this of the relationship between anger and violence, that Cicero used it for a discussion about anger and courage in his *Tusculan Disputations* (4.48).

It is worth comparing the gladiator's speech to another virtual attack, this time in Terence's *Adelphoe*. Geta has learned, falsely it turns out, that his mistress' daughter has been abandoned by Aeschinus, the boy who had impregnated and promised to marry her. Geta rehearses the punishment he would like to inflict on the family (*Ad.* 314–9):

> seni animam primum exstinguerem ipsi qui illud produxit scelus;
> tum autem Syrum inpulsorem, vah, quibus illum lacerarem modis!
> sublime[m] medium primum arriperem et capite in terra statuerem,
> ut cerebro dispergat viam;   315
> adulescenti ipsi eriperem oculos, post haec praecipitem darem;
> ceteros – ruerem agerem raperem tunderem et prosternerem.

> First I'd annihilate the old man who produced this curse, then Syrus who drove Aeschinus to it, how I'd tear him apart! I'd lift him up around the middle and stand him up on his head so that he scatters his brains upon the road. As for that young man, I'd rip his eyes out, then hurl him headlong. As for the rest, I'd fall on them, chase, seize, pound and throw them to the ground.

Like Lucilius' gladiator, Geta records the various steps in the attack, and with even greater detail and more colorful language. Nor is he just reciting his moves: as we learn from two characters who happen to be standing nearby, he acts them out as well in a full-blown performance (305, 308–9). Geta expresses his hostility not only with his acrobatics, but with his language as well (309–12):

> Ah
> me miserum, vix sum compos animi, ita ardeo iracundia.
> nil est quod malim quam illam totam familiam dari mi obviam,
> ut ego iram hanc in eos evomam omnem, dum aegritudo haec est recens.

> Ah, wretched me, I'm barely in control of my mind, I'm burning with so much rage. There is nothing I'd prefer than to have that whole household within reach, so that I could hurl my anger on them all while my anger is fresh.

In fact we have here another detailed illustration of the connection between anger and violence, and an analysis that reflects some philosophical awareness as well. When Geta says he needs to act quickly while the pain is fresh, he seems to allude to a feature of the Stoic theory of emotions. But in fact he has inverted their point: the Stoics recommend acting quickly in order to restrain, not give vent to, one's angry feelings.[30]

By juxtaposing passages like these from Terence and Lucilius, we can see features about each author that we might not notice otherwise. Both of the passages we have just discussed about anger and violence are memorable for their lively performative aspects and speakers' bravado. But their emphasis on anger also suggests that there may have been some influence from contemporary philosophy and theories of the emotions. Menander parodies philosophy, of course, and it could be that Terence draws upon a comic model for his humorous depic-

---

[30] Cic. *Tusc. Disp.* 3.83, Sen. *de ira* 2.4.1.

tion of Geta's rage.³¹ But given how often Lucilius pokes fun at the Stoics and Epicureans, it is just as likely that Geta's mis-reading of Stoic theory points to a Roman context for Terence's representation of anger.³² Similarly, the parasite Gnatho and his lessons on how to be successful may look somewhat different when read together with Lucilius' description of corruption in the Forum. Gnatho's advice about using flattery and pretense for one's own gain might have struck the audience not just as a comic scene, but as a very Roman one as well. At the same time, Lucilius' colorful descriptions of city life and its characters could also have been inspired by comedy and familiar types of dramatic scenes, just as we find with the erotic fragments in his early books.

Linguistic purity

I turn in conclusion to both writers' use of Greek. Terence's style is associated with purity, his language uncluttered by colloquialisms, abuse, or very much Greek.³³ Lucilius' style is spontaneous and conversational, full of obscenity and unusual words; the latter is one of the reasons that some of the fragments were preserved for us at all. He also uses Greek liberally, whether distinguishing between *poema* and *poiesis*, quoting from Homer, or referring to elements of Stoicism or Epicureanism.³⁴ But the approach is not at all monolithic, and including Greek in technical contexts or quotations from Greek authors is very different from using it to characterize other people's speech.³⁵ Here I survey a case of the latter from Book II of the satires, a set of fragments that concern the extortion trial of Mucius Scaevola. Although these fragments are often discussed in the

---

31 See Konstan 2012 on the relationship of Greek comedy and philosophy. Martin 1976 *ad* 319 points to the Latin style of the passage: 'The assonance of the verbs, emphasising Geta's rage, is much more a feature of Latin ... than of Menander's Greek, and it is probable that in this respect, as with a number of rhetorical features, T. goes beyond the simplicity of Menander's style.'
32 For parodies of philosophy in Lucilius, see e.g., W 507–8 and 1189–90. On Lucilius and philosophy, see Fiske 1920, *passim*, Muecke 2005, 43–4, Mayer 2005, Reinhardt 2013, 529, and most recently Dutsch 2014, 21–5.
33 Suetonius *Vit. Ter.* 7 quotes comments by both Cicero and Caesar on Terence's 'pure speech.' See Maltby 1985, 112–3 and cf. Müller 2007, who takes Caesar's phrase 'puri sermonis amator' to mean 'easy to understand' rather than pure or refined.
34 See Petersmann 1999 and Chahoud 2004 on the range of Lucilius' usage of Greek. Horace is critical of Lucilius' use of Greek at *Sat.* 1.10.20–4: see Gowers 2012 *ad loc.* and Hutchinson 2013, 15 on the inaptness of Horace's imagery of blended wine.
35 See Chahoud 2004, 7–11.

literature on Lucilius, they have not been considered together with Terence's use of Greek, so far as I know.

In the fragment below, Scaevola ridicules Albucius for his Philhellenism (W 87–93):[36]

> 'Graecum te, Albuci, quam Romanum atque Sabinum
> municipem Ponti, Tritani, centurionum,
> praeclarorum hominum ac primorum signiferumque,
> maluisti dici. Graece ergo praetor Athenis,
> id quod maluisti te, cum ad me accedes, saluto:
> 'chaere' inquam 'Tite.' Lictores, turma omnis chorusque:
> 'chaere, Tite.' Hinc hostis mi Albucius, hinc inimicus!'
>
> You prefer to be called a Greek, Albucius, rather than a Roman and a Sabine, a fellow-citizen of the centurions Pontus and Tritanus, outstanding men and first-rank standard-bearers. Therefore, as praetor at Athens, I greet you in Greek when you approach me, as you prefer: 'Chaere, Titus,' I say. And the whole troop and chorus say, 'Chaere, Titus.' This is why Albucius is my enemy, this is why he's hostile to me!

Albucius likes to be addressed in Greek, perhaps even wishes he *were* Greek: Scaevola implies that his desire to fit in at Athens is equivalent to a rejection of his Romanness.[37] What Albucius takes as a mark of superiority, Scaevola views as pretentious and disloyal.[38]

Other fragments from the same satire make a similar association between Greek and affectedness (W 84–6):[39]

> 'Quam lepide lexis conpostae ut tesserulae omnes
> arte pavimento atque emblemate vermiculato!
>
> How charmingly his words are put together, just like the little stones in a mosaic floor and inlaid pattern!

---

36 A much discussed fragment: see e.g., Gruen 1992, 290–1, Chahoud 2004, 31–4, Goldberg 2005, 161–2, Adams 2008, 353–4.

37 It is not the Greek *per se* that is the problem, but the fact that it is used in an official context rather than a private one with friends. On the complexity of Roman attitudes towards Greek in this period, see Gruen 1984, 256–9 and ch. 7, Petersmann 1999, 297–302, and Adams 2003, 353.

38 See Chahoud 2004, 5 on the use of Greek here as a form of 'mockery, distance, and hostility.' There may be a further layer of insult in the fact that Scaevola was a Stoic and Albucius an Epicurean: see Reinhardt 2013, 529 on this fragment and 'the pretentiousness of a self-styled Epicurean.'

39 Cicero quotes both fragments at *de orat.* 3.171. The use of *lexis* by Scaevola seems to be part of the mockery of Albucius here: see Adams 2003, 353–4.

> 'Crassum habeo generum, ne rhetoricoterus tu seis.
>
> I have Crassus for my son-in-law, so don't you be rhetorical.

Albucius cares not only about individual words, but their artistic arrangement. And while this attitude towards Albucius is expressed in Scaevola's voice, not Lucilius', presumably the satire would fail to be effective if readers, and perhaps Lucilius himself, were not sympathetic to the criticism. In fact, this view of Greek is not limited to the opposition between Scaevola and Albucius, but appears elsewhere in the satires as well.[40]

Terence's use of Greek is much more limited, as already mentioned. But that does not mean that he adopts a careless or casual manner towards it. In fact, Terence often incorporates Greek in order to mark differences in a character's social class and pretensions, though admittedly in a more subtle way than Lucilius. To begin with, Terence regularly includes Greek expressions and oaths in the speech of his servile characters, a touch that reflects the realism of his style.[41] Terence marks élite difference in his plays, then, but in the opposite manner to Lucilius, using it to distinguish characters of a lower, not higher, social status.

Terence's incorporation of Greek vocabulary is not limited to slaves. We also find it in the speech of free characters, not throughout the play as in the case of slaves, but in specific passages that play an important role in characterization. Here I look at two Terentian fathers, Simo from the *Andria* and Demea in the *Adelphoe,* who use Greek at significant moments in each play and in doing so, reveal their self-importance and sense of superiority.[42]

In the *Andria,* for example, Terence's first play, Simo is responsible for five of the eleven Greek words in the play.[43] Four of these occur in the very first scene of the play in a conversation with Sosia, Simo's freedman, while the fifth comes up in a confrontation with Crito towards the end of the play. Maltby takes the incidence of Greek in the opening scene as helping to establish the Greek setting of

---

40 See e. g., W 14, 15–6 (and Chahoud 2004, 28–9), which mock someone for choosing a Greek word when there is a straightforward Latin one available, as when English speakers include a French word or two to sound sophisticated. Other fragments criticize other adulerations of linguistic purity: Accius' spelling reforms, which would have approximated Greek more than Latin, and the use in Latin of provincial or other non-Latin words, on which see Petersmann 1999, 309 and Adams, 2003, 153 and 121, n. 53.
41 See Maltby 1985, 119 and Karakasis 2005, 83–4.
42 See Maltby 1985, 122.
43 I rely on the statistics in Maltby 1985. For a description of his methodology and what counts as a loan-word, see pp. 111–18. See also Chahoud 2004, 7–11 on the difference between Grecisms and code-switching.

the play. Yet it is more likely that it is directed at characterizing Simo and his hostile and skeptical attitude towards others.

Right from the start, Simo's portrayal is developed around the theme of *fides*: he first describes the loyalty he knows he can expect from Sosia, then goes on to detail his disappointments as far as his son Pamphilus is concerned.[44] Yet for all that he wants others to demonstrate their loyalty to him, he has great difficulty showing any himself: he consistently goes through intermediaries, for example, rather than speak to his son himself. The Greek words in his conversation with Sosia all concern Pamphilus: *ephebus* (51), *philosophus* (57), *symbola* (88), and *attat* (125), this last exclamation representing his sobering realization about the boy's love affair. By using Greek to describe his son in this opening scene, Simo indicates the detachment with which he views him. Terence allows us to see what kind of a father Simo is not only by what he says, but also by the diction he adopts.

Simo uses another Greek word before the play is over, yelling *sycophanta* (919) at Crito when the latter identifies the girl with whom Simo's son is in love as the daughter of their neighbour Chremes. Throughout the play, Simo has trusted only himself and his own interpretation of the situation at hand: perhaps the best example of this is when he takes his discovery of Pamphilus' baby to be part of a plot to trick him.[45] In accusing Crito of being an imposter in Greek, Simo reveals yet again his skepticism about other people's knowledge and authority.[46] Simo's reliance on Greek at the beginning and end of the play belongs to a pattern of name-calling and hostility that bolsters his need to feel superior.

A second example shows once again how a sudden increase in Greek vocabulary may emphasize a father's inflated sense of importance. In the *Adelphoe*, the highest proportion of Greek words occurs in the speech of the slave Syrus. But Demea uses seven words in the play as a whole and five in his remarkable turnaround at the end of the play, this compared to just one Greek word uttered by

---

[44] Simo has been spying on his son, and considers him blameworthy even though he can as of yet find no reason to fault him: see lines 149–50, 154, 164–5. See the excellent treatment of the opening of the play in McCarthy 2004. McGarrity 1978 addresses the theme of *fides* but takes a much more sympathetic view of Simo than I do here.
[45] See lines 471–2, 492–4, and Davos' response at 495: '*certe hercle nunc hic se ipsu' fallit, haud ego.*' As Goldberg puts it, 'The birth is genuine, and the laugh is on Simo, who throughout the play makes trouble for himself by refusing to accept the clear evidence of his senses' (1986, 20).
[46] See *An.* 814–6, where Crito anticipated a hostile reaction: *clamitent/me sycophantam, hereditatem persequi/mendicum.*

Micio.⁴⁷ At lines 855 and following, Demea decides that he will adopt Micio's indulgent approach to parenting in an attempt to win over his son's affection (*Ad.* 875–81):

> ita eos meo labore eductos maxumo hic fecit suos
> paullo sumptu: miseriam omnem ego capio, hic potitur gaudia.
> age age, nunciam experiamur contra ecquid ego possiem
> blande dicere aut benigne facere, quando hoc provocat.
> ego quoque a meis me amari et magni pendi postulo:
> si id fit dando atque obsequendo, non posteriores feram.   880
> deerit: id mea minime refert qui sum natu maxumus.

> While I raised them with enormous effort, he's made them his at little expense. I have all the misery, he enjoys all the pleasure. So come then, let me try to see now what I can do in return by speaking kindly and doing favors, since he challenges me to this. I want to be loved and appreciated by my children as well. If that happens by giving and indulging, I won't take last place. It will cost us, but that doesn't bother me much since I'm the older one.

Demea undergoes a transformation before our eyes, with every bit of gratitude he earns encouraging him to further acts of generosity.⁴⁸ At the same time that this change leads to a more affectionate relationship with the boys, it builds to a triumphal speech over Micio, something he may have desired just as deeply. Demea's linguistic shift reflects his growing sense of superiority and haughtiness as he sees himself outwitting Micio at his own game.⁴⁹

Terence's approach to Greek in these cases is deliberate and tied to social class and pretensions. He uses Greek for slaves' speech, where it contributes to the naturalism of the language of the play, as well as for free characters in specific passages, where it indicates their self-importance. It might seem as though these two dimensions of Terence's approach to Greek are in conflict with each other. But Terence probably wants us to see a connection between them. The free

---

47 *heia* (868), *hymenaeus* (907), *lampas* (907), *euge* (911), *opsono* (964). Note that this change in Demea is accompanied by one in meter as well: see Moore 2012, ch. 10 on the metre in the *Adelphoe* as a whole, and especially pp. 366–7 on Demea's speech at 855–81.
48 After insisting that Aeschinus be married on the spot, not without some damage to Micio's house (906–22), Demea arranges for Sostrata to marry Micio (929–45), gives some property to Hegio (947–56), frees Syrus (959–61), then frees Syrus' wife as well (972–7), and finally gives them both some money with which to get started (979–83).
49 See Moore 2012, 367: 'Each change in meter here reinforces Demea's power.' On the challenges of interpreting Demea's apparent change of heart at the end of the play, see Arnott 1963, Johnson 1968, Greenberg 1979/80, Goldberg 1986, 144, and Damen 1990.

characters who incorporate Greek words into their speech are speaking the language of slaves and thus debasing themselves. Terence suggests that fathers like Simo and Demea behave shamefully at the very moment when they consider themselves at their most astute and influential. And this is precisely the message of the trial scene from Lucilius' Book II. Scaevola implies that while Albucius thinks his adoption of Greek culture shows his sophistication, it in fact signals the abandonment of his Roman identity and good reputation.

Conclusions

It is easy to be influenced by Horace's picture of comedy and satire in the Republic, given the engaging first-person account of his development as a satirist and our need for guidance in making sense of Lucilius' fragmentary corpus. Horace's account helped shape a picture of Terence and Lucilius as very different sorts of poets, something their biographical traditions contributed to as well. But these assessments are misleading, as Terence and Lucilius clearly shared a great deal in terms of both content and style. Studying them together not only helps us understand the generic interplay between comedy and satire in the Republic, but also the ways in which poets from the same period responded to similar issues. It is likely that Lucilius was engaged with comedy throughout his entire career, not just in his earliest books, and that however much the satires are a reflection of Roman life, the depiction of Roman life itself was shaped by comic scenes and characters. As for Terence, the connections with Lucilius are another reminder of how distracting the prologues' focus on comic models has been. Terence's interest in language, emotion, and exploitation all point to a deep engagement with the literary and intellectual scene at Rome in the 2nd c. BCE.[50]

Acknowledgments

Many thanks to the organizers of the conference in Thessaloniki at which an earlier version of this paper was delivered, and especially to Stavros Frangoulidis for his kindness and generosity as host. I am also grateful to the audience for stimulating discussion and to the anonymous referee and Sander Goldberg for helpful criticism. Any remaining errors are of course my own.

---

50 On topical references in Terence's plays, see Starks, Jr., 2013.

Bibliography

Arnott, W. G. (1963), 'The End of Terence's "*Adelphoe*": A Postscript', *Greece & Rome* 10, 14–44.
Augoustakis, A. and Traill, A., (2013), (eds.), *A Companion to Terence*, Oxford.
Auhagen, U. (2001), 'Lucilius und die Komödie', in: G. Manuwald (ed.), *Der Satiriker Lucilius und seine Zeit*, 9–23.
Braund, S. (2004), '*Libertas* or *Licentia*? Freedom and Criticism in Roman Satire', in: I. Sluiter and R. M. Rosen (eds.), *Free Speech in Classical Antiquity*, Leiden, 409–28.
Breed, B. W and Rossi, A. (2006), 'Ennius and the Traditions of Epic', *Arethusa* 39, 397–425.
Chahoud, A. (2004), 'The Roman Satirist Speaks Greek', *Classics Ireland* 11, 1–46.
Damen, M. L. (1990), 'Structure and Symmetry in Terence's *Adelphoe*', *Illinois Classical Studies* 15, 85–106.
Damon, C. (1997), The *Mask of the Parasite: A Pathology of Roman Patronage*, Ann Arbor.
Dutsch, D. (2014), 'The Beginnings: Philosophy in Roman Literature before 155 BCE', in: M. Garani and D. Konstan (eds.), *The Philosophizing Muse: The Influence of Greek Philosophy on Roman Poetry*, Newcastle upon Tyne, 1–25.
Ferriss-Hill, J. L. (2015), *Roman Satire and the Old Comic Tradition*, Cambridge.
Fiske, G. C. (1920), *Lucilius and Horace: A Study in the Classical Theory of Imitation*, Madison.
Goldberg, S. M. (2005), *Constructing Literature in the Roman Republic*, Cambridge.
―――― (1986), *Understanding Terence*, Princeton.
―――― (1995), *Epic in Republican Rome*, Oxford.
―――― (2014), *Terence Hecyra*, Cambridge.
Gowers, E. (2012), *Horace Satires Book I*, Cambridge.
Greenberg, N. (1979–80), 'Success and Failure in the *Adelphoe*', *Classical World* 73, 221–36.
Gruen, E. S. (1984), *The Hellenistic World and the Coming of Rome*, Berkeley.
Gruen, E. S. (1992), *Culture and National Identity in Republican Rome*, Ithaca, N.Y.
Hanchey, D. P. (2013), 'Terence and the Scipionic *Grex*', in: A. Augoustakis and A. Traill (eds.), *A Companion to Terence*, Oxford, 113–31.
Hunter, R. L. (1985), 'Horace on Friendship and Free Speech', *Hermes* 113, 480–90.
Johnson, W. R. (1968), 'Micio and the Perils of Perfection', *California Studies in Classical Antiquity* 1, 171–86.
Karakasis, E. (2005), *Terence and the Language of Roman Comedy*, Cambridge.
Keane, C. (2005), *Figuring Genre in Roman Satire*, Oxford.
Konstan, D. (2014), 'Greek Comedy and Philosophy', in: M. Fontaine and A. Scafuro (eds.), *The Oxford Handbook of Greek and Roman Comedy*, Oxford, 278–97.
Maltby, R. (1985), 'The Distribution of Greek Loan-Words in Terence', *The Classical Quarterly* 35, 110–23.
Manuwald, G. (2001), (ed.), *Der Satiriker Lucilius und seine Zeit*, Munich (= Zetemata 110).
Martin, R. H. (1976), *Terence Adelphoe*, Cambridge.
Mayer, R. (2005), 'Sleeping with the Enemy: Satire and Philosophy', in: K. Freudenburg (ed.), *The Cambridge Companion to Roman Satire*, Cambridge, 146–59.
McCarthy, K. (2004), 'The Joker in the Pack: Slaves in Terence', *Ramus* 33, 100–19.
McGarrity, T. (1978), 'Thematic Unity in Terence's *Andria*', *Transactions of the American Philological Association* 108, 103–14.
McGill, S. (2012), *Plagiarism in Roman Literature*, Cambridge.

Muecke, F. (2005), 'Rome's First "Satirists": Themes and Genre in Ennius and Lucilius', in: K. Freudenburg (ed.), *The Cambridge Companion to Roman Satire,* Cambridge, 33–47.

Müller, R. (2007), '*Pura oratio* und *puri sermonis amator*: Zu zwei Begriffsklippen der Terenz-Forschung', in: P. Kruschwitz, W.-W. Ehlers, and F. Felgentreu (eds.), *Terentius Poeta,* München, 111–25.

Olson, D. S. (2014), (ed.), *Ancient Comedy and Reception,* Berlin.

Papaioannou, S. (2013), 'The Cultural Poetics of Terence's Literary Comedy', *Logeion* 3, 1–20.

Petersmann, H. (1999), 'The Language of Early Roman Satire: Its Function and Characteristics', *Proceedings of the British Academy* 93, 289–310.

Raschke, W. (1979), 'The Chronology of the Early Books of Lucilius', *Journal of Roman Studies* 69, 78–89.

Reinhardt, T. (2014), 'Philosophy Comes to Rome', in: F. Sheffield and J. Warren (eds.), *The Routledge Companion to Ancient Philosophy,* New York, 526–38.

Rosen, R. (2014), 'Comic *Parrhesia* and the Paradox of Repression', in: D. S. Olson (ed.), *Ancient Comedy and Reception,* Berlin, 13–28.

Ruffell, I. A. (2014), 'Old Comedy at Rome: Rhetorical Model and Satirical Problem', in: D. S. Olson (ed.), *Ancient Comedy and Reception: Studies on the Classical Tradition of Comedy from Aristophanes to the Twenty-First Century,* Berlin, 275–308.

Russo, A. (2007), *Quinto Ennio: Le opere minori,* Pisa.

Sharrock, A. (2009), *Reading Roman Comedy,* Cambridge.

Starks, Jr., J. (2013), 'Opera in bello, in otio, in negotio: Terence and Rome in the 160s BCE', in: A. Augoustakis and A. Traill (eds.), *A Companion to Terence,* Oxford, 132–55.

Umbrico, A. (2010), *Terenzio e i suoi nobiles: Invenzione e realtà di un controverso legame,* Pisa.

Dorota Dutsch
How to Do Things with Words – and Pictures: Text and Image in the Parisian Terence

In this essay I argue that the illustrated manuscripts of Terence (γ), descending from a lost late-antique codex, represent a medium of the reception of ancient drama that is still poorly understood.[1] Two habits of thought have shifted scholarly attention away from looking at the text and image of the illustrated Terence as a whole.[2] First, scholars tend to analyze the miniatures separately from the text, as a part of the iconographic tradition; second, and concomitantly, critics usually focus their attention on the Carolingian miniatures as 'witnesses' to absent images instead of looking at their material and textual context.[3] In order to exemplify the kind of insights one might gain from examining the interface of text and image, I offer a close reading of the introductory material and the first act of the *Andria* in Parisinus Latinus 7899 (P).[4]

---

1 Jones and Morey 1930, vol. 2, catalogue and compare the illustrated manuscripts. For detailed analysis of the textual tradition, see Grant 1986, 8–48; cf. Victor 2014 for a concise summary of more recent findings. Wright 2006 and Nervegna 2014 are the most recent proponents of the view that the illustrations were invented in late antiquity and have no earlier precedents. See contra, Dodwell 2000, Dutsch 2007, and Demetriou 2014; especially on the precedent of illustrated papyri of Menander (Agnoia P. Oxy. 2652, dated to 2nd or 3rd cent.). Whatever the date of their prototype, the Carolingian miniatures constitute an instance of reception of ancient performance tradition that goes back at least to late antiquity. The artists, patrons, and readers of illustrated manuscripts were undeniably concerned with the performance dimension of comedy. The inaccuracies in the Vatican manuscript (cf. Nervegna 2014, 729) might reflect the difficulty for the Carolingian artist, reproducing a body of 151 complex illustrations, and need not have been a feature of the late-antique codex.
2 I am grateful to Glenn Patten and Henrike Lähnemann for drawing my attention to recent work on the interaction of text and image in later medieval manuscripts. To cite two particularly important examples, Starkey 2004 analyzes the interaction of word, image, and performance in Wolfram von Eschenbach's *Willehalm*, contextualizing the manuscripts in the aesthetics of court-culture, while Hamburger 2006 explains how the frontpieces of late medieval *Bible historiale* function as theologically informed maps for both reading and viewing the manuscripts. The interpretation I propose here is germane to but independent from such readings. Because of the (at least) late-antique background of the Carolingian Terence, I do not draw on later medieval notions of reception of text and image, such as formulated in Pope Gregory's letter to Serenus (Hamburger 2006a, 17) or Thomasin von Zerclaere's comments on images and learning (Starkey 2004, 14–5).
3 Thus, Henri Omont's facsimile of the Parisian MS. 7899 reproduces only the illustrations, omitting the text. Wright 2006 reproduces almost exclusively the illustrated pages and rarely comments on the relationship between the image and the text; his brief comments on how the artist might have come up with his illustrations (2006, 212–4) are an exception.
4 In doing so, I will be relying on a glossary of gestures for this play, see Dutsch 2007.

This is not an obvious choice. The Parisian manuscript is usually considered of secondary importance to the Vaticanus Latinus 3868 (C), not only because of the Parisian manuscript's later date but also because of the expressive style of its drawings, typical of the school of Reims in the second half of the ninth century.[5] Thus, David H. Wright's recent reconstruction of the page layout and illustrations of the lost original, from which the γ manuscripts descend, relies chiefly on the Vatican copy (2006). Wright is distinctly unimpressed by the drawings in the Parisian manuscript: '[the] artists ... tended to exaggerate the lively qualities of their drawings, even sometimes at the expense of coherent anatomy and drapery' (2006, 192). Ironically, the same precise and expressive ink drawings make the Parisian manuscript an attractive 'witness' to performance tradition. C. R. Dodwell often resorts to this putatively inferior copy 'to clarify and correct' the older manuscript, because 'the drawings in the Paris manuscript often give a clearer rendering of the gestures than we find in the Vatican manuscript' (2000, 38).[6] Both Wright and Dodwell approach Carolingian illustrations with fixed expectations about what these illustrations ought to do. Wright assumes that they ought to be ornamental (hence his concern with draperies). Dodwell assumes that illustrations of drama ought to reveal ancient stage conventions. My own interest in the illustrated Terence was originally motivated by an impulse similar to Dodwell's: I wondered whether the gestures in the miniatures might represent performance practice of the late revivals of Terence and thought that the Parisian manuscript's precise drawings lent themselves well to representing details (Dutsch 2007). But such interpretations (including mine) are reductive: they constrain us to look *through* the codex as a physical object, wishing it to be transparent, and to look *toward* the absent 'Thing-in-itself', which is either the style of the original illustrations – considered apart from text – or the performance tradition.[7] In this essay I examine again the Parisian manuscript but this time focus on it as a material object and ask how drawings and text interact. In this process, the manuscript is no longer a transparent 'witness,' but an artifact that performs. The design for this performance is one that is hybrid, mingling the features of the late-antique model with the Carolingian aesthetics of the school of Reims.

As Gérard Genette proposed, a book can be conceived as a threshold; the book as a physical object enables the transition between the outside world and the

---

[5] On the historical context of the school of Reims see F. Mutherich 1996, and W. Wüstefeld, 105–16.
[6] See e. g. XIXb, XXXa, XXXVIa, XLVIa.
[7] The essentail contrast here is between Kant's ideal Thing-in-itself and the object of art as thing physically present for the viewer, as defined by Heidegger in *Poetry Language and Thought*. For Heidegger's critique of Kant, see especially (1971, 174–5).

Text and Image in the Parisian Terence — 455

imaginary space of the text.[8] The material properties of the book, its size, texture, illustrations, and font become integral to the experience of the person handling the book, or in our case, codex. It is impossible to escape abstraction entirely, as the task of historicizing a Carolingian reader's response to the codex and its hybrid aesthetics is beyond the scope of this paper. I will attempt, however, to outline how the Parisian copy engages readers' cognitive mechanics, and this analysis will stand as a sample of how the Carolingian copies integrate, and therefore how their late-antique model likely also integrated integrated text and image.

Let us begin with a brief description: the manuscript consists of 176 folios of parchment (261 mm by 215 mm), white on flesh side, darker on hair side.[9] The writing, a Carolingian minuscule, is in two different hands, in inks that vary from black to brown. There are about 25 lines of text on each page. In different sections of the folios, recto and verso, in principle at the beginning of each new scene, appear 151 ink drawings.[10] They show actors, costumed and masked, gesticulating and handling props, next to simple door-frames; captions in Rustic capitals above the drawings and occasional marginalia (in minuscule) break the iconographic illusion of performance. The present binding in calfskin bears the arms of Charles IX and was made in the 16th century.[11] But once we turn to the first folio, we come face to face with the Carolingian version of the late-antique codex. It opens grandly with a view of the title (folio 1v) and the portrait of Terence (on folio 2r). The title is written in Rustic capitals in red ink: 'P. TERENTI AFRI COMOEDIAE N VI.' A list of the names of plays in a column, in slightly smaller Rustic capitals: 'ANDRIA, EUNUCHUS, HEAUTONTIMOROUMENOS, ADELPHOE, HECYRA, PHORMIO,' maps out the sequence of the plays. At the bottom of 1v we read, in Rustic capitals the same size as Terence's name and the title: 'FELICITER CALLIOPIO,' (with best wishes to Calliopius). That the name of the scholar who most likely supervised the production of the late-antique codex was displayed as prominently as that of Terence speaks volumes about the importance of the codex as an artifact (and the connection between the Carolingian codex and its matrix).[12]

---

8 Genette (1987, 7; cf. *Paratexts* 1997, 2), drawing on Borges' vision of a library-universe (1941), proposed that a book functions as a threshold or vestibule.
9 So Wright (2006, 192; Omont 1907, 2) gives slightly different measurements: 260/220 mm.
10 It is worth noting that the illustrations have no frames. Wright points out that this is an unusual feature for late-antique illustrations, one more likely to occur when the illustration was copied from an earlier manuscript, as is the case with folio 1r of the famous Roman Vergil illustrating the first Eclogue (2001, 14).
11 See Omont (1907, 2–3) for a detailed description.
12 The inscription is ancient, but Calliopius need not have been simply a corrector of the text; see Victor 2014.

Fig. 1: Fol. 2r Actors holding Terence's portrait.

Facing the title page, on folio 2r, there is an ink drawing of two actors costumed as slaves holding a medallion portrait of a man, whose beard and haircut resemble those of third-century imperial portraits; obviously, this is Terence.[13] Such medallion portraits were customary; a very similar portrait of Menander can be found in the Villa of the Menander in Mitylene.[14] Here, the framed portrait surrounded by an ornament in Carolingian style reminds the reader that Terence is a classical playwright enshrined presently (in the late ninth century) as a master of ancient comic drama.[15] Terence's medallion is depicted as a heavy object, its mass

---

[13] On the features of Terence's portrait, see Dodwell 2000, 6–9; on consular portraits in medallions, see Wright 2001, 11.

[14] On these, see Charitonides and Kahil 1970, Dutsch 2007, Csapo 2010, Nervegna 2013: Chapter 3. On the relationship between the iconographic tradition of Menander and the illustrated manuscripts of Terence, see the section on manuscripts of Terence in Radden Keefe (forthcoming).

[15] By contrast, in the Vatican manuscript, the frame is late-antique: see Wright 2006, 6. On the importance of Terence in the Carolingian schools in general, see Riché 1989, 113–4. Beginning in the ninth century, Terence is usually found in the library-inventories of monasteries and cathedrals that had schools (Benjamin Victor, personal communication). Munk Olsen (vol. II, 1985, 578–635) lists plays and excerpts copied in between the ninth and tenth centuries. The plays were very likely subjects of careful analysis, and Munk Olsen (col. IV/1, 2009, 107–111) succinctly presents the evidence for the re-use of ancient exegesis on Terence (esp. Eugra-

supported by a pedestal and held up by two actors dressed as slaves. These trappings are important because they suggest that on the pages of the codex, the encounter with Terence, traditionally mediated by actors on stage, will be mediated through representations of actors. This portrait can be compared with the full body portraits of the sitting poet on folio 9r and 14r in the Roman Vergil, which frame the relationship between the viewer/reader and the poet as immediate and personal.[16] In contrast, the viewers/readers of the Terence manuscript are welcomed to a performance space, in which depictions of actors 'bring' them Terence's text.[17] This is, needless to say, an ambitious undertaking, but the folios introducing the *Andria* demonstrate how exactly the codex can work as a substitute performance space.

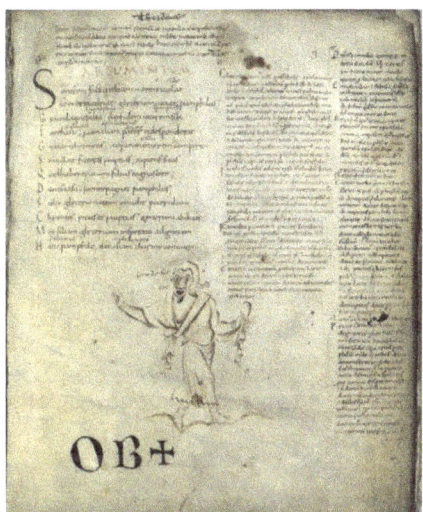

Figs. 2 and 3: Folio 2v: *armarium* and folio 3r: argumentum and the prologue.

Turning the leaf, the viewers face the first complex montage of text and image: an *armarium* (cupboard) to the left and the text of the argumentum and figure of the prologue to the right. The *armarium* (2v) contains thirteen masks placed on the shelves in order of their appearance on stage. Again, the masks are realistically

---

phius) and for the creation of new exegesis, from the ninth century on. As the references to Terence in Paschasius' lament on the Abbot Wala of Corbie suggest, even Carolingian theologians turned to Terence's plays for advice relevant to moral dilemmas (see Booker 2009, 44–9).
16 On portraits of Menander, see Nervegna 2013, 130–138.
17 The famous line from Plautus' *Menaechmi* (3) comes to mind: *apporto vobis Plautum, lingua non manu.*

drawn as objects placed on shelves; the mask on the lowest shelf shows a string by which the actor may attach it. Notably, the masks include one for Glycerium, who does not leave her house and would not have been visible on the classical stage, but who will appear on the page-turned-stage in the manuscript. On top of each mask there are floating letters: the scribe has added abbreviations suggesting which mask is needed for which character.[18] The single mask on the bottom shelf, for example, is identified as D-A-S, Davus. Clearly, the readers of the Parisian Terence are not just invited to imagine the characters of the play; they are invited to imagine actors playing them.[19]

Facing the masks are the *argumentum* and the figure of the Prologue (3r). The prologue speaker raises his right arm pointing towards the *argumentum* above him and further left towards 2v and the *armarium*.[20] This gesture invites the viewer to juxtapose the Prologue figure, the text of the *argumentum*, and the masks. We as readers and viewers may try to identify the features of the masks for the characters mentioned in the *argumentum*: Glycerium the pseudohetaira, Pamphilus, the youth who made her pregnant, Chremes, the father of the girl whom Pamphilus is expected to marry, and Charinus, the young man in love with her. The combination of folios 2v and 3r introduces the play as plot and also as visual material, as we are encouraged to look at the masks as part of the story.[21]

Terence's prologue to the *Andria* is written on folio 3v in the left-center of the page, surrounded on both sides by columns of commentary excerpted from Donatus,[22] and continues on 4r/v and on 6r.[23] Still reading the text of the prologue on 4v, the viewer now faces a particularly elaborate drawing on 6r.

---

18 This detail is absent from the Vatican Terence; cf. Wright 2006, 9.
19 This is, again, considerably different from the Vatican Vergil, which introduces the reader/viewer to the imaginary world of Vergil's poems; cf. Wright 2001, 54–6.
20 A prologue speaker, raising his right hand in a gesture that commands the spectator's attention: his arm, stretched out, points up and to the reader's/viewer's left.
21 These masks seem consistent in Parisinus, but see Nervegna (2014, 729) on the Vatican.
22 The *scholia* in P in general are a mixture of remarks from Donatus and another, unknown source (Muir and Turner 2010, 47); folios 3–9, discussed here, contain the opening of Donatus' commentary.
23 Folio 5 is misplaced, and should in fact be placed after folio 6.; see below on the conversation between Simo and Sosia.

Fig. 4: Fol. 6r: the beginning of the first scene of the *Andria*.

The drawing divides folio 6r into two horizontal sections. Vertically, the page is also divided into two columns; the last eight lines of the prologue and the first seven lines of the first scene of the *Andria* are written in the left one (above and below the miniature). The right column and spaces around the drawing are filled with excerpts from Donatus' commentary on this scene, densely written in far smaller minuscule. This page in particular, with the column of Terence's dialogue shifted to the left, rather than placed in the center, seems to have been designed to accommodate all three: text, image, and learned marginalia. This *mise en page* distinguishes the Parisian from the Vatican manuscript, in which the lines are filled without attention to meter, leaving only very small margins. The Parisian Terence, while less luxurious an edition than the Vatican, may be targeting a more learned readership, one aware of verse and interested in commentary, both written and (as I hope to demonstrate) visual. On folio 6r, Terence's text, Donatus' commentary, and the anonymous artist's drawing compete for the attention of the readers and viewers, allowing for different modes and patterns of cognitive engagement. One might consider all three elements in different order. One might or might not read Terence's text; one might choose to read the commentary, or not; one might pay close attention to the drawings or only glance at them. It is also possible to imagine the book read aloud (in meter or not) and the images displayed to the audience. In my sample reading, we will be moving from the image to Terence's text beneath and back to the image, in order to discuss it in some detail and analyze the figures' gestures.[24]

Below the final lines of the prologue, in the middle of the page, the ink drawing shows, from the viewer's left to right, an actor costumed as an old man and identified as Simo, another actor, wearing patched clothes and identified as Sosia, and two nameless figures, standing by a door. The text below the drawing reads:

> Si. Vos istaec intro auferte: abite. – Sosia,
> ades dum: paucis te volo. So. dictum puta:
> nempe ut curentur recte haec? Si. immo aliud. So. quid est 30
> quod tibi mea ars efficere hoc possit amplius?
> Si. nil istac opus est arte ad hanc rem quam paro,
> sed eis quas semper in te intellexi sitas,
> fide et taciturnitate. So. exspecto quid velis. (28–34)

> Si. Take these inside. Go! – Sosia,
> you stay: I want a few words. So. Consider them spoken:
> is it about taking proper care of the matter at hand? Si. No. Something else. So. Is there another matter in which my professional skill might assist you?
> Si. In my current undertaking, I have no use for your professional skill
> but for those skills I have always known you had:
> loyalty and discretion. Si. I await your orders.

Simo is upright and uses a gesture commanding attention (index and middle finger stretched out) which looks like that of the prologue speaker, though Simo's right arm is kept closer to his body, and is bent at the elbow, the hand at shoulder level. Sosia, hunched, his head between his shoulders, displays a posture that Roman orators routinely criticized as revealing subservience.[25] Sosia's gesture, performed with the right hand, is the reverse image of the instructing gesture of Simo, and signals compliance.[26] This beautifully emphasizes the nature of Sosia's responses to Simo in the text: 'it is as though I have already heard you' (*dictum puta*) and 'I am waiting for your orders' (*expecto quid velis*).[27] In his

---

[24] On the relationship between the gestures of an orator and those of an actor, see Fantham 1982, Graf 1992, Dutsch 2002, Fantham 2002.
[25] On the servile posture, see Quint. *Inst.* 11.3.83; cf. Donatus 83.1: 'sic cogitabam dixit nam ipsum gestum cogitationis exponit. Est igitur *mimesis*.'
[26] His index and middle finger slightly bent, he is pointing to the speaker, his other fingers folded. This gesture of compliance is typical of the way the miniatures portray slaves receiving orders from their masters. The 'hollow hand that moves frequently' that Quintilian associates with 'restraint verging on timidity' might have looked very much like this. See Dutsch 2007.
[27] HAEC deiktikos 3.3; 183.12; ASTUTE hoc et gestu et vultu servili cum agitatione capitis dixit.

left (!) hand Sosia is holding a ladle, which offers a clue to his occupation.[28] This detail is crucial for understanding what precisely Sosia is doing on stage. The text makes it clear that Sosia has a task to accomplish, but what this task is must be deduced from Sosia's brief reference to 'his art' (l. 31: *mea ars*). Terence would leave out such a detail from his performance script, precisely because his audience would learn from visual clues that Sosia is in fact a cook. The drawing supplies this missing piece of information.

The two figures represented to the right, standing at the door, also provide information that would have been conveyed through staging. Simo's first words would present no difficulty to a spectator, but are unclear to the reader: 'You carry these things inside.' The reader has to guess whom Simo is addressing and what needs to be carried inside. The illustrator explains by portraying two slaves carrying provisions: some fish, a tall plant, and a jar. He shows them standing on the right, by a door which must represent Simo's house. From now on this door will always be depicted stage right, while the other door will be placed stage left. The artist thus virtually transforms the page of the manuscript into a stage with fixed directions.

But this miniature is more than a pragmatic supplement to the text. The two figures at the door draw attention to the humor inherent in the scene, humor that depends on the conventions of ancient comedy. The slave who is holding the jar has his legs crossed and his hands on his hips; the other has merely stopped on the point of entering the house.[29] Their masked faces are turned towards the main scene to stage left. They are eavesdropping. These two are cheeky slaves, in the best tradition of Roman comedy; they have stopped to listen instead of obeying their master's orders. The posture of the cross-legged slave makes one think of another Simo, in Plautus' *Pseudolus* (485), and his comment on his own cheeky slave's royal pose (*status basilicus*). Further, by their upright posture, the slaves offer an amusing contrast with the submissive figure of Sosia. Although Sosia looks like a slave, he is a freedman – and a chef! His submissive posture and subservient speech play against the stereotype of the comic cook.[30] The two slaves also function as an internal audience, a model for spectators prefiguring the reader's/viewer's amused interest in the exchange between Simo and Sosia. The first miniature illustrating the *Andria* is definitely more than an ornament or

---

[28] The fact that Sosia uses his right hand for semantic gestures, leaving the left to hold the token of his work, links the drawing to the rhetorical tradition and its prohibitions on left-hand gestures, see Fantham 2002 and Dutsch 2002 and 2013.

[29] His posture brings to mind Plautus' *Pseudolus* and his *status basilicus* 457–8: *Simo: salve quid agitur? Ps. Statur hic ad hunc modum. Si. Statum uide hominis, Callipho, quam basilicum!*

[30] On the cook's traditional arrogance and eloquence, see Wilkins 2002, 387–407 in Greek comedy; cf. Gowers 1993, 92–108 on Roman Comedy.

a recording of a particular performance. It is something else altogether: a learned and humorous visual commentary on the text, with a particular focus on the kind of input that would have been supplied by staging and delivery. The image not only provides the general framework for the exchange, but also situates it within the generic tradition.

The next folios of the Parisian Terence demonstrate just how consistently this interplay of text and image is maintained. Turning the next leaf, the reader continues with the conversation between Simo and Sosia, dominated by Simo's account of Pamphilus' visits next door to the courtesan Chrysis and his secret affair with her foster sister (6v and 5r and 5v; the latter two should in fact be placed here). Simo explains that he now wants to test his son's true intentions by pretending that Pamphilus' wedding to another girl is to take place at once. (Finally the reader sees what Sosia's art must be.) Simo makes it clear that Davus is his son's accomplice (159–160).

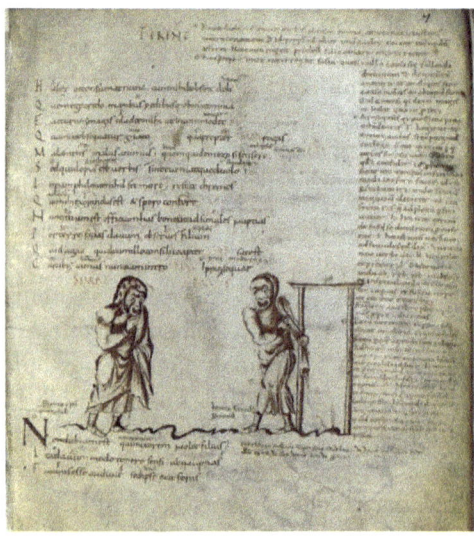

Fig. 5: Folio 7r: Simo and Davus.

Facing this exchange dominated by Simo, folio 7r contains the end of the conversation (160–71), a miniature representing two figures identified as Simo and Davus, and the initial three lines of the second scene:

> Si. Non dubiumst quin uxorem nolit filius.
> ita Davum modo timere sensi, ubi nuptias
> futuras esse audivit. sed ipse exit foras. (172–4)

> Si. There is no doubt my son doesn't want to get married.
> I have just noticed how scared Davus was when he
> heard about the coming wedding. But here he is, leaving the house.

The miniature features the old man and the slave; their self-contained hand-gestures suggest that drawing depicts the moment before Simo notices Davus. The change in Simo's posture from 6r is obvious. Head inclined slightly forward, Simo is thinking, his right hand touching his chin. Davus seems to be making a gesture that Quintilian associates with remorse and frustration (*Inst.* 3.11.104). He appears tense, but self-assured. The distance between the two figures and the angle of their masks suggest that they are both deep in thought. It is worth noting that Davus' posture goes directly against the instructions we find in Donatus' comment on this scene – that here Davus would make a *gestus servilis*.[31] The artist of the Parisian codex offers a more sophisticated reading of the situation, not only alerting the reader to the fact that Simo and Davus utter soliloquies (173–83), but also encapsulating the mistrust and subtle rivalry between the clever slave and his old master, whose secret ambition is to outsmart the *servus callidus*. This representation of Davus is consistent with the portrayal of other slaves on folio 6r, revealing the artist's interest in the figure of the cheeky slave. The text of the second scene and Davus' monologue (scene 3 in Lindsay's edition), which continue on folios 7v, 8rv and 9r, develop the theme of rivalry between master and the cheeky slave.

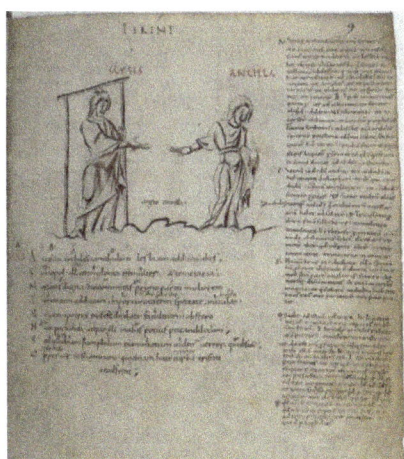

Fig. 6: Folio 9v: Mysis and Archylis.

---

31 183.12; ASTUTE hoc et gestu et vultu servili cum agitatione capitis dixit; 186.15 HOCCINE AGIS 1. Id est audis. 2. Demonstratiue veluti aurem suam tangens.

Once we turn the leaf, a new perspective emerges. The miniature on the upper half of folio 9v draws the reader's/viewer's attention to the door stage left, marking the position of the house of Glycerium. A female character is leaving; another one is standing in the door. The Parisian codex labels the scene *Mysis ancilla*. The figure leaving turns her back to the woman at the door; her mask, however, is facing the viewer, just as an actor's would. The woman walking away must be Mysis, who is the only speaker in the scene below. She addresses Archylis, who has just ordered her to fetch Lesbia the midwife. Mysis grumbles, because she does not trust Lesbia. The other woman depicted can only be Archylis.[32]

> My. Audivi Archylis iamdudum: Lesbiam adduci iubes.
> sane pol illa temulentast mulier et temeraria
> nec sati' digna quoi committas primo partu mulierem.   230
> tamen eam adducam? inportunitatem spectate aniculae
> quia compotrix eius est. di, date facultatem obsecro
> huic pariundi atque illi in aliis potiu' peccandi locum.
> sed quidnam Pamphilum exanimatum video? vereor quid siet.
> opperiar, ut sciam num quid nam haec turba tristitiae adferat.   (228–35)

> My. I have heard already Archylis: you are telling me to bring Lesbia.
> But, I swear, that woman really is a careless boozer,
> not solid enough to be trusted with woman's first childbirth.
> I should fetch her anyway? Look at the airs this old gal takes on,
> only because she is in charge of the girl. Gods, give the girl an easy childbirth
> and the midwife other opportunities to blunder!
> But why do I see Pamphilus so distraught? I fear that something is amiss.
> I will wait to see what sad news this trouble brings.

In the scene heading, Archylis is making a gesture often used in the miniatures by characters who are asking for something: the right hand, palm up, is at waist level, fingers curling into the palm.[33] Mysis's right hand is in a reverse position: index and middle finger stretched out, thumb bent in on the palm. This is a rare gesture, which occurs only here and in the heading of the scene in which Crito, having agreed to represent Pamphilus' and Glycerium's cause, and agrees to

---

32 The figure is identified as Archylis in the Bodleian manuscript, *Andria* 36; cf. Muir and Turner 2010.
33 In the *Domus Aurea* belonging to the Emperor Nero, there is an image representing the myth of Phaedra and Hippolytus in which the nurse pleads with Hippolytus making exactly this same gesture (Müller 1994, Fig. 2).

plead with Chremes and Simo (5.4, lines 904–81).[34] In both cases the character making this gesture has – despite initial reluctance – just agreed to do something at the request of the character making the pleading gesture.[35] If this is correct, the combination of pleading and agreement here provides a crucial piece of information, which is not evident from Mysis' rant: namely that, her objections notwithstanding, she is indeed going to go fetch Lesbia. In a live performance this would be made obvious by the direction of the movement of the actor playing Mysis. That Mysis does as she is asked becomes absolutely clear to the reader only much later (459), when she accompanies Lesbia into the house. As in the case of Sosia's huge spoon, then, this heading makes explicit information that is not made clear in the text beneath it. Particularly striking here is the mix of textuality and theatricality: in an effort to elucidate the text, the illustrator shows a stage with a silent character inside the house.

Fig. 7: Folio 10r: Pamphilus and Mysis.

Facing the heading and Mysis' monologue, 10r features another miniature in the upper half of the folio. To the left, the actor playing Pamphilus seems immersed in his thoughts; to the right Mysis stretches out her arms. Below this image is the text of the first eight lines of Scene 5 (the rest placed on 10v):

---

34 The same combination appears in the heading of the second to last scene, in which Crito speaks to Simo and Chremes at Pamphilus' request. Dodwell interpreted this rare gesture as denoting dissent. It occurs only here and later in the miniature illustrating *Andria* 904 ff.
35 This is confirmed by the presence of Pamphilus who has no speaking role in this scene.

Pa. Hoccinest humanum factu aut inceptu? hoccin[est] officium patris?
My. quid illud est? Pa. pro deum fidem quid est, si haec non
                                                  contumeliast?
uxorem decrerat dare sese mi hodie: nonne oportuit
praescisse me ante? nonne priu' communicatum oportuit?
My. miseram me, quod verbum audio!   240
Pa. quid? Chremes, qui denegarat se commissurum mihi
gnatam suam uxorem, id mutavit quia me inmutatum videt?
itane obstinate operam dat ut me a Glycerio miserum abstrahat?
quod si fit pereo funditus.
adeon hominem esse invenustum aut infelicem quemquam ut ego sum!   (236–45)

Pa. Is this a humane act or undertaking? Is that what a father ought to do?
My. What's that? Pa. As I trust the gods, what is it, if not an insult?
He announces that he will give me a wife tomorrow: shouldn't I
have known in advance? Should he not have told me earlier?
My. I am done for, what word did I hear?
Pa. What? Chremes who had refused to entrust his daughter
to me as my wife changed his mind because he saw that I hadn't changed mine?
And his is working tenaciously to drag my wretched person away from Glycerium?
May I die if this happens!
That any man can really be so ill-fated and unlucky as I am!

The miniature shows Pamphilus entering stage left;[36] his extreme agitation is obvious from the fact that, unlike almost all male figures in the miniatures, he gesticulates with both hands.[37] His right hand is moving towards his chest in a gesture of consternation (like Davus' on 7r); the left hand shows the reverse of the gesture of pleading or questioning (cf. Archylis above). Pamphilus' gestures convey both the grammatical form of the text below (a series of questions) and his utmost frustration with his father's authoritarian behavior and Chremes' change of mind.[38] To his right, Mysis is shown in the posture conveying despair, given in the miniatures to distraught female characters, typically exclaiming '*me miseram!*' I have argued that several drawings focus on Terence's efforts to play against the stock types. The miniature illustrating the first scene playfully emphasizes that Sosia is an atypical cook, while the one illustrating scene two alludes to an old man's ambitions as a plot-maker, usually, the domain of the clever slave. Conversely, the depiction of Pamphilus and Mysis seems to revel in the caricatural features of stock types rather than undermine them. Pamphilus'

---

[36] He is possibly imagined to be coming from Chremes' house rather than his father's, which would be stage right. Chremes is part of the plot to test Pamphilus' allegiances (166–70).
[37] The only analogous example I know is Chaerea in the miniatures illustrating *Eunuchus* 549ff.
[38] On automatic gestures linked to specific words or constructions, see Dutsch 2013.

unseemly confusion is strikingly typical of Terence's tormented lovers, while Mysis' outstretched arms bespeak a maid's notorious propensity for despair and her signature exclamation.[39] Translated into words, this image might read: 'Pamphilus utters a frustrated soliloquy, as comedic lovers often do, and Mysis, as befits an *ancilla*, pronounces herself utterly wretched.' But there is no need for translation: the image is sufficiently eloquent.

This extraordinary relationship between text and image in the Parisian Terence should caution us against thinking of its illustrations as either decorative or representing a specific performance in a naturalistic fashion. Instead, the miniatures seem to function as a visual commentary, supplying the kind of information that dramatic scripts leave to staging and delivery. The miniatures function, then, as rudimentary 'blocking' of the script. This blocking also reflects a learned tradition of Roman comedy in performance that is comparable to, but not coextensive with, the tradition represented in the comments on performance scattered throughout Donatus' commentary on Terence. Thanks to this clever montage of text and image, the reader/viewer can play a makebelieve theater game on the pages of the codex. The illustrated manuscript thus creates a space for imaginary performance and its multiple revivals, allowing Terence to be staged and restaged anew, each time a reader views the codex. The question of how this unique medium relates to ancient performance tradition must remain – for the moment – tantalizingly unanswered.

Acknowledgments

I would like to thank the organisers of 'Text, Illustration, Revival: Ancient Drama for Late Antiquity to 1550' Conference, Melbourne, 2011, Guilia Torello Hill and Andrew Turner, and the participants of the confernce for changing the way I think about masucripts. I am also very grateful to the organisers and participants of the 8th *Trends in Classics* Conference, Thessaloniki, June 2014 and to Carolyn Jones, Benjamin Victor, and Donna G. Williams for insightful comments on earlier versions of this paper.

---

39 Cf. Horace *Sat.* 1.1.130: *miseram se conscia clamet.*

Bibliography

Booker, C. M. (2009), *Past Convictions: The Penance of Louis the Pious and the Decline of the Carolingians*, Philadelphia.
Borges, J. L. (1941), 'La Bibliotheca de Babel', in: *El Jardin des senderos que se bifurcan*, Buenos Aires.
Bremmer, J. & Roodenburg, H. (1992), (eds.), *A Cultural History of Gesture*, Ithaca, New York.
Charitonides, S., Lilly K., and René G. (1970), *Les mosaïques de la maison du Ménandre à Mytilène*, Bern.
Csapo, E. (2010), *Actors and Icons of the Ancient Theatre*, Malden, MA.
Demetriou, C. (2014), 'Aelius Dontatus and his Commentary on Terence's Comedies', in: M. Fontaine and A Scafuro (eds.), *Oxford Handbook of Greek and Roman Comedy*, Oxford, 782–799.
Dodwell, C. R. (2000), *Anglo-Saxon Gestures and the Roman Stage*, Cambridge.
Dutsch, D. (2002), 'Towards a Grammar of Gesture: A Comparison Between the Types of Hand Movements of the Orator and of the Actor in Quintilian's *Institutio Oratoria* 11.3.85–184', *Gesture* 2, 259–81.
_____ (2007), 'Gestures in the Manuscripts of Terence and Late Revivals of Literary Drama', *Gesture* 7.1, 39–71.
_____ (2013), 'Towards a Roman Theory of Theatrical Gesture', in: G. W. M. Harrison and V. Liapis (eds.), *Performance in Greek and Roman Theater*, Leiden, 409–32.
Easterling, P. and Hall, E. (2002) (eds.), *Greek and Roman Actors*, Cambridge.
Fantham, E. (1982), 'Quintilian on Performance: Traditional and Personal Elements in *Institutio* 11.3', *Phoenix*. 36, 243–63.
_____ (2002), 'Orator and/et Actor', in: P. Easterling and E. Hall (eds.), *Greek and Roman Actors*, Cambridge, 362–76.
Genette, G. (1997), *Paratexts: Thresholds of Interpretation*, Cambridge; originally published as *Seuils* (1987) Paris.
Gowers, E. (1993), *The Loaded Table: Representations of Food in Roman Literature*, Oxford.
Graf, F. (1992), 'The Gestures of Roman Actors and Orators', in: J. Bremmer & H. Roodenburg (eds.), *A Cultural History of Gesture*, Ithaca, New York, 36–58.
Hamburger J. and Bouché, A. (2006) (eds.), *The Mind's Eye: Art and Theological Argument in the Middle Ages*, Princeton.
Hamburger, J. (2006), 'The Place of Theology in Medieval Art History: Problems, Positions, Possibilities', in: J. Hamburger and A. Bouché (eds.), *The Mind's Eye: Art and Theological Argument in the Middle Ages*, Princeton, 11–31.
_____ (2006a), 'The Medieval Work of Art: Wherein the 'Work?' 'Wherein the Art?'', in: J. Hamburger and A. Bouché (eds.), *The Mind's Eye: Art and Theological Argument in the Middle Ages*, Princeton, 372–412.
Heidegger, M. (1971), *Poetry Language and Thought*, trans. A. Hofstadter, New York.
Jones, L. W. and Morey, C. R. (1930–1), *The Miniatures of the Manuscripts of Terence prior to the Thirteenth Century*, Princeton.
Muir, B. and Turner, A. (2010), *A Facsimile Edition of Terence's Comedies. Oxford Bodleian Library MS Auct. F.2.13 CD ROM*, Oxford.
Müller, F. G. (1994), *The Aldobrandini Wedding*, Amsterdam.
Munk Olsen, B. (1982-), *L'Étude des auteurs classiques latins aux XIe et XIIe siècles*, Paris.

Mutherich, F. (1996), 'Carolingian Manuscript Illumination in Reims', in: K. Van der Horst, W. Noel and W. Wüstefeld (eds.), *The Utrech Psalter in Medieval Art*, Utrecht, 105–16.
Nervegna, S. (2013), *Menander in Antiquity: The Contexts of Reception*, Cambridge.
_____ (2014), 'Graphic Comedy Menandrian Mosaics and Terentian Miniatures', in: M. Fontaine and A. Scafuro (eds.), *Oxford Handbook of Greek and Roman Comedy*, Oxford, 717–143.
Omont, H. (1907), *Comédies de Térence; Reproduction des 151 dessins du Manuscrit latin 7899 de la Bibliothèque nationale*, Paris.
Radden, K. (forthcoming), 'The Textual Tradition and Manuscript Illustration of Plautus and Terence', in: M. Dinter (ed.), *Cambridge Companion to Roman Comedy*, Cambridge.
Riché, P. (1989), *Écoles et enseignement dans le haut moyen âge*, Paris.
Starkey, K. (2004), *Reading the Medieval Book: Word, Image and Performance in Wolfram von Eschenbach's* Willeham, Notredame IN.
Victor, B. (2014), 'The Transmission of Terence', in: M. Fontaine and A. Scafuro (eds.), *Oxford Handbook of Greek and Roman Comedy*, Oxford, 699–716.
Wilkins, J. (2000), *The Boastful Chef: The Discourse of Food in Ancient Greek Comedy*, Malden MA and Oxford.
Wright, D. H. (2001), *The Roman Vergil and the Origins of Medieval Book Design*, Toronto.
_____ (2006), *The Lost Late Antique Illustrated Terence*, Vatican.

Michael Fontaine
Is the Story of *Susanna and the Elders* Based on a Greek New Comedy?

The Evidence of Plautus' *Casina* and Burmeister's *Susanna*

> After many nights spent in vigil, after floods of tears called from my inmost heart, after the recollection of my past sins, I would once more take up Plautus. And when at times I returned to my right mind, and began to read the prophets, their style seemed rude and repellent. I failed to see the light with my blinded eyes.
> – St. Jerome (347 – 420), aged 37 [*]

Who wrote the Bible? I googled that question and got 72 million hits. I didn't check them all but I believe I am the first to argue that a comedian wrote part of it.

This paper is part of a larger project in which I advocate a new origin and understanding of the tale of *Susanna and the Elders*. In my view, the biblical story so closely resembles features regularly seen in Greek New Comedy that its author probably took an oral folktale from the Near East and reworked it along the narrative and ethical lines of Greek New Comedy, but did so in a Hellenistic-Jewish rather than Hellenistic-Roman setting. In that sense, and on the analogy of the name "Roman Comedy," I suggest we call *Susanna*, or at least think of it as, a "Jewish Comedy."

This paper comprises five sections. In the first three, I reconstruct a lost Neo-Latin comedy titled *Susanna* in order to show how it brought out many *inherently* comic features of the biblical *Susanna* story – and by "comic features," I mean specifically Greek New Comedy.[1] In the fourth, I argue that piety has led readers to overlook a pair of outrageous but very funny *double entendres* in the story, *double entendres* that point to the story's Greek origin. Last, I propose a new candidate for *Susanna*'s author: the Augustan-age historian and philo-Semite, Nicolaus of Damascus.

I begin with some background information.

---

[*] Letter 22.30 (384 CE).
[1] In a recent essay Erich Gruen (2009) also found 'comedic elements' in *Susanna* but by that term he simply meant 'funny.'

Susanna: Background, Date, and Summary

The tale of *Susanna and the Elders* is one of four additions to the Hebrew book of Daniel that survive only in Greek. Its assumed Semitic original, probably in Aramaic, was considered non-canonical, so it was not recopied and was eventually lost. The basic story as we know it survives in about ten oral variants in many languages, including two in Greek.

The less famous of the two Greek accounts is a crude outline called the Old Greek or Septuagint version. Despite its shared language, however, Fabrizio Pennacchietti, professor emeritus of Semitic philology at the University of Turin, has recently shown in a brilliant study that it has far more in common with the *Susanna* variants in other languages than it does with the more famous other account in Greek, which is the account I do discuss in this paper.[2] With one exception in §4 below, therefore, I shall say no more about the Old Greek version.

That *other* Greek account, the famous one, is the version that St. Jerome translated for the Vulgate. It is the version that became the basis for scores of dramatizations during the Reformation. It is the version everyone knows from art history. And until recently, it was attributed to an influential Hellenistic Jewish scholar, named Theodotion (fl. mid-2nd c. CE), who translated the Hebrew Bible into Greek. We now know, however, that it cannot be by him; it dates to the first century BCE at the latest. As one scholar puts it:

> The Greek translation of the Old Testament associated with the name Theodotion was formerly dated to the second century [sc. A.D.], but scholars have argued that this Greek version was available in the early first century A.D., even before 57 A.D. ... Much earlier, however, is the version of the Book of Daniel that survives within the Theodotion text: Theodotion-Daniel (as Alexander Di Lella has named it) dates to the first century B.C. ... Di Lella concludes that "Theodotion-Daniel essentially in its present state is a first-century B.C. production which was never reworked by Theodotion."[3]

In other words, Theodotion's version is a bastard child of a paradoxical kind – it is at least two centuries older than its purported Antonine-era father. This is the point we must grasp clearly and not lose sight of, since even Pennacchietti uncritically followed the older view and so mistakenly assigned it to the 2nd c. CE.[4]

---

2 Pennacchietti 2006.
3 Brown Tkacz 2006, 475–6.
4 Pennacchietti 2006. Actually, because Pennacchietti says so little about Theodotion's version – and precisely because, I believe, Theodotion's is so unlike the others in the details I will discuss below – that error *strengthens* rather than weakens his reconstruction of how the other

Who did write the version of *Susanna and the Elders* attributed to Theodotion (that is, "Theodotion-Daniel"), then, and when? Before I answer those questions, I shall summarize the story, anticipating parts of my discussion below by retaining in parentheses a number of key words in the Greek text.

> Susanna, the daughter of Hilkiah, was a beautiful and God-fearing Jewish woman. She lived in Babylon with her husband, Joakim, a wealthy, respected, and influential man. He owned a large house and attached garden, and each morning he put it at the public disposal of two appointed judges, called "elders of the people", to whom all brought their cases. One day the two see Susanna going into the garden for a walk and are filled with lust for her. They conspire to catch her alone and seduce her. Secretly entering the garden, the two lecherous elders peep on her when she comes in to bathe. When Susanna sends her handmaids out for oil and soap, they leap out and surprise her with a Hobson's choice of having sex with them or being falsely accused of adultery. "Look," they say, "the garden gates are shut, no one can see us, and we want you. So give in to our desire, and have sex with us. If you refuse, we will testify against you that a young man (νεανίσκος) was here with you and that is why you sent your maids away."
>
> At this Susanna groans (ἀνεστέναξεν) and exclaims, "I'm in a double bind! (στενά μοι πάντοθεν)."⁵ Realizing her answer means death, Susanna refuses, so the two elders leave and return the next day, where they accuse her in front of the people. She is sentenced to be stoned.
>
> As she is being led to execution, she shouts a loud prayer. God hears her and stirs up the holy spirit of the prophet Daniel, who was then a young boy (παιδάριον).⁶ Objecting that Susanna has been condemned without a proper investigation, he steps forth to interrogate the two elders himself. He separates them and asks each to name the kind of tree Susanna had lain under with the unknown young man. "Under a mastic tree (σχίνον)," says the one; "under an evergreen oak (πρίνον)," says the other. Catching them in the contradiction, Daniel convicts them of bearing false witness. He announces that an angel will cut (σχίσει) the first elder in two, and that the angel will saw (πρίσαι) the second elder in two. Outraged, the assembly reverses Susanna's sentence. They condemn the two elders to death and execute them in accordance with the Law of Moses. Susanna is saved, and from that day onward Daniel's reputation grows great among the people.

Susanna variants relate to one another. (In his stemmata of influences, dependence, and transmission, Theodotion's version stands out as the misfit.)

5 Verse 22, literally, "Things are narrow for me on all sides." Vulgate: *ingemuit Susanna, et ait: Angustiae sunt mihi undique.* Semitists say the locution is a Hebraism, pointing to its appearance in II Samuel 24:14 of the Septuagint, and consider it one piece of evidence that the Greek text presupposes a lost Semitic original. I have not seen it pointed out, however, that ἀνεστέναξεν and στενά are a pun in Greek.

6 Daniel is usually assumed to be a child, although παιδάριον can denote a little boy (Latin *puer*) or a young man in his teens or early twenties (Latin *adulescens* or *iuvenis*, corresponding to νεανίσκος).

New Comic Elements in the Story

In the past, features of *Susanna* have reminded scholars of the ancient novel. Many more remind me, however, of Greek New Comedy, both its peculiar structure and thematic concerns.

For example (and unlike in the novel), there is an Aristotelian unity of time and place (24 hours spread over two days, and a single house in Jewish Babylon, with an attached garden, where everything happens). There are a limited number of speaking characters and an omniscient prologue. There is the story's bourgeois or domestic focus, so reminiscent of New Comedy, which evokes stock characters and scenarios: an absent husband, a woman walking outdoors without a male chaperone (in Greek terms, a *kyrios*), who is therefore liable to be raped; a lovely woman attempting her toilette with handmaids; two lustful old men who eavesdrop on their victim; an attempt at adultery or seduction (*moicheia* – the word, like *moichos*, means both) that is tantamount to rape; a legal scenario at the heart of the story, whose jurors, the assembled people of Babylon, resemble a 'chorus'; and the miraculous intervention of a crafty young man or 'boy' who, with two plays on words, thwarts his corrupt elders and saves the day, thereby rescuing, reintegrating, and confirming the imperiled values of the household, or *oikos*.

Most of these features are found only in "Theodotion's" variant of the *Susanna* tale and, as I have said, they seem more reminiscent of Greek New Comedy than real life or ancient novels.

I am not entirely alone in that impression. Already in antiquity, some pious Christians felt *Susanna* could not be a true story, much less the Word of God. In an extant letter to Origen, Sextus Julius Africanus of Jerusalem (c. 160 – c. 240), an influential voice among the early historians of the Church, was the first in a series of ancient authors to call it forged or adulterated (κίβδηλος). Among other points, Africanus' suspicion was aroused by the puns that Daniel makes when he exposes the two corrupt elders and pronounces judgment on them. When the first elder says he saw Susanna and her lover under a mastic tree (σχῖνον), Daniel says an angel will cut (σχίσει) him in two. When the second says they were under an evergreen oak (πρῖνον – rhyming with σχῖνον), Daniel says an angel will saw (πρίσαι) him in two. Africanus felt sure that not even Philistion, the renowned mime-comedian (*mimographus*) of the Augustan age, would have written groaners like these:

ἔπειτα μετὰ τὸ θαυμασίως πως οὕτως ἀποφθέγξασθαι [sc. Δανιὴλ] καὶ παραδοξότατά πως αὐτοὺς ἀπελέγχει, ὡς οὐδὲ ὁ Φιλιστίωνος μῖμος. οὐ γὰρ ἐξήρκει ἡ διὰ τοῦ πνεύματος ἐπίπληξις, ἀλλ' ἰδίᾳ διαστήσας ἑκάτερον ἐρωτᾷ, ποῦ αὐτὴν ἐθεάσατο μοιχωμένην. ὡς δὲ ὁ μὲν ὑπὸ πρῖνον ἔφασκεν, ἀποκρίνεται πρίσειν αὐτὸν τὸν ἄγγελον, τῷ δὲ ὑπὸ σχῖνον εἰρηκότι σχισθῆναι παραπλησίως ἀπειλεῖ.

Then, after crying out in this extraordinary fashion, he [sc. Daniel] detects them in a way no less incredible, which not even Philistion the mime writer would have resorted to – not satisfied with rebuking them through the Spirit, he placed them apart, and asked them severally where they saw her committing adultery. And when the one said, "Under an evergreen oak tree" (*prinos*), he answered that the angel would saw him asunder (*prisein*); and in a similar fashion menaced the other who said, "Under a mastic tree" (*schinos*), with being rent asunder (*schisthenai*).[7]

Africanus objects that Daniel's puns work only in Greek, not Hebrew, but that is only one problem with Daniel's puns that he was the first to identify; I shall come back to it in §4.

Flash forward 1400 years. In northern Germany in 1621 a Neo-Latin poet and playwright named Joannes Burmeister of Lüneburg (1576 – 1638) noticed similarities between Plautus' *Casina* and "Theodotion's" account of the *Susanna* story. On that basis he created a Latin-language "inversion," or respectful parody, of *Casina*; he titled it *Susanna*. The play is lost and not even a single fragment survives. But having just edited one of Burmeister's other inversions of Plautus, and the fragments of a second that is based on Plautus' *moicheia*-themed *Amphitryo*, I am pretty sure I know what the *Casina-Susanna* play was like.[8] Let us consider how it developed.

Diphilus' *Kleroumenoi*, Plautus' *Casina*, "Theodotion's" *Susanna*, and Burmeister's *Susanna*

Burmeister called his play an "inversion" (*inversio*). What does that word mean? It means his new play about *Susanna* tracked Plautus' play about *Casina* in obsessive detail. He preserved the majority of Plautus' words verbatim, in the same order and meter as Plautus had them. When he did change a word, Burmeister often sought to pun on the original word. As he put it elsewhere, his goal was to offer readers an "imitation of Plautine Latin in the exercise of Christian piety." We can see how he did that by considering parallel plot summaries of *Casina* and

---

7 *Epistula ad Origenem*, found in Reichardt 1909, 78–80. The translation is that of Philip Schaff, modified.
8 Fontaine 2015.

the Bible's *Susanna* – the latter of which I shall briefly summarize again, this time emphasizing other details and quoting parts.

Adapted from a Greek original by Diphilus of Sinope (c. 360 – c. 300 BCE) titled *Kleroumenoi*, 'Men Drawing Lots,' *Casina* is among Plautus' most ribald comedies. In it an aged Athenian father and son are both secretly inflamed with desire for a foundling girl, named Casina, who lives in their house. Each hoping to conceal his passion from the other (and the rest of the family), the two men devise parallel schemes for sleeping with her. Each suborns a slave to marry Casina, on the understanding that the winning bridegroom will step aside for his master to enjoy her favors. The father's slave, Olympio, prevails, but he plans to cheat his master by sleeping with Casina first. Olympio is foiled, however, when upon arriving in his darkened bridal chamber he finds not Casina, but the other slave, Chalinus, in his bed (frustrating her husband's scheme, the son's mother has secretly substituted Chalinus for Casina). The farcical climax arrives when Olympio runs screaming from the house in terror and shame, and is persuaded by the complicit women to recount his unwitting homosexual experience. In the early modern period in which Burmeister wrote, the play was considered exceptionally obscene, influentially so by the German philologist Joachim Camerarius (1500–1574), who expurgated portions of it.[9]

At the start of *Susanna*, the two aged judges of Babylon are both secretly inflamed with desire for Susanna. Each hoping to conceal his passion from the other (and Susanna's family), the two men devise a scheme for sleeping with her. After parting company one day, each steals back to Joakim's house and, confronted by the other, confesses his passion. They then conspire to find a time when she will be alone, and to sleep with her. Upon catching her they offer her a dire choice (Daniel 13.20–21; in the following pages, I quote the Vulgate, not the Greek text, because this is what Burmeister used. I also quote the Douay-Rheims English translation of the Vulgate.):

> [20] Ecce ostia pomarii clausa sunt, et nemo nos videt, et nos in concupiscentia tui sumus: quam ob rem assentire nobis, et commiscere nobiscum. [21] Quod si nolueris, dicemus contra te testimonium, quod fuerit tecum juvenis, et ob hanc causam emiseris puellas a te.

> [20] "Behold the doors of the orchard are shut, and nobody seeth us, and we are in love with thee: wherefore consent to us, and lie with us. [21] But if thou wilt not, we will bear witness against thee, that a young man was with thee, and therefore thou didst send away thy maids from thee."

She refuses, they accuse her of adultery, and she is condemned to death.

---

[9] van der Poel 1999.

What prompted Burmeister to connect this story with *Casina*? The obvious points in common all derive from the relationship between the lechers and an unwilling woman, namely that when (1) two (2) rival (3) lechers, at least one of them (4) old, deviously (5) try to gratify their lust upon the (6) same woman (7) without the other finding out, they (8) fail and (9) get their comeuppance in the end.

These considerations make the character equations clear in broad outline. Casina becomes Susanna and Plautus' handmaids (e. g. Pardalisca in *Casina*) remain handmaids. The aged father Stalino (he is called Lysidamus or left anonymous in modern texts, but Burmeister knew him as Stalino) and his slave, Olympio, are combined to become one judge, while Chalinus becomes the other. Because they seek to conceal their lust from the other, both old men were drawn farcically as competitors or romantic rivals. Figures 1 and 2 – the one a 1st c. CE marble relief depicting a scene of New Comedy (based on earlier examples[10]), the other a painting of the Italian Baroque executed a decade before Burmeister was writing – show how easily Burmeister might have connected the inherent *senex amator* motif with *Susanna*'s elders.

Fig. 1: Scene of New Comedy (detail). One old man restrains another. Marble relief, first century CE, Naples, Museo Nazionale 6687. Reproduced by permission.

---

10 Csapo 2014, 117–9.

Fig. 2: *Susanna and the Elders* (1610), by Artemisia Gentileschi (1593 – c. 1656). Image is in the public domain @ http://en.wikipedia.org/wiki/Susanna.

The setting will have changed from Stalino's house to Joakim's house and walled garden, with its door playing a significant part. The timeline, too, of 24 hours divided by a single night – as in Terence's *Heauton Timorumenus* – stayed the same. Table 1 summarizes these equations.

Table 1: Equations between *Casina* and *Susanna*.

(1) of Character	
∴ Casina	→ Susanna
∴ *Senex amator* ("Stalino," "Lysidamus") + Olympio	→ one lecherous judge (*senex judex*)
∴ Chalinus (+ Alcesimus *senex* later)	→ the other lecherous judge (*senex judex*)
∴ Pardalisca *ancilla*	→ Susanna's handmaid (*puella*)
∴ [Euthynicus *adulescens*	→ Daniel *puer junior*]
(2) of Setting	
∴ Stalino's house	→ Joakim's house
∴ Attached garden (*hortum*)	→ walled garden (*pomarium*)
∴ House door	→ house door
∴ 24 hour timeline	→ 24 hours divided by a single night (as in Terence's *Heauton Timorumenus*)

Burmeister will have retained many lines verbatim or nearly so, such that the prologue's promise of Casina's chastity in 82–3 will have become a moralizing prediction of Susanna's fate:

> ... neque quicquam stupri
> faciet profecto in hac quidem comoedia.

> ... not a bit of fornication (*stupri*)
> will she be guilty of – at least not in *this* comedy.

Burmeister must also have noticed many structural parallels and coincidences of detail between *Casina* and the biblical narrative that go beyond the simple equations of character I just mentioned. It thus becomes easy to pick out certain lines that bring the contours of the Neo-Latin plot into view.

For example, in addition to the romantic rivals in *Casina*, the middle scenes of the play also feature (as in *Susanna*) a conspiracy of two old men against the unwilling Casina. Alcesimus, another old man, allows Stalino the use of his house in which to seduce Casina without his wife finding out. Furthermore, Plautus' Stalino, like the two aged judges in *Susanna*, is a man of high social standing and legal authority. He acts as lawyer (*advocatus*, 567) in a trial or litigation (*litem*, 568) for a relative of his. Other coincidences of structure include (1) the motivation of a *prandium* (lunch or dinner) that brings the lechers into contact with Casina/Susanna; (2) the relevance of unguents and a toilette scene; (3) the alternation of men and women in dialogue from scene to scene; (4) the significance of the house or garden door; and finally (5) a concluding ensemble scene, which can be used to represent the massed people (*multitudo*, *coetus*) in Daniel 13:41–62.

These coincidences of detail, which are summarized in Table 2, make it possible for us to identify cardinal points and to reconstruct how Burmeister went about altering Plautus' text. Let us look at some of them.

Table 2: Structural parallels between *Casina* and *Susanna*.

∴ a pair of romantic **rivals**
∴ a **conspiracy of two old men** – Stalino and his neighbour, Alcesimus – against the unwilling Casina.
∴ Stalino, like the two aged judges in *Susanna*, is **a man of high social standing** and legal authority.
∴ He acts as **lawyer or advocate** (*advocatus*, 567) in a **litigation** (*litem*, 568) for a relative of his.
∴ the motivation of a ***prandium*** that brings the lechers into contact with Casina/Susanna
∴ the relevance of **unguents** and a toilette scene
∴ the **alternation of men and women** in dialogue from scene to scene
∴ the significance of the **house** or **garden door**
∴ a **concluding ensemble scene**, which can represent the massed people in *Daniel* 13:41–62.

The two lechers in the biblical account first encounter Susanna by frequenting her house and seeing her enter the adjoining orchard (Daniel 13:8–12):

> ⁸ Et videbant eam senes quotidie ingredientem et deambulantem, et exarserunt in concupiscentiam ejus: ⁹ et everterunt sensum suum, et declinaverunt oculos suos ut non viderent caelum, neque recordarentur judiciorum justorum. ¹⁰ Erant ergo ambo vulnerati amore ejus, **nec indicaverunt sibi vicissim dolorem suum**: ¹¹ erubescebant enim indicare sibi concupiscentiam suam, volentes concumbere cum ea. ¹² Et observabant quotidie sollicitius videre eam.

> ⁸ And the old men saw her going in every day, and walking: and they were inflamed with lust towards her: ⁹ And they perverted their own mind and turned away their eyes that they might not look unto heaven, nor remember just judgments. ¹⁰ So they were both wounded with the love of her, yet **they did not make known their grief one to the other**: ¹¹ For they were ashamed to declare to one another their lust, being desirous to have sex with her. ¹² And they watched carefully every day to see her.

This portion formed the basis for reworking Act 1 of *Casina*. Plautus' play begins with a farcical dialogue between the two lecherous slaves, Olympio and Chalinus, each trying to keep his lust secret from the other – and those attempts, by another remarkable coincidence, enabled Burmeister to bring in the elders' judicial profession. Consider the opening lines of the scene, in which Olympio angrily whirls on Chalinus and asks him (89–90):

> OL. Non mihi licere meam rem me solum, ut volo,
> loqui atque cogitare, **sine ted arbitro**?

> OL. Can't I be allowed to talk and think over my own affairs,
> by myself, as I want, **without you spying on me** (*sine ted arbitro*)?

In Plautus' text *sine te arbitro* literally means "without you as my witness" or "judge" (*arbiter*) and it is a metaphor. If Burmeister left these words unchanged, as I suspect he did, then the metaphor becomes literalized as an ironic pun on the two elders' status as judges (*iudices*).

The whole scene proceeds in this farcical fashion and it concludes with the same pun applied in reverse. Chalinus, the rival of Olympio corresponding to the second judge, closes the scene by declaring (143–4):

> Te sequor.
> hic quidem pol certo nihil ages **sine me arbitro**.

> I'll follow you.
> By Pollux, you won't do anything here, that's sure, **without my spying on you** (*sine me arbitro*)!

The second event in the story is Susanna's visit to the garden bath with her handmaids (*Daniel* 13:15):

> Factum est autem, cum observarent diem aptum, ingressa est aliquando sicut heri et nudiustertius, cum duabus solis puellis, **voluitque lavari** in pomario: aestus quippe erat:

> And it fell out, as they [*sc. the judges*] watched a fit day, she went in on a time, as yesterday and the day before, with two maids only, **and was desirous to wash herself** (*voluitque lavari*) in the orchard: for it was hot weather.

This segment became *Casina*'s second act. It begins at lunchtime, with the entrance of Cleostrata, a matron, and her handmaid, Pardalisca, from Stalino's house (145–50):

> CLE. ego huc transeo in proximum ad meam vicinam.
> vir si quid volet me, facite hinc me arcessatis.
> PAR. **prandium** iusserat senex sibi parari.
> CLE. st, tace, atque abi. neque paro, neque hodie
> coquetur ...

> CLE. (*to servants within*) I am going over here next door to my neighbour's.
> If my husband wants me for anything, you are to come over here for me.
> PAR. Master said to have **lunch** (*prandium*) ready for him, ma'am.
> CLE. Hush! Be quiet and be off. I'm not preparing any and it won't be cooked today ...

As a side note, I should point out a feature of the biblical story that is inherently comic. Susanna's wish to bathe (*voluit lavari*) evokes the courtesan's famous toilette scene in Plautus' *Mostellaria* (I.iii = 312), in which her unguents are repeatedly mentioned. It also brings to mind the complaint of a young lover in Plautus' *Truculentus*, when he finds that the courtesan he is dying to see is not yet available (*Truculentus* 322–5):

> piscis ego credo, qui usque dum vivont **lavant**,
> minus diu **lavare** quam haec **lavat** Phrynesium.[11]
> si proinde amentur, mulieres diu quam **lavant**,
> omnes amantes balneatores sient.

> Even fish, who spend their whole lives **bathing**,
> don't **bathe** as long, I do believe, as this Phrynesium here **bathes**.
> If women would let you love 'em the length of time **their baths last**,
> lovers would all turn bathmen.

---

[11] The manuscripts call the courtesan Phronesium. I defend the spelling Phrynesium ("Little Phryne") in Fontaine 2010.

By a coincidence of detail, in the biblical account it is, as in *Casina*, the mention of lunchtime (*prandium*, translated 'dinner' in the Douay-Rheims version above) that brings about the initial meeting between Susanna and the lechers. In *Daniel* 13:13–4 one lecher says to the other,

> [13] Eamus domum, quia hora **prandii** est. Et egressi, recesserunt a se. [14] Cumque revertissent, venerunt in unum: et sciscitantes ab invicem causam, confessi sunt concupiscentiam suam: et tunc in communi statuerunt tempus quando eam possent invenire solam.

> [13] "Let us now go home, for it is dinner (***prandii***) time." So going out they departed one from another. [14] And turning back again, they came both to the same place: and asking one another the cause, they acknowledged their lust; and then they agreed upon a time, when they might find her alone.

This is how the correspondences will have gone with the whole play, until the conclusion. As with all adaptations, of course, we cannot easily guess where Burmeister might have added characters not found in the biblical account, as he does in his other inversions of Plautus. But I can say something about the ending and what it suggests about Daniel's role in Burmeister's play.

By another coincidence, *Casina* concludes with an unusual ensemble scene. It brings six characters onstage at the same time, and it must have formed the basis for the crowd that figures in the end of the biblical account, when Susanna is condemned to death. If Daniel appeared at all in Burmeister's play, structure suggests he can only have been in this scene, late in the play. But I suspect he did not appear at all. In a joke in the prologue of *Casina*, we learn that Plautus changed his Greek source text by cutting out the son's role entirely (64–6):

> is [*sc. the* adulescens *Euthynicus*], ne exspectetis, hodie in hac comoedia
> in urbem non redibit: Plautus noluit:
> interrupit pontem, qui erat ei in itinere.

> He will not return to the city today – do not expect him – during
> the course of this comedy. Plautus would not have it so –
> he broke down a bridge that lay on the youth's route.

In *Susanna*, it must have been Daniel that Burmeister dispensed with here. Even though his story occupies the second half of the biblical account, on my reconstruction of the play there is no room left for him. His role in the story was, I presume, told in a prediction in the final verses of the play, much as we see done in the prediction at the end of Plautus' *Amphitryo*.

About Daniel's puns …

So far I have sought to demonstrate Burmeister's insight into the inherent comic potential of the Susanna story. Now I want to flip that idea and ask a question. Is it possible that in turning *Susanna* into a comedy of his own, Burmeister unwittingly *reversed* the procedure that generated the *Susanna* story as we know it? Or to put the question more simply: Is *Susanna and the Elders* based on a Greek New Comedy?

On another occasion I plan to point out many more parallels among the *Susanna* story, New Comedy, Plautus' *Amphitryo* and *Rudens*, and late Euripidean tragedy. When I do, I shall highlight the themes of false testimony, of *moicheia* (adultery or seduction – the Greek word combines both), and of the similarities between *Susanna's* prologue and the *Rudens* prologue. Here I want to propose and pursue just one idea. I suggest that Daniel, the "boy" (often a word for "slave"!), could trace his characterization to a *servus callidus*, the crafty slave of New Comedy who is so famously fond of punning.[12]

That suggestion directs our attention back to Daniel's two puns, at the climax of the story, on σχῖνον and πρῖνον, each threat of punishment picking up and playing off the tree named by an elder. As we saw in §2, Sextus Julius Africanus grumbled that they are something that "not even Philistion the mime writer would have resorted to." For two reasons, his complaint is unjust.

His complaint is unjust firstly because it is an exaggeration. In Aristophanes' *Wasps* 897, the dog found guilty at trial is sentenced to don a collar made of σύκινος, figwood (897). Why σύκινος? Because, commentators tell us, it evokes the word συκοφάντης: professional blackmailers, malicious prosecutors – people, that is, like the two corrupt worthies in *Susanna*. There is no reason to think Philistion, whose reputation for humor became proverbial, would have eschewed this kind of thing.[13]

His complaint is also unjust because Africanus failed to notice the utter *irrelevance* of the puns. Neither of Daniel's threats is carried out. No angel of the Lord appears, and nobody splits or saws anyone in half. It is, rather, the assembled people who execute the corrupt elders "according to the Law of Moses," which means they stoned them. So why are the puns even here?

---

12 Scholars tend to credit Plautus rather than his Greek models with his crafty slaves' many puns, but that is true only in degree. Syrus in Terence's Menandrian *Heauton Timorumenus* is also fond of punning (*-ver-* in 372 and 356), *dom(i)na ~ damno*, 628).
13 Martial 2.41.15 refers to *ridiculi Philistionis*.

The only answer to that question I have seen anywhere is one that Erich Gruen has recently offered. He vaguely suggests that "Daniel also toys with them [sc. the elders] liberally in his questioning, twice employing puns to increase their discomfiture."[14] I fully agree, but the remark is truer than Gruen realizes. Consider Daniel's threats more closely.

After exposing each elder, Daniels tells the one that the angel of the Lord σχίσει σε μέσον, "will split you in two" (55) and the other that the angel πρίσαι σε μέσον, ὅπως ἐξολεθρεύσῃ ὑμᾶς, "will saw you (*singular*) in two, so that he may destroy you (*plural*)" (59). By those phrases everyone assumes Daniel is saying, in all seriousness, that the angel will cut or saw the man in two, as if μέσον were equivalent to δίχα, "in two pieces." Indeed, "in two" or "in half" is invariably how μέσον is rendered in English translations of *Susanna*. I think it is absurd.

True, we do find that conceit in New Comedy (cf. Plautus' *Aulularia* 282–8) and true, in the Old Greek version of *Susanna*, it is obviously what Daniel means. There he tells the one elder that the angel "will split your soul" (σχίσει σου τὴν ψυχήν) and the other that the angel "is standing by holding the sword, until the people destroy you, so that he can saw you up" (τὴν ῥομφαίαν ἕστηκεν ἔχων, ἕως ὁ λαὸς ἐξολεθρεύσει ὑμᾶς, ἵνα καταπρίσῃ σε).

To readers familiar with Greek or Roman New Comedy, however, and especially to readers of Plautus' *Miles Gloriosus*, it is obvious that in "Theodotion's" account we are dealing with two *double entendres*. In comedy, *castration* is the punishment one expects for a would-be *moichos* (adulterer or seducer). Plautus jokes about that several times, usually in puns.[15] Castration, or the facetious threat of it, is also the punishment par excellence in New Comedy for a lewd *senex amator*, or dirty old man, when you catch him acting naughty.[16] From that point of view, the threat of castration is precisely and *doubly* suitable for *Susanna's* two aged worthies.

The final scene of Plautus' *Miles Gloriosus* (1394–1426) is a burlesque of punitive castration. Earlier in the play, an amorous soldier had attempted *moicheia*; now he has been caught, causing puns and *double entendre* to fly thick and fast.[17] A group of slaves is now holding the soldier down while a cook, wielding a knife,

---

[14] Gruen 2009, 173.
[15] *Curculio* 23–8 (puns on *testes*); *Poenulus* 862–3 (puns on *vasa*). On *Miles Gloriosus*, see below.
[16] See *castrare* in Plautus' *Mercator* 272 and 275 – on which, by the way, *castigare* in v. 316 is a nice pun, both aurally and conceptually (*castus*), albeit unnoticed by commentators. In general, too, see Augoustakis 2008.
[17] Plautus intends puns on *abdomen*, *testes*, *dispennite*, and probably elsewhere: Fontaine 2010, 115–9.

steps up over him. In v. 1395 the slaves' master orders them to *discindere* the soldier. He means 'pull the soldier's legs apart' but the soldier – with a terrified glance, no doubt, at his private parts – takes it to mean 'tear him apart.' When the soldier pleads with the master to reconsider, repeating *obsecro* (1396, 1406), the cook whimsically echoes his word – exactly as Daniel does – to make a sinister counter-quip: *quam mox seco*, 'How soon shall I cut?' (1406)

The pairing of the cook and soldier could be a stock scenario. A cook in Plautus' *Truculentus* 614, also wielding a knife, threatens to stab a soldier. Although *moicheia* is not at issue, the cook does warn him *Tange modo, iam ego <te> hic agnum faciam et medium distruncabo*, "You just touch me, and I'll make you a lamb and – desunder you up the middle." The reader need not agree with me that *distruncabo* puns on *truncus*, in the sense "penis," to realize that the threat of *te ... medium distruncabo* alludes to castration in exactly the same manner that Daniel's σχίσει and πρίσαι σε μέσον do. In both cases, the word for "middle" (μέσον, *medium*) indicates the man's "midsection."[18]

In this connection those parallels are more important than they appear. When St. Jerome, who loved Plautus, translated *Susanna* for the Vulgate, he rendered σχίσει σε μέσον and πρίσαι σε μέσον as *scindet te medium* and *ut secet te medium*.[19] Comparing those choices, it is a shock to realize that (*di*)*scindere* and *secare* are the very same verbs we find in *Miles Gloriosus* and that *te medium distruncabo* is the wording of the threat in *Truculentus*. A conscious choice? Probably not, but Jerome's Latin does expose the inherent ambiguity and humor of Daniel's Greek.

What is so remarkable is that the conceit of punitive castration is decidedly non-Jewish. To pious readers of *Susanna* through the ages, the thought that Daniel is threatening castration as a punishment for attempted rape, even as a joke, would not occur. In Judaism, castration of any kind is literally anathema and in Christianity, punitive castration is metaphorically so. That is why no one has ever noticed it before.

This helps us see that Daniels' puns presuppose a Greek origin for not one but two reasons. The one, long known, is that they do not work in Semitic languages. The other, which I suggest here, is that it is only in Greek New Comedy, and not in Jewish literature, that the threat of punitive castration, and jokes and puns about it, are documented and deemed funny.[20]

---

18 ibid.
19 Jerome discusses the problems with translating Daniels' puns in his preface to *Susanna*. He suggests replacing them with puns on *ilex* (oak) and *illico* (on the spot) or *lentiscus* (mastic) and *lente* (slowly) or *lentus* (pliable, flexible).
20 Scafuro 1997, 222–3 discusses the legal reality or nonreality of punitive castration in Greece and Rome. In all of Jewish literature the only example of punitive castration one can find is a

Who wrote *Susanna*?

If *Susanna* really is indebted to Greek New Comedy, what is the nature of its debt? Let me state clearly that I am *not* arguing for a direct connection. Unlike the Roman comedies of Plautus or Terence, *Susanna* is not an adaptation or abridgment of a single Athenian comedy from the time of Menander, Diphilus, and Philemon. Rather, I envision a different process. Since we know there are parallels in Near Eastern folktales to the plot of Plautus' *Menaechmi* and to an episode in Plautus' *Miles Gloriosus*, I think *Susanna's* author, in similar fashion, borrowed a Near Eastern story that was circulating orally. He then recast it along the narrative and ethical lines of Greek New Comedy, just as those comedians who wrote the Greek models of *Menaechmi* and *Miles Gloriosus* did.[21]

The reason *Susanna* cannot descend directly from a classical Athenian comedy is that in her story, Susanna is put on trial for *moicheia* (adultery or seduction). That is not a Greek practice, and it means the characters in *Susanna* must have been Jewish, not Greek, from the beginning. In Athens and in Athenian comedy, married women were not prosecuted for adultery, much less stoned for it. When they were caught in adultery in real life, the matter was usually hushed up and such penalties as they did suffer were purely social, not legal, in nature. That is why *moicheia* scenarios are rare in New Comedy as we know it, featuring only in Plautus' *Miles Gloriosus* and the mythological *Amphitryo*.

Who might have written "Theodotion's" *Susanna*? I nominate the enigmatic Nicolaus of Damascus. Born in 64 BCE, one year after Horace, and later a friend of both Augustus and Herod the Great, he also tutored the children of Antony and Cleopatra. The date is a perfect match, if indeed our *Susanna* "essentially in its present state is a first-century B.C. production" (§1, above). The *Suda* credits him with writing comedies and tragedies, and modern scholars have ascribed to him the one and only Greek δρᾶμα on a Jewish theme whose existence, apart from Ezekiel's *Exagoge*, we know of.[22]

---

single opinion in the Babylonian Talmud (*Sotah* 13b), and it is decidedly eccentric. It claims that Potiphar, the palace guard of Genesis, attempted to rape Joseph and was in consequence castrated at God's behest by the angel Gabriel.
21 *Menaechmi*: Hansen 1977. *Miles Gloriosus*: Raffaelli 2009.
22 Kotlinska-Toma 2015, 159, 200, and 241–2. I agree with her that the ascription to Nicolaus of "the Damascene's *Susanna*" is likely, but it goes far past Felix Jacoby (1876–1959), whom she cites, to the 1634 Paris edition of Nicolaus' fragments by Henricus Valesius (1603–76).

What is that *drama*?[23] Its title is no more and no less than *Susanna*. Since its only fragment is the word Τίγριδος (genitive of the river Tigris), which does not appear in "Theodotion's" account, it has always seemed natural to assume that Nicolaus expanded "Theodotion's" account and dramatized it. I think that is getting it backwards. My guess is that "Theodotion's" account is actually a prose abridgement of Nicolaus' drama.

Or to put it differently: Where did Nicolaus' *Susanna* go? When we open the Bible, I think we are staring right at it.

Bibliography

Augoustakis, A. (2008), 'Castrate the He-goat! Overpowering the *Paterfamilias* in Plautus' *Mercator*', *Scholia* 17, 37–48.
Brown Tkacz, C. (2006), 'Ἀνεβόησεν φωνῇ μεγάλῃ: Susanna and the Synoptic Passion Narratives', *Gregorianum* 87, 449–86.
Csapo, E. (2014), 'The Iconography of Comedy', in: M. Revermann (ed.), *The Cambridge Companion to Greek Comedy*, Cambridge, 95–127.
Fontaine, M. (2010), *Funny Words in Plautine Comedy*, Oxford.
─────── (2015), *Joannes Burmeister: Aulularia and other Inversions of Plautus*, Leuven.
Gruen, E. (2009), *Diaspora: Jews Amidst Greeks and Romans*, Cambridge.
Hansen, W. F. (1977), 'An Oral Source for the Menaechmi', *CW* 70, 385–90.
Kotlinska-Toma, A. (2015), *Hellenistic Tragedy: Texts, Translations and a Critical Survey*, New York.
Pennacchietti, F. (2006), *Three Mirrors for two Biblical Ladies. Susanna and the Queen of Sheba in the Eyes of Jews, Christians, and Muslims*, Piscataway, New Jersey.
Rafaelli, R. (2009), 'Un racconto arabo, l'*Elena* di Euripide e la struttura del *Miles* di Plauto', in: R. Raffaelli/A. Tontini (eds.), *Lecturae Plautinae Sarsinates XII: Miles gloriosus*, Urbino, 135–56.
Reichardt, W. (1909), *Die Briefe des Sextus Julius Africanus an Aristides und Origenes*, Leipzig.
Rohde, E. (1876), *Der griechische Roman und seine Vorläufer*, Leipzig.
Scafuro, A. (1997), *The Forensic Stage: Settling Disputes in Graeco-Roman New Comedy*, Cambridge.
van der Poel, M. (1999), 'Lipsius as a Defender of Plautus', in: G. Tournoy/J. De Landtsheer/ J. Papy (eds.), *Iustus Lipsius, Europae Lumen Et Columen*. Proceedings of the International Colloquiium, Leuven, 17–19 September 1997, Leuven, 179–185.

---

[23] For later authors, like Photius, the word δρᾶμα might denote a tragedy, a comedy, or a Greek novel (Rohde 1876, 350–2).

Antony Augoustakis
Terence's Comedies in the *Terentius Christianus*: The Case of *Naaman*

The Dutch Neo-Latin dramatist Cornelius Schonaeus (Skoneus) was born in Gouda in 1541, studied at Leuven, and became rector of the Latin school of Haarlem in 1572, where he stayed until 1611, the year of his death.[1] Schonaeus is best known for his seventeen Latin plays, produced for the edification of his pupils at Haarlem, for which he received the honorary title *Terentius Christianus*, as the most prominent imitator and follower of the Latin comic poet in early modern times: these school plays remained very popular in Europe through the eighteenth century.[2] Schonaeus published other pieces as well, such as a *Liber Epigrammatum*, his schoolboy poems, in 1592, a book of elegies (*Carminum libellus*, 1569), and a Latin Grammar (*Rudimenta grammatices*, ca 1580). His seventeen Latin plays include biblical themes, such as *Tobaeus, Nehemias, Saulus Conversus, Naaman,*[3] *Iosephus, Iuditha, Susanna, Daniel, Triumphus Christi, Typhlus, Pentecoste, Ananias, Baptistes* (called a tragicomedy), but also some *fabulae iocosae atque ludicrae*, namely farces with various themes borrowed from the stock of Greek New and Roman Comedy, such as *Pseudostratiotae* (soldiers and their wives), *Cunae* (an unruly wife), *Vitulus* (a drunk merchant), and *Dyscoli* (pupils and their mothers).[4]

Building on recent studies on the Latin plays,[5] in this chapter I study the use of Terentian language and themes by Schonaeus in order to shed light on the Dutch playwright's choices as an imitator of Terence. As an example, I employ one of the early plays, *Naaman*, to trace the extent of Schonaeus' borrowing of Terentian language and context. In what follows, I would like to highlight how the selection process reflects Schonaeus' objective, namely to elide the pagan

---
[1] For biographical details, see Van de Venne 1983, 368–76, Verweij 2013, 95, and Bloemendal 2013, 332–5; the bibliography of printed works is given in detail in Van de Venne 1983, 1984, 1985, and 1986.
[2] Verweij 2013, 95.
[3] These first four plays were printed in the first edition in 1591 under the name *Terentius Christianus*, without Schonaeus' knowledge.
[4] All quotations of Schonaeus' plays come from the 1691 edition, a reissue of the 1652 edition, available through EEBO (Early English Books Online (eebo.chadwyck.com); the lines in the Latin text are not numbered in any edition, and all translations are my own. For Terence, I have used Barsby's 2001 Loeb edition.
[5] Most notably Verweij 2013.

context of the Terentian plays and replace it with a new, as he envisions it, overtly Christian agenda.

The production of Latin plays by schoolmasters was a wide phenomenon witnessed in the Low Countries as early as the 1530s, a tradition that endured and continued through the 1680s.[6] Most of the schoolmasters were conservative Catholics, even during the spread of Calvinism in most of the region.[7] Schonaeus was no exception. But unlike his predecessors, especially Guilielmus Gnapheus (1493–1568) and Georgius Macropedius (1486–1558), Schonaeus becomes more conservative in his choices:[8] in Schonaeus' plays, scenes of debauchery are reduced, the tone is far more tragic than comic, and the topics become almost exclusively religious;[9] the message (what we would call, "the lesson of the day") is closely tied to the nature of the plays.

It has been often pointed out that Schonaeus knows Terence by heart: it is very difficult to distinguish between conscious quotations from Terence and formulas of comic language.[10] In his study of the *Tobaeus/Tobias*, Michiel Verweij identifies quotations from Terence every five lines. As Verweij points out, many passages have a distinct Terentian flavour in terms of the elaborate adaptation of Terentian passages to suit particular characters in the Christian play. In addition, in his choice of meter, Schonaeus is once again "more orthodoxly

---

[6] Bloemendal 2013 discusses the socio-political context for the production of these plays at schools and universities as centers of humanism; on the beginnings of the tradition, see esp. 295–302. See Verweij 2013, 95–6 on the double pedagogical aim "of instilling moral lessons and teaching good Latin speech." Cf. also Parente 1987, 9–10: "they hoped not only to contribute to the spiritual and moral education of the pupil who watched or acted in the work, but also to broaden his command of Latin and later the vernacular in order to prepare him for a life of public service to the city or the state."
[7] Verweij 2013, 96: "in the second half of the sixteenth century, Protestants in the Low Countries were not so much Lutherans as Calvinists, and the Calvinist preachers were opposed to theatre in all its forms. It is then not to be wondered that Schonaeus's successors in Haarlem avoided anything realting to dramatic performance."
[8] Parente 1987, 9–60 studies the balance these authors try to achieve by rejecting episodes and characters from the ancient plays while reintroducing them in their own new works. On Macropedius and Gnapheus, major representatives of the first generation of Neo-Latin playwrights in the Low Countries, see Bloemendal 2013, 298–32.
[9] Verweij 2013, 96: "the earlier authors ... were far more liberal, including scenes set in taverns and brothels, seemingly without hesitation; the overall atmosphere was freer, somewhat more optimistic, more joyful, funnier, whereas school drama from the latter half of the sixteenth century was far more serious."
[10] Verweij 2013, 97; on Terentian language, see the excellent study by Karakasis 2005.

Terentian" than his predecessors.¹¹ And in terms of dramaturgy, Schonaeus' plays are much more static (*fabula stataria*) than those of his predecessors; the action takes place off-stage, it is reported by a messenger, the emphasis is on words and their power: "Schonaeus seems to represent a classical dramaturgy in which the accent is on words, not deeds."¹²

Let us look more closely at *Naaman*, a play published in 1572 and probably composed in 1571 at Haarlem. The play itself becomes very popular outside the confines of the Low Countries, as is attested by the recommendation in John Brinsley's *Ludus Literarius* (1627) to use the *Terentius Christianus* as a school book in England in order for the students to learn to speak Latin,¹³ as well as by the inclusion of a free translation of *Naaman* in the *Stonyhurst Pageants* ("The 18 Pageant of Naaman," ca. 1609, Lancashire). In the 1595 English translation of *Tobaeus*, *Iuditha*, and *Pseudostratiotes*, the editor addresses the reader observing, "Schonaeus, a very learned man, did something worth while: for the benefit of Christian boys he has clothed more chaste subject-matter in the pure language of Terence, in order that along with elegance of style boys may imbibe holiness and uprightness of character." In the 1652 Cologne edition of the *Terentius Christianus*, the foreword (by a certain Cornelius Loosaeus Callidius) addresses some of the challenges faced by Schonaeus in choosing the right author to imitate: it could not have been Plautus, he says, because of the loose morality presented in Plautine comedy. Terence, as he continues, is admittedly the right playwright: [sc. Terentius poeta] *puri sermonis Latini proprietatem exprimit optime, tum phrasi longe elegantissima miram eius linguae suavitatem et summum ornatum ostendit maxime* ("[the poet Terence] excellently expresses the quality of clean Latin speech, as well as especially displaying its marvelous sweetness and highest embellishment by means of his by extremely elegant diction"). And yet, no postclassical reception of Terence can be immune to the famous criticisms raised by Augustine in his *Confessions* (1.15–6), concerning the inherent dangers in Terentian comedy, and the foreword of the Cologne edition directly quotes from Augustine the well-known criticism of the rape scene in the *Eunuchus*.¹⁴ With this in mind, therefore, the foreword continues, Cornelius Schonaeus made certain choices: *quiquid in illo [sc. Terentio] laudem meretur, simul desumpsit: atque adeo felicissima aemuli studii imitatione, uberrimum illum ac nitidissimum Latinae eloquentiae fontem, totum in se transtulit* ("at once Schonaeus kept whatever was

---

11 Verweij 2013, 99; Schonaeus accompanies the text with marginal annotations on the various meters employed.
12 Verweij 2013, 102.
13 Craig 1923, 62.
14 See Augoustakis 2013 and Cain 2013.

praiseworthy in Terence and thus, by the most successful imitation of his rivalrous effort, he transferred to his work that famous, most plentiful and splendid, fountain of Latin eloquence"). Hence the reasonable conclusion that for language and meter one ought to look back to Terence to trace Cornelius' debts, but for the materials, one should look at the *Biblia Sacra*: *si Latini sermonis puritatem attendit, si phrasis elegantiam, Terentius ipse est. Si affectus, si gestus personis aptos spectat, si motus actionibus commodos, eundem videt ... Si vero metri harmoniam considerat, eundem ipsum audit. Si probatos mores, si pietatem denique observat, sic Ecclesiasten citius quam Comicum agnoscet* ("when he [Schonaeus] applies his mind to the purity of the Latin speech or the elegance of diction, he becomes Terence himself. When he considers the appropriate disposition and attitude of a character or the gestures suitable to the action, he looks back at the same author ... When he has in mind the harmony of meter, he listens to the same playwright. When finally he attends to upright morals and reverence, he will more readily use the Bible than the ancient comic poet"). As James Parente observes, "Christian schoolmasters developed a cautious approach to the ancients, lest they be accused by critics skeptical of the new curriculum of fostering impiety among students. To obviate these charges, the Christian humanists devised two methods of dealing with pagan drama. First, they defended the moral and stylistic utility of studying unexpurgated texts of the classical writers. Drawing on antique, patristic and contemporary sources, Christian humanists such as Philip Melanchthon (1497–1560) and Joannes Sturm (1507–89) zealously argued that the frank immorality of the pagan writers could nonetheless serve to deter young men from evil. At the same time, however, another group of schoolmen, disturbed by the religious controversies of the 1520s, drew on the same patristic and contemporary sources to argue the opposite case, namely, the banishment of all forms of pagan drama from the school stage. As a substitute for the pagan texts they offered their own original plays with plots based on biblical, hagiographical and medieval allegorical topics in the language of classical theater so as to uphold the stylistic ideal of the ancients without spiritual peril to the students."[15] In this context, Schonaeus' plays constitute no exception: the preface makes clear that the subject matter will be 'clothed' in Terentian language, without of course precluding the informed reader's response to the deft employment of context, as we shall see in the analysis below.

Cornelius' plucking from Terence's garden, however, is not done in the manner of a *florilegium*, an anthology of phrases and adaptations from the comic language of the famous playwright, but rather as an integration of the pagan

---

[15] Parente 1987, 11–2.

plays with the demands of the early modern period. In the foreword, we find reference to the alleged *malevoli* who might reproach Cornelius' selection of materials, a statement that is echoed from the Prologus to the *Naaman*, where Cornelius evokes the language of the Terentian *prologi* against the detractors:

> cum primum Schonaeus noster didascalus
> ad artem sese contulisset musicam,
> huc totus semper est enixus viribus,
> bonis uti placerent quas proferret fabulas ...
> nigros vero ac maleuolos qui obtrectant, nihil moratur ...

> As soon as our schoolmaster Schonaeus applied himself to the musical art, he strove with all his power so that the plays he produced would find approval among the worthy ... But he has nothing to say against those wicked and malicious ones who accuse him ...

The parallels with the *prologi* of Terence's plays are easy to detect, as for instance in *Hauton Timorumenos* (16) and *Adelphoe* (15) for the *maleuoli* or *Eunuchus* for the *boni* vs the detractors (1–3), but especially the opening of *Andria*:

> poeta quom primum animum ad scribendum appulit,
> id sibi negoti credidit solum dari,
> populo ut placerent quas fecisset fabulas.
> verum aliter evenire multo intellegit;
> nam in prologis scribundis operam abutitur,   5
> non qui argumentum narret sed qui malevoli
> veteris poetae maledictis respondeat.   (*An.* 1–7)

> When the playwright first turned his mind to writing, he believed that his only problem was to ensure that the plays he had created would win the approval of the public. He now realizes that the real outcome is quite different. He is wasting his time writing prologues, not to explain the plot but to respond to the slanders of the malicious old playwright.

Therefore, the opening of the first Terentian play becomes a tool in the hands of Cornelius Schonaeus in his beginning steps as a playwright.

But what about the subject matter of the play? The story of Naaman is narrated in a relatively minor episode in *2 Kings 5:* Naaman (whose name means "pleasantness" in Hebrew, נַעֲמָן), the Syrian commander of the armies of Ben-Hadad II, was afflicted with leprosy and urged by the Hebrew slave-girl of his wife to seek the help of the prophet Elisha in Samaria; he obtains a letter from Ben-Hadad to the king of Israel, Joram, but the Israelite becomes suspicious of the request (because of the ongoing war with Syria). Elisha sends for Naaman, who goes to see the prophet, but is received by the prophet's messenger who tells Naaman to cure his affliction by dipping himself seven times in the Jordan River.

Naaman is offended that the prophet does not take the time to come out and touch him to heal him. He is nevertheless cured and brings countless gifts to Elisha, who refuses them all (the unfaithful servant of Elisha runs after Naaman to receive the gifts but instead catches the disease, part of the story omitted by Schonaeus); in addition, the newly cured Naaman renounces his gods and accepts the God of Israel. The appealing nature of the story with its overt Messianic message, namely the prefiguration of Christ's baptism in the Jordan, must have indisputably presented an attractive prospect for Schonaeus.

The nucleus of the biblical story furnished the Dutch playwright with enough materials to turn this into a fully-fledged comedy in the manner of Terence: Naaman has a wife, Artemona, whose slave-girl, Phronesium, urges him on to visit Elisha; as her Greek name suggests, she is the voice of reason that ultimately leads Naaman to the right path of conversion. The house is run by slaves, some of them fulfilling the traditional role of the *servus currens*, craving food and trying to avoid hard work. Naaman is helped out in his journey by his *ministri nobiles*, Strato, Leonidas, and Storax: Strato opposes the trip to Samaria, since he suspects it to be part of the wife's and slave's collusive trick to lead Naaman astray and belittle him (as women would normally do, according to his thinking), while Leonidas supports and prods Naaman on to fulfill the prophet's command and finally wash in the Jordan.

In Act I, Scene I, Artemona delivers a monologue complaining of her unfortunate marriage to a leper, which turns into a discourse on unhappy marriage in general, full of the stereotypes we often encounter in comedic scenes of the type. In the following scene, Phronesium admonishes her mistress to avoid the common mistake of women who constantly complain about their spouses:

> PH. multa, mihi crede, mulierum sunt vitia: sed
> hoc e multis unum aiunt esse maximum,
> quod de maritis facile conqueruntur
> suis, hanc suspicionem oportet ut effugias,
> si honestam te probamque vis perhiberier.
>
> Believe me, women have many blemishes: but, as they say, this is the greatest of them all, namely that they easily complain about their husbands. You must avoid this mistrust, if you want to be called honorable and upright.

In this pastiche, Schonaeus has blended various stereotypical accounts of women in Terentian comedy, such as Clitipho's in the *Hauton Timorumenos*, Gnatho's in the *Eunuchus*, or Parmeno's description of the upright wife in the *Hecyra*:

>   CL. et nosti mores mulierum:
> dum moliuntur, dum conantur, annus est. (*Hau.* 239–40)

And you know how women are. While they're making their preparations and getting themselves going, a year goes by.

>   GN. novi ingenium mulierum:
> nolunt ubi velis, ubi nolis cupiunt ultro. (*Eu.* 812–13)

I know how women behave. When you want a thing they don't, and contrawise when you don't they do.

> PAM. haec, ita uti liberali esse ingenio decet,
> pudens modesta incommoda atque iniurias
> viri omnis ferre et tegere contumelias. (*Hec.* 164–66)

The wife as you would expect from a respectable character, was modest and restrained: she put up with all her husband's unkindness and ill-treatment, and she said nothing of his insulting behavior.

But Phronesium's rhetoric also adopts Hegio's discourse from the *Adelphoe* when he warns Demea that the more powerful and rich the two brothers are, the more they should strive to be fair-minded in order to be regarded as honorable:

> HEG. sed, Demea, hoc tu facito cum animo cogites.
> quam vos facillume agitis, quam estis maxume
> potentes, dites, fortunati, nobiles,
> tam maxume vos aequo animo aequa noscere
> oportet, si vos voltis perhiberi probos.   (*Ad.* 500–4)

All right, Demea, but be sure to keep this in mind: the easier your life is, the more powerful, rich, and prosperous you are, the higher the status you enjoy, the more it is your duty to be fair-minded and to act justly, if you want to be regarded as honorable men.

In Schonaeus' adaptation of the Terentian context then the girl's speech appropriates advice directed to men who aim at being *probi*. Such a tendency characterizes Schonaeus' comedy throughout, as the divide between men and women becomes more permeable than in the ancient plays while at the same time the traditional roles are upheld at the end.

As Artemona warns the slave girl that it does not befit a woman to tell all, when it is better to keep silent, Phronesium's Terentian language resurfaces, in adapting Chremes' famous lines from the *Hauton Timorumenos*.

ART. sed hoc
tecum facito uti cogites: in rebus istiusmodi,
quas celari magis, quam proferri expedit,
parum decere percontatricem esse iuvenculam.
PH. mulier sum, in alienis fortasse curiosior
quam par est, hera, vel me monere hoc, vel percontari puta.
quod etiam ne auderem quidem, nisi id tibi
ex usu fore confiderem. quapropter te obsecro,
da veniam, si hoc a me forte videatur
factum impudentius: et quicquid tandem est, tuum
quod excruciat animum, fac ut sciam.

ART. But about this do as you think: in matters of this sort, which it is better to hide than to display, it is ill-fitting that a young girl be inquisitive.
PH. I am a woman, perhaps more curious when it comes to other people's business than I should be, mistress; take it as advice or, if you like, as a question. I would never dare do this, except that I trust this to be of use to you. Therefore I ask you, be kind, if I seem to act shamelessly: and finally let me know what it is that bothers your heart.

Phronesium's exclamation that she is a busybody exemplifies Schonaeus' profitable exploration of Terentian language: *mulier* replaces *homo* of the original line and glosses it further by the addition of *curiosior*, echoing Menedemus' *aliena ut cures*, adding thus a comment on the Terentian play's proverbial encapsulation of the πολυπράγμων:

MEN. Chreme, tantumne ab re tuast oti tibi
aliena ut cures ea quae nil ad te attinent?
CHR. homo sum; humani nil a me alienum puto.
vel me monere hoc vel percontari puta.
rectumst, ego ut faciam; non est, te ut deterream. (*Hau.* 75–79)

MEN. Chremes, do you have so much free time from your own business that you concern yourself with other people's affairs when they nothing to do with you?
CHR. I'm human, and I regard no human business as other people's. Take it as advice or, if you like, as a question. If your behavior's right, I'll follow your example; if not, I'll try to dissuade you.

Phronesium invites her mistress to open up her heart and trust her by explaining the nature of her enormous problem; moving away from the model of the two men, Chremes and Menedemus, of the *Hauton Timorumenos*, here we encounter two women, perhaps intentionally, stereotypically presented as meddlers in one other's affairs; but most importantly, from the very beginning, Phronesium assumes Menedemus' role in facilitating the solution of the problem at hand, just as Menedemus does for his neighbour, Chremes, in the Terentian play. In Schonaeus' Christian play, the slaves are elevated to the protagonist's role, as it is Phronesium who facilitates Naaman's conversion.

Naaman's opening monologue in the first scene of Act II also mirrors similar complaints in classical comedy, as, for instance, Pamphilus' and Myrrhina's exclamations in the *Hecyra* (PAM. *an quisquam usquam gentiumst aeque miser?* 293; MY. *nullam pol credo mulierem me miseriorem vivere* ... , 566). Naaman explains his predicament by describing the terrible effects of his disease, as his whole body is covered by foul-smelling sores, affecting his inner organs as well:

> NA. an quisquam homo me vivit calamitosior,
> aut miserior? aut cui omnes bonae felicitates
> aeque aduersae sient? ...
>   nullone pacto
> ego abominabilem hanc pestem, luemque deterrimam
> e corpore excutere potero? nullumve erit dolorum finis? ...
> totum ulceribus, tuberibusque intumuit caput.
> corrosae pruriunt nares, capillus defluit,
> vox rauca est ...
> ad haec foetorem fauces eructant gravem: hinc
> adeo uno ore medici asserunt, ipsa quoque viscera
> interiora infecta et corrupta esse omnia ...

Is there anybody more afflicted or more wretched? Or one for whom all good luck is equally bad? ... Will I be able to shake out of my body this abominable pestilence, this most awful plague? Will there be an end to sorrow? My whole head is swollen with wounds and tumors. My nose, gnawed to pieces, itches; my hair falls out; my voice is hoarse ... Moreover, my mouth vomits an offensive stench: all doctors unanimously profess that all my interior organs are infected and ruined ...

A similar reaction to the unfolding of events is found in the fourth scene of the fourth act, when Naaman is frustrated by the king of Israel, after he had carried the letter to him regarding Elisha:

> NA. perii, quid nunc? quo fugiam, aut quo me recipiam miser?
> nullus sum, totus occidi: nam in eum mihi
> iam res rediit locum, ut si omnes omnia sua
> consilia conferant, atque huic subito malo
> salutem quaerant, auxilii nihil adferant! ...

I'm dead, what now? Where do I flee or where shall I betake myself, the wretched? I'm done for, I've perished. For, woe is me, the situation has now come back to such a point that if everybody put their head together and seek a remedy for his sudden evil, they wouldn't be able to help at all!

Perii and *nullus sum* or *occidi* and combinations thereof are common elements in such commiserations, part of the comedic register in similar scenes of comic despair in Plautus or Terence (*perii*: cf. *An.* 213, *Hau.* 404, *Eu.* 326; *nullus sum*: cf. *Eu.* 1023,

Hec. 319; also *Hec.* 319: PAM. *nullus sum* ... *perii*). The exclamation adds to the tragic tone of the narrative, turning the traditional *perii* into an expression of distress and ultimate frustration.[16] But in addition, Naaman's desperation alludes to and echoes the slave Geta's words from the *Adelphoe*, where he is up in arms when he finds out that Aeschinus is in love with someone other than Pamphila, his mistress' daughter:

> GE. nunc illud est quom, si omnia omnes sua consilia conferant
> atque huic malo salutem quaerant, auxili nil adferant,
> quod mihique eraeque filiaeque erilist. (*Ad.* 299–301)

> Now we're in a situation where, if everybody in the world put their heads together and tried to find a solution to the problem afflicting me and my mistress and my mistress's daughter, they wouldn't be able to help at all.

As such, the Terentian context adds a comic tone to the tragic nature of the narrative, namely Naaman's desperation at the lack of solution to his problem.

For his description of Naaman's meeting with the king, Schonaeus draws on Terence's *Eunuchus* and *Hecyra*; Naaman is received by the king in the traditional manner of foreign visitors and with the courtesy demanded by protocol:

> NA. ac primum quidem adventum mihi gratulatur [sc. rex].
> salutat, satis appellans familiariter,
> gaudebam. mox lectis a rege nostro quas
> illi adferebam literis, ibi homo subito
> furore iraque correptus vestes lacerat suas:
> torvisque me intuens oculis, quid inquit, an Deum me esse
> arbitratur, qui occidendae ac servandae vitae potestatem
> habeam? ut hic hominem a lepra sanandum mandet mihi?
> o indignum facinus!

> And at the first when I arrive, the king wishes me joy: he greets me, addressing me on friendly terms. I was happy. Soon when the letter I brought from my king was read, then the man suddenly tears his clothes, seized by fury and anger: looking at me with fierce eyes, he said: "What, does he think I am God who has the power to save a life or destroy it? He sends me this man to be healed from leprosy? Oh shameful deed!"

Gnatho is greeted similarly as he enters the market, by all the shopkeepers and sellers:

> GN. dum haec loquimur, interea loci ad macellum ubi adventamus,
> concurrunt laeti mi obviam cuppedenarii omnes,
> cetarii, lanii, coqui, fartores, piscatores,

---

16 On tragicomedy, see Herrick 1962.

quibus et re salva et perdita profueram et prosum saepe.
salutant, ad cenam vocant, adventum gratulantur. (*Eu.* 255–9)

In the course of this conversation we arrived at the market. Everybody ran up delighted to see me, the snack sellers, the fishmongers, the butchers, the cooks, the poulterers, the spratsellers, men who had profited by me in good times and in bad and often still do. They greeted me, invited me to dinner, congratulated me on my safe return.

The burlesque tone of Gnatho's narrative turns into a narrative of desperation by Naaman, as the initial meeting results in a disaster. But the narrative as it unfolds is reminiscent of the *Hecyra* as well: Naaman is reproached by the king who tears his clothes, indignant and enraged that someone could ever think he has the power to heal leprosy. In the *Hecyra*, Pamphilus hears the noise and voices from inside the house, where allegedly Philumena has some sort of disease, a *cotidiana febris* (she is shivering); upon closer inspection when Pamphilus comes into the house, he realizes that Philumena's real condition, the actual *morbus*, is her pregnancy. In the monologue that follows Pamphilus' exit from the house, he makes clear to the audience what was going on inside the house, in a narrative similar to Naaman's:

PAM. nequeo mearum rerum initium ullum invenire idoneum	
unde exordiar narrare quae necopinanti accidunt,	
partim quae perspexi hisce oculis, partim quae accepi auribus,	
qua me propter exanimatum citius eduxi foras.	
nam modo intro me ut corripui timidus, alio suspicans	365
morbo me visurum affectam ac sensi esse uxorem, ei mihi!	
postquam me aspexere ancillae advenisse, ilico omnes simul	
laetae exclamant "venit," id quod me repente aspexerant.	
sed continuo voltum earum sensi immutari omnium,	
quia tam incommode illic fors obtulerat adventum meum.	370
una illarum interea propere praecucurrit nuntians	
me venisse. ego eius videndi cupidus recta consequor.	
postquam intro adveni, extemplo eius morbum cognovi miser.	
nam neque ut celari posset tempus spatium ullum dabat	
neque voce alia ac res monebat ipsa poterat conqueri.	375
postquam aspexi, "o facinus indignum" inquam et corripui ilico	
me inde lacrumans, incredibili re atque atroci percitus.	(*Hec.* 361–77)

I can't think of a suitable point from which to begin to tell the things that have befallen me so unexpectedly – some seen with these very eyes, others head with these ears – and have sent me rushing out of the house so distraught. I dashed inside just now full of anxiety, expecting to see my wife suffering from an illness very different from the one I found, but oh dear! As soon as the maids saw I was back, they all cried out in one voice "He's come," full of joy because they had not expected to see me. But the next moment I noticed a change in all their expressions, because my return happened to have come at a most inconvenient time. Presently one of them ran ahead in a hurry to report my arrival. I followed straight behind her, eager to see my wife. When I got inside the room, I immediately recognized to my dismay what was wrong with her. The situation allowed them no time to cover it up, and she herself could only utter cries prompted by her pains. When I saw her, I cried out "It's outrageous!" and dashed out from the room at once in tears, overwhelmed by the terrible unbelievable turn of events.

The discovery of Philumena's condition makes Pamphilus exclaim *o facinus indignum*, a phrase that occurs elsewhere in Terence (cf. *An.* 145, *Eu.* 70, *Ph.* 511) and points to the idea "that people should behave in a manner worthy of themselves and treat others as they deserve."[17] As in the king's initial response, Pamphilus rejoices in his return, and so do the maids. Soon the change of mood is brought about by the discovery of the fake *morbus*, the pregnancy. In both cases, the situation is deemed beyond repair: the healing of leprosy is impossible, and so is the handling of childbirth in the *Hecyra*. Schonaeus masterfully exploits the Terentian monologue; as Sander Goldberg observes, "the richness of the monologue, full of genuine emotion, vivid description, and reported speech is especially effective at bringing the off-stage action to life."[18]

In the final scenes, the healed Naaman thanks his comrade, Leonidas, and recognizes his wife's and Phronesium's major roles in the process of his salvation:

> NA. O populares, ecquis me vivit fortunatior?
> venustatisque adeo, voluptatisque plenior?
> nemo hercule quisquam ...
> quid ego nunc commemorem primum, aut quem laudem maxime?
> illamne, quae prima hoc mihi consilium dedit
> ut facerem? an uxorem? an te mi Leonida? qui uti
> lavarer, auctor eras mihi, an Elisaeum potius?
> cuius ope nunc vivo et servatus sum planissime.
>
> Fellow countrymen, is there anyone alive today more fortunate than me? So full of grace and delight? By Hercules, no one ... Whom shall I mention first or praise the most? Her, who gave me the advice first to do this? Or my wife? Or you, my Leonidas, who were my instigator to wash in the river? Or rather Elisha, by whose power I now live and am most clearly saved?

The opening of the speech alludes to Pamphilus' joy in the *Hecyra* (PAM. *quis mest fortunatior venustatisque adeo plenior?/egon pro hoc te nuntio qui donem?* "Who is more fortunate than me or indeed luckier in love? What reward shall I

---

17 Barsby 1999, 96.
18 Goldberg 2013, 141.

give you in return for this news," 848–9) and repeats Chaerea's similar expression of thanks in the *Eunuchus*, where the supernatural is also mentioned, that is, Jupiter's role in human affairs, as God is responsible for Naaman's absolution in the waters of the Jordan:

> CH. o populares, ecquis me hodie vivit fortunatior?
> nemo hercle quisquam. nam in me plane di potestatem suam
> omnem ostendere, quoi tam subito tot congruerint commoda ...
> quid commemorem primum aut laudem maxume?
> illumne qui mihi dedit consilium ut facerem, an me qui id ausu' sim   1045
> incipere, an fortunam collaudem quae gubernatrix fuit,
> quae tot res tantas tam opportune in unum conclusit diem,
> an mei patris festivitatem et facilitatem? o Iuppiter,
> serva obsecro haec bona nobis!   (*Eu.* 1031–3, 1044–9)

> Fellow countrymen, is there anyone alive today more fortunate than me? Nobody at all. The gods have clearly manifested all their powers in my case; so many blessings have been heaped upon me so unexpectedly ... Who deserves to be named first or praised the most? The one who suggested the plan of action, or myself who dared to carry it out? Or should I praise Fortune the helmswoman who has packed so many favors into a single day? Or my father for his good humor and generosity? Oh Jupiter, I beseech you, preserve these blessings for us.

Naaman's mission, according to Schonaeus, is not complete until he persuades the unfaithful Strato, a new version of the mistrusting Thomas, that his salvation is the result of his washing his sins in the Jordan:

> NA. contemplare me sodes, Strato. Nosti
> qui fuerim, nunc quis sim vide: quae puritas,
> color, nitor, quae sit habitudo corporis.
> ST. o prodigium! quod evenire praedicant
> serpentibus, id ego nunc tibi accidisse conspicor:
> ut veteri pelle abjecta homo prorepseris
> novus. NA. plane novus, Strato: remiserunt
> se cruciatus. abiit dolor, membris suus rediit
> vigor: atque adeo intus prorsus me immutatum senti.
> ST. monstri simile, sed quo pacto isthuc accidit
> tibi? nulline es usus pharmacis? NA. nullis
> omnino, tantum me in Jordane immersi septies,
> quemadmodum ab Elisaeo praeceptum erat mihi.

> NA. Look at me, if you dare, Strato. You know how I was, now see how I am: my cleanliness, my complexion, my style, my physical condition.
> ST. What a miracle! What they say happens to snakes has happened to you, I see: so that you crawled out a new man, having cast aside your old skin.

NA. Brand new, Strato: the suffering has let up, the pain is gone, strength has returned to my limbs; I feel that I am completely changed inside also.
ST. Miraculous, but how did it happen to you? Have you used any drugs?
NA. No, not at all, I've only immersed myself seven times in the Jordan, as Elisha advised me to do.

Naaman's insistence on his *puritas*, his new *color* and *nitor* allude to Gnatho's digressive narrative in the *Eunuchus* of his meeting with another parasite, a beggar, who in comparison to him is dirty, shabbily dressed, and sick:

> GN. conveni hodie adveniens quendam mei loci hinc atque ordinis,
> hominem haud inpurum, itidem patria qui abligurrierat bona.   235
> video sentum, squalidum, aegrum, pannis annisque obsitum. "oh!
> quid istuc" inquam "ornatist?" "quoniam miser quod habui perdidi, em
> quo redactus sum. omnes noti me atque amici deserunt."
> hic ego illum contempsi prae me: "quid homo" inquam "ignavissume?
> itan parasti te ut spes nulla relicua in te sit tibi?   240
> simul consilium cum re amisti? viden me ex eodem ortum loco?
> qui color, nitor, vestitus, quae habitudost corporis!
> omnia habeo neque quicquam habeo; nil quom est, nil defit tamen."   (*Eu.* 234–43)

On my way here today I met a person of my own rank and station, a decent enough fellow, who had, like me, guzzled away his inheritance. He looked unkempt, dirty, sick, shabbily dressed, and senile. "Oh!" I said, "What sort of a get-up is that?" "I've lost what I had, unfortunately, and look what I'm reduced to. I'm abandoned by all my friends and acquaintances." I was full of contempt for him compared with myself. "What!" I said, "you spineless fellow! Have you managed your life in such a way as to leave yourself without hope? Have you lost your wits along with your wealth? I've come from the same background: look at me, my complexion, my style, my clothes, my physical condition. I have everything and I have nothing; no possessions but nothing lacking."

Gnatho takes pride in his better status with the line repeated by Naaman above. Gnatho underscores that the improvement of his status is not based on possessions, an element exploited by Schonaeus: Naaman changes internally, as well as externally; leprosy is healed but only through the revelation of the divine and the truth concerning the one God, the God of Israel. Strato is surprised at the *prodigium*, he calls it *monstri simile* (an expression that we find in Terence for grotesque, outrageous, unnatural occurrences, as in *Eu.* 334), and we can see here Schonaeus' innovation in the introduction of the imagery of the serpent changing its skin, here adapted to reflect Christian beliefs concerning rebirth after baptism.

In conclusion, the preceding analysis has offered but a glimpse into the breadth and wealth of materials found in Cornelius Schonaeus' reworking of Terentian comedy, written and produced to meet the needs of a Christian audience at Haarlem. Schonaeus aims at educating his pupils to follow the precepts of the Bible, to strive in imitation of the great figures of the Old and New Testament, and to seek repentance and forgiveness from the Creator. But his efforts could not have been as effective without the use of Terentian language and context: after all, the pagan themes of the classical playwright are not entirely abandoned but rather changed and adapted to something new that preserves the purity of Terentian language, a purity that is now transferred to a metaphorical level to reflect the desired purity of a Christian sermon that inspires and imbibes uprightness and holiness of character.

Acknowledgments

I would like to thank Stavros Frangoulidis for the invitation to participate in the Conference in Thessaloniki. This is part of a bigger project to edit Schonaeus' plays, with Latin text, English translation and commentary.

Bibliography

Augoustakis, A. (2013), 'Hrotsvit of Gandersheim Christianizes Terence', in: A. Augoustakis and A. Traill (eds.), *A Companion to Terence*, Malden, Mass., 397–409.
Barsby, J. (1999), *Terence: Eunuchus*, Cambridge.
_____ (2001), *Terence*, 2 vols, Cambridge, Mass.
Bloemendal, J. (2013), 'Neo-Latin Drama in the Low Countries', in: J. Bloemendal and H. B. Norland (eds.), *Neo-Latin Drama in Early Modern Europe*, Leiden, 293–364.
Cain, A. (2013), 'Terence in Late Antiquity', in: A. Augoustakis and A. Traill (eds.), *A Companion to Terence*, Malden, Mass., 380–96.
Craig, H. (1923), 'Terentius Christianus and the Stonyhurst Pageants', *Philological Quarterly* 2, 56–62.
Goldberg, S. (2013), *Terence: Hecyra*, Cambridge.
Herrick, M. (1962), *Tragicomedy: Its Origins and Development in Italy, France and England*, Urbana, Ill.
Karakasis, E. (2005), *Terence and the Language of Roman Comedy*, Cambridge.
Parente, J. A., Jr. (1987), *Religious Drama and the Humanist Tradition*, Leiden.
Schonaeus, C. (1691), *Terentius Christianus, seu Comoediae sacrae, tribus partibus distinctae Terentiano stylo*, Frankfurt am Main.
Van de Venne, H. (1983), 'Cornelius Schonaeus 1541–1611. A Bibliography of his Printed Works', *HumLov* 32, 367–433.
_____ (1984), 'Cornelius Schonaeus 1541–1611. A Bibliography of his Printed Works II', *HumLov* 33, 206–314.

———— (1985), 'Cornelius Schonaeus 1541–1611. A Bibliography of his Printed Works III', *HumLov* 34B, 1–113.
———— (1986), 'Cornelius Schonaeus 1541–1611. A Bibliography of his Printed Works IV', *HumLov* 35, 219–83.
Verweij, M. (2013), 'The *Terentius Christianus* at Work: Cornelius Schonaeus as a Playwright', in: P. Ford and A. Taylor (eds.), *The Early Modern Cultures of Neo-Latin Drama*, Leuven, 95–105.

Evangelos Karakasis
Petronian Spectacles: The Widow of Ephesus Generically Revisited

After dinner, in the course of Lichas' episode in Petronius' *Satyrica*, Eumolpus recites, in a refined Neronian Latin idiom,[1] a 'novella conviviale' (cf. Parca 1981, 100): it is the supposedly 'real-life' story[2] of the 'widow from Ephesus', a tale exemplifying female fickleness and instability. Despite Eumolpus' claims that he will carry his point without resorting to theatrical examples (110.8), he occasionally describes the widow of Ephesus and her character through terms with a particular theatrical and meta-theatrical semantic load (e. g. *fabula*, *spectaculum*, 111.5, 111.1).[3] Admittedly, Eumolpus is a good story-teller (Beck 1979, 239–53[4]) with a wide literary background, and one would, therefore, expect his narration to be influenced by various literary genres. Furthermore, the subject of his story is also, up to a point, expected to have a theatrical dimension: 'female instability' has an obvious comic touch,[5] as comedy is a literary genre where instances of misogyny or, in any case, criticisms of women abound (cf. e. g. Plaut. *Mil.* 187–94, Ter. *Hec.* 312);[6] what is more, these comic undertones are underscored by the way the story is received by a part of its Petronian audience, namely the laughing sailors (*risu excepere fabulam nautae*, 'the sailors received this tale with a laugh', 113.1).[7] All in all, the whole episode with its emphasis on the distinction between

---

[1] Cf. Adamik 2003, 1–10.
[2] For the widow tale as a real-life story, cf. esp. Herrmann 1927, 20–57.
[3] Cf. e. g. Slater 1990, 109, McGlathery 1998, 318; 2001, 122–4, Benz 2001, 100–1, Rimell 2002, 125, Castagna 2003, 33–4, Eickmeyer 2006, 78 and n. 14, Erasmo 2008, 24, Ragno 2009, 179, 354–7 vs. Anderson 2005, 48; see also Huber 1990, 52–3, Dickison 2013, 86–7.
[4] Cf. also Plaza 2000, 172–4, 180, Schmeling 2011, 427 vs. Eickmeyer 2006, 87 and n. 26.
[5] Cf. also Ure 1956, 1, 9, Parca 1981, 95.
[6] Cf. Watson and Watson 2014, 29–30.
[7] Cf. also Cicu 1986, 263. In terms of the novel's plot, open-endedness and ambivalence as to the reception of the tale is suggested by the different reactions to the story of the Petronian audience itself; contrast the soldiers' laughter, Tryphaena's embarrassment and Lichas' resentment (113.1–2; cf. Rastier 1971, 1027, Slater 1990, 110, Iribarren 2005, 119). For an open-ended, ambivalent text, able to generate a range of various reactions, e. g. depending on one's moral stance or the various focalisations/voices of the narrative, cf. esp. Rastier 1971, 1046–8, Huber 1990, Plaza 2000, 185 and the notion of 'relativisation'; see also Frings 1985, 60, Sega 1986, 67, Galand 1989, esp. 111–2, Fedeli–Dimundo 2000, 190–1, Ruiz Sánchez 2005, 171–2, Eickmeyer 2006, esp. 88 and n. 28, Ragno 2009, 285–6, Dickison 2013, 88. Readings which positively interpret the story as a victory of life over death include: Arrowsmith 1966, 328, Segal 1973, 90–3, Müller 1980, esp. 110–1, 114, Bakhtin 1981, 221–4, Cicu 1986, esp. 269, 271, Boldrini

Greek (e.g. the special mention of the Greek burial of the deceased husband, 111.2[8]) and Roman elements (e.g. the crucifixion and the mention of the provincial governor,[9] the *imperator provinciae*, 111.5, 113.2) resonates with and notably exploits the basic (ideological and structural) polarity of the Roman *palliata*. Lament, bewailing the death of a beloved husband, on the other hand, constitutes a typical tragic theme [e.g. Tecmessa weeping for the dead Ajax (in Sophocles' *Ajax*), Evadne grieving for Capaneus (in Euripides' *Suppliant Women*), or Hecuba mourning Priam (in Seneca's *Troades*), etc.[10]].

From this perspective, the present paper aims to read the story of the Ephesian beauty as a narrative where tragic and comic discourses interact and, thus, uncover layers of generic meaning. The Roman novel (Petronius and the episode in question included) have long been compellingly read in their relation to theatre, especially the mime;[11] building on and adding to this trend of thought, the basic purpose of the present paper is to reconsider the way this inset story is permeated by dramatic discourses, focusing, mainly, on the 'generic intrusion' of

---

1989, 129, Strunz 2001, esp. 447–8; see also Rastier 1971, 1031, Blume 1974, 48, Lefèvre 1997, 16–7, Fedeli–Dimundo 2000, 58 vs. e.g. Herzog 1989, 133–6 who sees an eventual 'corruption' of an exemplified and acclaimed initial *pudicitia*, Coccia 1989, 121–40, Conte 1996, 104–7, also viewing the story from a misogynistic angle, Rimell 2002, esp. 138 who compellingly contextualises the story within the overall Petronian narrative and its intertexts, and calls attention to a problematic 'happy end' (for the *status quaestionis*, see also Plaza 2000, 181–3, Slater 2009, 26–7). Frow 1986, 134, from a Marxist perspective, also reads the story as a progress from social propriety to 'profane values associated with bodily functions'. Garelli 1990, 51–9 as well compellingly examines the way irony is employed as the narrative means for underscoring female levity (esp. in the use of terms like *pudica*, *pudicitia* and *casta*, hyperbolic expressions, military diction and Vergilian citations); see also Perotti 2001–2, 247–8, 255–6. Whatever the case may be, i.e., irrespective of whether one reads the story positively, critically [i.e., as an attack against female moral weakness or hypocrisy (cf. esp. Pecere 1975, 106, Coccia 1989, 122 and n. 7, Courtney 2001, 166 and n. 11, Ragno 2009, 305–6 vs. La Penna 1985, 46–7, Cicu 1986, 265 for whom the widow eventually comes to her senses)], or even neutrally (e.g. simply or predominantly as a folk tale, cf. Slater 1990, 110, Borghini 2012, 121–9 and the 'specter bridegrooms' folktale type), a serious and rapid evolution of the lady's attitude towards life and spousal loyalty is evident (cf. Conte 1996, 106, Fedeli–Dimundo 2000, 68, Ragno 2004, 316 and n. 81), and it is on this very development that the story largely focuses.

8 Either avoidance of cremation, cf. Courtney 2001, 168, Ciaffi 2003, 287, or positioning on a stone block, not in the sarcophagus, cf. Pecere 1975, 52, D'Ambrosio 1994, 72–3; 1995, 69 and n. 3, Cavalca 2001, 98.

9 Cf. Vannini 2010, 242–3.

10 Cf. Cicu 1986, 260, Walcot 1991, 16; see also Ragno 2009, esp. 294–306, 312–6.

11 Cf. Fedeli 2009, 19 (with bibliography). For the theatrical associations of the Ephesian *matrona*-episode in particular, cf. especially the seminal work by Ragno 2009; see also Panayotakis 1995, 155–6 and n. 55, Fedeli–Dimundo 2000, 50.

'guest genres' like the mime, the Roman *palliata* and the Senecan tragedy, influenced, in turn, by Roman comedy in Greek dress, into the 'host' Roman novel. In particular I intend
- to examine the way comic, mimic and tragic generic rules, patterns and narrative sequences inform the Petronian tale, reinforcing Eumolpus' line of reasoning and
- to contextualise the story in the Neronian era, as a potential Petronian parody of Seneca and his tragic discourse.

Before proceeding, however, an initial observation is in order: several of the motifs, structures and narrative sequences[12] to be discussed below may be found in other, non-dramatic, literary genres as well (e. g. the adulterous erotic triangle, the erotic *furor*, etc.). However, what matters, in this case, is functionality vs. random instances: most of the subsequent themes constitute regular, central and essential features of the structure of either comic/mimic or tragic plots, to such an extent that they function as 'generic markers' defining a comic/mimic/tragic 'generic identity'. What is more, I am clearly arguing for a theatrical reading of the story on a cumulative basis; some of the following motifs and narratives evidently have a stronger comic, mimic or tragic colouring than others, but I believe that, in their concentration, they reinforce a theatrical reading of the tale.

Last but not least a further theoretical admission: following the seminal terminology of Harrison 2007, 16, the term 'host genre' denotes the main 'generic formation' under examination, the genre that keeps the 'dominant generic role', i. e., in the case in question, 'the novel'. A second 'generic formation', functioning on a secondary level within the 'host genre', is designated by the term 'guest genre', i. e., comedy, tragedy, mime, etc.

---

12 For a structural/semiotic analysis of the narrative's meaning, fashionable during the eighties, cf. esp. Sega 1986, 37–81 (with an emphasis on narrative sequences of the Russian formalist type, analysis according to Greimas and Genette, interest in interventions of the narrator, etc.), Pepe 1987, 210–28 (capitalising, in turn, on the theoretical tools developed by T. Todorov and B. Tomachevski). For further structural readings of the story, examining its association with other narrative parts of the *Satyrica*, cf. esp. Parca 1981, 100 (the reconciliation between Tryphaena and Giton), Cicu 1986, 249–71, Dupont 1977, 183–4 (the *Cena Trimalchionis*); see also Griton–Leroux 2003, 72–3, Vannini 2007, 306, 310. For a detailed study of mechanisms of 'inversion' in the story, cf. esp. Fedeli 1986, 9–35, for the narrative mechanism of 'triplication' (three interventions of the maid, for example), cf. esp. Fedeli 1987, 3–21, whereas for a thorough study of the various focalisations of the tale, cf. Iribarren 2005, 113–24.

Versions of the story and its stemma

The basic outline of the embedded narrative of the 'courted widow' is attested in three main Roman sources, Phaedrus (app. 15 Guaglianone = 13 Postgate), Petronius (111–2), and Romulus (3.9 = 59 Thiele), while a simpler Greek version is found in the *Vita Aesopi* (129 GW). The interrelation of the various versions to each other, especially of the Roman ones, has been the subject of a long and intense discussion, and various, often contradictory, views have been expressed. Some scholars, to give the basic trends in the debate, postulate Phaedrus' (and Romulus') dependence on Petronius, whose version must have been abridged by the Roman mythographer (Herrmann 1927, 21–41), others propose an expansion of Phaedrus' story by Petronius,[13] with Romulus following Phaedrus (Holzberg 2002, 45–6, Courtney 2001, 167; cf. also Müller 1980, 115–21), others claim that all three Latin versions owe a debt to an archetypical *argumentum* of a Hellenistic collection (Thiele 1908, 361–8), while others argue for a twofold tradition of an archetypical Latin version (probably Sisenna, translating Aristides' *Milesiaca*), with Petronius representing the first branch and the other two (Phaedrus and Romulus) deriving from a lost middle source, which constitutes the second branch of the extant Latin tradition (Weinreich 1931, 53–75). Lefèvre 1997, 15–32, while supporting the Milesian origin of an expanded Petronian story, is, on the other hand, of the view that the version of the *appendix Phaedriana* is simply an editorial construction by Perotti on the basis of Romulus' account, along with Petronian reminiscences. Vannini 2010, 23–38; 2013, 77–95 offers an excellent, thorough account of the *status quaestionis*, re-examines the issue afresh and comes to the compelling conclusion that all three extant Latin sources of the story may derive from an archetypal intermediary Latin account, probably derived from a collection of Aesopic *logoi*, as seems also to be the case with the Greek version of the *Vita Aesopi*.[14] Petronius is convincingly viewed, under this analysis, as developing and enriching a pre-existing basic narrative sketch, up to a point exemplified by Phaedrus' version. If so, the 'generic profile' of Petronius' alterations, within the framework of the extant tradition, may be indicative of the author's means of producing (generic) meaning.

---

13 Cf. also Fedeli–Dimundo 2000, 94, Schmeling 2011, 427.
14 Cf. also Pecere 1975, 7 and n. 10, Holzberg 2012, 130. For a detailed review of the literature on the origin of the story (Chinese, Indian or Asian in general (cf. esp. Grisebach 1889)/Western ancestry/real story) as well as the stemma of its various attestations, cf. esp. Cicu 1986, 249 and n. 1, Ragno 2004, 322 and n. 105; 2009, 135–8 (with the cited bibliography); see also Noia Campos 2005, 149–51, Ruiz Sánchez 2005, esp. 154–5, 170. For Vergil's *Aeneid* and Naevius' *Bellum Punicum* as key sources of the Petronian tale, cf. esp. Perotti 2001–2, 245, 248–51.

Comic discourses

To begin with, the description of the main Petronian character as a matron significantly does not occur in Phaedrus, where the handsome lady is simply described as a widow (*vidua*, vv. 21, 28) or as a *mulier* (vv. 10, 27), *femina* (v. 17) or even *domina* (v. 13).[15] *Matrona* as a characterisation, however, marks the Petronian heroine as a stock comic figure,[16] although comic matrons, as a general rule, are of an older age, dramatically functioning as the comic counterpart of the *senes*, i. e., old men. Exceptions, of course, occur, as is, for example, the case with Epidamnian Menaechmus' wife in Plautus' *Menaechmi*. Nevertheless, the way in which the lamenting widow is described in Petronius, especially as tearful with her hair loose, her face scratched and her beaten breast unclothed (111.1–3, 6–10), significantly associates her not only with typical mourning practices of the ancient world,[17] but also with bereaved New Comedy young women, especially pseudo-*meretrices*, of the type which will develop into a comic matron (and not a courtesan) with the passing of the time. This is, for example, the case with the young girl described in Terence's *Phormio*, who similarly laments her dead mother (vv. 106–7: *capillus passus, nudus pes, ipsa horrida, lacrumae, vestitus turpis*; cf. also *Haut.* 285–91)[18] and in so doing also inspires feelings of love and desire in a young man. The comic undertones of the label *matrona* are further highlighted by the narrator's option to set the plot in Ephesus, against the local vagueness of a simple folk tale,[19] i. e., at a location also absent from the shorter Phaedrean version.[20] Ephesus may, as already remarked, call to mind the probable Milesian origins of the tale[21] and the renowned moral looseness of Ephesian women,[22] but, on the other hand, Ephesus also func-

---

15 Cf. Massaro 1981, 220, Daviault 2003, 16, Perotti 2001–2, 246.
16 Cf. also Daviault 2003, 16–7.
17 Cf. Pecere 1975, 48–50, D'Ambrosio 1994, 55–73.
18 Cf. also D'Ambrosio 1994, 61 and n. 19, Corbeill 2004, 83, Schmeling 2011, 428.
19 Cf. Fedeli 1986, 10–1.
20 Cf. Herrmann 1927, 23, Massaro 1981, 220, Sega 1986, 44, 54, Huber 1990, 71, Perotti 2001–2, 246, Siewert 2007, 23.
21 Cf. Harrison 1998, 67–8, Daviault 2003, 17, Vannini 2010, 235, Schmeling 2011, 427–8; for the Milesian character of the story, claimed for as early as e. g. Collignon 1892, 349–50, cf. also esp. Sullivan 1968, 234, 246, Walsh 1970, 102, Müller 1980, 103–21, Conte 1996, 105–6, Benz 2001, 98–101, Courtney 2001, 166, Ciaffi 2003, 286 vs. Herrmann 1927, 47–50; for a concise account of the relevant criticism, see also Cicu 1986, 250 and n. 4, Lefèvre 1997, 15–6 and n. 33, Ragno 2009, 138 and n. 8 (with the relevant bibliography). As to the affinities of the Milesian production with the mime, cf. esp. Ragno 2009, 159–68 (again with an ample literature review).
22 Cf. Pecere 1975, 44–6, Cicu 1986, 256–7, Fedeli 1986, 11, Castagna 2003, 39–40, Ciaffi 2003, 287, Anderson 2005, 47; see also Fedeli–Dimundo 2000, 86, Perotti 2001–2, 260–1, Daviault

tions as the dramatic setting of New Comedy scenarios, e. g. of Plautus' *Bacchides*, and, most importantly, of Plautus' *Miles Gloriosus*, i. e., a comedy also involving a comic triangle consisting of three further stock comic characters, a young courtesan (Philocomasium), an *adulescens* (Pleusicles) and a rival soldier (Pyrgopolynices),[23] who in comedy, as here in Petronius, is significantly often focalised as a charmer of women.

Erotic triangles, which form the basis of several Roman comedies (e. g. Plautus' *Bacchides*, *Epidicus*, *Miles Gloriosus*, *Poenulus*, *Pseudolus*, *Truculentus*) and, as a comic legacy, of later elegiac discourses, appear, *mutatis mutandis*, in the Petronian story as well: a young lady, the sweetheart of a young man, is also courted by a young *miles*[24] who, being able to provide for the lady, functions as an agelast, a comic character disturbing the hero's 'peace' (e. g. Therapontigonus Platagidorus vs. Phaedromus for the love of Planesium in Plautus' *Curculio*, or Thraso vs. Phaedria, both in love with Thais in Terence's *Eunuchus*). A similar triangle develops in the Petronian tale with the important change that the dead husband functions here, up to a point at least, as the *adulescens* of the typical comic triangle. His lady, devoted to his memory, accordingly, makes him function as the rival of the soldier, who, again in keeping with his generic role, is able to provide for the object of his affection by bringing food and drink to the tomb, and eventually wins her favours. Obviously, the *miles* of the Petronian narrative is no longer the typical thick-headed, bragging and credulous Roman comic figure, but an efficient suitor (*nec deformis aut infacundus*, 'handsome and eloquent', 112.2) who does not show off but, instead, makes things happen in terms of erotic courtship; this, of course, is also true for some soldiers of the New Comic tradition as well. Conversely, the soldier is, in some cases, presented as a man with genuine erotic feelings, sincere passion and mental courtesy, who finally manages to overcome his erotic rival (e. g. Moschion in *Perikeiromene* and the *Sikyonioi*, perhaps also Kleinias in *Misoumenos*) and, consequently, to 'get the girl'. In these comic scenarios, though the soldier retains some typical features of his traditional buffoonery (military name, impulsive behaviour, melodramatic exaggeration), he is not the usual braggart any longer, the noisy target of comic ridicule. The soldier becomes instead an accredited lover who succeeds in his erotic affairs, while it is, conversely, the young man, his rival, who now plays the

---

2003, 17–8 and n. 9, who, however, brings to the fore the religious dimension of the city, adding to the alleged initial sanctity of the lady-heroine. Vannini 2013, 93 conclusively associates the city, as a Petronian innovation, with Eumolpus' professional career (Petr. 85.1).

23 Cf. also Daviault 2003, 21.
24 For the comic undertones of the soldier, cf. also Daviault 2003, 21, Ragno 2009, 320–1 and n. 581.

role of the agelast and, eventually, loses the girl. The development of the story in Petronius' tale is similar.

The Petronian wife, thus, stands in stark opposition to the faithful wives of Roman Comedy, as are, for example, the (although idealised up to a point) sisters of Plautus' *Stichus* (Panegyris and Pamphila of the Ambrosian palimpsest), who were urged by their father, Antipho, to abandon their husbands, absent for three consecutive years and hence possibly dead (cf. vv. 30–3), but without any success. The Petronian episode, on the contrary, develops along the line of an adultery story common not only in mime, as already observed in the literature on the episode (see below), but in the Roman *palliata* as well, where one comes across instances of either accomplished (e. g. in Plautus' *Amphitruo*, *Menaechmi* or in Terence's *Phormio*) or simply attempted adultery, chiefly on the part of comic men (e. g. in Plautus' *Miles Gloriosus*, *Truculentus*), especially in relation to comic lecherous *senes* (e.g. in Plautus' *Asinaria* with Demaenetus, *Casina* with Lysidamus, *Mercator* with Demipho and, up to a point, *Cistellaria* with Alcesimarchus' father, Nicobulus and Philoxenus in *Bacchides*, unless they are widowers). The Petronian husband is of course dead, but his physical presence in the tomb gives the whole situation a sense of spousal betrayal. Petronius thus toys in reverse with the sublime female Roman ideal of the *univira*.[25] It should, however, be noted here that in Roman Comedy adultery and erotic deception on the part of women appear only peripherally, although it plays an important role in the erotic novel. The only adulterous woman in Roman comedy actually appears in Plautus' *Amphitruo*, although the infidelity there is certainly unintentional: an innocent Alcmene is simply tricked by Zeus' miraculous transformation. It is thus another theatrical genre, namely the mime and its subspecies, the so-called adultery mime, which deals predominantly with female erotic faithlessness and infidelity. However, the notion of the adulterous *matrona* is far from absent from the comic scripts; in Plautus' *Miles Gloriosus*, Acroteleutium adopts the persona of an attractive, adulterous lady, the alleged wife of Periplectomenus, also purportedly in love with Pyrgopolynices, and in Terence's *Phormio*, the parasite's invitation to dinner by Nausistrata, out of spite for her husband's bigamy, may also create the impression of impending infidelity (vv. 1048–55, cf. also Plaut. *Cas.* 200–3). Female unfaithfulness is further not unknown in Old Comedy (cf. e. g. Ar. *Ec.* 225–6, *Lys.* 107–10, *Th.* 395–417, 473–519, *Ran.* 1043–4[26]).

And this brings us to Petronius' second key alteration to the model story, namely the expansion of the role of the *fidissima ancilla* (111.4),[27] who is another

---

25 Cf. also Strunz 2001, 443–4; see also Grimal 1985, 197.
26 Cf. also Habermehl 2006, 485.
27 Cf. Vannini 2010, 241; see also Herrmann 1927, 24, Pecere 1975, 11, 22, Müller 1980, 117–8, Fedeli 1986, 14, Sega 1986, 60, Huber 1990, 79, Perotti 2001–2, 258.

well-known stock character of comedy (e. g. Sophoclidisca or Giddenis in Plautus' *Persa* and *Poenulus* respectively). In Phaedrus' version the servant is simply assisting her mistress and brings the soldier water (vv. 12–5). The comic *ancilla*, as also happens later with the comic inheritance of the elegiac go-between, is regularly key to the consummation of a comic love affair (e. g. Pardalisca in Plautus' *Casina* putting off Lysidamus' scheme). This seems to be the case with the Petronian servant as well, who not only persuades her mistress to give in to the *miles*' erotic interest but also, unconsciously (e. g. Mysis in Terence's *Andria*, cf. vv. 737 ff.), works towards the narrative's goal and secures the meeting of the two lovers, by relighting the funeral candle and, thus, making the tomb visible to the soldier (111.4–6); significantly, this function of the maid seems to constitute a further Petronian innovation.[28] Milphidippa in Plautus' *Miles Gloriosus* is one more apposite comic parallel; for Acroteleutium's maid similarly functions as the agent of a (supposedly in this instance) love-struck character and, what is more, acts as a go-between facilitating the 'illicit' union of two 'lovers'. Following the equally comic generic pattern, it is the maid who first receives the *miles*' food and drink (also a Petronian novelty[29], cf. 111.10–3) in the course of his courtship; this practice is encapsulated by the meta-theatrical comment of Clitipho at Ter. *Haut*. 300–1, that 'it's standard practice for those who seek access to the mistress to give presents to the maid first'[30]/*nam disciplinast isdem munerarier/ancillas primum, ad dominas qui affectant viam*'.[31]

This Petronian *ancilla*, however, in her capacity as the catalyst of the erotic liaison between the lovers of the story, eventually assumes a further stock generic role, that of the comic *praeceptor amoris*, since, in the Petronian narrative, it is she who fashions a *suasoria* in the hopes of persuading her mistress to surrender erotically to her military suitor (111.10–3). Erotic counseling of this kind, however, is in Roman Comedy mostly associated with meretricious figures[32] of advanced age (*anus*), as is, for example, Scapha offering *erotodidaxis* to Philematium, aiming at persuading the young courtesan not to devote herself to one man as befits a *matrona*, at the beginning of Plautus' *Mostellaria* (vv. 158–294), or the protatic Syra similarly counseling the courtesan Philotis in the introductory scene of Terence's *Hecyra* (vv. 58–75). Petronius further stresses the 'comic generic descent' of the 'generic sub-role' adopted by the unnamed *ancilla* (that of a confidant attendant/erotic counselor) by picturing her, on a par with her celebrated mimic (e. g. Gyllis of Herodas' first

---

28 Cf. Vannini 2010, 242; 2013, 90–1; see also Müller 1980, 118–9.
29 Cf. Vannini 2010, 250.
30 Translated by Barsby, J. (2001), *Terence*, vol. 1, Cambridge, Mass. (Loeb), 209.
31 Cf. Ragno 2009, 320 and n. 581.
32 Cf. also Huber 1990, 46–7.

mime[33]) and comic predecessors, as having a soft spot for drinking. One could, for instance, mention here, with other commentators and critics of the passage as early as the seminal monograph of Pecere 1975, 90 and, more recently, Ragno 2009, 340–1 and n. 657, 349–50, the doorkeeper Leaena in Plautus' *Curculio*, similarly prostituting Planesium for the sake of Phaedromus' wine commission, Cleareta in *Asinaria*, Gymnasium's mother in *Cistellaria*, or even the very Scapha in *Mostellaria*; elegiac figures such as the Ovidian procuress Dipsas (*Am.* 1.8) with a 'speaking name' have also long been compellingly viewed as a comic heritage (cf. also Acanthis in Prop. 4.5).[34] The servant girl's *temulentia* seems also to be intentionally underscored by the *prothysteron* in *refecta potione et cibo*, 'refreshed with food and drink' (111.10), where drinking as a pleasure gains, also by word order, supremacy over food (Pecere 1975, 92[35]).

The role playing in the case of Petronius' *ancilla*, ultimately transforming herself from a comic faithful servant of moral principles (e. g. Syra in Plautus' *Mercator*) to a meretricious erotic counselor of the *palliata*[36] has further implications concerning the comic 'generic standing' of her mistress. The pretty widow finally falls under the influence of her meretricious *praeceptor amoris* and, at the end, chooses the soldier over the memory of her husband (112.2). However, in comic generic terms, it is not a matron who succumbs to the advice of a love counselor of the Petronian *ancilla* type but a *meretrix*; generically it is also the *meretrix* or the *pallake* who, as a rule, ends up with the *miles* as her lover (one should mention here Phronesium and Stratophanes in Plautus' *Truculentus*, Thais and Thraso in Terence's *Eunuchus*, and Menandrian heroines of *pallake*-status, Glykera and Krateia in Menander's *Perikeiromene* and *Misoumenos* respectively). Under this view, the Petronian widow, although described as a *matrona* at the beginning of the story (111.1), proves at the end of the story to assimilate the generic profile of a comic courtesan, i. e., to eventually adopt a generic role, manifestly opposed to that of a matron in terms of the comic generic world as well (cf. e. g. Plaut. *Cas.* 585, *Most.* 190; Ter. *Eun.* 37, *Ad.* 747).[37] This is another way Petronius employs to emphasise female levity and unpredictability, by following, in this case, the generic

---

33 Cf. also Pecere 1975, 20 and n. 23, Ragno 2009, 336–7, 349; see also Ragno 2004, 293–6.
34 Cf. also Boldrini 1989, 127 who also interestingly brings to the fore ancient views associating female drinking with adultery; see also Cicu 1986, 264 and n. 59, Huber 1990, 41, Courtney 2001, 170, Daviault 2003, 22 and n. 26, Ragno 2004, 295 and n. 12, Vannini 2010, 250–1, Schmeling 2011, 431, Holzberg 2012, 137.
35 See also Huber 1990, 41–2, Courtney 2001, 170, Vannini 2010, 251, Schmeling 2011, 431.
36 Cf. esp. Ragno 2009, 340–3; see also Sega 1986, 65, Pepe 1987, 220–1, Fedeli–Dimundo 2000, 81, Benz 2001, 98.
37 Cf. Focardi 1980, 158–9 and n. 1, Panayotakis 2010, 213; see also Grimal 1985, 195–203.

rules of Roman Comedy. Unlike a comic pseudo-*meretrix*, who develops into a *puella* and eventually becomes a *matrona*, Petronius' heroine takes exactly the opposite direction, defies the generic expectations that her initial presentation seems to generate, and develops into a comic *meretrix*, since it is comic courtesans who can regularly be accused of erotic fickleness and not comic *matronae* (see above). Thus, the many echoes and undertones of the comic *matrona* in the case of Petronius' young heroine create false generic prospects, further intensifying the comic effect through their falsification.

Additionally, in her effort to secure the union of the two lovers, the maid, as often remarked, makes use of epic language: she alludes to Anna's lines when urging Dido to succumb to Aeneas' love in the fourth book of Vergil's *Aeneid* (111.12: *id cinerem aut manes credis sentire sepultos?*, 'believest thou that the ashes or the spirit of the buried dead can feel thy woe?': based on Verg. *A.* 4.34 with *sentire* instead of the Vergilian *curare*, and 112.2: *placitone etiam pugnabis amori?*, 'wilt thou fight love even when love pleases thee?' also drawn from Verg. *A.* 4.38[38]). Eventually the Ephesian lady gives in to her suitor's endeavours and their euphemistic wedding (*nuptias fecerunt*, 112.3), as in the Vergilian intertext (*A.* 4.160–72),[39] is also consummated in a cave.[40] Not only bombastic language

---

38 The following line, *nec venit in mentem, quorum consederis arvis?*, 'or dost thou never remember in whose lands thou art resting?', a citation of Verg. *A.* 4.39, has been considered as an interpolation (e. g., on the basis of φ) and should, therefore, be deleted; cf. e. g. Fraenkel 1974, 690, Pecere 1975, 116–7, Fedeli 1986, 22, Vannini 2010, 256 vs. esp. Coccia 1989, 123 and n. 14, Garelli 1990, 57–8, Slater 1990, 170 and n. 21, McGlathery 1998, 327; 2001, 128, Rimell 2002, 208–9, Heuzé 2003, 54 and n. 1, Erasmo 2008, 25; see also Rose 1968, 257–8, Walsh 1970, 12 and n. 3. For a comprehensive literature review of the issue and the concomitant question of whether *arva* is used in obscene sense, cf. again Ragno 2009, 156–7.
39 Cf. Ragno 2009, 323 and n. 590.
40 For a Vergilian allusion here, variously interpreted as an epic parody or not, cf. Dell' Era 1970, 181, Walsh 1970, 12, 43–4, Colton 1975, 46–7, Pecere 1975, 115–7, Müller 1980, 109, Massaro 1981, 237, Parca 1981, 104, Frings 1985, 58–9, Cicu 1986, 266–7, Fedeli 1986, 27–9, Sega 1986, 65–6, Pepe 1987, 222, Coccia 1989, 123–4, Galand 1989, 112–4, Huber 1990, 43–4, Slater 1990, 109, 169–70, Fedeli–Dimundo 2000, 187–9, Courtney 2001, 170–2, Strunz 2001, 447, Rimell 2002, 128–37, Adamik 2003, 5, Castagna 2003, 36, Ciaffi 2003, 287, Daviault 2003, 21 and n. 23, Heuzé 2003, 53–8, Wolff 2003, 61, Ruiz Sánchez 2005, 172–3, Eickmeyer 2006, 93–7, Erasmo 2008, 25, Cipriani 2009, 42–4 and n. 109 on p. 42, Ragno 2009, 233–60 (also significantly pointing to a possible pantomimic or histrionic influence; cf. also Ragno 2004, 315 and n. 77), Vannini 2010, 252–3; 2013, 80 and n. 4, Schmeling 2011, 431–3, Holzberg 2012, 136, 138; see also Panayotakis 2009, 53–4. Through a Bakhtinian carnivalesque lens, McGlathery 1998, 313–36; 2001, 119–40 also discusses the Vergilian intertexts of the story, which, according to the scholar, brings epic down to novel (cf. also Garelli 1990, 57). Galand 1989, 113–4 reads in the Petro-

but also parodic use of elevated diction (epic, tragic and official language) is, crucially, yet another staple generic feature of Plautine slave figures, especially, although by no means exclusively, of the *servus callidus*, a figure often presiding, as is the case with the Petronian *ancilla* as well, over the erotic bliss of the young heroes of a comic narrative. Chrysalus and Pseudolus in Plautus' *Bacchides* and *Pseudolus* respectively are two well-known Plautine parallels, and this seems, up to a point, to hold true for Geta in Terence's *Phormio* too.[41] What is more, it has been claimed (Laird 1999, 245) that the Vergilian intertext (*A.* 4.9–54) alludes to New Comedy themes; if so, the Petronian reception further underlines the comic undertones of Vergil's lines (cf. also Ragno 2009, 260 and n. 344).

Next comes, at this juncture, a further alteration of Petronius in relation to the original account, namely the motif of *curiositas*. Whereas in Phaedrus' version it is the *miles*' feeling of thirst that leads him to the lady in the vault (vv. 11–2), in Petronius, where the soldier conquers his sweetheart by offering her a drink (thus thirst is out of the question as a motive, 111.13), curiosity accounts for his transposition in the location of the narrative (111.6: *vitio gentis humanae*, '[because of] a very human weakness').[42] Inquisitiveness is, of course, a habitual trait of the novel's hero,[43] yet it is also another staple comic motif, often exemplified in Roman comic drama through the eavesdropping routine[44] or through nosy comic characters like the busybody Chremes in Terence's *Hautontimorumenos*. The Petronian *miles* spies on the mourning beauty and, as occasionally in comedy (again, one should mention here Terence's *Phormio* and Antipho's infatuation with the bereaved Phanium, vv. 91–111), falls for the grieving girl at first sight. The comic colouring is further heightened here on the linguistic level as well: when starting to function as a comic lover, the narrator uses, with reference to the soldier, a well-attested comic linguistic option, namely the accumulated use of the interrogative pronoun in different genders, cases and syntactic functions (111.6): *vitio gentis humanae concupiit scire quis aut quid faceret*, 'a very human weakness made him curious to know who it was and what he was doing' (cf. also Plaut. *Amph.* 1028, *Trin.* 879, etc.[45]).

---

nian novel an influence of Ov. *Her.* 7 as well. For Verg. *A.* 6.450 ff. as an intertext of the soldier's initial mistaking of the lady as a ghost (111.7), cf. esp. Eickmeyer 2006, 96–7.
41 Cf. Karakasis 2014, 92.
42 Cf. Herrmann 1927, 24–5, Rastier 1971, 1049, Pecere 1975, 9, 17–9, Müller 1980, 117–8, Vannini 2010, 245; 2013, 90; see also Sega 1986, 73, Ruiz Sánchez 2005, 164.
43 Cf. Pecere 1975, 68–71, La Penna 1985, 45, Huber 1990, 27.
44 Cf. Duckworth 1952 [1994], 109–11.
45 Cf. Pecere 1975, 72, Ragno 2009, 321 and n. 581.

The two characters ultimately consummate their love (112.2); food and drink, a further Petronian innovation in relation to the archetypical story,[46] leads to sex, for as Chremes in Terence's *Eunuchus* remarks, *Eun.* 732: *sine Cerere et Libero friget Venus*, 'without food and wine love is cold'.[47] From this perspective, the matron's decision to die in loving memory of her husband, also a Petronian novelty following the novelistic ethos (cf. Charit. 8.1.4),[48] in fact is never executed. This is also, generically, in line with the comic *adulescentes*' expressed desire to commit suicide due to love woes and their separation from their beloved;[49] Charinus and Calidorus in Plautus' *Mercator* (vv. 471–3) and *Pseudolus* (vv. 85–95) respectively, as well as Phaedria in Terence's *Phormio* (vv. 551–4) are obvious examples of this comic practice.[50] In this last case, Phaedria's wish to commit suicide provides the incentive for the slave Geta's acts to promote his master's erotic interests, vv. 555–66; this seems also to be the case with the maid of the Petronian tale. What is more, the consummation of the love affair, as commonly in comedy again, is presented as the outcome of a deception carried out against bungling characters, who stand in the way of the couple's erotic bliss. As a first instance of deception, the lovers shut the door of the tomb, hoping to fool passers-by into believing that the bereaved lady has passed away out of sorrow (112.3). Moreover, when their erotic happiness is threatened by the *laxata custodia* (112.5) and the pilfering of the thief's corpse, the lovers, at the instigation of the matron, hang the late husband as a robber from the cross (112.5–8). Impersonation for erotic purposes constitutes a further established comic motif. However, before they hit upon this idea, the *miles* is crucially presented as willing to share the beloved lady's affections with her dead *adulescens*-husband, when he proposes to be buried along with the deceased rival in the same tomb (*sepulchra communia*, 112.6). The situation calls to mind a similar, less macabre of course, arrangement at the end of Terence's *Eunuchus*, where, yet again, a *miles*, Thraso, and an *adulescens*, Phaedria, are also supposed to share the favours of a common sweetheart, the *meretrix* Thais, vv. 1072–94 (for similar sharing agreements in the case of a comic courtesan, cf. also Plautus' *Asinaria*, *Bacchides* and *Trucu-*

---

46 Cf. Herrmann 1927, 24, Perotti 2001–2, 257 and n. 35.
47 Translated by Barsby, J. (2001), *Terence*, vol. 1, Cambridge, Mass. (Loeb), 397. Cf. also Blume 1974, 47, Huber 1990, 22 and n. 50, Courtney 2001, 171, Adamik 2003, 8, Vannini 2010, 255, Schmeling 2011, 432, Holzberg 2012, 137. For the association of food with sex, cf. esp. Boldrini 1988, 297–326; 1989, 121–31.
48 Cf. Vannini 2010, 33–4, 239; see also Pecere 1975, 17, 55 and n. 51, Boldrini 1989, 124, Müller 1980, 117, D'Ambrosio 1995, 71.
49 Cf. also Pecere 1975, 54–5.
50 Cf. Duckworth 1952 [1994], 239.

*lentus*⁵¹); in the novel the comic arrangement of a living triangle is transposed to the realm of the dead.

The widow immediately comes up with the solution: *malo mortuum impendere quam vivum occidere*, 'no, I would rather make a dead man useful, than send a live man to death', 112.7.⁵² Thus, the husband is presented as having ascended the cross by means of the expression *isset in crucem* (112.8), which, in a figurative sense, as an insult, is, as critics and commentators observe, particularly at home in Plautine comedy.⁵³ Could it be the case here that an overall comic situation (deception/impersonation) is also signalled though a hallmark of Plautine diction? In any case, crucifixion too appears in the background of Roman Comedy's 'generic realm', mostly as a threat to comic slaves (cf. Plaut. *Aul.* 59, *Mil.* 310, 372, *Pers.* 295, *Rud.* 1070, Ter. *Andr.* 621, 786), the *servus fallax* included, who thus faces the ultimate punishment (cf. Plaut. *Asin.* 548, *Most.* 348–62, 1133). This comic threat is, however, materialised only here in the case of Petronius' plot. This impersonation trick saves the *miles* from death by suicide; the Petronian lady thus dissuades her lover from killing himself with his sword (112.6, also a common accessory of the comic soldier's costume⁵⁴), in a scene reminiscent of the third act of Plautus' *Cistellaria*, where Selenium discourages her desperate lover, Alcesimarchus, from ending his life *per gladium* (vv. 639–50).

---

51 Cf. Barsby 1999, 281; see also Schmeling 2001, 434 speaking of a move 'into the sphere of comedy'.
52 For the ambiguity created by the infinitive *impendere*, which comes from *impendo* (= to expend), but may also allude to *suspendere* (= to hang), cf. esp. Buchwald 1964, 184, Lefèvre 1997, 18, Schmeling 2001, 434; more specifically, for an alleget ambivalence created by a confusion of *impendĕre* and *impendēre*, see Ragno 2009, 333–4 and n. 635 (with bibliography). For Daviault 2003, 24–5 one might see here an allusion to a hanged man's erection; for a similar (phallic), psychoanalytical reading of the story, cf. Rank 1913, 50–60; see also Fedeli 1986, 17 and n. 14, Griton–Leroux 2003, 76.
53 Cf. Pecere 1975, 143, Huber 1990, 51–2, Ragno 2009, 334–5 and n. 638, Vannini 2010, 263; vs. Courtney 2001, 173. For readings associating the story with Christian ideas, cf. esp. Cabaniss 1954, 98–102; 1960, 36–9; 1961, 41–53; 1962, 75–7; for an allusion to a mixture of water and vinegar (*posca*), given to the crucified, including Jesus Christ, cf. Colin 1953, 97–128. For the relevant *status quaestionis*, cf. esp. Ragno 2009, 329; see also Cicu 1986, 250 and n. 2 (again with the relevant bibliography).
54 Cf. Duckworth 1952 [1994], 90.

Mimic discourses

The episode has also been read as an instance of a mimic theatrical sequence; mimic features frequently discussed in the relevant literature include: a saucy and macabre subject-matter, a mimic triangle (lover – widow – a meretricious go-between), the crucifixion and drunkenness motif, the fake wedding theme, the closed doors setting, unexpected turns of the plot, parody of epic and 'literary parody' in general, sententious diction, apostrophe.[55]

However, there is sufficient evidence to construct an argument from a generic point of view, whereby, in terms of the well-known Neronian 'aesthetics of deviation' ('Aesthetik der Verkehrung'[56]) as well as in an effort to prove a point (Eumolpius' claim concerning the fickleness of women), basic features and sequences of an established adultery mime are notably altered in the Petronian story under discussion. The typical evolution of a common adultery mime is as follows:[57] a sly wife and her lover meet erotically, usually in her spouse's house, when the husband is absent. However, suddenly and without warning the latter appears and, consequently, the evil woman and her lover must devise a plan to escape discovery: either to keep the husband away, or to secretly allow the adulterous lover to leave the premises or, in any case, to prevent the husband from learning the truth. Variations of this basic pattern abound, especially as far as the cunning plan is concerned. Sometimes the husband is fooled, at other times he cottons on to the adulterous affair and drags the adulterers to court. In any case, the adulterers are eventually victorious and triumphant. In the Petronian tale many elements of this basic scheme occur, although in a modified form, once more with the aim of parading female instability:

- The story is set in a place which functions as the spousal residence; nonetheless, this is not a regular house but a grave, the last residence of a deceased spouse, also intended to be the final abode of the mourning lady, initially presented as the paradigm of pious widowhood (111.1).
- The cunning plan now aims to overcome the initial resistance of the lady (111.8–112.2). Unlike the sly adulteress of the traditional mime (the mimic *callida nupta*, Ov. *Tr.* 2.1.500), who appears lecherous and ready for philandering from the beginning, this Ephesian *matrona* starts as a model of fidel-

---

[55] Cf. Pecere 1975, 20 and n. 23, Sega 1986, 48, Wolff 2003, 61 and esp. Ragno 2009, 316–52, 358 and n. 714 (with the copious bibliography cited there). For the mime and its definition, cf. esp. Panayotakis 2010, 1–16.
[56] Cf. Karakasis 2011, 40 with the bibliography cited there.
[57] Cf. Konstantakos 2012, 19–20.

ity, and thus there is need for an organised plan in order to persuade her to commit adultery. Hence, the mimic stratagem here is not intended to cheat a cuckold (the mimic *stultus vir*, Ov. *Tr.* 2.1.500), but to seduce a lady.
- The husband appears in the Petronian narrative and is present in the action all along from the beginning; he does not show up after the meeting of the couple. But he is dead, and thus there is no need for a deception plan; adultery may well happen in front of him, as occasionally in adultery stories of mimic resonance (cf. Apul. *Met.* 9.5–7). The adulterer, as is also the case with the mimic *adulter* in general,[58] clearly faces the possibility of death (capital punishment for a poor sentry, 112.6), but, in the story in question, the new lover's threatened demise becomes the means for the eventual, outstanding transformation of the exemplary widow, 112.6–8.
- Last but not least, the one who is ultimately, secretly 'whisked away' from the action is not the smart adulterer, the *nec deformis aut infacundus iuvenis*, 'a young man, handsome and eloquent' (112.2), the *cultus … adulter* (Ov. *Tr.* 2.1.499), but the husband himself (his corpse is removed from the grave and furtively fixed to the cross, 112.8). The husband, although dead, ultimately falls victim to the astuteness of an 'adulterous wife', once again in line with mimic generic rules.

The *matrona* thus eventually acts out the role of a mimic *callida nupta* in securing her lover's safety and, as a result, Eumolpus' claim is also proven on the level of a mimic modal intrusion. A comparable transformation from a dignified, married *matrona* to an adulterous woman seems to be the focus of Laber. *com.* 20 as well.[59]

Tragic discourses

As already remarked, Petronius' *ancilla* undergoes a significant change of comic generic role, transforming herself from an honourable, upright maid (111.4) into a meretricious erotic counselor (111.10–112.2). This conversion to the role of the Ephesian widow's erotic confidante also led to her association with the myth of Hippolytus and Phaedra and its tragic representations, the *nutrix* in Seneca's *Phaedra* included. The most recent argument along these lines is developed by

---

58 Cf. Panayotakis 1995, 133–4.
59 Cf. Panayotakis 2010, 214.

Cipriani 2009, 12–6; 44–5,⁶⁰ who significantly speaks of a 'svolta meretricia' (op. cit., 12); a similar twist is also displayed both by the Ephesian beauty (see above) and the Cretan princess. Phaedra's *nutrix* is presented as undergoing a significant change of heart in the course of the dramatic action, not experienced by any other Senecan nurse; initially, she is presented as a spokesman for Phaedra's spousal fidelity and honour (vv. 129–249), whereas, later on, she assists with the union of Phaedra with Hippolytus, out of fear for Phaedra's life (vv. 267–73), when, at the end of the first act, the latter decides or, at least, pretends to have resolved, to commit suicide (vv. 250–66). Similarly, the Petronian maid, presented at the beginning as defender of connubial fidelity, when helping her mistress with the wake rituals, eventually becomes the instigator of the union of the novel's lovers, allegedly also as a result of her anxiety over her mistress' suicidal disposition (111.11). In Euripides' *Hippolytus*, on the other hand, there is no corresponding evolution in the dramatic function of the nurse: Phaedra's τροφὸς is from the outset ready to assist her mistress' illicit passion, after the latter reveals the object of her erotic desire and expresses her wish for death (cf. vv. 433–524), despite the expressions of despair the old maid utters, at the beginning at least (vv. 353–524). This so-called 'meretricious turn' is not, however, the only similarity between the Senecan and the Petronian figure: further structural and thematic correspondences may suggest not only a simple parallelism between the two characters but also an intertextual shaping of the Petronian maid as a Senecan tragic *ancilla*. To begin with, this similarity in dramatic function is further stressed by the Senecan philosophical discourse, to which both occasionally resort in order to structure their arguments, employing language crucially absent from the τροφὸς in Euripides' *Hippolytus*. For example, the tragic *nutrix* makes a crucial, Senecan distinction between *nefas* and *monstrum* (vv. 129–77) or bases her rhetoric on the presence of the Senecan divine providence (vv. 466–82, cf. also Coffey-Mayer 1990, 104–5, 134), whereas Petronius' *ancilla* similarly avails herself of Senecan philosophical consolatory diction in her function as a *praeceptor amoris*, as is, for example, the motif of the *dolor supervacuus*, the maxim *mortui nihil sentiunt*, etc. (111.11–2; cf. Sen. *Ep.* 63.13).⁶¹ This Senecan character

---

60 Cf. esp. Ragno 2009, 345 and n. 674 (with a literature review); see also Ragno 2009, 288–9 and n. 445. McGlathery 2001, 124–5 sees, instead, an influence of Euripides' *Hippolytus*; see also Pigeaud 2003, 50–3, pointing out the tragic colouring of the Petronian heroine's malaise and of her servant's assistance (the tragic προσεδρία). For the 'tragic' associations of the Petronian tale, cf. also Massaro 1981, 226, Perotti 2001–2, 258 viewing the novelistic protagonists as 'tragic' actors; see also Fedeli–Dimundo 2000, 49–50 persuasively identifying *populus* with a tragic chorus, 184.
61 Cf. Pecere 1975, 94–102, Cicu 1986, 263 and n. 58, Galand 1989, 112, Vannini 2010, 247, 251–3; see also Ragno 2009, 310–1 and n. 555. Cf. also Cipriani 2009, 14.

too, just like the Petronian *ancilla* as argued earlier, has convincingly been read as an adaptation of a stock comic figure, namely that of the *servus callidus*.⁶²

This association between Petronius' maid and Seneca's nurse ultimately suggests an intertextual colouring of Petronius' matron with traits of Seneca's Phaedra. Despite several differences in the circumstances of the two female protagonists, a basic narrative outline is observable in both instances: Seneca's Phaedra, like the Petronian heroine, faces a dilemma between fidelity to a (probably deceased) husband, on the one hand, and an (adulterous) love affair, on the other (cf. v. 112); Theseus, in Seneca, although not dead, is associated with death, since, at the outset of the drama, he is absent from the main action, accompanying his comrade Peirithous in the underworld, in search of the latter's beloved, Proserpina (vv. 91–8). Phaedra herself, in her argumentation in favour of her love for Hippolytus, points to the possibility that her lawful husband may never return from the realm of Dis (vv. 218–21), while, in act three, Theseus returns on stage half-dead and blesses his good fortune for Hercules' intervention which released him from a four-year-long captivity in the realm of the dead (vv. 835–53). In Euripides' *Hippolytus*, Theseus is absent from the tragic stage, because he is in charge of an embassy. Seneca's Hippolytus, whom Phaedra eventually chooses in terms of this tragic erotic triangle, is also described, as early as the introductory scene (vv. 1–84), as a *miles*, a robust *adulescens*, a victorious general performing a triumph after a significant victory, in opposition to Euripides' Hippolytus who lacks such evident military traits. This image of Seneca's Hippolytus as a military figure is further enhanced by the functional presence of his sword (cf. e.g. v. 706), which, in both stories (Petronius, Seneca), functions/is intended to function as a suicidal weapon associated with an affair of the heart. However, in Seneca it is the queen who thus meets her tragic death for having falsely accused and, as a result, led her beloved to his death (vv. 1197–8), while in Petronius, following the generic demands of a happy novelistic end, the matron (i.e., an intertextual Phaedra) dissuades her lover from killing himself with the lethal weapon (112.7–8). In Euripides, Phaedra in the end hangs herself (v. 777). This soldier-like Hippolytus may further remind the reader of the Petronian *miles* looking after the Ephesian lady, when, in the second act of Seneca's drama, he takes care of a worn out Phaedra (vv. 585–8), whereas the lament of Phaedra over the dead Hippolytus, with her loose and cut hair, and her determination to follow her beloved to the underworld, at the end of the Senecan play (vv. 1154–98), may also recall the similar disposition of the Ephesian matron at the beginning of the Petronian tale (111.1–9). In Euripides, Phaedra and Hippoly-

---

62 Cf. Frangoulidis 2009, 402–23.

tus never interact on stage. Last but not least, this association of the Petronian widow with the Senecan queen is further suggested on the level of Vergilian intertextuality; both figures have long been compellingly read as epigonal reappropriations of the Vergilian Dido, with their maids harking back to the Vergilian Anna.[63] Such a common intertextual ancestry further underlines the subtextual discourse of Petronius' widow with Seneca's protagonist.

All the above, accordingly, clearly point to an intertextual association of the Petronian inset story with Seneca's drama. This, of course, does not rule out various, further sub-textual links and references to other versions of Phaedra's story; an emphasis on Phaedra's desire, for example, to starve herself to death in Euripides' *Hippolytus* (vv. 131–40, 277) may bring the Petronian lady and her *inedia* (111.3) closer to the Euripidean heroine.[64] What is more, if Sophocles' *Phaedra*[65] and Euripides' *Hippolytus Veiled* had been substantially preserved, further allusions to these tragic versions could have been observable. Be that as it may, what matters here is that the Senecan drama is one of the primary tragic intertexts of Petronius' story. In terms of all previous sub-textual associations, Eumolpus' claim that female fickleness is betrayed by their all too prompt oblivion of their children (*quam cito etiam filiorum obliviscerentur*, 110.7) may, certainly, allude to famous (chiefly epic and tragic) examples like Helen, Klytaimestra or Medea,[66] but, in terms of a broader reading, may also point to Phaedra's mythical and tragic (also Senecan) paradigm, who, significantly, became neglectful of the filial status of her step-son Hippolytus [one should take notice of the word *filii* for denoting children, which, although not unattested elsewhere (cf. *OLD* s. v. 2), is crucially less inclusive than e. g. *liberi*, cf. *OLD* s.v. a]. A second indication of female levity is, according to Eumolpus, infatuation with a stranger (*peregrina libidine*, 110.7); this criterion is also met in the case of the Cretan Phaedra, who fell for the Troezenian Hippolytus.

Petronius' matron is, thus, related to a classical exemplum of a female figure yielding to passion, drawn, this time, from the generic realm of the tragic drama,

---

63 Seneca/Vergil, cf. Cipriani 2009, 11. Petronius/Vergil, cf. Pecere 1975, 22–3, Santoro L'Hoir 1992, 183, Strunz 2001, 444, Anderson 2005, 47, Richlin 2009, 95, Vannini 2010, 233, 251–2 (with the bibliography cited), 256, Holzberg 2012, 136. For an association of the unnamed widow, her military suitor, her maid and her dead husband with Dido, Aeneas, Anna and Sychaeus respectively, cf. esp. Siewert 2007, 20–3, Fedeli–Dimundo 2000, 94–6; see also D'Ambrosio 1995, 85–7, Conte 1996, 109, and n. 40 (above).
64 Cf. esp. Papadopoulou (forthcoming).
65 In Sophocles' *Phaedra*, Theseus was also absent in the underworld; cf. Coffey–Mayer 1990, 9.
66 For the possible associations of the widow of Ephesus with Helen and Medea, cf. esp. Ragno 2009, 204; see also Habermehl 2006, 487, Vannini 2010, 233.

and, what is more, from a tragic play written, in all probability, during the last years of Claudius' reign (cf. Coffey–Mayer 1990, 5), i.e., shortly before the Neronian *Satyrica*; what is more, a later, Neronian date has also been argued for.[67] The play, therefore, may still have had a significant impact within the Neronian literary circles of Rome. In this fashion, Petronius not only underlines female infidelity from a complementary tragic perspective, but also effectuates a parody of Seneca, in terms of his general satirical and parodic attitude towards Nero's pedagogue, evidenced throughout the novel.[68] This is especially evident elsewhere in the parodic modelling of Trimalchio on Maecenas' depiction by Seneca (*Ep.* 114.6) or even in the satirical presentation of various Senecan views as uttered by *Cena*'s host (e.g. 71.1 = Sen. *Ep.* 47.1).[69]

From this perspective, an association of Petronius' widow with Pompeia Paulina, Seneca's wife as sketched in Tacitus in particular, largely based on Seneca's companion Fabius Rusticus[70] [*Ann.* 15.63–4, cf. also Dio Cassius (62.25)], seems all the more appealing; it has long been pointed out that the ladies of both the Petronian and the Tacitean narratives are the recipients of comforting language, particularly at home with Seneca's consolatory discourse.[71] Several similarities between the 'wasting away' of Petronius' lady and Paulina's attempted suicide, after the allegations brought against her husband for taking part in the Pisonian conspiracy (65 AD), may be observed:
- both are presented as ideal paradigms of conjugal chastity, as they are willing to join their beloved husbands in death (Petr. 111.3, 5, Tac. *Ann.* 15.63.1–2);
- both are portrayed as ghostly, eerie figures due to their suicidal attempts (Petr. 111.7, 9–10), although in Paulina's case her ethereal build, her death-like pallor becomes a permanent feature of her external appearance (Tac. *Ann.* 15.64.2);
- both are dissuaded by their family and the authorities from lethal pain, from ending their lives (*parentes*, *propinqui* and the *magistratus* at Petr. 111.3,[72] Seneca and Nero in the case of Paulina, Tac. *Ann.* 15.63.1, 64.1);
- both in time surrender to the pleasures of life, despite their initial resolution to die in loving memory of their companions (Petr. 111.9, 112.1–4); in the case of Tacitus' Paulina, despite Tacitus' reserve, this is noticeably implied

---

67 Cf. Raios 2011, 182–99 (with an analysis of the *status quaestionis*).
68 For a general satirical attitude towards Seneca in the *Satyrica*, cf. esp. Ragno 2009, 289–90 and n. 450 (with the bibliography cited there).
69 Cf. Schmeling 2011, 114, 229, 290–1.
70 Cf. Habinek 2014, 16.
71 Cf. Ker 2009, 110–12.
72 For an allusion here to Coriolanus, cf. Cicu 1986, 259.

by the public rumours questioning her virtue, namely that she ultimately 'gave in to the attractions of life' (*spe blandimentis vitae*, *Ann.* 15.64.2[73]);
- both ladies are eventually saved from death and regain zest for life through crucial intermediaries of military figures and servants [the *miles* and the *fidissima ancilla* of Petronius' narrative (Petr. 111.4, 6); armed forces in command as well as slaves and freedmen binding Paulina's arms and checking her blood loss in Tacitus (*Ann.* 15.64.1)].

It may well be the case that Tacitus read in Petronius' tale an allusion to Paulina,[74] who, unlike other famous pious Roman wives (e.g. Paxaea, the wife of Pomponius Labeo, Sextia, the companion of Mamercus Scaurus, cf. Tac. *Ann.* 6.29, or Arria the elder, the spouse of Caecina Paetus, cf. also Plin. *Ep.* 3.16[75]), did not in fact follow her husband to the grave. This reaction of his may have been shared by others in the Neronian years or later, and thus may also point to an authorial objective as well. Petronius is parodying not only Senecan tragic and consolatory discourses, but also the alleged exemplary chastity of the philosopher's wife.

The fictional narrator of the story, Eumolpus, may also be using the story to poke fun at the erotic infidelity of a woman belonging to a member of his audience; as previously remarked, Lichas, in an animated emotional state, when recalling the infidelity of his wife, Hedyle, is of the view that the governor should have hanged the adulterous lady – *mulierem affigere cruci* (113.2–4; cf. also 106.2); the laughter of the *nautae* (113.1) thus may also originate from their associating the story with the elopement of Lichas' wife.[76] A similar objective may be claimed in the case of the real/historical narrator, Petronius, who, in the line of his textual mouthpiece, may also attack the wife of a historical figure, i.e., Seneca. If so, the widow of Ephesus inset story may have been written into the *Satyrica* narrative, or, in any case, revised during the last period of the author's life, after Seneca's death (April 65 AD) and before his suicide *invidia Tigellini*, according to the *communis opinio* (66 AD, cf. Tac. *Ann.* 16.17–20).

---

73 Cf. also Erasmo 2008, 30.
74 Cf. also Ker 2009, 112.
75 Cf. esp. D'Ambrosio 1995, 73–7.
76 Cf. Pecere 1975, 144, Fedeli–Dimundo 2000, 28–9, Ragno 2009, 270 and n. 384 (with further bibliography).

Conclusions

In the narrative, framing the widow story, the narrator, Eumolpus, maintains that he will exemplify female instability by resorting to a contemporary story, with no reference to famous names/examples or tragic plots (110.8). Despite this claim, the story he eventually recites is replete with tragic 'generic signs' and seems to recall the tragic exemplum of Seneca's *Phaedra*, i. e., a familiar, by the Neronian period, instance of female erotic *furor* obscuring a woman's decency, thus illustrating the main point of Eumolpus' narrative (110.7: *nullamque esse feminam tam pudicam quae non peregrina libidine usque ad furorem averteretur*, 'no woman was so chaste that she could not be led away into utter madness by a passion for a stranger'). However, the dramatic undertones of the Petronian narrative are not limited to tragedy; the story Eumolpus/Petronius chooses to narrate abounds in characters and motifs largely belonging, in their concentration, to the generic realm of Roman Comedy, well-known during the Neronian period both as a text and through re-performance[77] (e. g. the erotic triangle of an *adulescens*, a *puella* and a *miles*, or such comic motifs as love at first sight of a mourning beautiful young woman, the unfulfilled intention to kill oneself for love, deception and impersonation as a means of securing a happy erotic end, crucifixion). In addition, Petronius expands the initial comic matrix of the tale with topics and linguistic options further highlighting the story's branching out towards the generic sphere of Roman Comedy (e. g. the description of the Petronian lady as a *matrona*, the setting of the story in Ephesus, the expansion of the *ancilla*'s part, who adopts the function of a comic *lena* with a penchant for drinking, the *curiositas* topic moving forward the dénouement of the plot, as well as the occasional comic linguistic colouring of the narrative when the soldier starts to function as a comic lover). Female *levitas* is thus proven not only in the association of the Petronian lady with the relevant mythical and tragic example par excellence, i. e., the tragic Phaedra, but also in terms of the 'generic repertoire' of Roman Comedy: a lady, initially depicted as a comic *matrona*, ends up functioning as a comic *meretrix*, crucially under the influence of a young, honourable servant developing into a comic procuress. 'Female fickleness' is thus demonstrated on an inter-generic level, which includes comedy, mime (the *matrona* is eventually transformed into a mimic *callida nupta*, see above), tragedy, elegy[78]

---

77 For a significant influence of theatre/drama on Neronian literature in particular, cf. Castagna 2003, 37–8.
78 For possible 'elegiac undertones' (e. g. *miles* as an *exclusus amator*, his rhetoric as a kind of elegiac *Werbende Dichtung*, the *militia amoris* motif, the *ancilla* as the erotic go-between, the

and epic as well. This makes Eumolpus' point stronger, especially if there is also a moralising touch in the story, of the kind known mainly from satirical diatribe,[79] but also does justice to his ability to 'upgrade' a low and folkloric story to the level of a sophisticated text informed by mainstream Roman literature.

An overall note: as initially remarked, lamenting over a dead husband's body is a staple tragic motif; Evadne in Euripides' *Suppliant Women* even throws herself onto Capaneus' funeral pyre (cf. vv. 980–1071)[80] against her father's, Iphis', appeals, and, thus, follows her husband to death, as originally intended by the Petronian heroine as well, also dismissing her parents' intervention (111.3). In this respect and reading the story as a whole, Petronius' novel may also be understood, as often in the *Satyrica*, as an evolution from the tragic to the comic mode.[81] Despite the various, individual and specific comic/tragic reminiscences of the overall story on a micro-structural level, macro-structurally Petronius' *matrona* essentially starts playing a tragic heroine, acting, for example, as a new Evadne who follows her dead lover to death; this detail of the lady's willingness for suicide is crucially another Petronian innovation which may also allude both to novelistic[82] and 'tragic' practices. In the middle of the story, however, she largely switches, leaving aside her initial role of a predominantly tragic heroine, and eventually assumes that of a mainly comic courtesan. The narrative begins chiefly as a tragedy and largely ends as a comedy, with the turning point, i.e., the point of the generic transformation, being the maidservant's consolatory diction. This type of admonitory/didactic discourse, full of maxims and aphorisms of general truth, is a generic feature of both theatrical kinds: such sayings are plentiful in tragedy (especially Euripidean) and in New Comedy. Similarly, the role of the maidservant is common in the two genres. It is thus fitting that such a character with her diction (both inherently double-sided, i.e., of tragic and comic overtones) serves as an intermediary for the transition from the tragic to the comic. Once again 'generic interaction', 'generic transposition' in particular, makes Eumolpus' point crystal clear: *varium et mutabile semper femina*, 'a

---

slender, almost lifeless figure of the lady, the erotic implications of the lamp), cf. also La Penna 1985, 46, Galand 1989, 114, Huber 1990, 32, McGlathery 2001, 125–6, Rimell 2002, 125, 131, 148, 156, Castagna 2003, 36, Daviault 2003, 21–2 and n. 25, Eickmeyer 2006, 97–9, Ragno 2009, 320 and n. 581, Schmeling 2011, 429, 431–2, Holzberg 2012, 135.

79 Cf. e.g. Strunz 2001, 445 and n. 18.
80 Cf. Vannini 2010, 238; see also Prop.1.15.21–2.
81 Cf. also Castagna 2003, 39.
82 Cf. Vannini 2010, 239; 2013, 90.

fickle and changeful thing is woman ever'[83] (Verg. *A.* 569–70; see also Sen. *Dial.* 2.14.1).

Contextualising, as a final point, the story in the Neronian actuality, one could also read it as a parody of Senecan tragic and consolatory discourse; the Petronian widow seems to show resemblances not only to Seneca's famous tragic heroine (Phaedra) exemplifying a disastrous erotic *furor*, but also to Seneca's wife and her eventual surrender to the delights of life.

Acknowledgments

I wish to express my deepest thanks to Dr. I. Konstantakos and Dr. S. Papaioannou for their significant help and useful feedback on a previous draft of the present paper. I follow the text of Vannini 2010. All translations of Petronius come from: Heseltine, M., Rouse, W. H. D., Warmington, E. H. (1987), *Petronius Satyricon, Seneca Apocolocyntosis*, Cambridge, Mass. (Loeb). Occasional modifications are put in square brackets [ ].

Bibliography

Adamik, T. (2003), 'Sprache und Stil der Novelle von der Witwe von Ephesus (Petron. 111–112)', in: J. Herman and H. Rosén (eds.), *Petroniana. Gedenkschrift für Hubert Petersmann*, Heidelberg, 1–10.

Anderson, G. (2005), 'The novella in Petronius', in: H. Hofmann (ed.), *Latin Fiction. The Latin Novel in Context*, London and New York, 44–53.

Arrowsmith, W. (1966), 'Luxury and Death in the *Satyricon*', *Arion* 5, 304–31.

Bakhtin, M. M. (1981), *The Dialogic Imagination. Four Essays by M. M. Bakhtin* (transl. by C. Emerson and M. Holquist), Austin.

Barsby, J. (1999), *Terence: Eunuchus*, Cambridge.

Beck, R. (1979), 'Eumolpus *poeta*, Eumolpus *fabulator*: A Study of Characterization in the *Satyricon*', *Phoenix* 33, 239–53.

Benz, L. (2001), 'Die Fabula Milesia und die griechisch-römische Novellistik', in: L. Benz (ed.), *Script Oralia Romana. Die römische Literatur zwischen Mündlichkeit und Schriftlichkeit*, Tübingen, 43–137.

Blume, H. D. (1974), 'Petrons 'Witwe von Ephesus'', in: H. T. Johann and M. Lausberg (eds.), *Festgabe für Otto Hiltbrunner zum 60. Geburtstag*, Münster, 38–55.

---

[83] Translated by H. R. Fairclough/G. P. Goold (1999), *Virgil, Eclogues, Georgics, Aeneid 1–6*, Cambridge, Mass. (Loeb), 461.

Boldrini, S. (1988), 'Una vedova 'a pranzo': a proposito del cibo nel racconto della Matrona di Efeso e in alcune sue varianti', *Studi Urbinati di Storia, Filosofia e Letteratura* 61, 297–326.

────── (1989), 'Il pasto della vedova: cibo, vino, sesso, da Petronio a J. Amado', *GCN* 2, 121–32.

Borghini, A. (2012), 'Tipi o sottotipi narrativi nel racconto della matrona di Efeso: una schematizzazione folklorico-strutturale', in: A. Balbo, F. Bessone, E. Malaspina (eds.), *Tanti affetti in tal momento. Studi in onore di Giovanna Garbarino*, Alessandria, 121–30.

Buchwald, W. (1964), 'Die kluge Witwe von Ephesus (Petron. 112.7)', *WS* 77, 184.

Cabaniss, A. (1954), 'A Footnote to the 'Petronian Question'', *CPh* 49, 98–102.

────── (1960), 'The *Satyricon* and the Christian Oral Tradition', *GRBS* 3, 36–9.

────── (1961), 'The Matron of Ephesus Again: an Analysis', *University of Mississippi Studies in English* 2, 41–53.

────── (1962), 'The Matron of Ephesus: an Identification', *University of Mississippi Studies in English* 3, 75–7.

Castagna, L. (2003), 'La novella della *Matrona di Efeso*: meccanismi del riso', *CEA* 39, 27–42.

Cavalca, M. G. (2001), *I grecismi nel Satyricon di Petronio*, Bologna.

Ciaffi, V. (2003), *Petronio Satyricon*, Turin.

Cicu, L. (1986), 'La matrona di Efeso di Petronio', *SIFC* 4, 249–71.

Cipriani, G. (2009), 'Introduzione. Passioni 'prese in parola'. Adiuvanti, mezzane, ingiunzioni all' amore (Virgilio, Seneca e Petronio)', in: T. Ragno, *Il teatro nel racconto. Studi sulla fabula scenica della matrona di Efeso*, Bari, 9–50.

Coccia, M. (1989), '*Multa in muliebrem levitatem coepit iactare* ... (Le figure femminili del *Satyricon* di Petronio)', in: R. Uglione (ed.), *Atti del II convegno nazionale di studi su 'La donna nel mondo antico' (Torino 18–19–20 aprile 1988)*, Turin, 121–40.

Coffey, M. and Mayer, R. (1990), *Seneca: Phaedra*, Cambridge.

Colin, J. (1953), 'Il soldato della matrona d'Efeso e l'aceto dei crocefissi: Petronio 111', *RFIC* 31, 97–128.

Collignon, A. (1892), *Étude sur Pétrone. La critique littéraire, l'imitation et la parodie dans le Satiricon*, Paris.

Colton, R. (1975), 'The Story of the Widow of Ephesus in Petronius and La Fontaine', *CJ* 71, 35–52.

Conte, G. B. (1996), *The Hidden Author: An Interpretation of Petronius's Satyricon* (transl. by E. Fantham), Berkeley and Los Angeles.

Corbeill, A. (2004), *Nature Embodied: Gesture in Ancient Rome*, Princeton.

Courtney, E. (2001), *A Companion to Petronius*, Oxford.

D' Ambrosio, I. (1994), 'Scene da un funerale (Petron. 111, 2)', *Aufidus* 24, 55–73.

────── (1995), 'Suicidio al femminile', *Aufidus* 26, 69–90.

Daviault, A. (2003), 'La Matrone d'Éphèse, un personnage bien masculin', *CEA* 39, 15–26.

Dell' Era, A. (1970), *Problemi di lingua e stile in Petronio*, Rome.

Dickison, S. K. (2013), 'A Note on Fame and the 'Widow of Ephesus'', in: D. Lateiner, B. K. Gold, J. Perkins (eds.), *Roman Literature, Gender, and Reception: Domina Illustris. Essays in honor of Judith Peller Hallett*, London and New York, 85–9.

Duckworth, G. E. (1952), *The Nature of Roman Comedy: A Study in Popular Entertainment*, Princeton [2nd edn. with a foreword and bibliographical appendix by R. L. Hunter (1994), Bristol and Norman, OK].

Dupont, F. (1977), *Le Plaisir et la loi. Du Banquet de Platon au Satiricon*, Paris.

Eickmeyer, J. (2006), 'Eumolpus' fast cuts: Formen und Funktionen der Lesersteuerung in der 'Witwe von Ephesus' – Episode (*Satyrica* 110.6–113.5), mit einem Ausblick auf Petrons Poetik des Blicks', *GFA* 9, 73–104.

Erasmo, M. (2008), *Reading Death in Ancient Rome*, Columbus.
Fedeli, P. (1986), 'La matrona di Efeso. Strutture narrative e tecnica dell'inversione', *MCSN* 4, 9–35.
―――― (1987), 'Il cedimento dell' incrollabile eroe (da Omero a Livio a Petronio a S. Bernardo)', in: *Filologia e forme letterarie. Studi offerti a Francesco Della Corte*, Urbino, 3–21.
―――― (2009), 'Il romanzo petroniano: bilanci e prospettive', in: F. Gasti (ed.), *Il romanzo latino: modelli e tradizione letteraria*, Pavia, 13–29.
Fedeli, P. and Dimundo, R. (2000), *Petronio Arbitro. I racconti del Satyricon*, Rome.
Focardi, G. (1980), 'Il termine *maiestas* e la matrona', *SIFC* 52, 144–63.
Fraenkel, E. (1974), 'La matrona di Efeso e altri capitoli di Petronio', *Belfagor* 29, 687–95.
Frangoulidis, S. (2009), 'The Nurse as a Plot-maker in Seneca's *Phaedra*', *RFIC* 137, 402–23.
Frings, U. (1985), 'Lesedidaktisches zur 'Witwe'', *AU* 28.4, 54–64, 70–5.
Frow, J. (1986), *Marxism and Literary History*, Cambridge, Mass.
Galand, P. (1989), 'Le conte de la Matrone d'Éphèse: rhétorique de 'guidage' et réception: Pétrone lu par La Fontaine et Saint–Évremond', *GCN* 2, 109–19.
Garelli, M. (1990), 'La ironía en la Matrona de Éfeso', *REC* 21, 51–9.
Grimal, P. (1985), '*Matrona*. Les lois, les moeurs, le langage', *AFLNice* 50, 195–203.
Grisebach, E. (1889), *Die Wanderung der Novelle von der treulosen Witwe durch die Weltliteratur*, Berlin.
Griton, N. and Leroux, V. (2003), 'Lectures récentes du récit de Pétrone (110,6–113,5)', *CEA* 39, 71–80.
Habermehl, P. (2006), *Petronius, Satyrica 79–141. Ein philologisch-literarischer Kommentar*, Bd. 1: *Sat. 79–110*, Berlin and New York.
Habinek, T. (2014), '*Imago suae vitae*: Seneca's Life and Career', in: G. Damschen and A. Heil (eds.), *Brill's Companion to Seneca, Philosopher and Dramatist*, Leiden, 3–31.
Harrison, S. J. (1998), 'The Milesian Tales and the Roman Novel', *GCN* 9, 61–73.
―――― (2007), *Generic Enrichment in Vergil and Horace*, Oxford.
Herrmann, L. (1927), 'La matrone d'Éphèse dans Pétrone et dans Phèdre', *BAGB* 14, 20–57.
Herzog, R. (1989), 'Fest, Terror und Tod in Petrons Satyrica', in: W. Haug and R. Warning (eds.), *Das Fest* (Poetik und Hermeneutik 14), Munich, 120–50.
Heuzé, P. (2003), 'Sur un *color* virgilien du récit d'Eumolpe', *CEA* 39, 53–8.
Holzberg, N. (2002), *The Ancient Fable: An Introduction* (transl. by C. Jackson–Holzberg), Bloomington, Ind.
―――― (2012), 'Warum nicht auch einmal die 'Matrone von Ephesus'? Zu Interpretation und Rezeption von Petron 110,6–113,2', in: R. Kussl (ed.), *Altsprachlicher Unterricht: Kompetenzen, Texte und Themen* (Dialog Schule Wissenschaft – Klassische Sprachen und Literaturen, 46), Speyer, 129–44.
Huber, G. (1990), *Das Motiv der 'Witwe von Ephesus' in lateinischen Texten der Antike und des Mittelalters*, Tübingen.
Iribarren, V. I. (2005), 'Cuestión de punto de vista: análisis de la matrona de Éfeso (caps. 111–112)', in: J. Nagore (ed.), *Voces y lecturas de la novela latina*, Buenos Aires, 113–24.
Karakasis, E. (2011), *Song Exchange in Roman Pastoral*, Berlin and New York.
―――― (2014), 'Tragic and Epic Interactions in Terentian Comedy', in: S. Papaioannou (ed.), *Terence and Interpretation*, Newcastle upon Tyne, 75–93.
Ker, J. (2009), *The Deaths of Seneca*, Oxford.
Konstantakos, I. M. (2012), 'Divine Comedy: Demodocus' Song of Ares and Aphrodite and the Mythicization of an Adultery Tale', *Maia* 64, 12–34.

Laird, A. (1999), *Powers of Expression, Expressions of Power: Speech Presentation and Latin Literature*, Oxford.
La Penna, A. (1985), 'Tre note alla novella della matrona di Efeso in Petronio', *Maia* 37, 45–7.
Lefèvre, E. (1997), *Studien zur Struktur der 'Milesischen' Novelle bei Petron und Apuleius*, Stuttgart.
Massaro, M. (1981), 'La redazione fedriana della 'Matrona di Efeso'', *MCSN* 3, 217–37.
McGlathery, D. B. (1998), 'Petronius' Tale of the Widow of Ephesus and Bakhtin's Material Bodily Lower Stratum', *Arethusa* 31, 313–36.
―――― (2001), 'The Tomb of Epic: Bakhtinian Parody and Petronius' Tale of the Widow of Ephesus', in: P. Barta, P. A. Miller, C. Platter, and D. Shepherd (eds.), *Carnivalizing Difference: Bakhtin and the Other*, New York, 119–40.
Müller, C. W. (1980), 'Die Witwe von Ephesus. Petrons Novelle und die *Milesiaka* des Aristeides', *A&A* 26, 103–21.
Noia Campos, C. (2005), 'De la Matrona de Éfeso (A–Th 1510) a la compasiva viuda gallega', *RDTP* 60, 149–64.
Panayotakis, C. (1995), *Theatrum Arbitri: Theatrical Elements in the Satyrica of Petronius*, Leiden.
―――― (2009), 'Petronius and the Roman Literary Tradition', in: J. R. W. Prag and I. D. Repath (eds.), *Petronius: A Handbook*, Chichester/Malden, MA, 48–64.
―――― (2010), *Decimus Laberius: The Fragments*, Cambridge.
Papadopoulou, Th. (forthcoming), 'Euripidean Frenzy Goes to Rome: the Case of Roman Comedy and Novel', in: P. Kyriakou and A. Rengakos (eds.), *Wisdom and Folly in Euripides*, Berlin and Boston.
Parca, M. (1981), 'Deux récits milésiens chez Pétrone (*Satyricon*, 85–87 et 111–112). Une étude comparative', *RBPh* 59, 91–106.
Pecere, O. (1975), *Petronio: La novella della matrona di Efeso*, Padua.
Pepe, L. (1987), *Sermo Milesius*, Perugia.
Perotti, P. A. (2001–2), 'Note alla 'Matrona di Efeso' (Petronio 111–112)', *Rudiae* 13–4, 243–67.
Pigeaud, J. (2003), 'Sur quelques illustrations de l'épisode de la matrone d'Éphèse', *CEA* 39, 47–58.
Plaza, M. (2000), *Laughter and Derision in Petronius' Satyrica. A Literary Study*, Stockholm.
Ragno, T. (2004), 'Dal testo al gesto: la matrona di Efeso *ad scaenam*. Riflessioni su alcune esperienze di traduzione intersemiotica', *Kleos* 8, 293–344.
―――― (2009), *Il teatro nel racconto. Studi sulla fabula scenica della matrona di Efeso*, Bari.
Raios, D. (2011), Σενέκα Φαίδρα. Εισαγωγή, Κριτική Έκδοση, Μετάφραση, Ερμηνευτική Ανάλυση, Ioannina.
Rank, O. (1913), 'Die Matrone von Ephesus: Ein Deutungsversuch der Fabel von der treulosen Witwe', *Internationale Zeitschrift für ärztliche Psychoanalyse* 1, 50–60.
Rastier, F. (1971), 'La morale de l'histoire: notes sur la *Matrone d'Éphèse* (*Satiricon*, CXI–CXII)', *Latomus* 30, 1025–56.
Richlin, A. (2009), 'Sex in the *Satyrica*: Outlaws in Literatureland', in: J. R. W. Prag and I. D. Repath (eds.), *Petronius: A Handbook*, Chichester/Malden, MA, 82–100.
Rimell, V. (2002), *Petronius and the Anatomy of Fiction*, Cambridge.
Rose, K. F. C. (1968), 'Petroniana', *RhM* 111, 253–60.
Ruiz Sánchez, M. (2005), 'Rivales de la Matrona de Éfeso. Sobre algunos paralelos tradicionales y populares del relato de Petronio', *Myrtia* 20, 143–74.
Santoro L' Hoir, F. (1992), *The Rhetoric of Gender Terms. 'Man', 'Woman', and the Portrayal of Character in Latin Prose*, Leiden.

Schmeling, G. (2011), *A Commentary on the Satyrica of Petronius*, Oxford.
Sega, G. (1986), 'Due milesie: la matrona di Efeso e l'efebo di Pergamo', *MCSN* 4, 37–81.
Segal, E. (1973), 'Laughter in the House', *Horizon* 15, 90–3.
Siewert, W. (2007), 'Petrons 'Witwe von Ephesos' als Vergil-Parodie', *AU* 50, 20–6.
Slater, N. W. (1990), *Reading Petronius*, Baltimore.
_____ (2009), 'Reading the *Satyrica*', in: J. R. W. Prag and I. D. Repath (eds.), *Petronius: A Handbook*, Chichester/Malden, MA, 16–31.
Strunz, F. (2001), 'Wie untreu war die Witwe von Ephesus?', *Gymnasium* 108, 439–49.
Sullivan, J. P. (1968), *The Satyricon of Petronius: A Literary Study*, London.
Thiele, G. (1908), 'Phädrus-Studien', *Hermes* 43, 337–72.
Ure, P. (1956), 'The Widow of Ephesus: Some Reflections on an International Comic Theme', *DUJ* 18, 1–9.
Vannini, G. (2007), *Petronius 1975–2005: bilancio critico e nuove proposte*, Lustrum 49, Göttingen.
_____ (2010), *Petronii Arbitri »Satyricon« 110–115. Edizione critica e commento*, Berlin and New York.
_____ (2013), 'La Matrona di Efeso di Petronio e le altre versioni antiche dell'aneddoto', in: M. Carmignani, L. Graverini, and B. T. Lee (eds.), *Collected Studies on the Roman Novel = Ensayos Sobre La Novela Romana*, Cordoba, 77–95.
Walcot, P. (1991), 'On Widows and their Reputation in Antiquity', *SO* 66, 5–26.
Walsh, P. G. (1970), *The Roman Novel: The Satyricon of Petronius and the Metamorphoses of Apuleius*, Cambridge.
Watson, L. and Watson, P. (2014), *Juvenal: Satire 6*, Cambridge.
Weinreich, O. (1931), *Fabel, Aretalogie, Novelle. Beiträge zu Phädrus, Petron, Martial und Apuleius*, Heidelberg.
Wolff, É. (2003), 'Quelques remarques sur le succès de la *Matrone d'Éphèse*', *CEA* 39, 59–67.

Theodoros Antoniadis
Furor and Kin(g)ship in Seneca's *Thyestes* and Valerius Flaccus' *Argonautica* (1.700–850)

Introduction

The influence of Senecan drama on the literature of the Flavian Age remains, more or less, a rather uncharted area in recent bibliography, even if many critical studies have appeared in the last two decades suggesting that scholarly interest in (especially) the epic poetry of this period has almost reached its climax. This seems to be particularly true in the case of Valerius Flaccus, since Seneca has been found at the core of many interpretative works examining the intertextual landscape of his *Argonautica*.[1] However, the scholarship illustrating the presence of Senecan tragedy in his epic usually does not extend significantly beyond the multiple elements on a linguistic, generic or even philosophical level that the Flavian poet seems to have adopted and/or adapted from the *Medea* in delineating and, ultimately, refashioning the figure of the Colchian princess in his work.[2] Even so, Medea is neither the only character in the *Argonautica* to indicate the impact of Senecan drama (and other genres as well, particularly elegy) on Valerius' poem, nor the only ravaged figure in the work who exhibits a 'fearful and fearsome' rhetoric. In the last episode of the first book of the *Argonautica* (700–850), recognized as one of Valerius' most innovative moves within the poetic tradition,[3] the *furor/ira* of King Pelias (700–29), after discovering that his son Acastus has joined the expedition, presents a straightforward contrast to the virtues expounded by his brother (and Jason's

---

[1] On Valerius' self-conscious attempt as an epic successor to locate his work within a broader matrix of literary conventions and traditions, see the works of Hardie 1989, 1993 (especially 83ff.); Feeney 1991, 313–37; Hershkowitz 1998; Zissos 1999, 2002; Stover 2012, 181–218. On intertextuality in Roman Poetry, see the classic study of Hinds 1998.
[2] See the most recent works of Corrigan 2013, especially ch. 2 on 'Seneca's *Medea*' (pp. 99–190) and ch. 3 on 'Valerius Flaccus' Medea' (pp. 191–260); Buckley 2006, 132–93; Grewe 1998, 173–90 also focuses on Medea, but offers a useful list of references to all pre-existing scholarship on Senecan tragic influence (173–4). On Medea's character in the *Argonautica* note, however, the alternative approach of Zissos 2012, which distances the Colchian princess significantly from her counterpart as developed in Seneca's tragedy.
[3] See further Zissos 2008, 379ff.

father) Aeson in a mutual decision with his wife Alcimede to commit suicide, thereby seeking a decent and honourable death. While there are many other instances in the first book of Valerius' epic which have been found already to draw more or less emphatically on other Senecan tragedies too, especially the *Agamemnon*,[4] this article will maintain that this episode, through the various antitheses it shapes and the moral/ethic issues it raises, draws upon (sometimes even by negation) Seneca's *Thyestes*, recalling particularly the famous portrait of the ideal king as set out by the Chorus in the second ode (336–403).[5] Thus, on a metapoetic level, Valerius, while striving for innovation, effect and sensationalism in this particular episode, will emerge as subtle and delicate in his art of allusion and his tendency to redraw traditional generic boundaries.[6]

The mythological tradition

Before we turn to the exact parallels to be discussed, it is worth recalling the features the two fatal pairs of brothers, Pelias/Aeson and Atreus/Thyestes, share in the mythological tradition. In Homer's *Odyssey* (11.254–8) Pelias is a son of Neptune born from Tyro and a step-brother of Aeson, whose father was Cretheus. The beginning of the story, in the *Argonautica*, presents him further as a power-hungry king of Thessaly, who has gained dominion over the region from his earliest years (*Arg.* 1.22f.), a reference we find also in Hesiod (*Theog.* 995). Though Valerius does not mention this clearly, other versions of the myth, mainly Pindar's fourth *Pythian Ode*, suggest that there was a good deal of tension between the two brothers, and evidently Pelias usurped the throne from Aeson, excluding him from his share in the kingdom of Thessaly.[7] In order to strengthen his hold on the throne, Pelias is

---

[4] Note especially the catalogue of heroes (353–483) and the storm scene (574–692), both standard features of an epic, and the parallels found in the *Agamemnon* by Zissos 2008, 239–43, 253–4, 328–30 and Kleywegt 2005, 217–8, 339–40, 365–8. See also n. 54.
[5] To my knowledge, the first preliminary discussion concerning the influence of Seneca's plays on Valerius' sketch of the tyrannical portrait of Pelias in Book 1 was provided by Scaffai 1986, 233–7, followed more systematically by Galli 2002 and 2007 (see below).
[6] On Valerius' art of allusion, see Zissos 1999, 289–301 and Stover 2003, 123–47.
[7] See mostly Jason's words in Pind. *Pyth.* 4.108–10: πεύθομαι γάρ νιν Πελίαν ἄθεμιν λευ-/καῖς πιθήσαντα φρασίν/ἁμετέρων ἀποσυλᾶσαι βιαίως ἀρχεδικᾶν τοκέων· On this tradition see further Apollod. 1.9, 11, 16; Tzetz. ad Lycophr. 872; Diod. 4.50; Schol. ad Apollod 1.45; Schol. ad Hom. *Od.* 12.70. On the rivalry among brothers for the scepter of power, which had acquired a formulaic character in Latin poetry (note also the conflict between Eteocles and Polyneikes in Statius' *Thebaid*), see further Galli 2002, 234 and Frings 1992, 15–46.

said either to have expelled Aeson or locked him in a dungeon in Iolcus, and so the tale goes as we know it also from Apollonius Rhodius (3. 333–9) and Valerius Flaccus (*Arg.* 1.40–90) with Jason accepting eventually Pelias' challenge to obtain the Golden Fleece in order to claim the throne.[8] Turning to the episode examined here, Pelias becomes furious when he finds out that Jason has made his son Acastus join the expedition. Supposing that Jason will kill Acastus by tearing him apart (*Arg.* 718–9), he vindictively orders the execution/murder of Jason's parents, Aeson and Alcimede (*Arg.* 1.700–826). However, what is also significant for our purposes is the anticipation of Pelias' own notorious demise at his daughters' hands through Medea's agency and trickery, who persuaded them that by cutting him up and boiling him they could achieve his rejuvenation. This event, which falls well beyond the scope of Valerius' narrative,[9] is alluded to in Aeson's imprecation in the episode we examine here (*Arg.* 1.807–12, see below), where he wishes a most disgraceful death for Pelias.[10] Furthermore, in some versions of the myth, which Valerius probably had in mind, Medea is said to have dismembered the body of her brother Absyrtus (killed by Jason after another trap of hers) and scattered his limbs in the water, knowing that her father would stop chasing her and Jason with his fleet in order to retrieve his son's parts for proper burial.[11]

On the other hand, in the Greek myth as we know it mostly from Seneca's *Thyestes* (220–44), Atreus and his twin brother Thyestes are banished by their father Pelops, king of Elis, for murdering their half-brother Chrysippus in their desire for the throne, with a curse upon them that they and their descendants will perish at each other's hands. The brothers took refuge in Argos (Mycenae), where they ascended the throne in the absence of King Eurystheus, who was fighting the Heracleidae and eventually lost his life. Soon, Atreus claimed the throne exclusively for himself after he found a magical, gold-fleeced ram in his flocks, upon the possession of which the right to rule was deemed to rest.[12] Thy-

---

8 Note also Pind. *Pyth.* 4. 156–68 which Valerius seems especially to follow in his account of the initial confrontation between Pelias and Jason.
9 See, though, Ov. *Met.* 7.297–349 with Bömer's notes *ad loc.*, and Pind. *Pyth.* 4.350.
10 See further Hershkowitz 1998, 11–13; Kleywegt 2005, *ad loc.*; Zissos 2008, *ad loc.* Cf. Eur. *Med.* 486–7: Πελίαν τ' ἀπέκτειν', ὥσπερ ἄλγιστον θανεῖν,/παίδων ὑπ' αὐτοῦ, πάντα τ' ἐξεῖλον δόμον.
11 Cf. Apollod. 1.9.24; Ov. *Trist.* 3.9. The murder of Absyrtus is anticipated in Medea's words on several occasions in the *Argonautica* (note especially *Arg.* 7.339–40 and 8.106–7) while the idea that his corpse too will be dismembered is probably reinforced by the fate of Jason's brother, who is mutilated after Pelias' commands. Cf. *Arg.* 1.824–5: *te, puer, et visa pallentem morte parentum/diripiunt adduntque tuis*. See further Hull 1979, 407.
12 We follow here the main version of the myth as in Seneca's *Thyestes* 220–44. Cf. also Eur. *Or.* 11, Apollod. 2.10–4, 3.12; Paus. 2.18.1, 2.29.4, 6.20.7, Cic. *ND.* 3.27.68; Ov. *Ars* 1.327; *Trist.* 2.391; Stat.

estes, seeking to gain the throne even by the foulest means, seduced his brother's wife Aerope and by her assistance stole the ram from Atreus' flocks. For this act he was banished by Atreus, who, meanwhile, had managed to return from exile and recover the throne with the help of Hermes.[13] In the *Thyestes* Atreus, meditating a more complete revenge upon his brother, recalls him from exile, feigning friendship and offering him a place beside him upon the throne. His malicious plot is to kill his sons, cook them, save their hands and heads, and serve them to their own father, taunting him afterwards with the uneaten pieces.

The obvious resemblances between the myths can now be summarized as follows: the critical role of a ram's golden-fleece in the exercise of royal power [14] and a despicable king (Pelias-Atreus) who seeks by any, obviously iniquitous, means to banish his brother (Aeson-Thyestes) from his share in the kingdom. While these similarities, which ultimately refer to the common motif of 'fraternal odium', have been noticed,[15] the butchering and/or cooking of human limbs as a most cruel act of revenge (Medea against Absyrtus and Pelias – Atreus against Thyestes' children) has rather lacked the necessary attention. Furthermore, both Jason and Thyestes resort to the help of a woman (Medea and Aerope respectively), whom – more or less – they seduce, in order to get access to the golden fleece and claim regal power. Bearing in mind these mythological affinities, we may now turn to the passages from the *Argonautica* which, while not deviating from the standard version of the Argonautic saga, import specifically the 'tragedy of the *domus*' from the Senecan drama, focusing on the mythological elements (e. g. horrible death through dismemberment) common with the *Thyestes* and the concept of revenge through an unprecedented crime that dominates the thoughts and/or actions of members of the same family.

Theb. 4.306. On the similar function and connotations the Golden Fleece bears as an emblem of a dynasty in the *Thyestes* and the *Argonautica*, see Galli 2007, 26, 74.

13 Using advice he received from Hermes, Atreus made Thyestes agree to give the kingdom back when the sun moved backwards in the sky, a feat that Zeus accomplished.

14 Similarly Galli 2002, 239–40, who notes that the importance of the Golden Fleece for the sway of power is evident also in *Arg.* 5.228–37, where the shadow of Phrixus appears to Aeetes in a dream warning him that those who will request the fleece will also usurp his throne. The fact that Aeetes resorts to fraud in order to protect his power, promising Jason to give him the fleece and not just the fleece (*Arg.* 5.540–1: *Tum vellera victor/tam meritis nec sola dabo*), in order to enjoy his support at the war against his brother, brings to the reader's mind the similar tactics of Pelias towards Jason, with the figure of the Senecan Atreus always in the background.

15 See n. 7 and 14 above.

The poetics of revenge

Valerius' depiction of Pelias as a malicious and furious tyrant reaches its climax when the king of Thessaly becomes aware of Acastus' absence from the palace (*Arg.* 1.700–3, 716–25):[16]

> **Saevit atrox Pelias** inimicaque vertice ab alto   700
> vela videt nec qua se ardens effundere possit.
> nil animi, nil regna iuvant; fremit obice ponti
> clausa cohors, telisque salum facibusque coruscat.
> ... ...
> non Scythicas ferus ille domos nec ad ostia Ponti
> tendit iter, falsae sed captum laudis amore
> te, puer, in nostrae durus tormenta senectae
> nunc **lacerat**. Celsis an si freta puppibus essent
> pervia, non ultro iuvenes classemque dedissem?   720
> o domus, o freti nequiquam prole penates!'
> dixit et extemplo **furiis iraque** minaci
> terribilis: 'sunt hic etiam tua vulnera, praedo,
> sunt lacrimae carusque parens!' **simul aedibus altis
> itque reditque fremens rerumque asperrima versat.**   725

[700–3] Savage Pelias rages as from a lofty summit he sees the hateful sails- but not how he might give vent to his anger. Neither ardour nor royal power avail: the band of soldiers, held back by the barrier of ocean, growls: the salt water gleams with the reflection of weapons and firebrands ... [716–25] That brute journeys not to Scythian realms or the mouth of Pontus; instead, it is you, my child ensnared by the love of false glory, that he cruelly assails in order to bring anguish upon my old age. If the seas were navigable by lofty vessels, would I not have provided you with men and fleet of my own accord? O my household, o *penates* who trusted in your offspring to no avail!' He spoke, and continued hard upon, now terrible with madness and threatening anger: 'Plunderer, the means to wound you are still here: here are the tears and your beloved father.' Therewith he paces back and forth in the lofty palace, muttering to himself as he ponders the harshest of deeds.

The soliloquy of an anguished father lamenting the loss of his abducted child would definitely be more touching should the reader fail to read between the lines (719–20) and discover Pelias' malevolent intentions in his full knowledge that the expedition into which he forced Jason was doomed to end in disaster. Nevertheless, his assumption that at this very moment Jason is killing his son in

---

[16] For the text of Argonautica 1, I have consulted Liberman 1997 and Zissos 2008. All translations are from Zissos 2008.

such a brutal way (*te, puer, ... nunc lacerat*, 718–9) does not simply make him 'a typical tyrant expecting the worst from other people', like Aeetes later, in books 5 and 7.[17] It has been observed that the emphasis Valerius lays here on Pelias' absolute frenzy and enraged reaction (722–3: *furiis iraque minaci/terribilis*, 725: *fremens rerumque asperrima versat*, note also *furoribus* in line 727) evokes Senecan *furor* and *ira*.[18] Beyond the Neronian author's philosophical writings, where anger and its symptoms are featured most conspicuously,[19] and some of his tragedies, where passions of grief, anger and hatred are taken to the extreme,[20] the connotations of *lacerat* here (719) and elsewhere[21] in terms of the horrendous practice of dismemberment will turn my focus again to the *Thyestes*. In this play, the despicable image of a malicious tyrant, who derives a kind of perverse pleasure from being cruel, is attached to Atreus from the outset, particularly in the monologues of lines 192–204 and 267–78:[22]

Age, anime, fac quod nulla posteritas probet,
sed nulla taceat. Aliquod **audendum est nefas
atrox**, cruentum, tale quod frater meus
suum esse mallet. Scelera non ulcisceris, 195
nisi uincis. Et quid esse tam **saeuum** potest
quod superet illum? numquid abiectus iacet?
numquid secundis patitur in rebus modum,

Nescio quid animus maius et solito amplius
supraque fines moris humani tumet
instatque pigris manibus – haud quid sit scio,
sed grande quiddam est. Ita sit. Hoc, anime,
occupa 270
dignum est Thyeste facinus et dignum Atreo,
quod uterque faciat. Vidit infandas domus

---

17 The phrase is borrowed from Kleywegt 2005, *ad loc*. Kleywegt parallelizes Pelias here with Aeetes, who also gets furious over his failure to eliminate Jason by exposing him to danger, at *Arg.* 5.520: *furiis ignescit opertis* and 7.34: *effunditur ira*. Zissos 2008, 374 notes on lines 712–24 the curses of Dido towards Aeneas in *Aeneid* 4.590–629 and the anguished speech of Virgil's Mezentius to Lausus' corpse at *Aen.* 10.846–66.
18 See further Galli 2007, on 718–9, 725. Cf. especially *Arg.* 1.725: *rerum asperrima versat* with Sen. *De ira* 1.17.5: *crudelitatem et nova gener poenarum versaverat*.
19 Note especially his treatise *De ira* on how to alleviate anger. While other emotions may still have something calm about them, anger, according to Seneca, is all excitement, raging towards vengeance (*De ira* 1.1.1). On the content of *De ira* see Vogt 2006, 57–74 and Monteleone 2014. What is important in terms of what will follow here, is that Seneca in this treatise portrays most frequently the figure of the tyrant as the representative par excellence of people who, blinded by anger because they think they have been harmed, seek revenge with a totally disproportionate *scelus*. On this, as well as on the relationship between the *Thyestes* and Seneca's philosophical treatises (especially *De ira*), see Monteleone 2014, 130–1; Davis 2003, 69–79; Stanley 1981–83. For the passions in Seneca's *Thyestes* see the fruitful study of Schiesaro 2003.
20 Apart from the *Thyestes*, Zissos 2008, 376 quotes as paradigms Sen. *Her. F.* 381 and *Ag.* 903–6.
21 The verb is used again by Aeson in his curses against Pelias to have a disgraceful end, in lines 812–4: *quae fida manus, quae cara suorum/diripiat laceretque senem nec membra sepulchro/contegat*.
22 For the text of the *Thyestes* I have consulted Tarrant 1985 and Fitch 2004. All translations are from Fitch 2004.

fessis quietem? noui ego ingenium uiri	Odrysia mensas – fateor, immane est scelus,
indocile; flecti non potest- frangi potest. 200	sed occupatum; maius hoc aliquid dolor
proinde antequam se firmat aut vires parat,	inveniat. Animum Daulis inspira parens 275
petatur ultro, ne quiescentem petat.	sororque; causa est similis; assiste et manum
aut perdet aut peribit: in medio est **scelus**	impelle nostram. Liberos auidus pater
positum occupanti.	gaudensque **laceret** et suos artus edat.

[192–204] Come, my spirit, do what no future age will endorse, but none fail to talk about. I must dare some fierce, bloody outrage, such as my brother would have wished his own. You do not avenge crimes unless you surpass them. And what could be cruel enough to vanquish him? Does he lie downcast? Can he abide moderation in success, or inaction in failure? I know the man's intractable nature: he cannot be bent, but he can be broken. So, before he strengthens himself or marshals his powers, he must be attacked first, lest he attack me at rest. He will either destroy or be destroyed. Crime is set between us, for the one who seizes it first.

[267–78] Something greater, larger than usual, beyond normal human limits, is swelling in my spirit and jolting my sluggish hands. What it is I do not know, but is something mighty! So be it. Seize on it, my spirit! The deed is worthy of Thyestes and worthy of Atreus: let each perform it. The Odrysian house saw an unspeakable feast – that crime is monstrous, admittedly, but already taken. My bitterness must find something greater than this. Breathe your spirit into me, you Daulian mother and sister: Our cause is comparable. Stand by me, drive my hand. Let the father rend his children avidly, gleefully, and eat his own flesh.

Daniela Galli was the first to survey systematically the incorporation in *Arg.* 1 of the tyrant-model that Atreus represents in his relentless struggle to safeguard the sceptre of his throne in the *Thyestes*. Her introductory article in 2002 on this issue, followed by a stimulating commentary on *Arg.* Book 1 (2007), illustrates in various ways that Pelias' lust for power (*regni furor*) and the fear (*metus*) of losing it that haunts him throughout *Argonautica* 1 are largely inspired by Atreus' deceitful conduct as a despotic ruler and his wicked plans to eliminate his brother in the *Thyestes*.[23] After all, according to Galli, *regnum* is correlated with *fraus* in both works as Pelias and Atreus resort to fraud in order to mislead their enemies (Jason and Thyestes respectively) and implement their annihilation.[24] Nevertheless, while Galli

---

[23] See further Galli 2002, 231–42; 2007, 24–6, followed by Buckley 2014, 309.
[24] Galli 2002, 234–5. Cf. *Arg.* 1.22–3: *Haemoniam primis Pelias frenabat ab annis,/iam gravis et longus populis metus*, 29–32: *super ipsius ingens/instat fama viri virtusque haud laeta tyranno./ergo anteire **metus** iuvenemque exstinguere pergit/Aesonium letique vias ac tempora versat*, 38–9: *tum iuvenem tranquilla tuens nec fronte timendus/occupat et fictis dat vultum et pondera dictis* with *Thy.* 260–76. Galli stresses the significance of *metus*, i. e. the fear of losing power from which both Peleas and Atreus feel oppressed, as a source of the mortal plans they develop against Jason and Thyestes respectively. She also points to the common appearance of *occupare* (*Arg.* 1.39: *occupat* – *Thy.* 203–4: *in medio est **scelus**/positum occupanti*) in expressing the

primarily exemplifies Atreus' treacherous persuasiveness towards his brother as Valerius' constant point of reference in reshaping and actualizing the contrast between Pelias and Jason at the beginning of his epic when the former sends the latter off to destruction (*Arg.* 1.26–57), my focus here is rather on Valerius' tendency to implement Seneca's poetics of *furor/ira* and *nefas* as developed in the *Thyestes* in order to amplify the conflict between Pelias and his brother Aeson at the end of *Argonautica* 1. This direction is indicated, in my opinion, by some more precise verbal parallels and other descriptive echoes, which strengthen further the intertextual relationship between the two works. In the lines mentioned above, Atreus, presented as *iratus* (180), works himself up to a vengeful crime (193–4: *audendum est nefas/atrox*) against his twin brother. His trick as a whole (in fact a repeat of the family history of the Pelopids), with the intent to take further revenge on his brother by killing his sons and serving them to him as a meal (277–8), seems to be reflected in Pelias' resolution to turn his cruelty upon his brother Aeson as a reprisal for the latter's son's deeds. For our purposes, however, what matters most is not so much the verbal affinities (*Arg.* 1.700: *saevit* – *Thy.* 196: *saevum*) or the dire nuances of *lacerare* in both parallels (*Arg.* 1.719: *lacerat* – *Thy.* 278: *laceret*), but the shared wickedness and the obsession with *nefas*, a crime that will be 'atrocious' and unprecedented (cf. *Arg.* 1.725 with *Thy.* 267–70).[25] This may well explain why Valerius applies *atrox* to the portrait of Pelias in line 700. While, as Galli points out,[26] this adjective appears very rarely in Valerius' epic, in my opinion it cannot be accidental that it is used by Seneca to 'capture' the kind of crime that Atreus has in mind against his brother (see *Thy.* 194-5 quoted above).

The ode on the ideal king and the *Argonautica*

Eventually Pelias takes revenge on the absent Jason's elderly parents and Atreus on his brother's children, which makes the two tyrants equally despicable. This obviously presents a contrast to the Chorus' view of what an ideal king should be, in the famous second ode of *Thyestes* (336–52, 363–8, 388–403):

---

desire of both tyrants to anticipate and neutralize their enemies by premeditating their death, before Thyestes and Jason seize the chance to usurp their throne and destroy them. On my part, I discuss the opposing aspects of *metus* depicted in the actions of Pelias and Aeson, in relation to the Chorus' ode on the ideal king in the *Thyestes*.

25 Note also *commune nefas* that the Chorus applies to the Tantalids in the first ode (*Thy.* 139 with Tarrant 1985, *ad loc* and Davis 1989, 425–6).

26 See Galli 2007, on 700. The other occurrences in Valerius' epic are in *Arg.* 6.644 and 6.662.

Furor and Kin(g)ship in Seneca's *Thyestes* and Valerius Flaccus' *Argonautica* (1.700–850) — **541**

Tandem regia nobilis,
antiqui genus Inachi,
fratrum composuit minas.
Quis uos exagitat **furor**,
alternis dare sanguinem 340
et sceptrum scelere aggredi?
Nescitis, **cupidi arcium**,
regnum quo iaceat loco.
Regem non faciunt opes,
non vestis Tyriae color, 345
non frontis nota regia,
non auro nitidae fores:
Rex est qui posuit metus
et diri mala pectoris.

Quem non ambitio impotens 350
et numquam stabilis favor
uulgi praecipitis movet,
… … … … … … … … … ..
quem non lancea militis,
non strictus domuit chalybs,
qui tuto positus loco 365
infra se videt omnia
occurritque suo libens
fato nec queritur mori.
… … … … … … … … … ..
Rex est qui metuet nihil,
rex est qui cupiet nihil:
hoc regnum sibi quisque dat. 390

Stet quicumque volet potens
aulae culmine lubrico:
me dulcis saturet quies;
obscuro positus loco
leni perfruar otio,
nullis nota Quiritibus
aetas per tacitum fluat.
Sic cum transierint mei
nullo cum strepitu dies,
plebeius moriar senex.
Illi mors gravis incubat
qui, notus nimis omnibus,
ignotus moritur sibi.

[336–52] At last this famed royal house, issue of ancient Inachus, has arranged the brothers' threats. What is this frenzy that drives you to spill your blood by turns and beset the sceptre with crime? In your greed for strongholds, you mistake the place where kingship lies. A king is not made by wealth nor the colour of Tyrian robes nor the sign of royalty on his brow nor roofbeams gleaming with gold. A king is one rid of fear and the evil of an ugly heart; one that no wilful ambition or the ever shifting favour of the hasty mob can affect ... [363–8] one that no soldier's lance, no naked steel has subdued, one set in a place of safety who sees all things beneath him and willingly goes to meet his fate, with no protest at death. [388–403] A king is one who fears nothing, a king is one who will want nothing. Each grants himself this kingship. Who wishes may stand in power on a palace's slippery peak: let sweet repose sate me. Set in an obscure place let me bask in gentle leisure; unknown to any Quirites let my life flow on through peace. So, when my days have passed without turmoil, let me die an old plebeian man. Death weighs heavy on one who, too well known to all, dies unknown to himself.

Though the subject of the choral ode is the nature of kingship, the exact phraseology is pertinent to what the reader has just seen in the previous action[27] as it establishes a philosophical standard by which Atreus and Thyestes (and, as we

---

27 The incongruity between the preceding action in the play and the Ode's puzzling introduction (336–8), where brotherly reconciliation is announced at precisely the time when it has become impossible, can simply be overlooked if one follows the argument of Davis 1989, 423–6 that the Chorus is not present in Acts 1 and 2. Generally, Seneca's choral odes have often been asserted to be merely act-dividers due to their loose connection with the action in the plays, an issue which has to do with the possibility of stage production that Seneca may (or may not) have in mind concerning his tragedies. The two main threads of argument against and for the possibility of stage production in the case of the *Thyestes* can be traced in Zwierlein 1966, 78 and Sutton 1986, 37f. respectively. Tarrant 1985, 15 n. 77, while adopting Zwierlein's classic statement against the possibility of staging, accepts the likelihood of actual performances in Seneca's lifetime.

shall see later, Pelias and Aeson too) can be judged. Atreus embodies the very antithesis of all the virtues that the ideal king should represent according to the Chorus, and Thyestes, superficially at least, appears to espouse the values proclaimed.[28] In particular, while the generalized rebuke against those with lust for power (342: *cupidi arcium*) refers evidently to both brothers, the emphasis on *furor* (339) recalls either the Fury (*Furia*) who compelled the ghost of Tantalus in the first Act to drive the royal family mad with murderous rage (27: *furor*, 101: *furorem*) or the wrath which fills Atreus' heart (*Thy*. 23–9, 100, 250–4):[29]

FVRIA: Perge, detestabilis umbra, et penates impios **furiis** age. Certetur omni scelere et alterna vice 25 stringatur ensis; nec sit **irarum modus** pudorve, mentes caecus instiget **furor**, rabies parentum duret et longum **nefas** eat in **nepotes**;	Hunc, hunc **furorem** divide in totam domum. 100 **ATREUS. Dira Furiarum cohors** 250 discorsque Erinys veniat et geminas faces Megaera quatiens. **Non satis magno meum ardet furore pectus,** impleri iuvat maiore monstro.

[23–9] Proceed, loathsome shade: goad this unnatural house into vengeful rage, Let them compete in crime of every kind, and take turns to unsheathe the sword. Let there be no limit to their anger, no shame in it; let blind rage incite their minds, let parents' frenzy last and long-lived evil pass into the grandchildren. [100] Distribute *this* very frenzy throughout the house! [250–4] Let the dread band of Furies come, and the Erinys of strife and Megaera brandishing her twin torches. The madness firing my heart is not big enough, I want to be filled with some greater monstrosity.

By infecting the royal house of Argos anew with *furor* and *ira* (100), the Fury seems to verify and amplify the tragedy's status as a literary background or antecedent for any family crime (28: *nefas*) especially between descendants (29: *nepotes*) that are brothers.[30] At the same time, Atreus, though himself far from being tortured by the

---

28 However, as we shall see, in the ensuing scene Thyestes too will appear not to live up to the Chorus' ideal: despite his initial denouncement of wealth (457), kingship (442) and arms (468), in his opening speech he will betray the appeal to him of Argos, wealth (404) and the people's acclaim (411), and he will show fear towards death rather than being unafraid and undismayed (418f., 435). On the ode's relevance to the previous and future action in the play and its implications concerning the remoteness of both Atreus and Thyestes from true kingship see Tarrant 1985, 137f., 148f.; Davis 2003, 62–7.
29 Note also Thyestes' alleged *regni furor* (302). That Valerius is deeply influenced by Seneca's approach to the fatal results that the desire to rule brings in a family is apparent even in Aeetes' words, when referring to his brother's plot to ascend the throne (*Arg*. 5.536–7): *frater enim-/sceptri sic omnibus una cupido-/excidium parat et castris me ingentibus urget*). See n. 14.
30 On this, see further n. 7 and 14.

Furies, appeals to them in order to re-enact or confirm this kind of obsessive return of, and return to, the family crime. For the reader of Valerius, on the other hand, *furor, ira* and *nefas*, combined with the recurring notion of reciprocity in family bloodshed (note also *Thy.* 340: *alternis dare sanguinem*),[31] call to mind the action and the events taking place in the royal house in *Argonautica* 1. As we have seen, Pelias gets furious when he finds out that his son Acastus has joined Jason's enterprise and exacts his vengeance on Jason's parents (see lines 722–5 quoted above). What is more remarkable, however, is that Fury/Furia, not only as an emotion but also as a dreadful goddess of the Underworld, is manifested in the final episode of *Argonautica* 1 too, as she and her sisters are among the powers and divinities of retribution that even Aeson himself, despite his generally composed and unruffled stance (see below), will invoke in his desire to see his brother Pelias punished (*Arg.* 1. 794–8, 807–10):

> Tu, nuntia sontum
> **virgo** Iovi, terras oculis quae prospicis aequis, 795
> ultricesque deae Fasque et grandaeva **Furorum**
> Poena parens, meritis regis succedite tectis
> et saevas inferte faces!
> ... ...
> tum vobis siquod **inausum** 807
> **arcanumque nefas** et adhuc incognita leti
> sors superest, date fallaci pudibunda senectae
> exitia indecoresque obitus!

[794–8] And you, virgin, reporter of guilty deeds to Jupiter, who look upon the earth with impartial eyes ; and you avenging goddesses, and Right, and you, Retribution, ancient mother of the Furies : enter the guilty abode of the king and apply your harsh torches.

[807–10] Then, if you have at your disposal some secret crime not yet dared, some manner of death still unknown – provide a shameful end for this treacherous old age, an unseemly death!

Like Atreus, who had appealed to the *Dira Furiarum cohors* (*Thy.* 250), Aeson pleads with the *ultricesque deae Fasque et grandaeva Furorum/Poena parens* (796–7) to produce another atrocious, unprecedented crime in return for his brother's deeds.[32] In the event, the Fury appears to respond to Aeson's prayer

---

31 Note also *alterna vice* (25) in the Fury's curse and *alternae ... vices* (133) in the Chorus' earlier prayer.
32 Cf. *Thy.* 195: *audendum est nefas atrox* with *Arg.* 1.807: *inausum arcanumque nefas*. Galli 2007, *ad loc.* (796–7), attests the similarly personified figures in Sen. *Herc. Fur.* 98: *in se simper armatus Furor*; *Oed.* 590: *tum torva Erinys sonuit et caecus Furor*.

cursing Pelias with long years of unrelieved torment followed by a horrible death: *adstitit et nigro fumantia pocula tabo/contigit ipsa gravi Furiarum maxima dextra* 'The eldest of the Furies stood nearby; with her terrible right hand she touched the goblets foaming with black gore' (815–6).[33]

However, it is clear that Valerius has chosen to apply Atreus' portrait of a malicious tyrant to Pelias rather than to Aeson, as the main focus of his narrative is on the latter's choice of an honourable death for himself and Alcimede after consulting the shade of Cretheus in a necromancy. For our argument, it is significant to note here that this oracle does not take place close to a tomb, which was the customary spot in order to evoke the ghost of the deceased; the setting appears to be an area near or within a palace.[34] Andrew Zissos has determined that the same kind of location for a similar purpose (a necromantic ritual) is to be found only in Seneca's *Thyestes*.[35] Now, the ghost of Cretheus, summoned up to reveal Jason's destiny to his parents, while being very comforting about their son's fate, warns them of Pelias' wicked plans (*Arg.* 1.747–8):

> sed tibi triste nefas fraternaque turbidus arma
> rex parat et saevos irarum concipit ignes.
>
> But now the riled king prepares a grim crime, fraternal arms, against you, and ignites the fierce flames of his anger.

The combination of *nefas* with *fraterna arma*, the notion of a reciprocal crime, and the reference to 'burning rage' (*saevos irarum ... ignes*) should be enough to recall once again the fraternal *nefas* that *iratus* Atreus has been shown to be meditating against his brother (see above, *Thy.* 193–4), but Valerius suggests another link with the *Thyestes* in depicting the reaction of Jason's father upon the shocking revelation of the punishment that has been ordained for him and his wife (*Arg.* 1.755–70):

---

[33] As mentioned above (n. 9 and 10), this killing, though it falls well beyond the existing narrative of Valerius' epic, is supposed to be committed by his own daughters' hands after Medea's trickery and will involve a mutilation of his corpse, a mode of punishment initiated of course by Atreus in the *Thyestes*.

[34] Note *Arg.* 1.752–4: *Horruit interea famulum clamore supremo/maesta domus, regemque fragor per moenia differt/mille ciere manus et iam dare iussa vocatis* 'Meanwhile, the gloomy home shuddered with the servants' cries of lamentation; and through the walls of the city a shattering report spreads that the king is mustering a thousands troops, and that he is already giving orders to those summoned'. Similarly Strand 1972, 73.

[35] See Zissos 2008, 381 and cf. *Arg.* 1.752–4 with Sen. *Thy.* 641–56. In contrast, Galli 2007, on 755–6, quotes as parallel the similar landscape in Sen. *Oed.* 530, 523, 556–8, 574–5.

flagrantes aras vestemque nemusque sacerdos	755
praecipitat subitisque pavens circumspicit, Aeson	
quid moveat. – quam multa leo cunctatur in arta	
mole virum rictuque genas et lumina pressit,	
sic curae subiere ducem, ferrumne capessat	
imbelle atque aevi senior gestamina primi	760
an patres regnique acuat mutabile vulgus.	
contra effusa manus haerensque in pectore coniunx	
'me quoque' ait 'casus comitem quicumque propinquat	
accipies nec fata traham natumque videbo	
te sine, sat caeli patiens, cum prima per altum	765
vela dedit, potui quae tantum ferre dolorem.'	
talia per lacrimas. et iam circumspicit Aeson,	
praeveniat quo fine minas, quae fata capessat	
digna satis; magnos obitus natumque domumque	
et genus Aeolium pugnataque poscere bella.	770

The priestess overturns the flaming altars and casts down robe and foliage; and Aeson, in fear at these sudden developments, considers what to do. As a lion amidst a tight throng of men long hesitates, and presses together cheeks and eyes with its gaping jaw, so do anxious thoughts come upon the leader: should he seize the feeble sword and the weaponry of early youth, though an old man, or should he rouse the Fathers and the kingdom's fickle populace? But his wife, stretching forth her hands, clings to his breast, and says: 'You shall take me as a companion in whatever misfortune draws near, nor will I drag out my life or see my son without you, having endured long enough the sky above – I who was able to bear that great sorrow when first he set sail though the deep.' Such words she spoke through her tears. And now Aeson ponders by what end he might forestall the threats, what sufficiently worthy death to undertake: his son, his household, the Aeolian race, and his own achievements in war all demand a great demise.

Aeson's fear, which was hinted at earlier in his endeavour to hide his anxiety from his wife,[36] now becomes noticeable (756: *subitisque pavens*) after the foreboding events. Even more remarkable, however, is Valerius' effort to direct our attention to Aeson's prudent and sensible handling of his position in the face of the imminent threat, at least before the point at which we saw him turning his rage momentarily against his brother. The repetition of *circumspicit* (756, 767), instead of suggesting a kind of hesitation or fear, as some readers believe,[37] adds a rather 'philosophical' dimension to his reaction. Seneca himself uses the same verb in his treatise *De ira* to describe the virtue of a man who has looked guard-

---

36 Cf. *Arg.* 1.733–4: *ipsum etiam curisque parem talesque prementem/corde metus ducit, facilem tamen, Aesona coniunx.*
37 See Kleywegt 2005, 440–1, who believes that the verb, combined with *cunctatur* in the following simile (757–8), depicts someone who is looking urgently for safety.

edly about for a good long time and exercises self-control, before advancing slowly toward a determined goal (*De ira* 1.11.8): *Illa certissima est virtus quae se diu multumque circumspexit et rexit et ex lento ac destinato provexit.*[38] The fact that Seneca here refers to leaders and generals may not be accidental at all for the Valerian text, as Alcimede in her dramatic commitment to stand by her husband until the moment that fate strikes (761–2)[39] points to Aeson as a potential king, who, despite his old age, has to cope with anxious thoughts that came over him (759: *sic curae subiere ducem*). His final resolution is depicted as that of a true leader, whose family tradition and martial exploits for the sake of his kingdom and his people demand a glorious end (769–70: *magnos obitus natumque domumque/et genus Aeolium pugnataque poscere bella*). The choice of a decent death (786: *statuit leto*) not only confirms that he eventually manages to overcome his fleeting fears but in essence casts him as a Stoic hero comprising all those elements that constitute the portrait of the real king in the *Thyestes* (see especially lines 348–52, 365–8).[40] In particular, just like the true leader depicted by the Chorus (*Thy.* 348–9: *qui posuit metus/et diri mala pectoris*), Aeson manages to repress his fear and his evil thoughts in contrast to his brother Pelias, the purported malevolent king, who in his paranoid fear entrusted Jason with the quest of the fleece in the hope that the latter would lose his life during the expedition (*Arg.* 1.31–2: *ergo anteire* **metus** *iuvenemque exstinguere pergit/Aesonium* **letique** *vias ac tempora versat*). Furthermore, Aeson thrives as an ideal king, being himself a man free from intense ambition and a man who scorns the fickle support of the mob.[41] Thus, behind the emphatic recurrence of *circumspicit* (756,

---

[38] See also n. 19. The verb features prominently in Cicero's philosophical works meaning 'to ponder upon, weigh, consider', and is usually construed with an indirect question as here (757: *quid moveat*). Cf. Cic. *Par.* 4.2.30: *neque temere consulem saltatorem vocare, sed circumspicere, quibus praeterea vitiis adfectum esse necesse sit eum*; *Fam.* 5.13.3: *circumspicite celeriter animo, qui sint rerum exitus consecuti*; *Leg.* 2.17.42: *vide, quaere, circumspice, si quis est forte ex ea provincia qui te nolit perisse.*

[39] On Alcimede's stance in lines 762–6, which is thought to be modelled on Creusa's plea to Aeneas at *Aen.* 2.673–78, see Zissos 2008, *ad loc.*, and Hershkowitz 1998, 134–5, who regards her wifely devotion as befitting that of a Roman matron.

[40] On Aeson's behaviour as *exemplum* of a Stoic act, see also Hershkowitz 1998, 132 and Taylor 1994, 233–4. For the importance of suicide to Stoic thought with reference to Seneca's works see the classic study of Griffin 1975, 378–82 and Zissos 2008, 380, who quotes Cic. *Tusc.* 1.74, Sen. *Ep.* 24.3–5 and Luc. 4.474–520. On the suicides of Aeson and Alcimede see particularly McGuire 1997, 24–8 and Manuwald 2000.

[41] Cf. *Thy.* 350–2: *Quem non ambitio impotens/et* **numquam stabilis** *fauor/uulgi praecipitis mouet* with *Arg.* 1.761: *an patres regnique acuat* **mutabile** *vulgus.* Kleywegt 2005, *ad loc.*, notes that the possibility of inciting the archons and the folk to an armed insurrection had provoked Jason to similar deliberations, cf. *Arg.* 1.71–3: *heu quid agat? populumne levem veterique tyran-*

767) we can now discern a leader's careful assessment of his options and a calm approach to his critical and vulnerable situation before embracing his fate. The course of action that Aeson finally chooses suggests a typically Stoic paradigm which recalls the Chorus' portrait of the ideal king, who, while remaining unafraid and undismayed despite his misfortunes (*Thy.* 388–90: *Rex est qui metuet nihil,/rex est qui cupiet nihil:/hoc regnum sibi quisque dat*), looks down at his position with detachment (*Thy.* 366: *infra se videt omnia*) and gladly faces death (*Thy.* 367–8: *occurritque suo libens/fato nec queritur mori*).[42]

A similar Stoic approach is evident in Valerius' description of the gates of the Underworld upon the induction into Elysium of the shades of Aeson and Alcimede. While this katabasis is argued to be reminiscent in tone and content of Vergil's *Aen.* 6, the truth is that Valerius, in contrast to Vergil (*Aen.* 6.434–7), does not exclude people who, like Aeson and Alcimede, have committed suicide, from immediate entrance to Elysium.[43] Moreover, though there are some recognizable Stoic principles in the criteria said to reward virtuous people with admission to Elysium, no reference has been specifically made yet to the similar principles set by the Chorus in the *Thyestes* as prerequisites for the ideal king.

Valerius' ethical model identifies three eminent groups of people as eligible to enter Elysium (*Arg.* 1.832–9):

> hic geminae aeternum portae, quarum altera dura
> semper lege patens **populos regesque** receptat,
> ast aliam temptare nefas et tendere contra:
> rara et sponte patet, siquando pectore ductor   835
> vulnera nota gerens, galeis praefixa rotisque
> cui domus aut **studium mortales pellere curas,**
> culta fides, longe **metus** atque ignota **cupido**,
> seu venit in vittis castaque in veste sacerdos.

Here twin gates stand eternally, of which one is always open by stern decree, and it receives peoples and kings. But to try the other, to strive against it, is forbidden: it opens rarely and of its own accord, whenever there comes a leader bearing glorious wounds on

---

no/infensum atque olim miserantes Aesona patres/advocet, where *populum ... levem* closely corresponds to *mutabile vulgus* (*Arg.* 1.761).
42 On the influence of Stoicism on the second ode and the *Thyestes* in general, see Davis 2003, 61–9.
43 Cf. Virg. *Aen.* 6.434–7, and see further Summers 1894, 30 and Barich 1982, 143–4, who both suggest that Valerius' infernal topography is reworking three passages from *Aen.* 6.893–7 (twin gates of sleep), 660–5 (blessed souls) and 637–44 (Elysium). There are, however, some significant differences between Virgil's and Valerius' treatments; see especially Feeney 1991, 336–7, Hutchinson 1993, 300 and Ripoll 1998, 393–4.

his breast, whose home is affixed with helmets and chariot-wheels; or one whose concern was to banish the cares of mortals, who exalted truth, for whom fear was distant and desire unknown; or if there comes a priest in fillets and a pure robe.

The traditional association of the Underworld with doorways is reminiscent of Virgil's Gates of Sleep serving as an exit for Aeneas and the Sibyl at *Aen.* 6.893–6, which, in turn, draw upon Penelope's twin gates of dreams at *Od.* 19.562–7.[44] However, compared to Virgil, who had made Elysium potentially open to all humankind,[45] Valerius is rather more restrictive in his entry criteria as they are predicated upon activities and professions that are traditionally associated with the Roman aristocracy, as Zissos rightly notes.[46] Thus, while the first mentioned gate (*altera*) can receive almost everyone, from kings to peasants (833: *populos regesque*), the fact that it seems identical with the *porta sinistra* in line 847, which leads to the place where Pelias will be punished, creates the impression that those who enter it are subject at least to judgment, if not punishment.[47] On the other hand, the second gate which affords access to Elysium cannot be readily approached, let alone forced open (834): *ast aliam temptare nefas et tendere contra*. The use of the emblematic *nefas* not only stigmatizes every attempt to pass through this gate as profane, but presumably calls to mind evil people, like Pelias and Atreus, who have committed atrocious crimes. Moreover, this gate opens seldom and of its own accord only to distinguished groups of virtuous people: victorious military leaders who died for their country (835–7: *rara et sponte patet siquando pectore ductor/vulnera nota gerens, galeis praefixa rotisque/cui domus*), those who succeeded in dispelling mortal cares (837–8: *studium mortales pellere curas,/culta fides*) and, finally, priests (839). While especially the first and third categories of Elysian inductees have already been matched with their corresponding types in the *Aeneid*, critics are rather perplexed in identifying the people belonging to the intermediate category.[48] Zissos, following

---

[44] See further Zissos 2008, *ad loc.*, and Kleywegt 2005, *ad loc.* Both commentators agree that Valerius in 1.832 draws particularly on *Aen.* 6.893: *Sunt geminae Somni portae, quarum altera.*
[45] See the categories of virtuous people rewarded with admission to Elysium at *Aen.* 6.660–5 and Zissos 2008, 414.
[46] Zissos 2008, 414.
[47] This is what, according to Kleywegt 2005, *ad loc.*, the qualification *dura ... lege* (1.832–3) may be indicating.
[48] See further Kleywegt 2005, *ad loc.*, and Zissos 2008, *ad loc.* For those injured in the battlefield cf. especially *Aen.* 6.660: *hic manus ob patriam pugnando vulnera passi* while for the trophies adorning their houses (*galeis ... domus*) cf. *Aen.* 7.183ff., immediately following the same line repeated from *Aen.* 6.660. As for the second group of the so-called Stoic *proficientes*, Kleywegt 2005, *ad loc.*, suggests that it corresponds chiefly to the rather vague type of those who in Virgil

Ripoll, refers rather vaguely to those who have lived according to philosophical precepts, thus recognizing an allusion to Stoic *proficientes* in their imperviousness to fear and desire (*Arg.* 1.837: *longe* **metus** *atque ignota* **cupido**),⁴⁹ but has omitted to quote the second ode of the *Thyestes*, where the same virtues are attributed by the Chorus to the portrait of the real king, as already seen (*Thy.* 348, 388ff.): *rex est qui posuit metus ... Rex est qui metuet nihil,/rex est qui cupiet nihil*. Nevertheless, it is not only the capacity to put aside any fears and restless ambitions that makes Seneca's ideal king eligible to enter Valerius' Elysium. Above all, the real king of the Senecan chorus can claim his right to enter the gate of the Underworld like those people who have striven to cast out all mortal cares and live a peaceful life without titles or wealth (cf. *Thy.* 391–400 with *Arg.* 1.837: *studium mortales pellere curas*). From this point of view, Aeson meets the standards for entering the Underworld because he exemplifies the honesty and faith (*Arg.* 1.838: *culta fides*) of an ordinary man by having closed his eyes to any kind of glory bestowed upon him through acts of war or political manipulation (cf. again *Arg.* 1.759–61 with *Thy.* 350–2, as in n. 41). On the contrary, the horrendous end he imprecates for Pelias in essence condemns his brother to a life full of anxious worries resulting from martial struggles (*Arg.* 1.800–3): *classes et Pontica signa/atque indignatos temerato* **litore** *reges/***mente agitet** *semperque metu decurrat ad undas/arma ciens* – 'Rather may he be vexed in mind over the fleets and standards of Pontus and the kings angered by the violation of their coasts, and may he constantly rush down to the shore, calling his troops to arms.'). Pelias, thus, not only constitutes the tyrant whom infernal punishment awaits, but his fate is as determined as that of one of the warlike kings who are explicitly denounced by the Senecan chorus, as a result of their intense ambitions, in another passage from the second ode of the *Thyestes* (Sen. *Thy.* 369–80):

Reges conueniant licet		recludunt iuga Sarmatis,	
qui sparsos **agitant** Dahas,	370	certet Danuvii vadum	
qui rubri uada **litoris**		audet qui pedes ingredi	
et gemmis mare lucidis		et (quocumque loco iacent)	
late sanguineum tenent,		Seres uellere nobiles,	
aut qui Caspia fortibus		**mens** regnum **bona** possidet.	380

> Let kings forgather – those who rouse the scattered Dahae, who control the waters of the ruby coast, the sea blood-reddened far and wide by gleaming gems, or those who open the

---

are *sui memores ali(qu)os fecere merendo* (*Aen.* 6.664). For the category of priests (*Arg.* 1.839: *seu venit in vittis castaque in veste sacerdos*), cf. *Aen.* 6.661: *quique sacerdotes casti, dum vita manebat*.
49 See Zissos 2008, *ad loc.*, and Ripoll 1998, 394.

Caspian heights to the bold Sarmatians; let him compete, who dares to walk on the Danube River, and the Seres famed for silk (in whatever place they lie) wisdom secures the kingship.

Among the many warriors and their exploits in exotic places that the Chorus deprecates here in favour of a king with noble character (*Thy.* 380: *mens bona*) are to be found those who can claim to have reached places renowned for their 'vellus'. Even if Fitch (2004) is right in rendering *vellere* as 'silk' (*Thy.* 379: *Seres uellere nobiles*), the maritime exploits so keenly represented and denounced by Seneca in these lines (370: *agitant*, 371: *litoris*, 372–3: *mare ... sanguineum*, 373–5: *Caspia ... iuga*, etc.) may have influenced Valerius in representing with similar language the sea as the ultimate source of the punishment awaiting the power-hungry Pelias (cf. especially *Arg.* 1.801–2: ***litore*** *reges*/***mente agitet***).

Conclusions

While lines 369–80 of the *Thyestes*, and the second ode as a whole, seem to convey a political message (note especially the use of *Quirites* in line 396) to the Roman reader of the mid-first century A.D., hinting at the results of Rome's striving for power,[50] Valerius probably did not mean to go so far. Taking Roman power and expansion to distant lands in his own time rather for granted,[51] he seems merely to ask his readers to 'judge' his own protagonists according to the extent of their remoteness from the Stoic virtues, which, more or less, correlate with the portrait of the ideal king in the *Thyestes*. In this procedure, it is important to note that there are also some striking resemblances between Aeson's and Thyestes' stances. Just as Seneca presents Thyestes after the second ode accepting, full of fear (418f., 435), the crown and the luxury offered to him by his brother (531) and looking forward to the people's reception (411) despite his earlier opposing declarations,[52] similarly Valerius for a while distances Aeson from the Stoic paradigm of the ideal king, pointing, as we have seen, to his fears, his second thoughts and his reciprocal rage towards Pelias. But, in view of his final decision and his decent end, this may have been another way of 'variatio in imitando' on Valerius' part in order to make the admission to Elysium even more befitting for Aeson, whom death will not find 'unknown to himself', as the ode's concluding

---

50 On the political dimension of the ode, see Tarrant 1985, 137.
51 On the political references to the military achievements of Vespasian and Titus, which are commemorated in the proem (*Arg.* 1.5–21), see Zissos 2008, *ad loc.*
52 See n. 28.

sententia memorably puts it for people like him (*Thy.* 401–3): *illi mors gravis incubat/qui, notus nimis omnibus,/ignotus moritur sibi.*

To sum up, if Seneca's *Thyestes* is, as P. J. Davis fittingly put it,[53] 'a meditation on the dehumanising nature of the craving for revenge and the lust of power', then exactly the same might be said about Valerius' *Argonautica* 1. As mentioned above, this is not the only case, either in the first book or in the whole epic, where Valerius seems to be reading Senecan drama. Emma Buckley's recent contribution to *Brill's Companion to Valerius Flaccus* argues convincingly that Valerius draws upon other Senecan tragedies apart from the *Medea*, mainly *Hercules Furens*, in sketching the Tirynthian hero's portrait and Juno's wrathful revenge against him in the *Argonautica*.[54] What we may now conclude is that Valerius, appreciating perhaps the diachronic value of Seneca's portrait of the ideal king in the *Thyestes*, used it in a rather discreet and creative way in order to 'update' (with a Stoic flavouring) the character representation of Pelias and Aeson in the *Argonautica*. The common elements between the Argonautic saga and the myth of the Tantalids and, above all, the centrality of reciprocal crime in both myths, provided him with the necessary material and incentive to 'reconstruct' the well-known portrait of Seneca's ideal king in the figures of Pelias and Aeson and build his own epic on a more philosophical and rhetorical basis. At the same time, on the metapoetic level, one could say that Valerius seems to re-write Seneca's 'tragedy of *domus*' in an epic context. After all, for Valerius and his colleagues of the Flavian era, Seneca was something more than a philosopher and a dramatist. He was already a classical poet.[55]

Bibliography

Barich, M. J. (1982), *Aspects of the Poetic Technique of Valerius Flaccus*, PhD diss., Yale University, New Haven.
Bömer, F. (1976), *P. Ovidius Naso: Metamorphosen. Buch 6 – 7*, Heidelberg.
Buckley, E. L. (2006), *Valerius Flaccus' Argonautica: Post-Virgilian Literary Studies*, PhD diss., Cambridge University, Cambridge.

---

[53] Davis 2003, 76.
[54] Buckley 2014, 319–24 discusses mostly the Hylas episode (*Arg.* 3.459–86) as a kind of Senecan tragedy.
[55] I am grateful to professors Antony Augoustakis, Theodore Papanghelis and Stavros Frangoulidis as well as to the anonymous referee of *Trends in Classics* for their critical comments and suggestions on the final version of this article.

―――― (2014), 'Valerius Flaccus and Seneca's Tragedies', in: G. Manuwald and M. Heerink (eds.), Brill's Companion to Valerius Flaccus, Leiden, 307–25.
Corrigan, K. (2013), *Virgo to Virago. Medea in the Silver Age*, Cambridge.
Davis, P. J. (1989), 'The Chorus in Seneca's *Thyestes*', *CQ* 39, 421–35
―――― (2003), *Seneca: Thyestes*, London.
Feeney, D. C. (1991), *The Gods in Epic*, Oxford.
Fitch, J. G. (2004), *Seneca IX, Tragedies II: Oedipus, Agamemnon, Thyestes, Hercules on Oeta*, Cambridge, MA.
Frings, I. (1992), *Odia Fraterna als Manieristische Motiv. Beobachtungen zu Seneca's Thyest und Statius' Thebais*, Stuttgart.
Galli, D. (2002), 'Influssi del *Thyestes* di Seneca nel Libro I degli *Argonautica* di Valerio Flacco', *Aevum(ant)* 2, 231–42
―――― (2007), *Valerii Flacci Argonautica I: Commento*, Berlin.
Grewe, S. (1998), 'Der Einfluss von Senecas *Medea* auf die Argonautica des Valerius Flaccus', in: U. Eigler and E. Lefèvre, in Zsarb. mit G. Manuwald (eds.), '*Ratis omnia vincet.*' Neue Untersuchungen zu den Argonautica des Valerius Flaccus, München, 173–90.
Griffin, M. T. (1975), *Seneca: A Philosopher in Politics*, Oxford.
Hardie, P. (1989), 'Flavian Epicists on Virgil's Epic Technique', *Ramus* 18, 3–20.
―――― (1993), *The Epic Successors of Virgil: A Study in the Dynamics of a Tradition*, Cambridge.
Hinds, S. (1998), *Allusion and Intertext: Dynamics of Appropriation in Roman Poetry*, Cambridge.
Hutchinson, G. O. (1993), *Latin Literature from Seneca to Juvenal: A Critical Study*, Oxford.
Hershkowitz, D. (1998), *Valerius Flaccus' Argonautica. Abbreviated Voyages in Silver Latin Epic*, Oxford.
Hull, K. W. D. (1979), 'The Hero-Concept in Valerius Flaccus' *Argonautica*', in: C. Deroux (ed.), *Studies in Latin Literature and Roman History*, vol. 1, 379–407.
Kleywegt, A. J. (2005), *Valerius Flaccus, Argonautica Book 1*, Leiden.
Liberman, G. (1997), *Valerius Flaccus: Argonautiques, t. 1: Chants I–IV*, Paris.
Manuwald, G. (2000), 'Der Tod der Eltern Iasons. Zu Valerius Flaccus, *Arg.* 1,693–850', *Philologus* 144, 325–38
McGuire, D. T. (2007), *Acts of Silence: Civil War, Tyranny, and Suicide in the Flavian Epics*, Hildesheim.
Monteleone, M. (2014), '*De Ira*', in: G. Damschen and A. Heil (eds.), *Brill's Companion to Seneca. Philosopher and Dramatist*, Leiden, 127–34.
Ripoll, Fr. (1998), *La Morale Héroïque dans les Epopées Latines d' Epoque Flavienne. Tradition et Innovation*, Leuven.
Scaffai, M. (1986), 'Il Tiranno e le sue Vittime nel l. I degli 'Argonautica' di Valerio Flacco', in: *Munus amicitiae. Scritti in memoria di Alessandro Ronconi*, Florence, 233–61.
Schiesaro, A. (2003), *The Passions in Play: Thyestes and the Dynamics of Senecan Drama*, Cambridge.
Staley, G. A. (1981–3), 'Seneca's *Thyestes*: *Quantum mali habeat ira*', *GB* 10, 233–46.
Stover, T. (2003), 'Confronting Medea. Genre, Gender, and Allusion in the *Argonautica* of Valerius Flaccus', *CP* 98, 123–47.
―――― (2012), *Epic and Empire in Vespasianic Rome: A New Reading of Valerius Flaccus' Argonautica*, Oxford.
Strand, J. (1972), *Notes on Valerius Flaccus' Argonautica*, Stockholm.

Summers, W. C. (1894), *A Study of the Argonautica of Valerius Flaccus*, Cambridge.
Sutton, D. F. (1986), *Seneca on the Stage*, Leiden.
Tarrant, R. J. (1985), *Seneca's Thyestes: Edited with Introduction and Commentary*, Atlanta.
Taylor, P. R. (1994), 'Valerius' Flavian *Argonautica*', *CQ* 44, 212–35.
Vogt, K. M. (2006), 'Anger, Present Injustice and Future Revenge in Seneca's *De Ira*', in: G. Williams and K. Volk (eds.), *New Developments in Seneca Studies. Columbia Studies in the Classical Tradition*, Leiden, 57–74.
Zissos, A. (1999), 'Allusion and Narrative Possibility in the *Argonautica* of Valerius Flaccus', *CP* 94, 289–301.
─────── (2002), 'Reading Models and the Homeric Program in Valerius Flaccus', *Helios* 29, 69–96.
─────── (2008), *Valerius Flaccus' Argonautica, Book 1. Edited with Introduction, Translation, and Commentary*, Oxford.
─────── (2012), 'The King's Daughter: Medea in Valerius Flaccus' Argonautica', *Ramus* 41, 94–118.
Zwierlein, O. (1966), *Die Rezitationsdramen Senecas*, Meisenheim am Glan.

Emily Gowers
Noises Off: The Thyestes Theme in Tacitus' *Dialogus*

> THYESTES Quis hic tumultus uiscera exagitat mea?
> quid tremuit intus? sentio impatiens onus
> meumque gemitu non meo pectus gemit.   Sen. *Thy*. 999–1001

In the relentless final act of Seneca's *Thyestes*, as the truth begins to dawn, the tyrant who has ingested the bodies of his own children questions the urgency of his internal symptoms. 'What is this tumult that stirs up my entrails? What just trembled inside me? I feel a pressing burden and my chest groans with a groan that is not mine.' Most immediately, Thyestes is speaking of post-prandial discomfort. But these tremors, following as they do the 'eclipse' chorus (790–884), also encourage us to conceive of the tyrant's exploding body as microcosm of a disturbed universe. They remind us, too, that bodily unease is the physical analogue to a disturbed imagination. Thyestes' symptoms recall the earlier commotion, physiological *and* mental, in the other tyrant, Atreus, as he settles on his brother's horrible punishment:[1]

> ATREUS tumultus pectora attonitus quatit
> penitusque uoluit; rapior et quo nescio,
> sed rapior.   Sen. *Thy*. 260–2
>
> A frenzied tumult shakes my heart and turns it inside out; I am swept away, I know not where, but I am swept away.

Richard Tarrant's superb commentary has nothing specifically to say about Thyestes' words in line 1000: *quid tremuit intus?* 'What just trembled inside me?'. But it was Tarrant who pioneered the idea of a meta-dramatic dimension to Seneca's work, from the Fury's call for a revival of Tantalid revenge-drama in Act 1 to Atreus' staging of the play-within-a-play of which he is the crazed director in Act 5, in conscious competition with Medea's infanticidal murder and Procne's tragically staged crime in Book 6 of Ovid's *Metamorphoses*.[2] Is it out of the question

---

[1] Cf. also 1041–2 (Thyestes). This paper expands a paragraph in Gowers, forthcoming. Translations are my own unless otherwise indicated. My thanks to the anonymous reader for suggesting improvements.
[2] Ov. *Met*. 6.601–74, esp. 609–66. Both the Fury and Atreus seem conscious of the precedent: see Tarrant 1985 *ad Thy*. 56, 269–70, 272–7; see also Schiesaro 1994, Schiesaro 2003, 70–138.

that here, too, we are in the presence of a meta-theatrical joke? Inside the very stomach of Thyestes are relocated the familiar 'noises off' of Attic tragedy, as parodied by A. E. Housman in his famous 'Fragment of a Greek tragedy':[3]

> *Eriphyla (within).*   O, I am smitten with a hatchet's jaw!
>   And that in deed and not in word alone.
> *Cho.*   I thought I heard a sound within the house
>   Unlike the voice of one that jumps for joy.
> *Erip.*   He splits my skull, not in a friendly way,
>   Once more: he purposes to kill me dead.
> *Cho.*   I would not be reputed rash, but yet
>   I doubt if all be gay within the house.

The traditionally ominous sound 'within the house' here becomes the radical, even comic sound within the body – part of Seneca's experiment in taking the *Thyestes* drama as far as it had ever gone before, in challenging boundaries between traditional scenic insides (the house, the women's quarters, the inner grove) and outsides (the palace entrance, the woods, the gates of the city), in parallel with boundaries between bodily insides and outsides.[4] The playwright's daring may even stretch to the point where Thyestes – at least according to some scholars who believe the play was actually performed – is revealed on stage in the conventionally taboo act of eating his children (though I am inclined to believe, with Tarrant, that the famous belch at line 911, *eructat*, is meant to indicate specifically that the eating stage has finished).[5] Arguments for an internal *eccyclema*, a movable platform, are often wheeled out as a possibility for the final scene.[6] Is there really a whole inner stage for the director Atreus to spotlight, as he calls for more make-up, more lights, more action?

This paper will focus on another Roman *Thyestes*, one that may never have been written, let alone performed. But it is worth reflecting first on the capacity of this particular theme to beget agonistic or amplified successors and generate meta-theatrical play in line with the central features of its plot: fraternal conflict, generational rivalry and internal secrets. Seneca comes late in a long line of tragic Roman renderings of the plot in question: Ennius, Varius Rufus and Sempronius Gracchus each wrote a *Thyestes*, while the celebrated *Atreus* of Accius (130s

---

For specific echoes of Ovid's version, see Tarrant 1985 *ad Thy.* 103, 117, 127, 129, 154, 157, 192, 197, 199. On Seneca's emulation of Augustan poets in general, see Tarrant 1985, 18–9.
3 Raven and Housman 1959, 18.
4 On interiors and exteriors in Greek tragedy, see e. g. Padel 1992, Zeitlin 1996.
5 On the question of performance, see Fantham 1982, 34–49, Tarrant 1985, 13–5.
6 On the *eccyclema*, see Tarrant 1985 *ad* 885–919.

BC) was followed by those of Mamercus Aemilius Scaurus (c. 34 BC) and Pomponius Secundus (c. AD 60). Further back are the versions of *Thyestes* by Sophocles (which may or may not be the same as his *Atreus*), Euripides and at least six other Greek tragedians.[7] Having, as we do, only Seneca's version of the plot intact, it is hard to appreciate fully the pressure on each author to go one better, more violent – funnier, even – than the one before. Yet even from the few fragments that we have, it appears that from the start of the Roman tradition, at least, iteration and amplification were thematized:

> ATREUS iterum Thyestes Atreum adtractatum aduenit,
> iterum iam adgreditur me et quietum exuscitat:
> maior mihi moles, maius miscendumst malum,
> qui illius acerbum cor contundam et comprimam.   Accius *Atreus* fr. 198–201 Ribbeck^2

> Again Thyestes approaches Atreus to grapple with him, again he comes near me to disturb my peace. I must stir up a greater task, a greater crime, so I can pound and crush his bitter heart.

This Accian excerpt tells us that Seneca's opening *iterum* (Sen. *Thy*. 3–4: TANTALI UMBRA *quis male deorum Tantalo uisas domos | ostendit iterum?* 'Who perversely makes Tantalus look <u>again</u> on the homes of the gods?') is doubly meta-theatrical. Not only does it express Tantalus' accursed return to family violence along with Seneca's late arrival in the *Thyestes* tradition: it also echoes the *iterum* that Accius' Atreus voiced before them. Similarly, the Senecan Atreus' double *maius* at 267 and 274 not only challenges Tantalid and Ovidian precedent at once but also reiterates the Accian Atreus' *maior ... maius*:

> ATREUS nescioquid animus maius et solito amplius
>   ... maius hoc aliquid dolor
>   inueniat.   Sen. *Thy*. 267, 274–5

> My soul is plotting something greater, something grander than before ... let my pain find this greater solution.

It may, indeed, be particularly hard in the case of *Thyestes* to distinguish intertextual dialogue between different versions of the play from overall meta-literary inspiration arising from the plot itself.

The Thyestes plot also had a particularly rich history of being applied to topical outrages. Repercussions and recapitulations of the theme over many centuries in Rome demonstrate that it was a byword for the inflammatory revelation of

---

7 Tarrant 1985, 40. See also Lesky 1922–3.

tyranny, which could be manipulated in both dramatic and extra-dramatic contexts to collapse temporal boundaries between mythical past and nightmare present. The proviso uttered by Accius' Atreus, *oderint, dum metuant*, 'Let them hate me, so long as they fear me' (fr. 203–4 Ribbeck²), became shorthand for Roman *Realpolitik*, often cited by Cicero and later ascribed to the emperor Caligula.⁸ Matthew Leigh has given us a magnificent account of the percolation of the theme into late-republican political rhetoric.⁹ As for the empire, in Syme's words on Tacitus, 'Did not the tragedy of the Caesars embody a sequence of dramatic themes, with ambition, power and crime recalling the House of Atreus?'.¹⁰

Francesca Santoro L'Hoir has shown in more detail how Tacitus portrays his Julio-Claudian *domus* as an Argive palace, convulsed by the treachery and bloodlust of lurking women, and fills it with translated phrases from Aeschylus' *Agamemnon*.¹¹ As she also points out, Cicero had long before staged his *Pro Cluentio* and *Pro Caelio* as Argive dramas, reviving the Clytemnestra role for villainesses Sassia and Clodia.¹² In her view, Cicero's main inspiration for his *Clytemnestrae redivivae* is Aeschylus. However, it is also worth noting that the prosecutor in *Pro Cluentio*, in particular, gives Cicero's defence a particularly combative *Roman* meta-dramatic force: his name happens to be T. *Accius*. I would hazard a guess that, had we more to go on, we would find many quotations from the Accian *Atreus* embedded in the speech, beyond the obvious one that stands out at *Pro Clu.* 61.169: *inimicitias enim inter eos fuisse confiteor; sed homines inimicos suos morte adfici uolunt <u>aut quod [eos] metuunt aut quod oderunt</u>*, 'Men want their enemies dead <u>either because they fear them or because they hate them</u>'.¹³

The dramatic version of the theme that I focus on here is the first *Thyestes* we know of that succeeded Seneca's, the creation of one Curiatius Maternus. Nothing of this play remains – not surprisingly: we only know about it because Maternus is a character in Tacitus' *Dialogus*, who is discovered composing a *Thyestes* at the start of that work. Once an orator, now a dramatic poet, Maternus is among the principal speakers in a private debate about the proper medium for

---

8 Acc. fr. 203 Ribbeck²; Cic. *Phil.* 1.34.3, cf. *Cat.* 1.7.17; Sen. *Clem.* 12.4 *illo exsecrabili uersu*; Sen *De Ira* 1.20.3, who adds *Sullano scias saeculo scriptam*, 'You would know it was written in the time of Sulla'; Suet. *Gaius* 30.1. Cf. the muted variant ascribed to Tiberius at Suet. *Tib.* 59.2: *oderint dum probent*, 'Let them hate me so long as they know I am right'.
9 Leigh 1996.
10 Syme 1958, 363.
11 Santoro L'Hoir 2006, 33–70.
12 Santoro L'Hoir 2006, 158–73.
13 Maslowski 1982 discusses variants in the Ciceronian text at this point but not the allusion to Accius.

free speech in Vespasian's Rome: poetry or oratory, now that drama is confined to recitation and the scope of oratory has been curtailed? The *Dialogus* was written, it is generally thought, around AD 102, under Trajan, but set around AD 75, under Vespasian. As Roland Mayer points out, a play about Atreus and Thyestes might well have seemed topical just as Titus was consolidating his position as Vespasian's heir, to the detriment of his younger brother Domitian.[14]

The *Dialogus* has many problems – issues of interpretation along with uncertain dating and missing text. Its characters may be a mixture of historical and imagined (see below on Maternus). The dialogue is split into three pairs of speeches, in which Maternus speaks twice, both times on behalf of poetry. In this re-performance-with-a-difference of Plato's *Symposium*, he is often taken as the wise Socrates-figure, with the latecomer Messalla, who makes the case for oratory, as the flashier Alcibiades.[15] But Maternus appears to be inconsistent in his preaching and his practice. He dashes off anti-tyrannical plays while praising modern law and order over republican anarchy. Some scholars explain this by maintaining that the work does not just *discuss* the differences between republican freedom and imperial repression: it actually *enacts* them.[16] Shadi Bartsch, for example, argues that Maternus' speeches should be taken as a paradigm of imperial doublespeak: through him, Tacitus is not just nostalgically remembering poetry as a great republican phenomenon but actively proposing it as an imperial substitute for oratory, as the most suitable vehicle for resistance.[17] Nonetheless, as we have already seen, he chose prose for his own version of the Argive tragedies.[18]

What interests me here is the moment, early in the *Dialogus*, when two celebrated orators, Aper and Secundus, shadowed by a young and silent Tacitus, come to call on Maternus and find him brooding in his *cubiculum* over the plays he has either just recited publicly or is planning to write in future. We learn that he is splitting the risk between two dramatic genres: history plays, *fabulae praetextae* – in this case a *Domitius* and a *Cato* – and tragedies – a *Medea* and a *Thyestes*. 'Risk' is the operative word: all these plots, whether historical or mythological, had the potential to be understood as anti-tyrannical.[19] Here is Mayer's 2001

---

14 Mayer 2001, 96.
15 Allison 1999, Rutledge 2000, Breitenbach 2010.
16 Bartsch 1994, Penwill 2003, Dressler 2013.
17 Bartsch 1994, esp. 115–6. See also Strunk 2010.
18 Bartsch 1994, 121.
19 Bartsch 1994, 102. Cf. the similar substitution of Accius' tragedy *Tereus* for his *praetexta Brutus* at the *Ludi Apollinares* of 44 BC (following M. Brutus' assassination of Julius Caesar; Cic. *Phil.* 1.36, *Att.* 16.2.3, 16.5.1). Six of one, half a dozen of the other: see Henderson 1998, 81–2,

text, accompanied by Michael Winterbottom's revised Loeb translation (Hutton and Peterson 1980):

> 3.1 Igitur ut intrauimus cubiculum Materni, sedentem ipsum<que>, quem pridie recitauerat librum, inter manus habentem deprehendimus.
> 3.2 Tum Secundus 'nihilne te' inquit, 'Materne, fabulae malignorum terrent, quo minus offensas Catonis tui ames? an ideo librum istum adprehendisti, ut diligentius retractares et, sublatis si qua prauae interpretationi materiam dederunt, emitteres Catonem non quidem meliorem, sed tamen securiorem?'
> 3.3 Tum ille: 'leges' inquit 'quid Maternus sibi debuerit, et adgnosces quae audisti. quod si qua omisit Cato, sequenti recitatione Thyestes dicet: hanc enim tragoediam disposui iam et intra me ipse formaui. atque ideo maturare libri huius editionem festino, ut dimissa priore cura nouae cogitationi toto pectore incumbam.'
> 3.4 'Adeo te tragoediae istae non satiant' inquit Aper 'quo minus omissis orationum et causarum studiis omne tempus modo circa Medeam, ecce nunc circa Thyestem consumas.'
>
> <div align="right">Tac. <i>Dial.</i> 3</div>

Well, on entering Maternus's room we found him sitting with a book in front of him – the very same from which he had given his reading on the previous day; whereupon Secundus said, 'Has the talk of your detractors no terrors for you, Maternus? Does it not make you feel less enamoured of that exasperating Cato of yours? Or is it with the idea of going carefully over it that you have taken your drama in hand, intending to cut out any passages that may have given a handle for misrepresentation, and then to publish your 'Cato', if not better than it was at least not so dangerous?'

To this he rejoined, 'The reading of it will show you what Maternus considered his duty to himself; you will find it just as you heard it read. Yes, and if 'Cato' has left anything unsaid, at my next reading it shall be supplied in my 'Thyestes'; for so I call the tragedy which I have already planned and of which I have the outline in my head. It is just because I want to get the first play off my hands and to throw myself whole-heartedly into my new theme that I am hurrying to get this work ready for publication.'

'So then', said Aper, 'you have not had enough of those tragedies of yours? Otherwise you would not turn your back on your profession of speaker and pleader and spend your whole time on plays. The other day it was 'Medea', and now it is 'Thyestes'.'

And here, in addition, are two alternative English versions of 3.3 and 3.4, translated by John Penwill and David Levene, respectively:

Boyle 2006: 158 on the interchangeably irrepressible voices of a muted Brutus and a tongueless Philomela. An outspoken *Cato* would have been topical following the martyrdom of Stoic Helvidius Priscus in 74/5 (Syme 1958, 104, 110, 211–2, Mayer 2001, 92). Any earlier *Domitius* might have given offence to Nero, but Frank 1937 has argued that Maternus attacked Nero's courtier Vatinius (cf. *Dial.* 11.2) by portraying the Ciceronian conflict between L. Domitius (cos. 54 BC) and Caesar's favourite Vatinius; Mattingly 1959 identifies Maternus' play speculatively with the *Octavia*.

> You will read what Maternus owed to himself, and you will recognise what you heard. And if Cato left anything out, Thyestes will say it at my next recitation; for I have already planned this tragedy and have formed its outline in my mind. (Penwill 2003, 134)

> 'Those tragedies,' said Aper, 'do not weary you, to the point that you neglect your occupations in speeches and cases and spend all your time recently around Medea, and now around Thyestes.' (Levene 2004, 165)

For all their vigour and variety, all these translations have been forced to do some violence to the metaphors in the original Latin. 'In my head', 'in my mind', 'get it off my hands', 'throw myself into', 'turn your back on', 'weary yourself': these are new images introduced by the translators to fit better with English idiom. In due course, I will suggest a closer translation.

For a start, when I say that Maternus is 'brooding' over his play, I do not just mean in the sense of contemplating it. We are asked to imagine a particular scenario for the creation of these future tragedies. The choice of a *cubiculum* as setting is particularly apt for a dialogue about imperial repression. Spatial restriction elsewhere illustrates the cramping environment of modern oratory: the tight robes into which orators have to squeeze nowadays before their speeches (*adstricti et uelut inclusi*), the little consulting rooms (*auditoria et tabularia*) where they have to plan their cases, the cloistered rhetorical schools, and the hired halls where poets stage their recitations.[20] As Andrew M. Riggsby has revealed in a searching investigation, the Roman *cubiculum* was a multi-purpose room, always more than a bedroom, often used for study, private interviews, plotting, even murders.[21] Sociologist Erving Goffman would have classed it among the 'back-regions' of civic life, the kind of setting where future appearances on the public stage can be rehearsed or postponed.[22] It is hardly surprising, then, that when Messalla arrives as latecomer to this furtive symposium, he has to ask whether he is disturbing a secret party: *'num parum tempestiuus' inquit 'interueni secretum consilium et causae alicuius meditationem tractantibus?'*, 'I hope I've not come at the wrong time and interrupted you while you're involved in some private discussion or handling some case?'.

This confined setting is the domestic equivalent of the mysterious *arcana* of a tyrant's palace, whether in Argos or in Palatine Rome. As far as Neronian precedents go, we might also think of the darkened chamber where Persius lurks in *Satire* 1, muttering subversively and guarding his secrets, or of Seneca's Tantalus

---

20 *Dial.* 39.1, 35.1, 9.3.
21 Riggsby 1997.
22 Goffman 1959.

in his *Thyestes*, roused unwillingly from his *atrum cubile* in Hell.[23] Penwill, for one, has seen the sinister aspects of the *secretum consilium* that Messalla is 'accidentally' interrupting: the phrase primarily means 'private discussion', but it can also mean 'secret intrigue'. 'These,' he comments, 'are nervous times.'[24] For him, Maternus is the arch imperial dissimulator, who only pretends to love the poet's secluded retreat in woods and groves – a retreat all the better from which to launch his dramatic torpedoes. As passionate *uates* and committed defender of old liberties, Maternus makes an awe-inspiring role model for the young Tacitus – indeed, he is a martyr in the making, if Alan Cameron is right that, like so many other hosts and main speakers in ancient dialogues from Plato to Macrobius, he was to die soon after the imagined event.[25] Interestingly, Penwill detects a loose echo at the end of the *Dialogus*, as each speaker hands his audience over to the next generation, of the closing exchange of Seneca's *Thyestes*:

> ac simul assurgens et Aprum complexus 'ego' inquit 'te poetis, Messalla antiquariis criminabimur.'
> 'At ego uos rhetoribus et scholasticis' inquit.
> Cum arrississent, discessimus.   *Dial*. 42.2

> He [Maternus] rose and embraced Aper, saying 'We will both denounce you – I to the poets, Messalla to the antiquarians.'
> 'But I shall denounce both of you to the rhetoricians and the professors,' he [Aper] replied.
> After they had laughed at this, we left.   (Penwill 2003, 135)

> THYESTES uindices aderunt dei;
> his puniendum uota te tradunt mea.
> ATREUS Te puniendum liberis trado tuis.   Sen. *Thy*. 1110–12

> THYESTES Avenging gods will come.
> My prayers hand you to them for punishment.
> ATREUS I hand you to your children for punishment.   (Penwill 2003, 135)

Penwill concludes: 'Aper gets the joke, all right; he's read Seneca.'

---

23 Pers. *Sat*. 1.119–20 *me muttire nefas? nec clam? nec cum scrobe? nusquam?/ hic tamen infodiam*, 'Is it forbidden for me to mutter? Secretly? Into a hole? Anywhere? Here I shall bury my secret'; Sen. *Thy*. 70–1 (Tantalus) *abire in atrum carceris liceat mei /cubile*, 'Let me go back to the black lair of my prison-house'. Cf. Sen. *Phaed*. (Hippolytus) 522–3 *non in recessu furta et obscuro improbus / quaerit cubili seque multiplici timens / domo recondi*, 'He does not guiltily plot stealthy deeds in lair or dark chamber, nor does he hide away in fear in a labyrinthine palace'; Plin. *Pan*. 49.1 (Domitian) *arcana illa cubilia saeuique secessus, in quos timore, et superbia et odio hominum agebatur*, 'Those hidden lairs and cruel retreats into which he was driven by his fear, arrogance and hatred of his people'.
24 Penwill 2003, 131.
25 Cameron 1967: literary dialogues set just before the death of the host or principal interlocutor include Plato, *Phaedo*, *Crito* and *Theaetetus*, Cicero, *De Republica* and *De Oratore*, Athenaeus, *Deipnosophistae* and Macrobius, *Saturnalia*.

Let us see if we can 'get the joke' for our passage as well. There are several theories about who Curiatius Maternus actually was: perhaps a governor of Syria executed by Domitian for anti-tyrannical remarks (Dio 67.12.4) or a victim of Vespasian's informers.[26] But Bartsch admits to a sneaking suspicion that Tacitus' tragedian is no more than a fiction, a figure invented to tell us under what conditions literature can come into being once political freedoms have been curtailed.[27] Her suspicion is piqued by his name. Curiatius Maternus, she points out, is oddly reminiscent of a historical, or at least historiographical, figure in Tacitus' *Histories*, Curtius Montanus, who was exiled for libelling Nero and might have survived to become the Montanus who writes to Pliny (*Ep.* 7.29) and/or the aging courtier Montanus ridiculed by Juvenal in *Satire* 4, the one who drags his corpulent body into Domitian's council chamber: *Montani quoque uenter adest abdomine tardus* (4.107), 'Enter next Montanus' stomach, slowed down by its underbelly'.

But there is another reason altogether why 'Curiatius Maternus' might be *ben trovato*. It is a name that Maternus cannot resist bringing to our attention himself at 3.3, using the rhetorical figure of *emphasis* or *affectus*.[28] He says: *leges tu quid Maternus sibi debuerit*, 'You will read what (a) Maternus owed to himself'. Maternus has already been accused of being too much Cato, too absorbed into that most solipsistic of dramatic characters. Now, he uses his name to drive it home that, as bringer-to-birth of tragedies, he also has a quasi-*maternal* role. Mayer cites Virg. *Aen.* 6.510 and Luc. 8.80 as parallels for rhetorical self-naming, but he might equally have cited Seneca's Atreus or Medea, who do just this as they grow into their full selves as a result of their vengeful crimes: *Thy.* 180 *iratus Atreus*, 'irate Atreus'; *Med.* 171 *[Medea] fiam*, 'I will become [Medea]', 910 *Medea nunc sum*, 'now I am Medea'. In any case, we might note, Curiatius Maternus has already punned on his own name by drawing attention to his material, *materia*, at 3.2 and to his current preoccupation, his *cura*, at 3.3. More precisely, we might envisage him as 'mother [*mater*] of the senate [*curia*]', a republican figure who is not just venerable but also protective.

The notion of self-characterization through gender-switching is also particularly apt for the creative enterprise Maternus has chosen. Labour pains, both in devising a crime and enacting it, are central to the Thyestes plot, at least in Seneca's version of it. As Cedric Littlewood pointed out long ago, this is a play that, uniquely for Seneca, lacks parts for women. It pushes to the margins the adulter-

---

[26] See conveniently Bartsch 1994, 105–6. If he was Dio's anti-tyrannical victim (Syme 1958, 111, Cameron 1967, Barnes 1986), he would have been executed in 75/6, just after the implied date of the *Dialogus*.
[27] Bartsch 1994, 261.
[28] Mayer 2001, 96.

ous wife Aerope, who motivates Atreus' revenge, but makes her husband usurp female biological functions to gestate a very poetic revenge and then makes his brother, her lover, Thyestes, symbolically perform those functions. Thyestes will 'give birth' to his own offspring from his turbulent stomach, so anticipating the confused relationships of the next generation: Thyestes' incest with his own daughter results in the twisted offspring Aegisthus, future lover of his aunt-in-law, Clytemnestra.[29] Joe Park Poe, writing on the *Quis hic tumultus?* lines I quoted at the beginning, allowed a brief glimmer of this idea before brushing the possibility away: 'To a reader with a little sympathetic imagination these lines (999–1000, 1041–2) might suggest a teeming womb. However, this is a comparatively minor matter.'[30] Not so minor, surely, in a play where Tantalus and the Fury play midwives to an act of violence that grotesquely mimics illicit pregnancy: one man fills his sexual rival's stomach with his children's bodies (his *uiscera*, his flesh and blood, in his *uiscera*, his innards) in order to prove the paternity of his own sons. Meanwhile, the poet himself labours towards a monstrous, unwanted birth, his disgust enacted on stage both in ever-hungry Tantalus' lack of appetite for renewed revenge and in the messenger's lack of words to describe the horrors he has seen – before he launches in and describes them.[31] For all this, the tragic forerunner is *Medea*, the prototype of any play that involves the displacement of (pro)creative urges into infanticidal revenge. As Medea herself puts it: *parta ultio est: / peperi*, 'Vengeance is born: I have given birth' (Sen. *Med*. 25–6). For Seneca's Atreus, she is both an intertextual and an intratextual (intra-Senecan) model.[32] Thus Maternus even gets the order right in his account of his own dramatic output: first *Medea*, then *Thyestes*.

So we read that Tacitus' playwright has 'formed' his new play 'inside himself' (*intra me ipse formaui*) and, moreover, that he is hurrying (a concept common to Aeschylean and Tacitean intrigue[33]) to deliver one play to maturity, so that he can concentrate on incubating the new work, *Thyestes*, with all his heart:

---

29 Littlewood 1997.
30 Poe 1969, 372.
31 Schiesaro 2003, 27 calls Act 1 'a symbolic enactment of the birth of the play'; see further 26–69. On images of pregnancy for male creativity in Greek literature, see now Leitao 2012; in Roman literature, see Rimell 2002, 72, Gowers forthcoming.
32 See Tarrant 1985 for echoes of the Senecan Medea at *Thy.* 255 and 271, for inversion of Manilius on Medea's children (3.13 *male conceptos partus peiusque necatos*, 'offspring wickedly conceived and more wickedly murdered') at *Thy.* 41–2 and for a possible allusion to Ovid's tragic Medea at *Thy.* 269–70 (cf. *Her.* 12.212). On Seneca's self-consciously self-surpassing Medea, see also Schiesaro 2003, 16–8; on Ovid's, see Hinds 1993.
33 Santoro L'Hoir 2006, 41–2.

toto pectore incumbam. Now, *incumbere* does not exactly mean 'nest' or 'incubate', but something more like 'loom over', 'bear down on', an idiom that Cicero, for example, uses informally in his letters to denote strong enthusiasm.[34] However, the verb was previously used by none other than Seneca's *Medea* in her infanticidal speech, along with both *pectore ab imo* and *materia*:

> incumbe in iras teque languentem excita
> penitusque ueteres pectore ex imo impetus
> uiolentus hauri ...
> quaere materiam, dolor
>
> Sen. *Med.* 902–4, 914

> Bear down on your anger, stir your sluggish self, and drain your old urges violently from the depths of your heart ... find material, my pain

It is difficult, then, not to see gestational or obstetric imagery in Maternus' words, whether they recall Medea, or the tyrant Atreus, possessed by his brainchild, or his brother Thyestes, stuffed with his own children.[35]

Despite his complete absorption in his work, it soon becomes clear that the creation of the *fabula praetexta Cato* and the tragedy *Medea* has brought Maternus only temporary satisfaction. He is reported as being barely sated (3.4 *adeo non satiant*) and needing to produce another tragedy. Once again, his hunger for renewed creativity is similar to the genetically determined urges of his tragic characters, such that Maternus continues to function as an amalgam of three Senecan characters at once – Medea, whose post-partum crimes are 'greater', Thyestes, cursed by ancestral hunger, and Atreus, the dissatisfied plotter, whose rapid changes of appetite tell the history of the Tantalid house in the space of a line and a half:

> MEDEA maiora iam me scelera post partus decent.
>
> Sen. *Med.* 50

> Greater crimes are more fitting now I have given birth.

---

34 Cic. *Fam.* 10.10.2 *incumbe toto pectore*, 'apply yourself, heart and soul'. Seneca virtually glosses the word at *Ep.* 78.15: *quod premit, quod impendet, quod urguet, si subducere te coeperis, sequetur et grauius incumbet*, 'If you begin to withdraw your support from what presses you, leans over you and bears down on you, it will follow you and loom over you more heavily'. The related verb *incubare*, 'to brood (over)', is, as it happens, a favourite of Seneca's, appearing no fewer than five times in his *Thyestes*: 155 (Tantalus in Hell), 401 (death, *mors grauis*), 571 (night watchman), 733 (Atreus like a lion), 909 (Thyestes feasting).

35 For tyranny or *hubris* as a monstrous birth, cf. Solon fr. 6.3 West τίκτει γὰρ κόρος ὕβριν; Theog. fr. 39–42 ~ fr. 1081–82B (the city in labour with a tyrant); Soph. *OT* 872 (whether the ms. reading ὕβρις φυτεύει τύραννον is preferred or Blaydes's emendation ὕβριν φυτεύει τυραννίς).

ATREUS bene est, abunde est, iam sat est etiam mihi.
sed cur satis sit?   Sen. *Thy.* 889–90

It is enough, more than enough, it is enough even for me.
And yet, is it really enough?

Lurking in his *cubiculum* with his incipient play in his hands, Maternus also resembles the mad poet Eumolpus of Petronius' *Satyrica*, who groans below deck as he delivers a poem on the subject of the teeming Trojan Horse:

> audimus murmur insolitum et sub diaeta magistri quasi cupientis exire beluae gemitum. persecuti igitur sonum inuenimus Eumolpum sedentem membranaeque ingenti uersus ingerentem. mirati ergo quod illi uacaret in uicinia mortis poema facere, extrahimus clamantem, iubemusque bonam habere mentem. at ille interpellatus excanduit et: 'sinite me' inquit 'sententiam explere; laborat carmen in fine.' inicio ego phrenetico manum, iubeoque Gitona accedere et in terram trahere poetam mugientem.   Petr. *Sat.* 115

> We heard an unusual murmuring coming from below the captain's room, like the growl of a beast trying to get out. Following the sound, we found Eumolpus sitting scribbling verses onto a huge parchment. Amazed that he had time on the point of death to compose a poem, we dragged him out shouting and told him to cheer up. But he was furious at being interrupted, and said: 'Let me finish my last sentence; I'm struggling with the poem's ending.' I laid my hand on the lunatic and gave Giton instructions to go and drag the bellowing poet onto dry land.

Victoria Rimell has already pointed out similarities between Eumolpus and Thyestes and their painful labours,[36] while Charles Segal and Alessandro Schiesaro have stressed the connection in Senecan tragedy between the *arcana*, the hidden regions of royal palaces, and the invisible, portentous wombs of the female characters, Medea, Aerope and Jocasta.[37] As oracular *uates* pent up with thwarted emotions he is longing to expel, Maternus is as much Atreus and Thyestes, then, as he is their avenger. As a 'pregnant' recluse lurking in his *cubiculum*, he even recalls Plato's picture of a tyrant in the *Republic*: someone who hides away in the recesses of his house, 'like a woman'.[38]

---

[36] Rimell 2002, 81: 'Is our poet still the Trojan horse, pregnant with literature, bellowing like an animal as he is dragged to safety … ? Or has he lost control of the reins, the reverse of Agamemnon's 'free man' in *Sat.* 5, trapped within his own poetic material, inside the horse itself?'. Don Fowler, cited by Rimell 2002, 81, suggests that Eumolpus' groans are 'those of a woman in labour as well as of a madman'.
[37] Segal 1983, Schiesaro 2003, 88.
[38] Pl. *Rep.* 9.579b καταδεδυκὼς δὲ ἐν τῇ οἰκίᾳ τὰ πολλὰ ὡς γυνὴ ζῇ, 'He [the tyrant] lives for the most part lurking in his house like a woman'.

Here, then, is an attempt at a more accurate translation of 3.3–4:

> Then Maternus said: 'You will read what a Maternus owed to himself, and you will recognize what you have heard. But if 'Cato' has left anything out, 'Thyestes' will express it at the next reading. I have already planned this tragedy and <u>conceived it inside me</u>. And I am in a hurry to <u>get the book out</u>, so that once the other task is out of the way <u>I may brood with all my heart</u> over my new project.' Aper said: 'So far have those tragedies <u>not sated</u> you that you have given up on your devotion to oratory and lawsuits and now <u>consume</u> all your time, first on 'Medea' and then on 'Thyestes'.

On this reading, what we have here is a portrait of the playwright undergoing exactly the same processes as the central characters, Medea, Atreus and Thyestes, in the two plots he is devising: a sequence of lurking, inspiration, incubation, gestation, maturation, delivery and consumption or consummation – followed by renewed dissatisfaction and increased appetite.

After all this, it is no surprise to discover, later in the *Dialogus* (12.6), that Maternus refers to the two greatest tragedies of Augustan Rome, Varius' *Thyestes* and Ovid's *Medea*, as masterpieces to emulate.[39] Little of either play survives, and the brief mention here has only increased the tantalizing prestige of both among the chief casualties of Latin literature. The fact that they are mentioned at all might also lead us to suspect that Tacitus' description of Maternus in his chamber contains hidden allusions to them as well as to Seneca's play. The feminization of the playwright, for example, recalls the anecdote that preserves for us one famous line from Ovid's lost *Medea*, *feror huc illuc, uae, plena deo* (fr. 2 Ribbeck²), 'Alas, I am carried hither and thither, full of divine inspiration' – or, punningly, 'Alas, I am carried hither and thither, pregnant by the god' (of inspiration: Bacchus, or Apollo?), presumably spoken by Medea herself. Seneca the Elder (*Suas.* 3.6–7) attributes the line originally, and evidently erroneously, to Virgil and tells how the phrase was picked up by Ovid and became shorthand for enthusiastic speech, so that Junius Gallio, for example, always used to nickname the latest 'hot' declaimer as though he were a pregnant prophetess: 'How was so-and-so?' 'Oh, terribly *plena deo*.' Eliding as it does pregnancy and inspiration, being full of or by the god, the phrase is also used by Ovid of Carmentis in the *Fasti*, mother of Evander by Mercury, both prophetic goddess of *carmen* and patron of childbirth and midwives (*Fasti* 1.474 *carmina plena dei*; cf. 6.538 *fitque sui toto pectore plena dei*), while *plenus deo*, which assimilates oracular or oratorical male wisdom to vatic possession, is a term used by Lucan of none other than

---

39 He conspicuously overlooks Seneca's versions: Van den Berg 2014: 18 n. 1, 159.

Cato (*BC* 9.564; cf. 2.285, 9.255). It may well be significant that Maternus the Vespasianic *uates* has chosen prophetic characters for self-incarnation.

Are these Thyestean images of the imperial poet's labour pains any more than just a brief literary conceit? Clearly they tell us something about the cramped conditions under which post-republican authorship was possible: still ambitious, but increasingly frustrated, for inspired poets and fluent orators alike. When women are mentioned in the *Dialogus*, their role is always maternal, whether good or bad, genuine or artificial. Speaking of the business of educating and shaping children (*educandos formandosque liberos*), Messalla contrasts the wholesome republican matron, who used to fill her children with moral goodness along with her milk, with the hired Greek nurse of today, in her tiny maid's room (*cellula*), who feeds her young charges on a diet of rude jokes and trivia.[40] Ephemeral teenage passions for actors, gladiators and horses are said to be 'virtually conceived in the maternal womb' (29.3 *paene in utero matris concipi*). Male rhetorical training, on the other hand, must continue to channel creative instincts productively: breeding, rearing, nurturing, educating, forming and stocking the mind – even if its products are poured out fruitlessly in the confined spaces of dark lair and recitation hall.[41]

Somewhere along the way, the Thyestes story came to mean more than just a notorious Greek legend of domestic perversion and a dubious cannibalistic feast. It was also about sublimity, the irrepressible – tyrannical, even – sweep of poetic creation, particularly the kind that lays bare intimate passions under difficult, often tyrannical conditions.[42] At Horace's dinner of Nasidienus (*Sat.* 2.8), Varius, tragedian and author of an imminent *Thyestes*, stifles laughter in his napkin as the platters of burned and mangled limbs go by.[43] The spluttering satirist Persius reworks the Thyestes theme in *Sat.* 5, not just using the dramatically taboo image of the *olla Thyestae*, stewpot of Thyestes (5.8), and the hundred gobbets of vatic product (5.1–6), but also the idea of the private confabulation – 21 *secrete loquimur* (a phrase that Calder 1983 tweaks for the title of his discussion of Seneca's *Thyestes*) – as well as, significantly, the urge to expose intimate and inexpressible feelings on the outside:

---

40 *Dial.* 28.4.
41 Oratorical training in the old days as productive nurture: *Dial.* 33.2–4. Modern rhetorical fame compared to fruit picked too soon: *Dial.* 9.4. On the use of (masculine) agricultural imagery in the Roman theory of rhetoric, including *Dialogus*, see Connors 1997.
42 Leigh 1996, Schiesaro 2003, 127–32.
43 Gowers 1993, 177.

> excutienda damus praecordia ...
> hic ego centenas ausim deposcere fauces,
> ut quantum mihi te sinuoso in pectore fixi
> uoce traham pura, totumque hoc uerba resignent
> quod latet arcana non enarrabile fibra. Pers. *Sat.* 5.22–9

> I give you my heart to shake out ... Here I would dare to ask for a hundred throats, to draw out with pure voice how deeply I have fixed you in the folds of my heart, that my words might unseal all that hides untellable in my inmost fibre.

A suggestion, by way of a postscript. One other, more distant model for this conflation of tragedy, male creativity and female procreation springs to mind. Tacitus' repression-filled *Dialogus* and Horace's failed *Cena* both hark back to an idealized ancestor: Plato's *Symposium*. Many scholars, as I noted earlier, have seen the cryptic Maternus as a kind of Socrates.[44] But both he and Horace's sympotic Varius have another avatar: the tragedian Agathon, triumphant winner, the day before the party, with his first, unnamed drama, to which this gathering is satyr-play or tragicomic follow-up. In the all-male discussions and paeans to Eros that ensue, the *Symposium* notoriously allows half-admission to a token female, Diotima, someone with privileged access to female-only creative experience, if not to the party proper. Her vatic words are ventriloquized by Socrates, before he reduces her envied powers to *metaphors* of generation, the more easily to be adopted by men, who can then become 'pregnant' (without women's help) with beautiful ideas.[45]

What *was* the name of Agathon's successful tragedy, we might wonder? With no trace left in the text itself, it has been most commonly identified as the *Antheus*, a known play on a made-up theme (apt, it has been argued, for Plato's 'flowery' portrayal of Agathon here).[46] But of the handful of titles ascribed to this playwright, there is one other that might be worth considering as a rival. Plato gives us two clues. First, he tells us that Agathon, the day before winning the tragic *agon*, offered a *sacrifice* (ἔθυεν) for his victory.[47] Secondly, in his own speech Agathon twists a famous line from Sophocles: 'Ares is no match for Necessity' becomes 'Ares is no match for Eros'. The line in question comes from Sophocles' *Thyestes* (Θυέστης).[48]

---

[44] See above p. 4, with n. 15.
[45] Halperin 1990.
[46] Sider 1980, 50.
[47] Pl. *Symp.* 173a ὅτε τῇ πρώτῃ τραγῳδίᾳ ἐνίκησεν Ἀγάθων, τῇ ὑστεραίᾳ ᾗ ᾖ τὰ ἐπινίκια <u>ἔθυεν</u> αὐτός τε καὶ οἱ χορευταί, 'when Agathon won with his first tragedy, the day after he and his chorus members <u>offered</u> a victory <u>sacrifice</u>'.
[48] Soph. fr. 256 Radt πρὸς τήνδ' ἀνάγκην οὐδ' Ἄρης ἀνθίσταται; Pl. *Symp.* 196d (Agathon) Ἔρωτι 'οὐδ' Ἄρης ἀνθίσταται'.

Bibliography

Allison, J. (1999), 'Tacitus' *Dialogus* and Plato's *Symposium*', *Hermes* 127, 479–92.
Barnes, T. D. (1986), 'The Significance of Tacitus' *Dialogus de Oratoribus*', *HSCP* 90, 238–44.
Bartsch, S. (1994), *Actors in the Audience: Theatricality and Doublespeak from Nero to Hadrian*, Cambridge, MA.
Boyle, A. J. (2006), *An Introduction to Roman Tragedy*, London.
Breitenbach, A. (2010), 'Sokrates und Curiatius Maternus. Zur Bedeutung von Platons Symposium für den taciteischen *Dialogus de oratoribus*', *MH* 67, 146–63.
Calder, W. M. (1983), '*Secreti loquimur*: An Interpretation of Seneca's *Thyestes*', *Ramus* 12, 184–8.
Cameron, A. (1967), 'Tacitus and the Date of Curiatius Maternus' Death', *CR* 17, 258–61.
Connors, C. (1997), 'Field and Forum: Culture and Agriculture in Roman Rhetoric', in: W. Dominik (ed.), *Roman Eloquence: Rhetoric in Society and Literature*, London, 71–89.
Dressler, A. (2013), 'Poetics of Conspiracy and Hermeneutics of Suspicion in Tacitus's *Dialogus de Oratoribus*', *CA* 32, 1–34.
Fantham, E. (1982), *Seneca's Troades: A Literary Introduction*, Princeton.
Frank, T. E. (1937), 'Curiatius Maternus and his Tragedies', *AJP* 58, 225–9.
Goffman, E. (1959), *The Presentation of Self in Everyday Life*, New York.
Gowers, E. (1993), *The Loaded Table: Representations of Food in Roman Literature*, Oxford.
— (forthcoming), 'Girls will be Boys and Boys will be Girls, or, What is the Gender of Horace's *Epodes*?', in: P. Bather and C. Stocks (eds.), *Horace, Epodes: Literary Contexts*, Oxford.
Halperin, D. M. (1990), 'Why is Diotima a Woman?', in: *One Hundred Years of Homosexuality and Other Essays on Greek Love*, New York, 113–51 and 190–211.
Henderson, J. (1998), 'On Getting Rid of Kings: Horace, *Satires* 1.7', in: *Fighting for Rome: Poets and Caesars, History and Civil War*, Cambridge, 73–107.
Hinds, S. (1993) 'Medea in Ovid: Scenes from the Life of an Intertextual Heroine', *MD* 30, 9–47.
Hutton, M. and W. Peterson (1980), *Tacitus. Vol. 1: Agricola, Germania, Dialogus*, revised by R. Ogilvie, E. Warmington and M. Winterbottom, Cambridge, MA.
Leigh, M. (1996), 'Varius Rufus, Thyestes and the Appetites of Antony', *PCPS* 42, 171–97.
Leitao, D. D. (2012), *The Pregnant Male as Myth and Metaphor in Greek Literature*, Cambridge.
Lesky, A. (1922–3), 'Die griechischen Pelopidendrama und Senecas Thyestes', *WS* 43, 172–98.
Levene, D. (2004), 'Tacitus' *Dialogus* as Literary History', *TAPA* 134, 157–200.
Littlewood, C. (1997), 'Seneca's *Thyestes*: The Tragedy with no Women?', *MD* 38, 57–86.
Maslowski, T. (1982), 'On the Margin of Cicero, *Pro Cluentio* 169 and 170', *AJP* 103, 325–31.
Mattingly, H. (1959), 'The *Domitius* of Curiatius Maternus', *CR* 9, 104–7.
Mayer, R. (2001), *Tacitus Dialogus de Oratoribus*, Cambridge.
Padel, R. (1992), *In and Out of the Mind: Greek Images of the Tragic Self*, Princeton.
Penwill, J. (2003), 'What's Hecuba to him … ? Reflections on Poetry and Politics in Tacitus' *Dialogue on Orators*', *Ramus* 32, 122–47.
Poe, J. P. (1969), 'An Analysis of Seneca's *Thyestes*', *TAPA* 100, 355–76.
Raven, D. S. and Housman, A. E. (1959), 'Fragment of a Greek Tragedy', *G&R* 6, 14–9.
Riggsby, A. M. (1997), "'Public' and 'Private' in Roman Culture: The Case of the *cubiculum*", *JRA* 10, 36–56.
Rimell, V. (2002), *Petronius and the Anatomy of Fiction*, Cambridge.

Rutledge, S. H. (2000), 'Plato, Tacitus, and the *Dialogus de Oratoribus*', *Latomus* 254, 345–57.
Santoro L'Hoir, F. (2006), *Tragedy, Rhetoric, and the Historiography of Tacitus' Annales*, Ann Arbor, MI.
Schiesaro, A. (1994), 'Seneca's *Thyestes* and the Morality of Tragic *Furor*', in: J. Elsner and J. Masters (eds.), *Reflections of Nero: Culture, History and Representation*, London, 196–210.
Schiesaro, A. (2003), *The Passions in Play: Thyestes and the Dynamics of Senecan Drama*, Cambridge.
Segal, C. P. (1983), 'Boundary Violation and the Language of the Self in Senecan Tragedy', *A&A* 29, 172–87.
Sider, D. (1980), 'Plato's 'Symposium' as Dionysian Festival', *QUCC* 4, 41–56.
Strunk, T. E. (2010), 'Offending the Powerful: Tacitus' *Dialogus de Oratoribus* and Safe Criticism', *Mnemosyne* 62, 241–67.
Syme, R. (1958), *Tacitus*, Oxford.
Tarrant. R. J. (1985), *Seneca's Thyestes*, Atlanta, GA.
Van den Berg, C. (2014), *The World of Tacitus' Dialogus de Oratoribus*, Cambridge.
Zeitlin, F. I. (1996), 'The Power of Aphrodite: Eros and the Boundaries of the Self in Euripides' *Hippolytos*', in: *Playing the Other: Gender and Society in Classical Greek Literature*, Chicago, 219–84.

Roland Mayer
Seneca's Ted Hughes

The title of this chapter is not meant to be whimsical,[1] it aims rather to suggest that we may regard Seneca as having appropriated Hughes, not the other way round. That Hughes himself believed in this sort of entrapment is clear from the opening lines of 'Dreamers' in *Birthday Letters* (1998, 157):

> *We didn't find her – she found us.*
> *She sniffed us out. The Fate she carried*
> *Sniffed us out*
> *And assembled us, inert ingredients*
> *For its experiment. The Fable she carried*
> *Requisitioned you and me and her.*
> *Puppets for its performance.*

The genesis of Hughes's *Oedipus*

Some background information about Hughes's involvement in the play may further support a defence of the chapter's title. Hughes himself related in the Introduction to the published adaptation (1969, 7) that the original scheme was for a translation of Seneca's *Oedipus* by David Anthony Turner to be directed for the National Theatre by Sir Laurence Olivier.[2] Olivier fell ill and was replaced by Peter Brook, who was unhappy with Turner's version and turned to Hughes for a fresh adaptation.[3] And so on 19 March, 1968 at the Old Vic Theatre in London Hughes's version of Seneca's *Oedipus* was produced with some success (an extra week was added to the show's run of performances[4]), and it has occasionally been revived.[5]

---

[1] My title turns out to have been anticipated by Fleming 2013, 112, but I shall stick with it, since my strategy in the use of it is somewhat different from hers. Her article, focusing on the critique of modern rationalism in Hughes's work, is outstanding. I hope that what follows nonetheless makes some useful additions to the discussion.
[2] Turner's version is apparently to be found in Corrigan 1990 (not seen by me).
[3] For a fascinating insight into Hughes's use of Turner's version and his 'mythologized account' of how his adaptation came into being see Stead 2013.
[4] See Hunt 1995, 121–35 and Rosenthal 2013, 140–7 on the history of the production, and Marowitz 1977, 135–9 for a severe assessment of Brook's 'theatrical overlay' of the script, about which he has nothing to say apart from the interesting notion that Hughes had composed a sort of 'oratorio'; add Jacobs 1983, 165–9, Sagar-Tabor 1983a, 29–34 and Marshall 2009, 263, n. 3.

Thus the accidental replacement of both director and translator goes some way to justifying my notion that it was Seneca who requisitioned Hughes, rather than the other way round. It is above all one of the play's main themes, that of fate seizing its victim and moulding him to its pattern, which is far more significant, since it long resonated within Hughes's own mind-set. Seneca thus seemed to him to be a kindred spirit. Again, let me provide some further background.

Ted Hughes is one of the most important British poets of the post-war period (he became the Poet Laureate in 1984 and was awarded the Order of Merit). In 1967 his literary reputation was respectable; he had just published *Wodwo*, and he was working on the pieces that were to be published in the *Crow* collection in 1970. Still, he was a somewhat odd choice as the adapter of a Latin drama, since he was not trained in the Classics, though he had been taught Latin at school and must have passed the Latin examination required at that time for admission to the University of Cambridge (Talbot 2006). His comprehension of the language however was at best rusty (unlike that of the other great Yorkshire poet Tony Harrison), so he relied for guidance on both the repudiated version of Turner and the Loeb translation of Frank Justus Miller (indeed he lifted some phrases straight out of it). Now this might tempt us to hope that we will be treated to an 'innocent' engagement with the text. Granted Hughes was free of the academic baggage that weighs down a classical scholar (perhaps even with prejudice against Senecan drama), there is still no such thing as an 'innocent' reader. Hughes was no exception. Initially he read for the English Tripos at Cambridge, but disenchanted with the academic approach to literature, for the second part of his degree he transferred to the Archaeology and Anthropology Tripos. That programme did equip him with at least some of the 'baggage' he carried in his engagement with the tragedy of Seneca.[6] The aim of this chapter is to attempt to explain what it was in Seneca that gripped Hughes's imagination so powerfully, and what enabled him to produce a challenging reconfiguration of the Roman drama.

Reid 2007, 280–2 published a couple of Hughes's letters referring to his work on Seneca's script and the production of the play.

5 I saw the Royal Shakespeare Company's production in Islington's Almeida Theatre in August 1988. Boyle 2011, cxv, n. 275 lists further revivals.

6 The importance of this shift in his academic studies is also stressed by Fleming 2013, 109–10.

Hughes on the attractions of Seneca

Hughes himself explained in the Introduction to the printed script why he was happy to be adapting Seneca rather than Sophocles (1969, 8), guidance that is crucial to understanding his 'take' on the play. His leading idea was to make a text 'that would release whatever inner power this story, in its plainest, bluntest form, still has'. The implication of those words is clear: the drama's power is latent, hidden under accretions. Tellingly, he then uses an archaeologist's word, 'unearth': he wanted to 'unearth … the ritual possibilities' within the Senecan text (a point to be returned to later). He went on to note Seneca's 'tremendous rhetorical speeches and stoical epigrams', but clearly he regarded them as accretions masking the plain, blunt core. His adaptation will strip away the fashionable rind of rhetoric and Stoicism (along with most of the choral songs as well)[7] to expose the core. That core he identified as 'the raw dream of Oedipus, the basic, poetic, mythical substance of the fable'. This sounds like the typical anthropologist of the period working through layers or variations of accumulated matter to an imagined original version of a traditional tale. For instance, is it entirely fanciful to detect in the word 'raw' yet another anthropological notion, 'raw' being the primitive predecessor and antonym of the civilized 'cooked'? The Greek world of Sophocles was, according to Hughes, 'complete, fully explored … fully civilized' (clearly he hadn't read E. R. Dodds on the Greeks and the irrational, a work published in 1951). By contrast he found 'the figures in Seneca's *Oedipus* … Greek only by convention, by nature they are more primitive than aboriginals' (1969, 8). Surely here again we detect the student of 'Arch & Anth', repudiating the civilized world and eager to disclose a substrate of authenticity submerged beneath the bric-a-brac of high culture.[8] The phrase just quoted, 'more primitive than aboriginals', is of fundamental importance, since it reveals a quality upon which Hughes was fixated over the years.[9] For instance, in the letter accompanying the copy of the play he sent to Thom Gunn he referred to the ideal performers of the play as 'complete aboriginal barbarians' (Reid 2007, 300). Later in the *Prologue* to *Gaudete* (1977, 15), there will be the figures with 'primitive, aboriginal faces' who confront the Reverend Lumb. In *Birthday Letters* (1998, 23 and 62) he describes the 'aboriginal

---

[7] The first, third, and fifth choral songs are adapted and shortened. The second is given a title (1969, 30–1), 'Chorus to Bacchus', but its substance has 'nothing to do with Dionysus'. The fourth is omitted altogether.
[8] Fleming 2013, 111–12 also engages closely with Hughes's synkrisis of Sophocles and Seneca.
[9] See Gifford–Roberts 1981, 17 for the importance of the primitive in Hughes's work.

thickness' of his wife, Sylvia Plath's, lips as well as her 'prototype face', and he finds the chipmunk a 'midget aboriginal American'.[10]

Senecan psychology in Hughes: entrapment by fate, loss of control, fear, resignation, the mother-figure

To be on the safe side it had better now be confessed that I am no deep student of Hughes's work, so guidance regarding the salient psychological themes which recur in the poems has been sought from Gifford–Roberts 1981. With the aid of their analyses an attempt can now be made to show how Seneca's *Oedipus* harmonizes with some of them.

A persistent theme in the poems is 'the tormenting sense of not being in possession of one's own life and potentialities' (Gifford–Roberts 1981, 67), allied to which is a 'rejection of self-sufficient ego' (Gifford–Roberts 1981, 15). For Hughes, the agent of our dispossession is Fate. A passage from *Birthday Letters* has already been quoted at the outset which illustrates how Fate takes our lives out of our hands. To that can be added the opening line of 'Actaeon' from the earlier collection, *Tales from Ovid* (1997, 105),

> Destiny, not guilt, was enough
> For Actaeon.

Later in that poem (1997, 107), Actaeon is described as 'Steered by a pitiless fate'. In that same collection Atalanta too is driven by her fate (1997, 132), as are Pentheus (1997, 185 – the reference to his fate comes appropriately enough just after Tiresias [NB] has sketched to him what Bacchus has in store for him) and Midas (1997, 202).[11] Hughes's fatalism has also been identified as a factor in his later engagement with Aeschylus' *Oresteia*.[12]

Well before these poems were written Hughes had encountered in Seneca's Oedipus a figure who had fully internalized a sense that he was the victim of fate,

---

[10] To these may be added the following: 'In his reading of this poem ['The Long Tunnel Ceiling'] on radio Hughes said that the trout had 'a magical meaning for me'. It was an 'authentic aboriginal ... the holiest creature out there in its free unspoiled sacred world'; thus Keith Sagar on 'Ted Hughes, fishing and poetry' 2009 (available on Sagar's web site, item 12: http://www.keithsagar.co.uk/tedhughes.html).

[11] Niobe challenges Fate to reverse her happiness (1997, 215), Procne and Philomela have a sorry fate (1997, 232)

[12] See Silk 2007, 23 = 2009, 257–9; and especially n. 44 for Carey's identification of the crucial role played by Hughes's fatalism.

a sense made clear at the very beginning of the play (the word *fatum* appears over twenty-five times in it). We learn from Oedipus' opening speech that he fled Corinth because of the oracle that told him he would kill his father. He asks (1969, 14), 'what is fate preparing for me' and later describes himself as 'the man marked down by the god for the worst fate of all'.[13] Seneca's Oedipus is convinced that the plague afflicting Thebes is generated not by anything he has yet done (he has not killed Polybus, his presumed father), but by his still unrealized (for so he supposes it) fate. In this we detect a clue to something Hughes found uncongenial in the character of Sophocles' Oedipus. The Oedipus of Sophocles is not troubled by his destiny, but is presented as rational and pragmatic in the face of calamity; only gradually and incidentally does he come to learn of his own condition. But he is definitely not weighed down by any sense of doom, and at least initially his ego is all too self-sufficient. Not so the Oedipus of Seneca, who, conscious of his fate, is wracked by fear of its realization. Thus Hughes was able to introduce without discord into his characterization an acknowledgement of incapacity to deal with the situation. For instance, Hughes's Oedipus says 'you have put too much on to me' in his appeal to the gods (1969, 15), and to Jocasta he describes the plague as 'more than enough for any King' (1969, 16). The Oedipus of Sophocles could not have been made to speak thus, but such sentiments are entirely consistent with the original Senecan character, even though there is nothing similar in the Latin text.

The attraction of Seneca's fated Oedipus re-emerges in the third act, after Creon has related the speech of the revivified Laius. In the Latin original, Oedipus remarks in a two-line aside (659–60) that he is accused of having done what he has all along feared; he is afraid. Hughes describes in his own way the effects of this fear over six and a half lines (1969, 36).[14] Now granted verbal overload is one of Hughes's weaknesses as a poet,[15] the elaboration here is surely indicative of his interest in the theme of an impending fate that takes over a life. We can once again see why the Sophoclean Oedipus did not appeal, since he responds with anger, not fear, to Tiresias' accusation (*OR* 354–5), and he still has no sense of a fate that is waiting to pounce on him, has indeed already caught up with him. The ineluctability of fate is again enunciated in Hughes's, not Seneca's, opening lines of the fourth act (1969, 40 = lines 764–6 in the Latin text), where Oedipus is made to say,

---

[13] The eccentric layout of Hughes's version is here ignored. That layout, without traditional punctuation, proved a trial for the original Oedipus, Sir John Gielgud, but he triumphed over the adversity (Croall 2000, 452–3).
[14] The role of fear in the character of Oedipus is discussed by Fleming 2013, 112–3.
[15] So Gifford-Roberts 1981, 11 on 'excess'.

> *Before it was fear but now is it certainty*
> *how have I been trapped.*

'Trapped' is the operative word, and though Seneca didn't use it, Hughes's addition is not discordant with the characterization of the Roman Oedipus, who has been trapped from the beginning and he knows it. The speech that follows voices hitherto unspoken anxieties, something foreign to the character of Sophocles' Oedipus.

Finally, in the last choral song (1969, 52–3), beginning 'Fate is the master of everything' (= *fatis agimur*, 980), Hughes elaborated upon what is only sketched briskly in Seneca, the impracticability of trying to avoid or mitigate our destiny.[16]

Hughes, when writing his own poems, nonetheless adumbrated a means of negotiating with a dominant fate in the poem entitled 'A flayed crow in the hall of judgement' in the collection *Cave Birds* (1975). Gifford–Roberts 1981, 216–8 find in it a developing consciousness that though one is at the mercy of forces outside oneself, it is best to accept the outcome:

> *a great fear rests*
> *On the thing I am ... I shall not fight*
> *Against whatever is allotted to me.*

Hughes had already encountered that sentiment in Seneca's Oedipus, especially in his acceptance, one might almost say his embrace, of his blindness. Perhaps the most extraordinary scene in the whole play is the opening of the final act, when the self-blinded Oedipus re-appears on stage, to be joined by Jocasta. We all know that Sophocles did not provide the model for this confrontation. What surprises, even more than the on-stage suicide of Jocasta, is the serenity of Oedipus, a note struck by his opening words, *bene habet* 'all is well' (998). Hughes once again responded sympathetically to this characterization, and *more suo* elaborated it at some length in an aria of resignation (1969, 53–5). In the closing lines of the play he added something for which there is no model in the original text. Hughes's Oedipus addresses fate thus:

> *remorseless*
> *my enemy you are the friend I choose come with*
> *me.*

---

16 See Schofield 1983, 193 and Harrison 2009, 152–8.

Not Seneca, but entirely Senecan in sentiment: the wise man complies with fate, he does not fight it. Perhaps then the single most important link between Seneca's Oedipus and Hughes's poetic personae was their posture before the onslaught of one's personal doom.

The final scene of the play provides another clue to the attraction of Seneca's treatment of the myth. It will be remembered that in Sophocles' play before the moment when all is to be revealed by the herdsman Jocasta rushes into the palace, to appear no more. Seneca's Jocasta presumably leaves the stage at this point too, but he brings her back to confront her blinded son at the end. This strategy had an unexpected effect on Hughes. He saw that in Jocasta Seneca had given him a rather more complicated character than Sophocles. Like Seneca's Phaedra she wants to console and atone, but cannot find any way to do so except through suicide. Now here we touch on a matter that plagued Hughes, a bungler with his loves. Schofield 1983 has charted the difficulty Hughes had in particular with the mother-son theme, and has stressed the importance to him of the Oedipus myth, to which he reverted in the character or persona of Crow (1983, 189). Jocasta's re-appearance at the end of Seneca's play arguably generated the 'black Magnificat' Hughes composed for her towards its beginning (1969, 16–8), an aria of birth, for which Seneca provided no model. Schofield demonstrated how the song deploys themes later found in 'Crow and Mama', 'Song for a Phallus',[17] and 'Snake Hymn'.[18] In short, her first-act song is pure Hughes, especially in her sense that she bears Oedipus for a grim future. But the germ of the ideas and images elaborated there is to be found in her final speech, where Seneca has her call herself an accomplice in the crimes (*socia … scelerum* 1024). Horrifically she thrusts the sword up into her womb. Seneca precisely names the sword's goal, *uterum* 1039. Extraordinarily, Hughes does not, though the stage action must have made it clear where the sword was aimed. The reason for this suppression is twofold. First, Hughes had already given Jocasta the opportunity to concentrate on her womb in the first-act aria. Secondly, Seneca, unlike Sophocles, included a scene of failed sacrifice and extispicy; one of the victims is an unmated heifer, and yet to Manto's horror the beast is pregnant (1969, 28 = lines 371–5 in Seneca). Given the earlier focus on wombs there was no need for Hughes's Jocasta to be as specific as Seneca's at the end.

---

17 This was composed as a scabrous 'epilogue' or satyr-piece to Seneca's play.
18 'Examination at the Womb-Door' in the same collection is worth adding.

Ritual and drama

The scene just referred to illuminates two more points of contact between Seneca and Hughes. In his Introduction (1969, 8) Hughes observed that in Seneca's hands Oedipus' story had become 'something close to the scenario of a mystery play'. He didn't notice (why should he have?) that this is a feature of some of Seneca's other plays (*Medea* 670–842 for instance) and of the epos of his nephew Lucan (the famous Erichtho episode in the sixth book of the *Pharsalia*). Such outlandish rites were typical of the poetry of the period, and, as Hughes recognized, far removed from the 'radiant moral world of Sophocles'. What is striking is that a feature of Senecan dramaturgy which had left previous critics cold at last found a sympathetic response. It was noted at the outset that Hughes wanted to 'unearth ... the ritual possibilities' of the Senecan text.[19] The ritual and the scenario of the mystery play appealed creatively to Hughes, and clearly influenced the later *Gaudete*, which contains ritual of a spooky kind (like the extispicy [291–402] and the necromancy scenes in *Oedipus*), for example the sacrifice of the ox (1977, 17–9) and the drugging of Felicity (1977, 141–2).[20] But there is more to this: Seneca revelled in the chance such scenes offered to dwell upon the revolting aspects of sacrifice (or in other contexts, of wounding, such as the description of the laceration of Hippolytus in *Phaedra*). This too had nauseated older critics, but it struck a chord in Hughes, some of whose poems, for instance 'February 17th' in the collection *Moortown Elegies* (1978; republished as *Moortown* 1979, and then *Moortown Diary* 1989) or 'The Afterbirth' in *Birthday Letters* (1998, 130–1),[21] rival Seneca in their revolting physical detail.[22] Did Seneca somehow validate Hughes's personal attraction to the pornography of dismemberment and wounding, the internal made external?

---

19 Brook's original production emphasized the ritual aspect of the Senecan drama (Hunt 1995, 121–35).
20 Gifford-Roberts 1981, 181–2. Hughes started on *Gaudete* in about 1967, so his engagement with Seneca early on in its composition is significant.
21 'I pulled against | The corpse that would not come. Till it came. | And after it the long, sudden, yolk-yellow | Parcel of life | In a smoking slither of oils and soups and syrups – | And the body lay born, beside the hacked-off head.'
22 This is also noted by Slaney 2009, 60.

The Senecan legacy

As a sort of coda to this analysis it is worth noting that Seneca brought Hughes back to the Latin classics. Roughly thirty years later Hughes would turn, very successfully, for inspiration to Ovid, the Ovid of the *Metamorphoses*. It was that Ovid who provided tragic Seneca with so much of his own mythical material and verbal manner. Hughes himself didn't see the connection, obvious to the student of Latin poetry, but at some level he must have felt it. For in his Introduction to the twenty-four poems based on the *Metamorphoses* he noted the 'tortured subjectivity' (1997, viii) of the mythical characters and the 'catastrophic extremes of passion that border on the grotesque'. Ovid bequeathed to Seneca that strange fascination with the grotesque that for so long alienated the more po-faced classical scholar, so it is no surprise that once Hughes had found in one Roman poet, Seneca, something that appealed so strongly to his own imagination,[23] he appropriated the same quality from the work of Seneca's model, Ovid. As Hughes further explained (1997, ix) Ovid's characters are subjected to 'passion *in extremis*'[24] and their humanity is 'transformed' into the mythic or the supernatural or the divine. It will be recalled that it was in Seneca's *Oedipus*, not Sophocles', that Hughes recognized a truly mythic character. Finding something similar in Ovid was no accident. So the engagement with Seneca paved the way to his appreciation of Ovid.

It is time to draw these reflections to a close, and a final attempt to justify this chapter's non-whimsical title can now be made. The year, 1968, of the production of Hughes's adaptation ought to have been surprising. Back in the 1960s few professional classicists had any time for Senecan tragedy. For centuries it had been either vilified or ignored, with one or two remarkable exceptions.[25] What Seneca needed above all was a propitious time and a powerful advocate. The latter half of the twentieth century was certainly a propitious time, after the horrors of two world wars and under the threat of nuclear annihilation. Seneca's tragic world, oppressed by anguish and fixated on death,[26] was beginning to seem less remote and fanciful. But a voice was still needed with which he might speak to that newly propitious time. Scholarship was dragging its feet, so the voice had to be that of a contemporary poet. It was David Anthony Turner who

---

23 See Motto–Clark 1984.
24 That said, it is odd that the reader has to wait until the story of Myrrha for such a passion.
25 See Harrison 2009.
26 I allude of course to one of the few sympathetic voices raised in defence of Senecan tragedy's sensibility, the justly renowned Regenbogen 1927/8.

initiated the choice of Seneca's *Oedipus* for performance,[27] but in the event his was not the voice that Seneca wanted. By the working of unfathomable fate Seneca secured the voice he needed: Hughes did not choose Seneca, Seneca ensnared Hughes.[28]

Bibliography

Boyle, A. J. (2011), *Seneca, Oedipus*, Oxford.
Corrigan, R. W. (1990), *Classical Tragedy, Greek and Roman, 8 Plays*, New York.
Croall, J. (2000), *Gielgud, a Theatrical Life*, London.
Fleming, K. (2013), '"For Everybody must Answer the Sphinx", Ted Hughes's Translation of Seneca's *Oedipus*', *Canadian Review of Comparative Literature* 40.1, 105–21.
Gifford, T. and Roberts, N. (1981), *Ted Hughes, a Critical Study*, London.
Gifford, T. (2011), *The Cambridge Companion to Ted Hughes*, Cambridge.
Harrison, S. J. (2009), 'Modern Versions of Senecan Tragedy', *Trends in Classics* 1, 148–70.
Hunt, A. and Reeves, G. (1995), *Peter Brook*, Cambridge.
Hughes, T. (1969), *Seneca's Oedipus*, London.
_____ (1975), *Cave Birds*, London.
_____ (1977), *Gaudete*, London.
_____ (1997), *Tales from Ovid*, Twenty-four Passages from the Metamorphoses, London.
_____ (1978), *Moortown Elegies*, London.
_____ (1998), *Birthday Letters*, London.
_____ (2003), *Collected Poems*, ed. Paul Keegan, London.
Jacobs, F. R. (1983), 'Hughes and Drama', in: Sagar 1983b, 154–70.
Marowitz, C. (1977), *Confessions of a Counterfeit Critic*, London.
Marshall, H. (2009), 'The Hughes Version, Commercial Considerations and Dramatic Imagination', in: Rees 2009, 263–8.
Motto, A. L. and Clark, J. R. (1984), 'Grotesquery Ancient and Modern: Seneca and Ted Hughes', *Classical and Modern Literature* 5, 13–22.
Rees, R. D. (2009), *Ted Hughes and the Classics*, Oxford.
Regenbogen, O. (1927/8), 'Schmerz und Tod in den Tragödien Senecas', in: *Vorträge der Bibliothek Warburg*, 167–218 = *Kleine Schriften* 1961, Munich, 411–64.
Reid, C. (2007), *Letters of Ted Hughes*, London.
Rosenthal, D. (2013), *The National Theatre Story*, London.

---

[27] He explained his choice (in Hughes 1969, 9) somewhat negatively: no one else had chosen to put a Senecan drama into modern English for performance.
[28] My warm thanks for helpful observations at Thessaloniki go to Toph Marshall, Tim Moore, Costas Panayotakis, and Alessandro Schiesaro. A revised version of this paper was delivered at the Comparative Literature seminar in King's College London, where my colleagues and students – William Fitzgerald, Lucy Jackson, James Ryan, David Ricks, Michael Silk, Christopher Wintle and Rivkah Zim, all contributed to improvement of the information and the analysis offered here.

Sagar, K. (1978), *The Art of Ted Hughes*, Cambridge.
Sagar, K. and Tabor, S. (1983a), *Ted Hughes, a Bibliography 1946–1980*, London.
Sagar, K. (1983b), *The Achievement of Ted Hughes*, Manchester.
Schofield, A. (1983), 'The Oedipus Theme in Hughes', in: Sagar 1983b, 186–209.
Silk, M. (2007), 'Hughes, Plath and Aeschylus, Allusion and Poetic Language', *Arion* 14.3, 1–33 = 'Ted Hughes, Allusion and Poetic Language', in: Rees 2009, 234–62.
Slaney, H. (2009), 'Liminal's Kosky's Hughes's Artaud's Seneca's *Oedipus*', *New Voices in Classical Reception Studies* 4, 52–70.
Stead, H. (2013), '*Seneca's Oedipus*, by Hook or by Crook', *Canadian Review of Comparative Literature* 40.1, 88–104.
Talbot, J. (2006), '"I had Set Myself Against Latin", Ted Hughes and the Classics', *Arion* 13.3, 131–62.
_____ (2009), 'Eliot's Seneca, Ted Hughes's *Oedipus*', in: Rees 2009, 62–80.
Weissbort, D. (2006), *Ted Hughes, Selected Translations*, London.
Zajko, V. (2011), 'Hughes and the Classics', in: Gifford 2011, 107–20.

Stephen Harrison
Seneca's *Thyestes*: Three Female Translators into English

This paper looks at three verse translations by female writers of Seneca's only tragedy not to include a female human character, the *Thyestes*: that by the American scholar Ella Isabel Harris, in *The Tragedies of Seneca* (1904), the first English verse translation of all the tragedies by a single hand; that by the English poet Jane Elder (1982); and that by the London playwright Caryl Churchill (1995). The translation of Seneca's plays into English is a continuing topic of scholarly interest (see e. g. Share 1998, Fleming and Grant 2013); this paper is in some ways a sequel to my earlier investigation of the twentieth-century reception of Seneca's tragedies (Harrison 2009), and seeks to highlight the importance of female scholars and translators in the reception history of Seneca's tragedies, following alongside the recent work of scholars such as Judith Hallett on women's historic contribution to classical studies.[1] In what follows I will contextualise each version, and then compare the same sample passages for each author with the original Latin texts; the samples are drawn from three different kinds of context in Seneca's play: set-piece speech, dialogue between characters and choral lyric.[2]

Ella Isabel Harris, *The Tragedies of Seneca* (1904)

The record of the earliest female graduates of Yale graduate school has the following entry:[3]

> ELLA ISABEL HARRIS, B. A. Waynesburg College 1889, M. A. 1892. Upon receiving her degree in 1899, Miss Harris became Instructor at Vassar College. From 1900 to 1916 she was head of the department of English at the Washington State Normal School. Since 1917 she has been Associate Professor of English at Elmira College, Elmira, New York. Her dissertation, "Two Tragedies of Seneca Rendered into English Verse," with an Introduction, was published, without the Introduction, by Lamson, Wolffe & Company, Boston, in 1898; was republished by

---

[1] See e. g. Hallett 2013.
[2] I cite the relevant Latin text for each translator: Leo 1878 for Harris, and Miller 1917 for Elder and Churchill.
[3] Corwin 1920, 33 (this volume chronicles the earliest female Yale PhD graduates from the first in 1894).

Houghton, Mifflin Company in 1899 [as *Two Tragedies of Seneca: Medea and the Daughters of Troy*]; and was included in [her] "The Tragedies of Seneca Rendered into English Verse," Henry Frowde, London, 1904.

Harris was amongst the first few years of female PhD graduates from Yale (the first was in 1894); she received her doctorate in English, one of forty women to do so in the years 1894–1919, and her dissertation is one of those singled out for praise in 1920 by her former doctoral supervisor A. S. Cook, then Professor of English Language and Literature at Yale University and earlier one of the key advocates of female doctoral students.[4]

As already mentioned, Harris' translation in its 1904 version was pioneering in another way, providing the first complete verse translation of Seneca's tragedies by a single hand; it was soon to be followed by that of Frank Justus Miller (1907), who a decade later also provided a prose translation for his Loeb edition (1917).[5] That Harris' translation was well regarded in the US is suggested by its rapid reprinting in the two-play dissertation version and by its expansion into a complete version a few years later.[6] The brief review of the complete version in the *New York Times* of December 31 1904[7] spends most of its space objecting to Harris' view that Seneca is vital for Elizabethan drama, but states that the translation is close and therefore effective as a reading aid; the longer and more academic review in the *American Journal of Philology* for 1905 by Charles G. Osgood,[8] then professor of English at Princeton,[9] is much more positive about the link with Shakespeare, to be followed two decades later by the influential voice of T. S. Eliot,[10] and praises the translation's naturalness in English and its effective replication of key and diverse Senecan features. Much less positive is the characteristically acerbic review in *The Classical Review* of 1905 by the British Latinist W. C. Summers, then at Manchester and famous for his later negative characterisation of Seneca's dramas as 'contemptible … and full of morbid craving for the

---

4 For the praise, the forty and their publications and destinations see Corwin 1920, 26. Thirty-one of the forty dissertations were published, including the still-useful Goad 1898 on the 18C reception of Horace.
5 Miller 1907 and Miller 1917.
6 It is now available again in print (Harris 2011, the version cited here) and in a Kindle version.
7 Available online via http://www.nytimes.com/ref/membercenter/nytarchive.html (accessed 6.10.2014).
8 Osgood 1905.
9 For his career see conveniently http://pabook.libraries.psu.edu/palitmap/bios/Osgood__Charles_Grosvenor.html (accessed 6.10.2014).
10 See further Harrison 2009, 150–1.

horrible and disgusting'.[11] The review is condescending in the extreme; Summers considers only the first 600 lines of the *Hercules Furens*, the first play in the collection, pointing out a series of small mistranslations, and opens with a summary of his view: 'to translate Seneca is no easy task, and Dr. Harris has greatly overrated her strength'.[12] I hope to show that this is at least partly unfair.

Harris' own preface notes that she feels unable to render the lyric choruses in English lyric metres;[13] the metre used throughout is iambic pentameter, and the style is similarly Shakespearean, with some archaisms and elevated language. She also notes that the translation was mainly composed to help her own teaching, and that 'it is intended rather for the student of Seneca as an influence on modern drama than of Seneca for himself'.[14] Despite the Shakespearean colour, there is no indication that Harris intended the version for performance, or that she herself believed that the plays were intended for performance. She used Leo's edition, and no doubt shared his view that the plays were rhetorical declamations and not dramatic pieces (though she does insert stage directions in her version).[15]

Sample passages

A *Thyestes* 23–36 (the Fury reacts to the prologue-speech by the ghost of Tantalus):

Perge, detestabilis	Go, hated shade, and drive thy sin-stained home
umbra, et penates impios furiis age	To madness; let the sword try every crime,
certetur omni scelere et alterna uice	And pass from hand to hand; nor let there be
stringatur ensis; nec sit irarum modus	Limit to rage and shame; let fury blind
pudorue, mentes caecus instiget furor,	Urge on their thoughts; let parents' hearts be hard
rabies parentum duret et longum nefas	Through madness, long iniquity be heaped
eat in nepotes; nec uacet cuiquam uetus	Upon the children, let them never know
odisse crimen: semper oriatur nouum,	Leisure to hate old crimes, let new ones rise,
nec unum in uno, dumque punitur scelus,	Many in one; let sin while punished grow,
crescat. Superbis fratribus regna excidant	From the proud brothers let the throne depart,
repetantque profugos; dubia uiolentae domus	Then let it call the exiled home again.
fortuna reges inter incertos labet;	Let the dark fortunes of a violent house
miser ex potente fiat, ex misero potens,	Among unstable kings be brought to naught.
fluctuque regnum casus assiduo ferat.	Let evil fortune on the mighty fall,
	The wretched come to power; let chance toss
	The kingdom with an ever-changing swell
	Where'er it will.

---

11 Summers 1920, 58.
12 Summers 1905, 124.
13 Harris 2011, 3.
14 Harris 2011, 3.
15 Leo 1878, 147–59.

Here we can plainly see Harris' Shakespearean stylistic colour in operation (note the archaising 'thy' and 'naught'). Overall, there is a little expansion, but this perhaps reflects the greater conciseness of Latin in general; the translation is relatively close, even at time replicating the pointed word-order of the original, for example the parallel positioning of the two verbs *oriatur* and *puniatur* within their lines as 'rise' and 'grow', or the clause-opening phrase 'From the proud brothers', echoing *superbis fratribus*. Occasionally we find a change of metaphor or other looser rendering: *longum nefas/eat in nepotes* is intensified to 'let … long iniquity be heaped/Upon the children', while *certetur omni scelere et alterna uice/stringatur ensis* becomes 'let the sword try every crime,/And pass from hand to hand', modifying the verbs *certetur* and *stringatur* while clearly maintaining the general sense, *labet* ('totter') becomes the less subtle 'be brought to naught', and *regna excidant* becomes 'let the throne depart', changing the metaphor of 'dropping' the kingdom as something precious.[16]

B *Thyestes* 789–804 (the chorus react to the solar eclipse brought about by Atreus' monstrous crime):

Quo terrarum superumque potens,	Oh, whither, father of the earth and sky,
cuius ad ortus noctis opacae	Whose rising puts the glory of the night
decus omne fugit, quo uertis iter	To flight, oh, whither dost thou turn thy path
medioque diem perdis Olympo?	That light has fled at midday? Phoebus, why
cur, Phoebe, tuos rapis aspectus?	Hast thou withdrawn thy beams? The evening star,
nondum serae nuntius horae	The messenger of darkness, has not yet
nocturna uocat lumina Vesper,	Called forth the constellations of the night,
nondum Hesperiae flexura rotae	Nor yet the westward turning course commands
iubet emeritos soluere currus;	To free thy horses that have done their work,
nondum in noctem uergente die	The trumpet has not yet its third call given,
tertia misit bucina signum:	The signal of declining day, new night;
stupet ad subitae tempora cenae	The plowman is amazed at the swift fall
nondum fessis bubus arator.	Of supper-time, his oxen by the plow
Quid te aetherio pepulit cursu?	Are yet unwearied; from thy path in heaven,
quae causa tuos limite certo	What drives thee, O Apollo? What the cause
deiecit equos?	That forces from their wonted way thy steeds?

Here the translation picks up effectively the rhetorical repetitions which mark the dramatic moment of the original: 'oh, whither' renders *quo* twice, while the insistent *nondum*, repeated at the head of three different lines in Seneca, is elegantly redistributed in repetition by Harris to the beginning, middle and end of lines and varied in the middle occurrence ('not yet', 'Nor yet', 'not yet'), perhaps

---

[16] It is not inconceivable that Harris mistook *excidant* (certainly in Leo's text) for *excedant*: Seneca uses the latter verb in the sense of 'depart' twice in this play (249, 866).

an attempt to 'improve' the original which might have seemed unsubtle. On the other hand, 'plowman' and 'plow' introduces an unnecessary repetition not there in the original. Mild archaism is again present, again suggesting Shakespearean colour ('dost thou'), and there are some neat alliterative phrases which derive directly from the Bard himself ('declining day', 'wonted way').[17] In two places the version is loose: *medioque ... Olympo* is rendered 'midday' rather than 'in the middle of heaven', but since that position of the sun in the sky is parallel to the time-point of noon this is not misleading, while *tuos rapis aspectus* becomes 'withdrawn thy beams', perhaps avoiding the Christian-style personification for the pagan god's 'face'[18] rather than simply a mistranslation.

C *Thyestes* 995–1009 (dialogue between Atreus and Thyestes, revelation of Atreus' crime):

THY. *Quidquid est, fratri precor*	THY. Whate'er it is,
natisque parcat, omnis in uile hoc caput	I pray thee spare my sons, let all the storm
abeat procella. Redde iam natos mihi!	Break over my vile head. Give back my sons!
AT. *Reddam, et tibi illos nullus eripiet dies.*	AT. Yea, I will give them back, and never more
	Shalt thou be parted from them. [*Exit*]
[no marked break in Latin text]	
	SCENE IV [*Thyestes*]
THY. *Quis hic tumultus uiscera exagitat mea?*	THY. What distress
quid tremuit intus? sentio impatiens onus	Seizes my reins? Why shake my inmost parts?
meumque gemitu non meo pectus gemit.	I fear a burden that will forth, my breast
adeste, nati, genitor infelix uocat,	Groans with a groaning that is not my own.
adeste. Visis fugiet hic uobis dolor –	Come, children, your unhappy father calls;
unde obloquuntur?	Come, might I see you all this woe would flee.
	Whence come these voices?
[no marked break in Latin text]	SCENE V [*Atreus, Thyestes, slave with covered charger*]
AT. *Expedi amplexus, pater;*	AT. Father, spread wide thy arms, they come, they [come;
uenere. natos ecquid agnoscis tuos?	Dost thou indeed now recognise thy sons?
THY. *Agnosco fratrem. Sustines tantum nefas*	THY. I recognise my brother. Canst thou bear
gestare, Tellus? non ad infernam Styga	Such deeds, o earth? O Styx, wilt thou not break
tenebrasque mergis rupta et ingenti uia	Thy banks and whelm in everlasting night
ad chaos inane regna cum rege abripis?	Both king and kingdom, bearing them away
	By a dreadful path to chaos' awful void?

---

17 *Antony and Cleopatra* Act 5 Scene 1 (Octavian to Antony) 'I must perforce/Have shown to thee such a declining day', *Hamlet* Act 3 Scene 1 (Gertrude to Ophelia) 'So shall I hope your virtues/Will bring him to his wonted way again'.

18 Cf. e. g. KJV *Psalms* 13.1 'How long wilt thou forget me, O LORD? For ever? How long wilt thou hide thy face from me?'

In this climactic episode, Harris feels free to divide the text into short scenes not marked in the original, again in Shakespearean fashion. This changes the dramatic pace at times: the *antilabe* in line 1004, where Atreus finishes his brother's line with the wonderfully ironic encouragement to embrace his sons, is ignored and the two speeches are located in successive scenes; Harris chooses to reflect the dramatic moment by delay, where the original does it by sharp repartee. Conversely, Atreus' line 998 is a complete line in Seneca, but is incomplete in Harris, then being completed by Thyestes' reference to his digestive trouble, even though Harris has made Atreus exit mid-line. These choices suggest that Harris's scenes are formal insertions indicating where speakers and characters change or move rather than dramaturgical suggestions, and the complexities of working out how this episode might actually be staged are clear. In other modifications, Harris does seem to misinterpret lines 995–6, where Thyestes ironically prays that the threat of the storm be averted from his brother and sons (!); her 'I pray thee spare my sons' must be addressed to Atreus, whereas Thyestes' prayer is addressed more generally, and *parcat* refers to the storm and certainly not to Atreus who is indeed prayed for in the original (*fratri*). Stylistically, there is plenty of Shakespearean archaism at this dramatic moment,[19] and again Harris effectively renders key features of the original: the splendidly pointed *figura etymologica* at 1001 *meumque gemitu non meo pectus gemit* becomes the fine 'Groans with a groaning that is not my own', while the similar word-play *regna cum rege* (1009) becomes the neat 'Both king and kingdom'.

In sum, this is (for its time) a good and relatively faithful literary translation which tries to reflect in its diction Seneca's perceived affinity with and intellectual ancestry of Shakespeare, as one might expect of its author, a professor of English; it is at least as good as many early Loeb translations or Penguin Classics. Its literary modifications, the kind of features criticised by Summers as mistranslations, are at least in some cases arguably enhancements of the original, and are perhaps intended to make the text more attractive for a contemporary readership ('domesticating' rather than 'foreignising' in terms of translation theory), though it is indeed not always perfect in rendering the Latin. It merits our attention not just for its pioneering status as the first verse translation of Seneca's plays by a single hand, but also for its own intrinsic interest and qualities.

Jane Elder, Seneca: *Thyestes* (1982)

Jane Elder, a UK poet and teacher, studied Classics at Cambridge, and in the 1970s and early 1980s she worked on poetic versions of Seneca's *Hercules, Tro-*

---

[19] E.g. 'whelm', found at *Merry Wives of Windsor* Act 2 Scene 2, or 'reins' (= 'innards'), found at *Merry Wives of Windsor* Act 3 Scene 5.

ades and *Phaedra*.[20] These remain unpublished, but her version of *Thyestes* won the EEC Translation Competition in 1979–80 and was published by the then emerging poetry house Carcanet in 1982.[21] The play as published has no introduction, but a summary of the myth and a list of characters; as in the case of Harris' version, there is no sign of its being written for stage performance or of subsequent stage production, though it was produced on BBC radio in the year of its publication.[22]

Sample passages

A *Thyestes* 23–36 (the Fury reacts to the prologue-speech by the ghost of Tantalus):

FVRIA: *Perge, detestabilis*
umbra, et penates impios furiis age.
certetur omni scelere et alterna uice
stringatur ensis; nec sit irarum modus
pudorue, mentes caecus instiget furor,
rabies parentum duret et longum nefas
eat in nepotes; nec uacet cuiquam uetus
odisse crimen: semper oriatur nouum,
nec unum in uno, dumque punitur scelus,
crescat. Superbis fratribus regna excidant
repetantque profugos; dubia uiolentae domus
fortuna reges inter incertos labet;
miser ex potente fiat, ex misero potens,
fluctuque regnum casus assiduo ferat.

Go on, accursed   shadow
Drive your household even its gods too mad
let them compete in every crime let alternate
swords be drawn let there be no end to anger
no sense of shame let blind madness goad their
                                                                    hearts
the insanity of the fathers last become fixed
be passed down   a long line of wrong doing
in children and grandchildren let there never be
                                                                  leisure
for anyone to grow tired of old sins come to hate
                                                                    them
let new evil always be growing and not one
                                                              evil alone
but many in each one while the last is being
                                                      punished let
the next come
may the kingdoms fall out of the proud brothers'
                                                                    hands
may each in turn summon exiles home
may the changing fortunes of a violent house slip
                                                          totter among
insecure kings fall at last from power to misery
from misery to power may continual waves of
                                                chance carry the
realm away

---

20 According to the back cover of Elder 1982.
21 For Carcanet's history see http://www.carcanet.co.uk (accessed 6.10.2014).
22 See the data at http://www.apgrd.ox.ac.uk/productions/production/6696 (accessed 8.10.2014). For the context of classical plays performed on BBC radio in this period see Wrigley 2007.

The format of Elder's translation is clearly influenced by Ted Hughes' well-known 1968 version of Seneca's *Oedipus*,[23] using free form, short lines, breaks within lines, and showing no formal punctuation; this is not surprising as Hughes was by then one of the UK's leading poets, soon to become Poet Laureate (1984). The version is very close to the Latin, reflecting the author's classical education: 'shadow' renders *umbra* very literally, while 'alternate' clearly picks up *alterna* and *excidant* (contrast Harris) is closely translated as 'fall out of', *labet* doubly closely rendered as 'slip' and 'totter'. Some attention is paid to the original word order: thus 'swords be drawn' is placed at the start of its line like *stringatur ensis* (26); some original effects of style are reproduced in a different way, so that the multiple insistent Latin subjunctives of 25–36 (thirteen) are mirrored in the repetition of the modal elements 'let' (seven times) and 'may' (four times, three of them emphatically at the start of lines). The lexicon is modern but dignified, with no sign of colloquial elements.

B *Thyestes* 789–804 (the chorus react to the solar eclipse brought about by Atreus' monstrous crime):

CHORVS:
Quo terrarum superumque potens,
cuius ad ortus noctis opacae
decus omne fugit, quo uertis iter
medioque diem perdis Olympo?
cur, Phoebe, tuos rapis aspectus?

nondum serae nuntius horae
nocturna uocat lumina Vesper,
nondum Hesperiae flexura rotae
iubet emeritos soluere currus;
nondum in noctem uergente die
tertia misit bucina signum:
stupet ad subitae tempora cenae
nondum fessis bubus arator.
Quid te aetherio pepulit cursu?
quae causa tuos limite certo
deiecit equos?

Where
    Father of earth and sky
where have you gone
    you rise up and
    all glories of the night recede

why in midheaven
why
why destroy the day
    why wrench your face away,
Sun
not yet
    the Evening Star
        twilight's messenger
does not yet summon
    the fires of night
not yet
    the turning of your western wheel
does not yet give release
    to your tired team

---

[23] For this play see e. g. Harrison 2009, 152–8, Talbot 2009, Fleming 2013, Stead 2013, and the preceding chapter by Mayer in this volume.

                    their task completed   done
                    not yet as day turns towards dark
                                does the third trumpet sound
                                give the rest signal
                    the ploughman stands amazed
                                at supper-time's approach
                                                      too quick
                    his oxen not yet weary
                    what has driven you
                                from your course in heaven
                    what hurled your horses
                                aside from their fixed track

The use of short lines here slightly disguises the closeness of the translation to the Latin text; one mild exception is 'all glories of the night recede', which might owe something to the opening line of W. B. Yeats' 'Byzantium', 'The unpurged images of day recede' (this would explain the introduction of the plural and the choice of this verb at line-end). Again key rhetorical features of the original are successfully picked up: the triple initial *nondum* is echoed by the quadruple 'not yet', while the double *quo* (one in initial position) perhaps suggests the quadruple initial 'why'. There is also some elegant alliteration ('tired team', 'hurled your horses').

C *Thyestes* 995–1009 (dialogue between Atreus and Thyestes, revelation of Atreus' crime):

THY. *Quidquid est, fratri precor natisque parcat, omnis in uile hoc caput abeat procella. Redde iam natos mihi!*	THY. whatever this is may it spare
	my brother my sons
	                              let the whole storm
	break on my worthless head
	                              give back my sons

ATR.*reddam, et tibi illos nullus eripiet dies.*	ATR. I shall give them back no day shall tear them from you

THY. *Quis hic tumultus uiscera exagitat mea? quid tremuit intus? sentio impatiens onus meumque gemitu non meo pectus gemit. adeste, nati, genitor infelix uocat, adeste. Visis fugiet hic uobis dolor - unde obloquuntur?*	THY. what tumult what disturbance
	in my body here in my entrails
	what trembles in me
	                              I feel
	          a protesting burden my breast groans
	a groan that is not mine
	come my sons your ill-fated father calls you
	come this pain will end with your sight
	where are their voices
	                              I hear them
	                              they reproach me

AT. *Expedi amplexus, pater;*   AT.   Open your arms embrace them
uenere. natos ecquid agnoscis tuos?   you father
                                                        you recognise your sons?
                                                [*shows heads*]

THYESTES: *Agnosco fratrem. Sustines tantum nefas*   THY.I recognise
gestare, Tellus? non ad infernam Styga   my brother
tenebrasque mergis rupta et ingenti uia   O earth
ad chaos inane regna cum rege abripis?   can you endure
                                                        to bear so great a crime
                                                why don't you break   split open
                                                plunge down to hell the darkness
                                                make a huge road to the void to
                                                                            chaos
                                                for this kingdom for this king

Again the shorter lines conceal a close translation, with some especially faithful renderings of Seneca's epithets and metaphors (*vile*/'worthless', *tumultus*/'tumult'), of the *figura etymologica* of *gemitu ... gemit* ('my breast groans/a groan that is not mine', of the word-play *regna cum rege* ('for this kingdom for this king), and of the repetition *adeste ... adeste* ('come ... come', likewise both times in line-initial position). On the other hand, Elder dwells on and expands the tragic/grotesque moment where Thyestes appears to hear the voices of his sons: *unde obloquuntur?* becomes 'where are their voices/I hear them/they reproach me'; her translation of the verb is more attractive than the usual 'break in' or 'interrupt',[24] since Thyestes' children might well reproach their father for having eaten them, even if unawares (the irony would be fully Senecan).

In sum, this is a close and effective translation which is heavily influenced by the 1960s idiom for Seneca notably used by Hughes, modern but elevated and not colloquial; it is interesting that it like Hughes' version was performed on BBC radio, for which it (like Seneca's plays generally) is well suited. The author's good knowledge of Latin allows her to produce faithful renderings of the original, but without sacrificing interesting poetic and literary effects. It is to be regretted that her other Senecan versions did not reach publication.

---

24 Tarrant 1985 and Fitch 2004 respectively.

Caryl Churchill, *Seneca: Thyestes* (1994)

Caryl Churchill (b. 1938) is an English radical dramatist well known for hard-hitting plays on social issues, e. g. *Top Girls* (1982) on the heavy price of female success in the male-dominated environment of business, and *Serious Money* (1987), a verse satire on excesses in the London financial world; her most recent play (*Light Shining in Buckinghamshire*, 2015, National Theatre, London) is a historical drama on the English Civil War.[25] Her translation of *Thyestes* was produced at the Royal Court Theatre, London, in 1994; her only other direct translation amongst her more than thirty plays for the stage is her version of August Strindberg's *A Dream Play*, for the National Theatre in London in 2005, though in 1986 she collaborated with David Lan in *A Mouthful of Birds*, a play which owes something to Euripides' *Bacchae*. Her introduction to *Thyestes*[26] recounts how she was moved to translate the play by her experience of Ariane Mnouchkine's famous production of *Les Atrides* in Bradford in 1992,[27] which made her wonder whether there were Greek dramas which dealt with the origin of the feud in the House of Atreus there depicted: this led her to Seneca's Latin *Thyestes*, the only surviving ancient drama concerning this back-story.

In her introduction she also says that she had some Latin and worked from the already-mentioned Loeb prose translation of F. J. Miller (1917); she mentions the Elizabethan verse translations of Jasper Heywood and others and the links of Seneca and Shakespeare, which had made her expect Seneca to be grandiloquent, but on closer acquaintance 'I began to feel that he [Seneca] was far blunter, subtler and faster than I'd thought'.[28] This is the only one of the three versions considered here to be explicitly composed for the stage and by an established playwright. This clearly connects with Churchill's choice of shorter verse lines (often five and six syllables) to maintain dramatic pace. The general format of her translation seems again to be influenced by that of Ted Hughes, using free short lines and little punctuation; interestingly, she counted syllables and not stresses, thus in fact returning to Latin quantitative metre rather than employing the English dramatic tradition of accentual verse.[29]

---

[25] For key reference works on Churchill and her work cf. Aston and Diamond 2009 and Gobert 2014.
[26] See Churchill 1995, vii.
[27] For some orientation see Judet de la Combe 2005.
[28] Churchill 1995, vii-viii.
[29] Churchill 1995, viii.

A Thyestes 23–36 (Fury, speech)

FVRIA: *Perge, detestabilis*	Go on, detestable
umbra, et penates impios furiis age.	ghost, drive your gods mad.
certetur omni scelere et alterna uice	Let's have a wickedness
stringatur ensis; nec sit irarum modus	competition, swords
pudorue, mentes caecus instiget furor,	out in every street, no
rabies parentum duret et longum nefas	embarrassment at
eat in nepotes; nec uacet cuiquam uetus	being very angry –
odisse crimen: semper oriatur nouum,	blind fury. Then let
nec unum in uno, dumque punitur scelus,	rage harden and the long
crescat. Superbis fratribus regna excidant	wrong go into the
repetantque profugos; dubia uiolentae domus	grandchildren. No time for
fortuna reges inter incertos labet;	anyone to hate
miser ex potente fiat, ex misero potens,	old crimes because here come
fluctuque regnum casus assiduo ferat.	plenty of new ones

        and the punishments are
        even more wicked.
        whichever brother is
        triumphant will lose
        the kingdom, the exile
        get back in. Fortune
        will totter back and forth
        between them, power
follow misery and
        misery power
and waves of disaster
        batter the kingdom.

This version adds to the dramatic pace of its short metrical units (already noted) some colloquial expressions which likewise make it a lively piece for the modern stage ('Let's have a wickedness competition', 'Here come plenty of new ones'); similar in purpose is 'swords out in every street', with 'every street' not in the original but stressing violence in an urban landscape suitable to a modern metropolitan audience, while there is some expansion to make Seneca's terse and pointed style easier to understand aurally (e. g. adding 'whichever brother is triumphant'. At the same time, striking expressions in the original are closely reproduced: *detestabilis umbra* ~ 'detestable ghost', *longum nefas* ~ 'long wrong'.

B Thyestes 789–804 (Chorus, lyric)

CHORVS:	
Quo terrarum superumque potens,	Sun, where have you gone?
cuius ad ortus noctis opacae	how could you get lost
decus omne fugit, quo uertis iter	half way through the sky?

medioque diem perdis Olympo?
cur, Phoebe, tuos rapis aspectus?
nondum serae nuntius horae
nocturna uocat lumina Vesper,
nondum Hesperiae flexura rotae
iubet emeritos soluere currus;
nondum in noctem uergente die
tertia misit bucina signum:
stupet ad subitae tempora cenae
nondum fessis bubus arator.
Quid te aetherio pepulit cursu?
quae causa tuos limite certo
deiecit equos?

    The evening star's not here yet,
the chariot hasn't turned in the west
        and freed the horses,
the ploughman whose oxen still aren't tired
can't believe it's suppertime.

The key feature here is the abbreviation and simplification of Seneca's original, expressing the dramatic instant of the solar eclipse in a rapid reaction from the chorus; where the original builds up a series of time-indications, Churchill shortens the moment in a way which communicates effectively to the audience, halving the number of lines and using lively colloquial language ('how could you get lost', 'the ploughman whose oxen still aren't tired | can't believe it's suppertime'). This creates something of a piquant contrast between the drama of the moment and its homely reception by the chorus.

    C *Thyestes* 995–1009 (Atreus/Thyestes, dialogue)

THYESTES:
... Quidquid est, fratri precor
natisque parcat, omnis in uile hoc caput
abeat procella. Redde iam natos mihi!
ATREVS: Reddam, et tibi illos nullus eripiet dies.

    THY. Whatever it is
    I pray it spares my
    brother and children
and that the whole storm breaks
        on this vile head. Now
        give me back my sons.
        ATR. I'll give you them and
        the day shall never come
        to take them away.

THYESTES: *Quis hic tumultus uiscera exagitat mea?*
quid tremuit intus? sentio impatiens onus
meumque gemitu non meo pectus gemit.
adeste, nati, genitor infelix uocat,
adeste. Visis fugiet hic uobis dolor -
unde obloquuntur?

THY. What's this uproar churning
my stomach? What's this
shaking inside? I can't
    bear the load I feel
and my chest groans with a
    groaning that's not mine.
    Children, come here, your
    unhappy father's
    calling you, come here. This

	pain will go when I see your faces. Do I hear their voices? Where?
ATREVS: *Expedi amplexus, pater;* *uenere. natos ecquid agnoscis tuos?* THYESTES: *Agnosco fratrem. Sustines tantum nefas* *gestare, Tellus? non ad infernam Styga*	ATR. Open your arms, father they're coming now. Do you by any chance recognise your sons?
tenebrasque mergis rupta et ingenti uia *ad chaos inane regna cum rege abripis?*	[shows heads] THY. I recognise my brother. Earth how can you bear all this evil? Aren't you bursting open and plunging to the underworld and snatching kingdom and king down a vast road to chaos?

By contrast with the last extract, Churchill's rendering of this climactic scene sticks relatively closely to Seneca's original and has little colloquial colour (only the heavily ironic 'Do you by any chance | recognise your sons?', where the familiar tone creates an effective frisson at this moment of horror): some expressions are carefully reproduced (e. g. 'vile head' ~ *uile caput*), and in particular Churchill follows Seneca's insistent rhetoric, his repetitions (e. g. 'What's … What's' ~ *quis … quid*, 'come here … come here' ~ *adeste … adeste*), his use of the *figura etymologica* ('and my chest groans with a | groaning that's not mine' ~ *meumque gemitu non meo pectus gemit*, and 'kingdom and king', ~ *regna cum rege*), and his pair of insistent rhetorical questions in the passage's final lines, bolstered with an additional verbal ornament of three rather than two continuative present tenses ('bursting … plunging … snatching' ~ *rupta … mergis … abripis*). The drama of the key moment is effectively expressed in a dignified but vivid idiom aimed at gripping a theatrical audience.

In sum, this version naturally shows features which reflect its writing for the stage; like Elder's version, it is probably influenced by Ted Hughes' *Oedipus*, written and performed for the London stage at a time when Churchill was a London-based emerging dramatist writing for radio.[30] Though it naturally adapts Seneca's material for stage purposes (e. g. by abbreviation and greater colloquialism), as Churchill's introduction shows she appreciates the pointed nature of Seneca's verbal style and often reproduces its effects closely in her lexical and syntactic choices. The result is a version of real impact which is overdue for a stage revival.

---

30 For her early career see Aston and Diamond 2009, 3.

Conclusion

Women have played a full role in the revival of Senecan tragedy in the twentieth century:[31] the relative neglect of Seneca's dramas in the nineteenth century means that they have emerged into greater popularity at a time when women too have emerged into greater prominence in academic research, poetry and drama. Each of these texts shows the mark of its own particular context: Harris' translation is at least partly driven by her own role as an academic literary historian of her time and by her interest in Shakespeare as a scholar of English literature, while Elder reflects the taste and environment of her era of UK poetry, especially the idiom of Ted Hughes' version of Seneca's *Oedipus*. Neither of these versions is written for the stage, though Elder's was performed on radio; both stick relatively closely to Seneca's text and are by authors who are comfortable in translating Latin. Churchill's stage version clearly shows its function in its concern with making Seneca's text work as a drama for an audience, modifying some elements with this in mind; though Churchill is less of a Latinist than the other two writers, she is interestingly aware of the nature of Seneca's Latin style and exploits some of its key elements. All these versions are worth scholarly scrutiny and point to important elements in Seneca's tragedies as well as in their reception.

Bibliography

Aston, E. and Diamond, E. (eds.) (2009), *The Cambridge Companion to Caryl Churchill*, Cambridge.
Churchill, C. (1995), *Lucius Annaeus Seneca: Thyestes*, London.
Corwin, M. T. (1920), *Alumnæ, Graduate school, Yale University, 1894–1920*, New Haven.
Judet de la Combe, P. (2005), 'Ariane Mnouchkine and the History of the French Agamemnon', in: F. Macintosh, P. Michelakis, E. Hall and O. Taplin (eds.), *Agamemnon in Performance 458 BC to AD 2004*, Oxford, 273–89.
Elder, J. (1982), *Seneca: Thyestes*, Ashington.
Fantham, R. E. (1985), *Seneca's Troades*, Princeton.
Fitch, J. G. (2004), *Seneca: Tragedies* [2 vols], Cambridge, Ma.
Fleming, K. (2013), '"For everyone must answer the Sphinx": Ted Hughes' Translation of Seneca's *Oedipus*', in: Fleming and Grant, 105–21.
Fleming, K. and Grant, T. (eds.) (2013), *Seneca in the English Tradition* [special issue of *The Canadian Review of Comparative Literature* 40.1], Edmonton.

---

[31] This is true in scholarship as well as translation: see e.g. Fantham 1982, Henry and Henry 1985, Frank 1995.

Frank, M. (1995), *Seneca: Phoenissae*, Leiden.
Goad, C. M. (1898), *Horace in the English Literature of the Eighteenth Century*, New Haven.
Gobert, R. D. (2014), *The theatre of Caryl Churchill*, London.
Hallett, J. P. (2013), 'Investigating Women's Engagement with Graeco-Roman Antiquity, and Expanding the Circle of Classicists', in: L. Hardwick and S. J. Harrison (eds.), *Classics in the Modern World: A 'Democratic Turn'?*, Oxford, 131–40.
Harris, E. I. (1904), *The Tragedies of Seneca Rendered into English Verse*, London/New York.
―――― (2011), *The Tragedies of Seneca Rendered into English Verse*, Digireads (n. l.).
Harrison, S. J. (2009), 'Modern Versions of Senecan Tragedy', *Trends in Classics* 1, 148–70.
Henry, D. and Henry, E. (1985), *The Mask of Power: Seneca's Tragedies and Imperial Rome*, Warminster.
Leo, F. (1878), *L. Annaei Senecae Tragoediae*, Berlin.
Miller, F. J. (1907), *The Tragedies of Seneca, translated into English verse*, Chicago.
―――― (1917), *Seneca's Tragedies* [2 vols], London/Cambridge, Ma.
Osgood, C. G. (1905), review of Harris (1904), *AJP* 26, 343–6.
Share, D. (ed.) (1998), *Seneca in English*, Harmondsworth.
Stead, H. (2013), 'Seneca's *Oedipus*: By Hook or By Crook', in: Fleming and Grant, 88–104.
Summers, W. C. (1905), review of Harris (1904), *Classical Review* 19, 124–5.
―――― (1920), *The Silver Age of Latin Literature*, London.
Talbot, J. (2009), 'Eliot's Seneca, Ted Hughes' *Oedipus*', in: R. Rees (ed.), *Ted Hughes and the Classics*, Oxford, 62–80.
Tarrant, R. J. (1985), *Seneca's* Thyestes, Atalanta, Ga.
Wrigley, A. (2007), 'Stages of Imagination: Greek Plays on BBC Radio', in: C. Stray (ed.), *Remaking the Classics: Literature, Genre and Media in Britain, 1800–2000*, London, 57–73.

Notes on Contributors

Theodoros Antoniadis is Lecturer in Latin Literature at the Aristotle University of Thessaloniki. His doctoral dissertation *The Rhetoric of Belatedness: A Running Commentary on Ovid's Amores* (Thessaloniki, 2009) as well as a translation of Lucretius' *De Rerum Natura* have been published in Greek. He has also written various articles on Latin elegy, Senecan tragedy and Petronius' *Satyricon*. His current research focuses primarily on Flavian epic.

Antony Augoustakis is Professor of Classics at the University of Illinois (Urbana-Champaign, USA), Editor of *Illinois Classical Studies* and the College of Liberal Arts and Sciences Centennial Scholar. He is the author of *Statius, Thebaid 8* (Oxford, 2016), *Motherhood and the Other: Fashioning Female Power in Flavian Epic* (Oxford, 2010) and *Plautus' Mercator* (Bryn Mawr, 2009). He has edited *Brill's Companion to Silius Italicus* (Leiden, 2010), *Ritual and Religion in Flavian Epic* (Oxford, 2013), *Flavian Poetry and its Greek Past* (Leiden, 2014), *Oxford Readings in Flavian Epic* (Oxford, 2016), and co-edited with Carole Newlands *Statius' Siluae and the Poetics of Intimacy* (Arethusa, 2007) and with Ariana Traill the *Blackwell Companion to Terence* (Malden, MA, 2013). He is currently working on a monograph on *Death, Burial and Ritual in Flavian Epic* and a commentary on Silius Italicus' *Punica* 3 and pseudo-Seneca's *Hercules Oetaeus*.

Ruth Rothaus Caston is Associate Professor of Classical Studies at the University of Michigan. She has research interests in Augustan poetry, Roman comedy, Roman satire and ancient theories of the passions. She has published a book on jealousy in Roman Elegy (*The Elegiac Passion: Jealousy in Roman Love Elegy*, Oxford 2012) and is currently writing a monograph on Terence.

David Christenson is Professor of Classics at the University of Arizona. His main publications include an edition and commentary of Plautus' *Amphitruo* (Cambridge, 2000) and *Hysterical Laughter: Four Ancient Comedies about Women* (Oxford, 2014). He has published articles and chapters on Plautus and Terence, as well as other authors.

Catherine Connors is Professor of Classics at the University of Washington, Seattle, and is the author of *Petronius the Poet: Verse and Literary Tradition in the Satyricon* (Cambridge, 1998). Her current research focuses especially on representations of nature and geography in Roman and Greek literature.

Martin T. Dinter is Lecturer in Latin Literature and Language at King's College London. He is author of *Anatomizing Civil War – Studies in Lucan's Epic Technique* (Michigan, 2012) as well as co-editor of *A Companion to the Neronian Age* (Malden, 2013). He has published articles on Virgil, Horace, Lucan, Seneca and Flavian epic and is currently preparing a book-length study on Cato the Elder in literature as FAPESP research fellow at the University of Sao Paulo (USP), Brazil, as well as co-editing volumes on Seneca the Elder, Quintilian and Calpurnius Flaccus.

Dorota Dutsch is Associate Professor of Classics at the University of California, Santa Barbara. She is the author of *On Echoes and Voices: Feminine Discourse in Roman Comedy* (Oxford, 2008), co-editor with Sharon James and David Konstan of *Women in Roman Republican Drama* (Madison, 2015), with Ann Suter, of *Ancient Obscenities* (Ann Arbor, 2015), and with Mary Bachvarova and Ann Suter of *The Fall of Cities: Commemoration in Literature, Folksong and Liturgy* (forthcoming).

Michael Fontaine is Associate Professor of Classics and Associate Dean of the Faculty at Cornell University. He is the author of *Joannes Burmeister:* Aululario *and Other Inversions of Plautus* in the *Bibliotheca Latinitatis Novae* (Leuven, 2015) and co-editor of the *Oxford Handbook of Greek and Roman Comedy* (Oxford, 2014).

Stavros Frangoulidis is Professor of Latin at the Aristotle University of Thessaloniki. He has written articles on the Latin novel, Roman comedy and Senecan tragedy. He co-edited, with Stephen Harrison, *Narrative, Culture, and Genre in the Ancient Novel* (*Trends in Classics* 4.2, Berlin, 2012) and, with Theodore Papanghelis and Stephen Harrison, the *Generic Interfaces in Latin Literature* (Berlin, 2013). His books include: *Handlung und Nebenhandlung: Theater, Metatheater und Gattungsbewusstsein in der römischen Komödie* (Stuttgart, 1997); *Roles and Performances in Apuleius' Metamorphoses* (Stuttgart, 2001); and *Witches, Isis and Narrative: Approaches to Magic in Apuleius' Metamorphoses* (Berlin and New York, 2008).

T. H. M. Gellar-Goad is Assistant Professor of Classical Languages at Wake Forest University. His research focuses on ancient humor in Menander, Roman comedy and elegy, and Lucretius and Roman satire. In 2012 he served as composer-in-residence for the National Endowment for the Humanities Institute 'The Performance of Roman Comedy'.

Robert Germany is Assistant Professor of Classics at Haverford College. He has published work on Greek New and Roman Comedy and is currently at work on a monograph on the Unity of Time in ancient and early modern theater.

Lauren Donovan Ginsberg is Assistant Professor of Classics at the University of Cincinnati. Her work focuses on the interaction between Roman Imperial drama, epic and historiography from the perspective of intertextuality and cultural memory studies. She is especially interested in how Roman literature commemorates episodes of political strife and civil war. In addition to smaller projects on Seneca, Roman historical drama, Lucan and Tacitus, she is currently working on a monograph-length study of the anonymous historical drama *Octavia*.

Emily Gowers is Reader in Latin Literature at the University of Cambridge and Fellow of St John's College. She is author of *The Loaded Table: Representations of Food in Roman Literature* (Oxford, 1993) and *Horace: Satires I* (Cambridge, 2012) and co-editor (with William Fitzgerald) of *Ennius Perennis: The Annals and Beyond* (Cambridge, 2007).

Stephen Harrison is Professor of Latin Literature at the University of Oxford and Fellow and Tutor in Classics at Corpus Christi College. He has written widely on Horace, Vergil and the Roman novel, is the editor *of Living Classics: Greece and Rome in Contemporary Poetry in English* (Oxford, 2009) and co-editor of *Louis MacNeice: The Classical Radio Plays* (Oxford, 2013), and has contributed to the *Oxford History of Classical Reception in English Literature* on the nineteenth and twentieth centuries.

Richard Hunter is Regius Professor of Greek at the University of Cambridge and a Fellow of Trinity College. His most recent books include *Critical Moments in Classical Literature* (Cambridge, 2009), (with D. Russell) *Plutarch, How to Study Poetry (De audiendis poetis)* (Cambridge, 2011), *Plato and the Traditions of Ancient Literature* (Cambridge, 2012), *Hesiodic Voices: Studies in the Ancient Reception of Hesiod's Works and Days* (Cambridge, 2014) and *Apollonius of Rhodes, Argonautica IV* (Cambridge, 2015). Many of his essays have been collected in *On Coming After: Studies in Post-Classical Greek Literature and its Reception* (Berlin, 2008).

Evangelos Karakasis is Associate Professor of Latin at the University of Ioannina. He is the author of the following monographs: *Terence and the Language of Roman Comedy* (Cambridge, 2005, 2008), *Song Exchange in Roman Pastoral* (Berlin, 2011) and *Calpurnius Siculus: a Neronian Poet in Rome* (forthcoming with *Trends in Classics*, 2016) as well as of several papers on Roman comedy, pastoral, elegy/lyric poetry, epic and reception. He is also the editor of *Singing in the Shadow ... Pastoral Encounters in Post-Vergilian Poetry* (*Trends in Classics* 4.1, Berlin, 2012) and, with I. N. Perysinakis, of *Plautine Trends: Studies in Plautine Comedy and its Reception* (Berlin, 2015).

David Konstan is Professor of Classics at New York University. Among his publications are *Roman Comedy* (Ithaca, NY, 1983); *Sexual Symmetry: Love in the Ancient Novel and Related Genres* (Princeton, 1994); *Greek Comedy and Ideology* (Oxford, 1995); *Friendship in the Classical World* (Cambridge, 1997); *The Emotions of the Ancient Greeks: Studies in Aristotle and Classical Literature* (Toronto, 2006); *"A Life Worthy of the Gods": The Materialist Psychology of Epicurus* (Las Vegas, 2008); *Before Forgiveness: The Origins of a Moral Idea* (Cambridge, 2010); and *Beauty: The Fortunes of an Ancient Greek Idea* (New York, 2014). He has recently co-edited *Ancient Forgiveness* (Cambridge, 2012); *The Philosophizing Muse: The Influence of Greek Philosophy on Roman Poetry* (Newcastle upon Tyne, 2014); *Combat Trauma and the Ancient Greeks* (New York, 2014); and *Women in Roman Republican Drama* (Madison, 2015). He is a past president of the American Philological Association and a Fellow of the American Academy of Arts and Sciences and of the Australian Academy of the Humanities.

Ioannis M. Konstantakos studied Classics at the universities of Athens and Cambridge and is now Associate Professor of Ancient Greek Literature at the National and Kapodistrian University of Athens. His scholarly interests include ancient comedy, ancient narrative, folklore and the relations between Greek and Near-Eastern literatures and cultures. He has published four books and numerous articles on these topics. He has received scholarships from the Greek State Scholarships Foundation and the «Alexander S. Onassis» Public Benefit Foundation. In 2009 he was awarded the prize of the Academy of Athens for the best classical monograph published within the previous five years. In 2012 he was a finalist for the Greek state prize for critical essay.

Cedric Littlewood is Associate Professor at the University of Victoria, British Columbia. He is the author of articles, chapters and a book on Senecan tragedy, *Self-representation and Illusion in Senecan tragedy* (Oxford, 2004), but has also written on Persius, Juvenal and Lucan.

Gesine Manuwald is Professor of Latin at University College London. Her research interests cover Roman drama, Roman epic, Roman oratory and the reception of classical literature, especially in Neo-Latin poetry. Her publications include editions and monographs on Roman Republican drama, Ennius, Pacuvius and the genre of *fabula praetexta*.

C. W. Marshall is Professor of Greek at the University of British Columbia (Vancouver, Canada). He has published widely on ancient performance in Greece and Rome and modern popular culture, including comics and television. His books include *The Stagecraft and Performance of Roman Comedy* (Cambridge, 2006) and *The Structure and Performance of Euripides' Helen* (Cambridge, 2014).

Roland Mayer is Professor of Classics at King's College London. His scholarship has been focused on the literature of the early principate and on its reception in the Renaissance and the modern day.

Kathleen McCarthy is Associate Professor of Classics at the University of California, Berkeley. She is the author of *Slaves, Masters and the Art of Authority in Plautine Comedy* (Princeton, 2000).

Timothy J. Moore is the John and Penelope Biggs Distinguished Professor of Classics at Washington University in St. Louis. His primary scholarly interests are ancient Greek and Roman music, Latin literature and the history of dramatic comedy. His publications include *Artistry and Ideology: Livy's Vocabulary of Virtue* (Frankfurt, 1989), *The Theater of Plautus: Playing to the Audience* (Austin, 1998), *Music in Roman Comedy* (Cambridge, 2012), *Roman Theatre* (Cambridge, 2012), *Form and Meaning in Latin Drama* (ed., with Wolfgang Polleichtner, Trier, 2013), a translation of Terence's *Phormio*, and articles on Latin literature, the teaching of Greek and Latin, ancient music, American Musical Theatre and Japanese comedy.

Sophia Papaioannou is Associate Professor of Latin Literature at the National and Kapodistrian University of Athens. Her main research interests and publications are in the Literature of the Age of Augustus, ancient epic and Roman comedy. Her most recent book, *Terence and Interpretation* (Newcastle upon Tyne, 2014), is a collection of interpretive essays on Terence and the reception of Terence. She is currently preparing a book on the reception of Homeric orality in Vergil's *Aeneid*, a commentary on Plautus' *Curculio* and several articles on Latin epic, Roman comedy and Roman historiography.

Katerina Philippides is Lecturer in Roman drama at the Department of Theater Studies, University of Patras. She has published articles on Roman comedy and tragedy and also on Greek and Roman lyric poetry. She is currently working on a Greek translation and commentary of Plautus' *Mostellaria*.

Amy Richlin is Professor of Classics at UCLA. She has published widely on the history of sexuality and on Roman satire; her recent work includes articles on Plautus, and she has a book forthcoming from Cambridge University Press with the working title *Slave Theater in the Roman Republic*.

Alessandro Schiesaro is Professor of Latin Literature and Director of the School for Advanced Studies at Sapienza University of Rome. He has published especially on Lucretius, Virgil, Ovid and Seneca, including most recently *The Cambridge Companion to Seneca* (2015, co-edited with S. Bartsch).

Alison Sharrock is Professor of Classics at the University of Manchester. She is the author of *Reading Roman Comedy: Poetics and Playfulness in Plautus and Terence* (Cambridge, 2009) and of numerous papers on Roman comedy.

Niall W. Slater is the Samuel Candler Dobbs Professor of Latin and Greek at Emory University (Atlanta, Georgia). He focuses on ancient theatre and its production conditions, prose fiction and popular reception of classical literature. His books include *Spectator Politics: Metatheatre and Performance in Aristophanes* (Philadelphia, 2002); *Reading Petronius* (Baltimore, 1990); and *Plautus in Performance: The Theatre of the Mind* (Princeton, 1985; 2nd revised edition, 2000), as well as translations for *The Birth of Comedy* (ed. J. R. Rusten, Baltimore, 2011) and the *Bloomsbury Companion to Euripides' Alcestis* (London, 2013). Current work includes studies of Harley Granville Barker's productions of Greek tragedy and classical memories in C. S. Lewis's children's books.

Mario Telò is Associate Professor of Classics at the University of California, Los Angeles. He is the author of *Eupolidis Demi* (Florence, 2007) and *Aristophanes and the Cloak of Comedy: Affect, Aesthetics and the Canon* (forthcoming from the University of Chicago Press) as well as co-editor (with Emmanuela Bakola and Lucia Prauscello) of *Greek Comedy and the Discourse of Genre* (Cambridge, 2013).

Christopher Trinacty is Assistant Professor of Classics at Oberlin College. He is the author of *Senecan Tragedy and the Reception of Augustan Poetry* (Oxford, 2014) and articles on Seneca, Horace and Propertius. Currently he is co-editing a collection of essays on Senecan poetics for *Ramus* as well as beginning work on a commentary on Book 3 of Seneca's *Naturales Quaestiones*. His research interests include all things Senecan, Greek and Roman tragedy and Lucretius.

Bernhard Zimmermann is Professor of Classics at the Albert-Ludwigs-University of Freiburg. His research focuses particularly on ancient drama. He is the editor of several academic series, including the 'Handbuch der Altertumswissenschaft'.

General Index

A. Atilius Calatinus 282
abandoned child 276–7, 279, 284
Accius
– the tragic poet 342, 348–9, 352–7
– *Atreus* 556–9
– *Clytemestra* 397
accompaniment
– in Roman theatre 345–6, 354–5, 359
Achilles 348, 352
actor(s)/*grex* 206, 208–13, 215–16, 222–7
adulescens 254–5, 257–8, 260
adultery/adulterous 563–4
aemulatio 384, 389, 392
Aeneas 514, 522
Aerope 564, 566
Aeschylus 37
Aeson 534–6, 540, 542–7, 549–51
Aesopic fables 156–61
Aesopus 345
aesthetics
– of deviation 518
affect 312–14
Agamemnon
– death of 400–4
– dramatic tradition before Seneca 396–7
– king of Mycenae/Argos 395–407
Agathon 569
agnoia 208, 210, 212–13
agon 354
Ajax 348–9
Alcaeus 38
Alcesimarchus 278–9, 305–10, 312
Alcesimus 280
Alcibiades 559
Alcimede 534–5, 544, 546–7
Alcydonia 284
Alexander the Great 67–72, 81, 84, 88, 90, 92
Althaea 352
Ambrosian palimpsest 253
anagnorisis 350
ancient drama
– media of reception 453, 467
ancilla 511–13, 515, 519–21, 524–5

Andromache 345, 351
anger 439, 443–5
Anna 514, 522
Antiope 345
Antiphanes 14, 80–2, 85
anus 512
Appius Claudius Caecus 270
arcana 561–2, 566, 569
architecture 269
architectus 99, 103–5, 107–9, 113–16, 121–2
Arcturus 276–7
Argo 373–6
Argyrippus 253–61
aristocracy 98, 100
Aristophanes
– the comic playwright 13–14, 67, 80
– *Acharnians* 74
Aristotle
– *Poetics* 34
armarium 457–8
Artemona 494–5
Asinius Pollio 355
askoliasmos 33
Atalanta 349
Athenaeus 67–8, 72, 83–8, 90–2
Athens 263–7
Atreus 534–6, 538–45, 548, 555–9, 562–7
audience 203–13
Auxilium 276–7, 279, 312

Bacchanalia 26–8, 30, 32
Bacchants 353
Bacchic
– poetics 25–39 *see also* poetics
– rites 26–9
Bacchus/Dionysus 25–39, 353
Ballio 320
basilice/basileus 72
Bathyllus 318, 323
battle(s) 71, 73
bawd
– in Plautus' *Curculio* 322
Bible 471–2, 476, 487

brevis brevians 357
Brutus 354
Burmeister, Joannes 471–87

Caecilius Statius 38
Caligula
– the emperor 558
– murder of 406
callida nupta 518–9, 525
cannibalistic 568
canticum(a) 255, 320–5
Cappadox 231–2, 236–50
captatio benevolentiae 203–4
Capua 81
Carmentis 567
carmina Fescennina 33, 35–7
Casina 275–6, 279–81, 284, 286
Cassandra 351
– *vates* of Troy 405
castration 484–6
Cato the Elder 138–9
choragos 281
chorus 349, 354, 357–9, 555, 569
Christian drama 489–90
Cicero
– the orator 345, 354–6, 379, 382–3, 385, 443, 558, 562, 565
– on Greek and affectedness 446
– on Terence's 'pure speech' 445
– oratory and philosophy 331–43, *passim*
– *Pro Cluentio* 558
cinaedus 320
Circus Flaminius 268, 270–1
cistella 299–302, 304, 307–14
citizenship
– reproduction of 275–81, 283, 285–6
city 442–3
civic life 208–9, 211
civil war/political strife 417, 419–28
Claudius
– the emperor 523
– murder of 406–7
Cleanthes 379–86
Clearata 254, 257–9
Cleostrata 276, 279–81, 286
Clodia 558
columna rostrata 73

comedians 67–8, 71, 73–4, 77, 81, 83, 85–7, 89–92
comedy
– as a genre 505, 507, 509–12, 514–17, 525–6
– Roman 346–55
– tragic parody in 352–3
comoedia 15–23
coniectura 238–40
contaminatio 184, 380, 391–2
contiones 265
cook 101
Cornelius Schonaeus 489–503
corruption/deceit 442–3, 445
crepundia 302, 307, 309–10
crucifixion 506, 517–8, 525
cubiculum 559–61, 566
cultural memory 429
cultus adulter 519
cum (prefix) 305–6, 311
Curiatius Maternus
– character in Tacitus' *Dialogus* 558–69
curiositas 515, 525
Curtius Montanus 563

Danae 353
dance/dancing 32–5, 318–25, 355, 358
Daniel 74, 78–9, 81, 87, 472–6, 478–85
death 534–6, 540–7, 550
deception 511, 516–7, 519, 525
Demaenetus 256, 258–9
Demipho 276, 278
deus ex machina 31
Diabolus 253–60
Dido 514, 522
Dikaiopolis 74
Diotima 569
Diphilus 284, 475–82, 486
dismemberment 536, 538
Domitian 559, 562–3
Donatus
– commentary on performance 459, 467
doorposts 57–8
double entendre 471, 484
δρᾶμα 13–5
dramatic illusion 203–7, 212
dramaturgical 'failure' 167, 169–70, 181, 185, 192–6, 198

dream
- in Plautus' *Mostellaria* 53, 56, 60–1, 63
- in Roman theatre 353–4

East
- exotic 69
eccyclema/ekkyklema 50, 556
echo 388–90
elegy 97
Elisha 493–4, 497, 500, 502
Elysium 547–50
emotion
- and music in Roman theatre 354
- and theories of 443–4, 450
emphasis/*affectus* 563
empire
- and the aesthetics of containment 367–72, 376
empty stage 254–5
ending 301, 307, 309, 314
Ennius
- the poet 345–6, 351–6, 436–8, 556
- *Annales* 333, 337–8, 341
- *Epicharmus* 334, 336
- *fabulae praetextae* 337
- *Scipio* 338–41
- *Telephus* 74–5
- tragedies 334–6
entrance 254–5
epic 351
epilogues 215–17, 222–4, 228
Eratosthenes 34
erotic themes 439, 445
erotodidaxis 512
Etruria 31–2, 35
Euclio
- character of 146–61, 282–3, 286
Eumolpus 566
Euripides
- the playwright 13–4, 146–61, 387–92
- *Bacchae* 25, 30–1
- *Hippolytus* 520–2
- *Hippolytus Veiled* 522
- *Troades* 396–7, 401
Eurybates 399, 405
exclusus amator 255–6
exemplum 48, 57, 61–2

exodium 38
experimental dramaturgy 167–98

fables 67, 77, 79–82, 86–7
fabula
- as play 15–20
- *praetexta* 417, 559, 565
- *vs. res* 206, 210, 212
fate 573–4, 576–9, 582
Fauns 37–8
female solidarity 304, 307–8
feminisation 567
fetial 263, 267–72
Fides 275–7, 281–4, 286
finances 46, 54, 61
flattery 437, 442–3, 445
flute 319–21
folktale motifs 143–61
fraternal conflict 556
free will 414
furor 507, 525, 527
Fury 555, 564

Gates of the Underworld 547–8
generic
- boundaries 363–4
- enrichment 377
genre 307–9
gestures 355, 453–4, 458, 460–1, 463–6
gestus servilis 463
ghost
- of Thyestes 397–8, 403, 405
- story 52–3, 60, 63
gnomai 212
Greek 437, 445–50
Grumio 44, 46, 51, 56

Hagedorn, Friedrich von
- *Johann der Seifensieder* 147–8, 152, 156
Halcyon days 284–6
Halisca 307, 312–13
'Happy Poverty' narratives 143–61
Hecate 359
Helen 522
Hellenistic 68–9, 73, 80–3, 85–6, 90, 92
Herodas 76–7, 82, 85
Herodotus 13

heroic
- values 100
Hieron II
- the ruler of Syracuse 75–6
Hippolytus 390–2
history 333, 336–7, 339, 341–2, 417–30
Horace
- the poet 26, 30, 35, 37–9, 355–6
- *Epistle to Augustus* 35–6
- Nasidienus 568
    dinner of 568
- *Odes* 363–4, 366–8, 370–6
- *Satires* 369, 376, 435, 437, 440
Hughes, Ted
- 'aboriginal' 575–6
- *Birthday Letters* 573, 575–6, 580
- *Cave Birds* 578
- *Gaudete* 575, 580
- *Moortown Elegies* 580
- *Tales from Ovid* 576
- the translator of *Oedipus* 592, 594–5, 598–9
Hyginus 34, 350
hymns 351

ideal king 534, 540, 542, 546–7, 549–51
illusion
- dramatic 15, 20
impersonation 516–7, 525
impulse 414–15
incest 564
incumbere 560, 565
indictio belli 268–9, 271–2
induction 204
intertextuality 385–92, 417–30, 506, 514–5, 520–2, 533–4, 540
intratext/intratextuality 300, 307, 311, 380–8, 392
ira 533, 537–40
iterum 557
ius
- *commercii* 283
- *conubii* 283

Jason 354
Jerome 33
Jews 78, 81

joke 276, 282, 286
Julio-Claudian 558
Jupiter 353
Juvenal 72, 91, 563

king(s) 67–92
komos 321

Laberius 519
labour/pains 563, 568
lactaria columna 283
laments 351–3
Lampadio 278, 310–13
Lar/Lares 276–7
lena 254, 278, 303–4, 306–7, 310–11
leno 231–51
Libanius
- *Pro saltatione* 325
libertas 436–7
Lichas 505, 524
Livius Andronicus
- as father of Roman Drama 324, 346, 355–6
- *Aegisthus* 397
Livy 26–32, 34–5, 324
lovers
- in Roman comedy 352
Low Countries 489–503
Lucan 567
Lucian
- and pantomime 318, 321, 324–5, 358
- *De saltatione* 318, 321, 325
- Senecan performance and pantomime 324–5
Lucilius 379–85, *passim*
Lucretius
- the poet 368, 371, 374–5
- *De rerum natura* 39
ludi 32–3
Ludi Apollinares 271–2
ludificatio 259
lyric piety 364–8
Lysidamus 280–1

Machon 76–7, 82–6, 88–91
Macrobius 340–1, 562
Magna Graecia 324–5

maius 557
Mamercus Aemilius Scaurus 557
marriage
– *cum manu* 281
– *sine manu* 281
materiality 299–301, 304, 314
matron/wifes 216–17, 221, 228, 506, 509, 511–4, 516, 518–9, 521–2, 525–6
me miseram 466
Medea
– as character 350–1, 354, 357, 359–60, 522, 555, 560–1, 563–7
– and revenge, preceded by a ruse 399, 403
Melainis 278–9, 302–3, 307–8, 310, 312–3
Melanippe 351
melody 347, 356
memory 421, 429–30
Menander
– the comic playwright 15, 21, 276, 278, 280, 286, 513
– *Synaristosai* 278–9, 301–8
meretrix 253, 260, 509, 513–4, 516, 525
Messalla 559, 561–2, 568
messenger speeches 350, 353
metaliterary language 383, 386, 392
meta-play 399
metatheatre/metatheatrical 15–6, 23, 556–7
metre
– aeolic 357
– anapestic 349, 352–3, 356–60
– and accompaniment 346
– and rhythm 347
– as a determinant of music 346–7
– bacchiac 351–2, 357
– catalexis 352
– change in 449
– comic and tragic 346–50
– cretic 349, 351, 357
– dactylic 351, 357
– dramatic 435–6, 439
– iambic dimeter 359
– iambic octonarius 346, 349, 359
– iambic senarius 346–9, 351, 353–6, 358
– iambic septenarius 346

– iambic trimeter 355–6, 358–60
– iambo-trochaic 346–7, 355
– lyric 346–7
– non-iambo-trochaic 346–7, 352, 356–7
– polymetric 346–7, 351
– sapphic 357
– stichic 346–7
– trochaic octonarius 346, 352
– trochaic septenarius 346–50, 352–4, 359
– trochaic tetrameter 359
– variation for musical effects 346–50
miles 510, 512–3, 515–7, 521, 524–5
mime 188, 196, 506–7, 509, 511, 513, 518, 525
mirror 47–50, 54–5
mirum quin formula 70
miser 146–51, 154–60
monetary economy 43, 54
moneylender 53–4
monstrum 60, 62
moralising/amorality 216–18, 221, 223–5, 228
mosaics 278, 303–4
murder 555, 561, 564
music
– in pantomime 358
– in Roman comedy 347–54
– in Roman theatre 345–60
– in Roman tragedy 345–60
– in Roman tragedy, importance of 345
– in Seneca 358–60
music(al) 255–6
Myrrhina 276, 280–1

Naaman 489–503
Naevius 346, 353, 355–6
narrative inconsistency(ies) 254, 257
Near East 68, 79–82
nefas 364, 373, 538, 540, 542–4, 547–8
Nero/Neronian 417, 419–24, 426–9, 523, 560–1, 563
New Comedy 204
Nicolaus of Damascus 471, 486
Nietzsche 25
Novius 335
nutrix(ces) 70, 80

oaths
- in Roman theatre 352
oderint dum metuant 558
Odyssey-motif 187–94
Old Comedy 204
open-ended/open-endedness 255
oratory/oratorical 559, 561, 567–8
overtures 345
Ovid
- the poet 269–72, 387–92, 555–7, 564, 567
- *Fasti* 269–70
- *Heroides* 363–4
- *Metamorphoses* 363, 369–70, 581

Pacuvius
- the tragic poet 345, 349–56
- *Chryses* 331, 333
paidagogoi 80
Palaestrio 317, 319
Palatine manuscript 253
pallake 513
palliata 506–7, 511, 513
pantomime 317–25
- music in 358
papyri
- musical 358
parasite/*parasitus* 67–8, 70–3, 76, 81, 83–8, 90, 92, 101–2, 105, 115, 121
para-tragedy 308–10
Pardalisca 280
parody (legal) 225–7
parrhesia 440, 442
pater patratus 267–9
paterfamilias/patriarch 217, 219, 222, 224
patronage 436–9
Paulina 523–4
peiiurus 232, 238–9
performance 203–13
Peripatetic school 160–1
Periplectomenus 317–19
perjury 231–3, 238–43, 248, 250
Perseus 353
Persia 69, 74, 78
Persius 561–2, 568
perspective(s)
- Mycenaean 395–407
- Trojan 395–407

Petronius 505–6, 508–15, 517, 519–27, 566
Phaedra 519–22, 525, 527
Phaethon 369–70, 373, 376
Phanostrata 276, 278, 309, 311–13
Philaenium 253–5, 257–8, 260
Philematium 46–50, 55
Philip II 67, 69–71, 88, 90
Philoctetes 349, 353
Philolaches 43–51, 53–6, 60, 62–3
philosophy/philosophising 208, 331–3, 335, 337, 341–2, 354, 444–5
Phronesium 494–6, 500
Phrynichus
- *The Capture of Miletus* 13
pimps 231–52
Pindar
- *Olympians* 365–6
Planesium 243–6
Plato
- the philosopher 356
- *Symposium* 559, 569
Plautinisches 101, 106, 119
Plautus
- the comic playwright 15–23, 28–30, 38, 43–4, 50–1, 56–7, 59–60, 62, 67–9, 72–7, 80–2, 84–6, 88–9, 203–13, 275–9, 281–2, 284, 335–6, 342–3, 346, 349, 351–3
- *Aulularia* 102, 105–6, 116–25, 178–9, 182
  and folktales 143–61
  Greek model of 159–61
- *Casina* 275–86, 471–87
- *Mostellaria* 43–4, 48–9, 54, 59–60, 63
- *Persa* 102–16, 120, 124
- *Stichus* 167–8, 185–98
- *Trinummus* 167–85, 198
- *Truculentus* 263–73
Pliny the Younger 563
plot
- in Plautus' *Cistellaria* and Menander's *Synaristosai* 299–314, *passim*
- in the *Thyestes* tradition 556–7, 559, 563, 567
- of Clytemnestra and Aegisthus 395–407
- in Aeschylus' *Agamemnon* 396, 398
- in Seneca's *Agamemnon* 395–407
Plutarch 84–5, 87–8

poetics
- Callimachean 388
- of transgression 363–77 see also Bacchic
Polybius 75, 88
Pomponius 335
Pomponius Secundus 557
post-prandial discomfort 555
prayers 342
pre-emotion 413–14, 416
pregnancy 564, 567
pretention 446–9
Priam 352, 395–6, 400–4, 406
Procne 555
prologue(s)
- dramatic 15–9, 21–3, 203–13, 263–7, 271–2, 275–7, 279–81, 284, 286, 435–7, 439
- divine 275–81, 286
- fiction in 203–13
- of *Menaechmi* and *Captivi* 205–13
- Plautine 17, 21, 203–4
- Terentian 15–6
props 301–2, 304, 307–10
prosody 346, 357
prostitution/prostitutes 219, 223–7
protatic character 290
pseudo-*meretrix* 509, 514
Publilius Syrus 128–9
pudice 243–4
puella 299, 301–3, 307–9, 311–13
Punic War(s) 43, 63, 68, 75–6, 88
punishment 555, 562
puns 473–5, 480, 483–5
pure speech 445
Pylades 318, 323
Pyrgopolinices 510–11
Pyrrhus 268–71

rape 276, 278
Realpolitik, Roman
- cited by Cicero 558
recitative 323
recognitions
- in Plautus' *Epidicus* 289–90, 292–4, 297
- positive 292, 294, 296–8
- negative 292–3, 295–8

regicide(s) 398, 404–5, 407
Republican
- Roman 558–9, 563, 568
res divina 234, 236–7
resignation 576, 578
revenge 537–40, 555, 564
rex 67, 69–76, 83, 87, 92
Rhinthon of Tarentum 30
rhythm 347, 356–7
rich and poor 143–61
ritual 575, 580
rivalry 556
role-playing 211
Roman
- assemblies 264–6
- morals 127, 138–9
Romulus 37, 508

sacrifice/sacrificial 232–41, 244, 246–50, 569
sacruficare 234, 241
Sassia 558
satire 435–50, *passim*
satyr-play 569
Satyrs 37–8
scenic
- inside 556
- outside 556
scurra 73
secrecy 439, 442
Selenium 276, 278–9, 284, 302–11, 314
self-examination (philosophical) 48–9
self-interest 118–19
self-reflexivity 301, 308
Sempronius Gracchus 556
senatus consultum de Bacchanalibus 26
Seneca
- the philosopher 30–1, 345, 358–60, 379–92, 506–7, 519–25, 527
- *Agamemnon*
  colouring, Roman 397, 406
  dramatic tradition before Seneca 396–7
  resonances, political 406–7
- anapests in 359–60
- and pantomime 358
- iambic trimeters in 358–9
- *Medea* 363–4, 370, 373–7

- music in 358–60
- *Oedipus* 573, 575–6, 580–2
- performance of *senex amator* 345, 359
- *Thyestes* 363–6, 368–72, 376, 411, 415–16, 534–51, 555–7, 561–8
- tragedies 585–99
- translation in
    Senecan prose 382–7
    Senecan tragedy 387–92
sententia(e) 128–33, 136–9
servus
- *callidus/fallax* 313, 515, 517, 521
- *currens* 290
Shakespeare, William
- *Midsummer Night's Dream* 203, 206
shipwreck 276
Silenus 38
Silvanus 36
Simonides 285
slave(s) 68–70, 75, 77, 79–84, 86, 91–2, 97–116, 119–25
slavery 208, 212
social class 97–8, 100, 118–19
Socrates 559, 569
soldier(s) 70–1, 81, 85
solo performances 345, 358
song
- in Roman theatre 346–7
Sophocles 37
space
- Roman/Rome 264–9, 271, 273
- urban 263–73
sparagmos 31
stage
- and actors on 206, 209, 212
- and drama 207, 212
- arrangement and action 289
status 435–9, 447, 449–50
Stoic/Stoicism 380–5, 411–16, 444–6, 545–51
stultus vir 519
sublime ambition 371
Suda 323, 325
suffragium 265
symmetries
- in Plautus' *Epidicus* 289, 297
- symmetrical encounters 291

- symmetrical scenes 291
- repeated scenes 293, 297
Syphax 75
Syracuse 75–6, 88

Tacitus 523–4
- *Dialogus* 3 560
tale
- type 754 (Aarne-Thompson-Uther) 143–161
Tantalid(s) 555, 557, 565
Tantalus 365–6, 369, 411–16, 557, 561–2, 564–6
Tarquinius Superbus 353–4
technitai of Dionysus 25
Telamon 352
temple/*templum* 282–3, 286
- of Apollo Medicus 271–2
- of Bellona 268–73
- of Jupiter Optimus Maximus on the Capitoline Hill 282
Terence
- the comic playwright 15–7, 21, 335, 342, 351–3, 355, 357
- *Adelphoe* 130–2, 435, 437, 439, 442–4, 447–9
- *Andria* 133–6, 435, 447
- *Eunuchus* 441–3
- *Heauton Timoroumenos* 437, 439
- *Hecyra* 440–1
- illustrated manuscripts 453–4, 456, 467
- *Phormio* 455
Terentian dramaturgy 167, 169, 177–87, 194–5, 198
Terentius Christianus 489–503
Teucer 354
text
- and image 453, 455, 457, 462, 467
texture 301–2, 304, 307, 314
theatre Roman
- of Marcellus 272–3
- metre in 347–60
- origins 355
Theodotion 472–5, 484, 486–7
- *Susanna and the Elders* 471–87
Theopropides 44, 52–7, 59, 60–3
Theseus 521–2

Thespis 37
Thyestes
– as a theme 555–569
– character of 352
tibia 345–6
tibicen 256, 345–6, 355, 357
title 301–4, 306, 310
tollere 311–12
Toxilus 102–16, 120, 124
trade 68–9, 74, 79–84, 91–2
tragedy
– as a genre 97, 507, 525–6
– Attic 556
– messenger speeches in 350, 353
– Roman 345–60
    chorus in 349, 354, 357–8, 359
    development over time 355–358
    fragmentary nature of 345
    its relationship to comedy 347–54
    music and characterisation 347–9, 354
    philosophising in 354
– of *domus* 536, 551
tragicomic/tragicomedy 569, 551
Trajan 559
Tranio 43–4, 46, 51–63
translation 379–92, 585–99
Trimalchio 507, 523
Trojan
– Horse 566
– War 402, 404
– Women 388–90
Tryphaena 505, 507
tyrant 555, 561, 565–6

Ulysses 348–9, 353
univira 511
uxor dotata 177–9

Valerius Flaccus
– *Argonautica* 534–51
Varius Rufus 556
Varro 27, 29, 33–4
vates 562, 566, 568
verbum de verbo expressum 183–4
Vergil
– the poet 26, 32–7, 39, 340–1
– *Eclogues* 372, 375
– *Georgics* 367, 375–6
– *Aeneid* 371, 373, 375–6
Vespasian 559, 562, 568
violence 443–4
virtus 70, 76
Vita Aesopi 508

wealth
– as a theme in comedy 69, 73, 143–61
– in fables 77
wicker 301–2, 305, 314
widow of Ephesus 505–6, 508–9, 513, 517–19, 522–5, 527
women
– in classical scholarship 585–8, 599
wordplay 305, 307

Xenophon 318, 324

Yale University 585–6

Zosimus 323

Index locorum

The Index Locorum includes both ancient and modern sources. Fragmentary texts are cited by number and name of modern editor only (the relevant editions are to be found in the bibliography accompanying each article).

Accius
– *Aeneadae*
    Dangel 676–7 353
– *Armorum Iudicium*
    Dangel 164–8 348
    Ribbeck 169 349
    Dangel 171 349
    Warmington 103–8 348
    Warmington 109–14 348
    Warmington 115–17 348
– *Brutus*
    Dangel 651–72 353–4
    Dangel 674 354
    Ribbeck 1 429
    Ribbeck 2 429
– *Clytaemnestra*
    Dangel 291–3 353
– *Erigona*
    Dangel 320–3 354
– *Eurysaces*
    Dangel 335–8 353
    Dangel 360–6 354
– *Meleager*
    Dangel 517–18 352
– *Philoctetes*
    Dangel 195–211 349
    Dangel 214–30 349
    Dangel 237–40 353
– *Stasiastae*
    Dangel 403 353
Aeschylus
– *Ag.*
    1287 396
    1604 398
    1627 398
    1635 398
Aesop
– *Fables*
    Perry 225 157–8

Aristophanes
– *Acharn.*
    412–17 13–14
Aristotle
– Gigon fr. 783 144, 147, 154–5

Bonaventure des Périers
– *Nouvelles récréations et joyeux devis*
    19 143, 146–7, 152, 154, 156

Catullus
– *Carm.*
    49.1 382
    65.7 390
Cicero
– *De Or.*
    1.259 345
    3.102 345
    3.171 446
– *Div.*
    43–5 354
– *Leg.*
    2.39 356
– *Luc.*
    20 345
– *Off.*
    1.114 355
– *Opt. Gen.*
    14 385
– *Sen.*
    29 221
– *Tusc.*
    1.107 345
    3.83 444
    4.48 443

Donatus
– *ad Andr.*
    183.12 460, 463

Ennius
- *Achilles*
    Manuwald 2   353
- *Alexander*
    Manuwald 21   351
- *Andromacha*
    Manuwald 23   351
    Manuwald 33   353
- *Andromeda*
    Manuwald 40   353
- *Eumenides*
    Manuwald 52   354
    Manuwald 55   354
- *Hectoris Lytra*
    Manuwald 59   352
    Manuwald 66   352
- *Hecuba*
    Manuwald 80   353
- *Iphigenia*
    Manuwald 82   352
    Manuwald 84   354
- *Medea*
    Manuwald 92   354
- *Melanippa*
    Manuwald 104   351
- *Sabinae*
    Ribbeck 1   429
- *Thyestes*
    Manuwald 132   352
    Manuwald 133   352
Epictetus
- *Ench.*
    53.1   382
Étienne de Bourbon
- *Exempla*
    409   143, 147–8, 151, 153–5
    506   143, 147–8, 151, 153–5
Euripides
- *Hec.*
    1109–13   388–9
- *Hipp.*
    976–80   390
    1207–9   390
Florian
- *Fables*
    2.4   143, 150, 152, 154, 156
- *Gnomologium Vaticanum*
    72   144, 147, 154–5

Gracchus (writer of tragedies)
- *Peliades*
    Schauer 2   357

Herodotus
    6.21.2   13
Horace
- *A.P.*
    119   384
    131–5   385
    211   356
- *C.*
    1.1   370
    1.1.3–6   370
    1.1.7–10   370
    1.1.30–2   371
    1.1.36   372
    1.2.1   376
    1.2.17–20   376
    1.3   364, 373–6
    1.3.9–12   373
    1.3.23   373
    1.3.26   373
    1.3.28   373
    1.3.36–7   375
    1.4   370
    1.9.1–2   370
    1.9.5   370
    1.9.9   370
    1.12.5–8   370
    1.28.1–4   376
    2.1   364
    2.9.23–4   371
    2.19   364, 366, 368
    2.19.8   366
    2.19.9–16   366
    2.19.21–2   366
    2.19.29–32   366–7
    3.1.1   368, 371
    3.1.1–4   367
    3.1.45–8   367–8
    3.3.9–10   374
    3.4.6   368
    3.25   364
    3.27–8   373
    4.2   366
    4.7.25–8   392
    4.15.21–4   370

– *Ep.*
    1.7.46–95 144–5, 156
    2.1.139–55 35–6
– *S.*
    1.1.56–60 369
    1.1.68 369
    1.1.114–16 376
    1.2.31–5 224
    1.4 435
    1.4.11 369–70
    1.4.62 392
    1.6.6 435
    1.6.45 435
    1.6.56–61 440
    1.9 440
    1.10 435, 445
    1.10.42 355
    2.1 435
    2.1.30–4 440
    2.1.62–74 437
Hyginus
– *Fab.*
    27 350

Jacques de Vitry
– *Exempla*
    66 143, 147, 149–51, 153–4
Juvenal
    1.10–11 377
    1.149–50 374
    10.201 218
    12 373

Kirchhof, Hans Wilhelm
– *Wendunmuth*
    2.137 143, 147, 150, 152, 154

La Fontaine
– *Fables*
    8.2 143, 147–8, 152, 154–6
Livius Andronicus
– *inc.*
    Schauer 25 356
Livy
    7.2.3–8 355
    7.2.8–11 324
Lucan
    1.8 425

    1.666–9 424
    1.676–95 425
Lucilius (ed. Warmington)
    14 447
    15–16 447
    84–6 446
    87–93 446
    149–58 442
    159–71 442
    176–81 443
    412 435
    503 435
    507–8 445
    670–1 439
    672–3 439
    696–7 439
    698 435
    699 439
    737 439
    742 439
    793–803 439
    1145–51 442
    1189–90 445
Lucretius
    1.62–79 374–5
    1.76–7 375
    1.951–83 371
    3.3 384
    3.978–1023 415

Marius Victorinus
– Keil 6.60 358

Naevius
– *Danae*
    Schauer 12 353
– *Lycurgus*
    Schauer 22 353
Nonius Marcellus
    283L 350
Ovid
– *Fast.*
    3.261–6 392
    6.733–62 392
– *Her.*
    12.212 364
– *Ib.*
    29 390

– *Medea*
　Schauer 2　357
– *Met.*
　2.255–6　369
　2.296　370
　2.326–8　370
　3.377–8　389
　3.500–1　389
　6.424–674　363
　6.537　388
　11.743–8　285
　13.408–571　389
　15.531–2　392
　15.538–40　392
　15.543–6　391–2

Pacuvius
– *Armorum Iudicium*
　Schierl 21　353
– *Atalanta*
　Schierl 45–8　349–51
– *Chryses*
　Schierl 78–81　354
– *Iliona*
　Schierl 147　351
– *Medus*
　Schierl 168–76　350–1
– *Niptra*
　Schierl 199　353
– *Teucer*
　Schierl 238–41　353
　Schierl 249　352
Petronius
– *Sat.*
　110–12　505–27
Phaedrus
　1.27　158
　4.21　158
Pindar
– *Ol.*
　1.48–52　366
　1.55　366
– *P.*
　9　366
Plautus
– *Am.*
　50–63　18–9
　88–96　19

　203ff.　353
　861–8　22–3
　873–9　22
– *As.*
　78–86　219
　86　219
　96–7　219
　692–7　219
　846　225
　851–3　225
　853　220
　863　218
　871–5　219–22
　884–6　219
　888–9　219
　894–5　225
　903　225
　933–4　225
　934　217
　940–1　224
　942–7　224–5
– *Aul.*
　9–22　149, 156
　65f.　155
　67ff.　146, 150
　149ff.　216
　158–522　179
　172　146
　187　153
　192f.　152
　215f.　146, 148
　226–34　117–18
　228–35　161
　371–84　149–50, 158
　378　149
　449f.　147, 151
　465–72　148
　467　157
　587–94　120
　589　105–6
　616–23　121
　623　123
　661–2　123
　674　157
　677–81　121–2
　701–4　122
　709　157

Index Locorum

    808–10 122
    816–19 124
    822–8 124–5
    fr.iii 147, 154, 157
    fr.iv 147, 154–5
– *Bacch.*
    925–78 189
    1120–48 227
    1152 227
    1163 217
    1206 227
    1207–11 227
    1208 217, 220
    fr. vi 217
– *Capt.*
    1–3 209
    11–16 209–10
    21–2 211
    43–52 206, 210–11
    52 205–6
    54–62 17–8
    61–6 210
    1029–34 18
– *Cas.*
    1–4 276
    39–46 277
    82 223
    86 219, 223
    149–57 219
    155 220
    159 218
    189–96 221
    225–49 218
    240 217
    245–6 219
    248 219
    260 220
    452ff. 218
    466 218
    491–501 219
    497 220
    501 219
    517–19 217–18
    535 218
    550 218
    552 220
    559 218
    567–8 220
    727 218
    772–88 219
    780–7 219
    863 220
    937–1006 223
    978–81 28
    1009 224
    1012–18 222–4
    1015–19 216, 223–4
– *Cist.*
    1–3 304
    89–93 306
    139 307
    306ff. 216
    627–37 307
    647–50 308–9
    653–9 311
    671ff. 322
    686–9 312
    747 349
– *Curc.*
    1–6 172
    142 105, 172
    175–8 172–3
    280–95 173–4
    635 349
– *Ep.*
    449–51 293
    458–9 293
    576–7 295
– *Men.*
    3 207
    10 205
    7–12 16–7
    19–23 207
    45–6 208
    51–5 207
    56 207
    72–6 205
    753ff. 352
– *Merc.*
    230ff. 218
    255–65 221
    291 218
    304 220
    305 217

    313–14 218
    319–21 221
    374–5 130
    469–70 29
    525 217
    547–54 221
    574–6 218
    692–7 219
    700–4 219
    784 220
    784–6 219
    972–3 217
    983a–6 220
    1015–26 225–7
    1017 217, 226
– *Mil.*
    200ff. 317
    685–700 177–8
– *Most.*
    105–11 44–5
    135–43 45–6
    248–53 47–8
    265–71 49–50
    635–42 54–5
    750–7 55–6
    760–2 56–7
    818–40 57–60
    908–9 43, 57
    1149–51 21–2
    1178–9 115
– *Pers.*
    1–6 103
    7–12 105
    21–3 106
    24–5 107
    26–7 108
    28 108
    29 108
    251–6 110
    753–7 110
    757ff. 320
    833–43 111–12
    856–8 115
– *Poen.*
    126 215
    504ff. 320
    1370–1 17
– *Ps.*
    133ff. 320
    265–335 235–6
    1246ff. 321–2
    1323–5 115
– *Rud.*
    199ff. 351
    664ff. 351
    829ff. 216
    1249–53 138
– *Stich.*
    1–6 191
    60–5 192
    155–70 193
    539ff. 216
    673–82 197
    772ff. 320
– *Trin.*
    16–22 182
    236–43 171–2
    241a–54 178
    688–94 179–80
    705–7 20
    1008–16 173–4
    1015–16 175
    1028–45 170–1
Pomponius Secundus
– *inc.*
    Schauer 2–3 357
Propertius
    1.8 373

Quintilian
– *Inst.*
    9.2.42–4 386
    10.1.99–100 127–8
    10.1.122 384
Scaevus Memor
    Schauer 1 357
    Schauer 2 357
Seneca the Elder
– *Contr.*
    1.8 385
    2.5.3 385–6
    7.7.19 385
Seneca
– *Agam.*
    720–5 364

791–9 401–2
869b–71 395
1006b–9 404–5
– *Ben.*
  4.40.4 385
  6.10.1 385
  6.41.2 386
– *De ira*
  1.16 415–16
  2.1 413
  2.4.1 444
– *Dial.*
  1.5.6.7 386
– *Ep.*
  6.1 384
  47.1 380
  58.7 383
  75.1 379
  80.1 383
  106.12 381–2
  107.1 380, 384
  107.2 380–1
  107.3 381
  107.4 381–4
  107.7–8 383, 386
  107.9 383–4
  107.9–10 385
  107.10–12 382–3
  108.24–9 381
  114.1 384
  114.3 369
  118.1 382
– *Herc. Fur.*
  149 387–8
– *Med.*
  48–50 363
  261 373
  267 373
  275–6 373–4
  290 373
  306 374
  308 374
  318–21 374
  340 374
  340–5 374
  342 374
  347 373
  361–3 373

  372 375
  373–4 375
  375 375
  379–80 375
  587–90 370
  599–602 376
  667–8 376
  740–848 359–60
  866 376
– *Oedip.*
  223–32 359
  503–8 365
– *Phaedr.*
  820–4 392
  847–8 392
  959 386
  1022–4 390–1
  1201–12 359
  1223–5 390
  1256 392
– *Thyest.*
  23–9 542
  23–36 587
  56–7 363
  62–7 411
  68–83 365
  86 369
  95 369
  96–100 411
  100 542
  101–21 365
  108 369
  117–18 370
  120 370
  122–31 365
  132 369
  151 369
  174–5 369
  192–204 538–9
  250–4 542
  267–8 363, 368
  267–78 538–9
  281–4 365
  302 368
  336–52 541
  351–7 370
  363–8 541
  369–79 370

    369–80 549–50
    388–403 541
    391–403 370
    407–10 370
    412–20 412
    436–7 412
    489 412–13
    560–1 372
    648–52 371
    692 371
    789–804 588
    789–884 365
    885–6 372
    995–1009 589
– *Troad.*
    67–8 388
    95 389
    97–8 390
    108–13 389–90
    115–16 390
    993–4 385
    1122 390
    1160–1 390
[Seneca]
– *Oct.*
    462–9 419–20
    575–9 422
    778–88 423–4
    844–57 426–7
Shakespeare, William
– *Midsummer Night's Dream* III.1 203, 206
Sophocles
– *Ph.*
    219ff. 349
Statius
– *Theb.*
    12.817 384
Stobaeus
    4.31.78 144, 147, 154–5
    4.31.91 144, 147, 154–5
Suetonius
– *Vit. Ter.*
    7 445

Terence
– *Ad.*
    6–14 182–3
    15–21 437, 439
    19 439

    22–4 182–3
    155–96 249
    299–301 498
    305 444
    308–9 444
    309–12 444
    314–19 443
    411–29 131
    500–4 495
    833–5 132
    868 449
    875–81 449
    906–22 449
    907 449
    911 449
    929–45 449
    947–56 449
    952–4 132
    959–61 449
    964 449
    972–7 449
    979–83 449
– *And.*
    1–7 493
    9–12 21
    26 16
    28–34 460–1
    51 448
    57 448
    88 448
    99ff. 195
    125 448
    149–50 448
    154 448
    164–5 448
    172–4 462–3
    228–35 464–5
    236–45 465–6
    245ff. 352
    301ff. 352
    324 435
    471–2 448
    492–4 448
    495 448
    607ff. 352
    625 351
    814–16 448
    914 435
    919 448

– *Eun.*
    50–69 441
    79–80 441
    103–4 441
    121 441
    197–8 441
    234–43 502
    255–8 443
    255–9 498–9
    382–5 441
    812–13 495
    1031–3 501
    1044–9 501
– *Heaut.*
    22–4 437
    25–30 439
    75–9 496
    239–40 495
– *Hec.*
    164–6 495
    281ff. 352
    361ff. 353
    361–77 499
    865–7 441
    866–8 15
– *Phorm.*
    153ff. 352
    183 435
    338–42 436
    465ff. 352
Trag. Inc.
Schauer, *Tragicorum Romanorum Fragmenta* 1
    Adespota
        Schauer 22 351
        Schauer 56 351

Valerius Flaccus
    1.700–3 537
    1.716–25 537
    1.755–70 545–6
    1.794–8 543
    1.807–10 543
    1.832–9 547–9
Valerius Maximus
    2.4.4 355
Varius Rufus
– *Thyestes*
    Schauer 2 358
– *inc.*
    Schauer 3 357
Vergil
– *Ecl.*
    1.6 372
    1.62 375
– *G.*
    1.30–1 375
    1.501 376
    1.511–14 376
    2.380–96 32–3
– *Aen.*
    1.148–56 420
    1.278–96 376
    1.283 375
    2.550b–3 404
    2.557b–8 400, 404
    2.701–2 386
    4.670–1 403
    6.274–5 381
    7.761–82 392
    12.11 386

Waldis, Burkard
– *Esopus*
    4.82 143, 147, 152, 154, 156

Xenophon
– *Cyrop.*
    8.3.35–48 144, 147, 149–50, 154, 156

www.ingramcontent.com/pod-product-compliance
Lightning Source LLC
Chambersburg PA
CBHW070253240426
43661CB00057B/2550